Frommer's®

W9-BEB-370

POSTCARDS

FROM

MAUI

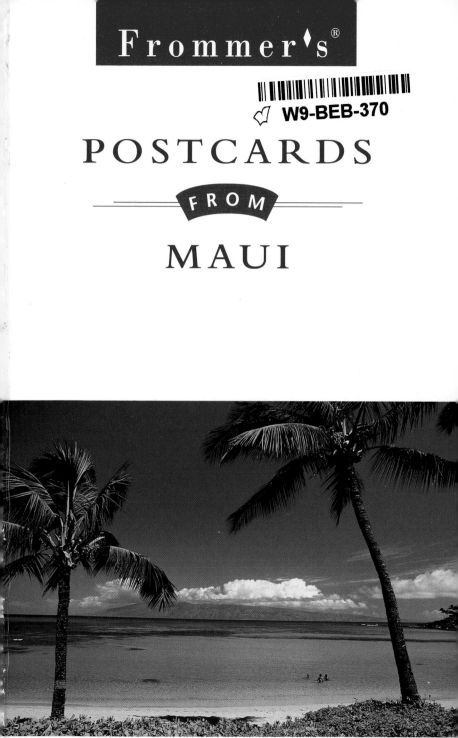

For coverage of the best beaches on Maui, see chapter 6. © David Olsen/Tony Stone Images.

You may spot a spinner dolphin while whale watching or ocean rafting, or even from shore. See chapter 6. © Stuart Westmorland/Tony Stone Images.

If you're lucky, you'll see a humpback whale breaching. See chapter 6. © Charla Thompson/ Photo Resource Hawaii.

Some of the many species visible to snorkelers and divers include the threadfin butterfly fish (© Jeff Hunter/Image Bank) and the green sea turtle (© Mike Severns/Tony Stone Images). See chapter 6.

Maluaka Beach (Makena Beach), a palm-fringed crescent of golden, grainy sand set between two black-lava points. See chapter 6. © Douglas Peebles Photography.

The Emerald Course at Wailea, designed by Robert Trent Jones, Jr. See chapter 6. © George Fuller/Photo Resource Hawaii.

Harbor in the historic whaling town of Lahaina. See chapter 7. © Chris Bryant/Tony Stone Images.

Sunrise at Haleakala National Park. See chapters 6 and 7. © Jim Cazel/Photo Resource Hawaii.

Cinder cones in the crater of Haleakala, the world's largest dormant volcano. See chapters 6 and 7. © Jon K. Ogata/Photo Resource Hawaii.

The snaky Haleakala Crater Road climbs from sea level to 10,000 feet, passing through puffy cumulus clouds like these. See chapters 6 and 7. © Robert Holmes Photography.

There are more than 25 miles of hiking trails in the crater, where the terrain ranges from burnt-red cinder cones to ebony-black lava flows. See chapters 6 and 7. © John Elk Photography.

Four-mile-long Kaanapali Beach, one of the best beaches on the island. See chapter 6. © Greg Vaughn/Tony Stone Images.

A snorkel cruise to Molokini, a natural sanctuary for tropical fish and one of the most popular snorkel spots. See chapter 6. © Mark E. Gibson Photography.

Hawaiian traditions live on in Maui. Luaus often feature hula performances. See chapter 9.
© Cliff Hollenbeck Photography.

Making traditional leis. See "The Welcoming Lei," in chapter 2.
© Hollenbeck Photography.

Driving through a verdant rain forest on the Road to Hana. See chapter 7. © Cliff Hollenbeck Photography.

On your way to Hana, you'll see sweet-smelling ginger everywhere. See chapter 7. © John Elk Photography.

Maui's rain forest is dotted with waterfalls. See chapter 7 for waterfall pools on the way to Hana. © Jerry Alexander/Tony Stone Images.

Taro and banana patches along the Hana coast. See chapter 7. © Greg Vaughn/Tony Stone Images.

Hamoa Beach, one of Hana's best beaches, is popular with sunbathers, surfers, and snorkelers alike. See chapters 6 and 7. © David Olsen/Tony Stone Images.

Oheo Gulch (often called Seven Sacred Pools) at Kipahulu, just beyond Hana. More than 20 water-fall pools and cataracts cascade into the sea. See chapter 7. © Cliff Hollenbeck Photography.

Iao Valley, a state park in the West Maui Mountains, offers easy trails perfect for family hikes. See chapter 7. © Mark E. Gibson Photography.

The highest sea cliffs in the world, along Molokai's north shore. See chapter 10. © Franco Salmoiraghi/Photo Resource Hawaii.

There's no better way to see Molokai's Kalaupapa National Historic Park than from the back of a mule. See chapter 10. © Douglas Peebles Photography.

The mule ride to Kalaupapa takes you down 26 switchbacks on a narrow, 3-mile trail. See chapter 10. © Franco Salmoiraghi/Photo Resource Hawaii.

Waterfall in the lush West Maui Mountains. See chapters 6 and 7. © *Randy Wells/Tony Stone Images.*

Frommer's® 2001

Maui

by Jeanette Foster & Jocelyn Fujii

IDG Books Worldwide, Inc.
An International Data Group Company
Foster City, CA • Chicago, IL • Indianapolis, IN • New York, NY

ABOUT THE AUTHORS

A resident of the Big Island, **Jeanette Foster** has skied the slopes of Mauna Kea (during a Fourth of July ski meet, no less) and gone scuba diving with manta rays off the Kona Coast. A prolific writer widely published in travel, sports, and adventure magazines, she's also a contributing editor to *Hawaii* magazine and *Arthur Frommer's Budget Travel* and the editor of this year's *Zagat Survey—Hawaii Restaurants.*

Jocelyn Fujii is the author of eight books on Hawaii and the Pacific, including *Under the Hula Moon: Living in Hawaii, The Best of Hawaii,* and *The Persis Collection of Contemporary Art.* Her articles have appeared in the *New York Times, National Geographic Traveler, Islands, Condé Nast Traveler, Travel Holiday,* and other national and international publications.

In addition to this guide, Jeanette and Jocelyn also coauthor *Frommer's Hawaii, Frommer's Hawaii from $60 a Day,* and *Frommer's Honolulu, Waikiki & Oahu.*

IDG BOOKS WORLDWIDE, INC.

An International Data Group Company
919 E. Hillsdale Blvd.
Suite 400
Foster City, CA 94404

Find us online at **www.frommers.com**

ISBN 0-02-863781-X
ISSN 1076-2817

Editor: Lisa Renaud/Dog-Eared Pages
Production Editor: Carol Sheehan
Photo Editor: Richard Fox
Design by Michele Laseau
Staff Cartographers: John Decamillis, Elizabeth Puhl, Roberta Stockwell
Page creation by: IDG Books Indianapolis Production Department

SPECIAL SALES

For general information on IDG Books Worldwide's books in the U.S., please call our Consumer Customer Service department at 1-800-762-2974. For reseller information, including discounts, bulk sales, customized editions, and premium sales, please call our Reseller Customer Service department at 1-800-434-3422.

Manufactured in the United States of America

5 4 3 2 1

Contents

List of Maps

AN INVITATION TO THE READER

In researching this book, we discovered many wonderful places—hotels, restaurants, shops, and more. We're sure you'll find others. Please tell us about them, so we can share the information with your fellow travelers in upcoming editions. If you were disappointed with a recommendation, we'd love to know that, too. Please write to:

Frommer's Maui 2001
IDG Books Worldwide, Inc.
909 Third Avenue
New York, NY 10022

AN ADDITIONAL NOTE

Please be advised that travel information is subject to change at any time—and this is especially true of prices. We therefore suggest that you write or call ahead for confirmation when making your travel plans. The authors, editors, and publisher cannot be held responsible for the experiences of readers while traveling. Your safety is important to us, however, so we encourage you to stay alert and be aware of your surroundings. Keep a close eye on cameras, purses, and wallets, all favorite targets of thieves and pickpockets.

WHAT THE SYMBOLS MEAN

✪ Frommer's Favorites

Our favorite places and experiences—outstanding for quality, value, or both.

The following abbreviations are used for credit cards:

AE	American Express	EURO	Eurocard
CB	Carte Blanche	JCB	Japan Credit Bank
DC	Diners Club	MC	MasterCard
DISC	Discover	V	Visa
ER	enRoute		

FIND FROMMER'S ONLINE

www.frommers.com offers up-to-the-minute listings on almost 200 cities around the globe—including the latest bargains and candid, personal articles updated daily by Arthur Frommer himself. No other Web site offers such comprehensive and timely coverage of the world of travel.

The Best of Maui

by Jeanette Foster & Jocelyn Fujii

Maui, also called the Valley Isle, is but a small dot in the vast Pacific Ocean, but it has the potential to offer visitors unforgettable experiences: floating weightless in a rainbowed sea of tropical fish, standing atop a 10,000-foot volcano watching the sunrise color the sky, listening to the raindrops in a bamboo forest.

From around the globe, travelers are drawn to Maui, each in search of a unique encounter. Next to Waikiki, Maui is Hawaii's most popular destination, welcoming some 2¹/₂ million people each year to its sunny shores. As soon as you arrive at Kahului Airport, a huge banner greets you with the news that the readers of *Condé Nast Traveler* voted Maui the best island *in the world*—and they've done so 5 years running. As a result, sometimes Maui feels a little *too* well known—especially when you're stuck in bumper-to-bumper traffic around the airport. However, the congestion here pales in comparison to that of big-city Honolulu; Maui is really just a casual collection of small towns. Once you move beyond the resort areas, you'll find a slower, more peaceful way of life, where car horns are used only to greet friends, posted store hours mean nothing if the surf's up, and taking time to watch the sunset is part of the daily routine.

Whether you want to experience the "real" Hawaii, go on a heart-pounding adventure, or simply relax on the beach, this book is designed to help you find the paradise of your dreams.

It can be bewildering to plan your trip with so many options vying for your attention; to make your task easier, this chapter highlights what we consider the very best that Maui has to offer.

1 The Best Beaches

- **D. T. Fleming Beach Park:** This quiet, out-of-the-way beach cove, located north of the Ritz-Carlton Hotel, starts at the 16th hole of the Kapalua golf course (Makaluapuna Point) and rolls around to the sea cliffs on the other side. Ironwood trees provide shade on the land side. Offshore, a shallow sandbar extends out to the edge of the surf. Generally, the waters are good for swimming and snorkeling, but sometimes, off near the sea cliffs, the waves are big enough to suit bodyboarders and surfers. See chapter 6.
- **Kapalua Beach:** On an island of many great beaches, this one takes the prize. A golden crescent with swaying palms protected from strong winds and currents by two outstretched lava-rock

promontories, Kapalua has calm waters that are perfect for snorkeling, swimming, and kayaking. Even though it borders the Kapalua Bay Hotel, the beach is long enough for everyone to enjoy. Facilities include showers, rest rooms, and lifeguards. See chapter 6.

- **Kaanapali Beach:** Four-mile-long Kaanapali stands out as one of Maui's best beaches, with grainy gold sand as far as the eye can see. Most of the beach parallels the sea channel, and a paved beach walk links hotels and condos, open-air restaurants, and the Whalers Village shopping center. Summertime swimming is excellent. The best snorkeling is around Black Rock, in front of the Sheraton; the water is clear, calm, and populated with brilliant tropical fish. See chapter 6.

- **Wailea Beach:** This is the best gold-sand, crescent-shaped beach on Maui's sun-baked southwestern coast. One of five beaches within Wailea Resort, Wailea is big, wide, and protected on both sides by black-lava points. It serves as the front yard for the Four Seasons Wailea, Maui's most elegant hotel, and the Grand Wailea Resort Hotel & Spa, its most outrageous. From the beach, the view out to sea is magnificent, framed by neighboring Kahoolawe and Lanai and the tiny crescent of Molokini. The clear waters tumble to shore in waves just the right size for gentle riding, with or without a board. While all of the beaches on the west and south coasts are great for spotting whales and watching sunsets, Wailea, with its fairly flat sandy beach that gently slopes down to the ocean, provides exceptionally good whale watching from shore in season (December through April), as well as unreal sunsets nightly. See chapter 6.

- **Maluaka Beach (Makena Beach):** On the southern end of Maui's resort coast, development falls off dramatically, leaving a wild, dry countryside punctuated by green kiawe trees. The wide, palm-fringed crescent of golden sand is set between two black-lava points and bounded by big sand dunes topped by a grassy knoll. Makena can be perfect for swimming when it's flat and placid, but it can also offer excellent bodysurfing when the waves come rolling in. Or, if you prefer, it can be a place of serenity, with vistas of Molokini Crater and Kahoolawe off in the distance. See chapter 6.

- **Waianapanapa State Park:** In east Maui, a few miles from Hana, the 120 acres of this state park offer 12 cabins, a caretaker's residence, a picnic area, a shoreline hiking trail, and, best of all, a black-sand beach (actually small black pebbles). Swimming is generally unsafe, though, due to strong waves breaking offshore, which roll into the beach unchecked, and strong rip currents. But it's a great spot for picnicking, hiking along the shore, and simply sitting and relaxing. See chapter 6.

- **Hamoa Beach:** This half moon–shaped, gray-sand beach (a mix of coral and lava) in a truly tropical setting is a favorite among sunbathers, snorkelers, and bodysurfers in Hana. The 100-foot-wide beach is three football fields long and sits below 30-foot black-lava sea cliffs. An unprotected beach open to the ocean, Hamoa is often swept by powerful rip currents. Surf breaks offshore and rolls ashore, making it a popular surfing and bodysurfing area. The calm left side is best for snorkeling in the summer. See chapter 6.

2 The Best Maui Experiences

- **Take the Plunge:** Don mask, fins, and snorkel, and explore the magical world beneath the surface of the ocean, where kaleidoscopic clouds of tropical fish flutter by exotic corals; a sea turtle might even come over to check you out. Molokini is everyone's favorite snorkeling destination, but the shores of Maui are lined with magical spots as well. Can't swim? No problem: Hop on the **Atlantis Submarine** (☎ **800/548-6262**) for a plunge beneath the waves without getting wet. See chapters 6 and 7.

- **Hunt for Whales on Land:** No need to shell out megabucks to go out to sea in search of humpback whales—you can watch these majestic mammals breach and spy hop from shore. We recommend scenic McGregor Point, at mile marker 9 along Honoapiilani Highway, just outside Maalaea in South Maui. The humpbacks arrive as early as November, but the majority travels through Maui's waters from mid-December to mid-April. See chapter 6.

- **Watch the Windsurfers:** Sit on a grassy bluff or stretch out on the sandy beach at Hookipa, on the north shore, and watch the world's top-ranked windsurfers twirling and dancing on the wind and waves like colorful butterflies. World championship contests are held at Hookipa, one of the greatest windsurfing spots on the planet. See chapters 6 and 7.

- **Experience Maui's History:** Wander the historic streets of the old whaling town of Lahaina, where the 1800s are alive and well thanks to the efforts of the Lahaina Restoration Society. Drive the scenic Kahekili Highway, where the preserved village of Kahakuloa looks much as it did a century ago. Stand in awe at Piilanihale, Hawaii's largest *heiau* (temple), located just outside Hana. See chapter 7.

- **Greet the Rising Sun from Haleakala's Summit:** Bundle up in warm clothing, fill a thermos full of hot java, and drive up to the summit to watch the sky turn from inky black to muted charcoal as a small sliver of orange forms on the horizon. Standing at 10,000 feet, breathing in the rarefied air, and watching the first rays of light streak across the sky is a mystical experience of the first magnitude. See chapter 7.

- **Explore a Different Hawaii—Upcountry Maui:** On the slopes of Haleakala, cowboys, farmers, ranchers, and other country people make their homes in serene, neighborly communities like Makawao, Kula, and Ulupalakua—worlds away from the bustling beach resorts. Acres of onions, lettuce, tomatoes, carrots, cabbage, and flowers cover the hillsides. Maui's only winery is located here, offering the perfect place for a picnic and a chance to sample the tropical varieties of paradise. See chapter 7.

- **Drive through a Tropical Rain Forest:** The Hana Highway is not just a "drive" but an adventure: Stop along the way to plunge into icy mountain ponds filled by cascading waterfalls; gaze upon vistas of waves pummeling soaring ocean cliffs; inhale the sweet aroma of blooming ginger; and take a walk back in time, catching a glimpse of what Hawaii looked like before concrete condos and fast-food joints washed ashore. See chapter 7.

- **Take a Day Trip to Lanai:** From Lahaina, join the snorkel cruise to Lanai offered by **Trilogy Excursions** (☎ **800/874-2666**), or take the **Expeditions Lahaina/Lanai Passenger Ferry** over and rent a four-wheel-drive Jeep on your own. It's a two-for-one island experience: Board in Lahaina Harbor and admire Maui from offshore, then get off at Lanai and go snorkeling in the clear waters, tour the tiny former plantation island, and catch the last ferry home. See chapters 6 and 11.

3 The Best of Natural Maui

- **Volcanoes:** Maui was born of two volcanoes (Puu Kukui, in the West Maui Mountains, and Haleakala, in the east) which flowed together to create the island. Don't miss seeing **Haleakala National Park.** A bird's-eye view into this long-dormant volcanic crater—big enough to contain Manhattan!—is more than just staring at a big hole in the ground. You'll see other-worldly swirls of burnt-red, orange, brown, and black cinders; lava tubes; and Haleakala's own minimountain range. See chapters 6 and 7.

- **Waterfalls:** Rushing waterfalls thundering downward into sparkling freshwater pools—they're some of Maui's most beautiful natural wonders. The Hana Highway offers numerous viewing opportunities and chances to stop for swims at the deep pools. At the end of the road you'll find **Oheo Gulch** (also known as the Seven Sacred Pools), some of the most dramatic and accessible waterfalls in the islands. See chapter 7.

- **Gardens:** The islands radiate the sweet smell of flowers. For a glimpse of Hawaii's spectacular range of tropical flora, we suggest spending an afternoon at one of Maui's lush gardens. At **Kula Botanical Garden,** you can take a leisurely self-guided stroll through more than 700 native and exotic plants, including orchids, proteas, and bromeliads. In Hana, numerous gardens display everything from tropical natives to exotics from around the globe. See chapter 7.

- **Marine Life Conservation Areas:** These preservation areas, submerged in a Neptunian underworld, possess a sensual serenity that's unmatched in the world above the waves. Four underwater parks are spread across Maui County: Honolua-Mokuleia Marine Life Conservation District and Ahihi-Kinau Natural Area Reserve, both off the shores of Maui (see chapters 6 and 7); Molokini Marine Life Conservation District, off Maui's southwest coast (see chapter 6); and Manele-Hulopoe Marine Life Conservation District, on Lanai (see chapter 11). Be sure to take your snorkel to at least one of these wonderful places.

- **A Garden of the Gods:** Out on Lanai's north shore lies the ultimate rock garden: a rugged, barren, beautiful place full of rocks strewn by volcanic forces and shaped by the elements into an infinite variety of shapes and colors—brilliant reds, oranges, ochers, and yellows. Scientists explain how these boulders got here with phrases like "ongoing posterosional event"; the ancient Hawaiians, however, considered this desolate, windswept place an entirely supernatural phenomenon. Natural badlands or mystical garden? Take a four-wheel-drive trip out here and see for yourself. See chapter 11.

4 The Best Maui Adventures

Branch out while you're in Maui; do something you wouldn't normally do—after all, you're on vacation. Below are a list of adventures we highly recommend. They may be a bit pricey, but these splurges are worth every penny.

- **Try Scuba Diving:** You're in love with snorkeling and the chance to view the underwater world, but it's just not enough—you want to get closer and see even more. Take an introductory scuba dive; after a brief lesson on how to use the diving equipment, you'll plunge into the deep to swim with the tropical fish and go eyeball to eyeball with other marine critters. See chapter 6.

- **Skim over the Ocean in a Kayak:** Glide silently over the water, hearing only the sound of your paddle dipping beneath the surface. This is the way the early Hawaiians traveled along the coastline. You'll be eye-level and up-close-and-personal with the ocean and the coastline, exploring areas you can't get to any other way. Venture out on your own, or go with an experienced guide—either way, you won't be sorry. See chapter 6.

- **Explore a Lava Tube:** Most people come to Maui to get outdoors and soak up some Hawaiian sunshine, but don't miss the opportunity to see firsthand how volcanic islands were formed. With **Maui Cave Adventures** (☎ **808/ 248-7308**), you can hike into the subterranean passages of a huge, extinct lava tube with 40-foot ceilings—an offbeat adventure and a geology lesson you won't soon forget. See chapter 6.
- **See the Stars from Inside a Volcanic Crater:** Driving up to see the sunrise is a trip you'll never forget, but to *really* experience Haleakala, plan to hike in and spend the night. To get a feel for why the ancient Hawaiians considered this one of the most sacred places on the island, you simply have to wander into the heart of the dormant volcano, where you'll find some 27 miles of hiking trails, two camping sites, and three cabins. See chapters 6 and 7.
- **Hike to a Waterfall:** There are waterfalls and there are waterfalls, but the hike to the magnificent 400-foot Waimoku Falls, in Oheo Gulch outside of Hana, is worth the long drive and the uphill hike. The falls are surrounded by lush green ferns and wild orchids, and you can even stop to take a dip in the pool at the top of Makahiku Falls on the way. See chapter 6.
- **Fly over the Remote West Maui Mountains:** Your helicopter streaks low over razor-thin cliffs, then flutters past sparkling waterfalls and down into the canyons and valleys of the inaccessible West Maui Mountains. There's so much beauty to absorb that it all goes by in a rush. You'll never want to stop flying over this spectacular, surreal landscape—and it's the only way to see the dazzling beauty of the prehistoric area of Maui. See chapter 7.
- **Take a Drive on the Wild Side:** Mother Nature's wild side, that is—on the Kahekili Highway on Maui's northeast coast. This back-to-nature experience will take you past ancient Hawaiian heiau (temples); along steep ravines; and by rolling pastures, tumbling waterfalls, exploding blowholes, crashing surf, and jagged lava coastlines. You'll wander through the tiny Hawaiian village of Kahakuloa and around the "head" of Maui to the Marine Life Conservation Area of Honolua-Mokuleia and on to the resort of Kapalua. You'll remember this adventure for years. See chapter 7.
- **Ride a Mule to Kalaupapa:** Even if you have only 1 day to spend on Molokai, spend it on a mule. The **Molokai Mule Ride** (☎ **800/567-7550**) trek from "topside" Molokai to the Kalaupapa National Historic Park (Father Damien's world-famous leper colony) is a once-in-a-lifetime adventure. The cliffs are taller than 300-story skyscrapers—but Buzzy Sproat's trustworthy mules plod up and down the narrow 3-mile trail daily, rain or shine, without ever losing a rider or mount on 26 switchbacks. See chapter 10.

5 The Best of Underwater Maui

An entirely different Maui greets anyone with a face mask, snorkel, and fins. Under the sea, you'll find schools of brilliant tropical fish, green sea turtles, quick-moving game fish, slack-jawed moray eels, and prehistoric-looking coral. It's a kaleidoscope of color and wonder.

- **Black Rock:** This spot, located on the Kaanapali Beach just off the Sheraton Maui Resort, is excellent for beginner snorkelers during the day and for scuba divers at night. Schools of fish congregate at the base of the rock and are so used to snorkelers that they go about their business as if no one were around. If you take the time to look closely at the crannies of the rock, you'll find lion fish in fairly shallow water. At night (when a few outfitters run night dives here), lobsters, Spanish dancers, and eels come out. See chapter 6.

- **Olowalu:** When the wind is blowing and the waves are crashing everywhere else, Olowalu, the small area 5 miles south of Lahaina, can be a scene of total calm—perfect for snorkeling and diving. You'll find a good snorkeling area around mile marker 14. You might have to swim about 50 to 75 feet; when you get to the large field of finger coral in 10 to 15 feet of water, you're there. You'll see a turtle-cleaning station here, where turtles line up to have small cleaner wrasses pick small parasites off. This is also a good spot to see crown-of-thorns starfish, puffer fish, and lots of juvenile fish. See chapters 6 and 7.

- **Hawaiian Reef:** Scuba divers love this area off the Kihei-Wailea coast because it has a good cross-section of topography and marine life typical of Hawaiian waters. Diving to depths of 85 feet, you'll see everything from lava formations and coral reef to sand and rubble, plus a diverse range of both shallow and deep-water creatures. See chapter 6.

- **Third Tank:** Scuba divers looking for a photo opportunity will find it at this artificial reef, located off Makena Beach at 80 feet. This World War II tank acts like a fish magnet: Because it's the only large solid object in the area, any fish or invertebrate looking for a safe home comes here. Surrounding the tank is a cloak of schooling snapper and goat fish just waiting for a photographer with a wide-angle lens. For its small size, the Third Tank is loaded with more marine life per square inch than any site off Maui. See chapter 6.

- **Molokini:** Shaped like a crescent moon that fell from the sky, this islet's shallow concave side serves as a sheltering backstop against sea currents for tiny tropical fish; on its opposite side is a deep-water cliff inhabited by spiny lobsters, moray eels, and white-tipped sharks. Neophyte snorkelers report to the concave side; experienced scuba divers, the other. Either way, the clear water and abundant marine life make this islet off the Makena coast one of Hawaii's most popular dive spots. See chapter 6.

- **Ahihi-Kinau Natural Preserve:** Fishing is strictly *kapu* (forbidden) in Ahihi Bay (at the end of the road in South Maui), and the fish know it; they're everywhere in this series of rocky coves and black-lava tide pools. The black, barren, lunar-like land stands in stark contrast to the green-blue water, which is home to a sparkling mosaic of tropical fish. Scuba divers might want to check out **La Pérouse Pinnacle** in the middle of La Pérouse Bay; clouds of damsel and trigger fish will greet you on the surface. See chapter 6.

6 The Best Golf Courses

- **Kaanapali Courses** (☎ **808/661-3691**): All golfers, from high handicappers to near-pros, will love these two challenging courses. The North Course is a true Robert Trent Jones Jr. design: an abundance of wide bunkers; several long, stretched-out tees; and the largest, most contoured greens on Maui. The South Course is an Arthur Jack Snyder design; although shorter than the North Course, it does require more accuracy on the narrow, hilly fairways. Just like its sibling course, it has a water hazard on its final hole, so don't tally up your score card until the final putt is sunk. See chapter 6.

- **Kapalua Resort Courses** (☎ **877/527-2582**): Kapalua is probably the best nationally known golf resort in Hawaii, due to the PGA Kapalua Mercedes played here each January. The Bay Course and the Village Course are vintage

Arnold Palmer designs; the new Plantation Course is a strong entry from Ben Crenshaw and Bill Coore. All are sited on Maui's windswept northwestern shore, at the rolling foothills of Puu Kukui, the summit of the West Maui Mountains. See chapter 6.

- **Wailea Courses** (☎ **888/328-MAUI**): On the sunbaked south shore of Maui stands Wailea Resort, *the* hot spot for golf in the islands. You'll find great golf at these three resort courses: the Blue course is an Arthur Jack Snyder design, and the Emerald and Gold courses are both by Robert Trent Jones Jr. All boast outstanding views of the Pacific and the mid-Hawaiian Islands. See chapter 6.
- **Makena Courses** (☎ **808/879-3344**): Here you'll find 36 holes by "Mr. Hawaii Golf"—Robert Trent Jones Jr.—at his best. Add to that spectacular views: Molokini islet looms in the background, humpback whales gambol offshore in winter, and the tropical sunsets are spectacular. The South Course has magnificent views (bring your camera) and is kinder to golfers who haven't played for a while. The North Course is more difficult but also more spectacular. The 13th hole, located part way up the mountain, has a view that makes most golfers stop and stare. The next hole is even more memorable: a 200-foot drop between tee and green. See chapter 6.
- **The Lanai Courses:** For quality and seclusion, nothing in Hawaii can touch Lanai's two golf-resort offerings. **The Experience at Koele** (☎ **808/565-4600**), designed by Ted Robinson and Greg Norman, and **The Challenge at Manele** (☎ **808/565-2222**), a wonderful Jack Nicklaus effort with ocean views from every hole, both rate among Hawaii's best courses. Both are tremendous fun to play, with the Experience featuring the par-four 8th hole, which drops some 150 yards from tee to fairway, and the Challenge boasting the par-three 12th, which plays from one cliff side to another over a Pacific inlet—one of the most stunning holes in Hawaii. See chapter 11.

7 The Best Luxury Hotels & Resorts

- **Sheraton Maui** (☎ **800/STAY-ITT**): Offering the best location on Kaanapali Beach, the most recent renovations, and a great "hassle-free" experience, the Sheraton is our pick of Kaanapali hotels. This is the place for travelers who just want to arrive, have everything ready for them, and get on with their vacation. (Sheraton has a "no hassle" check-in: The valet takes you and your luggage straight to your room, which means no time wasted standing in line at registration.) See chapter 4.
- **Ritz-Carlton Kapalua** (☎ **800/262-8440**): With its great location, style, and loads of hospitality, this is the best Ritz anywhere. Situated on the coast below the picturesque West Maui Mountains, this grand, breezy hotel overlooks the Pacific and Molokai across the channel. The natural setting, on an old coastal pineapple plantation, is the picture of tranquillity. The service is legendary; the golf courses are daunting; and the nearby beaches are perfect for snorkeling, diving, and just relaxing. See chapter 4.
- **Four Seasons Resort Wailea** (☎ **800/334-MAUI [6284]**): This is the ultimate beach hotel for latter-day royals, offering excellent cuisine, spacious rooms, gracious service, and Wailea Beach—one of Maui's best gold-sand beaches, right outside the front door. Every room has at least a partial ocean view from a private lanai. The luxury suites are as big as some Honolulu condos, and full of marble and deluxe appointments. See chapter 4.

- **Kea Lani Hotel, Suites and Villas** (☎ 800/659-4100): This all-suite luxury hotel in Wailea has 840-square-foot suites with microwave kitchenette and coffeemaker, living room with high-tech media center and pullout sofa bed (great if you have the kids in tow), a marble wet bar, and a spacious bedroom. The oversized marble bathrooms have separate showers big enough for a party. Your own large lanai off the bedroom and living room overlooks the pools and lawns, with a view that sweeps right down to the white-sand beach. See chapter 4.
- **Manele Bay Hotel** (Lanai; ☎ 800/321-4666): This is Lanai's only hotel at the beach—not just any beach, but overlooking Hulopoe Beach, one of Hawaii's best stretches of golden sand. The U-shaped, Mediterranean-style hotel steps down the hillside to the pool and that great beach, then fans out in oceanfront wings separated by gardens with lush flora, man-made waterfalls, lotus ponds, and streams. Bordered on the other side by golf greens on a hillside of dry land scrub, the hotel is a real oasis against the dry Arizona-like heat of Lanai's arid south coast. See chapter 11.

8 The Best Moderately Priced Accommodations

- **Aston Maui Islander** (☎ 800/367-5226): This wooden complex isn't on the beach, but it is on a quiet side street (a rarity in Lahaina) and within walking distance to restaurants, shops, attractions, and, yes, the beach (just 3 blocks away). The good-sized, comfortable, and quiet units—especially those with kitchenettes—are one of Lahaina's great buys. The entire complex is spread across 10 landscaped acres and includes tennis courts (with night lights until 10pm), pool, sundeck, barbecue, and picnic area. See chapter 4.
- **Lahaina Inn** (☎ 800/669-3444): If the romance of historic Lahaina catches your fancy, a stay here will really complete the experience. Built in 1938 as a general store, it has been restored as a charming, Victorian antique-filled inn right in the heart of town. Downstairs you'll find one of Hawaii's most popular storefront bistros, David Paul's Lahaina Grill. See chapter 4.
- **Plantation Inn** (☎ 800/433-6815): Attention, romantic couples: You need look no further. This charming Lahaina hotel looks like it's been here 100 years or more, but looks can be deceiving. The Victorian-style inn is actually of 1990s vintage—an artful deception. The rooms are romantic to the max, tastefully done with period furniture, hardwood floors, stained glass, ceiling fans, and four-poster canopy beds. The rooms wrap around the large pool and deck; also on site are a spa and an elegant pavilion lounge, where breakfast is served. See chapter 4.
- **Napili Bay** (☎ 888/661-7200): One of Maui's best-kept secrets (until now, that is), this intimate, two-story condo complex is located right on half-mile-long white-sand Napili Beach. The beach here is so beautiful that people staying at the much more expensive resort down the street frequently haul all their beach paraphernalia here to set up for the day. The studio apartments, which are compact but have everything you need, start at just $75—unbelievable! See chapter 4.
- **Maui Coast Hotel** (☎ 800/426-0670): This off-beach midrise is one of the only moderately priced hotels in Kihei (though the Kihei area has lots of affordable condo complexes). One chief advantage of this hotel is its location: It's about a block from Kamaole Beach Park I, with plenty of bars, restaurants, and shopping within walking distance (Jamison's Grill & Bar is next door). A $2.5 million renovation of all the furniture and soft goods in the rooms plus the remodeled public areas (lobby, pool, restaurant, bar) has made this moderate hotel into a luxury resort with a reasonable price tag. See chapter 4.

- **Punahoa Beach Apartments** (☎ 800/564-4380): This small ocean-side Kihei condo complex is hidden on a quiet side street; the grassy lawn out front rolls about 50 feet down to the beach. You'll find great snorkeling just offshore and a popular surfing spot next door, with shopping and restaurants all within walking distance. Every well-decorated unit features a lanai with fabulous ocean views. See chapter 4.

9 The Best Bed-and-Breakfasts

- **Old Wailuku Inn at Ulupono** (☎ 800/305-4899): Located in historic Wailuku, the most charming town in central Maui, this restored, 1924 former plantation manager's home is the place to stay if you're looking for a night in the old Hawaii of the 1920s. The guest rooms are wide and spacious, with exotic ohia-wood floors and traditional Hawaiian quilts. The morning meal is a full gourmet breakfast served on the enclosed back lanai, or on a tray delivered to your room if you prefer. See chapter 4.
- **Guest House** (☎ 800/621-8942): This is one of the great bed-and-breakfast deals in Lahaina: a charming inn offering more amenities than the expensive Kaanapali hotels just down the road. The spacious home features floor-to-ceiling windows, parquet floors, and a large swimming pool. Guest rooms have quiet lanais and romantic hot tubs. Breakfasts are a gourmet affair. See chapter 4.
- **What a Wonderful World B&B** (☎ 808/879-9103): One of Kihei's best B&Bs offers a great central location in town—just a half mile to Kamaole II Beach Park, 5 minutes from Wailea golf courses, and convenient to shopping and restaurants. All rooms boast cooking facilities and private entrances, bathrooms, and phones. A family style breakfast (eggs Benedict, Alaskan waffles, skillet eggs with mushroom sauce, fruit blintzes) is served on the lanai, which has views of white-sand beaches, the West Maui Mountains, and Haleakala. See chapter 4.
- **Makena Landing** (☎ 808/879-6286): This gem, one of the island's best B&Bs, offers a fabulous location (right on the ocean at Makena Landing); incredible views (sunsets to die for); and excellent swimming, snorkeling, diving, and shoreline fishing just outside your bedroom. To complete the picture, add private entrances, full kitchens, and the nicest hosts you'll ever meet. See chapter 4.
- **Olinda Country Cottages & Inn** (☎ 800/932-3435): Breathe the crisp, clean air of Olinda at this charming B&B, located on an 8¹/₂-acre protea farm on the slopes of Haleakala and surrounded by 35,000 acres of ranch lands (with miles of great hiking). The 5,000-square-foot Tudor mansion, refurbished and outfitted with priceless antiques, has large windows with incredible panoramic views of all of Maui. In addition to the guest rooms in the country house, two cozy cottages and a romantic country suite are also available. See chapter 4.
- **Silver Cloud Ranch** (☎ 800/532-1111): Old Hawaii lives on at Silver Cloud Ranch, founded in 1902 by a sailor who jumped ship when he got to Maui. Located in Kula at 2,800 feet, the former working cattle spread offers a commanding view of four islands and features antique-filled guest rooms, quaint studios, and even a romantic honeymooners' cottage. See chapter 4.
- **Kili's Cottage** (☎ 800/262-9912): If you're looking for a quiet getaway in the cool upcountry elevation of Kula, this sweet, three-bedroom cottage with a large lanai, situated on 2 acres, is the perfect place. Not only is the price right for families, but the amenities are numerous: full kitchen, gas barbecue, washer/dryer, views, even toys for the kids. See chapter 4.

- **Huelo Point Flower Farm** (☎ 808/572-1850): Here's a little Eden by the sea in remote Huelo, on a spectacular 300-foot sea cliff near a waterfall stream. The 2-acre estate, which overlooks Waipio Bay in East Maui, contains two guest cottages, a guest house, and a main house, all available for rent. Facilities include a pool and an oceanfront hot tub. Homemade scones, tree-ripened papayas, and fresh-roasted coffee are available to start your day, and you're welcome to pick fruit, vegetables, and flowers from the extensive garden. See chapter 4.
- **Ekena** (☎ 808/248-7047): Situated on 8^1/$_2$ acres in the hills above Hana, this Hawaiian-style wooden pole house, with 360-degree views of the coastline, the ocean, and Hana's verdant rain forest, is perfect for those in search of a quiet, peaceful vacation. Inside, the elegantly furnished home features floor-to-ceiling sliding-glass doors and a fully equipped kitchen; outside, hiking trails into the rain forest start right on the property. Beaches, waterfalls, and pools are mere minutes away. See chapter 4.
- **Hamoa Bay Bungalow** (☎ 808/248-7884): This enchanting retreat sits on 4 verdant acres within walking distance of Hamoa Beach, just outside Hana. The romantic, 600-square-foot, Balinese-style cottage has a full kitchen and hot tub. This very private place is perfect for honeymooners—even the tropical breakfast of fruit, yogurt, and muffins is left out daily to eat at your leisure. See chapter 4.

10 The Best Restaurants

- **A Saigon Cafe** (☎ 808/243-9560): Jennifer Nguyen's unmarked dining room in an odd corner of Wailuku is always packed, a tribute to her clean, crisp Vietnamese cuisine—and the Maui grapevine. Grab a round of rice paper and wrap your own Vietnamese "burrito" of tofu, noodles, and vegetables. Lemongrass shrimp, curries, and the Nhung Dam, the Vietnamese version of fondue, are among the solid hits. See chapter 5.
- **Maui Bake Shop** (☎ 808/242-0064): Guiltless gourmets flock to Wailuku for these European pastries, homemade soups, sandwiches on fresh-baked bread, buttery brioches, and other simple pleasures. The brick oven is one of Maui's oldest, installed in 1935. There are a couple of tables as well as a counter, where regulars pick up their birthday cakes and then try, unsuccessfully, to leave without the white-chocolate macadamia-nut cheesecake, the ultimate dessert. See chapter 5.
- **David Paul's Lahaina Grill** (☎ 808/667-5117): Tirelessly popular and universally appreciated for its consistently high quality, David Paul's is still most folks' favorite Maui eatery. No one seems to tire of his kalua duck, Kona coffee–roasted rack of lamb, or tequila shrimp. We love the Kula salad, eggplant napoleon, and marvelous presentations of fresh Maui produce. The menu changes often, but thank goodness the room doesn't; its pressed-tin ceilings and 1890s decor continue to satisfy. See chapter 5.
- **Gerard's** (☎ 808/661-8939): Proving that French is fabulous, particularly in the land of sushi and sashimi, Gerard Reversade is the Gallic gastronome who delivers ecstasy with every bite. From the rack of lamb to the spinach salad and oyster mushrooms in puff pastry, you will never forget his cooking. Like Piaf on the sound system, his food has integrity and a searing beauty. The fairy lights on the veranda in the balmy outdoor Lahaina setting are the icing on the gâteau. See chapter 5.
- **Hula Grill** (☎ 808/667-6636): You can wander straight off the beach into this Whalers Village restaurant in Kaanapali, where you'll be met by the welcoming

embrace of Peter Merriman's firecracker mahimahi, crab and corn cakes, and, at lunch, down-home sandwiches and salads. During the day, watch sailboats bob on the horizon; at night, flickering torchlight warms the koa walls and Hawaiian canoes. Hula Grill is not intimate—in fact, it's big and bustling—but it's an upbeat place to enjoy top-notch island cookery with a storybook view. See chapter 5.

- **Sansei Seafood Restaurant** (☎ 808/669-6286): Furiously fusion and relentlessly popular, Sansei serves sushi, and then some: hand rolls warm and cold, udon and ramen, and the signature Asian rock-shrimp cake with the oh-so-complex lime chile butter and cilantro pesto. This Kapalua choice is flavor central—simplicity is not the strong suit, so be prepared for some busy tasting. See chapter 5.
- **A Pacific Cafe Kihei** (☎ 808/879-0069): Executive chef George Gomes's pan-seared mahimahi with garlic and sesame, pan-seared scallops, tiger-eye sushi tempura, and roster of daily specials are only part of the reason diners flock to this Kihei magnet. You never know what to expect here, only that it will be good. Curry is king: The red Thai curry soup and curry-fried oysters are too good to miss. See chapter 5.
- **Casanova Italian Restaurant** (☎ 808/572-0220): Yes, we still love Casanova in upcountry Makawao, and for more than one reason: garlic spinach topped with Parmesan and pine nuts, polenta with radicchio, tiramisu, the spaghetti fradiavolo. This is pasta heaven and the center of nightlife on this half of the island. See chapter 5.
- **Café 'O Lei** (☎ 808/573-9065): What Casanova is to Makawao's nightlife, Café 'O Lei is to lunch: reliable, exciting, and tirelessly creative. Makawao merchants come daily for the rainbow of salads (Asian, greens, quinoa) and the breathtaking sandwiches that use fresh Maui vegetables marinated and grilled, served on focaccia with goat cheese. Served on hand-painted ceramic dinnerware, on a narrow terrace cooled by mountain breezes and with wild chickens eyeing your lunch, the meal is a Maui adventure. See chapter 5.
- **Haliimaile General Store** (☎ 808/572-2666): It's an oasis in the middle of the pineapple fields, an erstwhile plantation-style house that has been one of Maui's most popular upcountry haunts for a decade. Bev's boboli topped with crab dip, paniolo ribs, ahi tartare, and the house salad—with Mandarin oranges, toasted walnuts, and blue-cheese crumble—are part of the Haliimaile legend. See chapter 5.
- **Pele's Other Garden** (Lanai; ☎ 808/565-9628): It's a tough call on Lanai, where two formal, expensive restaurants are world-class and not to be missed, but in the end, we give the nod to the everyday good thing—a place where you can return every day of your stay and not get tired of the food, a New York–style deli run by conscientious, dedicated owners. The sandwiches and pizzas are excellent, made of top-quality (and wholesome) ingredients such as free-range turkey and fresh organic produce. It's mostly take-out, but plans call for more tables, and with the people lining up at the counter, they need the extra space—a good sign. See chapter 11.

11 The Best Shops & Galleries

- **Summerhouse** (☎ 808/871-1320): Bright and sassy tropical wear, and the jewelry and accessories to go with them, are a cut above at Kahului's Summerhouse. T-shirts are tailored and in day-to-evening colors, while dresses are good for both the office and a night out. See chapter 8.
- **Bailey House Gift Shop** (☎ 808/244-3920): You can travel Hawaii and peruse its past with the assemblage of made-in-Hawaii items at this museum gift shop

A Night to Remember: Maui's Top Luau

The **Old Lahaina Luau** (☎ 808/667-1998) has always been at the leading edge of cultural entertainment in Hawaii; it's $^1/_3$ entertainment, $^1/_3$ good food, and $^1/_3$ ambience. At its new and more spacious location at the northern end of Lahaina, there's more of everything, particularly those qualities we've come to love: authenticity, intimacy, hospitality, cultural integrity, and sheer romantic beauty. This is Maui's top luau and one of our two favorites in the state. With the expansion of the luau in its 1-acre site just ocean-side of the Lahaina Cannery, what was peerless has become even better.

Local craftspeople display their wares only a few feet from the ocean. Seating is provided on lauhala mats for those wishing to dine as the traditional Hawaiians did, but there are tables for everyone else. Staging has been thoughtfully planned, so that the audience faces the ocean as well as the show; hidden underground dressing rooms allow the dancers dramatic entrances and exits. Thatched buildings, amphitheater seating, and the backdrop of a Lahaina sunset are among the event's unforgettable features.

The luau begins at sunset and features Tahitian and Hawaiian entertainment, including ancient hula, hula from the missionary era, modern hula, and an intelligent narrative on the dance's rocky course of survival into modern times. The sophisticated entertainment is both educational *and* riveting, even for jaded locals, and the top-quality food is as much Pacific Rim as authentically Hawaiian, served from an open-air thatched structure. Dishes include imu-roasted kalua pig, baked mahimahi in Maui onion–cream sauce, guava chicken, teriyaki sirloin steak, lomi salmon, poi, dried fish, poke, Hawaiian sweet potato, sautéed vegetables, seafood salad, and the ultimate taste treat, taro leaves with coconut milk. (No watered-down mai tais, either; these are the real thing.) You won't soon forget the genuine hospitality and enthusiasm of the staff. The cost is $69 for adults, $39 for children, plus tax.

Although the Old Lahaina Luau is an integral part of the Maui experience, they're taking the show beyond Hawaii's shores, to become the first hula troupe ever to have its own float in the 74th annual Macy*s Thanksgiving Day Parade™ in 2000. It will also be the first time that hula has been performed in front of Macy's during the parade.

in Wailuku. Tropical preserves, Hawaiian music, pareus, prints by esteemed Hawaii artists, cookbooks, hatbands, and magnificent wood bowls reflect a discerning standard of selection. Unequaled for Hawaiian treasures on Maui. See chapter 8.

- **Brown-Kobayashi** (☎ 808/242-0804): At this quiet, tasteful, and elegant Asian shop in Wailuku, the selection of antiques and collectibles changes constantly but reflects an unwavering sense of gracious living. There are old and new European and Hawaiian objects, from koa furniture (which disappears fast) to lacquerware, Bakelite jewelry, Peking glass beads, and a few priceless pieces of antique ivory. Every square inch is a treasure trove. See chapter 8.
- **Sig Zane Designs** (☎ 808/249-8997): This Hilo icon didn't skip a beat in winning the hearts of Maui residents when he moved to Wailuku. It's just like the time he moved to the Hilo Bayfront from his first, more obscure location; his

presence brought an infusion of energy to the area and the whole neighborhood came alive. Located on Wailuku's Market Street, his new shop of aloha wear and Hawaiian lifestyle treasures is a boon to historic Wailuku. See chapter 8.

- **Hui No'eau Visual Arts Center** (☎ **808/572-6560**): Half the experience is the center itself, one of Maui's historic treasures: a strikingly designed 1917 *kamaaina* (native-born or old-timer) estate on 9 acres in Makawao; two of Maui's largest hybrid Cook and Norfolk pines; and an art center with classes, exhibitions, and demonstrations. The gift shop is as memorable as the rest of it. You'll find one-of-a-kind works by local artists, from prints to jewelry and pottery. See chapter 8.

- **Ka Piko O Lele** (☎ **808/662-0207**): This strictly Hawaiian gallery in Lahaina has it all: first-rate works in all media, a higher purpose (fund-raising for the restoration of Moku'ula, considered the spiritual and political power center of the old Hawaiian kingdom in Lahaina), and a strong dose of cultural integrity. Books, jewelry, sculptures, specialty food items—the top-quality selection is by Maui artists exclusively. See chapter 8.

- **Village Galleries** (☎ **808/661-4402** in Lahaina, or 808/669-1800 in Kapalua): Maui's oldest galleries have maintained high standards and the respect of a public that is increasingly impatient with clichéd island art. On exhibit are the finest contemporary Maui artists in all media, with a discerning selection of handcrafted jewelry. In Lahaina, the new contemporary gallery has a larger selection of jewelry, ceramics, glass, and gift items, as well as paintings and prints. See chapter 8.

- **Ola's** (☎ **808/573-1334**): Imaginative, bright, and impeccably tasteful, the selection represents the work of more than 100 artists from Hawaii and the mainland. Ola's celebrates craftsmanship at its finest, from studio glass to wood turning, painting, porcelain, fabrics, and jewelry. A good dose of whimsy spices up this Makawao shop; it's a romp through the joys of the creative spirit. See chapter 8.

- **Viewpoints Gallery** (☎ **808/572-5979**): We love this airy, well-designed Makawao gallery and its helpful staff, which complement the fine Maui art: paintings, sculpture, jewelry, prints, woods, and glass. This is Maui's only fine-arts cooperative, showcasing the work of dozens of local artists. See chapter 8.

2

Planning Your Trip: The Basics

by Jeanette Foster

Maui has so many places to explore, things to do, sights to see—where do you start? That's where we come in. In the pages that follow, we've compiled everything you need to know to plan your ideal trip to Maui: information on airlines, seasons, a calendar of events, how to make camping reservations, and much more (even how to get married in the islands).

1 The Island in Brief

CENTRAL MAUI

This flat, often windy corridor between Maui's two volcanoes is where you'll most likely arrive—it's the site of the main airport. It's also home to the majority of the island's population, the heart of the business community, and the local government (courts, cops, and county/state government agencies). You'll find good shopping and dining bargains here, but very little in the way of accommodations.

KAHULUI   This is "Dream City," home to thousands of former sugarcane workers who dreamed of owning their own homes away from the plantations. A couple of small hotels located just 2 miles from the airport are convenient for 1-night stays if you have a late arrival or early departure, but this is not a place to spend your vacation.

WAILUKU   With its faded wooden storefronts, old plantation homes, and shops straight out of the 1940s, Wailuku is like a time capsule. Although most people race through on their way to see the natural beauty of **Iao Valley,** this quaint little town is worth a brief visit, if only to see a real place where real people actually appear to be working at something other than a suntan. This is the county seat, so you'll see men and women in suits on important missions in the tropical heat. Beaches surrounding Wailuku are not great for swimming, but the old town has a spectacular view of Haleakala, a couple of hostels and an excellent historic B&B, great budget restaurants, a tofu factory, some interesting bungalow architecture, a Frank Lloyd Wright building on the outskirts of town, and the always-endearing Bailey House Museum.

WEST MAUI

This is the fabled Maui you see on postcards. Jagged peaks, green valleys, a wilderness full of native species—the majestic West Maui Mountains are the epitome of earthly paradise. The beaches here are some of the islands' best. And it's no secret: This stretch of coastline along Maui's "forehead," from Kapalua to the historic port of Lahaina, is the island's most bustling resort area (with South Maui close behind).

If you want to book into a resort or condo on this coast, first consider which community you'd like to make your base. Starting at the southern end of West Maui and moving northward, the coastal communities are as listed below.

LAHAINA   This old whaling seaport teems with restaurants, T-shirt shops, and a gallery on nearly every block, but there's still lots of real history to be found amid the tourist development. This vintage village is a tame version of its former self, when whalers swaggered ashore in search of women and grog. The town is a great base for visitors: A few old hotels (like the newly restored 1901 Pioneer Inn on the harbor), quaint B&Bs, and a handful of oceanfront condos offer a variety of choices, most within walking distance to the beach as well as town. This is the place to stay if you want to be in the center of things—oodles of restaurants, shops, and nightlife—but note that town is rather congested and doesn't have enough parking.

KAANAPALI   Farther north along the West Maui coast is Hawaii's first master-planned resort. Pricey midrise hotels, which line nearly 3 miles of lovely gold-sand beach, are linked by a landscaped parkway and separated by a jungle of plants. Golf greens wrap around the slope between beachfront and hillside properties. **Whalers Village**—a seaside mall with such fancy names as Tiffany and Louis Vuitton, plus the best little whale museum in Hawaii—and other restaurants are easy to reach on foot along the waterfront walkway or via resort shuttle, which also serves the small West Maui airport just to the north. Shuttles also go to Lahaina, 3 miles to the south, for shopping, dining, entertainment, and boat tours. Kaanapali is popular with convention groups and families— especially those with teenagers, who will like all the action.

FROM HONOKOWAI TO NAPILI   In the building binge of the 1970s, condominiums sprouted along this gorgeous coastline like mushrooms after a rain. Today, these older ocean-side units offer excellent bargains for astute travelers. The great location—along sandy beaches, within minutes of both the Kapalua and the Kaanapali resort areas, and close enough to the goings-on in Lahaina town—makes this area a great place to stay for value-conscious travelers. It feels more peaceful and residential than either Kaanapali or Lahaina.

In **Honokowai** and **Mahinahina,** you'll find mostly older units that tend to be cheaper; there's not much shopping here aside from convenience stores, but you'll have easy access to the shops and restaurants of Kaanapali.

Kahana is a little more upscale than Honokowai and Mahinahina. Most of the condos here are big high-rise types, built more recently than those immediately to the south. You'll find a nice selection of shops and restaurants in the area, and Kapalua West Maui Airport is nearby.

Napili is a much-sought-after area for condo seekers: It's quiet; has great beaches, restaurants, and shops; and is close to Kapalua. Units are generally more expensive here (although we've found a few hidden gems at affordable prices; see the Napili Bay entry in chapter 4).

KAPALUA   North beyond Kaanapali and the shopping centers of Napili and Kahana, the road starts to climb and the vista opens up to fields of silver-green pineapple and manicured golf fairways. Turn down the country lane of Pacific pines toward the sea, and you could only be in Kapalua. It's the very exclusive domain of two gracious, and expensive, hotels, set on one of Hawaii's best gold-sand beaches, next to two bays that are marine-life preserves (with fabulous surfing in winter).

Maui

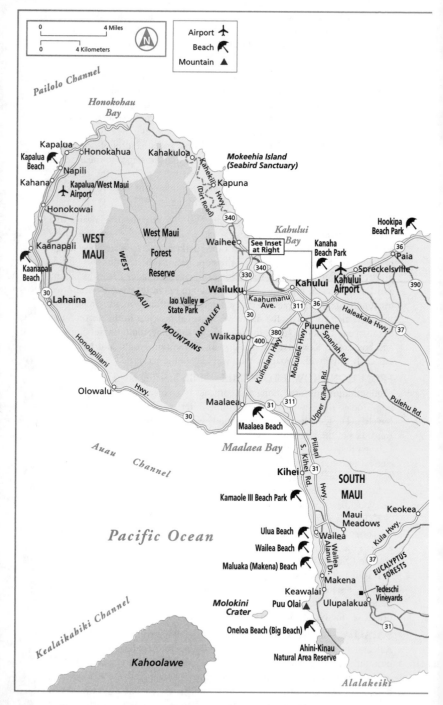

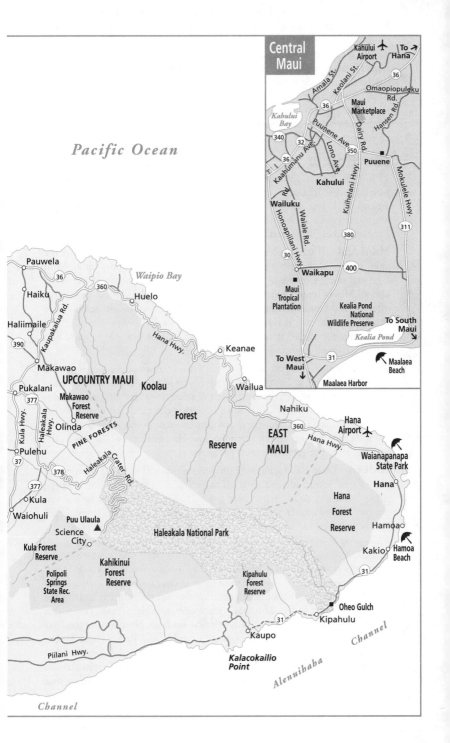

Pacific Ocean

Central Maui

Kahului Airport
To Hana
36
Omaopiopuleku Rd.
Amala St.
Keolani St.
Maui Marketplace
36
Kahului Bay
Puunene Ave.
Hansen Rd.
340
32
350
Kaahumanu Ave.
Lono Ave.
Dairy Rd.
Puuene
Kuihelani Hwy.
Kahului
Mokulele Hwy.
Wailuku
Honoapiilani Hwy.
Waiale Rd.
380
311
30
Waikapu
400
Maui Tropical Plantation
Kealia Pond National Wildlife Preserve
To South Maui
Kealia Pond
To West Maui
31
Maalaea Beach
Maalaea Harbor

Pauwela
36
360
Waipio Bay
Haiku
Huelo
Haliimaile
Kaupakalua Rd.
Hana Hwy.
Keanae
390
Makawao
UPCOUNTRY MAUI
Koolau
Wailua
Pukalani
377
Forest
Nahiku
Hana Airport
Makawao Forest Reserve
360
Olinda
Hana Hwy.
Kula Hwy.
Haleakala Hwy.
PINE FORESTS
Reserve
EAST MAUI
Waianapanapa State Park
Pulehu
37
Haleakala Crater Rd.
Hana
378
Hana
377
Kula
Forest
Waiohuli
Puu Ulaula
Reserve
Hamoa
Science City
Haleakala National Park
Kakio
Hamoa Beach
Kula Forest Reserve
Kahikinui Forest Reserve
Polipoli Springs State Rec. Area
Kipahulu Forest Reserve
31
Oheo Gulch
Kipahulu
Piilani Hwy.
31
Kaupo
Channel
Kalacokailio Point
Alenuihaha
Channel

17

Even if you don't stay here, you're welcome to come and enjoy Kapalua. Both of the fancy hotels provide public parking and beach access. The resort champions innovative environmental programs; it also has an art school, a golf school, three golf courses, historic features, a collection of swanky condos and homes (many available for vacation rental at astronomical prices), and wide-open spaces that include a rain-forest preserve—all open to the general public. Kapalua is a great place to stay put. However, if you plan to "tour" Maui, know that it's a long drive from here to get to many of the island's highlights; you might want to consider a more central place to stay, because even Lahaina is a 15-minute drive away.

SOUTH MAUI

This is the hottest, sunniest, driest, most popular coastline on Maui for sun worshippers—Arizona by the sea. Rain rarely falls, and temperatures stick around 85°F year-round. On former scrubland from Maalaea to Makena, where cacti once grew wild and cows grazed, are now four distinct areas— Maalaea, Kihei, Wailea, and Makena—each appealing to a different crowd.

MAALAEA If the western part of Maui is a head, Maalaea is just under the chin. This windy oceanfront village centers around the small boat harbor (with a general store, a couple of restaurants, and a huge new mall) and the newly opened **Maui Ocean Center,** an aquarium/ocean complex. This quaint region offers several condominium units to choose from, but visitors staying here should be aware that it is often—as in 350 days a year—very windy (all the wind from the Pacific is funneled between the West Maui Mountains and Haleakala, coming out in Maalaea).

KIHEI Kihei is less a proper town than a nearly continuous series of condos and mini-malls lining South Kihei Road. This is Maui's best vacation bargain: Budget travelers flock to the eight sandy beaches along this scalloped, condo-packed, 7-mile stretch of coast. Kihei is neither charming nor quaint, but it does offer sunshine, affordability, and convenience. If you want latte in the morning, fine beaches in the afternoon, and Hawaii Regional Cuisine in the evening, all at budget prices, head to Kihei.

WAILEA Only 2^1/$_2$ decades ago, this was wall-to-wall scrub kiawe trees, but now Wailea is a manicured oasis of multimillion-dollar resort hotels strung along 2 miles of palm-fringed gold coast. It's like Beverly Hills by the sea, except California never had it so good: warm, clear water full of tropical fish; year-round sunshine and clear blue skies; and hedonistic pleasure palaces on 1,500 acres of black-lava shore. Amazing what a billion dollars can do.

This is the playground of the stretch-limo set. The planned resort development—practically a well-heeled town—has a shopping village, three prized golf courses of its own and three more in close range, and a tennis complex. A growing number of large homes sprawl over the upper hillside (some offering excellent bed-and-breakfast units at reasonable prices). The resorts along this fantasy coast are spectacular, to say the least. Next door to the Four Seasons, which is the most elegant, is the Grand Wailea Resort Hotel & Spa, a public display of ego by Tokyo mogul Takeshi Sekiguchi, who dropped $600 million in 1991 to create his own minicity. There's nothing like it in Hawaii, maybe even on the planet. Stop in and take a look—it's so gauche you've gotta see it.

Appealing natural features include the coastal trail, a 3-mile round-trip path along the oceanfront with pleasing views everywhere you look—out to sea and to the neighboring islands, or inland to the broad lawns and gardens of the hotels. The trail's south end borders an extensive garden of native coastal plants, as well as ancient lava-rock house ruins juxtaposed with elegant ocean-front condos. But the chief attractions, of course, are those five outstanding beaches (the best is Wailea).

MAKENA   Suddenly, the road enters raw wilderness. After Wailea's over-manicured development, the thorny landscape is a welcome relief. Although beautiful, this is an end-of-the-road kind of place: It's a long drive from Makena to anywhere on Maui. If you want to tour a lot of the island, you might want to book somewhere else, or resign yourself to spending a lot of time in your car. But if you crave a quiet, relaxing respite, where the biggest trip of the day is from your bed to the gorgeous, pristine beach, Makena is your place.

Beyond Makena you'll discover Haleakala's last lava flow, which ran to the sea in 1790; the bay named for French explorer La Perouse; and a chunky lava trail known as the King's Highway, which leads around Maui's empty south shore past ruins and fish camps. Puu Olai stands like Maui's Diamond Head on the shore, where a sunken crater shelters tropical fish, and empty golden-sand beaches stand at the end of dirt roads.

UPCOUNTRY MAUI

After a few days at the beach, you'll probably take notice of the 10,000-foot mountain in the middle of Maui. The slopes of Haleakala ("House of the Sun") are home to cowboys, farmers, and other country people who wave back as you drive by. They're all up here enjoying the crisp air, emerald pastures, eucalyptus, and flower farms of this tropical Olympus—there's even a misty California redwood grove. You can see a thousand tropical sunsets reflected in the windows of houses old and new, strung along a road that runs like a loose hound from Makawao, an old paniolo-turned–New Age village, to Kula, where the road leads up to the crater and **Haleakala National Park.** The rumpled, two-lane blacktop of Highway 37 narrows on the other side of Tedeschi Winery, where wine grapes and wild elk flourish on the Ulupalakua Ranch, the biggest on Maui. A stay upcountry is usually affordable, a chance to commune with nature, and a nice contrast to the sizzling beaches and busy resorts below.

MAKAWAO   Until recently, this small, two-street upcountry town consisted of little more than a post office, gas station, feed store, bakery, and restaurant/bar serving the cowboys and farmers living in the surrounding community; the hitching posts outside storefronts were really used to tie up horses. As the population of Maui started expanding in the 1970s, a health-food store popped up, followed by boutiques, a chiropractic clinic, and a host of health-conscious restaurants. The result is an eclectic amalgam of old paniolo Hawaii and the baby-boomer trends of transplanted mainlanders. **Hui No'eau Visual Arts Center,** Hawaii's premier arts collective, is definitely worth a peek. The only accommodations here are reasonably priced bed-and-breakfasts, perfect for those who enjoy great views and don't mind slightly chilly nights.

KULA   A feeling of pastoral remoteness prevails in this upcountry commu-nity of old flower farms, humble cottages, and new suburban ranch houses with million-dollar views that take in the ocean, isthmus, West Maui Mountains, Lanai and Kahoolawe off in the distance, and, at night, the string of pearls that lights the gold coast from Maalaea to Puu Olai. Kula sits at a cool 3,000 feet (bring a jacket), just below the cloud line, and from here, a winding road snakes its way up to Haleakala National Park. Everyone here grows something—Maui onions, carnations, orchids, and proteas, that strange-looking blossom that looks like a *Star Trek* prop. The local B&Bs cater to guests seeking cool tropic nights, panoramic views, and a rural upland escape. Here you'll find the true peace and quiet that only rural farming country can offer—yet you're still just 30 to 40 minutes away from the beach and an hour's drive from Lahaina.

EAST MAUI

THE ROAD TO HANA   When old sugar towns die, they usually fade away in rust and red dirt. Not **Paia.** The tangle of electrical, phone, and cable wires hanging overhead symbolizes the town's ability to adapt to the times—it may look messy, but it works. Here, trendy restaurants, eclectic boutiques, and high-tech windsurf shops stand next door to the ma-and-pa grocery, fish market, and storefronts that have been serving customers since the plantation days. Hippies took over in the 1970s; although their macrobiotic restaurants and old-style artists' co-op have made way for Hawaii Regional Cuisine and galleries featuring the works of renowned international artists, Paia still manages to maintain a pleasant vibe of hippiedom. The town's main attraction, though, is **Hookipa Beach Park,** where the wind that roars through the isthmus of Maui brings windsurfers from around the world, who come to fly over the waves on gossamer wings linked to surfboards. A few B&Bs are located just outside Paia in the tiny community of **Kuau.**

Ten minutes down the road from Paia and up the hill from the Hana Highway—the connector road to the entire east side of Maui—sits **Haiku.** Once a pineapple-plantation village, complete with cannery (today a shopping complex), Haiku offers vacation rentals and B&Bs in a quiet, pastoral setting: the perfect base for those who want to get off the beaten path and experience a quieter side of Maui, but don't want to feel too removed (the beach is only 10 minutes away).

About 15 to 20 minutes past Haiku is the largely unknown community of **Huelo.** Every day, thousands of cars whiz by on the road to Hana. But if you take the time to stop, you'll discover a hidden Hawaii, where Mother Nature is still sensual and wild, where ocean waves pummel soaring lava cliffs, and where serenity prevails. Huelo is not for everyone, but if you want the magic of a place still largely untouched by "progress," check into a B&B or vacation rental here.

HANA   Set between an emerald rain forest and the blue Pacific is a village probably best defined by what it lacks: golf courses, shopping malls, and McDonald's. Except for two gas stations and a bank with an ATM, you'll find little of what passes for progress here. Instead, you'll discover fragrant tropical flowers, the sweet taste of backyard bananas and papayas, and the easy calm and unabashed small-town aloha spirit of old Hawaii. What saved "Heavenly" Hana from the inevitable march of progress? The 52-mile **Hana Highway,** which winds around 600 curves and crosses more than 50 one-lane bridges on its way from Kahului. You can go to Hana for the day—it's a 3-hour drive (and a half century away)—but 3 days are better. The tiny town has one hotel, a handful of great B&Bs, and some spectacular vacation rentals (where else can you stay in a tropical cabin in a rain forest?).

2 Visitor Information

For advance information on traveling in Maui, contact the **Maui Visitors Bureau,** 1727 Wili Pa Loop, Wailuku, Maui, HI 96793 (☎ **800/525-MAUI** or 808/244-3530; fax 808/244-1337; www.visitmaui.com). If you want to stop by once you're on the island, here are directions from the airport: Go right on Highway 36 (the Hana Hwy.) to Kaahumanu Avenue (Hwy. 32); follow it past Maui Community College and Wailuku War Memorial Park onto East Main Street in Wailuku; at North Market Street, turn right, and then right again on Mill Street; go left on Imi Kala Street and left again onto Wili Pa Loop.

The **Kaanapali Beach Resort Association** is at 2530 Kekaa Dr., Suite 1-B, Lahaina, HI 96761 (☎ **800/245-9229** or 808/661-3271; fax 808/661-9431; www.maui.net/~kbra).

The state agency responsible for tourism is the **Hawaii Visitors and Convention Bureau** (HVCB), Suite 801, Waikiki Business Plaza, 2270 Kalakaua Ave., Honolulu, HI 96815 (☎ **800/GO-HAWAII** or 808/923-1811; www. gohawaii.com).

If you want information about working and living in Hawaii, contact **The Chamber of Commerce of Hawaii,** 1132 Bishop St., Suite 200, Honolulu, HI 96815 (☎ **808/545-4300**).

INFORMATION ON MAUI'S PARKS

NATIONAL PARKS Both Maui and Molokai have one national park each: **Haleakala National Park,** P.O. Box 369, Makawao, HI 96768 (☎ **808/ 572-4400;** www.nps.gov/hale); and **Kalaupapa National Historical Park,** P.O. Box 2222, Kalaupapa, HI 96742 (☎ **808/567-6802;** www.nps.gov/ kala). For more information, see "Hiking & Camping" in chapters 6 and 10.

STATE PARKS To find out more about state parks on Maui and Molokai, contact the **Hawaii State Department of Land and Natural Resources,** 54 S. High St., Wailuku, HI 96793 (☎ **808/984-8109;** www.hawaii.gov), which provides information on hiking and camping, and will send you free topographic trail maps on request.

COUNTY PARKS For information on Maui County Parks, contact **Maui County Parks and Recreation,** 1580-C Kaahumanu Ave., Wailuku, HI 96793 (☎ **808/270-7230;** www.mauimapp.com).

3 Money

Hawaii pioneered the use of **ATMs** more than 2 decades ago, and now they're everywhere. You'll find them at most banks, in supermarkets, at Long's Drugs, and in some resorts and shopping centers like Whalers Village in Kaanapali. **Cirrus** (☎ **800/424-7787;** www.mastercard.com/atm) and **Plus** (☎ **800/ 843-7587;** www.visa.com/atms) are the two most popular networks; check the back of your ATM card to see which network your bank belongs to (most banks belong to both these days).

With the convenience of ATMs, **traveler's checks** seem less necessary. But you may want to go with traveler's checks if you want to avoid ATM withdrawal charges, or if you still prefer the security they offer—provided you don't mind showing identification every time you want to cash one.

You can get traveler's checks at almost any bank. **American Express** offers checks in denominations of $10, $20, $50, $100, $500, and $1,000. You'll pay a service charge ranging from 1% to 4%. You can also get American Express traveler's checks over the phone by calling ☎ **800/221-7282** or **www. americanexpress.com**. AmEx gold or platinum cardholders can avoid paying the fee by ordering over the telephone; platinum cardholders can also purchase checks fee-free in person at AmEx Travel Service locations (check the Web site for the office nearest you). American Automobile Association members can obtain checks fee-free at most AAA offices.

Visa offers traveler's checks at Citibank branches and other financial institutions nationwide; call ☎ **800/227-6811** to locate the purchase location near you. **MasterCard** also offers traveler's checks through **Thomas Cook Currency Services;** call ☎ **800/223-9920** for a location near you.

Credit cards are accepted all over the island. They're a safe way to carry money and keep track of your expenses. Still, be sure to keep some cash on hand for small expenses, or for that rare occasion when a restaurant or small shop doesn't take plastic.

4 When to Go

Most visitors don't come to Maui when the weather's best in the islands; rather, they come when it's at its worst everywhere else. Thus, the **high season**—when prices are up and resorts are booked to capacity—generally runs from mid-December through March or mid-April. The last 2 weeks of December in particular are the prime time for travel to Maui; if you're planning a holiday trip, make your reservations as early as possible, count on holiday crowds, and expect to pay top dollar for accommodations, car rentals, and airfare. Whale-watching season begins in January, and continues through the rest of winter, sometimes lasting into May.

The **off-seasons,** when the best bargain rates are available, are spring (from mid-April to mid-June) and fall (from September to mid-December)—a paradox, since these are the best seasons in terms of reliably great weather. If you're looking to save money, or if you just want to avoid the crowds, this is the time to visit. Hotel rates tend to be significantly lower during these off-seasons. Airfares also tend to be lower—again, sometimes substantially—and good packages and special deals are often available.

Note: If you plan to come to Maui between the last week in April and mid-May, be sure to book your accommodations, interisland air reservations, and car rental in advance. In Japan, the last week of April is called Golden Week, because three Japanese holidays take place one after the other; the islands are especially busy with Japanese tourists during this time.

Due to the large number of families traveling in **summer** (June through August), you won't get the fantastic bargains of spring and fall. However, you'll still do much better on packages, airfare, and accommodations than you will in the winter months.

THE WEATHER

Because Maui lies at the edge of the tropical zone, it technically has only two seasons, both of them warm. The dry season corresponds to summer, and the rainy season generally runs during the winter from November to March. It rains every day somewhere in the islands at any time of the year, but the rainy season can cause "gray" weather and spoil your tanning opportunities. Fortunately, it seldom rains for more than 3 days straight, and rainy days often just consist of a mix of clouds and sun, with very brief showers.

The **year-round temperature** usually varies no more than 15°F, but it depends on where you are. Maui is like a ship in that it has leeward and windward sides. The **leeward** sides (the west and south) are usually hot and dry, whereas the **windward** sides (east and north) are generally cooler and moist. If you want arid, sunbaked, desert-like weather, go leeward. If you want lush, often wet, junglelike weather, go windward. Your best bets for total year-round sun are the Kihei-Wailea and Lahaina-Kapalua coasts.

Maui is also full of **microclimates,** thanks to its interior valleys, coastal plains, and mountain peaks. If you travel into the mountains, it can change from summer to winter in a matter of hours, because it's cooler the higher up you go. In other words, if the weather doesn't suit you, go to the other side of the island—or head into the hills.

HOLIDAYS

When Hawaii observes holidays, especially those over a long weekend, travel between the islands increases, interisland airline seats are fully booked, rental cars are at a premium, and hotels and restaurants are busier than usual.

Federal, state, and county government offices are closed on all federal holidays: January 1 (New Year's Day); third Monday in January (Martin Luther King Jr. Day); third Monday in February (Presidents' Day, Washington's Birthday); last Monday in May (Memorial Day); July 4 (Independence Day); first Monday in September (Labor Day); second Monday in October (Columbus Day); November 11 (Veterans' Day); fourth Thursday in November (Thanksgiving Day); and December 25 (Christmas).

State and county offices also are closed on local holidays, including Prince Kuhio Day (March 26), honoring the birthday of Hawaii's first delegate to the U.S. Congress; King Kamehameha Day (June 11), a statewide holiday commemorating Kamehameha the Great, who united the islands and ruled from 1795 to 1819; and Admission Day (third Friday in August), which honors Hawaii's admission as the 50th state in the United States on August 21, 1959.

Other special days celebrated by many people in Hawaii but that do not involve the closing of federal, state, or county offices are Chinese New Year (in January or February), Girls' Day (March 3), Buddha's Birthday (April 8), Father Damien's Day (April 15), Boys' Day (May 5), Samoan Flag Day (in August), Aloha Festivals (in September or October), and Pearl Harbor Day (December 7).

Maui, Molokai, & Lanai
Calendar of Events

Please note that, as with any schedule of upcoming events, the following information is subject to change; always confirm the details before you plan your schedule around an event. For a complete and up-to-date list of events throughout Maui, Molokai, and Lanai, point your Internet browser to www.visitmaui.com.

January

- **PGA Kapalua Mercedes Championship,** Kapalua Resort, Maui. Top PGA golfers compete for $1 million. Call ☎ 808/669-0244 for information, or 888/310-4653 for tickets. First weekend after New Year's Day.
- **Maui Pro Surf Meet,** Hookipa Beach and Honolua Bay, Maui. The top professional surfers from around the globe compete for some $40,000 in prize money. Call ☎ 808/575-9264. Mid-January.
- **Hula Bowl Football All-Star Classic,** War Memorial Stadium, Maui. An annual all-star football classic featuring America's top college players. Call ☎ 888/716-HULA or 808/947-4141. Sunday before the Super Bowl.
- ✪ **Ka Molokai Makahiki,** Kaunakakai Town Baseball Park, Mitchell Pauole Center, Kaunakakai, Molokai. Makahiki, a traditional time of peace in ancient Hawaii, is re-created with performances by Hawaiian music groups and hula halau (dance troupes), ancient Hawaiian games and

sporting competitions, and Hawaiian crafts and food. A wonderful chance to experience the Hawaii of yesteryear. Call ☎ **800/800-6367** or 808/553-3876. Late January.

❂ **Chinese New Year,** Lahaina, Maui. Lahaina town rolls out the red carpet to this important event with a traditional lion dance at the historic Wo Hing Temple on Front Street, accompanied by fire works, food booths and a host of activities. Call ☎ **808/667-9175** or e-mail: action@maui.net. January 24 in 2001 (the year of the snake).

• **Celebration of Whales,** Four Seasons Resort, Wailea, Maui. Cetacean experts host discussions, whale-watching excursions, social functions, art exhibits, and entertainment. Call ☎ **808/847-8000.** Last weekend in January.

February

• **Whale Week,** Wailea. The weeklong activities start out with an island-wide whale count, done from shore, facilitated by the Pacific Whale Founda-tions. Volunteers are always welcome. Other events during the week include a parade, regatta and celebrations throughout Wailea. Call ☎ **808/879-8860.** Mid- to late February.

March

• **Whalefest Week,** West Maui. A weeklong celebration with seminars, art exhibits, sailing, snorkeling and diving tours, and numerous events for children to celebrate Maui's best-known winter visitors, the humpback whales. Call ☎ **808/667-9194,** or go to www.visitmaui.com. Usually early March.

• **Maui Marathon,** Kahului to Kaanapali, Maui. For nearly 3 decades, runners have lined up at the Maui Mall before daybreak and headed off for Kaanapali, some 26.2 miles across the island. Call ☎ **808/ 871-6441.** Usually early to mid-March.

• **St. Patrick's Day Parade,** Kaanapali Parkway, Kaanapali Resort, Maui. Everyone becomes Irish for a day when this hometown parade makes its way through the Kaanapali Resort area. Call ☎ **808/661-3271.** March 17.

• **East Maui Taro Festival,** Hana, Maui. Here's your chance to taste taro in its many different preparations, from poi to chips. Also on hand are Hawaiian exhibits, demonstrations, and food booths. Call ☎ **808/ 248-8972.** Usually the last weekend in March.

• **Queen Kaahumanu Festival,** Kaahuman Center, Kahului, Maui. A day of celebration for Kamehameha's first wife, with Hawaiian exhibits, entertainment, games, and storytelling. Call ☎ **808/877-3369.**

• **Prince Kuhio Celebration.** Various festivals throughout the state com-memorate the birth of Jonah Kuhio Kalanianaole, born March 26, 1871. He might have been one of Hawaii's kings, if not for the U.S. overthrow of the monarchy and Hawaii's annexation to the United States. Prince Kuhio was elected to Congress in 1902. Molokai has a daylong event; call ☎ **808/553-5215.** End of March.

• **Molokai Hawaiian Paniolo Heritage Rodeo,** Molokai Rodeo Arena, Maunaloa, Molokai. A celebration of Hawaii's *paniolo* (cowboy) heritage. Call ☎ **808/552-2791.**

April

• **Buddha Day,** Lahaina Jodo Mission, Lahaina, Maui. This historic mis-sion holds a flower-festival pageant honoring the birth of Buddha. Call ☎ **808/661-4303.** Usually the first Sunday in April.

- **Molokai Earth Day,** Mitchell Pauole Center, Kaunakakai, Molokai. A daylong event honoring the natural resources and beauty of the island of Molokai. Call ☎ **808/553-5236.** Mid-April.
- ✪ **Annual Ritz-Carlton Kapalua Celebration of the Arts,** Ritz-Carlton Kapalua, Maui. Contemporary and traditional artists give hands-on lessons. Call ☎ **808/669-6200.** Weekend before Easter.
- **Da Kine Hawaiian Pro Am Windsurfing,** Hookipa Beach Park, Maui. The top competitors from around the globe flock to the world-famous windsurfing beach for this annual competition. Call ☎ **800/827-7466** or 808/575-9264.
- **David Malo Day,** Lahaina. Lahainaluna High School celebrates its famous Hawaiian scholar with a luau and hula performances. Call ☎ **808/662-4000.** Usually mid- to late April.
- ✪ **That Ulupalakua Thing! Maui County Agricultural Trade Show and Sampling,** Ulupalakua Ranch and Tedeschi Winery, Ulupalakua, Maui. The name might be long and cumbersome, but this event is hot, hot, hot. Local product exhibits and sampling, food booths, and live entertainment. Call ☎ **808/875-0457** or 808/878-1266 for this year's schedule.
- **Banyan Tree Birthday Party,** Lahaina. Come celebrate the 128th birthday of Lahaina's famous Banyan Tree with a weekend of activities. Call ☎ **808/667-9194.** Usually the end of April.

May

- ✪ **Annual Lei Day Celebration.** May Day is Lei Day in Hawaii, celebrated with lei-making contests, pageantry, arts and crafts, and concerts throughout the islands. Call ☎ **808/879-1922** for Maui events. May 1.
- **Molokai Kayak Challenge,** Molokai to Oahu. Kayakers race 38 grueling miles from Kaluakoi Resort on Molokai to Hawaii Kai's Koko Marina. Call ☎ **808/537-8660.** Mid-May.
- ✪ **Molokai Ka Hula Piko,** Papohaku Beach Park, Kaluakoi, Molokai. A daylong celebration of the creation of hula on the island where it was born, featuring performances by hula halau, musicians, and singers from across the state. See demonstrations of Hawaiian crafts, including quilting, woodworking, feather work, and deer-horn scrimshaw. Hawaiian foods, including Molokai specialties, are also available. Call ☎ **800/800-6367** or 808/553-3876. Third weekend in May.
- **Outrigger Canoe Season,** all islands. From May to September, nearly every weekend, canoe paddlers across the state participate in outrigger canoe races. Call ☎ **808/961-5797.**
- **In Celebration of Canoes,** Front Street, Lahaina, Maui. This street festival features daylong events with food booths, music, parades, cultural demonstrations, and more, all in celebration of the Hawaiian canoe. Call ☎ **808/667-9194.**
- **Maui Music Festival,** Kapalua Resort, Maui. Weekend of events featuring the top musicians in the state. Call ☎ **800/628-4767** or 808/661-3271.

June

- **Maui Film Festival,** Wailea. Premieres and special screenings at this week-long film festival, where traditional Hawaiian storytelling, chanting, and hula precede each screening every night. Call ☎ **808/579-9996.** Usually the first week in June.
- ✪ **King Kamehameha Celebration,** statewide. It's a state holiday with a massive floral parade, *hoolaulea* (party), and much more. Call ☎ **808/ 661-5304** for Maui events, or **808/552-2791** for Molokai events. First weekend in June.

Ongoing Events

Every Friday night from 7 to 10pm, as part of **Friday Night is Art Night** in Lahaina, the town's galleries open their doors for special shows, demonstrations, and refreshments; there are even strolling musicians wandering the streets.

On the first and third weekends of the month, Hawaiian artists sell and share culture, arts, and crafts under the famous landmark **Banyan Tree** in Lahaina. On the other weekends, the Lahaina Arts Society has an exhibit and sale of various works of art in the same place.

Every Wednesday and Friday, at 4:30 and 7:30pm, outstanding contemporary and art films are shown at the Maui Arts & Culture Center in Kahului, as part of the **Maui Film Festival**.

You don't have to spend a good chunk of change and order two drinks to experience the Hawaiian art of hula. There are **free hula performances** every week. In **Lahaina:** every Sunday at 1pm in the Lahaina Cannery Mall; and every Wednesday at 2pm, and every Friday at 2 and 6pm at the Lahaina Center. In **Kaanapali:** Every Monday, Wednesday, and Friday at 7pm at the Whalers Village. In **Kapalua:** Every Thursday at 10am at the Kapalua Shops.

It's also fun to check out Maui's **outdoor markets,** where you can find good deals on gifts to bring home, try the local produce, and meet the locals. Every Saturday from 7am to 1pm, the **Maui Swap Meet** is held next to the Post Office on Puunene Avenue in Kahului. This is Maui's largest outdoor market, filled with everything from produce to Hawaiian art. The **Hana Farmer's and Crafter's Market,** Hasegawa Service Station, Hana Highway, Hana, is a chance to meet local artists and farmers every Thursday from 9:30am to 3:30pm. The parking lot of the **Kaahumanu Shopping Center,** Kaahumanu Avenue, Kahului, is filled with bargains every Friday from 9am to 5pm. At the **Kahului Shopping Center,** also on Kaahumanu Avenue in Kahului, you'll get great deals on produce every Wednesday morning from 7am to noon. Arrive early to get the best bargains at the **Suda Store,** on Kihei Road in Kihei, which hosts an outdoor market every Monday, Wednesday, and Friday from 1:30 to 5:30pm. On Lower Honoapiilani Road in **Honokowai,** you'll find a great farmers market and other items for sale every Monday, Wednesday, and Friday from 7 to 11am.

- **Cowhorse Classic,** Molokai Rodeo Arena, Maunaloa, Molokai. The island's cowboys celebrate Hawaii's paniolo heritage. Call ☎ **808/552-2791.**
- **Bankoh Slack Key Guitar Festival,** Maui Arts & Cultural Center, Kahului. Free concert featuring Hawaii's top guitarists. Call ☎ **808/242-7469.**

July

✪ **Pineapple Festival,** Lanai City, Lanai. Some of Hawaii's best musicians participate in Lanai's liveliest event, celebrating the golden fruit with everything from fishing tournaments to pineapple-cooking contests, food and craft booths, water activities, entertainment, and demonstrations by well-known chefs. Call ☎ **808/565-7600.** Held in July or August.

- **Bon Dance and Lantern Ceremony,** Lahaina. This colorful Buddhist ceremony honors the souls of the dead. Call ☎ **808/661-4304.** Usually early July.
- **Fourth of July,** Kaanapali. A grand ole celebration with live music, children's activities and fireworks. Call ☎ **808/661-3271.**
- **Polo Season,** Olinda Polo Field, Makawao, Maui. Polo matches featuring Hawaii's top players, often joined by famous international players. Call ☎ **808/572-7326.** Most weekends throughout the summer.
- **Makawao Parade and Rodeo,** Makawao, Maui. The annual parade and rodeo event has been taking place in this upcountry cowboy town for generations. Call ☎ **808/572-9565** or 808/572-2076 for this year's date. It's usually held on the weekend closest to July 4.
- ✪ **Hoolaulea O Ke Kai—A Molokai Sea Fest,** Kaunakakai, Molokai. Canoe races, windsurfing competition, and Hawaiian music and food at this daylong celebration of the sea. Call ☎ **800/800-6367** or 808/553-3876 for this year's date and schedule.
- ✪ **Kapalua Wine Symposium,** Kapalua, Maui. Famous wine and food experts and oenophiles gather at the Ritz-Carlton and Kapalua Bay hotels for formal tastings, panel discussions, and samplings of new releases. Call ☎ **800/669-0244** for this year's dates and schedule.

August

- **Maui Onion Festival,** Whalers Village, Kaanapali, Maui. Everything you ever wanted to know about the sweetest onions in the world. Food, entertainment, tasting, and Maui Onion Cook-Off. Call ☎ **808/661-4567.** First week in August.
- **Admission Day,** all islands. Hawaii became the 50th state on August 21, 1959, so the state takes a holiday; all state-related facilities will be closed. Third Friday in August.
- **Molokai Museum and Cultural Center Annual Music Festival,** Meyer Sugar Mill and Museum Grounds, Kalae, Molokai. An outdoor music festival featuring top Hawaiian musicians. Call ☎ **808/567-6436.** Saturday following Admissions Day (which is the third Friday in August).

September

- ✪ **Aloha Festivals,** various locations statewide. Parades and other events celebrate Hawaiian culture. Call ☎ **800/852-7690,** or 808/545-1771 for a schedule of events.
- ✪ **Great Molokai Mule Drag and Hoolaulea,** Kaunakakai, Molokai. As part of the Aloha Festivals celebration on Molokai, the local residents honor the importance of the mule to the island's heritage with a mule race (which is sometimes a mule-dragging contest) down the main street of Kaunakakai. Call ☎ **800/800-6367** or 808/553-3876.
- **Maui Writer's Conference,** Grand Wailea Resort, Wailea, Maui. Workshops, lectures, and panel discussions with writers, agents, and publishers. Call ☎ **808/879-0061.** Labor Day Weekend.
- ✪ **Earth Maui,** Kapalua Resort, Kapalua, Maui. A weeklong series of events to encourage appreciation of Maui's natural environment, plus hiking and snorkeling trips. Call ☎ **800/527-2582** or 808/669-0244 for this year's schedule of events.
- **A Taste of Lahaina,** Lahaina Civic Center, Maui. Some 20,000 people show up to sample 35 signature entrees of Maui's premier chefs during the weekend-long festival, which includes cooking demonstrations, wine tastings, and live entertainment. The weekend kicks off with "Maui

Chefs Presents" on Friday, an elegant dinner by Maui's top chefs. Call ☎ 808/667-9175 or send an e-mail to action@maui.net. Usually mid-September.

- **Hana Relays,** Hana Highway. Hundreds of runners, in relay teams, will crowd the Hana Highway from Kahalui to Hana (you might want to avoid the road this day). Call ☎ **808/871-6441.** Usually the third Saturday in September.
- **Na Wahine O Ke Kai,** Molokai to Waikiki. A women's 40.8-mile outrigger canoe race from Molokai to Oahu. Departs from Hale O Lono, Molokai, and finishes at Duke Kahanamoku Beach, Hilton Hawaiian Village, Waikiki. Call ☎ **808/262-7567.** End of September.
- **Tour of Champions Mountain Bike Race,** Molokai Ranch, Molokai. Invited elite mountain-bike racers flock to Molokai to compete for some $100,000 in prize money in this prestigious race. Call ☎ **808/552-2791.**

October

- **Run to the Sun,** Paia to Haleakala, Maui. The world's top ultramarathoners make the journey from sea level to the top of 10,000-foot Haleakala, some 37 miles. Call ☎ **808/871-6441.**
- **Maui County Fair,** War Memorial Complex, Wailuku, Maui. The oldest county fair in Hawaii features a parade, amusement rides, live entertainment, and exhibits. Call ☎ **808/242-0909.** Early October.
- ✪ **Aloha Classic World Wavesailing Championship,** Hookipa Beach, Maui. The top windsurfers in the world gather for this final event in the Pro Boardsailing World Tour. If you're on Maui, don't miss it—it's spectacular to watch. Call ☎ **808/575-9151.**
- **Molokai Hoe,** Molokai to Oahu. The season's biggest canoe race, this men's 40.8-mile outrigger contest crosses the channel from Molokai to finish at Fort DeRussy Beach in Waikiki. Call ☎ **808/261-6615.** Mid-October.
- ✪ **Halloween in Lahaina,** Maui. There's Carnival in Rio, Mardi Gras in New Orleans, and Halloween in Lahaina. Come to this giant costume party (some 20,000 people show up) on the streets of Lahaina; Front Street is closed off for the party. It'll be the greatest memory of your trip. Call ☎ **808/667-9175.**

November

- **Hawaii International Film Festival,** various locations on Maui. A cinema festival with a cross-cultural spin, featuring filmmakers from Asia, the Pacific Islands, and the United States. Call ☎ **800/752-8193** or 808/528-FILM or point your Web browser to www.hiff.org. Mid-November.
- **Molokai Ranch Rodeo and Great Molokai Stew Cookoff,** Molokai Rodeo Arena, Maunaloa, Molokai. The island's cowboys celebrate Hawaii's paniolo heritage. Call ☎ **800/800-6367** or 808/552-2791.
- **Festival of Art & Flowers,** Lahaina, Maui. Look for cut flower displays, floral arrangements, demonstrations, lei-making contests, art exhibits, and entertainment. Call ☎ **808/667-9175** or e-mail action@maui.net. Weekend before Thanksgiving.
- **Maui Invitational Basketball Tournament,** Lahaina Civic Center, Maui. Top college teams vie in this annual pre-season tournament. Call ☎ **312/755-3504.** Usually held around Thanksgiving.
- **Kapalua Betsy Nagelsen Pro Am Tennis Invitational,** Kapalua Tennis Garden, Maui. Top women pro tennis players compete in this prestigious event. Call ☎ **808/669-5677.**

- **Old-Fashioned Holiday Celebration,** Lahaina, Maui. The Banyan Tree Park on Front Street hosts a day of Christmas carolers, Santa Claus, live music and entertainment, a crafts fair, baked goods, and activities for children. Call ☎ **808/667-9175** or e-mail action@maui.net. Second Saturday in December.
- **Festival of Lights,** island-wide. Festivities include parades and tree-lighting ceremonies. Call ☎ **808/667-9175** on Maui or 808/567-6361 on Molokai. Early December.
- ✪ **First Night,** Maui Arts and Cultural Center, Maui. Hawaii's largest festival of arts and entertainment takes place on three different islands. For 12 hours, musicians, dancers, actors, jugglers, magicians, and mimes perform, food is available, and fireworks bring in the New Year. Alcohol-free. Call ☎ **808/242-7469.** December 31.

5 What to Pack

Maui is very informal: You'll get by with shorts, T-shirts, and sneakers at most attractions and restaurants; a casual dress or a polo shirt and khakis is fine even in the most expensive places. Dinner jackets are required only at a very few resorts, such as the Lodge at Koele on Lanai, and they'll cordially provide a jacket if you don't bring your own. Don't forget a long-sleeved cover-up (to throw on at the beach when you've had enough sun for the day), rubber water shoes or flip-flops, and hiking shoes and several pairs of good socks if you plan to do any hiking. If you have them, you might also bring binoculars for whale-watching.

Be sure to bring **sun protection:** sunglasses, strong sunscreen, a light hat (like a baseball cap or a sun visor), and a canteen or water bottle if you'll be hiking—you'll easily dehydrate on the trail in the tropic heat, so figure on carrying 2 liters of water per day on any hike. Campers should bring water purification tablets or devices. Also see "Staying Healthy," below.

Don't bother overstuffing your suitcase with 2 whole weeks' worth of shorts and T-shirts: Maui has **laundry facilities** everywhere. If your accommodation doesn't have a washer and dryer or laundry service, there will most likely be a laundry nearby. The only exception to this is Hana; the tiny town has no Laundromat, so either check with the place you're staying beforehand, or do a load of laundry before you arrive.

One last thing: **It really can get cold on Maui.** If you plan to see the sunrise from the top of Haleakala, bring a warm jacket—even in summer, when it's 80°F at the beach, 40°F upcountry temperatures are not uncommon. It's always a good idea to bring long pants and a windbreaker, sweater, or light jacket. And be sure to bring along rain gear if you'll be in Maui from November to March.

6 Health & Insurance

STAYING HEALTHY

Maui is one of the healthiest places in the world to visit. People who live here have a longer life expectancy than anywhere else in the United States (74 years for men and 79 years for women). However, you should be aware of a few natural hazards so that, if necessary, you can take the proper steps to prevent them from blooming into full-scale problems.

ON LAND

As in any tropical climate, there are lots of bugs in Maui. Most of them won't harm you; however, three insects—mosquitoes, centipedes, and scorpions—do sting, and they can cause anything from mild annoyance to severe swelling and pain.

MOSQUITOES   These pesky insects aren't native to Hawaii, but arrived as larvae stowed away in the water barrels on the ship *Wellington* in 1826. There's not a whole lot you can do about them, except to apply commercial repellent to keep them off you, or burn mosquito punk or citronella candles to keep them out of your area. If they've bitten you, head to the drugstore for sting-stopping ointments (antihistamine cremes like Benadryl or homeopathic creams like Sting Stop or Florasone); they'll ease the itching and swelling. Most bites disappear in anywhere from a few hours to a few days.

CENTIPEDES   These segmented insects with a jillion legs come in two varieties: 6- to 8-inch-long brown ones and the smaller 2- to 3-inch-long blue guys; both can really pack a wallop with their sting. Centipedes are generally found in damp, wet places, like under wood piles or compost heaps; wearing closed-toe shoes can help prevent stings if you accidentally unearth a centipede. If you're stung, the reaction can range from something similar to a mild bee sting to severe pain; apply ice at once to prevent swelling. See a doctor if you experience extreme pain, swelling, nausea, or any other severe reaction.

SCORPIONS   Rarely seen, scorpions are found in arid, warm regions; their stings can be serious. Campers in dry areas should always check their boots before putting them on, and shake out sleeping bags and bed rolls. Symptoms of a scorpion sting include shortness of breath, hives, swelling, and nausea. In the unlikely event that you're stung, apply diluted household ammonia and cold compresses to the area of the sting and seek medical attention immediately.

Hiking Safety

In addition to taking the appropriate cautions regarding Maui's bug population (see above), hikers should always let someone know where they're heading, when they're going, and when they plan to return; too many hikers get lost on Maui because they don't inform others of their basic plans.

Always check weather conditions with the **National Weather Service** (☎ 808/877-5111) before you go. Hike with a pal, never alone. Wear hiking boots, a sun hat, clothes to protect you from the sun and from getting scratches, and high-SPF sunscreen on all exposed areas of skin. Take water. Stay on the trail. Watch your step. It's easy to slip off precipitous trails and into steep canyons, with often disastrous, even fatal, results. Incapacitated hikers are often plucked to safety by fire and rescue squads, who must use helicopters to gain access to remote sites. Many experienced hikers and boaters today pack a cellular phone in case of emergency; just dial ☎ 911.

Vog

The volcanic haze dubbed "vog" is caused by gases released when molten lava—from the continuous eruption of the volcano on the flank of Kilauea on the Big Island—pours into the ocean. This hazy air, which looks like urban smog, limits viewing from scenic vistas and wreaks havoc with photographers trying to get clear panoramic shots. Some people claim that long-term exposure to vog has even caused bronchial ailments.

There actually is a "vog" season in Hawaii: the fall and winter months, when the trade winds that blow the fumes out to sea die down. The vog is felt not only on the Big Island, but also as far away as Maui and Oahu.

OCEAN SAFETY

Because most people coming to Maui are unfamiliar with the ocean environment, they're often unaware of the natural hazards it holds. But with just a few precautions, your ocean experience can be a safe and happy one. An excellent book to get is *All Stings Considered: First Aid and Medical Treatment of Hawaii's Marine Injuries* (University of Hawaii Press, 1997), by Craig Thomas (an emergency-medicine doctor) and Susan Scott (a registered nurse). These avid water people have put together the authoritative book on first aid for Hawaii's marine injuries.

SEASICKNESS   The waters off Maui can range from calm as glass to downright frightening (in storm conditions), and they usually fall somewhere in between; in general, expect rougher conditions in winter than in summer.

Some 90% of the population tends toward seasickness. If you've never been out on a boat or if you've gotten seasick in the past, you might want to heed the following suggestions:

- The day before you go out on the boat, avoid alcohol; caffeine; citrus and other acidic juices; and greasy, spicy, or hard-to-digest foods.
- Get a good night's sleep the night before.
- Take or use whatever seasickness prevention works best for you— medication, an acupressure wristband, gingerroot tea or capsules, or any combination—*before* you board; once you set sail, it's generally too late.
- Once you're on the water, stay as low and as near the center of the boat as possible. Avoid the fumes (especially if it's a diesel boat); stay out in the fresh air and watch the horizon. Do not read.
- If you start to feel queasy, drink clear fluids like water, and eat something bland, such as a soda cracker.

STINGS   The most common stings in Hawaii come from jellyfish, particularly Portuguese man-of-war and box jellyfish. Since the poisons they inject are very different, you need to treat each sting differently.

A bluish-purple floating bubble with a long tail, the **Portuguese man-of-war** causes thousands of stings a year. Stings, although painful and a nuisance, are rarely harmful; fewer than one in a thousand requires medical treatment. The best prevention is to watch for these floating bubbles as you snorkel (look for the hanging tentacles below the surface). Get out of the water if anyone near you spots these jellyfish.

Reactions to stings range from mild burning and redness to severe welts and blisters. *All Stings Considered* recommends the following treatment: First, pick off any visible tentacles with a gloved hand, a stick, or anything handy; rinse the sting with salt or fresh water; and apply ice to prevent swelling and to help control pain.

Hawaii folklore advises using vinegar, meat tenderizer, baking soda, papain, or alcohol, or even urinating on the wound. Studies have shown that these remedies may actually cause further damage. Most Portuguese man-of-war stings will disappear by themselves within 15 to 20 minutes if you do nothing to treat them. Still, be sure to see a doctor if pain persists or if a rash or other symptoms develop.

Box jellyfish, transparent, square-shaped bell jellyfish, are nearly impossible to see in the water. Fortunately, they seem to follow a monthly cycle: 8 to 10 days after the full moon, they appear in the waters on the leeward side of the island and hang around for about 3 days. Also, they seem to sting more in the morning hours, when they're on or near the surface. The best prevention is to get out of the water.

Stings range from no visible marks to red, hive-like welts, blisters, and pain (a burning sensation) lasting from 10 minutes to 8 hours. *All Stings Considered* recommends the following course of treatment: First, pour regular household vinegar on the sting; this may not relieve the pain, but it will stop additional burning. Do not rub the area. Pick off any vinegar-soaked tentacles with a stick. For pain, apply an ice pack. Seek additional medical treatment if you experience shortness of breath, weakness, palpitations, muscle cramps, or any other severe symptoms. Again, ignore any folk remedies. Most box jellyfish stings disappear by themselves without treatment.

PUNCTURES Most sea-related punctures come from stepping on or brushing against the needlelike spines of sea urchins (known locally as *wana*). Be careful when you're in the water; don't put your foot down (even if you have booties or fins on) if you cannot clearly see the bottom. Waves can push you into wana in a surge zone in shallow water (the wana's spines can even puncture a wet suit).

A sea urchin sting can result in burning, aching, swelling, and discoloration (black or purple) around the area where the spines have entered your skin. The best thing to do is to pull out any protruding spines. The body will absorb the spines within 24 hours to 3 weeks, or the remainder of the spines will work themselves out. Again, contrary to popular wisdom, do not urinate or pour vinegar on the embedded spines—this will not help.

CUTS All cuts obtained in the marine environment must be taken seriously, because the high level of bacteria present can quickly cause the cut to become infected. The most common cuts are from **coral.** Contrary to popular belief, coral cannot grow inside your body. However, bacteria can—and very often does—grow inside a cut. The best way to prevent cuts is to wear a wet suit, gloves, and reef shoes. Never, under any circumstances, should you touch a coral head; not only can you get cut, but you can also damage a living organism that took decades to grow.

The symptoms of a coral cut can range from a slight scratch to severe welts and blisters. *All Stings Considered* recommends gently pulling the edges of the skin open and removing any embedded coral or grains of sand with tweezers, or rinsing well with fresh water. Next, scrub the cut well with fresh water. Never use ocean water to clean a cut. If the wound is bleeding, press a clean cloth against it until it stops. If bleeding continues, or the edges of the injury are jagged or gaping, seek medical treatment.

TRAVEL INSURANCE

There are three kinds of travel insurance: trip-cancellation, medical, and lost-luggage coverage. **Trip-cancellation insurance** is a good idea if you have paid a large portion of your vacation expenses up front (say, by purchasing a package deal). The other two types of insurance, however, don't make sense for most travelers. Rule number one: Check your existing policies before you buy any additional coverage.

Your existing health insurance should cover you if you get sick while on vacation—though if you belong to an HMO, you should check to see whether you are fully covered when away from home. For independent travel health-insurance providers, see below.

Don't Get Burned: Smart Tanning Tips

Tanning just ain't what it used to be. Hawaii's Caucasian population has a higher incidence of deadly skin cancer, malignant melanoma, than anywhere else in the United States. But none of us are safe from the sun's harmful rays: People of all skin types and races can burn when exposed to the sun too long.

To ensure that your vacation won't be ruined by a painful, throbbing sunburn, here are some helpful tips on how to tan safely and painlessly:

- **Wear a strong sunscreen at all times, and use lots of it.** Use a sunscreen with a sun-protection factor (SPF) of 15 or higher; people with a light complexion should use 30. Apply sunscreen as soon as you get out of the shower in the morning, and at least 30 minutes before you're exposed to the sun. No matter what the label says—even if the sunscreen is waterproof—reapply it every 2 hours and immediately after swimming.

- **Read the labels.** To avoid developing allergies to sunscreens, avoid those that contain para-aminobenzoic acid (PABA). Look for a sunscreen with zinc oxide, talc, or titanium dioxide, which reduce the risk of developing skin allergies. For the best protection from UVA rays (which can cause wrinkles and premature aging), check the label for zinc oxide, benzophenone, oxybenzone, sulisobenzone, titanium dioxide, or avobenzone (also known as Parsol 1789).

- **Wear a hat and sunglasses.** And make sure that your sunglasses have UV filters.

- **Avoid being in the sun between 9am and 3pm.** Use extra caution during these peak hours. Remember that a beach umbrella is not protection enough from the sun's harmful UV rays; in fact, with the reflection from the water, the sand, and even the sidewalk, some 85% of the ultraviolet rays are still bombarding you.

- **Protect children from the sun, and keep infants out of the sun altogether.** Infants under 6 months should not be in the sun at all. Older babies need zinc oxide to protect their fragile skin, and children should be slathered with sunscreen every hour. The burns that children get today predict what their future will be with skin cancer tomorrow.

If you start to turn red, **get out of the sun.** Contrary to popular belief, you don't have to turn red to tan; if your skin is red, it's burned—and that's serious. The redness from a burn may not show until 2 to 8 hours after you get out of the sun, and the full force of that burn may not appear for 24 to 36 hours. During that time, you can look forward to pain, itching, and peeling. The best **remedy** for a sunburn is to get out of the sun immediately and stay out of the sun until all the redness is gone. Aloe vera (straight from the plant or from a commercial preparation), cool compresses, cold baths, and anesthetic benzocaine may also help with the pain of sunburn.

If you've decided to get a head start on your tan by using a self-tanning lotion that dyes your skin a darker shade, remember that this will not protect you from the sun. You'll still need to generously apply sunscreen when you go out.

Your homeowner's or renter's insurance should cover stolen luggage. The airlines are responsible for losses up to $2,500 on domestic flights if they lose your luggage (finally upped in early 2000 from the old 1984 limit of $1,250); if you plan to carry anything more valuable than that, keep it in your carry-on bag.

The differences between **travel assistance** and insurance are often blurred, but in general, the former offers on-the-spot assistance and 24-hour hot lines (mostly oriented toward medical problems), while the latter reimburses you for travel problems (medical, travel, or otherwise) after you have filed the paperwork. The coverage you should consider will depend on how much protection is already contained in your existing health insurance or other policies. Some credit- and charge-card companies may insure you against travel accidents if you buy plane, train, or bus tickets with their cards. Before purchasing additional insurance, read your policies and agreements over carefully. Call your insurers or credit-card companies if you have any questions.

If you do require additional insurance, try one of the companies listed below. But don't pay for more than you need. If you need only trip-cancellation insurance, don't purchase coverage for lost or stolen property, which should be covered by your homeowner's or renter's policy. Trip-cancellation insurance costs approximately 6% to 8% of the total value of your vacation.

Among the reputable issuers of travel insurance are **Access America** (☎ **800/ 284-8300;** www.accessamerica.com); **Travel Guard International** (☎ **800/ 826-1300;** www.travel-guard.com); and **Travelex Insurance Services** (☎ **888/457-4602;** www.travelex-insurance.com).

7 Tips for Travelers with Special Needs

FOR TRAVELERS WITH DISABILITIES

Travelers with disabilities are made to feel very welcome in Maui. Hotels are usually equipped with wheelchair-accessible rooms, and tour companies provide many special services. The **Hawaii Center for Independent Living,** 414 Kauwili St., Suite 102, Honolulu, HI 96817 (☎ **808/522-5400;** fax 808/ 586-8129; www.hawaii.gov/health/cpd; e-mail: cpdppp@aloha.net), can provide information and send you a copy of the *Aloha Guide to Accessibility* ($15).

A World of Options is a 658-page book of resources for travelers with disabilities. It costs $35 and is available from **Mobility International USA,** P.O. Box 10767, Eugene, OR 97440 (☎ **541/343-1284,** voice and TDD; www.miusa.org). For information on travel destinations, services, accommodations, and transportation contact: **Access/Abilities,** P.O. Box 458, Mill Valley, CA 94942 (☎ **415/388-3250;** www.accessabil.com).

Travel services for travelers with disabilities include: **Enable Travel Services,** New Frontiers, 7545 S. University Blvd., Littleton, CO 80122, which plans trips for travelers with disabilities; the **Society for the Advancement of Travel for the Handicapped,** 347 Fifth Ave., Suite 610, NY, NY 10016 (☎ **212/ 447-7284;** e-mail: sathtravel@aol.com), a nonprofit educational organization that serves as a central clearinghouse for the exchange of information on travel facilities for people with disabilities; and **Travelin' Talk Network,** P.O. Box 3534, Clarksville, TN 37043-6670 (☎ **615/552-6670**), which has a directory of members willing to share their knowledge of certain areas with travelers with disabilities.

Publications for travelers with disabilities include **Annual Directory of Travel Agencies for the Disabled,** Twin Peaks Press, P.O. Box 129, Vancouver,

WA 98666-0129 (☎ **360/694-2462**); **Travel Resources for Deaf and Hard of Hearing People,** c/o Gallaudet University, 800 Florida Ave, NE, Washington DC 20002-3695 (☎ **202/651-5051** or TTY 202/651-5052; www.gallaudet.edu/~nicd); and **The Wheelchair Traveler,** 123 Ball Hill Rd., Milford, NE 03055 (☎ **603/673-4539**), which has information on hotels, restaurants, and sightseeing for wheelchair users.

Resources on the internet include **Access-Able Travel Source (www.access-able.com)**, where you'll also find relay and voice numbers for hotels, airlines, and car-rental companies on Access-Able's user-friendly site, as well as links to accessible accommodations, attractions, transportation, tours, local medical resources and equipment repairers, and much more. **Moss Rehab ResourceNet (www.mossresourcenet.org)** is a great source for information, tips, and resources relating to accessible travel. Here you'll find links to a number of travel agents who specialize in planning trips for disabled travelers.

For travelers with disabilities who wish to do their own driving, hand-controlled cars can be rented from **Avis** (☎ **800/331-1212;** www.avis.com) and **Hertz** (☎ **800/654-3131;** www.hertz.com). The number of hand-controlled cars in Hawaii is limited, so be sure to book well in advance—at least a week. For wheelchair-accessible vans, contact **Accessible Vans of Hawaii,** 186 Mehani Circle, Kihei, HI 96753 (☎ **800/303-3750** or 808/879-5521; fax 808/879-0640; www.accessiblevans.com). Maui recognizes other state's windshield placards indicating that the driver of the car is disabled, so be sure to bring yours with you.

Vision-impaired travelers who use a Seeing Eye dog can now come to Hawaii without the hassle of quarantine. A recent court decision ruled that visitors with Seeing Eye dogs only need to present documentation that the dog is a trained Seeing Eye dog and has had rabies shots. For more information, contact the **Animal Quarantine Facility** (☎ **808/483-7171;** www.hawaii.gov).

FOR GAY & LESBIAN TRAVELERS

Known for its acceptance of all groups, Hawaii welcomes gays and lesbians just as it does anybody else.

The best guide for gay and lesbian visitors is Matthew Link's *Rainbow Handbook Hawaii,* which not only covers travel on every island, but also has information on Hawaii's gay history, gay and lesbian businesses in the state, and interviews with Hawaii residents. The book is available for $14.95 by writing P.O. Box 100, Honaunau, HI 96726 (☎ **800/260-5528;** www.rainbowhandbook.com).

To get a sense of the local gay and lesbian community, contact **Both Sides Now,** P.O. Box 5042, Kahului, HI 96733-5042 (☎ **808/244-4566;** fax 808/874-6221; www.maui-tech.com/glom; e-mail: gaymaui@maui.net), which publishes a monthly newspaper on news, issues, and events for Maui's gay, lesbian, bisexual, and transgender communities.

For the latest information on the gay marriage issue, contact the **Hawaii Marriage Project** (☎ **808/532-9000**).

Pacific Ocean Holidays, P.O. Box 88245, Honolulu, HI 96830 (☎ **800/735-6600** or 808/923-2400; www.gayhawaii.com), offers vacation packages that feature gay-owned and gay-friendly lodgings. It also publishes the *Pocket Guide to Hawaii: A Guide for Gay Visitors & Kamaaina,* a list of gay-owned and gay-friendly businesses throughout the islands. Send $5 for a copy (mail order only; no phone orders, please), or access the online version on the Web site.

FOR SENIORS

Discounts for seniors are available at almost all of Maui's major attractions, and occasionally at hotels and restaurants. Always inquire when making hotel reservations, and especially when you're buying your airline ticket—most major domestic airlines offer senior discounts.

Members of the **American Association of Retired Persons** (AARP), 601 E St. NW, Washington, DC 20049 (☎ **800/424-3410** or 202/434-2277; www.aarp.org), are usually eligible for such discounts; AARP also puts together organized tour packages at moderate rates. The **National Council of Senior Citizens,** 8403 Colesville Dr., Suite 1200, Silver Spring, MD 20910 (☎ **301/578-8800;** www.ncscinc.org), a nonprofit organization, offers members hotel, condominium, and car-rental discounts, as well as a 24-hour emergency alert service for accident, injury, or illness.

Some great, low-cost trips to Hawaii are offered to people 55 and older through **Elderhostel,** 75 Federal St., Boston, MA 02110 (☎ **617/426-8056;** www.elderhostel.org), a nonprofit group that arranges travel and study programs around the world. You can obtain a complete catalog of offerings by writing to Elderhostel, P.O. Box 1959, Wakefield, MA 01880-5959.

If you're planning to visit Haleakala National Park, you can save sightseeing dollars if you're 62 or older by picking up a **Golden Age Passport** from any national park, recreation area, or monument. This lifetime pass has a one-time fee of $10 and provides free admission to all of the parks in the system, plus a 50% savings on camping and recreation fees. You can pick one up at any park entrance; be sure to have proof of your age with you.

FOR FAMILIES

Maui is paradise for children: beaches to frolic on, water to splash in, unusual sights to see, and a host of new foods to taste. Be sure to check out "Family-Friendly Accommodations" in chapter 4, "Family-Friendly Restaurants" in chapter 5, and "Especially for Kids," in chapter 7.

The larger hotels and resorts have supervised programs for children and can refer you to qualified baby-sitters. You can also contact **People Attentive to Children (PATCH)** (☎ **808/242-9232**), which will refer you to individuals who have taken their training courses on child care.

Baby's Away (☎ **800/942-9030** or 808/875-9093; www.babysaway.com) rents cribs, strollers, high chairs, playpens, infant seats, and the like, to make your baby's vacation (and yours) much more enjoyable.

Remember that Maui's sun is probably much stronger than what you're used to at home, so it's important to protect your kids from the sun, and keep infants out of the sun altogether. Infants under 6 months should not be in the sun at all. Older babies need zinc oxide to protect their fragile skin, and children should be slathered with sunscreen every hour.

Condo rentals are a great option for families; the convenience of having your own kitchen is great for Mom and Dad. See "Types of Accommodations" at the beginning of chapter 4. Our favorite condo complexes are reviewed throughout that chapter.

8 Getting Married on Maui

Whatever your budget, Maui is a great place for a wedding. Not only does the entire island exude romance and natural beauty, but after the ceremony, you're only a few steps away from the perfect honeymoon. And the members of your wedding party will most likely be delighted, since you've given them the perfect excuse for their own island vacation.

It happens every day in Hawaii, where more than 20,000 marriages are performed each year. Nearly half of the couples married here are from somewhere else. This booming business has spawned dozens of companies that can help you organize a long-distance event and stage an unforgettable wedding, Hawaiian style or your style.

The easiest way to plan your wedding is to let someone else handle it at the resort or hotel where you'll be staying. All of the major resorts and hotels (and even most of the small ones) have wedding coordinators, whose job is to make sure that your wedding day is everything you've dreamed about. They can plan everything from a simple (relatively) low-cost wedding to an extravaganza that people will remember and talk about for years. Remember that resorts can be pricey—catering, flowers, musicians, and so on, may cost more in a resort than outside a resort, but sometimes you can save money because the resort will not charge a room rental fee if they get to do the catering. Be frank with your wedding coordinator if you want to keep costs down.

You can also plan your own island wedding, even from afar, and not spend a fortune doing it.

THE PAPERWORK

The state of Hawaii has some very minimal procedures for obtaining a marriage license. The first thing you should do is contact the **Marriage License Office,** State Department of Health Building, 54 S. High St., Wailuku, HI 96793 (☎ 808/984-8210; www.hawaii.gov), open Monday through Friday from 8am to 4pm. The staff will mail you a brochure, *Getting Married,* and direct you to the marriage licensing agent closest to where you'll be staying on Maui.

Once on Maui, the prospective bride and groom must go together to the marriage licensing agent to get a license. A license costs $50 and is good for 30 days; if you don't have the ceremony within the time allotted, you'll have to pay another $50 for another license. The only requirements for a marriage license are that both parties are 15 years of age or older (couples 15 to 17 years old must have proof of age, written consent of both parents, and the written approval of the judge of the family court) and are not more closely related than first cousins. That's it.

Contrary to some reports from the media, gay couples cannot marry in Hawaii. After a protracted legal battle, and much discussion in the state legislature, in late 1999, the Hawaii Supreme Court ruled the state won't issue a marriage license to a couple of the same sex. For the latest information on this issue, contact the **Hawaii Marriage Project** (☎ 808/532-9000).

PLANNING THE WEDDING

DOING IT YOURSELF The marriage licensing agents, which range from the governor's satellite office to private individuals, are usually friendly, helpful people who can steer you to a nondenominational minister or someone who's licensed by the state of Hawaii to perform the ceremony. These marriage performers are great sources of information for budget weddings. They usually know great places to have the ceremony for free or for a nominal fee.

If you don't want to use a wedding planner (see below) but want to make arrangements before you arrive on Maui, our best advice is to get a copy of the daily newspaper, the *Maui News,* P.O. Box 550, Wailuku, HI 96793 (☎ **808/ 244-7691**). People willing and qualified to conduct weddings advertise in the classifieds. They're great sources of information, because they know the best places to have the ceremony and can recommend caterers, florists, and everything else you'll need.

USING A WEDDING PLANNER Wedding planners—many of whom are marriage licensing agents as well—can arrange everything for you, from a small, private, outdoor affair to a full-blown formal ceremony in a tropical setting. They charge anywhere from $450 to a small fortune—it all depends on what you want.

Planners on Maui include **A Wedding Made in Paradise,** P.O. Box 986, Kihei, HI 96753 (☎ 800/453-3440 or 808/879-3444; fax 808/874-1278; www.wedinparadise.com; e-mail: wedmaui@maui.net); **A Dream Wedding: Maui Style,** 143 Dickenson St., Suite 201, Lahaina, HI 96761 (☎ 800/743-2777 or 808/661-1777; fax 808/667-2042; www.maui.net/~dreamwed/dream.html; e-mail: dreamwed@maui.net); **A Romantic Maui Wedding,** P.O. Box 13232, Lahaina, HI 96761 (☎ 800/808-4144 or 808/874-6444; fax 808/879-5525; www.justmauied.com; e-mail: sandy@justmauied.com); **Dolphin Dream Weddings,** P.O. Box 10546, Lahaina, HI 96761 (☎ 800/793-2WED or 808/661-8535; www.maui.net/~dolphin; e-mail: dolphin@maui.net); and **Simply Married,** 2718 Iolani St., Pukalani, HI 96768 (☎ 800/291-0110 or 808/572-7898; fax 800/368-6933 or 808/572-1240; www.maui.net/~married; e-mail: married@maui.net).

9 Money-Saving Package Deals

Booking an all-inclusive travel package that includes some combination of airfare, accommodations, rental car, meals, airport and baggage transfers, and sightseeing can be the most cost-effective way to travel to Maui.

Package tours are not the same as escorted tours. They are simply a way to buy airfare and accommodations (and sometimes extras like sightseeing tours and rental cars) at the same time. When you're visiting Hawaii, a package can be a smart way to go. You can sometimes save so much money by buying all the pieces of your trip through a packager that your transpacific airfare ends up, in effect, being free. That's because packages are sold in bulk to tour operators, who then resell them to the public at a cost that drastically undercuts standard rates.

Packages, however, vary widely. Some offer a better class of hotels than others. Some offer the same hotels for lower prices. With some packagers, your choice of accommodations and travel days may be limited. Which package is right for you depends entirely on what you want.

Read this guide. Do a little homework; read up on Maui so that you can be a smart consumer. Compare the rack rates that we've published to the discounted rates being offered by the packagers to see what kinds of deals they're offering—if you're actually being offered a substantial savings, or if they've just gussied up the rack rates to make their offer *sound* like a deal. If you're being offered a stay in a hotel we haven't recommended, do more research to learn about it, especially if it isn't a reliable franchise. It's not a deal if you end up at a dump.

Read the fine print. Make sure you know *exactly* what's included in the price you're being quoted, and what's not. Are hotel taxes and airport transfers included, or will you have to pay extra? Before you commit to a package, make sure you know how much flexibility you have, say, if your kid gets sick or your boss suddenly asks you to adjust your vacation schedule. Some packagers require iron-clad commitments, while others will go with the flow, charging only minimal fees for changes or cancellations.

The best place to start looking for a package deal is in the travel section of your local Sunday newspaper. Also check the ads in the back of such national travel magazines as *Arthur Frommer's Budget Travel* and *Travel Holiday*. **Liberty Travel** (☎ **888/271-1584;** www.libertytravel.com), for instance, one of the biggest packagers in the Northeast, usually boasts a full-page ad in Sunday papers. You won't find much in the way of service, but you will get a good deal. **American Express Travel** (☎ **800/AXP-6898;** www.americanexpress.com/travel) can also book you a well-priced Hawaiian vacation; it also advertises in many Sunday travel sections.

Excellent deals, like airfare, rental car, and 7 nights in a Maui condo starting at $470 per person (based on double occupancy), can be found at **More Hawaii For Less** (☎ **800/967-6687;** www.hawaii4less.com), a California-based company that specializes in air-condominium packages at unbelievable prices.

Hawaii is such an ideal destination for vacation packages that some packagers book Hawaiian vacations as the majority of their business. **Pleasant Hawaiian Holidays** (☎ **800/2-HAWAII** or 800/242-9244; www.pleasantholidays.com or www.2hawaii.com) is by far the biggest and most comprehensive packager to Hawaii; it offers an extensive, high-quality collection of 50 condos and hotels in every price range.

Other reliable packagers include the airlines themselves, which often package their flights together with accommodations. Among the airlines offering good-value package deals to Hawaii are **American Airlines FlyAway Vacations** (☎ 800/321-2121; www.aavacations.com), **Continental Airlines Vacations** (☎ 800/634-5555 or 800/301-3800; www.coolvacations.com), **Delta Dream Vacations** (☎ 800/872-7786; www.deltavacations.com), **TWA Getaway Vacations** (☎ 800/GETAWAY or 800/438-2929; www.twa.com), and **United Vacations** (☎ 800/328-6877; www.unitedvacations.com). If you're traveling to the islands from Canada, ask your travel agent about package deals through **Air Canada Vacations** (☎ 800/776-3000; www.aircanada.ca).

GREAT DEALS AT HAWAII'S TOP HOTEL CHAINS

Hawaii's three major hotel chains—which together represent nearly 100 hotels, condominiums, resorts, a historic B&B, and even restored plantation homes—have a host of packages that will save you money.

With four properties on Maui, the **Outrigger Hotels and Resorts** (☎ **800/ OUTRIGGER;** fax 800/622-4852; www.outrigger.com) offers excellent, moderately priced, luxury-resort accommodations. Package deals include a car package, bed-and-breakfast, golf packages, deals on multinight stays, family plans, cut rates for seniors, and even a package for island hopping where you save up to 20% when you stay 7 nights at any Outrigger resort on any island.

The **Aston** chain (☎ **800/92-ASTON;** fax 808/922-8785; www.aston-hotels.com), which celebrated 50 years in Hawaii in 1998, has some 31 hotels, condominiums, and resort properties scattered throughout the islands, with nine on

Package-Buying Tip

For one-stop shopping on the Web, go to **www.vacationpackager.com**, a search engine that can link you up to many different package-tour operators, who can then help you plan a custom-tailored trip to Maui. Be sure to look under "Maui," "Hawaii," and the "Hawaiian Islands."

Maui. They range dramatically in price and style, from the elegant Maui Hill to the economical Aston Maui Islander. Aston offers package deals galore, including family plans; discounted senior rates; car, golf, and shopping packages; and deals on multinight stays, including a wonderful "Island Hopper" deal that allows you to hop from island to island and get 25% off on 7 nights or more at Aston properties.

10 Getting There

If possible, fly directly to Maui; doing so can save you a 2-hour layover in Honolulu and another plane ride. If you're headed for Molokai or Lanai, you'll have to connect through Honolulu.

If you think of the island of Maui as the shape of a head and shoulders of a person, you'll probably arrive on its neck, at **Kahului Airport.**

At press time, six airlines fly directly from the mainland to Kahului: **United Airlines** (☎ 800/241-6522; www.ual.com) offers daily nonstop flights from San Francisco and Los Angeles; **Aloha Airlines** (☎ 800/367-5250; www.alohaair.com) has daily flights from Oakland, California; **Hawaiian Airlines** (☎ 800/367-5320; www.hawaiianair.com) has direct flights from Los Angeles (daily) and Seattle (four times a week); **American Airlines** (☎ 800/433-7300; www.americanair.com) flies direct from Los Angeles; **Delta Airlines** (☎ 800/221-1212; www.delta-air.com) offers direct flights from San Francisco and Los Angeles; and **American Trans Air** (☎ 800/435-9282; www.ata.com) has direct flights from Los Angeles, San Francisco, and Phoenix.

The other carriers—including **Continental** (☎ 800/525-0280; www.continental.com), which offers nonstop service from Newark to Honolulu—fly to Honolulu, where you'll have to pick up an interisland flight to Maui. Both **Aloha Airlines** and **Hawaiian Airlines** offer jet service from Honolulu. See "Interisland Flights," below.

For information on airlines serving Hawaii from places other than the U.S. mainland, see chapter 3, "For Foreign Visitors."

FLY FOR LESS: TIPS FOR GETTING THE BEST AIRFARES

- Keep your eye out for periodic **sales.** You'll almost never see a sale during the peak winter vacation months, and especially not around the holidays, but before fuel prices went through the stratosphere last year, deals in the off-season were as low as $300 round-trip from Los Angeles to Maui. Just before we went to press that rate had climbed to $360. Note, however, that the lowest-priced fares are often nonrefundable, require advance purchase of 1 to 3 weeks and a certain length of stay, and carry penalties for changing dates of travel. So when you're quoted a fare, make sure you know exactly what the restrictions are before you commit.
- If your schedule is flexible, you can almost always get a cheaper fare by **staying over a Saturday night** or by **flying during midweek.** Many airlines won't volunteer this information, so be sure to ask.
- **Consolidators,** also known as bucket shops, are a good place to find low fares, often below even the airlines' discounted rates. There's nothing shady about the reliable ones—basically, they're just big travel agents that get discounts for buying in bulk and pass some of the savings on to you. But be aware that consolidator tickets are usually nonrefundable or come with stiff cancellation penalties.

  We've gotten great deals on many occasions from ✪ **Cheap Tickets** (☎ 800/377-1000; www.cheaptickets.com). **Council Travel** (☎ 800/

226-8624; www.counciltravel.com) and **STA Travel** (☎ **800/ 781-4040;** www.sta.travel.com) cater especially to young travelers, but their bargain-basement prices are available to people of all ages. Other reliable consolidators include **Lowestfare.com** (☎ **888/278-8830;** www. lowestfare.com); **1-800-AIRFARE** (www.1800airfare.com); **Cheap Seats** (☎ **800/451-7200;** www.cheapseatstravel.com); and **1-800-FLY CHEAP** (www.flycheap.com).

- **Search the Internet for cheap fares**—though it's still best to compare your findings with the research of a dedicated travel agent, if you're lucky enough to have one, especially when you're booking more than just a flight. My favorite site, which has consistently offered the lowest airfares for Hawaii, is **Expedia** (www.expedia.com). See **"Planning Your Trip: An Online Directory,"** which contains lots of guidance on how to make the Web work for you.

LANDING AT KAHULUI AIRPORT

If there's a long wait at baggage claim, step over to the state-operated **Visitor Information Center,** where you can pick up brochures and the latest issue of *This Week Maui,* which features great regional maps of the islands, and ask about island activities. After collecting your bags from the poky, automated carousels, step out, take a deep breath, proceed to the curbside rental-car pick-up area, and wait for the appropriate rental-agency shuttle van to take you a half mile away to the rental-car checkout desk. (All major rental companies have branches at Kahului; see "Getting Around," below.)

If you're not renting a car, the cheapest way to get to your hotel is **Speed-iShuttle** (☎ **808/875-8070**), which can take you between Kahului Airport and all the major resorts between 5am and 11pm daily. Rates vary, but figure on $24 for two passengers to Wailea (one way) and $48 for two to Kapalua (one way). Be sure to call before your flight to arrange pickup.

If you're staying in the Lahaina-Kaanapali area, transportation service is available through **Airporter Shuttle** (☎ **800/259-2627** or 808/877-7308), which runs every half hour from 9am to 4pm; the cost is $13 one way, $19 round-trip.

You'll see taxis outside the airport terminal, but note that they are quite expensive—expect to spend around $60 to $75 for a ride from Kahului to Kaanapali and $50 from the airport to Wailea.

If possible, avoid landing on Maui between 3 and 6pm, when the working stiffs on Maui are "pau work" (finished with work) and a major traffic jam occurs at the first intersection.

Your Departure: Agricultural Screening at the Airports

All baggage and passengers bound for the mainland must be screened by agricultural officials before boarding. This takes a little time, but isn't a problem unless you happen to be carrying a football-sized local avocado home to Aunt Emma. Officials will confiscate fresh avocados, bananas, mangoes, and many other kinds of local produce in the name of fruit-fly control. Pineapples, coconuts, and papayas inspected and certified for export, boxed flowers, leis without seeds, and processed foods (macadamia nuts, coffee, jams, dried fruit, and the like) will pass. Call federal agricultural officials (☎ 808/877-8757) before leaving for the airport if you're not sure about your trophy.

The Welcoming Lei

Nothing makes you feel more welcome than a lei. The tropical beauty of the delicate garland, the deliciously sweet fragrance of the blossoms, the sensual way the flowers curl softly around your neck—there's no doubt about it: Getting lei'd in Hawaii is a sensuous experience.

Leis are much more than just a decorative necklace of flowers; they're also one of the nicest ways to say hello, good-bye, congratulations, I salute you, my sympathies are with you, or I love you. The custom of giving leis can be traced back to Hawaii's very roots: According to chants, the first lei was given by Hiiaka, the sister of the volcano goddess, Pele, who presented Pele with a lei of lehua blossoms on a beach in Puna.

During ancient times, leis given to *alii* (royalty) were accompanied by a bow, since it was *kapu* (forbidden) for a commoner to raise his arms higher than the king's head. The presentation of a kiss with a lei didn't come about until World War II; it's generally attributed to an entertainer who kissed an officer on a dare, then quickly presented him with her lei, saying it was an old Hawaiian custom. It wasn't then, but it sure caught on fast.

Lei-making is a tropical art form. All leis are fashioned by hand in a variety of traditional patterns; some are sewn of hundreds of tiny blooms or shells, or bits of ferns and leaves. Some are twisted, some braided, some strung. Every island has its own special flower lei. On Oahu, the choice is *ilima,* a small orange flower. Big Islanders prefer the *lehua,* a large, delicate red puff. Maui likes the *lokelani,* a small rose. On Kauai, it's the *mokihana,* a fragrant green vine and berry. Molokai prefers the *kukui,* the white blossom of a candlenut tree. And Lanai's lei is made of *kaunaoa,* a bright yellow moss, while Niihau uses its abundant seashells to make leis that were once prized by royalty and are now worth a small fortune.

Leis are available at the Kahului Airport, from florists, and even at supermarkets.

Leis are the perfect symbol for Hawaii: They're given in the moment, their fragrance and beauty are enjoyed in the moment, and when they fade, their spirit of aloha lives on. Welcome to the islands!

AVOIDING KAHULUI   You can avoid Kahului Airport altogether by taking an **Island Air** (☎ **800/323-3345;** www.alohaair.com) flight from Honolulu or the Big Island to **Kapalua–West Maui Airport,** which is convenient if you're planning to stay at any of the hotels in Kapalua or at the Kaanapali resorts. If you're staying in Kapalua, it's only a 10- to 15-minute drive to your hotel; it takes 10 to 15 minutes to Kaanapali (as opposed to 35 or 40 minutes from Kahului). Island Air also flies into tiny **Hana Airport,** but you have to make a connection at Kahului to get there.

INTERISLAND FLIGHTS

Don't expect to jump a ferry between any of the Hawaiian islands. Today, everyone island-hops by plane. In fact, almost every 20 minutes of every day from just before sunrise to well after sunset (usually around 8pm), a plane takes off or lands at the Kahului Airport on the interisland shuttle service. If you miss a flight, don't worry; they're like buses—another one will be along soon.

Aloha Airlines (☎ **800/367-5250** or 808/244-9071; www.alohaaair.com) is the state's largest provider of interisland air transport service. It offers 180 regularly scheduled daily jet flights throughout Hawaii, utilizing an all-jet fleet of Boeing 737 aircraft. Aloha's sibling company, **Island Air** (☎ **800/323-3345** or 808/484-2222; www.hawaiianair.com), operates deHavilland DASH-8 and DASH-6 turboprop aircraft and serves Hawaii's small interisland airports on Maui, Molokai, and Lanai, with flights connecting them to Oahu and the Big Island.

Hawaiian Airlines (☎ **800/367-5320** or 808/871-6132; www.hawaiianair. com), Hawaii's first interisland airline, has carried more than 100 million passengers to and around the state. It's one of the world's safest airlines, having never had a fatal incident since it began operations in 1929.

A newcomer on the interisland commuter scene is Kahului-based **Pacific Wings** (☎ **888/873-0877** or 808/575-4546; fax 808/873-7920; www. pacificwings.com), which flies eight-passenger, twin-engine Cessna 402C aircraft. It currently offers flights between Kahului and Hana, Molokai, Lanai, Waimea (on the Big Island), and Honolulu.

MULTI-ISLAND PASSES At press time, the standard interisland fare was around $100 one way between islands. However, both airlines offer multiple-flight deals that you might want to consider.

Aloha Airlines offers the **Seven-Day Island Pass,** which allows visitors unlimited travel on Aloha and Island Air flights for 7 consecutive days. The price is $321. And for $330, you can buy a **Coupon Book,** which contains six blank one-way tickets that you can use—for yourself or any other traveler— any time within 1 year of purchase. If you and a companion are island-hopping two or three times during your stay, this is an excellent deal.

Hawaiian Airlines offers the **Hawaiian Island Pass,** which gives you unlimited interisland flights for $299 per person for 5 consecutive days, $349 for 7 days, $369 for 10 days, and $409 for 2 weeks.

11 Getting Around

The only way to really see Maui is by rental car. There's no real islandwide public transit.

Maui has only a handful of major roads: One follows the coastline around the two volcanoes that form the island, Haleakala and Puu Kukui; one goes up to Haleakala's summit; one goes to Hana; one goes to Wailea; and one goes to Lahaina. It sounds simple, right? Well, it isn't, because the names of the few roads change en route. Study the foldout map in the back of this book before you set out.

The best and most detailed road maps are published by *This Week Magazine,* a free visitor publication available on Maui. Most rental-car maps are pretty good, too.

CAR RENTALS

Maui has one of the lowest car-rental rates in the country. The average nondiscounted, unlimited-mileage rate for a 1-day rental for an intermediate-sized car was $39 in 2000 (plus the $3 state tax). That's the fourth-lowest rate in the country, compared with the national average of $53.50 a day. Cars are usually plentiful on Maui, except on holiday weekends, which in Hawaii also means King Kamehameha Day, Prince Kuhio Day, and Admission Day (see "When to Go," earlier in this chapter). Rental cars are usually at a premium on Molokai and Lanai, so be sure to book well ahead.

The road from Central Maui to Kihei and Wailea, **Mokulele Highway (Hwy. 311),** is a dangerous strip that's often the scene of head-on crashes involving intoxicated and speeding drivers; be careful. Also, be alert on the **Honoapiilani Highway (Hwy. 30)** en route to Lahaina, because drivers who spot whales in the channel between Maui and Lanai often slam on the brakes and cause major tie-ups and accidents.

If you get into trouble on Maui's highways, look for the flashing blue strobe lights on 12-foot poles; at the base are emergency, solar-powered call boxes (programmed to dial 911 as soon as you pick up the handset). There are 29 emergency call boxes on the island's busiest highways and remote areas, including along the Hana and Haleakala highways and on the north end of the island in the remote community of Kahakuloa.

Another traffic note: Buckle up your seat belt—Hawaii has stiff fines for noncompliance.

Maui is a great place to tool around in a convertible! You might ask your car-rental company about rates and try to reserve one in advance.

All the major car-rental agencies have offices on Maui, usually at both Kahului and West Maui Airports. They include: **Alamo** (☎ 800/327-9633; www.goalamo.com), **Avis** (☎ 800/321-3712; www.avis.com), **Budget** (☎ 800/935-6878; www.budgetrentacar.com), **Dollar** (☎ 800/800-4000; www.dollarcar.com), **Hertz** (☎ 800/654-3011; www.hertz.com), and **National** (☎ 800/227-7368; www.nationalcar.com).

There are also a few frugal car-rental agencies offering used cars at discount prices. **Word of Mouth Rent-a-Used-Car,** in Kahului (☎ **800/533-5929** or 808/877-2436, www.mauirentacar.com), offers a four-door compact without air-conditioning for $115 a week, plus tax; with air-conditioning, it's $140 a week, plus tax. **LTAR,** 1993 S. Kihei Rd., Suite 214-B Kihei (☎ **877/874-4800** or 808/874-4800; www.maui.net/~ltar), leases used economy cars at a weekly rate from $88, plus tax. LTAR provides no airport pickup, however; you'll have to make your own way to Kihei (it's about $20 in the SpeediShuttle van; see "Other Transportation Options," below, for details).

To rent a car in Hawaii, you must be at least 25 years old and have a valid driver's license and a credit card. Your valid home-state license will be recognized here.

MULTI-ISLAND DEALS   If you're going to visit multiple islands, it's usually easiest—and cheapest—to book with one company and carry your contract through on each island for your entire stay; just drop off your car on the island you're leaving, and there will be one waiting for you on the next island with the same company. By booking your cars this way, as one interisland rental, you can usually take advantage of weekly rates that you'd be excluded from if you treated each rental separately. Both **Avis** (☎ **800/321-3712;** www.avis.com) and **Hertz** (☎ **800/654-3011;** www.hertz.com) can do this for you; inquire about interisland rental arrangements when booking.

INSURANCE   Hawaii is a no-fault state, which means that if you don't have collision-damage insurance, you are required to pay for all damages before you leave the state, whether or not the accident was your fault. Your personal car insurance back home may provide rental-car coverage; read your policy or call your insurer before you leave home. Bring your insurance identification card if you decline the optional insurance, which usually costs from $12 to $20 a day. Obtain the name of your company's local claim representative before you go. Some credit-card companies also provide collision-damage insurance for their customers; check with yours before you rent.

EASY RIDING AROUND MAUI

Don black denim and motorcycle boots and ride around Maui on a hog, available for $100 to $150 a day at **Island Riders,** 126 Hinau St. (by Pizza Hut), Lahaina (☎ **800/529-2925** or 808/661-9966; www.islandriders.com). Forget the greasy Hell's Angels image; latter-day Wild Ones are buttoned-down corporate types, or California Highway Patrol officers on holiday. Whether you blast up Haleakala's grand corniche or haul ass to Hana, it's the most fun you can have on two wheels. This toy store for big boys and girls also rents exotic cars (Dodge Vipers, Cobras, Prowlers, Ferraris, Porches, Corvettes, and Jeeps), which start at about $200 a day and top out around $400. Island Riders offers free pickup from most Maui hotels—convenient if you're throwing caution to the wind for just a day (half-day rentals are available, too).

MOPEDS

Mopeds are available for rent from **Wheels USA,** at any of their three locations: 741 Wainee St., Lahaina (☎ **808/667-7751**); 75 Kaahumanu Ave., Kahului (☎ **808/871-6858**); or in Kihei, Rainbow Mall, 2439 S. Kihei (☎ **808/875-1221**). Mopeds, which start at $25 for 4 hours, are little more than motorized bicycles that get up to around 35mph (with a good wind at your back), so we suggest using them only locally (to get to the beach or to go shopping). Don't take them out on the highway, because they can't keep up with the traffic.

OTHER TRANSPORTATION OPTIONS

TAXIS   For island-wide 24-hour service, call **Alii Taxi** (☎ 808/661-3688 or 808/667-2605). You can also try **Kihei Taxi** (☎ 808/879-3000), **Wailea Taxi** (☎ 808/874-5000), or **Yellow Cab of Maui** (☎ 808/877-7000) if you need a ride.

SHUTTLES   SpeediShuttle (☎ **808/875-8070**) can take you between Kahului Airport and all the major resorts from 5am to 11pm daily (for details, see "Landing at Kahului Airport" under "Getting There," above).

Free shuttle vans operate within the resort areas of Kaanapali, Kapalua, and Wailea; if you're staying in those areas, your hotel can fill you in on exact routes and schedules.

12 The Active Vacation Planner

If you want nothing more on your vacation than a fabulous beach and a perfectly mixed mai tai, you're in luck—Maui has some of the most spectacular beaches (not to mention the best mai tais) in the world. But Maui's wealth of natural wonders is hard to resist; the year-round tropical climate and spectacular scenery tend to inspire even the most committed desk jockeys and couch potatoes to get outside and explore.

If you have your own snorkel gear or other water-sports equipment, bring it if you can. However, if you don't have it, don't fret; everything you'll need is available for rent. We discuss all kinds of places to rent or buy gear in chapter 6.

Safety Tip

Be sure to see "Health & Insurance," earlier in this chapter, before setting out on any adventure; it includes useful information on hiking, camping, and ocean safety. Even if you just plan to lie on the beach, check out the box called "Don't Get Burned: Smart Tanning Tips," on page 33, to learn how to protect yourself against the sun's harmful rays.

SETTING OUT ON YOUR OWN VS. USING AN OUTFITTER

There are two ways to go: Plan all the details before you go and schlepp your gear 2,500 miles across the Pacific, or go with an outfitter or a guide and let them worry about the details.

Experienced outdoor enthusiasts can follow their noses to coastal campgrounds or even trek into the rain forest on their own, but it's often preferable to go with a local guide who is familiar with the conditions at both sea level and the summit, knows the land and its flora and fauna in detail, and has all the gear you'll need. It's also good to go with a guide if time is an issue. If you really want to see native birds, for instance, an experienced guide will take you directly to the best areas for sightings. And many forests and valleys in the interior of the islands are either on private property or in wilderness preserves that are accessible only on guided tours. If you go with a guide, plan on spending at least $100 a day per person; we recommend the best local outfitters and tour-guide operators in chapter 6.

But if you have the time, already own the gear, and love doing the research and planning, try exploring on your own. Chapter 6 discusses the best spots to set out on your own, from the best offshore snorkel and dive spots to great daylong hikes, as well as the federal, state, and county agencies that can help you with hikes on public property; we also list references for spotting birds, plants, and sea life. We recommend that you always use the resources available and inquire about weather, trail or surf conditions, water availability, and other conditions before you take off on your adventure.

For hikers, a great alternative to hiring a private guide is taking one of the guided hikes offered by the **Nature Conservancy of Hawaii,** 1116 Smith St., Honolulu, HI 96817 (☎ **808/573-4147** on Maui; 808/553-5236 on Oahu; or 808/524-0779 on Molokai), and the **Hawaii Chapter of the Sierra Club,** P.O. Box 2577, Honolulu, HI 96803 (☎ **808/573-4147** on Maui; www. hi.sierraclub.org). Both organizations offer guided hikes on preserves and special places during the year, as well as 1- to 7-day work trips to restore habitats and trails and root out invasive plants like banana poka, New Zealand flax, non-native gorse, and wild ginger. It might not sound like a dream vacation to everyone, but it's a chance to see the "real" Maui—including wilderness areas that are usually off-limits.

All Nature Conservancy hikes are free. However, you must reserve a spot, and a deposit is required for guided hikes to ensure that you'll show up; your deposit is refunded once you do. The hikes are generally offered once a month on Maui, Molokai, and Lanai (call the Oahu office for reservations). There's also no charge for the trips to restore habitats. Write for a schedule of guided hikes and other programs.

The Sierra Club offers weekly hikes on Maui. Hikes are led by certified Sierra Club volunteers and are classified as easy, moderate, or strenuous. These half-day or all-day affairs cost $1 for Sierra Club members, $3 for nonmembers (bring exact change). For a copy of the newsletter, which lists all outings and trail repair work, send $2 to the address above.

Fun for Less: Don't Leave Home Without an AOA Gold Card

Almost any activity you can think of—from taking a helicopter ride to enjoying a Polynesian luau—can be purchased at discount prices with the **Activity Owners Association Gold Card.** (The AOA's offices are at 355 Hukilike St., no. 202, Kahului, HI 96732; ☎ **800/398-9698** or 808/871-7947; fax 808/877-3104; e-mail aoa@maui.net; www.maui.org). The AOA Gold Card, accepted by members on Maui, Molokai, and Lanai, offers 10% to 25% discounts off activities and meals. The card costs $30 and can be used for discounts for up to four people at a time.

You can save big bucks with the Gold Card. For example, if you have your heart set on taking a helicopter ride that goes for $149, you'll pay only $119.20 with your Gold Card, saving you nearly $30 per person— almost $120 in savings for a family of four. With just one activity alone, you've gotten the cost of the card back in savings. And there are hundreds of activities to choose from: air tours, attractions, bicycling tours, dinner cruises, fishing, guided tours, helicopter tours, horseback riding, kayaking, luaus, snorkeling, rafting, sailing, scuba diving, submarine rides, and more. It even gets you discounts on rental cars, restaurants, and golf!

Here's how it works: You contact AOA via mail, e-mail, fax, phone, or Internet (see above). They issue you the card, good for discounts for one year after the date you purchased it. You contact the activity (restaurant, rental car, etc.) directly, give them your AOA Gold Card number, and get discounts ranging from 10% to 25%.

Another great option for AOA Gold Card members is the opportunity to purchase certain activities at half price. At the beginning of every month, a list of activities, called Owners Tickets, is posted (at the AOA office and also available via phone, fax, mail, or the Web site: www. hawaiifun.org/ot). The hottest Owners Ticket is half off the Trilogy "Discover Lanai" snorkel/sail trip, which retails for $159 and is available to a limited number of AOA members for just $79.50. The half-price Owners Tickets are available only to AOA Gold Card members, and the activities are good for up to one year from the date of purchase.

USING ACTIVITIES DESKS TO BOOK YOUR ISLAND FUN

If you're interested in an activity that requires an outfitter or a guide, such as horseback riding, whale watching, or sportfishing, you might want to consider booking through a discount activities center or activities desk. These agents—who act as a clearinghouse for activities, just as a consolidator functions as a discount clearinghouse for airline tickets—can often get you a better price than you'd get by booking an activity directly with the outfitter yourself.

Discount activities centers will, in effect, split their commission with you, giving themselves a smaller commission to get your business—and passing, on average, a 10% discount on to you. In addition to saving you money, good activities centers should be able to help you find, say, the snorkel cruise that's right for you, or the luau that's most suitable for both you *and* the kids.

But it's in the activity agent's best interest to sign you up with outfitters from which they earn the most commission; some agents have no qualms about booking you into any old activity if it means an extra buck for them. If an agent tries to push a particular outfitter or activity too hard, be skeptical. Conversely, they'll try to steer you away from outfitters that don't offer big commissions. For example, Trilogy, the company that offers Maui's most popular snorkel cruises to Lanai (and the only one with rights to land at Lanai's Hulupoe Beach), offers only minimal commissions to agents and does not allow agents to offer any discounts at all; as a result, most activities desks on Maui will automatically try to steer you away from Trilogy even if you say you want to book with it.

Another important word of warning: Be careful to avoid those activities centers offering discounts as fronts for timeshare sales presentations. Using a free snorkel cruise or luau tickets as bait, they'll suck you into a 90-minute presentation—and try to get you to buy into a Maui timeshare in the process. Not only will they try to sell you a big white elephant you never wanted in the first place, but—since their business is timeshares, not activities—they also won't be as interested, or as knowledgeable, about which activities might be right for you. These shady deals seem to be particularly rampant on Maui. Just do yourself a favor and avoid them altogether.

On Maui, we recommend **Tom Barefoot's Cashback Tours** (e-mail: barefoot@ maui.net), at Dolphin Shopping Center, 2395 S. Kihei Rd., Kihei (☎ **808/ 879-4100**), and at 834 Front St., Lahaina (☎ **808/661-8889**). Tom offers a 10% discount on all tours, activities, and adventures when you pay in cash or with traveler's checks. If you pay with a credit card or personal check, he'll give you a 7% discount. The two showrooms are loaded with pictures and maps of all the activities the company books. We found Tom's to be very reliable and honest.

OUTDOOR ETIQUETTE

Carry out what you carry in. Find a trash container for all your litter (including cigarette butts). Litterbugs anger the gods.

Observe *kapu* (taboo) and NO TRESPASSING signs. Don't climb on ancient Hawaiian *heiau* (temple) walls or carry home rocks, all of which belong to the Hawaiian volcano goddess Pele. Some say it's just a silly superstition, but each year the National and State Park Services get boxes of lava rocks in the mail, sent back to Hawaii by visitors who have experienced unusually bad luck.

Fast Facts: Maui

American Express For 24-hour traveler's check refunds and purchase information, call ☎ **800/221-7282.** Local offices are located in South Maui, at the **Grand Wailea Resort** (☎ **808/875-4526**), and in West Maui, at the **Ritz-Carlton Kapalua** (☎ **808/669-6018**) and the **Westin Maui** at Kaanapali Beach (☎ **808/661-7155**).

Area Code All of the islands are in the **808** area code. Note that if you're calling one island from another, you must dial 1-808 first, and you'll be billed at long-distance rates (which can be more expensive than calling the mainland).

Business Hours Most offices are open from 8am to 5pm. The morning commute usually runs from 6 to 8am, and the evening rush is from 4 to

6pm. Bank hours are Monday through Thursday from 8:30am to 3pm, Friday from 8:30am to 6pm; some banks are open on Saturday. Shopping centers are open Monday through Friday from 10am to 9pm, Saturday from 10am to 5:30pm, and Sunday from noon to 5 or 6pm.

Dentist Emergency dental care is available at **Maui Dental Center,** 162 Alamaha St., Kahului (☎ **808/871-6283**).

Doctor No appointment is necessary at **West Maui Healthcare Center,** Whalers Village, 2435 Kaanapali Pkwy., Suite H-7 (near Leilani's Restaurant), Kaanapali (☎ **808/667-9721;** fax 808/661-1584), which is open 365 days a year, nightly until 10pm. In Kihei, call **Urgent Care,** 1325 S. Kihei Rd., Suite 103 (at Lipoa Street, across from Star Market), Kihei (☎ **808/879-7781**), open daily from 6am to midnight; doctors are on call 24 hours a day.

Emergencies Dial ☎ **911** for the police, ambulance, and fire department. District stations are located in Lahaina (☎ **808/661-4441**) and in Hana (☎ **808/248-8311**). For the **Poison Control Center,** call ☎ **800/362-3585.**

Hospitals For medical attention, go to **Maui Memorial Hospital,** in Central Maui at 221 Mahalani, Wailuku (☎ 808/244-9056); and East Maui's **Hana Medical Center,** on Hana Highway (☎ 808/248-8924).

Liquor Laws The legal drinking age in Hawaii is 21. Beer, wine, and liquor are sold in grocery and convenience stores at any hour, 7 days a week. It's illegal (though rarely prosecuted) to have an open container on the beach.

Newspapers The *Honolulu Advertiser* and the *Honolulu Star Bulletin* are circulated statewide. The *Maui News* is the island's daily paper.

Post Offices To find the nearest post office, call ☎ **800/ASK-USPS.** In Lahaina, there are branches at the Lahaina Civic Center, 1760 Honoapiilani Hwy., and at the Lahaina Shopping Center, 132 Papalaua St.; in Kahului, there's a branch at 138 S. Puunene Ave.; and in Kihei, there's one at 1254 S. Kihei Rd.

Radio The most popular stations are KHPR (88.1 or 90.7 FM), the **National Public Radio** station; KGU (760 AM), for **news and talk radio;** KUMU (94.7 FM), for **easy listening;** and KSSK (590 AM), the **pop-music station** and the top morning-drive DJs.

Safety Although Hawaii is generally a safe tourist destination, visitors have been crime victims, so stay alert. The most common crime against tourists is rental car break-ins. Never leave any valuables in your car, not even in your trunk. Thieves can be in and out of your trunk faster than you can open it with your own key. Be especially careful at high-risk areas such as beaches and resorts. Never carry large amounts of cash with you. Stay in well-lighted areas after dark. Don't hike on deserted trails alone. See also "Health & Insurance," earlier in this chapter, for other safety tips.

Smoking It's against the law to smoke in public buildings, including airports, grocery stores, retail shops, movie theaters, banks, and all government buildings and facilities. Hotels have no-smoking rooms available, restaurants have no-smoking sections, and car-rental agencies have smoke-free cars. Most bed-and-breakfasts prohibit smoking indoors.

Taxes   Hawaii's sales tax is 4%. Hotel occupancy tax is 7.25%, and hoteliers are allowed by the state to tack on an additional .001666% excise tax. Thus, expect taxes of about 11.42% to be added to every hotel bill.

Time   Hawaii standard time is in effect year-round. Hawaii is 2 hours behind Pacific standard time and 5 hours behind eastern standard time. In other words, when it's noon in Hawaii, it's 2pm in California and 5pm in New York during standard time on the mainland. There's no daylight saving time here, so when daylight saving time is in effect on the mainland, Hawaii is 3 hours behind the West Coast and 6 hours behind the East Coast—so in summer, when it's noon in Hawaii, it's 3pm in California and 6pm in New York.

Hawaii is east of the international date line, putting it in the same day as the U.S. mainland and Canada, and a day behind Australia, New Zealand, and Asia.

Weather   For the current weather, call ☎ **808/871-5111;** for recreational activities call ☎ **808/871-5054;** for Haleakala National Park weather, call ☎ **808/871-5111;** for marine weather and surf and wave conditions, call ☎ **808/877-3477.**

Planning Your Trip: An Online Directory

This Online Directory will help you take better advantage of the travel planning information available online. Part 1 lists general Internet resources that can make any trip easier, such as sites for obtaining the best possible prices on airline tickets. In part 2, you'll find some top online guides specifically for Maui.

Please keep in mind that this is not a comprehensive list, but rather a discriminating selection to get you started. Recognition is given to sites based on their content value and ease of use. Inclusion is not paid for—unlike some Web-site rankings, which are based on payment. Finally, remember this is a press-time snapshot of leading Web sites; some undoubtedly will have evolved, changed, or moved by the time you read this.

1 Top Travel-Planning Web Sites

by Lynne Bairstow

Lynne Bairstow is the co-author of *Frommer's Mexico,* and the editorial director of *e-com* magazine.

WHY BOOK ONLINE?

Online agencies have come a long way over the past few years, now providing tips for finding the best fare, and giving you suggested dates or times to travel that yield the lowest price if your plans are at all flexible. Other sites even allow you to establish the price you're willing to pay, and they check the airlines' willingness to accept it. However, in some cases, these sites may not always yield the best price. Unlike a travel agent, for example, they may not have access to charter flights offered by wholesalers.

Online booking sites aren't the only places to reserve airline tickets— all major airlines have their own Web sites and often offer incentives (bonus frequent-flyer miles or net-only discounts, for example) when you buy online or buy an e-ticket. (See "Getting There" in chapter 2, "Planning Your Trip: The Basics" for a complete list of the airlines serving Maui, with their Web sites.)

The new trend is toward conglomerated booking sites. By mid-2000, a consortium of U.S. and European-based airlines is planning to launch an as-yet unnamed Web site that will offer fares lower than those available through travel agents. United, Delta, Northwest, and

Check Out Frommer's Site

We highly recommend **Arthur Frommer's Budget Travel Online** (**www.frommers.com**) as an excellent travel-planning resource. Of course, we're a little biased, but you'll find indispensable travel tips, reviews, monthly vacation giveaways, and online booking. Among the most popular features of this site are the regular "Ask the Expert" bulletin boards, which feature Frommer's authors answering your questions via online postings.

Subscribe to Arthur Frommer's Daily Newsletter (**www.frommers. com/newsletters**) to receive the latest travel bargains and inside travel secrets in your e-mailbox every day. You'll read daily headlines and articles from the dean of travel himself, highlighting last-minute deals on airfares, accommodations, cruises, and package vacations.

Search our Destinations archive (**www.frommers.com/destinations**) of more than 200 domestic and international destinations for great places to stay and dine, and tips on sightseeing. Once you've researched your trip, the online reservation system (**www.frommers.com/booktravelnow**) takes you to Frommer's favorite sites for booking your vacation at affordable prices.

Continental have initiated this effort, based on their success at selling airline seats on their own sites.

The best of the travel-planning sites are now highly personalized; they store your seating preferences, meal preferences, tentative itineraries, and credit-card information, allowing you to quickly plan trips or check agendas. In many cases, booking your trip online can be better than working with a travel agent. It gives you the widest variety of choices, control, and the 24-hour convenience of planning your trip when you choose.

WHO SHOULD BOOK ONLINE?

Online booking is best for travelers who want to know as much as possible about their travel options, for those who have flexibility in their travel dates, and for bargain hunters.

One of the biggest successes in online travel for both passengers and airlines is the offer of last-minute specials, such as American Airlines' weekend deals or other Internet-only fares that must be purchased online. Another advantage is that you can cash in on incentives for booking online, such as rebates or bonus frequent-flyer miles.

Business and other frequent travelers also have found numerous benefits in online booking, as the advances in mobile technology provide them with the ability to check flight status, change plans, or get specific directions from handheld computing devices, mobile phones, and pagers. Some sites will even e-mail or page a passenger if their flight is delayed.

TRAVEL-PLANNING & -BOOKING SITES

The following sites offer domestic and international flight, hotel, and rental car bookings, plus news, destination information, and deals on cruises and vacation packages. Free (one-time) registration is required for booking.

✪ **Expedia. expedia.com**

Expedia is known as the fastest and most flexible online travel planner for booking flights, hotels, and rental cars. It offers several ways of obtaining the best possible fares: **Flight Price Matcher** service allows your preferred airline to match an available fare with a competitor; a comprehensive **Fare Compare** area shows the differences in fare categories and airlines; and **Fare Calendar** helps you plan your trip around the best possible fares. Its main limitation is that like many online databases, Expedia focuses on the major airlines and hotel chains, so don't expect to find too many budget airlines or one-of-a-kind B&Bs here.

Personalized features allow you to store your itineraries, and receive weekly fare reports on favorite cities. You can also check on the status of flight arrivals and departures, and through MileageMiner, track all of your frequent-flyer accounts.

Expedia also offers packages, cruises, and information on specialized travel (like casino destinations, and adventure, ski, and golf travel). There are also special features for travelers accessing information on mobile devices.

Travelocity (incorporates Preview Travel). www.travelocity.com; www.previewtravel.com

Travelocity uses the SABRE system to offer reservations and tickets for more than 400 airlines; you can also reserve and purchase from more than 45,000 hotels and 50 car-rental companies. An exclusive feature of the SABRE system is their **Low Fare Search Engine,** which automatically searches for the three lowest-priced itineraries based on a traveler's criteria. Last-minute deals and consolidator fares are included in the search. If you book with Travelocity, you can select specific seats for your flights with online seat maps, and also view diagrams of the most popular commercial aircraft. Their hotel finder provides street-level location maps and photos of selected hotels.

Travelocity features an inviting interface for booking trips, though the wealth of graphics involved can make the site somewhat slow to load, and any adjustment in your parameters means you'll need to completely start over.

This site also has some very cool tools. With the **Fare Watcher** e-mail feature, you can select up to five routes for which you'll receive e-mail notices when the fare changes by $25 or more. If you own an alphanumeric pager with national access that can receive e-mail, Travelocity's **Flight Paging** can alert you if your flight is delayed. You can also access real-time departure and arrival information on any flight within the SABRE system.

Note to AOL Users: You can book flights, hotels, rental cars, and cruises on AOL at keyword: Travel. The booking software is provided by Travelocity/ Preview Travel and is similar to the Internet site. Use the AOL "Travelers Advantage" program to earn a 5% rebate on flights, hotel rooms, and car rentals.

TRIP.com. www.trip.com

TRIP.com began as a site geared for business travelers, but its innovative features and highly personalized approach have broadened its appeal to leisure travelers as well. It is the leading travel site for those using mobile devices to access Internet travel information.

TRIP.com provides the average and lowest fare for the route requested, in addition to the current available fare. An on-site "newsstand" features breaking news on airfare sales and other travel specials. Among its most popular features are Flight TRACKER and intelliTRIP. **Flight TRACKER** allows users to track any commercial flight en-route to its destination anywhere in the

Online Directory

More people still look online than book online, partly due to fear of putting their credit-card numbers out on the Net. Secure encryption, and increased experience buying online, has removed this fear for most travelers. In some cases, however, it's simply easier to buy from a local travel agent who can deliver your tickets to your door (especially if your travel is last-minute or if you have special requests). You can find a flight online and then book it by calling a toll-free number or contacting your travel agent, though this is somewhat less efficient. To be sure you're in secure mode when you book online, look for a little icon of a key (in Netscape) or a padlock (in Internet Explorer) at the bottom of your Web browser.

United States, while accessing real-time FAA-based flight monitoring data. **intelliTRIP** allows you to identify the best airline, hotel, and rental-car fares in less than 90 seconds.

In addition, trip.com offers e-mail notification of flight delays, plus city resource guides, currency converters, and a weekly e-mail newsletter of fare updates, travel tips, and traveler forums.

Yahoo Travel. www.travel.yahoo.com
Yahoo is currently the most popular of the Internet information portals, and its travel site is a comprehensive mix of online booking, daily travel news, and destination information. Their **Best Fares** area offers what it promises, and provides feedback on refining your search if you have flexibility in travel dates or times. There is also an active section of Message Boards for discussions on travel in general, and to specific destinations.

LAST-MINUTE DEALS & OTHER ONLINE BARGAINS
There's nothing airlines hate more than flying with lots of empty seats. The Net has enabled airlines to offer last-minute bargains to entice travelers to fill those seats. Most of these are announced on Tuesday or Wednesday and are valid for travel the following weekend, but some can be booked weeks or months in advance. You can sign up for weekly e-mail alerts at **the airlines' own sites** (see "Getting There," in chapter 2) or check sites that compile lists of these bargains, such as **Smarter Living** or **WebFlyer** (see below). To make it easier, visit a site that will round up all the deals and send them in one convenient weekly e-mail.

Cheap Tickets. www.cheaptickets.com
Cheap Tickets has exclusive deals that aren't available through more mainstream channels. One caveat about the Cheap Tickets site is that it will offer fare quotes for a route, and later show this fare is not valid for your dates of travel—most other Web sites, such as Expedia, consider your dates of travel before showing what fares are available. Despite its problems, Cheap Tickets can be worth the effort because its fares can be lower than those offered by its competitors.

❂ 1travel.com. www.1travel.com
Here you'll find deals on domestic and international flights and hotels. 1travel.com's **Saving Alert** compiles last-minute air deals so you don't have to scroll through multiple e-mail alerts. A feature called "Drive a little using low-fare airlines" helps map out strategies for using alternate airports to find lower fares. And **Farebeater** searches a database that includes published fares,

consolidator bargains, and special deals exclusive to 1travel.com. *Note:* The travel agencies listed by 1travel.com have paid for placement.

Bid for Travel. www.bidfortravel.com
Bid for Travel is another of the travel auction sites, similar to Priceline (see below), which are growing in popularity. In addition to airfares, Internet users can place a bid for vacation packages and hotels.

LastMinuteTravel.com. www.lastminutetravel.com
Suppliers with excess inventory come to this online agency to distribute unsold airline seats, hotel rooms, cruises, and vacation packages. It has great deals, but an excess of advertisements and slow-loading graphics.

Moment's Notice. www.moments-notice.com
As the name suggests, Moment's Notice specializes in last-minute vacation deals. You can browse for free, but if you want to purchase a trip you have to join Moment's Notice, which costs $25.

✪ Priceline.com. http://travel.priceline.com
Priceline lets you "name your price" for domestic and international airline tickets and hotel rooms. You select a route and dates, guarantee with a credit card, and make a bid for what you're willing to pay. If one of the airlines in Priceline's database has a fare lower than your bid, your credit card will automatically be charged for a ticket.

But you can't say when you want to fly—you have to accept any flight leaving between 6am and 10pm on the dates you selected, and you may have to make a stopover. No frequent-flyer miles are awarded, and tickets are non-refundable and can't be exchanged for another flight. So if your plans change, you're out of luck. Priceline can be good for travelers who have to take off on short notice (and who are thus unable to qualify for advance purchase discounts). But be sure to shop around first, because if you overbid, you'll be required to purchase the ticket—and Priceline will pocket the difference between what it paid for the ticket and what you bid.

Priceline says that more than 35% of all reasonable offers for domestic flights are being filled on the first try, with much higher fill rates on popular routes (New York to San Francisco, for example). They define "reasonable" as not more than 30% below the lowest generally available advance-purchase fare for the same route.

Smarter Living. www.smarterliving.com
Best known for its e-mail dispatch of weekend deals on 20 airlines, Smarter Living also keeps you posted about last-minute bargains.

SkyAuction.com. www.skyauction.com
An auction site with categories for airfare, travel deals, hotels, and much more.

Travelzoo.com www.travelzoo.com
At this Internet portal, more than 150 travel companies post special deals. It features a Top 20 list of the best deals on the site, selected by its editorial staff each Wednesday night. This list is also available via an e-mailing list, free to those who sign up.

WebFlyer. www.webflyer.com
WebFlyer is a comprehensive online resource for frequent flyers and also has an excellent listing of last-minute air deals. Click on "Deal Watch" for a round-up of weekend deals on flights, hotels, and rental cars from domestic and international suppliers.

TOP VACATION PACKAGE SITES

Both **Expedia** and **Travelocity** (see above) offer excellent selections and searches for complete vacation packages. Travelers can search by destination and desired dates coupled with how much they are willing to spend.

Pleasant Hawaiian Holidays (www.pleasantholidays.com) is by far the biggest and most comprehensive packager to Hawaii, and now offers its low-cost deals on the Web; check out the site's 360° "Surround Video" tours of hotels and destinations. **The Hottest Airfares on Earth** (www.etn.nl/hotfares.htm) is a clearinghouse of information on airfares, packages, and hotel deals from low-cost ticket suppliers, tour operators, and travel agents. **Travel Shop** (www.aonestoptravel.com) has access to consolidated rates on every aspect of travel to Hawaii, and promises to meet or beat any quote you get from a travel agent or airline. Finally, check out the Hawaii package deals at **Travelzoo.com** (www.travelzoo.com) and **More Hawaii For Less** (www.hawaii4less.com).

Other reliable packagers include the airlines themselves, which often package their flights together with accommodations. Among the airlines offering good-value package deals to Hawaii are **American Airlines FlyAway Vacations** (www.aavacations.com), **Continental Airlines Vacations** (www.coolvacations.com), **Delta Dream Vacations** (www.deltavacations.com), **TWA Getaway Vacations** (www.twa.com), **United Vacations** (www.unitedvacations.com), and **Air Canada Vacations** (www.aircanada.ca).

2 Top Web Sites for Maui

by Jeanette Foster

ISLAND, SIGHTSEEING & ENTERTAINMENT GUIDES

EastMaui.Com. www.eastmaui.com
The island photos and dining reviews on this independent guide to Maui's eastern side make it a fine site to preview your stay on the windward side of the island.

Ecological Guide to Maui Hawaii Vacations. http://supak.com/ecomaui/ecomaui.htm
Visitors seeking environmentally friendly hiking and diving tours find links to tour operators as well as articles on preserving the region's natural ecosystem. The "Virtual Tours" section includes links to photo galleries and QuickTime video clips that show off the local beauty.

✪ **Hawaii Visitors & Convention Bureau: Maui.** www.gohawaii.com/hokeo/islands/maui.html
The Maui section of the Visitors and Convention Bureau's online guide is especially strong for its lodging lists. It provides links to individual accommodations, including bed and breakfasts, condos, vacation rentals, hotels, and resorts, with a brief description of each facility. A solid Points of Interest section explains many of the island's attractions. Looking to get hitched? Link to the island's wedding planners.

Ka Olelo Hawaii E Komo. www.geocities.com/TheTropics/Shores/6794
Learn to speak Hawaiian on this easy-to-use Web site that has excellent information on pronunciation, sayings, songs, basic conversations, and so on. In no time you'll be speaking like a native.

Maui Arts & Cultural Center. www.maui.net/~macc/macc/macc12.html
Learn about Maui culture and read the event schedule to catch an exhibition or performance from the local ethnic art scene.

Check Your E-mail While You're on the Road

You don't have to be out of touch just because you don't carry a laptop while you travel. Web browser-based free e-mail programs make it much easier to stay in e-touch.

Just open a freemail account at a browser-based provider, such as **MSN Hotmail (hotmail.com)** or **Yahoo! Mail (http://mail.yahoo.com)**. AOL users should check out AOL Netmail, and **USA.NET (www.usa.net)** comes highly recommended for functionality and security. You can find hints, tips and a mile-long list of freemail providers at www.emailaddresses.com.

Be sure to give your freemail address to the family members, friends, and colleagues with whom you'd like to stay in touch while you're on Maui. All you'll need to check your freemail account while you're away from home is a Web connection, easily available at net cafes, copy shops, and some hotels. After logging on, just point the browser to **www.hotmail. com, www.yahoo.com**, or the address of any other service you're using. Enter your user name and password, and you'll have access to your mail, both for receiving and sending messages to friends and family back home, for just a few dollars an hour. From these sites, you can download all of your e-mail (even from office accounts); there will be a section generally called "check other mail" that allows you to add the names of other e-mail servers.

Maui Cheetah. www.mauigateway.com/~rw/cheetah.htm
This home-grown site, put together by a Lahaina resident and shop owner, has some great ideas on how to save money on your trip, some tips on driving on Maui, and a listing of his favorite restaurants, activities, and accommodations.

Maui Community Events Calendar. http://calendar.maui.net/cgi/ calendar.pl
Just about everything you need to know about what's happening on Maui: from the arts to entertainment and from sports to government hearings.

✪ **Maui Island Currents. www.islandcurrents.com**
Specializing in arts and culture, Island Currents gives the most detailed low-down on current exhibitions and the performing arts. Gallery listings are organized by town and in-depth articles highlight local artists. Consult restaurant reviews from the Maui News 1998 "Best of Maui" for suggestions and prices.

✪ **Mauimapp: Maui Island Guide. www.mauimapp.com/**
Though this well-rounded guide serves primarily as a directory of links, you'll find (if you look hard) a link to critical restaurant reviews written by readers and a schedule of events. A map section describes hikes and camping spots around the island. You'll find articles from the Maui Historical Society covering aspects of Hawaiian culture, from prestate history to the slack-key guitar.

✪ **Maui Net. www.maui.net**
Extensive directory of links to accommodations, island activities, and shopping. Activity Desk has links to golf, hiking, airborne activities, and ocean adventures, such as scuba and snorkeling. These links lead to outfitters where you can learn more and set up excursions before you arrive in paradise.

Maui Visitors Bureau. www.visitmaui.com
In addition to providing ad-driven links to lodging, dining, outdoor activities, and shopping, the "More for Less" section offers a decent list of budget attractions and excursions. Web cams and photos let you virtually experience the ocean and downtown Lahaina.

The Valley Isle. http://pages.prodigy.net/plantsman/contents.htm
This practical resource provides ideas for packing, tips for taking photos, directions around the island, and a calendar of events. Photos offer a preview to the coast and mountains.

Weather. http://hawaiiweathertoday.com/mwt
An easy-to-use, friendly site with no fuss info on the weather on Maui and other islands. You can also try the **Weather Channel** at **www.weather.com**.

DINING GUIDES

Maui Guide to Vegan Dining. www.mauidiningguide.com
Organized by region, find descriptions, addresses, and phone numbers for consuming strictly vegetarian meals. Also see the World Guide to Vegetarianism's listings for Hawaii (**www.veg.org/veg/Guide/USA/Hawaii/index.html**).

Zagat Survey: Hawaii Restaurant Reviews. www.zagat.com
The popular reader-written restaurants review book on-line with hundreds of Maui eateries arranged by cuisine, neighborhood, or price.

MUSIC

✪ **Hawaiian Jamz. www.mauigateway.com/~jamz**
This excellent site is dedicated to the preservation and promotion of Hawaiian music and culture and has a wide range of Hawaiian music. Each hour-long show has a theme and is archived (so you can listen to them anytime you wish).

Internet Hawaii Radio. www.hotspots.hawaii.com
If you are looking for a site to get you into the mood of seeing Hawaii, this eclectic site features some of the best Hawaiian music, with opportunities to buy the CD or cassette. A respectable assortment of Hawaiian historical/cultural books is available to purchase online.

Radio Station KPOA. www.kpoa.com
Maui's local Hawaiian station, playing island music all day and night long. Listen to the live broadcasts.

NEWSPAPERS & MAGAZINES

Maui News. www.mauinews.com
The best thing about this online site for the local daily newspaper on Maui is the entertainment section, with listings of ongoing events and reviews of plays, dances, movies, and restaurants.

Maui's Free Press. www.mauisfreepress.com
Maui's weekly community newspapers, the *Haleakala* and *Kihei Times,* offer a sizable listing section on local events.

This Week Magazine. www.thisweek.com/maui/twm.mainhtml
The island-by-island visitor publication is now online, filled with links to its advertisers for accommodations, dining, entertainment, shopping, and more. Its listings are somewhat limited, but the maps are outstanding.

BEACHES & OUTDOOR PURSUITS

✪ **Beach and Activity Guide. www.beachactivityguide.com/Maui**
The online version of this free print visitor's publication offers listings for activities, dining, golfing, lodging, shopping, and water sports, plus great maps. You can even book all your activities online. Click on "On the House" for a nice roundup of free activities on Maui.

Fun and Adventure on Maui. www.mauitoday.com
The Activity Owners Association of Hawaii outlines specific tours and suggests tour operators (within the association) for all kinds of outdoor excursions, including biking, jet-skiing, scuba diving, and more. Visitors seeking less strenuous fun will find information on whale watching, sunset dinner cruises, and helicopter rides.

Haleakala National Park. www.nps.gov/hale/
The National Park Service offers directions, accommodations, history, and information about park activities.

Maui A-Z: Beaches. www.maui.net/~tkern/mauiatoz.html
The detailed descriptions and photos of local beaches, organized by region, make this the best section of the Maui A-Z guide. It includes comprehensive tips on scuba diving, snorkeling, and kayaking.

State Parks on the Island of Maui. www.hawaii.gov/dlnr/dsp/maui.html
The Hawaii state government posts acreage, brief descriptions, and opening hours for the island's state-managed parks.

GETTING AROUND

Aloha Air. www.alohaair.com
This interisland airline shares flight schedules, and information on budget passes. Reserve online.

Hawaiian Airlines. www.hawaiianair.com
Check schedules and reserve online for transpacific or interisland service. Also find rental car deals and frequent-flyer facts.

Lanai/Lahaina Expeditions. www.maui.net/~paradise/expeditions/ expeditions.html
Get rates, schedules, and special golf and hotel tour packages for this passenger ferry to Lanai.

Pacific Wings. http://pacificwings.com
Flight schedules, prices, and contact information for this small interisland airline.

Trans-Hawaii's Airport Shuttle. www.transhawaiian.com/discount/htm
Not only will you find pricing for the Airport Shuttle, but also you can print out discount coupons to save you money on your trip.

SpeediShuttle. www.speedishuttle.com/mservoff.html
A very handy chart on the cost of SpeediShuttle on Maui to various destinations around the island, plus online reservations.

MOLOKAI

Kalaupapa National Historic Park. www.nps.gov/kala
From the National Park Service comes this official guide to this place of refuge for sufferers of leprosy. The site gives you everything you need to know about the park, including who can visit, when, how to get there, fees, the facilities,

activities, recommendations, special events, programs, even adjacent visitor attractions.

✪ Molokai: The Most Hawaiian Island. **visitmolokai.com**
This is a very complete site for activities, events, night life, accommodations, and family vacations. Enjoy the landscape from a virtual photo tour. Get driving times between various points and learn about local history.

Molokai Visitors Association. **www.molokai-hawaii.com**
Descriptions of lodging, island attractions and events, and restaurant contact information will give you some ideas for relaxing or taking an adventure.

LANAI

Destination Lanai. **www.visitmaui.com**
Most of the accommodations, restaurants, shops, and activities that this tiny island has to offer on one Web site, including information on weddings and honeymoons.

For Foreign Visitors

by Jeanette Foster

3

The pervasiveness of American culture around the world may make you feel that you know the USA pretty well, but leaving your own country for the States—especially the unique island state of Hawaii—still requires some additional planning.

1 Preparing for Your Trip

ENTRY REQUIREMENTS

Immigration laws are a hot political issue these days; the following requirements may have changed somewhat by the time you plan your trip. Check at any U.S. embassy or consulate for current information and requirements. You can also plug into the U.S. State Department's Internet site at **www.state.gov**; click on VISA SERVICES for the latest entry requirements.

DOCUMENT REGULATIONS   Canadian citizens may enter the United States without visas; they need only proof of residence.

The U.S. State Department has a **Visa Waiver Pilot Program** allowing citizens of certain countries to enter the United States without a visa for stays of up to 90 days. At press time, these countries included Andorra, Argentina, Australia, Austria, Belgium, Brunei, Denmark, Finland, France, Germany, Iceland, Ireland, Italy, Japan, Liechtenstein, Luxembourg, Monaco, the Netherlands, New Zealand, Norway, San Marino, Slovenia, Spain, Sweden, Switzerland, and the United Kingdom. (Greece has been preliminarily approved, but at press time visas were still required.) Citizens of these countries need only a valid passport and a round-trip air or cruise ticket in their possession upon arrival. If they first enter the United States, they may then visit Mexico, Canada, Bermuda, and/or the Caribbean islands and return to the United States without needing a visa. Further information is available from any U.S. embassy or consulate.

Citizens of all other countries must have (1) a valid **passport** with an expiration date at least 6 months later than the scheduled end of their visit to the United States, and (2) a **tourist visa,** which may be obtained without charge from the nearest U.S. consulate.

To obtain a visa, you must submit a completed application form (either in person or by mail) with a $1^{1}/_{2}$-inch-square photo, and you must demonstrate binding ties to a residence abroad. Usually, you can obtain a visa at once or within 24 hours, but it may take longer during the summer rush from June to August. If you cannot go in person, contact the nearest U.S. embassy or consulate for directions on applying by mail. Your travel agent The U.S. consulate or embassy that issues your visa will determine whether you will be issued a multiple- or-single-entry visa and any restrictions regarding the length of your stay. Inquiries about visa cases and the application process can be made by calling ☎ **202/663-1225.**

U.K. citizens can obtain up-to-date passport and visa information by calling the **U.S. Embassy Visa Information Line** at ☎ **0891/200-290** or the **London Passport Office** at ☎ **0990/210-410** (for recorded information).

Foreign driver's licenses are recognized in Hawaii, although you may want to get an international driver's license if your home license is not written in English.

MEDICAL REQUIREMENTS   Inoculations are not needed to enter the United States unless you are coming from or have stopped over in areas known to be suffering from epidemics, particularly cholera or yellow fever. If you have a disease requiring treatment with medications containing narcotics or requiring a syringe, carry a valid signed prescription from your physician to allay suspicions that you are smuggling drugs.

For HIV-positive visitors, requirements for entering the United States are somewhat vague and change frequently. If an HIV-positive noncitizen applying for a nonimmigrant visa knows that HIV is a communicable disease of public health significance but checks "no" on the question about communicable diseases, INS may deny the visa because it thinks the applicant committed fraud. If a nonimmigrant visa applicant checks "yes," or if INS suspects the person is HIV positive, it will deny the visa unless the applicant asks for a special waiver for visitors. This waiver is for people visiting the United States for a short time, to attend a conference, for instance, to visit close relatives, or to receive medical treatment. For up-to-the-minute information concerning HIV-positive travelers, contact the **HIV/AIDS Treatment Information Service** (☎ **800/HIV-0440** or 301/519-0459; www.hivatis.org), or the Center for Disease Control and Prevention's **National AIDS Hotline** (☎ **800/342-2437,** or 800/ 344-7432 in Spanish; www.cdc.org).

CUSTOMS

WHAT YOU CAN BRING IN   Every adult visitor may bring in the following free of duty: 1 liter of wine or hard liquor, 200 cigarettes or 100 cigars (but no cigars from Cuba) or 3 pounds of smoking tobacco, and $100 worth of gifts. These exemptions are offered to travelers who spend at least 72 hours in the United States and who have not claimed exemptions within the preceding 6 months. It is forbidden to bring into the country foodstuffs (particularly cheese, fruit, cooked meats, and canned goods) and plants (vegetables, seeds, tropical plants, and so on). Foreign tourists may bring in or take out up to $10,000 in U.S. or foreign currency with no formalities; larger sums must be declared to customs on entering or leaving, which involves filing form CM 4790. For more information, call the U.S. Customs office at ☎ **202/927-1770** or check out www.customs.ustreas.gov.

In addition, you cannot bring fresh fruits and vegetables into Hawaii, even if you're coming from the U.S. mainland and have no need to clear customs. Every passenger

Travel Tip ───────────────────────────────────

Be sure to keep a copy of all your travel papers separate from your wallet or purse, and leave a copy with someone at home should you need it faxed in an emergency.

is asked shortly before landing to sign a certificate declaring that he or she does not have fresh fruits and vegetables in his or her possession.

WHAT YOU CAN BRING HOME   Check with your country's Customs or Foreign Affairs department for the latest guidelines—including information on items that are not allowed to be brought in to your home country—just before you leave home.

U.K. citizens should contact HM Customs & Excise Passenger Enquiries (☎ **0181/ 910-3744**) or visit www.open.gov.uk.

For a clear summary of **Canadian** rules, visit the comprehensive Web site of the **Canada Customs and Revenue Agency** at **www.ccra-adrc.gc.ca**.

Citizens of **Australia** should request the helpful Australian Customs brochure *Know Before You Go,* available by calling ☎ **1-300/363-263** from within Australia, or 61-2/6275-6666 from abroad. For additional information, go online to **www.dfat. gov.au** and click on HINTS FOR AUSTRALIAN TRAVELLERS.

For **New Zealand** customs information, contact the New Zealand Customs Service at ☎ **09/359-6655,** or go online to www.customs.govt.nz.

INSURANCE

The United States has no nationwide health system, and the cost of medical care in Hawaii is extremely high. In most cases, doctors and hospitals will require advance payment or proof of coverage before they render their services. We strongly advise you to secure health-insurance coverage before setting out. You may even want to take out a comprehensive travel policy that covers (for a relatively low premium) sickness or injury costs (medical, surgical, and hospital); loss or theft of your baggage; trip-cancellation costs; guarantee of bail in case you're arrested; and costs of accident, repatriation, or death. See "Health & Insurance" in chapter 2 for more information. Packages such as **Europ Assistance** in Europe are sold by automobile clubs and travel agencies at attractive rates. **Worldwide Assistance Services, Inc.** (☎ **800/ 777-8710,** ext. 409, or 703/204-1897; www.worldwideassistance.com) is the agent for Europ Assistance in the United States.

U.K. travelers might call the **Association of British Insurers** (☎ **0171/ 600-3333**), which gives advice by phone and publishes the free *Holiday Insurance,* a guide to policy provisions and prices. You might also shop around for better deals: Try **Columbus Direct** (☎ **0171/375-0011;** www.columbusdirect.co.uk).

Canadians should check with their provincial health plan offices or call **Health-Canada** (☎ **613/957-2991**) to find out the extent of their coverage and what documentation and receipts they must take home in case they are treated in the United States.

Though lack of health insurance may prevent you from being admitted to a hospital in nonemergencies, don't worry about being left on a street corner to die: The American way is to fix you now and bill the living daylights out of you later.

MONEY

CURRENCY   The American monetary system has a decimal base: 1 U.S. **dollar** ($1) = 100 **cents** (100¢). The most common bills (all ugly, all green) are the $1 (colloquially, a "buck"), $5, $10, and $20 denominations. There are also $2 bills (seldom encountered), $50 bills, and $100 bills (the last two are usually not welcome as payment for small purchases). Note that redesigned $100, $50, and $20 bills were introduced in the last few years, but the old-style bills are still legal tender. Expect to see redesigned $10 and $5 notes by the time you arrive.

There are six denominations of coins: 1¢ (1 cent, or a penny); 5¢ (5 cents, or a nickel); 10¢ (10 cents, or a dime); 25¢ (25 cents, or a quarter); 50¢ (50 cents, or a half dollar); and the rare $1 piece (the older, large silver dollar and the newer, small Susan B. Anthony coin). By the end of 2000, a new gold-toned $1 piece will be introduced.

EXCHANGING CURRENCY   Exchanging foreign currency for U.S. dollars can be painless on Maui. Most banks will exchange your foreign currency for U.S. dollars, as will the big hotels; the banks generally offer better rates. Aside from desks at banks and hotels, there is just one currency-exchange service on Maui: **Trans Peso,** 1000 Limahana Pl., Unit D, Lahaina (☎ **808/667-0354**), but it only handles pesos from the Philippines. There are currency services at the Honolulu International Airport.

TRAVELER'S CHECKS   It's actually cheaper and faster to get cash at an **automatic teller machine** (ATM) than to fuss with traveler's checks. As noted in "Visitor Information & Money" in chapter 2, Hawaii has ATMs almost everywhere. Traveler's checks are, however, readily accepted at most hotels, restaurants, and large stores. But *make sure that they're denominated in U.S. dollars,* as foreign-currency checks are often difficult to exchange. The three traveler's checks that are most widely recognized—and least likely to be denied—are **Visa, American Express,** and **Thomas Cook/MasterCard.** Be sure to record the numbers of the checks, and keep that information separately in case they get lost or stolen. Remember: You'll need identification, such as a driver's license or passport, to change a traveler's check.

CREDIT CARDS   Credit cards are widely used in Hawaii: **Visa** (BarclayCard in Britain), **MasterCard** (EuroCard in Europe, Access in Britain, Chargex in Canada), **American Express, Diners Club, Discover,** and **Carte Blanche;** some vendors may also accept international cards like **enRoute, Eurocard,** and **JCB,** but not as universally as AmEx, MasterCard, or Visa. You can save yourself trouble by using "plastic" rather than cash or traveler's checks in most hotels, restaurants, and retail stores (nearly every food and liquor store now accepts credit cards, too). You must have a credit card to rent a car in Hawaii. There are, however, a handful of stores and restaurants that do not take credit cards, so be sure to ask in advance. Most businesses display a sticker near their entrance to let you know which cards they accept. And be aware that often businesses require a minimum purchase price, usually around $10 or $15, to use a credit card.

SAFETY
GENERAL   While tourist areas are generally safe, visitors should always stay alert, even in laid-back Maui (and especially in resort areas). It's wise to ask the island tourist office if you're in doubt about which neighborhoods are safe. Avoid deserted areas, especially at night. Generally speaking, you can feel safe in areas where there are many people and open establishments.

Avoid carrying valuables with you on the street, and don't display expensive cameras or electronic equipment. Hold onto your pocketbook, and place your billfold in an inside pocket. In restaurants and on the beach, keep your possessions in sight.

Remember also that hotels are open to the public and that, in a large hotel, security may not be able to screen everyone entering. Always lock your room door—don't assume that once inside your hotel, you're automatically safe.

DRIVING   Safety while driving is particularly important. Ask your rental agency about personal safety, or ask for a brochure of traveler safety tips when you pick up your car. Get written directions or a map with the route marked in red from the agency showing you how to get to your destination.

Recently, more crime has involved burglary of tourist rental cars in hotel-parking structures and at beach parking lots. Park in well-lighted and well-traveled areas if possible. Never leave any packages or valuables in sight in the car. If someone attempts to rob you or steal your car, do not try to resist the thief/carjacker—report the incident to the police department immediately.

For more information on hiking safety and ocean safety, see chapter 2.

2 Getting to & Around the United States

Airlines serving Hawaii from places other than the U.S. mainland include **Air Canada** (☎ 800/776-3000; www.aircanada.ca); **Canadian Airlines** (☎ 800/426-7000; www.cdnair.ca); **Canada 3000** (☎ 888/CAN-3000; www.canada3000.com); **Air New Zealand** (☎ 0800/737-000 in Auckland, 64-3/379-5200 in Christchurch, 800/926-7255 in the U.S.; www.airnewzealand.co.nz), which runs 40 flights per week between Auckland and Hawaii; **Qantas** (☎ 008/177-767 in Australia, 800/227-4500 in the U.S.; www.qantas.com.au), which flies between Sydney and Honolulu daily (plus additional flights 4 days a week); **Japan Air Lines** (☎ 03/5489-1111 in Tokyo, 800/525-3663 in the U.S.; www.jal.com); **All Nippon Airways** (ANA; ☎ 03/5489-1212 in Tokyo, 800/235-9262 in the U.S.; www.ana.co.jp); **China Airlines** (☎ 02/715-1212 in Taipei, 800/227-5118 in the U.S.; www.china-airlines.com); **Air Pacific,** serving Fiji, Australia, New Zealand and the South Pacific (☎ 800/227-4446; www.airpacific.com); **Korean Airlines** (☎ 02/656-2000 in Seoul, 800/223-1155 on the East Coast, 800/421-8200 on the West Coast, 800/438-5000 from Hawaii; www.koreanair.com); and **Philippine Airlines** (☎ 631/816-6691 in Manila, 800/435-9725 in the U.S.; www.philippineair.com).

Travelers coming from Europe can take advantage of the **APEX (Advance Purchase Excursion)** fares offered by all major U.S. and European carriers. Aside from these, attractive values are offered by **Icelandair** (☎ 354/5050-100 in Reykjavik, 0171/388-5599 in London, 800/223-5500 in the U.S.; www.icelandair.is) on flights from Luxembourg to New York and by **Virgin Atlantic Airways** (☎ 0293/747-747 in Britain, 800/862-8621 in the U.S.; www.fly.virgin.com) from London to New York/Newark. You can then catch a connecting domestic flight to Honolulu.

The visitor arriving by air should cultivate patience and resignation before setting foot on U.S. soil. Getting through immigration control may take as long as 2 hours on some days, especially summer weekends. Add the time it takes to clear customs, and you'll see that you should make a very generous allowance for delay in planning connections between international and domestic flights—an average of 2 to 3 hours at least.

For further information about travel to Hawaii, see "Getting There" and "Getting Around" in chapter 2.

Fast Facts: For the Foreign Traveler

Also see the Fast Facts in chapter 2 for more information.

Business Hours   See "Fast Facts: Maui" in chapter 2.

Climate   See "When to Go" in chapter 2.

Currency & Currency Exchange   See "Money" under "Preparing for Your Trip," earlier in this chapter. Also see "Money," in chapter 2. For the latest market conversion rates, point your Internet browser to **www.x-rates.com**.

Electricity   Hawaii, like the U.S mainland and Canada, uses 110–120 volts (60 cycles), compared to the 220–240 volts (50 cycles) used in most of Europe and in other areas of the world, including Australia and New Zealand. Small

---

Money-Saving Tip

The **ETN (European Travel Network)** operates a Web site offering discounts on international airfares to the United States, as well as on accommodations, car rentals, and tours; point your Internet browser to **www.discount-tickets.com**.

---

appliances of non-American manufacture, such as hair dryers or shavers, will require a plug adapter with two flat, parallel pins; larger ones will require a 100-volt transformer. Downward converters that change 220–240 volts to 110–120 volts are difficult to find in the United States, so bring one with you.

Embassies & Consulates   All embassies are located in Washington, D.C. Some consulates are located in major cities, and most nations have a mission to the United Nations in New York City. Listed here are the embassies and some consulates of the major English-speaking countries. If your country isn't listed below, call for directory information in Washington, D.C. (☎ **202/555-1212**) or point your Web browser to **www.embassy.org/embassies** for the location and phone number of your national embassy.

The embassy of **Australia** is at 1601 Massachusetts Ave. NW, Washington, D.C. 20036 (☎ **202/797-3000;** www.austemb.org). There is also an Australian consulate in Hawaii at 1000 Bishop St., Penthouse Suite, Honolulu, HI 96813 (☎ **808/524-5050**).

The embassy of **Canada** is at 501 Pennsylvania Ave. NW, Washington, D.C. 20001 (☎ **202/682-1740;** www.canadianembassy.org). Canadian consulates are also at 1251 Avenue of the Americas, New York, NY 10020 (☎ **212/596-1628**), and at 550 South Hope St., 9th floor, Los Angeles, CA 90071 (☎ **213/346-2700**).

The embassy of **Japan** is at 2520 Massachusetts Ave. NW, Washington, D.C. 20008 (☎ **202/238-6700;** www.embjapan.org). The consulate general of Japan is located at 1742 Nuuanu Ave., Honolulu, HI 96817 (☎ **808/543-3111;** www.embjapan.org/honolulu).

The embassy of **New Zealand** is at 37 Observatory Circle NW, Washington, D.C. 20008 (☎ **202/328-4800;** www.emb.com/nzemb). The only New Zealand consulate in the United States is at 780 Third Ave., New York, NY 10017 (☎ **212/328-4800**).

The embassy of the **Republic of Ireland** is at 2234 Massachusetts Ave. NW, Washington, D.C. 20008 (☎ **202/462-3939;** www.irelandemb.org). There's a consulate office in San Francisco at 44 Montgomery St., Suite 3830, San Francisco, CA 94104 (☎ **415/392-4214**).

The embassy of the **United Kingdom** is at 3100 Massachusetts Ave. NW, Washington, D.C. 20008 (☎ **202/588-6640;** www.fco.gov.uk/directory). British consulates are at 845 Third Ave., New York, NY 10022 (☎ **212/745-0200**), and 11766 Wilshire Blvd., Suite 400, Los Angeles, CA 90025 (☎ **310/477-3322**).

Emergencies   Call ☎ **911** to report a fire, call the police, or get an ambulance. This is a toll-free call (no coins are required at public telephones).

Gasoline (Petrol)   One U.S. gallon equals 3.8 liters, while 1.2 U.S. gallons equals 1 Imperial gallon. You'll notice there are several grades (and price levels) of gasoline available at most gas stations. And you'll also notice that their names change from company to company. The ones with the highest octane are the most expensive, but most rental cars take the least expensive "regular" gas, with an octane rating of 87.

Holidays   See "When to Go" in chapter 2.

Legal Aid   The ordinary tourist will probably never become involved with the American legal system. If you're pulled over for a minor infraction (for example, driving faster than the speed limit), never attempt to pay the fine directly to a police officer; you may wind up arrested on the much more serious charge of attempted bribery. Pay fines by mail or directly into the hands of the clerk of the court. If accused of a more serious offense, it's wise to say and do nothing before consulting a lawyer (you have a right to both remain silent and to consult an attorney under the U.S. Constitution). Under U.S. law, an arrested person is allowed one telephone call to a party of his or her choice; call your embassy or consulate.

Mail   Mailboxes are generally found at intersections, are blue with a blue-and-white eagle logo, and carry the inscription "U.S. Postal Service." If your mail is addressed to a U.S. destination, don't forget to add the five-figure postal code, or zip code, after the two-letter abbreviation of the state to which the mail is addressed. The abbreviation for Hawaii is HI.

International airmail rates, as we went to press, are 60¢ for half-ounce letters (40¢ for letters going to Mexico and 46¢ for letters to Canada) and 50¢ for postcards (35¢ to Mexico and 40¢ to Canada). All domestic first-class mail goes from Hawaii to the U.S. mainland by air.

Taxes   The United States has no VAT (value-added tax) or other indirect taxes at a national level. Every state, and every city in it, has the right to levy its own local tax on all purchases, including hotel and restaurant checks, airline tickets, and so on. In Hawaii, sales tax is 4% (note that food is taxed just like other purchases). There's also a 7.25% hotel-room tax and a small excise tax, so the total tax on your hotel bill will be 11.42%.

Telephone & Fax   The telephone system in the United States is run by private corporations, so rates, particularly for long-distance service and operator-assisted calls, can vary widely—especially on calls made from public telephones. Local calls—that is, calls to other locations on the island you're on—made from public phones in Hawaii cost 35¢. The international-country code for Hawaii is 1, just as it is for the rest of the United States and Canada.

Generally, hotel surcharges on long-distance and local calls are astronomical. You are usually better off using a **public pay telephone,** which you will find clearly marked in most public buildings and private establishments as well as on the street. Many convenience stores and newsstands sell **prepaid calling cards** in denominations up to $50; these can be the least expensive way to call home. Even if you purchase a phone card (where the long distance charges are prepaid), you still might want to use the public pay phone, as most hotels add a surcharge on toll-free calls.

Most **long-distance and international calls** can be dialed directly from any phone. For calls to Canada and other parts of the United States, dial 1, followed by the area code and the seven-digit number. For international calls, dial 011, followed by the country code, city code, and telephone number of the person you wish to call.

In Hawaii, interisland phone calls are considered long-distance and are often as costly as calling the U.S. mainland.

For **reversed-charge or collect calls,** and for **person-to-person calls,** dial 0 (zero, not the letter "O"), followed by the area code and number you want; an operator will then come on the line, and you should specify that you are calling collect, person-to-person, or both. If your operator-assisted call is international, ask for the overseas operator.

Note that all phone numbers with the area code 800, 888, or 877 are toll-free.

For **local directory assistance** ("information"), dial 411; for **long-distance information,** dial 1, then the appropriate area code and 555-1212; for **directory assistance for another island,** dial 1, then 808, then 555-1212.

Fax facilities are widely available and can be found in most hotels and many other establishments. Try **Mail Boxes, Etc.** (check the local Yellow Pages) or any photocopying shop.

Telephone Directories There are two kinds of telephone directories in the United States. The general directory, the so-called *White Pages,* lists private and business subscribers in alphabetical order. The inside front cover lists the emergency numbers for police, fire, and ambulance, and other vital numbers (like the Coast Guard, poison-control center, crime-victims hot line, and so on). The first few pages are devoted to community-service numbers, including a guide to long-distance and international calling, complete with country codes and area codes.

The second directory, printed on yellow paper (hence its name, *Yellow Pages*), lists all local services, businesses, and industries by type of activity, with an index at the front. The listings cover not only such obvious items as automobile repairs or drugstores (pharmacies), but also restaurants by type of cuisine and geographical location, bookstores by special subject and/or language, places of worship by religious denomination, and other information that the visitor might otherwise not readily find. The *Yellow Pages* also include detailed maps, postal zip codes, and a calendar of events.

Time See "Fast Facts: Maui" in chapter 2.

Tipping It's part of the American way of life to tip. Many service employees receive little direct salary and must depend on tips for their income. In fact, the U.S. government imposes income taxes on service personnel based on an estimate of how much they should have earned in tips relative to their employer's total receipts. In other words, they may have to pay taxes on a tip you didn't give them! The following are some general rules:

In **hotels,** tip bellhops at least $1 per piece of luggage ($2 to $3 if you have a lot of luggage), and tip the housekeeping staff at least $1 per person, per day. Tip the doorman or concierge only if he or she has provided you with some specific service (for example, calling a cab for you or obtaining difficult-to-get theater tickets). Tip the valet parking attendant $1 every time you get your car.

In **restaurants, bars, and nightclubs,** tip service staff 15% to 20% of the check, tip bartenders 10% to 15%, and tip valet-parking attendants $1 per vehicle. Tip the doorman only if you were provided with some specific service (such as calling a cab for you). Tipping is not expected in cafeterias and fast-food restaurants.

Tip **cab drivers** 15% of the fare.

As for **other service personnel,** tip skycaps at airports at least $1 per piece ($2 to $3 if you have a lot of luggage), and tip hairdressers and barbers 15% to 20%. Tipping ushers at movies and theaters and gas-station attendants is not expected.

Toilets Foreign visitors often complain that public toilets are hard to find in most U.S. cities. True, there are none on the streets, but visitors can usually find one in a bar, fast-food outlet, restaurant, hotel, museum, or department store—and it will probably be clean. (The cleanliness of toilets at service stations, parks, and beaches is more open to question.) Note, however, a growing practice in some restaurants and bars of displaying a notice that "toilets are for customers only." You can ignore this sign, or better yet, avoid arguments by paying for a cup of coffee or soft drink, which will qualify you as a patron.

4

Accommodations

by Jeanette Foster

Maui has accommodations to fit every taste and budget, from luxury ocean-front suites and historic bed-and-breakfasts to reasonably priced condos that will sleep a family of four.

Remember to consider *when* you will be traveling to the islands. Maui has two seasons—high and low. The highest season, during which rooms are always booked and rates are at the top end, runs from mid-December to March. The second high season, when rates are high but bookings are somewhat easier, is summer, June to September. The low season, with fewer tourists and cheaper rates, is April to June and September to mid-December.

Finally, remember to add Maui's 11.42% accommodations tax to your final bill. Parking is free unless otherwise noted.

Important Note: Before you book, be sure to read "The Island in Brief," in chapter 2, which will help you choose your ideal location. Also check out the accommodations categories in chapter 1, "The Best of Maui," for a quick look at our absolute favorites.

TYPES OF ACCOMMODATIONS

HOTELS   In Hawaii, "hotel" can indicate a wide range of options, from few or no on-site amenities to enough extras to qualify as a miniresort. Generally, a hotel offers daily maid service and has a restaurant, on-site laundry facilities, a pool, and a sundries/convenience–type shop (as opposed to the shopping arcades that most resorts have). Top hotels also provide activities desks, concierge service, business centers, a bar and/or lounge, and perhaps a few more shops. The advantages of staying in a hotel are privacy and convenience; the disadvantage is generally noise: either thin walls between rooms or loud music from a lobby lounge late into the night.

RESORTS   In Hawaii, a resort offers everything a hotel offers and more. What you get varies from property to property, of course, but expect facilities, services, and amenities such as direct beach access, with cabanas and chairs; pools (often more than one) and a Jacuzzi; a spa and fitness center; restaurants, bars, and lounges; a 24-hour front desk; concierge, valet, and bell services; room service (often around the clock); an activities desk; tennis and golf (some of the world's best courses are at Hawaii resorts); ocean activities; a business center; children's programs; and more.

The advantage of staying at a resort is that you have everything you could possibly want in the way of services and things to do; the disadvantage is that the price generally reflects this. Don't be misled by a name—just because a place is called "ABC Resort" doesn't mean it actually *is* a resort. Make sure you're getting what you pay for.

CONDOS   The roominess and convenience of a condo—which is usually a fully equipped multiple-bedroom apartment—makes this a great choice for families. Condominium properties in Hawaii are generally several apartments set in either a single high-rise or a cluster of low-rise units. Condos generally have amenities such as some degree of maid service (ranging from daily to weekly; it may or may not be included in your rate, so be sure to ask), a pool, laundry facilities (either in your unit or in a central location), and an on-site front desk or a live-in property manager. The advantages of a condo are privacy, space, and conveniences—which usually include a fully equipped kitchen, a washer and dryer, a private phone, and perhaps your own lanai or balcony. The downsides include the absence of an on-site restaurant and the density of the units (perhaps more private than a B&B or hotel, but not quite like renting your own cottage, villa, or house, either).

Condos vary in price according to size, location, and amenities. Many of them are located on or near the beach, and they tend to be clustered in resort areas. While there are some very high-end condos, most tend to be quite affordable, especially if you're traveling in a group that's large enough to require more than one bedroom.

BED-AND-BREAKFASTS   Maui has a wide variety of places that fall under this category: everything from the traditional B&B—several bedrooms in a home (which may or may not share a bathroom), with breakfast served in the morning—to what is essentially a vacation rental on an owner's property that comes with fixings for you to make your own breakfast. Make sure that the B&B you're booking matches your own mental picture. Would you prefer conversation around a big dining-room table as you eat a hearty breakfast, or just a muffin and juice to enjoy in your own private place? Laundry facilities and a private phone are not always available at B&Bs. We've reviewed lots of wonderful places in this chapter. If you have to share a bathroom, we've spelled it out in the listings; otherwise, you can assume that you will have a private bathroom.

The advantage of a traditional B&B is its individual style and congenial atmosphere. B&Bs are great places to meet other visitors, and the host is generally very happy to act as your own private concierge, offering tips on where to go and what to do. In addition, B&Bs are usually an affordable way to go (though fancier ones can run $150 or more a night). The disadvantages are lack of privacy, usually a set time for breakfast, few amenities, generally no maid service, and the fact that you'll have to share the quarters beyond your bedroom with others. In addition, B&B owners usually require a minimum stay of 2 or 3 nights, and it's often a drive to the beach.

VACATION RENTALS   This is another great choice for families, as well as for long-term stays. "Vacation rental" usually means there will be no one on the property where you're staying. The actual accommodation can range from an apartment in a condominium building to a two-room cottage on the beach to an entire fully equipped house. Generally, vacation rentals are the kinds of places you can settle into for a while: They have kitchen facilities (which can be either a complete kitchen or just a kitchenette with microwave, fridge, burners, and coffeemaker), on-site laundry facilities, and phone; some also have such extras as TV, VCR, and stereo. The advantages of a vacation rental are complete privacy, your own kitchen (which can save you money on meals), and lots of conveniences. The disadvantages are a lack of an on-site property manager, no organized ocean activities, and generally no maid service; often, a minimum stay is required (sometimes as much as a week). If you book a vacation rental, be sure you have a 24-hour contact so that when the toilet won't flush or you can't figure out how to turn on the air-conditioning, you'll have someone to call.

BARGAINING ON PRICES

Rates can sometimes be bargained down, but it depends on the place. In general, each type of accommodation allows a different amount of latitude in bargaining on their rack (or published) rates.

The best bargaining can be had at **hotels** and **resorts.** Hotels and resorts regularly pay travel agents as much as 30% of the rate they're getting for sending clients their way; if business is slow, some hotels might give you the benefit of at least part of this commission if you book directly instead of going through an airline or travel agent. Most also have *kamaaina* or "local" rates for islanders, which they might extend to visitors during slow periods. It never hurts to ask politely for a discounted or local rate; a host of special rates are also available for the military, seniors, members of the travel industry, families, corporate travelers, and long-term stays.

Ask about package deals, which might include a car rental or free breakfast for the same price as a room. Hotels and resorts offer packages for everyone: golfers, tennis players, families, honeymooners, and more. See "Money-Saving Package Deals," in chapter 2.

We've found that it's worth the extra few cents to make a local call to the hotel; sometimes the local reservationist knows about package deals that the toll-free operators are unaware of.

If all else fails, try to get the hotel or resort to upgrade you to a better room for the same price as a budget room, or to waive the parking fee or the extra fees for children. Persistence and polite inquiries can pay off.

It's harder to bargain at **bed-and-breakfasts.** You may be able to bargain down the minimum stay, or negotiate a discount if you're staying a week or longer. But generally, a B&B owner has only a few rooms and has already priced the property at a competitive rate; expect to pay what's asked.

You have somewhat more leeway to negotiate on **vacation rentals** and **condos.** In addition to asking for a discount on multinight stays, also ask whether the condo or vacation rental can throw in a rental car to sweeten the deal; believe it or not, they often will.

What to Do If Your Dream Hotel Turns Out to Be a Nightmare

To avoid any unpleasant surprises, ask lots of questions when you make your reservation. Find out exactly what the accommodation is offering you: the cost, minimum stay, included amenities. Ask if there's a penalty fee for leaving early. Read the small print in the contract—especially that on cancellation fees. Discuss the cancellation policy ahead of time with the B&B, vacation rental, condominium agent, or booking agency so you'll know what your options are if the accommodation doesn't meet your expectations. Get this in writing (so there are no misunderstandings later).

When you arrive, if the room you're given doesn't meet your expectations, notify the front desk, rental agent, or booking agency immediately. Approach the management in a calm, reasonable manner, and suggest a constructive solution (such as moving to another unit). Be reasonable and be willing to compromise. Do not make threats or leave; if you leave, it may be harder to get your deposit returned.

USING A BOOKING AGENCY VS. DOING IT YOURSELF

Sometimes you can save money by making arrangements yourself—not only can you bargain on the phone, but some accommodations may also be willing to pass on a percentage of the commission they would normally have to pay a travel agent or a booking agency.

However, if you don't have the time or money to call several places to make sure they offer the amenities you'd like and to bargain for a price you're comfortable with, then you might consider using a booking agency. The time the agency spends on your behalf might well be worth any fees you'll have to pay.

The top reservations service in the state is **Hawaii's Best Bed & Breakfasts,** P.O. Box 563, Kamuela, HI 96743 (☎ 800/262-9912 or 808/885-4550; fax 808/885-0559; www.bestbnb.com; e-mail: bestbnb@aloha.net). This service charges $15 to book the first two locations and $5 for each additional location. Barbara and Susan Campbell personally select the traditional homestays, cottages, and inns, based on each one's hospitality, distinctive charm, and attention to detail.

Another great statewide booking agent is **Ann and Bob Babson,** 3371 Keha Dr., Kihei, HI 96753 (☎ 800/824-6409 or 808/874-1166; fax 808/879-7906; www.maui.net/~babson; e-mail: babson@maui.net), who can steer you in the right direction for both accommodations and car rentals. Not only do they personally inspect the units they recommend, but the Babsons are also impeccably honest and dedicated to matching you up with the place that's right for you.

For vacation rentals, contact **Hawaii Beachfront Vacation Homes** (☎ 808/247-3637 or 808/235-2644; www.hotspots.hawaii.com/beachrent1.html; e-mail: hibeach@lava.net). **Hawaii Condo Exchange** (☎ 800/442-0404; http://hawaiicondoexchange.com) acts as a consolidator for condo and vacation-rental properties.

1 Central Maui

KAHULUI

If you're arriving late at night or have an early morning flight out, the best choice near Kahului Airport is the **Maui Seaside Hotel,** 100 Kaahumanu Ave. (near Lono Ave.), Kahului, HI 96732 (☎ 800/367-7000 or 808/877-3311; www.sand-seaside.com). The rooms are small and somewhat dated, but they're clean and cheap ($98 to $125 double), and some come with kitchenettes. Otherwise, try the **Maui Beach Hotel,** 170 Kaahumanu Ave. (Hwy. 32, at Hwy. 340), Kahului, HI 96732 (☎ 808/877-0051). The nondescript, motel-like rooms go for $93 to $115 and include free airport shuttle service. These two places are okay for a night, but not a place to spend your vacation.

WAILUKU

MODERATE

✪ **Old Wailuku Inn at Ulupono.** 2199 Kahookele St. (at High St., across from the Wailuku School), Wailuku, HI 96732. ☎ 800/305-4899 or 808/244-5897. Fax 808/242-9600. www.mauiinn.com. 7 units. A/C TV TEL. $120–$180 double. Rates include gourmet breakfast. Extra person $20. AE, DISC, MC, V.

This 1924 former plantation manager's home, lovingly restored by innkeepers Janice and Thomas Fairbanks, offers a genuine old Hawaii experience. Inspired by Hawaii's poet laureate, Don Blanding, the theme is Hawaii of the 1920s and 1930s. Guest rooms are wide and spacious, with exotic ohia-wood floors, high ceilings, and traditional Hawaiian quilts. The mammoth bathrooms (some with claw-foot tubs, some with Jacuzzis) have plush towels and "earth-friendly" toiletries on hand. A full gourmet breakfast is served on the enclosed back lanai or, if you prefer, delivered to your room. You'll feel right at home lounging on the generously sized living-room sofa, or watching the world go by from an old wicker chair on the lanai.

Located in the old historic area of Wailuku, the inn is just a few minutes' walk from the Maui County seat, the state building, the courthouse, and a wonderful stretch of antiques shops. It's fully equipped to handle business travelers, with automated message service, modem jacks, and multiple phones in each room; fax and copy services and computers are available for guest use.

INEXPENSIVE

Backpackers, head for **Banana Bungalow Maui,** a funky Happy Valley hostel at 310 North Market St., Wailuku, HI 96793 (☎ **800/846-7835** or 808/244-5090; fax 808/244-3678; www.bananabungalowmaui.com), $16 dorms rooms and some private rooms ($29 single, $35 double). Dorm-style accommodations ($18) and private rooms ($30 single, $44.60 double) are also available at the **Northshore Inn,** in old Wailuku, at 2080 Vineyard St., Wailuku, HI 96793 (☎ **800/647-6284** or 808/242-8999; fax 808/244-5004; http://hostelhawaii.com). Note, however, that women traveling alone might not feel safe in either of these areas after dark.

2 West Maui

LAHAINA
MODERATE

If you dream of an oceanfront condo but your budget is on the slim side, also consider **Lahaina Roads,** 1403 Front St. (a block north of the Lahaina Cannery Shopping Center). Reservations can be made c/o Klahani Travel, Lahaina Cannery Mall, 1221 Honoapiilani Hwy., Lahaina, HI 96761 (☎ **800/669-MAUI** or 808/667-2712; fax 808/661-5875; www.klahani-travel.com). The 17 units here go for $100 for a one-bedroom unit (for up to four), and $200 for a two-bedroom unit (for up to six). There's a 3-night minimum.

Also consider the condos at the **Lahaina Shores Beach Resort,** 475 Front St. (near Shaw Street; ☎ **800/628-6699;** www.lahaina-shores.com). This large oceanfront complex has studio and one-bedroom units priced from $165 to $275.

✪ **Aston Maui Islander.** 660 Wainee St. (between Dickenson and Prison sts.), Lahaina, HI 96761. ☎ **800/92-ASTON,** 800/367-5226, or 808/667-9766. Fax 808/661-3733. www.aston-hotels.com. 372 units. A/C TV TEL. High season $108 double, $132–$142 studio with kitchenette, $162 1-bedroom with kitchen (for up to 4 guests), $227 2-bedroom with kitchen (for 6 guests), $276 3-bedroom with kitchen (for 8 guests). Off-season $98 double, $118–$128 studio with kitchenette, $138 1-bedroom with kitchen, $198 2-bedroom with kitchen, $248 3-bedroom with kitchen. Extra rollaway bed $18, cribs free. AE, CB, DC, DISC, JCB, MC, V. Parking $1.

The units here are one of Lahaina's great buys, especially those with kitchenettes; the larger ones are perfect for families on a budget. This wooden complex isn't on the beach, but it's on a quiet side street (a rarity in Lahaina) and within walking distance of restaurants, shops, attractions, and, yes, the beach (just 3 blocks away). All of the good-sized rooms, decorated in tropical-island style, are comfortable and quiet. The entire complex is spread across 10 landscaped acres and includes tennis courts

Lahaina & Kaanapali Accommodations

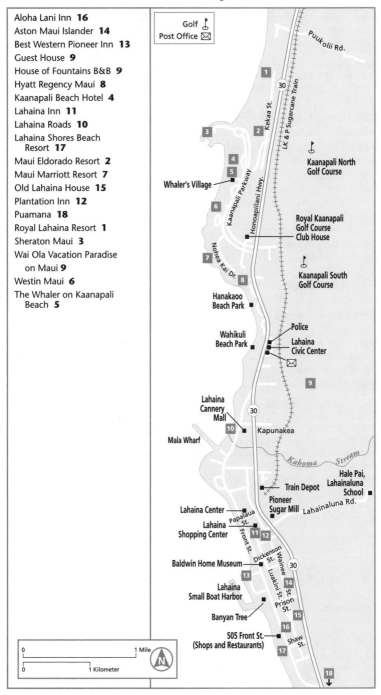

Aloha Lani Inn **16**
Aston Maui Islander **14**
Best Western Pioneer Inn **13**
Guest House **9**
House of Fountains B&B **9**
Hyatt Regency Maui **8**
Kaanapali Beach Hotel **4**
Lahaina Inn **11**
Lahaina Roads **10**
Lahaina Shores Beach
    Resort **17**
Maui Eldorado Resort **2**
Maui Marriott Resort **7**
Old Lahaina House **15**
Plantation Inn **12**
Puamana **18**
Royal Lahaina Resort **1**
Sheraton Maui **3**
Wai Ola Vacation Paradise
    on Maui **9**
Westin Maui **6**
The Whaler on Kaanapali
    Beach **5**

Golf
Post Office ✉

Puukolii Rd.

Kekaa St.

LK & P Sugarcane Train

Kaanapali North
Golf Course

Kaanapali Parkway

Honoapiilani Hwy.

Whaler's Village

Royal Kaanapali
Golf Course
Club House

Nohea Kai Dr.

Kaanapali South
Golf Course

Hanakaoo
Beach Park

Police

Wahikuli
Beach Park

Lahaina
Civic Center

✉

Lahaina
Cannery
Mall

Kapunakea

Mala Wharf

Kahoma Stream

Hale Pai,
Lahainaluna
School

Train Depot

Pioneer
Sugar Mill

Lahainaluna Rd.

Lahaina Center

Papalaua St.

Lahaina
Shopping Center

Front St.

Baldwin Home Museum

Dickenson St.

Wainee

Luakini St.

Lahaina
Small Boat Harbor

Prison St.

Banyan Tree

505 Front St.
(Shops and Restaurants)

Shaw St.

0   1 Mile
0   1 Kilometer

N

(with lights for night play until 10pm), a pool, a sundeck, a barbecue, and a picnic area. The aloha-friendly staff will be happy to take the time to answer all of your questions.

Best Western Pioneer Inn. 658 Wharf St. (in front of Lahaina Pier), Lahaina, HI 96761. ☎ **800/457-5457** or 808/661-3636. Fax 808/667-5708. www.bestwestern.com. 50 units. A/C TV TEL. $102–$120 double. Extra person $15. AE, CB, DC, DISC, MC, V. Parking $4 in lot 2 blocks away.

This historic hotel has come a long way from its origins as a turn-of-the-century whalers' saloon and inn. Until the 1970s, a room at the Pioneer Inn overlooking Lahaina Harbor went for $20 and included a can of Raid insect repellent; folks partied at the bar downstairs until the wee hours of the morning, so no one slept. But those days are long gone—and this old waterfront hotel has never looked better. You can surf on the waves out front. If you want a beach for sunbathing in the sand, walk down Front Street about 3 to 4 blocks (10 minutes) to the "Beach Access" sign across from Kauaula Road.

This once-rowdy home-away-from-home for sailors and whalers now seems almost respectable, like visiting your great-grandma's house—old but nice, even charming (a word never before associated with this relic). The hotel is a two-story plantation-style structure with big verandas that overlook the streets of Lahaina and the harbor. All rooms have been totally remodeled, with vintage bathrooms and new curtains and carpets; they even have TVs, VCRs, and direct-dial phones now. There's a new outdoor pool, three restaurants, the historic whalers' saloon (without the honky-tonk music), 20 shops, and the Lahaina Harbor just 50 feet away. The quietest rooms face either the garden courtyard—devoted to refined outdoor dining accompanied by live (but quiet) music—or the square-block-sized banyan tree next door. We recommend room no. 47, over the banyan court, with a view of the ocean and the harbor. If you want a front-row seat for all the Front Street action, book no. 48.

House of Fountains Bed & Breakfast. 1579 Lokia St. (off Fleming Rd., north of Lahaina town), Lahaina, HI 96761. ☎ **800/789-6865** or 808/667-2121. Fax 808/667-2120. www.alohahouse.com. 7 units (private bathrooms have shower only). A/C TV. $95–$145 double. Rates include full breakfast. Extra person $20. AE, DISC, MC, V. From Hwy. 30, take the Fleming Rd. exit; turn left on Ainakea; after 2 blocks, turn right on Malanai St.; go 3 blocks, and turn left onto Lokia St.

Talk about escape: A young German couple ran away to Maui for their honeymoon, fell in love with the island, bought a big house above Lahaina, and turned it into one of the area's best B&Bs. Their 7,000-square-foot contemporary home, in a quiet residential subdivision at the north end of town, is popular with visitors from around the world. This place is immaculate (hostess Daniela Clement provides daily maid service). The oversized rooms are fresh and quiet, with white ceramic-tile floors, bright tropical fabrics, and wicker furnishings; the four downstairs rooms all open onto flower-filled private patios. Guests share a pool, a Jacuzzi, a well-equipped guest kitchen, and a barbecue area. You're welcome to curl up on the living-room sofa facing the fireplace (not really needed in Lahaina) with a book from the library. Breakfast is served in the sunny dining room. Self-service laundry facilities are available for $2. The nearest beach is about 10 minutes away.

✪ **Lahaina Inn.** 127 Lahainaluna Rd. (near Front St.), Lahaina, HI 96761. ☎ **800/669-3444** or 808/661-0577. Fax 808/667-9480. www.lahainainn.com. 12 units (most bathrooms have shower only). A/C TEL. $99–$169 double. Extra person $20. Rates include continental breakfast. AE, DC, JCB, MC, V. Next-door parking $5. No children under 14.

A stay here really captures the romance of historic Lahaina. Built in 1938 as a general store, swept by fire in the mid-1960s, and reopened as a hotel in the 1970s, this place deteriorated into a fleabag with an eyesore of a bar at street level. Then, in 1986, rescue came in a classy way: It was saved from extinction by Rick Ralston, the Waikiki airbrush artist who became the Crazy Shirts mogul—and a one-man historic restoration society. About a million dollars of T-shirt money has brought this place back to life as a charming, antique-filled inn right in the heart of Lahaina. It doesn't have its own beach, but you can walk or drive to a good beach in just a few minutes.

If you like old hotels that have genuine historic touches, you'll love this place. As in many old hotels, some of these Victorian antique-stuffed rooms are small; if that's a problem for you, ask for a larger unit. All come with private bathrooms and lanais. The best room in the house is no. 7 ($99), which overlooks the beach, the town, and the island of Lanai; you can watch the action below or close the door and ignore it. Downstairs is one of Hawaii's finest bistros, David Paul's Lahaina Grill (see chapter 5).

✪ **Plantation Inn.** 174 Lahainaluna Rd. (between Wainee and Luakini sts., 1 block off Hwy. 30), Lahaina, HI 96761. ☎ **800/433-6815** or 808/667-9225. Fax 808/667-9293. www. theplantationinn.com. 18 units (some bathrooms have shower only). A/C TV TEL. $135–$215 double. Rates include full breakfast. AE, CB, DC, DISC, JCB, MC, V.

Attention, romance-seeking couples: Look no further. This charming inn looks like it has been here 100 years or more, but looks can be deceiving: The Victorian-style hotel is actually of 1990s vintage—an artful deception. The rooms are romantic to the max, tastefully done with period furniture, hardwood floors, stained glass, and ceiling fans; there are four-poster canopy beds and armoires in some rooms, brass beds and wicker in others. All come equipped with soundproofing (a plus in Lahaina), TV, VCR, fridge, private bathroom, and lanai; the suites have kitchenettes. The rooms wrap around the large pool and deck. You're a few minutes' walk or drive from a good beach.

Also on the property are a spa and an elegantly decorated pavilion lounge, as well as Gerard's, an excellent French restaurant (see chapter 5). It can be pricey, but hotel guests get a discount on dinner (you'll kick yourself if you don't eat here). Breakfast is served around the pool and in the pavilion lounge; ours featured fresh fruit, followed by a choice of Gerard's French toast or his homemade yogurt and granola.

Puamana. Front St. (at the extreme southern end of Lahaina, a half mile from downtown). Reservations c/o Klahani Travel, Lahaina Cannery Mall, 1221 Honoapiilani Hwy., Lahaina, HI 96761. ☎ **800/669-6284** or 808/667-2712. Fax 808/661-5875. www.klahani.travel.com. 40 units. TV TEL. $100–$175 1-bedroom unit, $140–$250 2-bedroom unit, $300–$500 3-bedroom unit. 3-night minimum. AE, DC, DISC, MC, V.

These 28 acres of town houses situated right on the water are the ideal choice for those who want the option of retreating from the crowds and cacophony of downtown Lahaina into the serene quiet of an elegant neighborhood. (Puamana is on the water, but the shoreline here is rocky. There's a good beach right next door at Paunau Beach Park.)

Private and peaceful are apt descriptions for this complex: Each unit is a privately owned individual home, with no neighbors above or below. Most are exquisitely decorated, and all come with a full kitchen, TV, lanai, barbecue, and at least two bathrooms. There are three pools (one for adults only), a tennis court, table tennis, and on-site laundry facilities (some units have washers and dryers as well). Puamana was once a private estate in the 1920s, part of the sugar plantation that dominated Lahaina; the plantation manager's house has been converted into a clubhouse with oceanfront lanai, library, card room, sauna, and office.

Wai Ola Vacation Paradise on Maui. Kuuipo St. (P.O. Box 12580), Lahaina, HI 96761. ☎ **800/492-4652** or 808/661-7901. Fax 808/661-7901. www.waiola.com. 3 units. A/C TV

TEL. $95–$115 studio, $100–$120 suite, $115–$135 1-bedroom apt. 5-night minimum high season, 3-night minimum low season. Extra person $15. AE, CB, DC, DISC, JCB, MC, V.

Just 2 blocks from the beach, in a quiet, residential development behind a tall concrete wall, lies Maui's version of Shangri-la: shade trees, sitting areas, gardens, a pool, an ocean mural, and a range of accommodations—a suite inside the 5,000-square-foot home, a separate studio cottage, and a one-bedroom apartment. Hostess Julie Frank owned and operated Julie's Bed-and-Breakfast in Half Moon Bay, California, for years; as a veteran innkeeper, she knows how to provide comfortable accommodations and memorable vacations. The Kuuipo (Sweetheart) Suite comes complete with deck and sweeping views of the Lahaina coastline. Downstairs, just off the pool, hot tub, and deck, is the 1,000-square-foot one-bedroom apartment, which has a full kitchen, a queen bed, a sofa bed, a private phone, TV/VCR, and air-conditioning. The 500-square-foot studio cottage, located in the courtyard, has a full kitchen and tasteful white wicker furniture. Guests have full access to the pool, barbecue facilities, and outdoor wet bar.

INEXPENSIVE

In addition to the following choices, also consider value-priced **Old Lahaina House** (☎ **800/847-0761** or 808/667-4663; fax 808/667-5615; www.mauiweb.com/maui/olhouse), which features comfy twin- and king-bedded doubles for $60 to $95.

Aloha Lani Inn—A Maui Guest House. 13 Kauaula Rd. (at Front St.), Lahaina, HI 96761. ☎ **800/57-ALOHA** or 808/661-8040. Fax 808/661-8045. www.maui.net/~tony. 3 units (all with shared bathroom). $69 double. 3-night minimum. AE, MC, V.

If you're on a fixed budget and don't mind sharing a bathroom, this clean, casual guesthouse, just a block from the beach, is the place for you. Host Melinda Mower, who took over the operation formerly known as Aloha Tony's in June 1996, has livened up the place with tropical and floral interior decor. The entire house is guest-friendly: The living room is stuffed with books on the flora, fauna, history, and marine life of the islands, along with menus from dozens of nearby restaurants; all the drawers and cabinets in the communal kitchen are labeled with their contents; a map of Maui pinpoints great things to do; and loads of brochures are available to help you plan your stay. The guest rooms are small, but the location is dynamite: a stone's throw from the beach and within walking distance of downtown Lahaina (no parking woes), yet in a quiet residential neighborhood.

✪ **Guest House.** 1620 Ainakea Rd. (off Fleming Rd., north of Lahaina town), Lahaina, HI 96761. ☎ **800/621-8942** or 808/661-8085. Fax 808/661-1896. www.mauiguesthouse. com. 4 units. A/C TV TEL. $115 double. Rates include full breakfast. AE, DISC, MC, V. Take Fleming Rd. off Hwy. 30; turn left on Ainakea; the house is 2 blocks down.

This is one of Lahaina's great bed-and-breakfast deals: a charming house with more amenities than the expensive Kaanapali hotels just down the road. The roomy home features parquet floors, floor-to-ceiling windows, and a pool—surrounded by a deck and comfortable lounge chairs—that's larger than some at high-priced condos. Every guest room is air-conditioned and has a ceiling fan, small fridge, TV, and private phone; four of the rooms each have a quiet lanai and a romantic hot tub. The large kitchen (with every gadget imaginable) is available for guests' use. The Guest House also operates Trinity Tours and offers discounts on car rentals and just about every island activity. It doesn't have its own beach, but it's a 10-minute walk to Wahihuli State Wayside Park.

KAANAPALI
VERY EXPENSIVE

Another option to consider is the **Royal Lahaina Resort,** 2780 Kekaa Dr., Lahaina, HI 96761 (☎ **800/44-ROYAL** or 808/661-3611; fax 800/432-9752 or 808/ 661-6150; www.hawaiihotels.com). But skip the overpriced hotel rooms; stay here only if you can get one of the 122 cottages tucked among the well-manicured grounds ($295 to $385 double).

If you aren't looking for something uniquely Hawaiian and you like the Marriott chain's style, consider the **Maui Marriott Resort,** 100 Nohea Kai Dr., Lahaina, HI 96761 (☎ **800/228-9290** or 808/667-1200; fax 808/667-8181; www.marriott. com). Rates are $200 to $360 double, from $400 suite; ask about packages.

♻ **Sheraton Maui.** 2605 Kaanapali Pkwy., Lahaina, HI 96761. ☎ **800/STAY-ITT** or 808/661-0031. Fax 808/661-9991. www.sheraton-maui.com. 510 units. A/C TV TEL. $340–$500 double, from $625 suite. Extra person $45. Children 17 and under stay free in parent's room using existing bedding. AE, CB, DC, DISC, MC, V. $7 optional "resort amenties package," includes self parking, "free" local phone calls, "free" credit-card calls, "free" in-room safe, fresh-flower lei greeting on arrival, daily coffee and newspaper, use of fitness center and "free" kids program. Valet parking $12.

Terrific facilities for families and fitness buffs and a premier beach location make this beautiful resort an all-around great place to stay. The first to set up camp in Kaanapali (in 1963), the hoteliers took the best location on the beach: the curving white-sand cove next to Black Rock (a lava formation that rises 80 feet above the beach), where they built into the side of the cliff. Some of the island's best snorkeling is right offshore. The grand dame of Kaanapali Beach reopened in 1997 after a $160 million, 2-year renovation; the resort is virtually new, with six buildings set in well-tended tropical gardens. The lobby has been elevated to take advantage of panoramic views, and a new lagoonlike pool features lava-rock waterways, wooden bridges, and an open-air spa.

The new emphasis is on family appeal, with a class of rooms dedicated to those traveling with children (665-square-foot units with two double beds and a pull-down wall bed) and other kid-friendly amenities. Every room is outfitted with all the comforts that make for easy travel—from minifridges and free Kona coffee for the coffeemakers to irons, hair dryers, and even toothbrushes and toothpaste. Other pluses include a "no hassle" check-in policy: The valet takes you and your luggage straight to your room, so no standing in line at registration. But not everything has changed, thankfully. Cliff divers still swan-dive off the torch-lit lava-rock headland in a traditional sunset ceremony—a sight to see. And the views of Kaanapali Beach, with Lanai and Molokai in the distance, are some of the best in Kaanapali.

Dining/Diversions: Three restaurants, with cuisine ranging from teppanyaki to steaks and seafood, plus a snack bar and three bars and cocktail lounges.

Amenities: Two pools, three tennis courts, summer children's program, room service (6:30am to 10:30pm), fitness center, game center, full beach services and water sports, 24-hour coin-op laundry, hospitality suite for early arrivals or late departures, massage, valet laundry, baby-sitting, express checkout, in-house doctors' office, conference facilities, activities desk.

Westin Maui. 2365 Kaanapali Pkwy., Lahaina, HI 96761. ☎ **800/228-3000** or 808/ 667-2525. Fax 808/661-5831. www.westin.com. 793 units. A/C MINIBAR TV TEL. $265– $495 double, from $800 suite. Extra person $30 ($50 in Royal Beach Club rooms). Special wedding/honeymoon and other packages available. AE, DC, DISC, ER, JCB, MC, V. "Resort fee" of $8 includes such amenities as "free" local phone calls, use of fitness center, "complimentary" coffee and tea, "free" parking, and "free" local paper.

ⓘ　Family-Friendly Accommodations

If you're traveling with the kids, you'll be welcomed with open arms at many of Maui's accommodations. Our favorites are listed below. Note that by state law, hotels that offer supervised activity programs can accept only children ages 5 to 12.

WEST MAUI

Embassy Vacation Resort *(see p. 84)*　　Kids will love this place. The all-suite property features a mammoth 1-acre pool with a 24-foot water slide and a great beach for swimming and snorkeling. Every unit has a complete entertainment center that will satisfy even the surliest teenager: 35-inch TV (with HBO), VCR (a vast video library is on site), and stereo. With roomy condolike suites (ranging from 820 to 1,100 square feet) that feature hotel-style amenities, all-you-can-eat breakfasts, and free daily cocktail parties included in the price, Mom and Dad will be happy, too.

Hale Kai *(see p. 85)*　　This small condo complex is ideally located for families: right on the beach, next door to a county park, and a 10-minute drive to Lahaina's attractions. Kids can hang out at the pool, swim in the ocean, or play in the park. There's a TV and VCR in every unit, and the well-equipped kitchens (with dishwasher, microwave, even a blender) allow Mom and Dad to save money on eating out.

Maui Park *(see p. 87)*　　Located directly across the street from Honokowai Beach Park, the roomy apartments at this three-story complex are a good value for families. Extras include a large swimming pool, a jet spa, and barbecue and picnic areas.

Noelani Condominium Resort *(see p. 88)*　　If your kids love to swim, head to this Kahana condo on the ocean. Right next door is great snorkeling at a sandy cove, frequented by spinner dolphins and turtles in summer and humpback whales in winter. On site are two freshwater pools (one heated for night swimming). The units feature complete kitchens and entertainment centers.

Ritz-Carlton Kapalua *(see p. 91)*　　The Ritz Kids is a daytime program offering both educational activities (exploring the ecosystems in streams, learning the hula) and sports (from golf to swimming). The cost for the program is $15 per child (which includes lunch); it's complimentary for the half-day program (actually, it's covered by your $10 per day "resort fee").

Sheraton Maui *(see p. 79)*　　The Sheraton Maui, on Kaanapali Beach, offers "family suites," which have three beds (two double beds and one pull-down double wall bed), a sitting room with full-sized couch, and two TVs, both

The "Aquatic Playground"—an 87,000-square-foot pool area with five free-form heated pools joined by swim-through grottoes, waterfalls, and a 128-foot-long water slide— sets this resort apart from its peers along Kaanapali Beach. Thanks to megahotelier Christopher Hemmeter, who waved his magic wand over the property in the late 1980s, this is the Disney World of water-park resorts—and your kids will be in water-hog heaven. The fantasy theme extends from the estate-like grounds into the interior's public spaces, which are filled with the shrieks of tropical birds and the splash of waterfalls. The oversized architecture, requisite colonnade, and $2 million art collection make a pleasing backdrop for all of the action. We think it's a bit over the top, but equipped with Nintendo. In addition, there's the Keiki Aloha program for children, with fun activities ranging from Hawaiian games to visits to nearby attractions. Children 12 and younger enjoy free meals (breakfast, lunch, and dinner) when dining with one adult in the Kids Eat Free program.

SOUTH MAUI

Koa Resort *(see p. 94)*   Right across the street from the ocean in Kihei, this deluxe condo complex is great for active families, with its two tennis courts, pool, hot tub, and 18-hole putting green. The spacious, privately owned units are fully equipped and have plenty of room for even a large brood.

Mana Kai Maui Resort *(see p. 96)*   This complex, an unusual combination of hotel and condominium, sits on a beautiful white-sand cove that's one of the best snorkeling beaches on the south coast. Families will like the condo units, which have full kitchens and open living rooms; sliding-glass doors lead to small lanai overlooking the sandy beach and ocean.

✪ **Four Seasons Resort Wailea** *(see p. 98)*   This is a real standout, the most kid-friendly hotel on Maui. The *keikis* will feel welcome with such amenities as free milk and cookies on the first day, children's menus in all restaurants (including room service), and complimentary infant needs (crib, stroller, high chair, playpen, car seats) and child-safety features (toilet-seat locks, plug covers, security gates). The resort can also prepurchase a range of necessities (such as diapers and baby food) for you before your arrival. Kids and teens have a huge list of recreational activities and equipment to choose from, including a game room (with Super Nintendo, Sony PlayStation, foosball, and more); a free scuba clinic (for ages 12 and up); children's videos; and a host of sailing, snorkeling, and whale-watching activities.

UPCOUNTRY

Kili's Cottage *(see p. 106)*   In the cool elevation of Kula, this sweet three bedroom/two-bathroom cottage, situated on two acres, is a great place for families. The price is right—$95 double—and the amenities are numerous: a large lanai, a full kitchen, a gas barbecue, a washer/dryer, great views, and even toys for the kids. The hostess, Kili Namau'u, who is the director of a Hawaiian language immersion school, greets each guest with royal aloha, from the house filled with flowers (picked from the garden) to the welcome basket filled with tropical produce grown on the property.

---

guests seem to love it: The resort has taken top honors in various readers' surveys, from *Condé Nast Traveler* to *Travel & Leisure*. With lots of indoor and outdoor meeting spaces, it's also a big hit with wedding parties and groups.

Most rooms in the two 11-story towers overlook the aquatic playground, the ocean, and the island of Lanai in the distance. In addition to the standard features, each comes with a safe, an iron and board, a coffeemaker, and its own lanai. The latest addition to the rooms are new beds, not just any old beds but Westin's custom-designed "heavenly bed," a 900 coil, pillow-topped mattress by Simmons (plus a choice of five different pillows). If that doesn't give you sweet dreams, nothing will.

Dining/Diversions: Several outdoor restaurants and lounges, ranging from a sushi bar to a seafood buffet. The hotel's Villa restaurant is currently being renovated, soon to be replaced with another upscale choice.

Amenities: Five pools, Jacuzzi, water exercise classes, scuba lessons for beginners and refresher courses, guided hikes, extensive health club and spa facilities, extensive supervised kids' program weekdays, twice-daily maid service, nightly turndown, multilingual staff, American Express and Hertz desks, secretarial services, coin-op laundry, ATM, hospitality suite for early check-ins and late departures, beauty salon, retail shops, business center, and conference facilities. Guest Services will help you plan sightseeing and activities. Golf, tennis, and shopping are all at hand. A wedding coordinator, known as the director of romance, can help you throw an unforgettable wedding.

EXPENSIVE

Hyatt Regency Maui. 200 Nohea Kai Dr., Lahaina, HI 96761. ☎ **800/233-1234** or 808/661-1234. Fax 808/667-4714. www.hyatt.com. 815 units. A/C MINIBAR TV TEL. $235–$495 double, from $600 suite. Extra person $30 ($50 in Regency Club rooms). Children 18 and under stay free in parent's room using existing bedding. Packages available. AE, DC, DISC, JCB, MC, V. Valet parking $8, free self-parking.

People either absolutely love or hate this fantasy resort. One of several built by Christopher Hemmeter for Hyatt in the 1980s, this hotel—the southernmost of the Kaanapali properties—has lots of imaginative touches: a collection of exotic species (flaming pink flamingos, unhappy-looking penguins, and an assortment of loud parrots and macaws in the lobby), nine waterfalls, and an eclectic Asian and Pacific art collection. This huge place covers some 40 acres; even if you don't stay here, you might want to walk through the expansive tree-filled atrium and the parklike grounds, with their dense riot of plants and fantasy pools with grottoes, slides, and a suspended walking bridge. There's even a man-made beach in case the adjacent public beach is just too crowded.

All the rooms are pleasantly decorated in rich colors, floral prints, and Asian lamps—a welcome change from the typical beiges—and feature separate sitting areas and private lanai. In-room extras include safes, hair dryers, coffeemakers, and irons and ironing boards. Two Regency Club floors have private concierge, complimentary breakfast, sunset cocktails, and snacks.

Dining/Diversions: Swan Court is a romantic setting for dinner (see chapter 5 for a full review); the Cascades Grille and Sushi Bar serves steak, seafood, and sushi; and Spats offers Italian fare. There's also the casual poolside Pavilion, numerous lounges, a swim-up cocktail bar, and the "Drums of the Pacific" dinner show.

Amenities: The Great Pool; health club with weight and exercise rooms, Jacuzzi, sauna, and massage studio; six hard-surface tennis courts; three nearby golf courses; game room; small lending library; twice-daily maid service; concierge; room service; activities desk; baby-sitting. Snorkeling gear, bicycles, kayaks, boogie boards, and video and underwater cameras are available for rent. *Kiele V,* the Hyatt's 55-foot catamaran, sponsors snorkel trips, whale-watching excursions, and evening cruises. The Camp Hyatt kids' program offers daytime and evening supervised activities for 3-to 12-year-olds.

✪ **Maui Eldorado Resort.** 2661 Kekaa Dr., Lahaina, HI 96761. ☎ **800/688-7444** or 808/661-0021. Fax 808/667-7039. www.outrigger.com. 98 units. AC TV TEL. $195–$210 studio double, $250–$275 1-bedroom (for up to 4), $350–$375 2-bedroom (for up to 6). Numerous packages available, including 7th night free, car packages, senior rates, and more. AE, CB, DC, DISC, JCB, MC, V.

These spacious condominium units—all with full kitchens, washer/dryers, and daily maid service—were built at a time when land in Kaanapali was cheap, contractors took pride in their work, and visitors expected large, spacious rooms with views from every window. You'll find it hard to believe that this was one of Kaanapali's first properties in the late 1960s—this first-class choice still looks like new. The Outrigger chain has managed to keep prices down to reasonable levels, especially if you come in spring or fall. It's a great place for families, with its big units, grassy areas that are perfect for running off excess energy, and a beachfront that's usually safe for swimming.

Amenities include daily maid service, a travel desk, fax services, your own personal safe, three pools, a beach cabana, barbecue areas, shops, and laundry facilities.

✪ **The Whaler on Kaanapali Beach.** 2481 Kaanapali Pkwy. (next to Whalers Village), Lahaina, HI 96761. ☎ **800/367-7052** or 808/661-4861. Fax 435-655-4844. www.ten-ten.com/vri. 360 units (150 in rental pool). A/C TV TEL. High season $195–$210 studio double, $260–$390 1-bedroom (sleeps up to 4), $430–$510 2-bedroom (sleeps up to 6). Off-season $195–$205 studio, $235–$355 1-bedroom, $370–$480 2-bedroom. 2-night minimum. Extra person $15; crib $10. Packages available. AE, MC, V.

Location, location, location—in the heart of Kaanapali, right on the world-famous beach, lies this oasis of elegance, privacy, and luxury. The relaxing atmosphere strikes you as soon as you enter the open-air lobby, where light reflects off the dazzling koi in the meditative lily pond. No expense has been spared on these gorgeous accommodations; all have full kitchens, washer/dryers, marble bathrooms, 10-foot beamed ceilings, and blue-tiled lanai. Add to that a rarity in Kaanapali these days: free parking. Every unit boasts spectacular views, which include vistas of both Kaanapali's gentle waves and the humpback peaks of the West Maui Mountains.

Dining/Diversions: Next door is Whalers Village, where you'll find Peter Merriman's terrific Hula Grill (see chapter 5) and a handful of other restaurant and bar choices.

Amenities: Daily maid service, pool and spa, exercise room, five tennis courts. The Kaanapali Golf Club's 36 holes are across the street, and all the ocean activities Maui has to offer are just out back.

MODERATE

Kaanapali Beach Hotel. 2525 Kaanapali Pkwy., Lahaina, HI 96761. ☎ **800/262-8450** or 808/661-0011. Fax 808/667-5978. www.kaanapalibeachhotel.com. 433 units. A/C TV TEL. $145–$265 double; from $215 suite. Extra person $25. Free car, bed-and-breakfast, golf, and romance packages available, as well as discount rates for seniors. AE, CB, DC, DISC, JCB, MC, V.

This old beach hotel, set in a garden by the sea, is Maui's most genuinely Hawaiian place to stay—you *live* aloha here. It isn't a luxury property, but it's not bad, either. Three low-rise wings are set around a wide, grassy lawn with coco palms and a whale-shaped pool, bordering a fabulous stretch of beach. The spacious, spotless motel-like rooms are done in wicker and rattan, with Hawaiian-style bedspreads and a lanai that looks toward the courtyard and the beach. The beachfront rooms are separated from the water only by Kaanapali's landscaped walking trail.

The Kaanapali Beach Hotel is older and less high-tech than its upscale neighbors, but it has an irresistible local style and a real Hawaiian warmth that are absent in many other Maui hotels. Old Hawaii values and customs are always close at hand, and in true aloha style, the service is some of the friendliest around. Tiki torches, hula, and Hawaiian music create a festive atmosphere in the expansive open courtyard every night. As part of the hotel's extensive Hawaiiana program, you can learn to cut pineapple, weave lauhala (the leaf of the hala tree), and even dance the *real* hula; there's also an arts-and-crafts fair three days a week, a morning welcome reception weekdays, and a Hawaiian library.

The hotel's three restaurants feature native Hawaiian dishes as well as modern Hawaiian cuisine (see chapter 5 for a review of the Tiki Terrace); there's also a poolside bar that fixes a mean piña colada. Amenities include a concierge, baby-sitting, a United Airlines desk, coin-op laundry, in-room movies, convenience shops and salon, conference rooms, beach-equipment rentals, free scuba and snorkeling lessons, access to tennis and Kaanapali golf, and ice, drink, and snack machines.

HONOKOWAI, KAHANA & NAPILI
VERY EXPENSIVE

Embassy Vacation Resort. 104 Kaanapali Shores Pl. (in Honokowai), Lahaina, HI 96761. ☎ **800/669-3155** or 808/661-2000. Fax 808/661-1353. www.maui.net/~embassy. 413 units. A/C TV TEL. $290–$445 1-bedroom suite (for 4, can sleep up to 5), $560 2-bedroom suite (for 4, can sleep up to 5). Rates include full breakfast and 2-hour cocktail party daily. Extra person $20. Children 18 and under stay free in parent's room using existing bedding. AE, CB, DC, DISC, MC, V. Parking $5. Take the first turn off Hwy. 30 after Kaanapali onto Lower Honoapiilani Rd.; turn left at Kaanapali Shores Place.

You can't miss this place; the shockingly pink pyramid-shaped building is visible from the highway. It's composed of three towers, each set around a central atrium amidst tropical gardens with interlocking waterfalls and waterways; a huge wooden deck overlooks the koi-filled ponds and streams. Kaanapali's shops, golf, tennis, and restaurants are just minutes away.

Kids will love it here. The all-suite property features a mammoth 1-acre pool with a 24-foot water slide, a great beach for swimming and snorkeling, and complete entertainment centers in every unit with 35-inch TVs (with HBO), VCRs (a vast video library is on site), and stereos. Mom and Dad will appreciate the roomy condolike suites (ranging from 820 to 1,100 square feet), hotel-style amenities, all-you-can-eat breakfasts, and free daily cocktail parties. Every unit has a full-sized sofa bed, a good-sized lanai, a minikitchen (microwave, small fridge, wet bar, and coffeemaker with free Kona coffee), two phones, a soaking tub big enough for two, and a second TV in the bedroom.

Dining/Diversions: There are three on-site dining choices: the oceanfront North Beach Grille, the poolside Ohana Bar and Grill, and a sandwich/snack bar, The Deli Planet.

Amenities: Pool, health club, Jacuzzi, sauna, sundeck, 18-hole minigolf, concierge, laundry facilities, dry cleaning, tour desk, children's program (during holidays and in summer).

EXPENSIVE

Families might want to consider the **Sands of Kahana,** 4299 Lower Honoapiilani Rd. (☎ **888/669-0400** or 808/669-1199; fax 808/669-8409; www.sands-of-kahana. com). Despite the austere appearance of the high-rise buildings, these units offer many amenities, including pools and a playground. Rates are $165 to $335 in high season, $145 to $305 in low season; there's a 5-night minimum.

✪ **Napili Kai Beach Club.** 5900 Honoapiilani Rd. (at the extreme north end of Napili, next door to Kapalua), Lahaina, HI 96761. ☎ **800/367-5030** or 808/669-6271. Fax 808/669-0085. www.napilikai.com. 162 units. TV TEL. $185–$275 double studio, $320–$395 1-bedroom suite (sleeps up to 4), $475–$600 2-bedroom (sleeps up to 6). Extra person $15. Packages available. AE, MC, V.

Just south of the Bay Club restaurant in Kapalua, nestled in a small, white-sand cove, lies this comfortable oceanfront complex. Clusters of one- and two-story units with

Accommodations from Honokowai to Kapalua

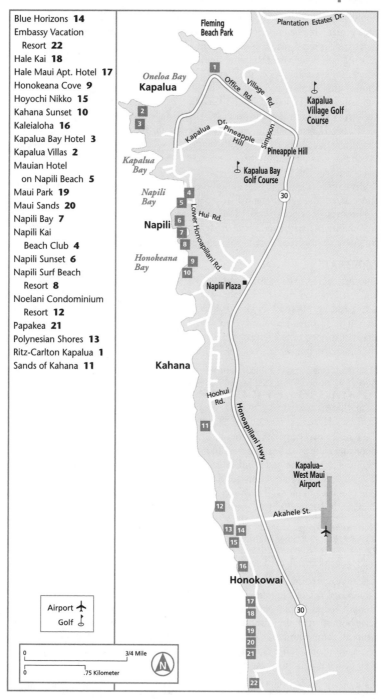

double-hipped Hawaii-style roofs face their very own gold-sand, safe-swimming beach; many have a view of the Pacific, with Molokai and Lanai in the distance. The older beachfront Lahaina Building units, with ceiling fans only, are a good buy at $215. Those who prefer air-conditioning should book into the Honolua Building, where, for the same price, you'll get a fully air-conditioned room set back from the shore around a grassy parklike lawn and pool. All units (except eight hotel rooms) have fully stocked kitchenettes with full-sized fridges, stoves, microwaves, toaster ovens, and coffeemakers; some have dishwashers. There's daily maid service.

Dining/Diversions: The Sea House Restaurant serves three meals (see chapter 5); the Whale Watcher's Bar takes care of cocktails. There's complimentary coffee at the beach pagoda every morning, free tea in the lobby every afternoon, and a free mai tai party once a week.

Amenities: Beach pagoda; complimentary beach chairs, mats, swim masks, and snorkels; complimentary tennis rackets and golf putters; two shuffleboard courts; barbecue areas; four pools; two 18-hole putting greens; laundry facilities; dry cleaning; free children's activities (available Easter, June 15 to August 31, and Christmas); activities desk. Tennis courts are nearby, and golf is just minutes away.

MODERATE

Another option is **Polynesian Shores,** 3975 Lower Honoapiilani Rd. (near Kahana, and just 2 minutes from the Kapalua–West Maui Airport), Lahaina, HI 96761 (☎ 800/433-6284 or 808/669-6065; fax 808/669-0909; www.maui.net/~polyshor). Every unit (one to three bedrooms, from $110 to $200) has floor-to-ceiling sliding-glass doors that open onto a private lanai with an ocean view; there's great snorkeling off the beach out front.

Hale Kai. 3691 Lower Honoapiilani Rd. (in Honokowai), Lahaina, HI 96761. ☎ 800/446-7307 or 808/669-6333. Fax 808/669-7474. www.halekai.com. 40 units. TV TEL. High season $115 1-bedroom, $145–$150 2-bedroom (rates for up to 4), $185 3-bedroom (for up to 6). Off-season $100 1-bedroom, $130–$135 2-bedroom, $185 3-bedroom. 3-night minimum. Extra person $10. Children 3 and under stay free in parent's room. MC, V.

This small, two-story condo complex is ideally located, right on the beach and next door to a county park; shops, restaurants, and ocean activities are all within a 6-mile radius. The units are older but in excellent shape, and come with a full kitchen and TV/VCR. Many guests clamor for the oceanfront pool units, but we find the park-view units cooler, and they still have ocean views (upstairs units also have cathedral ceilings). Book early, because units fill up fast; repeat guests make up most of the clientele.

Honokeana Cove. 5255 Lower Honoapiilani Rd. (in Napili), Lahaina, HI 96761. ☎ 800/237-4948 or 808/669-6441. Fax 808/669-8777. www.honokeana-cove.com. 33 units. A/C TV TEL. $110 1-bedroom, $154 2-bedroom (sleeps up to 4), $183 3-bedroom (sleeps up to 6). 3-night minimum. Extra person $10–$15. MC, V.

These large, secluded units—cozily set around a pool in a lush tropical setting—have fabulous views of Honokeana Cove. The beach here isn't sandy (it's composed of smooth round rocks), but the water just offshore is excellent for snorkeling (turtles have been spotted just offshore) and for whale watching in winter. The well-appointed units all come with a full kitchen, TV (including Spectra Vision at no extra charge), VCR, and lanai. Amenities include laundry, barbecues, and deck chairs. All in all, a well-priced option in an expensive neighborhood.

✪ **Kahana Sunset.** 4909 Lower Honoapiilani Rd. (at the northern end of Kahana, almost in Napili), c/o P.O. Box 10219, Lahaina, HI 96761. ☎ **800/669-1488** or 808/669-8011. Fax 808/669-9170. www.kahanasunset.com. 79 units (49 in rental pool). A/C TV TEL. High season

$160–$180 1-bedroom (sleeps up to 6), $165–$265 2-bedroom (sleeps up to 6). Low season $95–160 1-bedroom, $140–$200 2-bedroom. 3-night minimum. AE, MC, V. From Hwy. 30, turn makai (toward the ocean) at the Napili Plaza (Napilihau St.), then left on Lower Honoapiilani Rd.

Lying in the crook of a sharp horseshoe curve on Lower Honoapiilani Road is this series of wooden condo units, stair-stepping down the side of a hill to a postcard-perfect white-sand beach. The unique location, nestled between the coastline and the road above, makes Kahana Sunset a very private place to stay. A small pool and Jacuzzi sit in the midst of a grassy lawn; down by the sandy beach are gazebos and picnic areas. The units feature full kitchens, washer/dryers, large lanai with terrific views, and sleeper sofas. This is a great complex for families: The beach out front is safe for swimming, the grassy area is away from traffic, and the units are roomy enough for all. The two-bedroom units have parking just outside, making carrying luggage and groceries that much easier.

Maui Park. 3626 Lower Honoapiilani Rd. (in Honokowai), Lahaina, HI 96761. ☎ **800/367-5004** or 808/669-6622. Fax 800/477-2329 or 808/669-9647. www.castle-group.com. 288 units. A/C TV TEL. High season $119 double room, $141–$149 studio double with kitchen, $159–$171 1-bedroom (sleeps up to 4), $207 2-bedroom (sleeps up to 6). Low season $109 double room, $120–$127 studio double with kitchen, $137–$149 1-bedroom, $185 2-bedroom. AE, DC, DISC, MC, V.

Directly across the street from Honokowai Beach Park, this three-story, six-building complex is a good choice for families. The property features a large pool, a jet spa, and barbecue and picnic areas; a convenience store is just next door, and coin-op laundry facilities are on site. The roomy units all come with balconies and kitchens. There are no elevators, but wheelchair-accessible rooms are available on the ground level.

Maui Sands. Maui Resort Management, 3600 Lower Honoapiilani Rd. (in Honokowai), Lahaina, HI 96761. ☎ **800/367-5037** or 808/669-1902. Fax 808/669-8790. www.mauigetaway.com. 76 units. A/C TV TEL. $90–$154 1-bedroom (sleeps up to 3); $125–$187 2-bedroom (sleeps up to 5). Extra person $9. 7-night minimum. MC, V.

The Maui Sands was built back when property wasn't as expensive and developers took the extra time and money to surround all their condo units with lush landscaping. It's hard to get a unit with a bad view: All face either the ocean (with views of Lanai and Molokai) or tropical gardens blooming with brilliant heliconia and sweet-smelling ginger. Each roomy unit has a big lanai and full kitchen. With two big bedrooms plus space in the living room for a fifth person (or even a sixth), the larger units are good deals for families (though note that they only have one bathroom). There's a narrow beach out front and a pool and laundry facilities on site. In case you have any problems or questions, the management agency is just across the street.

Mauian Hotel on Napili Beach. 5441 Lower Honoapiilani Rd. (in Napili), Lahaina, HI 96761. ☎ **800/367-5034** or 808/669-6205. Fax 808/669-0129. www.mauian.com. 44 units. High season $160–$190 double; off-season $140–$170 double. Rates include free continental breakfast. Extra 3rd or 4th person $10 each. Children under 5 stay free in parent's room. AE, DISC, MC, V.

The Hawaiian family that built this low-rise hotel in 1961 now own it again, and they've restored the studio units to their original old Hawaiian style. This is a great place to get away from it all: The Mauian is perched above a beautiful half-mile-long, white-sand beach with great swimming and snorkeling; there's a pool with chaise longues, umbrellas, and tables on the sundeck; and the verdant grounds are bursting with tropical color. The renovated rooms feature hardwood floors, Indonesian-style furniture, and big lanai with great views. Return guests are drawn back by the small touches, such as the fresh flowers in rooms upon arrival (plus chilled champagne for guests celebrating a special occasion). There are no phones and no TVs in the rooms (this place really is about getting away from it all), but the large Ohana (family) room does have a TV with VCR and an extensive library for those who can't bear the solitude, plus complimentary coffee; phones and fax service are available in the business center. Great restaurants are just a 5-minute walk away, Kapalua Resort is up the street, and the nightly sunsets off the beach are spectacular.

Napili Surf Beach Resort. 50 Napili Pl. (off Lower Honoapiilani Rd., in Napili), Lahaina, HI 96761. ☎ 800/541-0638 or 808/669-8002. Fax 808/669-8004. www.napilisurf.com. 53 units (some with shower only). TV TEL. $99–$159 studio (sleeps up to 3), $179–$229 1-bedroom (sleeps up to 4). No credit cards.

This well-maintained, superbly landscaped condo complex has a great location on Napili Beach. Facilities include two pools, three shuffleboard courts, and three gas barbecue grills. The well-furnished units (all with full kitchen) were renovated in 1997, and free daily maid service—a rarity in condo properties—keeps the units clean. Management encourages socializing: In addition to weekly mai tai parties and coffee socials, the resort hosts annual shuffleboard and golf tournaments, as well as gettogethers on July 4th, Thanksgiving, Christmas, and New Year's. Many guests arrange their travel plans around these events at the Napili Surf.

✪ **Noelani Condominium Resort.** 4095 Lower Honoapiilani Rd. (in Kahana), Lahaina, HI 96761. ☎ 800/367-6030 or 808/669-8374. Fax 808/669-7904. www.noelani-condo-resort. com. 50 units. TV TEL. $107–$127 studio double, $147–$157 1-bedroom (sleeps up to 4), $197–$207 2-bedroom (sleeps up to 4), $237–$257 3-bedroom (sleeps up to 6). Rates include continental breakfast on 1st morning. Extra person $10. Children under 18 stay free in parent's room. Packages for honeymooners, seniors, and AAA members available. 3-night minimum. AE, MC, V.

This oceanfront condo is a great value, whether you stay in a studio or a threebedroom unit (ideal for large families). The top-notch property is AAA approved and, after extensive exterior and interior renovations, has just been awarded a three-diamond designation. Everything is first class, from the furnishings to the oceanfront location, with a sandy cove next door at the new county park. There's good snorkeling off the cove, which is frequented by spinner dolphins and turtles in the summer and humpback whales in winter. All units feature full kitchens, entertainment centers, and spectacular views. Our favorites are in the Antherium building, where the one-, two-, and threebedrooms have oceanfront lanai just 20 feet from the water. There are two freshwater swimming pools (one heated for night swimming) and an oceanfront Jacuzzi. Guests are invited to a continental breakfast orientation on their first day and mai tai parties at night.

INEXPENSIVE

Another option is **Hoyochi Nikko,** 3901 Lower Honoapiilani Rd. (in Honokowai), Lahaina, HI 96761 (☎ 800/487-6002 or 808/669-8343; fax 808/669-3937;www. mauilodging.com), which has just 17 older (but well maintained) one- and two-bedroom units sharing 180 feet of oceanfront ($75 to $115 double).

Frugal travelers should also consider the **Hale Maui Apartment Hotel** (☎ 888/ 621-1736 or 808/669-6312; fax 808/669-1302), a wonderful tiny apartment hotel run by Hans and Eva Zimmerman, whose spirit is 100% aloha. All their one-bedroom suites, which run $75 to $95 double, come with ceiling fans, private lanai, and complete kitchens. There's no pool, but a private path leads to a great swimming beach.

Blue Horizons. 3894 Mahinahina Dr. (2 blocks from the Kapalua–West Maui Airport), Lahaina, HI 96761. ☎ 800/669-1948 or 808/669-1965. Fax 808/665-1615. 4 units. A/C

TV TEL. $79–$99 double. 2-night minimum. Rates include breakfast Mon–Sat. Extra person $15. AE, MC, V.

The only bed-and-breakfast on the west side of the island outside of Lahaina, Blue Horizons is about a 10-minute drive to Lahaina and about a 5-minute walk to sandy beaches. The four units, in a custom-built home in a subdivision, range from compact to spacious suites with separate bedrooms and a living-room area with sofa bed. Three units have kitchenettes and all four are air-conditioned, which helps not only with the heat of Mahinahina but also with the noise of the subdivision. A lavish breakfast is served in the screened dining area, where the ocean view may distract you from the banana pancakes. Amenities on site include a tile lap pool, washer/dryer, gas barbecue, and video library.

Kaleialoha. 3785 Lower Honoapiilani Rd. (in Honokowai), Lahaina, HI 96761. ☎ **800/ 222-8688** or 808/669-8197. Fax 808/669-2502. E-mail: kaleialoha@maui.net. 26 units. TV TEL. $105–$115 1-bedroom double. Extra person $10. 3-night minimum. MC, V.

This condo complex for the budget-minded has recently been upgraded, with new paint, bedspreads, and drapes in each unit. The advantage of the one-bedroom units—besides the ocean view—is the sofa bed in the living room, which allows the apartments to comfortably sleep four (and makes them ultra-affordable). All the island-style units feature fully equipped kitchens, with everything from dishwashers to washers and dryers (the only thing they do not supply is beach towels; bring your own). The complex has a pool, and there's great ocean swimming just off the rock wall (no sandy beach); a protective reef mows waves down and allows even timid swimmers to relax.

✪ Napili Bay. 33 Hui Dr. (off Lower Honoapiilani Hwy., in Napili), c/o Maui Beachfront Rentals, 256 Papalaua St., Lahaina, HI 96767. ☎ **888/661-7200** or 808/661-3500. Fax 808/661-5210. www.mauibeachfront.com. 33 units. TV TEL. $75–$100 for up to 4. 5-night minimum. MC, V.

One of Maui's best secret bargains is this small, two-story complex, located right on Napili's half-mile white-sand beach. It's perfect for a romantic getaway: The atmosphere is comfortable and relaxing, the ocean lulls you to sleep at night, and birdsong wakes you in the morning. The beach here is one of the best on the coast, with great swimming and snorkeling—in fact, it's so beautiful that people staying at much more expensive resorts down the road frequently haul all their beach paraphernalia here for the day. The studio apartments are compact but all have everything you need to feel at home: a full kitchen (including microwave, coffeemaker, toaster, blender, and more), a big TV, a comfortable queen bed, and a roomy lanai that's great for watching the sun set over the Pacific. Louvered windows and ceiling fans keep the units cool during the day.

Within walking distance of restaurants and a convenience store, the complex is just a mile from a shopping center, 10 minutes from world-class golf and tennis, and 15 minutes from Lahaina. A resident on-site manager is a walking encyclopedia of information on where to go and what to do while you're on Maui. All this for as little as $75 a night—unbelievable! Book early, and tell 'em Frommer's sent you.

Napili Sunset. 46 Hui Rd. (in Napili), Lahaina, HI 96761. ☎ **800/447-9229** or 808/669-8083. Fax 808/669-2730. www.napilisunset.com. 42 units. TV TEL. High season $105 studio double, $195 1-bedroom double, $285 2-bedroom (sleeps up to 4). Off-season $85 studio, $175 1-bedroom, $235 2-bedroom. Extra person $12. Children under 3 stay free in parent's room. 3-night minimum. MC, V.

Housed in three buildings (two on the ocean and one across the street) and located just down the street from Napili Bay (see above), these clean, older, but well-maintained units offer good value. At first glance, the plain two-story structures don't look like much, but the location, the bargain prices, and the friendly spirit of the staff are the real hidden treasures here. In addition to daily maid service, the units each have a free in-room safe, a full kitchen (with dishwasher), ceiling fans, a sofa bed in the living room, a small dining room, and small bedrooms. Laundry facilities are on site (you provide the quarters, they provide the free detergent). The beach, one of Maui's best, can get a little crowded, because the public beach access is through this property (and everyone on Maui seems to want to come here). The studio units are all located in the building off the beach and a few steps up a slight hill; they're good-sized, with complete kitchens and either a sofa bed or a queen Murphy bed, and they overlook the small swimming pool and garden. The one- and two-bedroom units are all on the beach (the downstairs units have lanai that lead right to the sand). The staff makes sure each unit has the basics—paper towels, dishwasher soap, coffee filters, condiments—to get your stay off to a good start.

Papakea. Maui Resort Management, 3600 Lower Honoapiilani Rd. (in Honokowai), Lahaina, HI 96761. ☎ **800/367-5037** or 808/669-1902. Fax 808/669-8790. www.mauigetaway. com. 28 units. TV TEL. $90–$125 studio double, $105–$184 1-bedroom (sleeps up to 4), $126–$220 2-bedroom (sleeps up to 6). 7-night minimum. Extra person $9. MC, V.

Just a mile down the beach from Kaanapali lie these low-rise buildings, surrounded by manicured, landscaped grounds and ocean views galore. Palm trees and tropical plants dot the property, a putting green wraps around two kidney-shaped pools, and a foot bridge arches over a lily pond brimming with carp. Each pool has its own private cabana with sauna, Jacuzzi, and barbecue grills; a poolside shop rents snorkel gear for exploring the offshore reefs. As if that weren't enough, there are three private tennis courts on the grounds for guests' use. All units have big lanai, dishwashers, and washer/ dryers. The studios have pull-down beds to save space during the day. Definitely a good value.

KAPALUA
VERY EXPENSIVE

Kapalua Bay Hotel & Villas. 1 Bay Dr., Kapalua, HI 96761. ☎ **800/367-8000** or 808/669-5656. Fax 808/669-4694. www.kapaluabayhotel.com. 209 units. A/C MINIBAR TV TEL. $360–$610 double, from $1,000 ocean villa suite, from $400 1- and 2-bedroom bay suites. Extra person $60. Children 17 and under stay free in parent's room using existing bedding. AE, CB, DC, JCB, MC, V.

Few Hawaiian resorts have the luxury of open space like this one. It sits seaward of 23,000 acres of green fields lined by spiky Norfolk pine windbreaks. The 1970s-style rectilinear building sits down by the often windy shore, full of angles that frame stunning views of ocean, mountains, and blue sky. The tastefully designed maze of oversized rooms fronts a palm-fringed gold-sand beach that's one of the best in Hawaii, as well as an excellent Ben Crenshaw golf course. The Kapalua Shops are within easy walking distance.

Each guest room has a sitting area with a sofa, a king or two double beds, and an entertainment center; plantation-style shutter doors open onto private lanai with a view of Molokai across the channel. The renovated bathrooms each feature two granite vanities, a large soaking tub, and a glass-enclosed shower. The one- and two-bedroom villas are situated on the ocean at the very private Oneloa Bay. Each one has several lanai, a full kitchen, a washer/dryer, ceiling fans, an oversized tub, and access to three swimming pools with cabanas and barbecues.

Dining: The most appealing dining spot is the classic Bay Club (see chapter 5), in its own plantation-style building overlooking the sea, specializing in seafood for lunch and dinner. The casual Gardenia Court serves three meals daily.

Amenities: Two pools, exercise room, a famous trio of golf courses (each with its own pro shop), 10 Plexi-pave tennis courts for day and night play (villa guests have access to two additional tennis courts), 24-hour room service, twice-daily maid service, ice service every afternoon and on request, massage, resort shuttle, complimentary transfer to Kapalua–West Maui Airport, secretarial services, and baby-sitting. Kamp Kapalua, for kids ages 5 to 12, offers activities ranging from snorkeling and surfing to lei making and cookie baking. Adults can plan similar activities through the hotel's Beach Activity Center.

✪ **Ritz-Carlton Kapalua.** 1 Ritz-Carlton Dr., Kapalua, HI 96761. ☎ **800/262-8440** or 808/669-6200. Fax 808/665-0026. www.kapaluamaui.com. 548 units. A/C MINIBAR TV TEL. $295–$395 double, from $375 suite. Extra person $40 ($80 in Club Floor rooms). Wedding/ honeymoon, golf, and other packages available. AE, DC, DISC, MC, V. Valet parking $10, free self-parking.

Of all the Ritz-Carltons in the world, this is probably the best. It's in the best place (Hawaii), near the best beach (Kapalua), and it has a friendly staff who go above and beyond the call of duty. The Ritz is a complete universe, one of those resorts where you can sit by the pool with a book for two whole weeks. It rises proudly on a knoll, in a singularly spectacular setting between the rain forest and the sea. During construction, the remains of hundreds of early Hawaiians were discovered buried in the sand, so the hotel was moved inland to avoid disrupting the graves. The setback actually improved the hotel's outlook, which now has a commanding view of Molokai. The hotel follows the formula of Ritz-Carltons everywhere, which many people love; some of you may find its slightly formal air a little out of place in tropical Hawaii.

The style is fancy plantation, elegant but not imposing. The public spaces are open, airy, and graceful, with plenty of tropical foliage and landscapes by artist Sarah Supplee that recall the not-so-long-ago agrarian past. Rooms are up to the usual Ritz standard, outfitted with marble baths, private lanai, in-room fax capability, and voice mail. The private club floors have their own concierge and private lounge; guests here get continental breakfast, afternoon drinks, and other extras. Hospitality is the keynote here; you'll find the exemplary service you expect from Ritz-Carlton seasoned with good old-fashioned Hawaiian aloha.

Dining/Diversions: Dining is excellent at the Anuenue Room (also great for elegant Sunday brunch; see chapter 5), the outdoor Terrace (for breakfast and dinner), and poolside (for lunch). It's a small hike to the beach, so fortunately, the Beach House serves daytime drinks and light fare right on the sands. Cocktails are served in the Lobby Lounge, which doubles as an espresso bar in the morning. A new pool bar serves drinks by the three pools.

Amenities: Three top-rated golf courses, a tennis complex, three pools, a nine-hole putting green, a croquet lawn, beach volleyball, fitness center, salon offering massage and spa treatments, guests-only full-day guided backcountry hikes, historic plantation-style wedding chapel, 24-hour room service, twice-daily towels, nightly turndown, airport and golf shuttle, secretarial services, daily kids' programs, lei greetings, and multilingual staff.

EXPENSIVE

If you're interested in a luxurious condo or townhouse, also consider **Kapalua Villas** (☎ **800/545-0018** or 808/669-8088; www.kapaluavillas.com). These palatial units dotting the oceanfront cliffs and fairways of this idyllic coast are a relative bargain, especially if you're traveling with a group. The one- and two-bedroom condos go for $189 to $475; three-bedroom homes are $1,095 to $1,395; four-bedroom homes are $2,500 to $3,500; and a five-bedroom home ranges from $4,000 to $5,500.

3 South Maui

MAALAEA

Contact **Maalaea Bay Rentals,** 280 Hauoli St., Wailuku, HI 96793 (☎ **800/ 367-6084** or 808/244-7012; fax 808/242-7476; www.maalaeabay.com), which has a variety of units in nearly every condominium in Maalaea, ranging from a low of $70 for a one-bedroom garden unit in an older building to $195 for a two-bedroom ocean-front unit. If your stay is shorter than 5 nights, an extra charge will be added for cleaning. Laundry facilities are on site, and all units have full kitchens and complete furnishings down to the TV, phones, linens, and beach towels.

KIHEI

We recommend two booking agencies that represent a host of condominiums and unique homes in the Kihei/Wailea area: **Kihei Maui Vacation,** P.O. Box 1055, Kihei, HI 96753 (☎ **800/541-6284** or 808/879-7581; www.kmvmaui.com), and **Condominium Rentals Hawaii,** 362 Huku Lii Place, Suite 204, Kihei, HI 96753 (☎ **800/ 367-5242** or 808/879-2778; www.crhmaui.com).

EXPENSIVE

In addition to the choices below, also consider the **Aston at the Maui Banyan** (☎ **800/92-ASTON** or 808/875-0004; www.aston-hotels.com), a very nice condo across the street from Kamaole Beach Park II. The one- to three-bedroom units are all nicely done and feature full kitchens (with microwaves), air-conditioning, and washer/ dryers. There's a tennis court and a Jacuzzi on site. Rates are $155 to $400 in high season, $130 to $340 in low season; be sure to ask about packages.

Maalaea Surf Resort. 12 S. Kihei Rd. (at S. Kihei Rd. and Hwy. 350), Kihei, HI 96743. ☎ **800/423-7953** or 808/879-1267. Fax 808/874-2884. 34 units in rental pool. A/C TV TEL. $205 1-bedroom double, $277 2-bedroom (sleeps up to 6). Extra person $15. MC, V.

Located at the quiet end of Kihei Road, this two-story condominium complex sprawls over 5 acres of lush tropical gardens. This is the place for people who want a quiet, relaxing vacation on a well-landscaped property, with a beautiful white-sand beach right outside. The large, luxury town houses all have ocean views, big kitchens, air-conditioning, cable TV, VCRs, and phones. Maid service (Monday through Saturday) is included in the price.

✪ **Maui Hill.** 2881 S. Kihei Rd. (across from Kamaole Park III, between Keonekai St. and Kilo-hana Dr.), Kihei, HI 96753. ☎ **800/92-ASTON** or 808/879-6321. Fax 808/879-8945. www.aston-hotels.com. 140 units. A/C TV TEL. High season $230 1-bedroom, $285 2-bedroom, $400 3-bedroom. Off-season $190 1-bedroom, $245 2-bedroom, $340 3-bedroom. AE, CB, DC, DISC, JCB, MC, V.

If you can't decide between the privacy of a condominium unit and the conveniences a hotel offers, this place will solve your dilemma. Managed by the respected Aston chain, Maui Hill gives you the best of both worlds. Located on a hill above the heat of Kihei town, this large, Spanish-style resort (with white stucco buildings, red-tile roof, and arched entries) offers large luxury condos with full kitchens, lots of space, and plenty of privacy; you also get all the amenities and activities of a hotel—large pool, hot tub, tennis courts, daily maid service, concierge, Hawaiiana classes, and more. Nearly all units have ocean views, a dishwasher, a washer/dryer, a queen sofa bed, and a big lanai. Beaches are within easy walking distance; a variety of restaurants and shops is just a short walk away along South Kihei Road. The management here goes out of their way to make sure that your stay is wonderful.

South Maui Accommodations

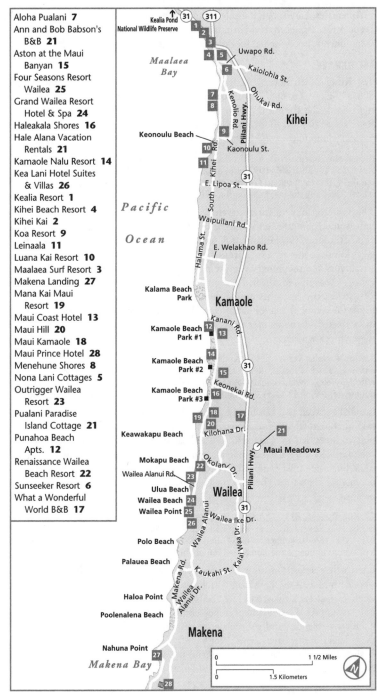

Kealia Pond National Wildlife Preserve

Maalaea Bay

Uwapo Rd.

Kaiolohia St.

Ohukai Rd.

Kenolio Rd.

Piilani Hwy.

Kihei

Keonoulu Beach

Kaonoulu St.

South Kihei Rd.

E. Lipoa St.

Pacific

Waipuilani Rd.

Ocean

Halama St.

E. Welakhao Rd.

Kalama Beach Park

Kamaole

Kanani Rd.

Kamaole Beach Park #1

Kamaole Beach Park #2

Keonekai Rd.

Kamaole Beach Park #3

Keawakapu Beach

Kilohana Dr.

Maui Meadows

Mokapu Beach

Okolani Dr.

Wailea Alanui Rd.

Ulua Beach

Piilani Hwy.

Wailea Beach

Wailea

Wailea Point

Wailea Ike Dr.

Wailea Alanui

Polo Beach

Palauea Beach

Kaukahi St.

Kalai Waai Dr.

Makena Rd.

Wailea Alanui Dr.

Haloa Point

Poolenalena Beach

Makena

Nahuna Point

Makena Bay

0   1 1/2 Miles

0   1.5 Kilometers

93

Amenities: Large pool, hot tub, putting green, tennis courts, shuffleboard, 14 barbecue areas, classes in Hawaiiana such as lei making and crafts, concierge, weekly complimentary continental breakfast, and weekly manager's party.

MODERATE

The **Kihei Beach Resort,** 36 S. Kihei Rd., Kihei, HI 96753 (☎ **800/367-6034** or 808/879-2744; fax 808/875-0306; www.kiheibeachresort.com), has spacious condos right on the beach, but the downside is the constant traffic noise from Kihei Road. Rates are $110 to $140 for a one-bedroom, $145 to 170 for a two-bedroom; there's a 3-night minimum.

Haleakala Shores. 2619 S. Kihei Rd. (across from Kamaole Park III, at Keonekai St.), Kihei, HI 96753. ☎ **800/869-1097** or 808/879-1218. Fax 808/879-2219. 144 units (76 in rental pool). TV TEL. High season (7-night minimum) $125–$175 double; off-season (5-night minimum) $80–$130 double. Extra person $10. MC, V.

This is a great buy for frugal travelers, especially for families on a budget. Each large unit (some 1,200 square feet) sleeps up to six people and comes with two bedrooms, two bathrooms, private lanai, full kitchen with dishwasher, and washer/dryer. The great location, just across the street from Kamaole Park III, makes it an easy walk to restaurants and shopping. Even the parking situation is ideal: There's a free covered garage. Okay, now for the bad news: The units were built in 1974, and most still sport '70s-style decor. Also, they can be noisy, thanks to traffic on Kihei Road (ask for a unit inside the complex) and thin walls (you can hear your neighbors' TV and conversations quite clearly). If you manage to get a quiet unit and can overlook the nostalgic decor, these units are winners.

Kamaole Nalu Resort. 2450 S. Kihei Rd. (between Kanani and Keonekai rds., next to Kamaole Beach Park II), Kihei, HI 96753. ☎ **800/767-1497** or 808/879-1006. Fax 808/879-8693. www.mauigateway.com/~kamaole. 36 units. TV TEL. High season $145–$165 double; off-season $100–$130 double. 3-night minimum. Extra person $10–$15. MC, V.

Located between two beach parks, Kamaole I and Kamaole II, this six-story condominium boasts fabulous ocean views. The property, right across the street from a shopping complex, has an ocean-side pool and barbecue facilities that are great for a sunset cookout. The units have large living rooms and private lanai; the kitchens are a bit small but come fully equipped. Try to get no. 306, which has a wonderful bird's-eye ocean view. Be warned: Because the building is located on Kihei Road, the units can be noisy.

✪ **Koa Resort.** 811 S. Kihei Rd. (between Kulanihakoi St. and Namauu Place), c/o Bello Realty, P.O. Box 1776, Kihei, HI 96753. ☎ **800/541-3060** or 808/879-3328. Fax 808/875-1483. www.bellomaui.com. 54 units (some with shower only). TV TEL. High season $105–$180 double; off-season $85–$160 double. No credit cards.

Located just across the street from the ocean, Koa Resort consists of five two-story wooden buildings on more than 5¹/₂ acres of landscaped grounds. The spacious, privately owned one-, two-, and three-bedroom units are decorated with care and come fully equipped. Each kitchen comes complete with fridge, dishwasher, disposal, microwave, blender, and coffeemaker. The larger units have both showers and tubs; the smaller units have showers only. All feature large lanai, ceiling fans, and washer/dryers. The property has two tennis courts, a pool, a hot tub, and an 18-hole putting green. For maximum peace and quiet, ask for a unit far from Kihei Road.

✪ **Maui Coast Hotel.** 2259 S. Kihei Rd. (1 block from Kamaole Beach Park I), Kihei, HI 96753. ☎ **800/426-0670** or 808/874-6284. Fax 808/875-4731. www.westcoasthotels. com. 265 units. A/C TV TEL. $145–$155 double, $165–$195 suite, $205 1-bedroom (sleeps up to 4), $299 2-bedroom (sleeps up to 6). Children 17 and under stay free in parent's room if using existing bedding. Rollaway bed $18. Room-car packages available. AE, DC, DISC, JCB, MC, V.

This off-beach midrise stands out as one of the only moderately priced hotels in Kihei (which is largely full of affordable condo complexes rather than traditional hotels or resorts). Ask about the room-car packages: For the price of a room (or a one- or two-bedroom apartment), the Maui Coast's Extra Value package gives you a rental car for just a few dollars more. The other chief advantage of this hotel is its location: about a block from Kamaole Beach Park I, with plenty of bars, restaurants, and shopping within walking distance (Jamison's Grill & Bar is next door). A $2.5 million renovation of all the furniture, upholstery, carpets, and linens in the rooms plus the remodeled public areas (lobby, pool, restaurant, bar) has made this moderately priced hotel into a luxury resort and a terrific value. The rooms offer extras such as sitting areas, coffee-makers and free coffee, hair dryers, whirlpool tubs, minifridges, safes, ceiling fans, and furnished, private lanai. There's a casual restaurant, a sushi bar, and a poolside bar with nightly entertainment. Additional amenities include room service (7am to 9pm), an activities desk, complimentary laundry (you buy the soap), two pools (one for the kids), two Jacuzzis, tennis courts, and a gift shop. This ain't the Ritz, but you'll be very comfortable here—and your wallet will thank you.

Maui Kamaole. 2777 S. Kihei Rd. (between Keonekai and Kilohana rds., at the Wailea end of Kihei), Kihei, HI 96753. ☎ **800/367-5242** or 808/874-5151. Fax 808/879-6900. www.crhmaui.com. 210 units. A/C TV TEL. High season $142–$172 1-bedroom (sleeps up to 4), $182–$227 2-bedroom (rates are for 4, sleeps up to 6). Off-season $107–$117 1-bedroom, $137–$152 2-bedroom. Extra person $12. 4-night minimum. AE, JCB, MC, V.

You'll find this complex right across the street from the Kihei Public Boat Ramp and beautiful Kamaole Beach Park III, which is great for swimming, snorkeling, and beachcombing. Each roomy, fully furnished unit comes with a private lanai, two bathrooms (even in the one-bedrooms), washer/dryer, and all-electric kitchen. The one-bedroom units, which can comfortably accommodate four, are quite a deal, especially if you're traveling with the kids in the off season. The grounds are nicely landscaped and offer two swimming pools, hot tub, two tennis courts, and barbecues. Restaurants are within walking distance.

INEXPENSIVE

Additional choices include **Aloha Pualani,** 15 Wailana Place, Kihei, HI 96753 (☎ **800/PUALANI** or 808/874-9265; fax 808/874-9127; www.alohapualani.com), which offers five suites surrounding a heated pool. Rates are $89 to $150, with a 3-night minimum.

Luana Kai Resort, 940 S. Kihei Rd., Kihei, HI 96753 (☎ **800/669-1127** or 808/879-1268; fax 808/879-1455; www.luanakai.com), is an older condo complex with 113 one- and two-bedroom units ($79 to $149 for a one-bedroom, $99 to $169 for a two-bedroom; 4-night minimum).

Kihei Kai, 61 N. Kihei Rd., Kihei, HI 96753 (☎ **800/735-2357** or 808/879-2357; fax 808/874-4960; www.maui.net/~kiheikai), has one-bedroom apartments ($80 to $115) that are ideal for families.

Finally, the **Sunseeker Resort,** 551 S. Kihei Rd., P.O. Box 276, Kihei, HI 96753 (☎ **800/532-MAUI** or 808/879-1261; fax 808/874-3877; www.maui.net/~sunseeker), offers older, sometimes noisy budget units with great ocean views—somewhat of a rarity on Maui. Rates are $60 for a studio, $70 for a one-bedroom, $125 for a two-bedroom; there's a 3-night minimum.

○ **Ann and Bob Babson's Bed & Breakfast and Sunset Cottage.** 3371 Keha Dr. (in Maui Meadows), Kihei, HI 96753. ☎ **800/824-6409** or 808/874-1166. Fax 808/879-7906. www.mauibnb.com. 4 units. TV TEL. $85–$110 double room (including breakfast Mon–Sat), $125 cottage double (sleeps up to 4). Extra person $15. 5-night minimum. MC, V.

We highly recommend staying right here on this landscaped half-acre, which boasts 180° views of the islands of Lanai, Kahoolawe, and Molokini and sunsets not to be missed. (The nearest good beach is about a 5-minute drive away.) Accommodations include two rooms in the house (one with panoramic ocean views, skylights, and a whirlpool tub), a one-bedroom suite downstairs, and a two-bedroom cottage. The Babsons have three adorable cats (if you're allergic, you might want to book elsewhere).

Hale Alana Vacation Rentals—Palm & Ginger Cottages. 490 Mikioi Place (Maui Meadows), Kihei, HI 96753. ☎ **800/871-5032** or 808/875-4840. Fax 808/879-3998. www.maui.net/~kstover. 2 units. TV TEL. $80 double (plus a $40 cleaning fee). 4-night minimum. Extra person $15. MC, V.

Tucked into the residential neighborhood of Maui Meadows (and a 5-minute drive from the nearest good beach) is an oasis of fruit trees, a vegetable garden, and a sundeck with picnic table, chairs, and a hot tub overlooking the ocean. Both rental cottages have their own TVs, VCRs, CD players, and washer/dryers. The two-bedroom Ginger Cottage is best for families, while the one-bedroom Palm Cottage makes a cozy honeymoon cottage (though it does have a sofa bed). Guests are welcome to pick dinner from the thriving vegetable garden and gather fresh fruits for their breakfast. Occasionally Karen will waive the 4-night minimum for last-minute bookings.

Kealia Resort. 191 N. Kihei Rd. (north of Hwy. 31, at the Maalaea end of Kihei), Kihei, HI 96753. ☎ **800/265-0686** or 808/879-0952. Fax 808/875-1540. www.apmimaui.com. 51 units. TV TEL. $65–$90 studio double, $85–$130 1-bedroom double, $145–$185 2-bedroom (for up to 4). Extra person $10. Children 12 and under stay free in parent's room. 4-night minimum. MC, V.

This oceanfront property at the northern end of Kihei is well maintained and nicely furnished—and the price is excellent. As tempting as the $65 studio units may sound, don't give in: they face noisy Kihei Road and are near a major junction, so big trucks downshifting can be especially noisy at night. Instead, go for one of the ocean-view units, which all have full kitchens, washer/dryers, and private lanai. The grounds, which abut a 5-mile stretch of beach, feature a recently retiled pool with sundeck. The management goes out of its way to provide opportunities for guests to meet; social gatherings include free coffee-and-doughnut get-togethers every Friday morning and pupu parties on Wednesdays.

Leinaala. 998 S. Kihei Rd., Kihei, HI 96753. ☎ **800/334-3305** or 808/879-2235. Fax 808/879-8366. www.maui-condo-rentals.com. 24 units. TV TEL. $110 1-bedroom double, $145 2-bedroom (sleeps up to 4). 4-night minimum. Extra person $10. MC, V.

From Kihei Road, you can't see Leinaala amid the jumble of buildings, but this oceanfront boutique condo offers excellent accommodations at 1980s prices. The building is set back from the water, with a county park—an oasis of green grass and tennis courts—in between. The units are compact, but filled with everything you need: a full kitchen, a sofa bed, and an ocean-view lanai. Hide-a-beds are available if you need them. On site are laundry facilities and a freshwater swimming pool.

Mana Kai Maui Resort. 2960 S. Kihei Rd. (between Kilohana and Keonekai rds., at the Wailea end of Kihei), Kihei, HI 96753. ☎ **800/367-5242** or 808/879-2778. Fax 808/876-5042. www.crhmaui.com. 132 units. A/C TV TEL. $89–$130 double, $165–$235 1-bedroom (sleeps up to 4), $205–$290 2-bedroom (sleeps up to 6). AE, DC, DISC, MC, V.

This eight-story complex, on a beautiful white-sand cove, is an unusual combination of hotel and condominium. The hotel rooms, which constitute half of the total number of units, are small but nicely furnished. The condo units feature full kitchens and open living rooms with sliding-glass doors that lead to small lanai overlooking the sandy beach and ocean. Some units are beginning to show their age, but they're all clean and comfortable. There are laundry facilities on each floor. Guests enjoy an open-air restaurant called Five Palms (see chapter 5) and a pool. One of the best beaches on the coast for snorkeling is just steps away.

Menehune Shores. 760 S. Kihei Rd. (between Kaonoulu and Hoonani sts.), P.O. Box 1327, Kihei, HI 96753. ☎ **800/558-9117** or 808/879-3428. Fax 808/879-5218. www. menehunereservation.com 70 units. TV TEL. $90–$110 1-bedroom double, $105–$135 2-bedroom double, $120–$150 2-bedroom (sleeps up to 4), $145–$185 3-bedroom (sleeps up to 6). 3-night minimum. Weekly car/condo package $789 1-bedroom double, $905 2-bedroom double, $1,067 2-bedroom (sleeps up to 4), $1,389 3-bedroom (sleeps up to 6). Extra person $7.50. No credit cards.

If you plan to stay on Maui for a week, you might want to look into the car/condo packages here; they're a real deal, especially for families on a budget. The six-story Menehune Shores is about 30 years old and is showing its age in some places, but all units are well maintained and have ocean views. The design is straight out of the 1970s, but the view from the private lanai is timeless. The kitchens are fully equipped, all units have washer/dryers, and the oceanfront location guarantees a steady breeze that keeps the rooms cool (there's no air-conditioning). The U-shaped building sits in front of the ancient Hawaiian fish ponds of Kalepolepo; some Hawaiians still fish them using traditional throw nets, but generally the pond serves as protection from the ocean waves, making it safe for children (and those unsure of their ability) to swim in the relatively calm waters. There's also a heated pool, shuffleboard courts, and a whale-watching platform on the roof garden.

✪ **Nona Lani Cottages.** 455 S. Kihei Rd. (just south of Hwy. 31), P.O. Box 655, Kihei, HI 96753. ☎ **800/733-2688** or 808/879-2497. Fax 808/891-0273. www.nonalanicottages. com. 11 units. A/C TV. $68–$75 double room, $78–$88 cottage. Extra person $10. 2-night minimum for rooms, 4-night minimum for cottages. No credit cards.

Picture this: a grassy expanse dotted with eight small cottages tucked among palm trees, fruit trees, and sweet-smelling flower trees, right across the street from a white-sand beach. This is one of the great "hidden" deals in Kihei: the 400-square-foot cottages are tiny but contain everything you'll need: a small but complete kitchen, twin beds that double as couches in the living room, a separate bedroom with queen bed, and a lanai with table and chairs—ideal for watching the ocean waves as you eat your break-fast. The cottages were totally renovated in 1999 with new carpet, new flooring, new furniture, and repainted. The real attraction is the garden setting next to the beach. The prices are beyond affordable. There are no phones in the cabins (a blessing if you're trying to escape civilization), but there's a public one near the coin-op laundry.

If the cabins are booked, or if you just want a bit more luxury, you might opt for one of the private guest rooms in host David Kong's main house. Each beautiful room features cathedral-like open-beam ceilings, plush carpet, koa bed frames, air-conditioning, glass tile shower, separate lanai outside, and a private entrance.

Pualani Paradise Island Cottage. 3134 Hoomua Dr. (in Maui Meadows), Kihei, HI 96753. ☎ **800/800-8608** or 808/874-1048. Fax 808/879-6932. www.mauisuncoast.com. 1 cottage. TV TEL. $75–$95 double. 4-night minimum. No credit cards.

Tucked away on a quiet street in the residential area above Wailea known as Maui Meadows (about a 5-minute drive from the nearest good beach), you'll find this quaint cottage, surrounded by lush landscaped grounds and a large swimming pool. The cozy cottage, with a fully equipped kitchen, has all the comforts of home, including a VCR and stereo. Some guests return again and again to the immaculate grounds, the charming cottage, and the cool pool. Host Jack St. Germain also has a real estate company specializing in vacation rentals (condos, cottages, and homes), ranging from $40 to $175 a day; check the Web site (above) for details.

✪ **Punahoa Beach Apartments.** 2142 Iliili Rd. (off S. Kihei Rd., 100 yards from Kamaole Beach I), Kihei, HI 96753. ☎ **800/564-4380** or 808/879-2720. Fax 808/875-3147. E-mail: punahoares@aol.com. 12 units. TV TEL. High season $111 studio, $152–$162 1-bedroom, $156 2-bedroom. Off-season $79 studio, $98–$104 1-bedroom, $108 2-bedroom. All are double rates; extra person $15. 5-night minimum. AE, MC, V.

Book this place: We can't put it any more simply than that. The location—off noisy, traffic-ridden Kihei Road, on a quiet side street with ocean frontage—is fabulous. A grassy lawn rolls about 50 feet down to the beach; there's great snorkeling just offshore and a popular surfing spot next door; and shopping and restaurants are all within walking distance. All of the beautifully decorated units in this small, four-story building have lanai with great ocean views and fully equipped kitchens. Rooms go quickly during winter, so book early.

✪ **What a Wonderful World B&B.** 2828 Umalu Pl. (off Keonakai St., near Hwy. 31), Kihei, HI 96753. ☎ **800/943-5804** or 808/879-9103. Fax 808/874-9352. http://thesupersites. com/wonderfulworld. 4 units. A/C TV TEL. $65 double, $75 studio, $85–$95 1-bedroom apt. Rates include full breakfast. Children 11 and under stay free in parent's room. AE, MC, V.

We couldn't believe what we'd discovered here: an impeccably done B&B with thought and care put into every room, a great location, and excellent rates. Then we met hostess Eva Tantillo, who has not only a full-service travel agency, but also a master's degree in hotel management, along with several years of experience. The result? One of Maui's finest bed-and-breakfasts, centrally located in Kihei (a half mile to Kamaole II Beach Park, 5 minutes from Wailea golf courses, and convenient to shopping and restaurants). Choose from one of four units: the master suite (with small fridge, coffeemaker, and barbecue grill on the lanai), studio apartment (with fully equipped kitchen), or two one-bedroom apartments (also with fully equipped kitchens). Each has a private entrance. Guests are welcome to use the barbecue, laundry facilities, and hot tub. Eva serves a gourmet family style breakfast (eggs Benedict, Alaskan waffles, skillet eggs with mushroom sauce, fruit blintzes, and more) on her lanai, which has views of white-sand beaches, the West Maui Mountains, and Haleakala.

WAILEA

For a wide selection of condos throughout Wailea and Makena, contact **Destination Resorts Hawaii,** 3750 Wailea Alanui Dr., Wailea, HI 96753 (☎ **800/367-5246** or 808/879-1595; fax 808/874-3554; www.destinationresortshi.com). Their luxury units include studio doubles priced from $140 to $200; one-bedroom doubles from $150 to $450; two-bedrooms from $180 to $550; and three-bedrooms from $500 to $700. Children under 16 stay free. Minimum stays vary by property.

VERY EXPENSIVE

✪ **Four Seasons Resort Wailea.** 3900 Wailea Alanui Dr., Wailea, HI 96753. ☎ **800/334-MAUI** or 808/874-8000. Fax 808/874-6449. www.fshr.com. 463 units. A/C MINIBAR TV TEL. $305–$745 double, from $575 suite. Packages available. Extra person $80 ($150 in Club Floor rooms). Children under 18 stay free in parent's room using existing bedding. AE, DC, JCB, MC, V. Free valet parking.

All of the luxury hotels in Wailea are fabulous, boasting terrific views and luxurious accommodations. What sets the Four Seasons apart is its relaxing, casual atmosphere, combined with service so seamless that you hardly notice it. If money's no object, this is the place to spend it. And bring the kids, too: There's a complete activities program designed just for them.

It's hard to beat this modern version of a Hawaiian palace by the sea. Although it sits on the beach between two other hotels, you won't feel like you're on chockablock resort row: The Four Seasons inhabits its own separate world, thanks to an open courtyard of pools and gardens. The spacious (about 600 square feet) rooms feature furnished private lanai (nearly all with ocean views) that are great for watching whales in winter and sunsets year-round. The grand bathrooms have deep marble tubs, showers for two, and lighted French makeup mirrors. Other room amenities include safes, voice mail, irons and ironing boards, hair dryers, and plush terry robes. Guests on Club Floors enjoy special perks, including breakfast, afternoon tea and snacks, cocktails, pupus, and an open bar.

Service is attentive but not cloying. At the pool, guests lounge in Casbah-like tents, pampered with special touches like iced Evian and chilled towels. And you'll never see a housekeeping cart in the hall: The cleaning staff work in teams, so they're as unobtrusive as possible and in and out of your room in minutes.

This ritzy neighborhood is home to great restaurants and shopping, the Wailea Tennis Center (known as Wimbledon West), and six golf courses—not to mention that great beach, with gentle waves and islands framing the view on either side.

Dining: Seasons, the signature restaurant of the resort, features French-International seafood in a memorable setting. The Seaside Restaurant offers a casual atmosphere overlooking the Pacific by day; at night, it's transformed into Ferraro's at Seaside, serving authentic Italian fare. The poolside Pacific Grill offers lavish breakfast buffets and dinners featuring Pacific Edge cuisine. See chapter 5 for full reviews of most of these choices.

Amenities: Beach pavilion with snorkels, boogie boards, kayaks, and other watersports gear; 1 hour free use of snorkel equipment; complimentary use of bicycles; complimentary exercise and tennis attire on loan; two pools (one for adults only); 41 pool and beach cabanas; two whirlpools (one for adults only); fitness center with weight room and steam room; tennis (two lighted Plexi-pave courts with rackets and tennis balls provided); putting green; terrific spa offering massage and other treatments; game room; video library; salon; shops; conference facilities; twice-daily maid service; 24-hour room service; same-day dry cleaning and laundry, 1-hour and overnight pressing; free overnight shoe shine or sandal repair; shuttle service around the resort; airport limousine service; rental cars at concierge desk; 24-hour medical service; lei greeting and oshibori towel on arrival; and early arrival/late departure facility. The year-round kids' program features loads of activities and a complete children's facility, plus a teen recreation center; there's a children's video library and toys.

Grand Wailea Resort Hotel & Spa. 3850 Wailea Alanui Dr., Wailea, HI 96753. ☎ **800/ 888-6100** or 808/875-1234. Fax 808/879-4077. www.grandwailea.com. 814 units. A/C MINIBAR TV TEL. $390–$675 double, from $1,100 suite. Extra person $25 ($75 in Napua Club rooms). AE, CB, DC, DISC, JCB, MC, V. Free valet parking.

Here's where grand becomes grandiose. The pinnacle of Hawaii's brief fling with fantasy megaresorts, this monument to excess is extremely popular with families, incentive groups, and conventions; it's the grand prize in Hawaii vacation contests and the dream of many honeymooners.

This hotel really is too much. It has a Japanese restaurant decorated with real rocks hewn from the slopes of Mount Fuji; 10,000 tropical plants in the lobby; an intricate pool system with slides, waterfalls, rapids, and a water-powered elevator to take you up to the top; Hawaii's most elaborate spa (not even the Romans had it this good); Hawaii's most expensive hotel suite, a 5,500-square-foot pad with a 180° view of paradise; a restaurant in a man-made tide pool; a floating New England–style wedding chapel; and nothing but ocean-view rooms, outfitted with every amenity you could ask for. (The 100 Napua Club rooms offer extras like their own attendants, and complimentary continental breakfast, cocktails, and tea service.) And it's all crowned with a $30 million collection of original art, much of it created expressly for the hotel by Hawaii artists and sculptors. There's also a fantastic beach out front. Five golf courses, including two 18-hole championship courses, are nearby.

Dining/Diversions: Six restaurants and 12 bars range from fine dining to casual poolside snacks, serving everything from Japanese and Italian specialties to local seafood and spa cuisine. See chapter 9 for a description of the Tsunami nightclub. There's also luau grounds for 300.

Amenities: Hawaii's largest spa, the 50,000-square-foot Spa Grande, with a blend of European-, Japanese-, and American-style treatments and techniques; the 2,000-foot-long Action Pool, featuring a 10-minute swim/ride through mountains and grottoes; complimentary dive and windsurf lessons; lei greeting; 24-hour room service; twice-daily towel service; same-day laundry and dry cleaning; multilingual concierge; infant care center; art and hotel tours; Budget Rent-A-Car and American Express tour desks; seaside wedding chapel; conference facilities. Kids enjoy a computer center, video game room, arts and crafts, a 60-seat children's theater, and an outdoor playground.

✪ **Kea Lani Hotel, Suites and Villas.** 4100 Wailea Alanui Dr., Wailea, HI 96753. ☎ **800/ 659-4100** or 808/875-4100. Fax 808/875-1200. www.kealani.com. 450 units. A/C TV TEL. $295–$590 suite for 4, from $1,400 villa. AE, CB, DC, DISC, MC, V.

At first glance this blinding white complex of arches and turrets may look a bit out of place in tropical Hawaii (actually it's a close architectural cousin of Las Hadas, the Arabian Nights fantasy resort in Manzanillo, Mexico). But once you enter the flower-filled lobby and hear the soft murmuring of the fountain and see the big blue Pacific Ocean outside, there's no doubt that you're in Hawaii.

The price may be high, but you get what you pay for here, plus a few extras: This all-suite luxury hotel has 840-square-foot suites, each with a microwave kitchenette and a coffeemaker, a living room with a high-tech media center and a pull-out sofa bed (great if you have the kids in tow), a marble wet bar, an oversized marble bathroom (with a separate shower that's big enough for a party), and a spacious bedroom. Plus there's a large lanai off the bedroom and living room that overlooks the pools, the lawns, and the white-sand beach.

The villas are definitely the stuff of fantasy. Here's where the rich and famous stay—in the 2,000-square-foot, two- and three-bedroom individual beach bungalows, each with its own plunge pool and gourmet kitchen.

Dining/Diversions: Romantic Nick's Fishmarket Maui features the freshest seafood in its innovative cuisine (see chapter 5 for a full review). Breakfast is served at Kea Lani Restaurant, and you can grab lunch at the poolside Polo Beach Grille & Bar. Excellent Mediterranean food and healthy cuisine is served at the Caffé Ciao (also see chapter 5). The Lobby Lounge features sunset cocktails and nightly entertainment.

Amenities: An excellent full-service spa offering the latest in body treatments, facials, and massage; professionally managed fitness center; two large swimming "lagoons" connected by a 140-foot water slide and swim-up bar, plus an adult lap pool; 14 tennis courts and full-service pro shop; access to Wailea Golf Course's three championship courses; complimentary limo service within Wailea Resort; room service; range of unique boutique shops; tour activity desk; rental-car desk; laundry facilities; ATM.

Renaissance Wailea Beach Resort. 3550 Wailea Alanui Dr., Wailea, HI 96753. ☎ **800/ 9-WAILEA** or 808/879-4900. Fax 808/879-6128. www.renaissancehotels.com. 345 units. A/C TV TEL. $320–$550 double, from $900 suite. Extra person $40. Children 18 and under stay free in parent's room using existing bedding. AE, CB, DC, DISC, MC, V. Parking $5.

This is the place for visitors in search of the luxury of a Wailea hotel, but in a smaller, more intimate setting. Located on 15 acres of rolling lawn and tropical gardens, the Renaissance Wailea feels like a small boutique hotel. Perhaps it's the resort's U-shaped design, the series of small coves and beaches, or the spaciousness of the rooms— whatever the reason, it just doesn't feel crowded here. Wailea's golf, tennis, and shopping are right at hand.

Each room has a sitting area, a large lanai, a VCR, three phones (with data ports), a fridge, and a safe; you'll get complimentary in-room coffee and a daily newspaper. The bathrooms include such extras as double vanities (one with lighted makeup mirror) and *hapi* coats (Japanese-style cotton robes). Bedspreads, drapes, and towels in all rooms have recently been upgraded. Rooms in the Mokapu Beach Club, an exclusive two-story building just steps from a crescent-shaped beach, feature such extras as private check-in, in-room continental breakfast, and access to a private pool and beach cabanas.

Dining/Diversions: The casual, open-air Palm Court offers buffets and oven-baked pizzas. Hana Gion features a sushi bar and teppanyaki grill. Maui Onion, a casual poolside restaurant surrounded by lush gardens and a cascading waterfall, serves breakfast and lunch. Every Monday, there's a traditional luau at sunset.

Amenities: Complete fitness center, two freshwater swimming pools, two whirlpools, shopping arcade, hair salon, basketball court, Ping-Pong, shuffleboard, room service (6am to 11pm), lei greeting, concierge, complimentary video library, traditional Hawaiian craft classes, massage therapy, baby-sitting, Camp Wailea children's program.

EXPENSIVE

Outrigger Wailea Resort. 3700 Wailea Alanui Dr., Wailea, HI 96753. ☎ **800/OUTRIGGER** or 808/879-1922. Fax 800/622-4852. www.outrigger.com. 516 units. A/C TV TEL. $255–440 double, from $550 suite. Packages available. AE, CB, DC, DISC, JCB, MC, V.

This classic 1970s-style hotel is like a tropical garden by the sea. It was the first resort built in Wailea (in 1976), yet it remains the most Hawaiian of them all. Airy and comfortable, with touches of Hawaiian art throughout and a terrific aquarium that stretches forever behind the front desk, it just feels right.

What's truly special about this hotel is how it fits into its environment without overwhelming it. Eight buildings, all low-rise except for an eight-story tower, are spread along 22 gracious acres of lawns and gardens spiked by coco palms, with lots of open space and a half mile of oceanfront on a point between Wailea and Ulua beaches. The vast, parklike expanses are a luxury on this now-crowded coast. Three championship golf courses are nearby.

In 2000, the resort went through a $25 million renovation. Its entry was expanded into a 32,000-foot open-air courtyard with a waterfall and carp pond. The south pool was transformed into a water activity area, complete with two water slides, a children's recreation center, and more deck space. And the rooms were refurbished and upgraded to include refrigerators, safes, 25-inch televisions, coffeemakers, data ports, and other items.

Dining/Diversions: The restaurants and lounges also were renovated in 2000: A new lounge called Mele Mele was added, serving cocktails and pupu; the Hula Moons Restaurant was remodeled and additional outdoor dining was added; and the oceanfront pool restaurant was redesigned for casual lunches and dinners.

Amenities: Three pools, room service (6:30am to 11pm), massage (which you can even have outdoors by the water!), same-day laundry and valet, multilingual concierge, gift shop, newsstand, beauty salon, barber shop.

MAKENA
EXPENSIVE

Maui Prince Hotel. 5400 Makena Alanui, Makena, HI 96753. ☎ **800/321-MAUI** or 808/874-1111. Fax 808/879-8763. www.westin.com. 304 units. A/C MINIBAR TV TEL. $230–$395 double, $440–$840 suite. Packages available. AE, DC, JCB, MC, V. Free valet parking.

If you're looking for a vacation in a beautiful, tranquil spot with a golden-sand beach, here's your place. But if you plan to do a lot of touring on Maui, you might try another hotel. The Maui Prince is at the end of the road, far, far away from anything else on the island, so sightseeing in other areas would require a lot of driving. When you first see the stark white hotel, it looks like a high-rise motel stuck in the woods—but only from the outside. Inside, you'll discover an atrium garden with a koi-filled waterfall stream and an ocean view from every room. There's a simplicity to the furnishings that makes some people feel uncomfortable and others blissfully clutter-free. Rooms are small but come with private lanai with great views.

Dining/Diversions: Japanese cuisine tops the menu at the elegant Hakone, which has a sushi bar (see chapter 5 for a full review). The Prince Court specializes in Hawaii Regional Cuisine (also see chapter 5); the casual Cafe Kiowai offers seasonal and international specialties. There's also a casual spot serving lunch and snacks, and local Hawaiian music nightly in the lounge.

Amenities: Six Plexi-pave tennis courts (two lit for night play), 36 holes of golf (designed by Robert Trent Jones), adults' and children's pools, fitness center, massage, nature trail, library, shell lei greeting, multilingual concierge, same-day dry cleaning and laundry, daily kids' program, early arrival and late-departure services.

INEXPENSIVE

✪ **Makena Landing.** 5100 Makena Rd. (next to the county beach park), Makena, HI 96753. ☎ **808/879-6286.** 2 units. TV TEL. $120 double. 3-night minimum. Extra person $10. No credit cards.

This has to be the most fabulous location for a bed-and-breakfast: right on the ocean at Makena Landing. Once you settle in, you might not want to leave. (In fact, you're pretty removed from the rest of the island. If you want to do a lot of touring, resign yourself to spending a lot of time in your car.) The view is incredible; the sunsets are to die for; some of the best swimming, snorkeling, diving, and shoreline fishing are within walking distance; and the hosts are the nicest people you'll ever meet. The property has been in the Lu'uwai family for seven generations; hosts Boogie and Vi are both native Hawaiians, and they're brimming with generosity.

To ensure privacy, the two units are at opposite ends of the two-story cedar house. Both have private entrances, full bathrooms, kitchens, and private balconies that overlook the ocean, with Molokini and Kahoolawe off in the distance. The kitchens have everything you can think of, and Vi makes sure that you have all the fixings for breakfast. Outside are a barbecue area and a sundeck; here you'll have the ocean splashing at your feet, and a ringside seat to watch the humpback whales from December to April.

4 Upcountry Maui

MAKAWAO, OLINDA & HALIIMAILE

When you stay in the cooler upcountry climate of Makawao, Olinda, and Haliimaile, on the slopes of Maui's 10,000 foot Haleakala volcano, you'll be (relatively) close to Haleakala National Park. Makawao and Olinda are approximately 90 minutes from the entrance to the park at the 7,000-foot level (you still have 3,000 feet and another 30 to 45 minutes to get to the top). Haliimaile, which is about 10 to 15 minutes driving time from Makawao, adds additional time to your drive up to the summit. Accommodations in Kula are the only other options that will get you closer to the summit so you can make the sunrise.

MODERATE

✪ **Olinda Country Cottages & Inn.** 2660 Olinda Rd. (near the top of Olinda Rd., a 15-minute drive from Makawao), Makawao, HI 96768. ☎ **800/932-3435** or 808/572-1453. Fax 808/573-5326. www.mauibnbcottages.com. 5 units. TV TEL. $120 double (includes continental breakfast), $130 double suite (includes 1st morning's breakfast in fridge), $175–$195 double cottage (sleeps up to 5; includes 1st morning's breakfast in fridge). Extra person $15. 2-night minimum for rooms and suite, 3-night minimum for cottages. No credit cards.

Set on the slopes of Haleakala in the crisp, clean air of Olinda (just 15 minutes from the restaurants and shops of Makawao), this charming B&B is on an 8¹/₂-acre protea farm, surrounded by 35,000 acres of ranch lands (with miles of great hiking trails). The 5,000-square-foot country home, outfitted with a professional eye to detail, has large windows with incredible panoramic views of all of Maui. Upstairs are two guest rooms with antique beds, private full bathrooms, and a separate entryway. Connected to the main house but with its own private entrance, the Pineapple Sweet has a full kitchen, an antique-filled living room, a marble-tiled full bathroom, and a separate bedroom. A separate 1,000-square-foot cottage is the epitome of cozy country luxury, with a fireplace, a bedroom with a queen bed, cushioned window seats (with great sunset views), and open-beam cathedral ceilings. The 950-square-foot Hidden Cottage (in a truly secluded spot surrounded by protea flowers) features three decks, 8-foot French glass doors, a full kitchen, a washer/dryer, and a private tub for two on the deck. Beaches are about a half-hour drive away.

INEXPENSIVE

If you'd like your own private cottage, consider **Peace of Maui,** 1290 Haliimaile Rd. (just outside Haliimaile town), Haliimaile, HI 96768 (☎ **888/475-5045** or 808/572-5045; www.peaceofmaui.com), which has a full kitchen, a bedroom, a day bed, and a large deck; the cottage goes for $75. Children are welcome. The owners also have rooms in the main house (with shared bathroom and kitchen facilities) from $40.

Banyan Tree House. 3265 Baldwin Ave. (next to Veteran's Cemetery, less than a mile below Makawao), Makawao, HI 96768. ☎ **808/572-9021.** Fax 808/573-5072. www.banyantreehouse.com. 4 units. $75–$85 cottage double, $225 three-bedroom/three-bathroom house (sleeps up to 6). Extra person $10 (children up to 12 free). 3-night minimum for house. MC, V.

Huge monkeypod trees (complete with swing and hammock) extend their branches over this 2¹/₂-acre property like a giant green canopy. The restored 1920s plantation manager's house is decorated with Hawaiian furniture from the 1930s. The large guest rooms have big, comfortable beds and private, marble-tiled bathrooms. A fireplace stands at one end of the huge living room, a large lanai runs the entire length of the house, and the hardwood floors shine throughout. The three guest cottages have been totally renovated and also feature hardwood floors and marble bathrooms. The small cottage has a queen bed, a private bathroom, a microwave, a coffeepot, and access to the fridge in the laundry room. The larger cottages have two beds, private bathrooms, and TVs; one has a kitchenette, the other has a full kitchen. Guests have use of laundry facilities. The quiet neighborhood and nostalgic Old Hawaii ambiance give this place a comfortable, easygoing atmosphere. Restaurants and shops are just minutes away in Makawao, and the beach is a 15-minute drive—but this place is so relaxing that you may find yourself wanting to do nothing more than lie in the hammock and watch the clouds float by.

Hale Ho'okipa Inn Makawao. 32 Pakani Place, Makawao, HI 96768. ☎ **808/572-6698.** www.mauinet/visions/halehoo/htm. 4 units (2 with shower only). $75–$95 double, $130 suite with full kitchen. Rates include continental breakfast. Extra person $8. No credit cards. From Haleakala Hwy., turn left on Makawao Ave., then turn right on the fifth street on the right off Makawao Ave. (Pakani Place); go to the last house on the right (green house with white picket fence and water tower).

Step back in time at this 1924 plantation-style home, rescued by owner Cherie Attix in 1996 and restored to its original charm. Cherie lovingly refurbished the old wooden floors, filled the rooms with antique furniture from the 1920s, and hung works by local artists on the walls. The result is a charming, serene place to stay, just a 5-minute walk from the shops and restaurants of Makawao town, 15 minutes from beaches, and a 1^1/2-hour drive from the top of Haleakala. The guest rooms have separate outside entrances and private bathrooms. The house's front and back porches are both wonderful for sipping tea and watching the sunset. The Kona Wing is a two-bedroom suite with private bathroom and use of the kitchen.

KULA

Lodgings in Kula are the closest options to the entrance of Haleakala National Park (about 60 minutes away).

MODERATE

If you'd like to stay in a former sea captain's cottage, consider **Country Garden Cottage** (☎ **888/878-2858** or 808/878-2858; fax 808/876-1458; www.countrygardencottage. com), a meticulously restored 1940s home on the slopes of Haleakala ($120 double; 3-night minimum). Another good choice is the romantic **Bloom Cottage** (☎ and fax **808/878-1425;** http://bizweb.lightspeed.net/bloomcottagemaui), with a fireplace and tasteful furnishings ($115 double; 3-night minimum); the three-bedroom house next door goes for $140 a night double, $10 for each extra person (it sleeps up to 6).

✪ **Silver Cloud Ranch.** Old Thompson Rd. (1.2 miles past Hwy. 37). RR 2, Box 201, Kula, HI 96790. ☎ **800/532-1111** or 808/878-6101. Fax 808/878-2132. www.silvercloudranch. com. 12 units. $85–$135 double in main house, $105–$145 double studio in bunkhouse, $150 double cottage. Rates include full breakfast. Extra person $15. AE, DC, DISC, MC, V.

Old Hawaii lives on at the Silver Cloud Ranch, founded in 1902 by a sailor who jumped ship when he got to Maui. The former working cattle spread has a commanding view of four islands, the West Maui Mountains, and the valley and beaches below. The best rooms in the main house are on the second floor: the King Kamehameha Suite (with king bed) and the Queen Emma Suite (with queen bed). The Lanai Cottage, a honeymoon favorite nestled in a flower garden, has an ocean-view lanai, a claw-foot bathtub, a full kitchen, and a wood-burning stove to warm chilly nights; a futon is available if you're traveling with a third person. One-lane Thompson Road makes

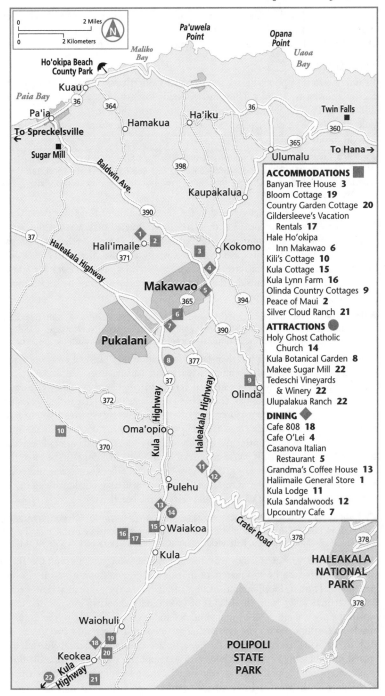

ACCOMMODATIONS ■
Banyan Tree House **3**
Bloom Cottage **19**
Country Garden Cottage **20**
Gildersleeve's Vacation
  Rentals **17**
Hale Ho'okipa
  Inn Makawao **6**
Kili's Cottage **10**
Kula Cottage **15**
Kula Lynn Farm **16**
Olinda Country Cottages **9**
Peace of Maui **2**
Silver Cloud Ranch **21**

ATTRACTIONS ●
Holy Ghost Catholic
  Church **14**
Kula Botanical Garden **8**
Makee Sugar Mill **22**
Tedeschi Vineyards
  & Winery **22**
Ulupalakua Ranch **22**

DINING ◆
Cafe 808 **18**
Cafe O'Lei **4**
Casanova Italian
  Restaurant **5**
Grandma's Coffee House **13**
Haliimaile General Store **1**
Kula Lodge **11**
Kula Sandalwoods **12**
Upcountry Cafe **7**

an ideal morning walk (about 3 miles round-trip), and you can go horseback riding next door at Thompson Ranch. There's a TV available if you feel visually deprived, but after a few Maui sunsets, you won't even remember why you bothered to ask.

INEXPENSIVE

In addition to the options below, also consider **Gildersleeve's Vacation Rentals,** formerly known as Elaine's Upcountry Guest Rooms (☎ **808/878-6623;** fax 808/878-2619); the warm and welcoming hosts rent three rooms in their spacious pole house ($65 double), plus a wonderful cottage that sleeps up to four ($110; 3-night minimum).

✪ **Kili's Cottage.** Kula, c/o Hawaii's Best Bed & Breakfasts, P.O. Box 563, Kamuela, HI 96743. ☎ **800/262-9912** or 808/885-4550. Fax 808/885-0559. www.bestbnb.com. 1 cottage. TV TEL. $95 double. 2-night minimum. Rate includes breakfast fixings. Extra person $10. No credit cards.

If you're looking for a quiet getaway in the cool elevation of Kula, this sweet three-bedroom/two-bathroom cottage with a large lanai, situated on 2 acres, is the perfect place. The amenities are numerous: full kitchen, gas barbecue, washer/dryer, views, even toys for the kids. Hostess Kili Namau'u, who is also the director of a Hawaiian-language immersion school, greets each guest with royal aloha—from the flowers (picked from the garden outside) that fill the house to the welcome basket of tropical produce grown on the property.

Kula Cottage. 206 Puakea Place (off Lower Kula Rd.), Kula, HI 96790. ☎ **808/878-2043** or 808/871-6230. Fax 808/871-9187. www.gilbertadvertising.com/kulacottage. 1 cottage. TV TEL. $95 double. 2-night minimum. Rate includes continental breakfast. No credit cards.

We can't imagine having a less-than-fantastic vacation here. Tucked away on a quiet street amid a half-acre of blooming papaya and banana trees, Cecilia and Larry Gilbert's romantic honeymoon cottage is very private—it even has its own driveway and carport. The 700-square-foot cottage has a full kitchen (complete with dishwasher), washer/dryer, and three huge closets that offer enough storage space for you to move in permanently. An outside lanai has a big gas barbecue and an umbrella table and chairs. Cecilia delivers a continental breakfast daily (visitors rave about her homemade bread in the guest book). If you're an animal lover, Hana, the dog, will be more than happy to be a surrogate pet to you during your vacation; otherwise, Cecilia makes sure that Hana stays out of your way. Groceries and a small take-out lunch counter are within walking distance; it's a 30-minute drive to the beach.

✪ **Kula Lynn Farm Bed & Bath.** 2114 Naalae Rd., Kula, HI 96790. ☎ **800/874-2666,** ext. 300, or 808/878-6176. Fax 808/878-6320. E-mail: captcoon@gte.net. 1 unit. TV TEL. $85 double. 3-night minimum. Rate includes breakfast fixings. Extra person $10. AE, MC, V.

The Coons, the same great family that runs Maui's best sailing adventure on the *Trilogy,* offer this spectacular 1,600-square-foot unit on the ground floor of its custom-built pole house. From its location on the slopes of Haleakala, the panoramic view—across Maui's central valley, with the islands of Lanai and Kahoolawe in the distance—is worth the price alone. Wall-to-wall windows and high ceilings add to the feeling of spaciousness throughout. The two bedrooms, two bathrooms, and two queen sofa beds in the living room make this the perfect place for a family. No expense has been spared in the European-style kitchen, with top appliances and Italian marble floors. This place should appeal to those who enjoy a quiet location and such activities as barbecuing on the lanai and watching the sun set.

5 East Maui: On the Road to Hana

KUAU

INEXPENSIVE

Kuau Cove Plantation. 2 Wa'a Place (on the ocean side off Hana Hwy., 1 mile from stop-light in Paia), Paia, HI 96779. ☎ **808/579-8988.** Fax 808/579-8710. www.maui. net/~kuaubnb. 4 units. TV TEL. $85 double, $95 studio apt. 2-night minimum. Rates include continental breakfast. Extra person $10 (a rollaway bed is available). MC, V.

This 1930s plantation doctor's home has been restored and decorated with antiques, wicker, and rattan furniture. An old-fashioned porch greets you upon arrival, and Douglas fir floors run throughout the house. The dining room overlooks a large lawn with two ancient monkeypod trees and lots of exotic blooming plants. Two large bedrooms in the main house each have a queen bed, private bathroom, TV, and phone. Each of the two studios (separate from the main house) has a small kitchenette, bedroom, sitting area, and full bathroom. Our favorite is the upstairs studio, which has its own small lanai with an ocean view. A continental breakfast is served buffet style in the dining room from 7:30 to 9am every day; breakfast is delivered to the two studio apartments.

Quiet accommodations, gorgeous surroundings, and the real coup: the private path leading to a secluded ocean cove lined with coconut palms (access is tricky, so you generally have this beach all to yourself). There's world-class windsurfing just a short walk away at Hookipa Beach, restaurants within a 5-minute drive, and great boutiquing a mile away in Paia; it's just 10 minutes to Kahului Airport.

⭐ **Mama's Beachfront Cottages.** 799 Poho Place (off the Hana Hwy., in Kuau), Paia, HI 96779. ☎ **800/860-HULA** or 808/579-9764. Fax 808/579-8594. www.mamasfishhouse. com. 6 units. A/C TV TEL. $135 1-bedroom (sleeps up to 4), $260–$300 2-bedroom (sleeps up to 6). AE, DC, DISC, MC, V.

The fabulous location (nestled in a coconut grove on the secluded Kuau beach), beautifully decorated interior (with island-style rattan furniture and works by Hawaiian artists), and plenty of extras (Weber gas barbecue, 27-inch TVs, and all the beach toys you can think of) make this place a must-stay for people looking for a centrally located vacation rental. It has everything, even Mama's Fish House next door (where guests get a 20% discount). The one-bedrooms are nestled in a tropical jungle, while the two-bedrooms face the beach. Both have terra-cotta floors, complete kitchens, sofa beds, and laundry facilities. We love Mama's sense of humor: We opened the closet in one unit and found a grass hula skirt complete with a coconut-shell top tacked to the back wall.

HAIKU

MODERATE

Honopo'u Lodge. Haiku, c/o Hawaii's Best Bed & Breakfasts, P.O. Box 563, Kamuela, HI 96743. ☎ **800/262-9912** or 808/885-4550. Fax 808/885-0559. www.bestbnb.com. 3 units. TV TEL. $100–$175 double. Rates include breakfast fixings. 3–5 night minimum. No credit cards.

Hidden on Maui's north shore, next door to a 750-acre ranch, is this upscale vacation retreat: a unique 4,000-square-foot architect-designed octagonal house, with native ohia posts and cedar wood. The entire downstairs of the octagonal-shaped house was decorated with veteran B&B owner Dr. Fred Fox's impeccable sense of color and design; it comes complete with a spacious atrium and a kitchenette (with microwave, small fridge, stove, and coffeemaker). Rates start at $175 for two ($225 if four people take both bedrooms). Upstairs is a smaller studio with its own private entrance and small kitchenette ($100 for two). There are ocean views from every room and waterfalls nearby. Amenities include a large (32 feet by 16 feet) pool, Jacuzzi, sundeck, barbecue, laundry facilities, and satellite TV.

Maui Tradewinds. Haiku, c/o Hawaii's Best Bed & Breakfasts, P.O. Box 563, Kamuela, HI 96743. ☎ **800/262-9912** or 808/885-4550. Fax 808/885-0559. www.bestbnb.com. 1 unit. TV TEL. $145 double. 3-night minimum. Extra person $15. No credit cards.

No expense was spared in the construction of this 1,000-square-foot studio apartment, located on the lower level of a custom-built home in the rolling hills of Haiku. Maui Tradewinds distinguishes itself from other accommodations with its floor-to-ceiling windows that capture the ocean view, blonde-wood floors, recessed lighting, bamboo furniture, laundry facilities, top-of-the-line kitchen equipment, outdoor Jacuzzi, and full bathroom with dry/steam sauna. With the sofa bed, the unit sleeps up to four adults.

✪ **Pilialoha B&B Cottage.** 2512 Kaupakalua Rd. (0.7 miles from Kokomo intersection), Haiku, HI 96708. ☎ **808/572-1440.** Fax 808/572-4612. www.pilialoha.com. 1 cottage. TV TEL. $130 double. 3-night minimum. Rates include continental breakfast. Extra person $20. No credit cards.

The minute you arrive at this split-level country cottage, located on 2 acres of eucalyptus trees, you'll see owner Machiko Heyde's artistry at work. Just in front of the cottage is a garden blooming with some 200 varieties of roses. You'll find more of Machiko's handiwork inside the quaint cottage, which is great for couples but can sleep up to five: There's a queen bed in the master bedroom, a twin bed in a small adjoining room, and a queen sleeper sofa in the living room. A large lanai extends from the master bedroom. You'll find a great movie collection for rainy days or cool country nights, a washer/dryer, beach paraphernalia (including snorkel equipment), and a garage. Machiko delivers breakfast daily; if you plan on an early morning ride to the top of Haleakala, she'll make sure you go with a thermos of coffee and her homemade bread. *Pilialoha* translates as "friendship," which is how you will feel about your hostess by the time you leave.

INEXPENSIVE

For a peaceful retreat, try the **Bamboo Mountain Sanctuary,** 1111 Kaupakalua Rd., Haiku, HI 96708 (☎ **808/572-4897;** www.planet-hawaii.com/zen), a 1940s plantation house that has served as a Zen monastery for 17 years; it offers five rooms (all with shared bathroom) on the edge of the Koolau Forest Reserve ($75 double).

Conveniently located near Twin Falls and Baldwin Beach is the **Golden Bamboo Ranch,** Kaupakalua Road (at Holokai Rd.), Haiku (☎ **800/262-9912** or 808/ 885-4550; fax 808/885-0559; www.bestbnb.com), set on 7 acres covered with fruit trees and boasting wonderful views ($85 to $95 double).

Maui Dream Cottages. 265 W. Kuiaha Rd. (1 block from Pauwela Cafe), Haiku, HI 96708. ☎ **808/575-9079.** Fax 808/575-9477. www.planet-hawaii.com/haiku. 2 cottages (with showers only). TV. $70 for up to 4. 7-night minimum. MC, V.

Essentially a vacation rental, this 2-acre country estate is located atop a hill overlooking the ocean. The grounds are dotted with fruit trees (bananas, papayas, and avocados, all free for the picking), and the front lawn is comfortably equipped with a double hammock, chaise longues, and table and chairs. One cottage has two bedrooms, one bathroom, full kitchen (with microwave and coffeemaker), washer/dryer, and entertainment center. The other is basically the same, but has only one bedroom (plus a sofa bed in the living room). They're both very well maintained, comfortably outfitted with furniture that's not only attractive but also casual enough for families with kids. The Haiku location is quiet and restful and offers the opportunity to see how real islanders live. However, you'll have to drive a good 20 to 25 minutes to restaurants in Makawao or Paia for dinner. Hookipa Beach is about a 20-minute drive, and Baldwin Beach (good swimming) is about 25 minutes away.

TWIN FALLS
INEXPENSIVE

Also consider the off-the-beaten-path **Tea House Cottage** (☎ **808/572-5610;** www.mauiteahouse.com): You park your car and follow a fern-lined path to a secluded hideaway in the jungle, powered by alternative energy (no power poles!). Here's your chance to get away from it all while still having utilities, phone, TV—you can even plug in your laptop ($110 double).

Budget travelers might consider the very affordable **Halfway to Hana House** (☎ **808/572-1176;** www.maui.net/~gailp), an adorable studio (complete with kitchenette), nestled in among the ferns and flowers in the jungle, just past Twin Falls, with rates starting at $75 double (without breakfast) and $85 double with breakfast.

⭘ **Maluhia Hale.** P.O. Box 687 (off Hana Hwy., nearly a mile past Twin Falls bridge), Haiku, HI 96708. ☎ **808/572-2959.** Fax 808/572-2959. www.maui.net/~djg/index.html. 2 units. TV. $105 cottage double, $110 suite double. 3-night minimum. Rates include continental breakfast. Extra person $20. No credit cards.

Diane and Robert Garrett design and build homes that are works of art. Here, they've created a private country cottage that has the feeling of a gracious old Hawaiian plantation home. A sense of peace and orderliness reigns in the cottage: You enter through an open and airy screened veranda, which leads to a glassed-in sitting room, a bed in lacy white linen, and a kitchenette. Hand-selected antiques fill the cottage, and Diane's exquisite flower arrangements add splashes of color. A traditional Hawaiian bathhouse is adjacent, with an old claw-foot tub and separate shower. In the main house is a romantic suite complete with a small kitchenette and screened porch. Diane does light housekeeping daily; no matter which accommodation you choose, at the end of the day, you'll return to a softly lit place filled with sweet-smelling tropical flowers. A simply wonderful place.

HUELO
MODERATE

⭘ **Huelo Point Flower Farm.** Off Hana Hwy., between mile markers 3 and 4. P.O. Box 1195, Paia, HI 96779. ☎ **808/572-1850.** www.maui.net/~huelopt. 4 units. $135 cottage double, $150 carriage house double, $275 guest house double. $2,800 per week for main house for 6. Extra person $25. 2-night minimum, except for main house, which has a 7-night minimum. No credit cards.

Here's a little Eden by the sea on a spectacular, remote 300-foot sea cliff near a waterfall stream: a 2-acre estate overlooking Waipio Bay with two guest cottages, a guest house, and a main house available for rent. The studio-sized Gazebo Cottage has a glass-walled ocean front, a koa-wood captain's bed, TV, stereo, kitchenette, private ocean-side patio, private hot tub, and a half-bathroom with outdoor shower. The new 900-square-foot Carriage House apartment sleeps four and has glass walls facing the mountain and sea, plus a kitchen, den, decks, and a loft bedroom. The two-bedroom main house contains an exercise room, fireplace, sunken Roman bath, cathedral ceilings, and other extras. There's a natural pool with a waterfall and an oceanfront hot tub. You're welcome to pick fruit, vegetables, and flowers from the extensive garden. Homemade scones, tree-ripened papayas, and fresh-roasted coffee start your day. Despite its seclusion, off the crooked road to Hana, it's just a half hour to Kahului, or about 20 minutes to Paia's shops and restaurants.

✪ **Huelo Point Lookout B&B.** Off Hana Hwy. (between mile markers 3 and 4), c/o Hawaii's Best Bed & Breakfasts, P.O. Box 563, Kamuela, HI 96743. ☎ **800/262-9912** or 808/885-4550. Fax 808/885-0559. www.bestbnb.com. 4 units. TV TEL. $105–$325 double. Rates include a welcome breakfast basket. Extra person $20–$30. 3-night minimum. No cards.

About a quarter-mile from the 300-foot cliffs of Waipio Bay is this lovely B&B, situated on 2 acres of tropical jungle with a hot tub, 40-foot free-form swimming pool, and a view all the way down the coastline to Hana. The main house has pentagonal glass walls that offer sweeping views of the ocean and up the side of Haleakala. It has two private entrances, a large bedroom with king bed, a kitchenette, a big bathroom with a tub for two, and a lotus pond and waterfall outside on the private deck. The Honey-moon Cottage is a totally renovated old fisherman's residence, with an upstairs bedroom, a full kitchen, a sitting room, and a solarium with lots of windows, skylights, and a deck. The bathroom has a Victorian tub and glass all around, with views of Haleakala on one side and the ocean on the other. The Halekala Cottage is smaller but full of amenities, including a full kitchen, king bed, and tiled bathroom that extends outside into the garden so that you can actually take a hot shower under the stars, surrounded by white lattice and tropical flowers. The newest cottage, Rainbow, located next to the swimming pool, features 25-foot-high glass walls with nothing but views. Other unique amenities include a private indoor hot tub, glass-ceilinged bathroom, and work-of-art wooden staircase. The owners, Jeff and Sharyn, also own a video store in Paia, so they can get you the movies of your choice.

INEXPENSIVE

Hale Akua Shangri-la Retreat Center. Star Rte. 1, Box 161 (off Hana Hwy., between mile markers 3 and 4), Haiku, HI 96708. ☎ **888/368-5305** or 808/572-9300. Fax 808/572-6666. www.haleakua.com. 12 units (some with shared bathroom). $55–$150 double room, $100–$125 cottage double. Rates include breakfast and yoga class. Extra person $20. AE, DISC, MC, V.

This place isn't for everyone; the hang-loose atmosphere might or might not be your style. Way off the beaten path, Hale Akua is a collection of eclectic buildings on 2 tropical acres where, at certain times of the year, guests can choose to go "clothing optional" (translation: nude). The main house on the property has breathtaking ocean views and private lanai off most rooms; guests share the living room, bathroom, and kitchen. The Cabana building, next to the 60-foot pool, is a two-story house with five separate rooms, two kitchens, and a dining area. Also on the property is a cottage with two rooms, one pyramid-shaped. Other on-site features include a hot tub, fountain, lily pond, hammock, trampoline, and maze formed by panex trees. Yoga classes are available.

6 At the End of the Road in East Maui: Hana

Picture Shangri-La, Hawaiian-style: 66 acres rolling down to the sea in a remote Hawaiian village, with a wellness center, two pools, and access to one of the best beaches in Hana. It all adds up to the **Hotel Hana-Maui** (☎ **800/321-HANA** or 808/248-8211; fax 808/248-7202; $425 double, $475 suite, $550 to $795 cottage). However, this once-gorgeous luxury resort has been suffering from neglect of late. As we went to press, a new management company just acquired the hotel. We hope they do some maintenance (like cleaning up the 4-inch high weeds growing in the rain gutters), bring the once-sterling dining room back to a level of excellence in both food and service, work on the attitude of the employees (which was once open and friendly, but in the last few years has soured somewhat), and do some major renovations to all the buildings. Until this happens, you might want to look elsewhere for accommodations in Hana. We recommend the following.

MODERATE

✪ **Ekena.** Off Hana Hwy., above Hana Airport (P.O. Box 728), Hana, HI 96713. ☎ **808/248-7047.** Fax 808/248-7047. www.maui.net/~ekena. 2 units. TV TEL. $165 double, $215–$300 for 4. 3-night minimum. Extra person $25. No credit cards.

Just one glance at the 360° view, and you can see why hosts Robin and Gaylord gave up their careers on the mainland and moved here. This 8^1/$_2$-acre piece of paradise in rural Hana boasts ocean and rain-forest views; the floor-to-ceiling sliding-glass doors in the spacious Hawaiian-style pole house bring the outside in. The elegant two-story home is exquisitely furnished, from the comfortable U-shaped couch that invites you to relax and take in the view to the top-of-the-line mattress on the king bed. The kitchen is fully equipped with every high-tech convenience you can imagine (guests have made complete holiday meals here). Only one floor (and one two-bedroom unit) is rented at any one time to ensure privacy. The grounds are impeccably groomed with tropical plants and fruit trees. Hiking trails into the rain forest start right on the property, and the beaches and waterfalls are just minutes away. Robin places fresh flowers in every room and makes sure you're comfortable; after that, she's available to answer questions about what Hana has to offer, but she also respects your privacy and lets you enjoy your vacation in peace.

✪ **Hamoa Bay Bungalow.** P.O. Box 773, Hana, HI 96713. ☎ **808/248-7884.** Fax 808/248-7047. www.hamoabay.com. 2 units. TV TEL. $175 cottage (sleeps only 2); main house $200 double, $300 for 4. 3-night minimum. No credit cards.

Down a country lane guarded by two Balinese statues stands a little bit of Indonesia in Hawaii: a carefully crafted bungalow, plus an Asian-inspired two-bedroom house overlooking Hamoa Bay. This enchanting retreat is just 2 miles beyond Hasegawa's general store on the way to Kipahulu. It sits on 4 verdant acres within walking distance of Hamoa Beach (which James Michener considered one of the most beautiful in the Pacific). The 600-square-foot Balinese-style cottage is distinctly tropical, with giant Elephant bamboo furniture from Indonesia, batik prints, a king bed, full kitchen, and screened porch with hot tub and shower. Hidden from the cottage is a 1,300-square-foot home with a soaking tub and private outdoor stone shower. There's an elephant bamboo king bed in one room, a queen bed in the other; there's also a screened-in sleeping porch, a full kitchen, and wonderful ocean views.

Hana Hale Malamalama. Across from the Mormon Church in Hana, c/o Hawaii's Best Bed & Breakfasts, P.O. Box 563, Kamuela, HI 96743. ☎ **800/262-9912** or 808/885-4550. Fax 808/885-0559. www.bestbnb.com. 6 units. $130–$275 double. Extra bedroom $60. 2-night minimum. No credit cards.

Located on a historic site with ancient fish ponds and a cave mentioned in ancient chants, this place definitely exudes the spirit of Old Hawaii. Host John takes excellent care of the ponds (you're welcome to watch him feed the fish at 5pm daily) and is fiercely protective of the hidden cave ("it's not a tourist attraction, but a sacred spot"). There's access to a nearby rocky beach, which isn't good for swimming but makes a wonderful place to watch the sun set. All accommodations include fully equipped kitchens, private bathrooms, bedrooms, living/dining areas, and private lanai. With two duplex suites—one with more than 1,800 square feet of living space—the main house is an architectural masterpiece, built entirely of Philippine mahogany with 4-foot-wide skylights the entire length of the house. The separate two-level Tree House cottage is nestled between a kamani tree and a coconut palm. Downstairs is the bathroom with a Jacuzzi tub for two, while upstairs is a Balinese bamboo bed, small kitchen/living area, and a small deck. Also on the property is the ocean-view Bamboo Inn, with two units, and the Pond Side Bungalow, with a private outdoor Jacuzzi tub and shower.

Hana Kai Maui Resort. 1533 Uakea Rd. (P.O. Box 38), Hana, HI 96713. ☎ **800/346-2772** or 808/248-8426. Fax 808/248-7482. www.hanakai.com. 17 units. $125–$145 studio double, $145–$195 1-bedroom (sleeps up to 4). Children under 8 stay free in parent's room. AE, MC, V.

Hana's only vacation condo complex, Hana Kai offers studio and one-bedroom units overlooking Hana Bay. All units have large kitchens and private lanai. The one-bedroom units each have a sliding door that separates the bedroom from the living room, plus a sofa bed that sleeps two additional guests. There are no phones or TVs in the units (a pay phone is located on the property), so you can really get away from it all. Ask for a corner unit with wraparound ocean views.

✪ Heavenly Hana Inn. P.O. Box 790, Hana, HI 96713. ☎ and fax **808/248-8442.** www.placestostay.com. E-mail: hanainn@maui.net. 4 units. TV TEL. $100 double studio $185–$250 suite. Rates include complimentary continental breakfast; full gourmet breakfast available at $12.50 per person. 2-night minimum. AE, DISC, JCB, MC, V. Children under 15 discouraged.

Owners Robert Filippi and Sheryl Murray understatedly describe their B&B as a "Japanese-style inn at secluded and beautiful Hana." That's a little like saying a Four Seasons hotel is a big building with rooms. This impeccably thought-out accommodation is a little bit of heaven, where no detail has been overlooked. The suites each have a sitting room with a futon and couch, polished hardwood floors, and a separate bedroom with a raised platform bed (with an excellent, firm mattress). The black-marble bathrooms contain huge tubs and separate glassed-in showers. Flowers are everywhere, ceiling fans keep the rooms cool, and the daily gourmet breakfast (a fruit course and a main entree plus homemade breads and pastries) is not only delicious, but also served in a setting filled with art, including the hand-crafted dining table and matching chairs. The 2 acres of grounds are done in Japanese style with a bamboo fence, tiny bridges over a meandering stream, and Japanese gardens.

Papalani. Star Route 27 (4 miles past Hasegawa's General Store), Hana, HI 96713. ☎ **808/248-7204.** Fax 808/248-7285. 2 units. TEL. $150 double. 3-night minimum. Extra person $25. No credit cards. No children under 8.

These luxurious, romantic accommodations are hidden from the road, offering privacy and quiet in a first-class setting. There's only one drawback: mosquitoes—swarms of them, in fact. A stream runs through the property, and although hostess Cybil has done everything possible to eliminate this nuisance (like providing screened-in lanai so that you can enjoy the outdoors without experiencing these biting pests), you'll want to bring your insect repellent.

Otherwise, Papalani lives up to its name, which means "heaven and all the spiritual powers." The apartment and the cottage, both professionally decorated, have white leather couches, wood floors, and expensive artwork. Everything is first-class, from the appliances in the kitchen to the faucets in the bathroom. The apartment has a kitchenette with minifridge, blender, and coffeemaker, while the separate cottage has a full kitchen. Both units have their own laundry facilities and private hot tubs. This is a TV-free environment, so you can really get in touch with nature. The great location means you're just a 5-minute walk to Waioka Stream (where there's good swimming in the pools), a mile from beautiful Hamoa Beach, and 5 minutes from Hana. Cybil asks that guests not smoke on the property and that meat be cooked on a barbecue outside.

INEXPENSIVE

If you'd like your own cottage, consider the simple but adequately furnished **Aloha Cottages,** 83 Keawa Pl., P.O. Box 205, Hana, HI 96713 (☎ **808/248-8420**), which go for $62 to $95 double.

✪ **Hana's Tradewinds Cottage.** 135 Alalele Place (P.O. Box 385), Hana, HI 96713. ☎ **800/327-8097** or 808/248-8980. Fax 808/248-7735. www.hanamaui.net. 2 cottages. TV. $110 studio double, $135 two-bedroom double. Extra person $10. 2-night minimum. AE, DISC, MC, V.

Nestled among the ginger and heliconias on a 5-acre flower farm are these two separate cottages, each with complete kitchen, carport, barbecue, hot tub, TV, ceiling fan, and sleeper sofa. The studio cottage sleeps up to four; a bamboo shoji blind separates the sleeping area (with queen bed) from the sofa bed in the living room. The Tradewinds cottage has two bedrooms (with queen bed in one room and two twins in the other), one bathroom (with shower only), sleeper sofa, and huge front porch. The atmosphere is quiet and relaxing, and host Rebecca Buckley, who has been in business for a decade, welcomes families (she has two children, a cat, and a very sweet golden retriever). You can use their laundry facilities at no extra charge.

Waianapanapa State Park Cabins. Off Hana Hwy., c/o State Parks Division, 54 S. High St., Rm. 101, Wailuku, HI 96793. ☎ **808/984-8109.** 12 cabins. $45 for 4 (sleeps up to 6). Extra person $5. 5-night maximum. No credit cards.

These 12 rustic cabins are the best lodging deal on Maui. Everyone knows it, too—so make your reservations early (up to 6 months in advance). The cabins are warm and dry and come complete with kitchen, living room, bedroom, and bathroom with hot shower. Furnishings include bedding, linen, towels, dishes, and very basic cooking and eating utensils. Don't expect luxury—this is a step above camping, albeit in a beautiful tropical jungle setting unlike any other in the islands. The key attraction at this 120-acre state beach park is the unusual horseshoe-shaped black-sand beach on Pailoa Bay, popular for shore fishing, snorkeling, and swimming. There's a caretaker on site, along with rest rooms, showers, picnic tables, shoreline hiking trails, and historic sites. But bring mosquito protection—this *is* the jungle.

5 Dining

by Jocelyn Fujii

Maui's soaring visitor statistics translate into good eats at every turn and healthy competition among restaurants.

In the island's dizzying scenario of musical (dining) chairs, some things haven't changed: You can still dine well at Lahaina's open-air waterfront watering holes, where the view counts for 50% of the experience. There are still budget choices, but not many; Maui's old-fashioned, multigenerational mom-and-pop diners are disappearing by attrition, eclipsed by the flashy newcomers, or clinging to the edge of existence in the older neighborhoods of central Maui, such as lovable Wailuku. You'll have to work harder to find them in the resort areas. But you won't have to go far to find creative cuisine, pleasing style, and stellar dining experiences in upcountry, south, and west Maui.

The few restaurant closures have been more than offset by the opening of several new notables, particularly on the west and south shores. In between, in Maalaea, be on the lookout for culinary guru Peter Merriman's new paean to "tropas," his take on tapas and the "shared dining" concept. Scheduled to open in June 2000, Maui's new Merriman's (Merriman's Bamboo Bistro in Maalaea Harbor Village, next to the Maui Ocean Center) will carry the classics that made his Merriman's on the Big Island such a culinary icon.

In the listings below, reservations are not necessary unless otherwise noted.

1 Central Maui

KAHULUI
EXPENSIVE

Sam Choy's Kahului. At Kaahumanu Center, 275 Kaahumanu Ave. (5 min. from Kahului Airport on Hwy. 32), Kahului. ☎ **808/893-0366.** Reservations recommended. Breakfast main courses $4–$10, lunch main courses $7–$12, dinner main courses $20–$35. AE, DC, DISC, JCB, MC, V. Mon–Thurs 8am–9pm, Fri 8am–9:30pm, Sat 7am–9:30pm, Sun 7am–9pm. LOCAL/HAWAII REGIONAL.

Sam Choy's cooking, which the *Wall Street Journal* calls "blue-collar chow," has spread from Hawaii to Tokyo—loco moco, poke, and all. It's still poke paradise. His seared poke salad remains a lunchtime staple (vastly overrated, in our opinion), and his seafood laulau, macadamia-nut-crusted ono, and rib eye steak are some of the evening attractions. At breakfast, residents gather for poke omelettes, spinach and shiitake mushroom omelettes, the morning's fresh catch, taro cakes, and other local favorites.

MODERATE

Marco's Grill & Deli. In the Dairy Center, 395 Dairy Road, Kahului. ☎ **808/877-4446.** Main courses $10.95–$22. AE, DC, DISC, JCB, MC, V. Daily 7:30am–10pm. ITALIAN.

Located in the elbow of central Maui, where the roads to upcountry, west, and south Maui converge, Marco's is popular among area residents who like its homemade Italian fare and friendly informality. This is one of those comfortable neighborhood fixtures favored by all generations. Locals stop here for breakfast, lunch, and dinner, before and after movies, on the way to and from baseball games and concerts.

Everything—from the meatballs, sausages, and burgers to the sauces, salad dressings, and raviolis—is made in-house. The 35 different choices of hot and cold sandwiches and entrees are served all day. They include vodka rigatoni with imported prosciutto, *pasta e' fasio* (a house specialty, smoked ham hock simmered for hours in tomato sauce, with red and white beans), and simple pasta with marinara sauce. The antipasto salad, vegetarian lasagna, and roasted peppers are taste treats, but it's the meatballs and Italian sausage that are famous in central Maui.

INEXPENSIVE

The **Kaahumanu Center,** the structure that looks like a white *Star Wars* umbrella in the center of Kahului, at 275 Kaahumanu Ave. (5 minutes from Kahului Airport on Hwy. 32), has a very popular food court. The **Juiceland** kiosk near the top of the elevator offers vitamin-rich (and delicious!) vegetable and fruit juices in creative combinations, as well as smoothies made from the legendary fresh fruits of Maui. **Maui Tacos,** one of the string of palate-pleasing Mexican diners sprinkled throughout Maui (see p. 129), offers green burritos; painted naturally with spinach, they're the best this side of the Rio Grande. **Edo Japan** teppanyaki is a real find; its flat Benihana-like grill dispenses marvelous, flavorful mounds of grilled fresh vegetables and chicken teriyaki for $4.15. **Yummy Korean B-B-Q** offers the assertive flavors of Korea; **Panda Cuisine** serves tasty Chinese food; and **The Coffee Store** (see p. 133) sells sandwiches, salads, pasta, and nearly two dozen coffee drinks. When you leave Kaahumanu Center, take a moment to gaze at the West Maui Mountains to your left from the parking lot. They are one of Maui's wonders.

Ichiban. In the Kahului Shopping Center, 47 Kaahumanu Ave., Kahului. ☎ **808/871-6977.** Main courses $4.25–$5.25 at breakfast, $4.25 and up at lunch (combination plates $8.50), $4.95–$26.95 at dinner (combination dinner $11.95, dinner specials $8.95 and up). DC, MC, V. Mon–Fri 6:30am–2pm, Sat 10:30am–2pm; Mon–Sat 5–9pm. JAPANESE/SUSHI.

What a find: an informal neighborhood restaurant that serves inexpensive, home-cooked Japanese food *and* good sushi at realistic prices. Local residents consider Ichiban a staple for breakfast, lunch, or dinner and a haven of comforts: egg-white omelettes, great saimin, combination plates (teriyaki chicken, teriyaki meat, *tonkatsu* (pork cutlet), rice, and pickled cabbage), chicken yakitori, and sushi—everything from unagi and scallops to California roll. The sushi items may not be inexpensive, but like the specials, such as steamed opakapaka, they're a good value. We love the tempura, miso soup, and spicy ahi hand roll.

Restaurant Matsu. In the Maui Mall, 70 E. Kaahumanu Ave., Kahului. ☎ **808/871-0822.** Most items less than $6. No credit cards. Mon–Thurs 9am–6pm, Fri 9am–9pm, Sat 9am–5:30pm, Sun 10am–4pm. JAPANESE/LOCAL.

Customers have come from Hana (more than 50 miles away) just for Matsu's California rolls, while regulars line up for the cold saimin (julienned cucumber, egg, Chinese-style sweet pork, and red ginger on noodles) and the bento plates (various assemblages of chicken, teriyaki beef, fish, and rice). The nigiri sushi items are popular, especially for the don't-dally lunch crowd. The katsu pork and chicken, breaded and deep-fried, are other specialties of this casual Formica-style diner. We love the tempura udon and the saimin, steaming mounds of wide and fine noodles swimming in homemade broths and topped with condiments. The daily specials are a changing lineup of home-cooked classics: roast pork with gravy, teriyaki ahi, miso butterfish, and breaded mahimahi.

WAILUKU
MODERATE

✪ **A Saigon Café.** 1792 Main St., Wailuku. ☎ **808/243-9560.** Main courses $6.50–$16.95. DC, MC, V. Mon–Sat 10am–9:30pm, Sun 10am–8:30pm. VIETNAMESE.

How's this for attitude: There's no sign. Jennifer Nguyen can afford to be elusive, because, difficult as this restaurant is to find, diners drive all the way from Kula and beyond to savor her famous soups and curries. But first you have to get there: Heading into Wailuku from Kahului, go over the bridge and take the first right on Central Avenue, then the first right on Nani Street. At the next stop sign, look for the building with the neon sign that says "Open." You've arrived at A Saigon Café, where the menu runs the gamut, from a dozen different soups to cold and hot noodles (including the popular beef noodle soup called *pho*) and chicken and shrimp cooked in a clay pot.

Wok-cooked Vietnamese specialties—sautéed, with spicy lemongrass and sweet-and-sour sauces—highlight the produce of the season, and the fresh catch (ono, opakapaka) comes whole and crisp or steamed with ginger and garlic. You can create your own Vietnamese "burritos" from a platter of tofu, noodles, and vegetables that you wrap in rice paper and dip in garlic sauce. Among our favorites are the shrimp lemongrass, piquant and refreshing, and the tofu curry, swimming in herbs and vegetables straight from the garden. Fans are raving about the new Kona lobster dish (flash fried, tossed with ginger, onion, garlic, and chili sauce, and rearranged back in the lobster shell) and the clams with black bean sauce, as well as the house-made peanut-garlic sauce that will soon be bottled and sold, by popular demand.

INEXPENSIVE

Class Act. At Maui Community College, 310 Kaahumanu Ave., Wailuku. ☎ **808/984-3480.** Reservations recommended. 5-course lunch $15. No credit cards. Wed and Fri 11am–12:15pm (last seating). Menu and cuisine type change weekly.

Part of a program run by the distinguished Food Service Department of Maui Community College, this restaurant has a growing following. Student chefs show their stuff with a flourish in their "classroom," where they pull out all the stops as if it were their own place. Linen, china, servers in ties and white shirts, and a five-course lunch make this a five-star value.

The appetizer, soup, salad, and dessert are set, but you can choose between the regular entree and a heart-healthy entree prepared in the culinary tradition of the week. The filet mignon of French week is popular, and so are the Thai curries; Chinese stir-fry; pastas; and Japanese, Austrian, Moroccan, and other international menus. Tea and soft drinks are offered—and they can get pretty fancy, with fresh fruit and spritzers—but otherwise it's BYOB. Chris Speere, chef instructor, is the owner-chef of the excellent and beloved Pauwela Cafe (see section 5 of this chapter).

✪ **Maui Bake Shop.** 2092 Vineyard St., Wailuku. ☎ **808/242-0064.** Most items under $5. AE, CB, DISC, MC, V. Mon–Fri 6am–4pm, Sat 7am–2pm. BAKERY/DELI.

Baker José Krall (who was trained in the South of France and throughout Europe) and his wife, Maui native Claire Fujii-Krall, turn out buttery brioches, healthy nine-grain and two-tone rye breads, focaccia, strudels, sumptuous fresh-fruit gâteaux, puff pastries, and dozens of other baked goods and confections. The breads are baked in one of Maui's oldest brick ovens, installed in 1935; a high-tech European diesel oven handles the rest. The front window displays the more than 100 bakery and deli items, among them salads, a popular eggplant marinara focaccia, quiches, and a moist, inexpensive calzone. Homemade soups team up nicely with sandwiches on freshly baked bread. The food here is light enough (well, almost) to justify the Ultimate Dessert: white-chocolate macadamia-nut cheesecake.

Norm's Cafe. 740 Lower Main St., Wailuku. ☎ **808/242-1667.** Main courses $5.35–$7.95. AE, MC, V. Mon–Sat 5am–2pm, Thurs–Sat 5–9pm, Sun 6am–2pm. AMERICAN/LOCAL.

Norm's welcomes you with a plaid yellow concrete-block entrance lined with lava rock—an apt foreshadowing of the old-fashioned, Formica-table celebration that awaits inside. Hot-pink paper menus issue the call for Norm's signature Paukukalo Burger, an 8-ounce hamburger with blue-cheese dressing and all the trimmings; Fran's Club, a turkey-bacon-avocado fantasy on grilled sourdough; and the universal fave, bamboo-steamed ono, fabulous and cheap at $6.45. There's always a gaggle of regulars somewhere in the far corner, trying to decide between saimin, dry mein, a BLT, and the humongous hamburger.

Sam Sato's. Millyard, 1750 Wili Pa Loop, Wailuku. ☎ **808/244-7124.** Plate lunches $5.50–$5.90. No credit cards. Mon–Sat 7am–2pm. NOODLES/PLATE LUNCHES.

Sam Sato's is a Maui institution, not only for its noodles (saimin, dry noodles, chow fun), but also its flaky baked *manju*, filled with sweetened lima beans or adzuki beans. Sam opened his family eatery in 1933, and his daughter, Lynne Toma, still makes the broth the old-fashioned way: from scratch. The saimin and the dry noodles, with broth that comes in a separate bowl, are big sellers. One regular comes to the counter, with its wooden stools and homemade salt and pepper shakers, for his "usual": two barbecued meat sticks, two scoops of rice, and three macaroni salads. The peach, apple, coconut, and pineapple turnovers fly out the door, too, as do take-out noodles by the tray. *Tip:* If you want them to hold the MSG, be sure to make your request early.

Wei Wei BBQ and Noodle House. Millyard Plaza, 210 Imi Kala St., Wailuku. ☎ **808/242-7928.** Combination plates $4.95–$6.95; main courses $5.95–$8.50. No credit cards. Daily 10am–9pm. CHINESE/NOODLES.

Noodles are rapidly gaining on Big Macs as the fast-food choice of Hawaii, and Wei Wei is the darling of the on-the-go, no-nonsense, noodle-loving Maui crowd. You order at the counter, fast-food style, from a menu that includes Chinese classics: saimin with roast duck, shrimp-vegetable chow mein, dim sum, and the extremely popular house fried noodles. American favorites—hamburgers, a teriyaki chicken burger, a turkey sandwich, and the popular chicken katsu burger—are winning fans, too.

2 West Maui

LAHAINA
EXPENSIVE

✪ **David Paul's Lahaina Grill.** 127 Lahainaluna Rd. ☎ **808/667-5117.** Reservations required. Main courses $19–$38. AE, CB, DC, DISC, MC, V. Daily 5:30–10pm. Bar daily 5:30pm–midnight. NEW AMERICAN.

David Paul's chic restaurant, with its pressed-tin ceilings, black-and-white tile floors, Southwestern flavor, and eclectic 1890s decor, is a long way from the dank barroom that used to be in this same location. Today it's the favorite restaurant of most Maui diners. On an island where excellent dining is as ubiquitous as ocean views, that's high praise, and well deserved.

A special custom-designed chef's table can be arranged with 48-hour notice for larger parties, but the daily menu is enticement enough: tequila shrimp with firecracker rice, Kona lobster–crab cakes in a sesame-Dijon sauce, Kona coffee–roasted rack of lamb, kalua duck in a plum wine reduction, seared ahi encrusted in Maui onion, and many other seductions. The bar is the busiest spot in Lahaina, even without an ocean view.

✪ **The Feast at Lele.** 505 Front St. ☎ **808/667-5353.** Reservations strongly recommended. Set menu $89 for adults, $59 for children 2–12. AE, CB, DC, DISC, MC, V. Apr 1–Sept 30 Tues, Thurs, and Sat 6–9pm. Oct 1–Mar 31 Tues, Thurs, and Sat 5:30–8:30pm. POLYNESIAN.

The owners of the Old Lahaina Luau (see chapter 9, "Maui After Dark"), I'o and Pacific'o have outdone themselves with their lavish cultural concoction, The Feast at Lele. This dining experience sizzles, with chef James McDonald's wonderful food, an outdoor oceanfront setting, and dancers from the Old Lahaina Luau in a high-voltage combination. As if the sunset weren't heady enough, there are white tablecloths and candles on tables set on the sand, where dances from Hawaii, Tonga, Tahiti, and Samoa (complete with fire dancing) are presented, up close and personal, in full ti-leafed, costumed splendor. Unlike a luau, where the seating is en masse, you sit as in a restaurant, at a table with your companions. Chanting, singing, drums, dancing, the swish of fresh ti leaf skirts, the scent of plumeria—it's intoxicating. The opening is particularly mesmerizing, as a softly lit canoe carries three people ashore to the sound of conch shells on the beach.

The courses, like the entertainment, are well-timed, so the mini-feasts from the island nations are presented in sync with the entertainment from those cultures. The kalua pig is greaseless, the steamed moi comes whole and tasty, and the pohole ferns and hearts of palm are crisp and savory. From Tonga there's lobster-ogo (seaweed) salad and grilled steak; from Tahiti, steamed chicken and taro leaf in coconut milk; and from Samoa, grilled fish in banana leaf.

✪ **Gerard's.** In the Plantation Inn, 174 Lahainaluna Rd. ☎ **808/661-8939.** Reservations recommended. Main courses $26.50–$32.50. AE, CB, DC, DISC, JCB, MC, V. Daily 6–9pm. FRENCH.

The charm of Gerard's—fairy lights on the veranda, soft lighting, French doors, Edith Piaf on the sound system, excellent service from bow-tied servers—is matched by a menu of uncompromising standards. Gerard Reversade never runs out of creative offerings, yet stays true to his French roots.

A frequent winner of the *Wine Spectator* Award of Excellence, Gerard's offers roasted opakapaka with star anise, fennel fondue, and hints of orange and ginger, a stellar entree on a menu of winners. If you're feeling extravagant, the Kona lobster ragout with pasta and morels promises ecstasy, and the grilled rack of lamb with its mint crust and roasted garlic, served with an eggplant charlotte, is the ultimate for lamb lovers. At the other end of the calorie count, the spinach salad with scallops, discreet shavings of Parmesan, and a hint of browned butter is among the finest we've tasted. Gerard's has an excellent appetizer menu, too, with shiitake and oyster mushrooms in puff pastry, fresh ahi and smoked salmon carpaccio, and a very rich, highly touted escargot ragout with burgundy butter and garlic cream.

Lahaina & Kaanapali Dining

Aloha Mixed Plate **4**

Beachside Grill and Leilani's on the Beach **2**

Cheeseburger in Paradise **9**

Compadres Bar & Grill **5**

David Paul's Lahaina Grill **10**

The Feast at Lele **16**

Gerard's **11**

Groovy Smoothies **12**

Hard Rock Cafe **6**

Hula Grill **2**

I'o **16**

Kimo's **7**

Lahaina Coolers **13**

Lahaina Fish Company **9**

Pacific'o Restaurant **16**

Pizza Paradiso Express **2**

Sam Choy's Lahaina Restaurant and Big Aloha Brewery **6**

Swan Court **3**

Swiss Cafe **14**

Tiki Terrace **1**

Village Pizzeria **16**

Woody's Island Grille **8**

Zoolu Grille & Bar **15**

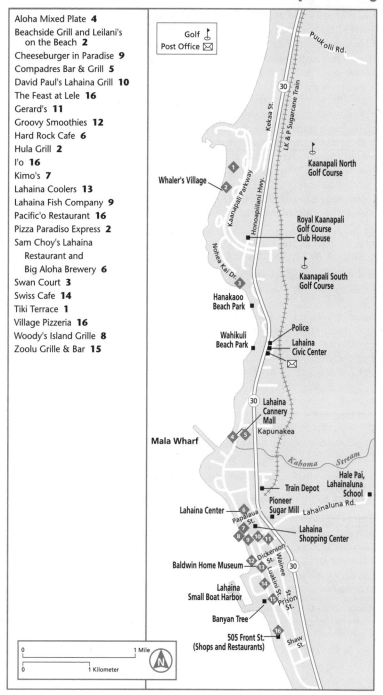

119

I'o. 505 Front St. ☎ **808/661-8422.** Reservations recommended for dinner. Main courses $23–$30. AE, DC, MC, V. Daily 5:30–10pm. PACIFIC RIM.

Although we wish they'd lose their overly self-conscious names with accents and apostrophes in strange places, we like the food and the view at I'o and its neighboring sister restaurants, The Feast at Lele and Pacific'o. I'o is a fantasy of sleek curves and etched glass, co-owned by chef James McDonald. He offers an impressive selection of appetizers (his strong suit) and some pretty lavish Asian-Polynesian interpretations of seafood, such as stir-fried lobster with mango-Thai curry sauce; fresh ahi in a nori panko crust; and lemongrass coconut fish. Our advice is to go heavy on the appetizers, because they're superb, especially the silken purse, a brilliant, seamless concoction of tricolored pot stickers stuffed with roasted peppers, mushrooms, spinach, macadamia nuts, and silken tofu. The Box also captures our loyalty: grilled skewers of fresh fish in miso sabayon are presented in a lacquer box and unveiled like a tasty surprise. Oyster lovers: the Pan Asian Rockefellers are baked on a bed of spinach and kai choy and served with a hint of star anise coconut cream, and they are memorable.

✪ **Pacific'o Restaurant.** 505 Front St. ☎ **808/667-4341.** Reservations recommended. Main courses $9–$14 at lunch, $19–$38 at dinner. AE, DC, MC, V. Daily 11am–4pm, 5:30–10pm. PACIFIC RIM/CONTEMPORARY PACIFIC.

If you like seafood, sunsets, and touches of India and Indonesia in your fresh-from-the-sea dining choices, you should be happy here. The tables are literally on the beach; you can't get closer to the ocean than award-winning Pacific'o. With good food complementing this sensational setting, foodies and aesthetes have much to enjoy. The split-level dining starts at the top, near the entrance, with a long, cordial bar (where you can also order lunch or dinner) and a few tables along the railing. Steps lead to the outdoor tables, where the award-winning seafood dishes come to you with the backdrop of Lanai across the channel.

If the Asian gravlax is still on the menu, don't miss it: house-cured salmon comes on warm sweet potato applejacks with wasabi chive sour cream and caviar. The prawn and basil wontons, the wok-fried oysters, and the Tandoori-spiced fresh moonfish are fine examples of Pacific'o's style. We've always enjoyed the vegetarian special: a marinated, roasted tofu steak crowned with quinoa, Maui onions, and red lentils, with a heavenly dose of shiitake mushrooms.

Sam Choy's Lahaina Restaurant and Big Aloha Brewery. Lahaina Center, 900 Front St. ☎ **808/661-3800.** Reservations recommended for dinner. Main courses $22–$32. AE, DC, DISC, JCB, MC. V. Daily 5–9:30pm. HAWAII REGIONAL/SEAFOOD.

Sam Choy's second Maui restaurant features a marine motif, a garden terrace, an open kitchen, and 210 seats—like everything else associated with Sam Choy, it's big. Choy's extensive appetizer menu includes barbecued spareribs, fried poke, steamed clams with miso-sake sauce, crab cakes with ginger pesto, and the noodles, rib-eye steak, and fresh fish dishes that are his menu staples statewide. His well-known seafood laulau and king crab legs are among his dinner staples. There are happy hour specials from 5 to 7pm.

Zoolu Grille & Bar. 666 Front St. ☎ **808/667-6200.** Reservations recommended. Main courses $16–$28. AE, DC, JCB, MC, V. Daily 11:30am–2:30pm and 5–9:30pm. CALIFORNIA ECLECTIC.

The bamboo handrails, rattan chairs, and Hawaiian tapa-printed upholstery are a clue: This place is friendly and hip. Tropical interior accents, a second-floor bar and dining room with three open sides, and birds singing in the banyans across the street are some of the reasons for Zoolu's immediate popularity. The pupu we loved: blackened ahi, tempura ahi wrapped in nori with Thai curry sauce, and the pot stickers, generous with the shiitakes and prepared in a spicy ginger-lemon soy sauce. The salads are elaborate, from falafel and mixed greens to tomato-Maui onion-pimiento, and they include the option to add giant shrimp or chicken. You can also choose "entree salads" of ahi Nicçoise and charbroiled diver scallops on Kula greens. "Double-edged swordfish" is the Zoolu specialty—assertive, steaklike cuts, in lemongrass-caper or blackened Cajun-style preparations. Zoolu may be trendy verging on theme-ish, but it still won us over.

MODERATE

Maui's branch of the **Hard Rock Cafe** is in Lahaina at 900 Front St. (☎ **808/667-7400**).

Compadres Bar & Grill. In Lahaina Cannery Mall, 1221 Honoapiilani Hwy. ☎ **808/ 661-7189.** Main courses $10–$18.50. AE, DC, DISC, JCB, MC, V. Daily 8am–10pm. MEXICAN.

Despite its concrete floors and high industrial ceilings, Compadres exudes good cheer. And that cheer has burgeoned lately with a new open-air dining area and a take-out taqueria window for diners on the run. The food is classic Tex-Mex, good any time of the day, beginning with huevos rancheros, egg burritos, hotcakes, and omelettes (the Acapulco is heroic) and progressing to enchiladas and appetizers for the margarita-happy crowd later on. Stay spare (vegetable enchilada in fresh spinach tortilla) or get hefty (Texas T-bone and enchiladas). This is a carefree place with a large capacity for merrymaking.

Kimo's. 845 Front St. ☎ **808/661-4811.** Reservations recommended for dinner. Lunch main courses $5.95–$10.95; dinner main courses $12.95–$23.95. AE, DC, DISC, MC, V. Daily 11am–3pm and 5–10:30pm. STEAK/SEAFOOD.

Although it's a formula restaurant (sibling to Leilani's and Hula Grill), Kimo's has a loyal following and several features that set it apart from the plethora of restaurants serving surf-and-turf with great sunset views. Its oceanfront patio and upstairs dining room, with views of Molokai, Lanai, and Kahoolawe, are desirable spots from morning until after sunset. The menu doesn't dazzle you with creativity, but it's consistently well-executed. The burgers and sandwiches are affordable, and you can count on the fresh fish in various preparations (garlic-lemon and a sweet-basil glaze) to be cooked to perfection. The waistline-defying hula pie—macadamia-nut ice cream in a chocolate-wafer crust with fudge and whipped cream—originated here.

Lahaina Fish Company. 831 Front St. ☎ **808/661-3472.** Main courses $9.99–$23.99. AE, JCB, MC, V. Daily 11am–midnight. SEAFOOD.

The open-air dining room here is literally over the water, with flickering torches after sunset and an affordable menu that covers the seafood-pasta basics. Head to an ocean-side table and order a cheeseburger, chicken burger, fish burger, a generous basket of peel-and-eat shrimp, or sashimi; lingering is highly recommended. The light lunch/grill menu offers appetizers (sashimi, seared ahi, spring rolls, and pot stickers), salads, and soups. The restaurant has spiffed up its dinner selections to include hand-carved steaks, several pasta choices, and local fare such as stir-fry dishes, teriyaki chicken, and luau-style ribs. Fresh seafood is the specialty: four types of fresh fish are offered nightly, in three preparations, and Pacific Rim specials include fresh ahi, seared spicy or cooked in a sweet ginger-soy sauce.

Woody's Island Grill. 839 Front. St. ☎ **808/661-8788.** Reservations recommended. Main courses $8–$22. AE, DISC, JCB, MC, V. Daily 11am–10pm. AMERICAN.

The owners of Cheeseburger in Paradise closed the Aloha Cantina and replaced it with Woody's, and it's a big improvement. You'll walk through a socko aloha shirt shop called Gary's to enter the open-air oceanfront room, where a wood-burning grill cooks

ⓘ   Family-Friendly Restaurants

In addition to Kahului's **Food Court at Kaahumanu Center,** where children have their pick of everything from tacos to teriyaki chicken, here's a sampling of places that go the extra mile for families:

CENTRAL MAUI

Koho Grill & Bar (Kaahumanu Center, 275 Kaaahumanu Ave.; ☎ **808/ 877-5588**)   A family of four can eat inexpensively here, and the kids have their own menus (with drawings for coloring) that change regularly. Sandwiches (grilled cheese, cheeseburger, hamburger) and fries go for $3.50 and under, and the ever-popular keiki quesadilla is a friendly $3.75. It's casual, a good value, and crayons are provided for the artists-in-the-making.

WEST MAUI

David Paul's Lahaina Grill *(see p. 117)*   You won't find a cheeseburger on the sophisticated menu, but kids get more than their share of attention. The food is fabulous, and the keiki (children's) menu offers soup, salad, and a choice of pasta marinara (spaghetti), fried-chicken strips with french fries, beef kabobs, mahimahi and shrimp sautéed or baked, and other entree choices—for $12. If they have the ingredients (no hamburger or hot dog buns in the pantry), the kitchen will accommodate special requests. Crayons, a coloring sheet, and the usual boosters and high chairs are part of the package.

Hula Grill *(see p. 125)*   Behind the scenes, children sort of run this place. Chef Peter Merriman, who put Hula Grill on the map, is the father of three, and the general manager's 10-year-old keeps him on his toes and the menu sensitive to keiki wants and needs. Children can play freely on the grassy lawn and the sandy beach in front of the restaurant, in full view of the outdoor tables. Besides free pasta for kids under 3, the menu (a coloring page of a gecko surfing, a smiling sun, a hula girl under a palm tree) includes keiki cheese pizza, grilled chicken and fries, cheeseburger and fries, fish and chips, pasta with Parmesan and butter, and other choices for $3.95 to $8.95.

Maui Tacos *(see p. 129)*   The four Maui Tacos on Maui are all kid-friendly. The menu is cheap to begin with, the place is largely take-out, but those who eat in have a fast-food type of environment that goes with the keiki menu: $2.75 keiki burritos; $2.99 for the tacos with churro (pastry) and a small drink; $3.99 for the ever-popular cheese quesadilla without lettuce or tomatoes, and minisized combination plates. In all Maui Tacos except Kaahumanu Center, there's a candy machine with everything from Chiclets to Gummi Bears.

---

fresh ono, mahimahi (with mango ginger butter), ribs, New York steak, and other surf-and-turf choices. There are sandwiches, including an excellent blackened ahi with wasabi aioli, and Cajun fish tacos, and coconut shrimp with sweet-sour sauce. The grilled opakapaka with a lemon-caper-butter sauce is very popular, teamed with the coconut shrimp for $20.

INEXPENSIVE

✪ **Aloha Mixed Plate.** 1285 Front St. ☎ **808/661-3322.** Main courses $4.95–$9.95. MC, V. Daily 10:30am–10pm. PLATE LUNCH/BEACHSIDE GRILL.

Look for the festive turquoise-and-yellow wooden, plantation-style front with the red corrugated-iron roof and adorable bar, tiny and busy, directly across from the Lahaina

SOUTH MAUI

Hakone *(see p. 136)*   Kids checking into the Westin Maui Prince Hotel receive a "tippy cup" and a coloring book if they're 4 to 6 years old and a sports cup and coloring book if they're 7 to 12 years old. They can then bring their cups to any of the Prince's restaurants and receive complimentary juice, milk, or soda. Drawings on the menus are for coloring, and pint-size orders of chicken teriyaki, shrimp tempura, and udon noodle soup with shrimp tempura can be ordered at dinner for $9 to $12.

Pacific Grill, Four Seasons Resort Maui at Wailea *(see p. 135)*   This restaurant rolls out the red carpet for the little ones. Keiki-friendly features at Pacific Grill include a special buffet at a lower-than-usual height, with finger foods and mini-sandwiches, that children can walk up to themselves while their parents wait for their orders. The menus aim to please: everything from chicken noodle soup and roasted chicken to hot dogs, hamburgers, and pizza ($4 to $7.50). Even older kids are pampered here. At dinner, the "I'm Not a Kid Anymore" menu, addressing preteens and teens, offers Chinese-style barbecue ribs for $6, burgers for $9, and grilled steak, chicken, and fish for $13 to $16.

Peggy Sue's *(see p. 134)*   Since this is a malt-burger-and-fries kind of place, kids fit in naturally. There are high chairs and booster seats, of course, but the real draw is the food: $3.95 for a choice of half of their famous hamburger, a small hot dog, or a peanut-butter-and-jelly or grilled-cheese sandwich, served with fries, a small drink, and a junior sundae for dessert. The atmosphere is carefree, with a tongue-in-cheek, teenybopper quality. The keiki menu has a full page of coloring ("Surf's Up at Peggy Sue's!") with a find-a-word game for fun.

UPCOUNTRY MAUI

Haliimaile General Store *(see p. 138)*   A beautiful drawing of the plantation storefront is great coloring material for keiki, who are given crayons and a pleasing keiki menu for lunch and dinner. From "kid cocktails" (chocolate and banana with milk; strawberry, banana, and cherry soda; kiwi soda; and lemonade) to the cheese pizza, barbecue ribs, chicken, and spaghetti and meatballs, this is the mother lode for families. With the ice-cream-and-cookie dessert, these are splashy choices for $8 at lunch, $15 at dinner.

Cannery Mall. You can have a fabulous plate lunch served to your aqua-colored picnic table at ocean's edge, in the shade of large kiawe and milo trees. (On the upper level, there are umbrellas and plumeria trees—just as charming.) In this wonderful setting, you can tuck into inexpensive mahimahi, kalua pig and cabbage, shoyu chicken, teriyaki beef, and other local plate-lunch specials, all at budget-friendly prices, with macaroni salad and rice. The shoyu chicken is the best we've had, fork tender and tasty. We don't know of anywhere else where you can order a mai tai, enjoy table service, and eat out of Styrofoam plates—and with an ocean view, too.

Cheeseburger In Paradise. 811 Front St. ☎ **808/661-4855.** Burgers $6.50–$9.95. AE, DISC, MC, V. Daily 8am–10pm. AMERICAN.

There are good reasons why this two-story green-and-white building next to the sea-wall is always packed: good value, good grinds, and a great ocean view. Wildly successful, always crowded, highly visible, and very noisy with its live music in the evenings, Cheeseburger is a shrine to the American classic. The home of three-napkin cheeseburgers with attitude, this is burger country, tropical style, with everything from tofu and garden burgers to big, juicy beef and chicken burgers, served on whole-wheat and sesame buns baked fresh daily. The Cheeseburger In Paradise—a hefty hunk with Jack and Cheddar cheeses, sautéed onions, lettuce, fresh tomatoes, and Thousand Island dressing—is a paean to the basics. You can build your own burger by adding sautéed mushrooms, bacon, grilled ortega chiles, and other condiments for an extra charge. Onion rings, chili-cheese fries, and cold beer complete the carefree fantasy.

Groovy Smoothies. 708 Front St. ☎ **808/661-8219.** Smoothies less than $4.50. No credit cards. Daily 9am–9:30pm. SMOOTHIES.

This closet-size take-out stand makes the best smoothies in Lahaina. The peanut butter–chocolate is over-the-top wonderful, a good jolt of energy for all that walking on Front Street. Fruit lovers can choose the mango-and-banana smoothie, but others may pine for the piña colada, the Peachy Keen, or any of the berry delights. Protein powders, bee pollen, and other nutritious ingredients can be blended into these tasty, healthy treats. If they're too pure for you, there are always muffins, high-octane espresso shots, and Danishes.

Lahaina Coolers. 180 Dickensen St. ☎ **808/661-7082.** Most items less than $14. AE, CB, DC, DISC, MC, V. Daily 8am–2am. AMERICAN/INTERNATIONAL.

A huge marlin hangs above the bar, and epic wave shots and wall sconces made of surfboard fins line the walls at this ultracasual (laid back) indoor/outdoor restaurant. Open windows on three sides take advantage of the shade trees to create a cordial, cheerful ambience. (If it gets too hot, a mister outside goes off periodically to cool off the plants and people.) New wood floors and teak chairs have added a fresh look to this restaurant, where the bar is open until 2am and the full menu can carry you from breakfast to bedtime.

The specialty, evil jungle pasta, comes with Thai peanut sauce and chicken breast, and although it's very popular, to us it was underwhelming. The breakfast items range from omelettes to fried rice and huevos rancheros. We've heard raves over the Moroccan Benedict (with spinach and feta cheese) and the fresh fish and kalua pork tacos. Pizzas, pastas, fresh catch, steak, and enchiladas round out the entrees, and everything can be prepared vegetarian upon request.

Swiss Café. 640 Front St. ☎ **808/661-6776.** 8-inch pizzas $5.95–$7.95; sandwiches $5.95–$7.95. No credit cards. Daily 9am–6pm. SANDWICHES/PIZZA.

This tiny café, a take-out stand with a few outdoor tables just off Lahaina's main drag, serves a Swiss breakfast, but it's mainly a sandwich and pizza shop. It's cheap, and its sandwiches, particularly the signature melts (using Emmentaler cheese baked on Italian Parmesan crust), score high in quality and value. Ice cream is another attraction, $2 a scoop for made-on-Maui Roselani and other top mainland brands. The tables are on the asphalt, so there's not much ambience—but the Lavazza coffee, top-quality breads baked fresh daily at Caffé Ciao at Kea Lani, and keen attention to the sandwich fillings and pizza toppings are noticeable and endearing. Most popular are the turkey-broccoli melt; spicy chicken with mushrooms, onions, and tomatoes and a Dijon herb spread; and our favorite, the veggie melt, with thin slices of tomatoes, cheese, broccoli, and zucchini on freshly baked bread, served warm. The Swiss owner, Dominique Martin, has imbued this corner of Lahaina with a European flavor, down to the menus printed in English and German and the Swiss breakfast of sliced ham, Emmentaler cheese, hard-boiled egg, and freshly baked croissant.

Village Pizzeria. 505 Front St. ☎ **808/661-8112.** Salad and pizza $4.50; $7.95–$22 for main courses and special pizzas. AE, DC, DISC, MC, V. Daily 11am–9:30pm. PIZZA.

With thin or thick crust, more than a dozen toppings, and the signature clam-and-garlic pizza that you can smell from around the corner, this pizzeria draws a steady stream of diners to its corner cafe at the popular shopping complex called 505 Front. Appetizers, sandwiches (on homemade bread), pasta, and famous tiramisu make this more than a pizza joint.

KAANAPALI
EXPENSIVE

Swan Court. In the Hyatt Regency Maui, 200 Nohea Kai Dr. ☎ **808/661-1234.** Reservations recommended for dinner. Main courses $28–$36. AE, DC, DISC, JCB, MC, V. Daily 6:30–11:30am and 6–10pm. CONTINENTAL.

A dance floor and new furnishings have been added to this romantic restaurant in the Hyatt Regency. Come here as a splurge or on a bottomless expense account, and enjoy its continental menu in incomparable surroundings. The combination of waterfalls, ocean view, Japanese gardens, and swans and flamingos serenely gliding by is hopelessly romantic, especially with alfresco dining and appropriately extravagant fare. The menu changes nightly in this tiered dining room. Hunan marinated lamb chops and the island-style bouillabaisse are perennial favorites, but many other seafood and game specials will make it hard to decide.

MODERATE

Beachside Grill and Leilani's on the Beach. In Whalers Village, 2435 Kaanapali Pkwy. ☎ **808/661-4495.** Reservations recommended for dinner. Lunch and dinner (Beachside Grill) $5.95–$10.95; dinner (Leilani's) $14.95 and up. AE, DC, DISC, MC, V. Beachside Grill daily 11am–11pm (bar daily until 12:30am); Leilani's daily 5–10pm. STEAK/SEAFOOD.

The Beachside Grill is the informal, less-expensive room downstairs on the beach, where folks wander in off the sand for a frothy beer and a beachside burger. Leilani's is the dinner-only room, with more expensive but still not outrageously priced steak and seafood offerings. At Leilani's, you can order everything from affordable spinach, cheese, and mushroom raviolis to lobster and steak at the higher market price. Still, children can order a quarter-pound hamburger for less than $5 or a broiled chicken breast for a couple of dollars more—a value, for sure. Pasta, rack of lamb, filet mignon, and Alaskan king crab at market price are among the temptations in the upstairs room. Although the steak-and-lobster combinations can be pricey, the good thing about Leilani's is the strong middle range of entree prices, especially the fresh fish for around $20.

All of this, of course, comes with an ocean view. There's live Hawaiian music every afternoon except Fridays, when the Rock 'n' Roll Aloha Friday set gets those decibels climbing. Free concerts are usually offered on a stage outside the restaurant from 2pm to sunset on the last Sunday of the month. The popular Music on the Beach program is always a big draw—and another big reason to love Leilani's. Any way you cut it, the view, food, prices, and location make this a hard-to-beat Kaanapali staple.

✪ **Hula Grill.** In Whalers Village, 2435 Kaanapali Pkwy. ☎ **808/667-6636.** Reservations recommended for dinner. Lunch and Barefoot Bar menus $5.95–$11.95; dinner main courses $12.95 and up. AE, CB, DC, DISC, MC, V. Daily 11am–11pm. HAWAII REGIONAL/SEAFOOD.

Who wouldn't want to tuck into banana-glazed opah, crab and corn cakes, or ahi poke rolls under a thatched umbrella, with a sand floor and palm trees at arm's length and

The Tiki Terrace

Bravo to the **Kaanapali Beach Hotel** for the low-salt, employee-tested Native Hawaiian Diet served in its Tiki Terrace, 2525 Kaanapali Parkway (☎ **808/ 661-0011**). Titled Kulaiwi Cuisine, the menu features the healthy, traditional Hawaiian diet of fresh fish and taro greens, flavored with herbs and spices. The use of salt is kept to a minimum, but you can always add your own. The Kulaiwi menu consists of pohole fern shoots from Keanae Valley (on the way to Hana), marinated with onions and seaweed and served with ginger-tomato dressing. (We think that with their freshness, pleasing crunch, and mild flavor, fern shoots are one of the most underused greens of Hawaii.) Entree choices might be oven-poached chicken breast or fresh catch, served with puréed taro tops (like spinach, but better), grilled bananas, steamed sweet potato, taro, and fresh poi made on the premises. The seafood can be ordered with shrimp, scallops, spinach, and sweet potatoes, cooked in ti leaves laulau style, or in a Hawaiian seafood stew. The vegetable laulau is another stroke of genius: fresh vegetables with tofu and sweet potato, with the coconut sauce prudently served on the side. If this is too tame for you, the à la carte menu offers baked prawns stuffed with crab and mushrooms, chicken baked or filled with shiitake mushrooms and fresh spinach, and many other choices. Fish can be grilled, sautéed, steamed, baked, or poached in roasted garlic, ginger teriyaki, sherried peppercorn, shallot, and other sauces. The dining room is old-fashioned Hawaii, not fancy, with tables on a terrace ringed with plumeria and palm trees.

The regular Tiki Terrace breakfast menu presents a good opportunity to sample Hawaiian food in a familiar context: taro hash browns; three-egg lomi salmon omelette with sweet potato home fries ($11.95); a fruit plate of banana baked in ti leaf with lehua honey and macadamia nuts, served with yogurt; and French toast made with taro bread. There are even Hawaiian taro pancakes, and they're wonderful.

At the buffet-style **Mixed Plate** on the same property, the Hawaiian Friday lunch is widely touted among residents, who voted this the best Hawaiian food in the *Maui News:* fresh poi, lomi salmon, laulau, kalua pig, ahi poke, and pohole fern salad, $8.95 for the works. The hotel also sponsors **Aunty Aloha's Breakfast Luau** at 8am weekdays, with live music, hula, breakfast (scrambled eggs, Portuguese sausage, and rice), and the inimitable and hilarious Aunty Aloha, who does a fire-knife dance with cigarette lighters and will tell you how to save money on your Maui vacation. Her slide show of Maui activities lasts about 1¹/₂ hours.

The emphasis on Hawaiian food is only one part of a pervasive spirit of aloha that distinguishes this hotel. The poi made by the hotel's employees is well known on Maui, and sells out regularly.

Reservations are recommended for dining in the Tiki Terrace. Main courses run $5.95 to $29; American Express, Discover, Japan Credit Bank, MasterCard, and Visa are accepted. Dinner is served daily from 5:30 to 9pm.

a view of Lanai across the channel? Peter Merriman, a culinary guru and one of the originators of Hawaii Regional Cuisine, segued seamlessly from his smallish, Big Island upcountry enclave to this large, high-volume dining room on the beach. He has redefined chain-restaurant cuisine with this 300-seat, open-air restaurant in the style of a 1930s kamaaina beach house. Hula Grill offers a wide range of prices and choices; although it can be expensive, it doesn't have to be. The superb menu includes Merriman's signature wok-charred ahi; firecracker mahimahi; seafood pot stickers; crab and corn cakes; and several different fresh-fish preparations, including his famous ahi poke rolls, lightly sautéed rare ahi wrapped in rice paper with Maui onions. The macadamia nut/crab wontons arrive in a bamboo steamer and are topped with veggies, accompanied with a very hot dip—with a Mango Rita (mango margarita), they're sensational. At lunch, order burgers, sandwiches, or gourmet appetizers from the Barefoot Bar menu. There's happy-hour entertainment and Hawaiian music daily.

INEXPENSIVE

Pizza Paradiso Express. In Whalers Village, 2435 Kaanapali Pkwy. ☎ **808/667-0333.** Gourmet pizza $3.35–$4.25 (by the slice); whole pizzas $11.95–$24.95. No credit cards. Daily 11am–10pm. PIZZA.

Pizza Paradiso has hit upon a simple but effective formula: good crust, true-blue sauces, and toppings loyal to tradition but with just enough edge for those who want it. Create your own pizza with roasted eggplant, mushrooms, anchovies, artichoke hearts, spicy sausages, cheeses—and a slew of other toppings—and enjoy it in this mallish fast-food atmosphere or take it to Kaanapali Beach, just a few steps away. Voted the best pizza in a *Maui News* readers' poll, Pizza Paradiso offers some heroic choices, from the Veg Wedge to the Maui Wowie (with ham and Maui pineapple), the Jimmy Hoffa (pepperoni and mozzarella), and the God Father (roasted chicken, artichoke hearts, sun-dried tomatoes, the works). These pizzas are always described in superlatives, even by jaded New Yorkers.

Pizza Paradiso's Honokowai location has all this and more, including an expanded menu of award-winning pastas (see listing below).

HONOKOWAI, KAHANA & NAPILI
EXPENSIVE

A Pacific Café Honokowai. Honokowai Marketplace, 3350 Lower Honoapiilani Rd. ☎ **808/669-2800.** Reservations recommended. Main courses $19–$30. AE, DC, JCB, MC, V. Daily 5–10pm. HAWAII REGIONAL.

The Honokowai Marketplace is a mix of everyday good things for the neighborhood: a supermarket, the first 1-hour Martinizing dry cleaner in Hawaii, ice cream, pizza, health foods, and this, Jean-Marie Josselin's newest Hawaii restaurant. A large rotisserie with an open, U-shaped kitchen, a 1,000-square-foot lanai, and a menu of Josselin staples add up to another great Maui restaurant. The menu changes daily, but you can always count on fresh island ingredients; innovative soups, such as the "creamless" asparagus soup with seared sea scallops and white truffle oil; grilled items (ahi steak au poivre, Mongolian rack of lamb); house specialties (wok-charred mahimahi with sesame garlic crust); and meats and pizzas baked in the tandoor oven. The seared lobster poke in wasabi lemon sauce is highly recommended. This branch of A Pacific Café is still not as tested as the Kihei branch, though, which is a more mature, established, and consistent restaurant.

✪ Roy's Kahana Bar & Grill/Roy's Nicolina Restaurant. Kahana Gateway, 4405 Honoapiilani Hwy. ☎ **808/669-6999.** Reservations strongly suggested. Main courses $13–$26. AE, CB, DC, DISC, JCB, MC, V. Roy's Kahana, daily 5:30–10pm; Roy's Nicolina, daily 5:30–10pm. EURO-ASIAN.

These two sibling restaurants are next door to each other, have the same menu, and are busy, busy, busy. They bustle with young, hip servers impeccably trained to deliver blackened ahi or perfectly seared lemongrass *shutome* (broadbill swordfish) hot to your table, in rooms that sizzle with cross-cultural tastings. Both are known for their rack of lamb and fresh seafood (usually eight or nine choices), and for the large, open kitchens that turn out everything from pizza to sake-grilled New York steak and roasted half-chickens in garlic and orange, glistening in Cabernet sauce. If pot stickers are on the menu, don't resist. Large picture windows open up Roy's Kahana but don't quell the noise, which reaches boisterous levels in all of Roy Yamaguchi's restaurants. Roy's Nicolina now features dining on the lanai.

Sea House Restaurant. At the Napili Kai Beach Club, 5900 Honoapiilani Hwy. ☎ **808/ 669-1500.** Reservations required for dinner. Main courses $15–$26, appetizer menu $4–$13. AE, MC, V. Sat–Thurs 8–11am, noon–2pm (pupu menu 2–9pm), and 5:30–9pm (6–9pm in summer); Fri Polynesian Show 6–9pm. STEAK/SEAFOOD.

The Sea House is not glamorous, famous, or hip, but it's worth mentioning for its gorgeous view of Napili Bay. The Napili Kai Beach Club, where Sea House is located, is a charming throwback to the days when hotels blended in with their surroundings, had lush tropical foliage, and were sprawling rather than vertical.

Dinner entrees come complete with soup or salad, vegetables, and rice or potato. The lighter appetizer menu is a delight—more than a dozen choices range from sautéed or blackened crab cake to crisp Pacific Rim sushi of ahi capped in nori and cooked tempura-style. On Friday nights, a Polynesian dinner show features the children of the Napili Kai Foundation, an organization devoted to supporting Hawaiian culture. The top attraction here, however, is the million-dollar view.

MODERATE

Fish & Game Brewing Co. & Rotisserie. In Kahana Gateway Shopping Center, 4405 Honoapiilani Hwy. ☎ **808/669-3474.** Reservations recommended for dinner. Main courses $6.95–$12.95 at lunch, $13.95–$30.95 at dinner. AE, CB, DC, DISC, JCB, MC, V. Daily 11am–3pm, happy hour 3–5:30pm, dinner 5:30–10pm, late-night menu 10:30pm–2am. SEAFOOD.

Large microbrew vats have been installed to one side of what used to be Fish & Game Sports Grill, a popular spot in Kahana, notable for its overabundance of testosterone. Television sets are ubiquitous in the restaurant, which includes an oyster bar, deli counter and retail section, and tables. The small retail section sells fresh seafood, and the menu for sit-down covers basic tastes: salads (Caesar, Oriental chicken with wontons), fish-and-chips, fresh fish sandwiches, cheeseburgers, and beer—lots of it. At dinner, count on heavier meats and the fresh catch of the day (ahi, mahimahi, ono), with rotisserie items such as grilled chicken, steaks, and duck. The special late-night menu offers shrimp, cheese fries, quesadillas, and other light fare.

INEXPENSIVE

Hawaiian Moons Community Market & Deli. 3636 Lower Honoapiilani Road. ☎ **808/ 665-1339.** Menu items $5.50–$14.95. AE, DC, JCB, MC, V. Mon–Sat 7am–5pm (health-food store until 8pm), Sun 7am–6pm; hot foods served Mon–Sat 10:30am–5pm, Sun 10:30am–6pm. NATURAL FOOD DELI.

Our favorite south Maui health-food store has set out its shingle in west Maui with this natural foods deli that also offers fresh fish specials, chili, soups, sushi, salad bar, and sandwiches (not to mention an ATM machine!). The ingredients are wholesome: eggless mayonnaise, grain mustard, organic and free-range turkey, "mock chicken" made of seasoned tofu, garden burgers, whole-wheat bread, fresh marlin soup, and a gourmet tuna sandwich made with capers, red peppers, fresh dill, celery, and seasonings. This is an all-purpose natural foods market and deli, a supermarket for the health-conscious, with a large selection of Maui products and produce. Hint: The selection of Chinese herbs, soaps, and beauty products is outstanding.

Maui Tacos. In Napili Plaza, 5095 Napili Hau St. ☎ **808/665-0222.** Most items less than $6.95. No credit cards. Mon–Sat 9:30am–9pm, Sun 9:30am–8pm. MEXICAN.

Mark Ellman's Maui Tacos chain is growing faster than you can say "Haleakala." Ellman put gourmet Mexican on paper plates and on the island's culinary map. Barely more than a take-out counter with a few tables, this and the several other Maui Tacos on the island are the rage of hungry surfers, discerning diners, burrito buffs, and Hollywood glitterati. Choices include excellent fresh-fish tacos (garlicky and flavorful!), chimichangas, and mouth-breaking compositions such as the Hookipa, a "surf burrito" of fresh fish, black beans, and salsa. The green-spinach burrito contains four kinds of beans, rice, and potatoes—it's a knockout, requiring a siesta.

You'll find other branches in the Kaahumanu Center, Kahului (☎ **808/871-7726**); Lahaina Square, Lahaina (☎ **808/661-8883**); and Kamaole Beach Center, Kihei (☎ **808/665-0222**).

Pizza Paradiso Italian Caffe. Honokowai Marketplace, 3350 Lower Honoapiilani Rd. ☎ **808/667-2929.** Pizzas $11.95–$24.95, pastas $5.95–$8.95. DISC, MC, V. Daily 11am–10pm. PIZZA/ITALIAN.

Owner Paris Nabavi had such success with his Pizza Paradiso in Whalers Village (see listing above) that he opened up in the new marketplace—and can hardly keep up with demand. The pasta sauces—marinara, pescatore, Alfredo, Florentine, and pesto, with options and add-ons—are as popular as the pizzas and panini sandwiches. The Greek salad with Parmesan crostini, roasted garlic, fresh-baked panini, and zucchini crostini are as good as the pizzas that launched this Italian cafe. The Massimo, a pesto sauce with artichoke hearts, sun-dried tomatoes, and capers, comes with a choice of chicken, shrimp, or clams; it's so good it was a Taste of Lahaina winner in 1999. Take out or dine in; this hot spot also offers free neighborhood delivery.

KAPALUA
EXPENSIVE

The Anuenue Room. In The Ritz-Carlton Kapalua. 1 Ritz-Carlton Dr. ☎ **808/669-6200.** Reservations recommended. Two courses $55, three courses $65, four courses $75, five courses $85. AE, CB, DC, DISC, MC, V. Tues–Sat 6:30–9p.m. GRASSROOTS HAWAIIAN.

You can see 100-year-old Cook pines from the dining room and terrace, and beyond them, seeming like a stone's throw away, the ocean and Molokai. With the torches flickering and palm trees rustling, it's an exquisite setting for a romantic dinner.

Chef de cuisine Craig Connole has taken the bold step of devising a menu that melds indigenous Hawaiian ingredients with sophisticated European elements. To wit: ahi, sweet potato, taro, pohole ferns, *wana* (sea urchin), *opihi* (limpets), breadfruit, freshwater shrimp, and coconut milk, presented in gourmet versions such as seared ahi-foie gras poke and lomi salmon with poi and Beluga caviar. Moi, the fish of the moment, is prepared lau lau style, steamed in ti leaves, and lobster is spiced up and mated with taro in a soup that is delectable. The fresh Keahole lobster salad—served with hearts of palm, lettuce, and chilled mango—is an explosion of flavors and textures, cool and simple and splendid.

The Bay Club. In the Kapalua Bay Hotel & Villas. ☎ **808/669-5656.** Reservations recommended for dinner. Dress code at dinner: evening resort wear, slacks and collared shirts requested (no shorts, jeans, or casual T-shirts). Main courses $24–$38. AE, CB, DISC, JCB, MC, V. Daily 11:30am–2pm, 6–9:30pm. SEAFOOD.

Tried and true, The Bay Club is one of Maui's lasting pleasures. The classic enjoyments—a stellar view, beatific sunsets, attentive service from bow-tied dinner servers—are matched by a seafood menu that has lost none of its luster with the years. The Caesar salad is still tossed table-side, the seafood is fresh, the peppered steak just so, the vegetarian dishes quite elegant. At lunch, a soup-salad-seafood bar costs $16.95 and includes shrimp, artichoke, and taco salads, smoked salmon, and other light choices. At dinner the menu cranks up several notches and the rack of lamb, fresh fish, and fancier fare prevail.

Plantation House Restaurant. 2000 Plantation Club Dr. (right at Kapalua Plantation Golf Course). ☎ **808/669-6299.** Reservations recommended. Main courses $18–$26. AE, MC, V. Daily 8am–3pm and 5:30–10pm. SEAFOOD/HAWAIIAN-MEDITERRANEAN.

With its teak tables, fireplace, and open sides, the Plantation House gets stellar marks for atmosphere. The 360° view from high among the resort's pine-studded hills takes in Molokai and Lanai, the ocean, the rolling fairways and greens, the northwestern flanks of the West Maui Mountains, and the daily sunset spectacular. Readers of the *Maui News* have deemed this the island's "Best Ambience"—a big honor on this island of wonderful views.

Choices change constantly but may include fresh fish prepared several ways— among them, Mediterranean (seared), Upcountry (sautéed with Maui onions and vegetable stew), Island (pan-seared in sweet sake and macadamia nuts), and Rich Forest (with roasted wild mushrooms), the top seller. The wonton napoleon with tofu or ahi is a tangy, high-rise phenom, and the curried spinach pot stickers, topped with coconut peanut sauce, a great take on Indian samosas.

MODERATE

Jameson's Grill & Bar at Kapalua. 200 Kapalua Dr. (at the 18th hole of the Kapalua Golf Course). ☎ **808/669-5653.** Reservations recommended for dinner. Lunch $5.95–$11.95; main courses $6.95–$12.95 on the cafe menu, $15.95–$39.95 at dinner. AE, DC, DISC, JCB, MC, V. Daily 8am–10pm; breakfast and lunch available 8am–3pm, cafe menu 3–10pm, dinner 5–10pm daily. AMERICAN.

This is the quintessential country-club restaurant, in the open air with views of Lanai, the mountains, coconut trees, and Cook pines. The glass-enclosed room is across from the Kapalua pro shop, a short lob from the tennis courts and golf course. The familiar Jameson's mix of fresh fish (sautéed, wok-seared, or grilled), stuffed shrimp, prawns, rack of lamb, ahi steak, and other basic surf-and-turf selections prevail at dinner. At lunch, for duffers dashing to make tee time, inexpensive "golf sandwiches" are a pleasing alternative if you're not in the mood for fish-and-chips or crab cakes. Breakfasts here are terrific; perhaps you'll choose the eggs Kapalua (crab cakes topped with poached egg and wild-mushroom sauce).

✪ **Sansei Seafood Restaurant and Sushi Bar.** At the Kapalua Shops, 115 Bay Dr. ☎ **808/669-6286.** Reservations recommended. Main courses $15.95–$22. AE, DISC, JCB, MC, V. Sat–Wed 5:30–10pm, sushi bar until 11pm; Thurs–Fri 5:30pm–2am. PACIFIC RIM.

Furiously fusion, part Hawaii Regional Cuisine, and all parts sushi, Sansei is tirelessly creative, with a menu that scores higher with the adventurous than with the purists. Maki is the mantra here. If you don't like cilantro, watch out for those complex spicy crab rolls. Other choices include Panko-crusted ahi sashimi, sashimi trio, ahi carpaccio, noodle dishes, lobster, Asian rock-shrimp cakes, traditional Japanese tempura, and sauces that surprise, in creative combinations such as ginger-lime chile butter and cilantro pesto. But there's simpler fare as well, such as pastas and wok-tossed upcountry vegetables. Desserts include tempura-fried ice cream with chocolate sauce, crème brûlée, and a special autumn phenom, persimmon crème brûlée, made with Kula persimmons (don't miss it!).

3 South Maui

KIHEI/MAALAEA

EXPENSIVE

Carelli's on the Beach. 2980 S. Kihei Rd. ☎ **808/875-0001.** Reservations recommended. Main courses $22–$38. MC, V. Daily 6–10pm, bar until 11pm. ITALIAN/SEAFOOD.

Kihei's well-tanned, chicly attired trendies come here for pasta, seafood, celebrity-watching, and, of course, the view. With its prime on-the-sand location at Keawakapu Beach, you can watch the sun set in ravishing surroundings over cioppino (the most popular item), fresh fish specials, seafood ravioli, carpaccio, peppercorn-crusted filet mignon, an outstanding rack of lamb with truffle sauce, and other Italian favorites. The wood-burning brick oven turns out great pizzas, and the food is a match for this dazzling setting on a broad, gentle white-sand beach.

Five Palms. In the Mana Kai Resort, 2960 S. Kihei Rd. ☎ **808/879-2607.** Reservations recommended for dinner. Main courses $17.95–$49. AE, DC, JCB, MC, V. Daily 8am–2:30pm, 5–9pm. PACIFIC RIM.

This is the best place in Kihei for lunch in the open air. The tables are a few feet from Keawakapu Beach (where Carelli's is located) and the views of Kahoolawe and Molokini are up close and personal. You'll have to walk through a nondescript parking area and the modest entrance of the Mana Kai Resort to reach this unpretentious place. At lunch, salads, sandwiches, and pasta are the hot items. Look for Kula greens; burgers; sandwiches on homemade focaccia with burly fries; capellini with shiitake mushrooms, sun-dried tomatoes, and white wine sauce; and other appealing choices, including a perfectly grilled vegetable platter. At dinner, with the torches lit on the beach and the main dining room open, the ambience shifts from daytime casual to evening romantic, still casual but much more elegant.

Merriman's Bamboo Bistro. Maalaea Harbor Village, corner of Old Maalaea Rd. and Honoapiilani Hwy., next to Maui Ocean Center. ☎ **808/243-7374.** Reservations recommended. Prices not available at press time. Daily 11:30am–2pm and 5–9:30pm. HAWAII REGIONAL CUISINE.

As of this writing, the long-awaited opening of Merriman's Bamboo Bistro was slated for June 2000. Culinary guru Peter Merriman says his new bistro will encourage "shared dining," with variable portions of the things we've come to expect from him—clean flavors, fresh local products, and creative preparations on the cutting edge of Hawaii Regional Cuisine. "We want to encourage lots of small plates," he says, calling his version of tapas "tropas." Some of the same menu items from his Big Island restaurant will be offered here: sesame-crusted fish with spicy lilikoi sauce, kiawe-grilled beef, house-baked artisan breads, dewy-fresh produce from Maui and the Big Island. The "low-commitment dining" and thoughtful flexibility in pricing and portions will enable diners to spend as much or as little as they want while they linger over the harbor view. The three-level, 160-seat restaurant will feature an exhibition kitchen with a rotisserie and floor-to-ceiling glass. There will be indoor-outdoor seating, and every seat will have an ocean view.

✪ **A Pacific Cafe Kihei.** In Azeka Place II, 1279 S. Kihei Rd. ☎ **808/879-0069.** Reservations recommended. Main courses $24.75–$32. AE, DC, DISC, JCB, MC, V. Tues–Sat 8am–2pm, daily 6–9pm. HAWAII REGIONAL.

This restaurant is busy every night of the week, so make your reservations as early as possible. Chef-partner George Gomes, a culinary icon with a huge following, sets this restaurant apart from others in Jean-Marie Josselin's chain. The food is consistent and excellent. You'll dine on rattan chairs at hammered-copper tables, under very high ceilings, in a room bordered with windows overlooking the parking lot of a strip mall (but you'll be so busy enjoying the food, you won't notice the lack of view). From the open kitchen and a menu that changes monthly comes a stream of marvels: the signature tiger-eye ahi sushi tempura, light and delectable; garlic-sesame, pan-seared mahimahi, a Pacific Cafe staple; salmon firecracker rolls; misoyaki salmon; and a sumptuous roster of starters. Standout starters include the red Thai curry soup, sometimes with fish and occasionally with lobster, rich, creamy, and spicy; and the curry fried oysters with a cilantro scallion sauce.

The Waterfront at Maalaea. Maalaea Harbor, 50 Hauoli St. ☎ **808/244-9028.** Reservations recommended. Main courses $18–$54. AE, DC, DISC, JCB, MC, V. Daily 5pm–closing. SEAFOOD.

The Waterfront has won awards for wine excellence, service, and seafood, but its biggest boost is word of mouth. Loyal diners rave about the friendly staff and seafood, served in simple surroundings with a view you'll never forget, especially at sunset. You have nine choices of preparations for the several varieties of fresh Hawaiian fish, ranging from *en papillote* (baked in buttered parchment) to Southwestern (smoked chile and cilantro butter) to light cuisine (broiled or poached, then topped with steamed, fresh vegetables). Other choices: Kula onion soup, an excellent Caesar salad, lobster chowder, and grilled eggplant layered with Maui onions, tomatoes, and spinach, served with red-pepper coulis and Big Island goat cheese.

MODERATE

Buzz's Wharf. Maalaea Harbor, 50 Hauoli St. ☎ **808/244-5426.** Reservations suggested. Main courses $10.95–$24.95. AE, CB, DC, DISC, JCB, MC, V. Daily 11am–9pm. AMERICAN.

Buzz's is another formula restaurant that offers a superb view, substantial sandwiches, meaty french fries, and surf-and-turf fare—it's satisfying but not sensational. Still, this bright, airy dining room is a fine way station for whale-watching over a cold beer and a fresh mahimahi sandwich with fries, or if you're feeling extravagant, the house specialty, Prawns Tahitian. Some diners opt for several appetizers (stuffed mushrooms, steamer clams, clam chowder, onion soup) and a salad, then splurge on dessert. Buzz's prize-winning dessert—Tahitian Baked Papaya, a warm, fragrant melding of fresh papaya with vanilla and coconut—is the pride of the house.

The Greek Bistro. 2511 S. Kihei Rd. ☎ **808/879-9330.** Reservations recommended. Combination and family style dinners $14.95–$21.95 per person; family style platter $35 for 2. Children's portions also available. AE, CB, DC, JCB, MC, V. Daily 5–10pm. GREEK.

Especially in chaotic Kihei, the banana trees, yellow ginger, and hibiscus that surround the tile-floored terrace add a lot of character to the dining experience at this indoor/outdoor bistro. Homemade pita bread, quality feta and spices, classic spanakopita and chicken and lamb *souvlaki* (the Greek version of shish kebab) are some of the authentic and popular Mediterranean offerings. The family style combination platters include lamb kabobs and the fresh fish of the day. Also popular are the Greek lasagna and the Mediterranean chicken breast, an elaborate platter of mushroom-and-wine-infused organic skinless chicken, served with linguine and vegetables.

Hapa's Rockin' Sushi. In the Lipoa Shopping Center, 41. E. Lipoa St. ☎ **808/891-1555.** Reservations not accepted. Sushi $3 to $15 each. AE, DISC, JCB, MC, V. Daily 6pm–2am. SUSHI.

Right next door to Hapa's Brew Haus, on the other side of the glass windows, the new sushi bar is a Kihei hotspot, serving up traditional and fusion sushi at a small sushi bar and a few small tables. There's often a line waiting to crowd into the boîte, where you can see and hear the musicians and deejays who appear nightly next door as a key component of the Hapa's scene. Sushi rolls (California, salmon skin, spicy hamachi) and sashimi (13 choices, from jumbo clam to sweet shrimp) are the headliners, with hot and cold sake to go with them.

Jacques on the Beach. 760 Kihei Rd. ☎ **808/875-7791.** Reservations recommended. Main courses $13.95–$21. MC, V. Daily 5–10pm. AMERICAN/PACIFIC RIM.

Jacques in Paia (see section 5 of this chapter) is such a hit that they've expanded to the shoreline, where a stunning sunset is the centerpiece—a pleasant surprise in a nondescript condo building that's covered with ersatz petroglyphs. The restaurant is adjacent to a natural fishpond, with glass windows on three sides and glass doors that open to the sea and views that encompass the West Maui Mountains. Clearly this location is a sleeper, and the sensitive lighting and excellent Hawaiian music on the sound system further enhance the room.

The menu that made Jacques in Paia so successful prevails here, too. The Greek salad is a meal in itself, and the ceviche is outstanding, tangy and perfect with lime, cucumbers, tomatoes, radishes, red onion, and fresh cubes of ahi. The seared ahi is prepared just so, served with Molokai sweet potatoes and topped with a basil-infused vegetable saute. *Caveat:* Stay away from the Beef Bistro; the braised beef was much too greasy and gristly.

Stella Blues Cafe. In Long's Center, 1215 S. Kihei Rd. ☎ **808/874-3779.** Main courses $9.95–$17.95. DISC, MC, V. Daily 8am–9pm. AMERICAN.

Stella Blues gets going at breakfast and continues through to dinner with something for everyone—vegetarians, children, pasta and sandwich lovers, hefty steak eaters, and sensible diners who go for the inexpensive fresh Kula green salad. Indoor seating is no-smoking; there's lanai seating for smokers (though note that the location is in a strip mall). At the time of this writing, there are plans for a renovation that will include a new counter and awnings for the outdoor seating. Grateful Dead posters line the walls of this corner cafe, and a covey of gleaming motorcycles is invariably parked outside. It's loud and lively, casual, irreverent, and unpretentious.

Sandwiches are the highlight, ranging from Tofu Extraordinaire to Mom's egg salad on croissant to garden burgers and grilled chicken. Daily specials include fresh seafood and other surprises—all home-style cooking, made from scratch, down to the pesto mayonnaise and homemade herb bread. At dinner, selections are geared toward good-value family dining, from affordable full dinners to pastas and burgers.

INEXPENSIVE

✪ **Alexander's Fish & Chicken & Chips.** 1913 S. Kihei Rd. ☎ **808/874-0788.** Fish-and-chips $6.75–$9.50. MC, V. Daily 11am–9pm. FISH & CHIPS/SEAFOOD.

This may be the most popular restaurant on the south shore. Look for the ocean mural in front, Kalama Park across the street, and a marketplace next door: This is Alexander's, a friendly neighborhood take-out stand with patio seating outside and a very busy kitchen. Beachwear is welcome here. Fresh ono, mahimahi, and ahi, broiled or fried, are all popular, as are the 13-piece shrimp, chicken, oyster, calamari, rib, or fish baskets. Other offerings include fresh fish, Cajun chicken, calamari, teriyaki chicken, barbecued beef, and shrimp sandwiches, along with onion rings, fries, cornbread, chicken wings, and other side orders in a light and tasty batter.

The Coffee Store. In Azeka's Place II, 1279 Kihei Rd. ☎ **808/875-4244.** All items less than $8.50. AE, CB, DC, DISC, MC, V. Sun–Thurs 6am–10pm, Fri–Sat 6am–10pm. COFFEEHOUSE.

This simple, classic coffeehouse for caffeine connoisseurs serves two dozen different types of coffee and coffee drinks, from mochas, lattes, and frappés to cappuccino, espresso, and toddies. Breakfast items include smoothies, lox and bagels, quiches, granola, and assorted pastries. Pizza, salads, vegetarian lasagna, veggie-and-shrimp quesadillas, and sandwiches (garden burger, tuna, turkey, ham, grilled veggie panini) also move briskly from the take-out counter. If that's too tame, the turkey and veggie tortilla-wrapped sandwiches are a local legend. There are only a few small tables and they fill up fast, often with musicians and artists who spent the previous evening entertaining at the Wailea and Kihei resorts.

Peggy Sue's. In Azeka Place II, 1279 S. Kihei Rd. ☎ **808/875-8944.** Burgers $6–$11, plate lunches $5–$10. DC, MC, V. Sun–Thurs 11am–9pm, Fri–Sat 11am–10pm. AMERICAN.

Just for a moment, forget that diet and take a leap. Peggy Sue's, a 1950s-style diner with oodles of charm, is a swell place to spring for a chocolate malt and french fries. Pink, yellow, and green old-fashioned soda-shop stools; an ELVIS PRESLEY BOULEVARD sign; and jukeboxes on every Formica table provide the visuals. You'll find the best chocolate malt on the island here, as well as sodas, milkshakes, floats, and egg creams. The burgers are famous—more round than flat, brushed with teriyaki sauce, served with all the goodies. There are also garden burgers for the cautious.

Shaka Sandwich & Pizza. 1295 S. Kihei Rd. ☎ **808/874-0331.** Sandwiches $3.75–$8; pizzas $12.95–$25.95. Sun–Thurs 10:30am–9pm, Fri–Sat 10:30am–10pm (deliveries, daily 10:30am–9pm). PIZZA.

How many "best pizzas" are there on Maui? It depends on which shore you're on, the west or the south. At this south-shore old-timer, award-winning pizzas share the limelight with New York–style heroes and Philly cheese steaks, calzones and salads, homemade garlic bread, and homemade meatball sandwiches. Shaka uses fresh Maui produce, long-simmering homemade sauces, and homemade Italian bread. Choose thin or Sicilian thick crust with gourmet toppings: Maui onions, spinach, anchovies, jalapeño peppers, and a spate of other vegetables. Don't be misled by the whiteness of the white pizza; with the perfectly balanced flavors of olive oil, garlic, and cheese, you won't even miss the tomato sauce. Clam-and-garlic pizza, spinach pizza (with olive oil, spinach, garlic, and mozzarella), and the Shaka Supreme (with at least 10 toppings!) will satisfy even the insatiable.

WAILEA

Due to open in late summer 2000, the restaurant-dining complex called **The Shops at Wailea** is expected to bring a giant infusion of new possibilities to the formerly moribund center. Four restaurants and dozens of shops, most of them upscale, are among the new tenants of this complex, located between the Outrigger Wailea Resort and the Grand Wailea Hotel. Some things to watch for: the Tommy Bahama Café/Emporium (a first for Hawaii), Ruth's Chris Steak House, Hapa Grill & Bar, and Longhi's.

Next door at the Outrigger Wailea, massive changes are also taking place. **Hula Moons,** the retro-Hawaiian themed restaurant, is undergoing a $3 million renovation and moving to the upper level of the lobby building, where it will serve mid-priced steak and seafood with an ocean view.

EXPENSIVE

Ferraro's at Seaside. In the Four Seasons Resort Maui at Wailea, 3900 Wailea Alanui Drive. ☎ **808/874-8000.** Reservations recommended. Main courses $21.50–$32; 3-course dinner $41. AE, CB, DC, DISC, MC, V. Daily 6–9pm. ITALIAN.

Serving authentic Italian fare in an outdoor tropical setting, with a drop-dead gorgeous view of the ocean and the West Maui Mountains, was a master stroke for Four Seasons. For lunch or dinner, Ferraro's is an excellent choice. It's not inexpensive but the ambience is casual, and the food is first-rate, whether it's the oregano-marinated shrimp with avocado or the linguine puttanesca. Mango margaritas, excellent salads such as Maine lobster with avocado and toasted sourdough, and sandwiches and half-pound burgers keep the poolside crowd happy at lunch, but at dinner the choices intensify. The fish selection is noteworthy: pepper-crusted ahi with kalamata olive ragout, grilled sea scallops and steamed mussels with saffron risotto cake, poached snapper with red onion-orange marmalade. Duck ravioli, cannellini bean soup, and garlic shrimp papardelle are among the evening's temptations. It won't be easy to choose.

Joe's Bar & Grill. At the Wailea Tennis Club, 131 Wailea Ike Place. ☎ **808/875-7767.** Reservations recommended. Main courses $17–$30. AE, DC, MC, V. Daily 5:30–10:30pm. AMERICAN GRILL.

The 360° view spans the golf course, tennis courts, ocean, and Haleakala—a worthy setting for Beverly Gannon's inspiring and inimitable style of American home-cooking with a regional twist. The hearty staples include excellent mashed potatoes, lobster, fresh fish, and filet mignon, and appetizers such as ahi tartare in a sesame caper sauce. Favorites include the crisp calamari with spicy Thai fish sauce and the ahi with farfalle in basil, garlic, and tomato. The chocolate cake is memorable.

✪ Nick's Fishmarket Maui. In the Kea Lani Hotel, 4100 Wailea Alanui. ☎ **808/ 879-7224.** Reservations recommended. Main courses $23.95–$38. AE, CB, DC, DISC, JCB, MC, V. Daily 5:30–10pm, bar until 11pm. SEAFOOD.

Hawaii's newest Nick's has the perfect balance of visual sizzle and memorable food. A private room with attractive murals seats 50, and the round bar, where you can sit facing the ocean, is highlighted with unobtrusive, minimalist, dangling amber lights, one of the friendliest touches in Wailea. Stefanotis vines create shade on the terrace, where the sunset views reveal the best of Wailea. We love the lavish wine list; torch-lighting at sunset; onion vichyssoise with taro swirl and a hint of *tobiko* (flying fish roe); Maui Wowie Greek salad with hearts of palm, Kula tomatoes, avocados, feta cheese, Maui onions, and rock shrimp; opah in phyllo crust; and the mahimahi, done to perfection. Bow-tied waiters and almond-scented cold towels add an extra touch to this ocean-side phenomenon.

Pacific Grill. In the Four Seasons Resort Wailea, 3900 Wailea Alanui Dr. ☎ **808/874-8000.** Reservations recommended. Main courses $18.50–$29.50. AE, CB, DC, DISC, JCB, MC, V. Daily 6–11:30am (buffet Mon–Sat 6:30–11am, Sun 6:30am–noon); daily 6–9:30pm. AMERICAN/ PACIFIC RIM.

For those wanting something between very casual and superluxe, Pacific Grill is the ticket. Open for lunch only occasionally, the Grill is the place for ingenious tropical drinks (try the Kamaaina, a blend of rum, coconut milk, and fresh banana!) in an open-air room that looks out over the pool and ocean, with views of the West Maui Mountains. The cross-cultural appetizers command center stage: slipper lobster spring rolls; chilled lemongrass shrimp; a basket of crab claw, shrimp and vegetable tempura; and a spinach salad nonpareil, a fantastic medley of spinach, grilled shiitake mushrooms, and toasted almonds. Three of the appetizer selections can be combined into one super sampler to go with those Kon Tiki and Honi Honi cocktails, or as a light entree. In a marriage of island favorites with American classics, the entrees range from the familiar (vegetarian stir-fry, New York steak, rotisserie chicken) to the exotic (steamed snapper with shiitake mushrooms and ginger, crisped shutome with miso ginger sauce). The sides are stellar: sautéed mushrooms with caramelized onions, seared spinach and arugula with garlic, steamed asparagus, baby bok choy—nothing fancy, but prepared with typical Four Seasons finesse.

Seasons. In the Four Seasons Resort Wailea, 3900 Wailea Alanui Dr. ☎ **808/874-8000.** Reservations recommended. Main courses $32–$42; prix-fixe $78–$85. AE, CB, DC, DISC, JCB, MC, V. Tues–Sat 6–9:30pm. CONTEMPORARY AMERICAN/HAWAIIAN.

This is the ultimate dining room in Wailea, the superluxe, special-occasion restaurant with soft piano music, sunset view, crisp service, and a fantasy menu. You'll find everything from Petrossian caviar and seared foie gras to Keahole lobster meunière, hamachi sashimi, and steamed kumu (goatfish) with seaweed and lime broth. Exotic sauces (caper raisin, cumin-scented carrot juice, fennel) and the most upscale fresh fishes of Hawaii (kumu and moano, two types of goatfish; onaga, ruby snapper; opakapaka, pink snapper) are presented in delicate preparations, with innovative accompaniments such as caramelized endive and watercress foam. Luxurious and pricey, Seasons marries the best of local produce and seafood with cross-cultural touches, but with its rack of lamb, pheasant, beef tenderloin, and vegetarian specials, there's enough diversity for all tastes.

MODERATE

Caffé Ciao. In the Kea Lani Hotel, 4100 Wailea Alanui. ☎ **808/875-4100.** Reservations recommended. Main courses $14.95–$29.95, pizzas $15–$21. AE, CB, DC, DISC, JCB, MC, V. Daily 11am–10pm; bar until 11pm. ITALIAN.

There are two parts to this charming trattoria: the deli and take-out section, and the tables under the trees, next to the bar. Rare and wonderful wines, such as Vine Cliff, are sold in the deli, along with ultraluxe rose soaps and other bath products. You'll find assorted pastas, pizza, roasted potatoes, vegetable panini, vegetable lasagna, abundant salads, and an appealing selection of microwavable and take-out goodies for those nights when room service or going out won't do. On the terrace under the trees, the tables are cheerfully accented with Italian herbs growing in cachepots, and there's friendly service to go with the pizzas and pastas. Our fave is the linguine pomodoro, with fresh tomatoes, spinach-tomato sauce, and a dollop of mascarpone.

SeaWatch. 100 Wailea Golf Club Dr. ☎ **808/875-8080.** Reservations required for dinner. Lunch $4.50–$12; dinner main courses $21 and up. AE, DC, MC, V. Daily 8am–3pm, 3–5:30pm (grille menu), and 5:30–10pm. ISLAND CUISINE.

The people who own Kapalua's Plantation House also own SeaWatch, which means there's a great view and high standards in the use of fresh Maui produce and island fish in pan-Pacific preparations. SeaWatch is a good choice from morning to evening, and it's one of the more affordable stops in tiny Wailea. You'll dine on the terrace or in a high-ceilinged room, on a menu that carries the tee-off-to-19th-hole crowd with ease. From breakfast on, it's a celebration of island bounty: Maui onions on the lox and bagel, kalua pork and Maui onions in the scrambled eggs, crab cake Benedict with roasted pepper hollandaise. Lunchtime sandwiches, pastas, salads, wraps, and soups are moderately priced, and you get 360° views to go with them. The cashew chicken wrap with mango chutney is a winner, as is the grilled fresh catch sandwich with Kula lime aioli. At dinner, the nightly fresh catch, the Seawatch signature, can be ordered in one of three preparations. *Hint:* Save room for the bananas Foster.

MAKENA

Hakone. In the Maui Prince Hotel, 5400 Makena Alanui. ☎ **808/874-1111.** Reservations recommended. Complete dinner $32–$45; kaiseki $58; Mon night buffet $38, sushi bar. AE, JCB, MC, V. Mon 6–9pm, Tues–Sat 6–9:30pm. JAPANESE.

The Prince Hotels always emphasize Japanese cuisine, so it's no wonder that they spared no effort in creating a slice of Kyoto in Makena, complete with sandalwood walls and pillars assembled by Japanese craftsmen. Hakone offers superluxe Japanese fare, gorgeously presented and pricey. The popular Sunday-night sushi buffet and Monday-night Japanese dinner buffet offer a sampling of this elegant cuisine. Whether it's from the buffet, a kaiseki menu, the sushi bar, or à la carte, the food comes elegantly presented, be it miso soup, a hand-roll sushi, broiled miso butterfish, shrimp tempura, or sashimi.

Prince Court. In the Maui Prince Hotel, 5400 Makena Alanui. ☎ **808/874-1111.** Reservations recommended. Main courses $27–29; Sun brunch $36. AE, JCB, MC, V. Sun 9am–1pm, Thurs–Mon 6–9:30pm. HAWAII REGIONAL.

Half of the Sunday brunch experience here is the head-turning view of Makena Beach, the crescent-shaped islet called Molokini, and Kahoolawe island. The other half is the sumptuous buffet, spread over several tables: pasta, omelettes, cheeses, pastries, sashimi, crab legs, smoked salmon, fresh Maui produce, and a smashing array of ethnic and continental foods. The dinner menu changes regularly but the consistent best seller remains the trio of mixed fish. Taro, local corn, and the bountiful array of fruits and vegetables from upcountry Maui make frequent appearances in the Pacific Rim menu. If the seafood risotto with poi is on the menu, don't miss it.

4 Upcountry Maui

MAKAWAO & HALIIMAILE
MODERATE

✪ **Casanova Italian Restaurant.** 1188 Makawao Ave. ☎ **808/572-0220.** Reservations recommended for dinner. Main courses $8–$23; 12-inch pizzas $10 and up. DC, MC, V. Mon–Sat 11:30am–2pm and 5:30–9pm, Sun 5:30–9pm. Lounge daily 5:30pm–12:30 or 1am; deli daily 8am–6:30pm. ITALIAN.

The nexus of upcountry dining and nightlife, Casanova is Makawao's center of hip. The food and music are great, and the tiny veranda with its few stools in front of the deli is always full at Makawao's busiest intersection. Casanova consists of a stage, dance floor, restaurant, and bar—and food to love and remember. This is pasta heaven; try the spaghetti fradiavolo (seafood in a caper, Greek olive, and tomato sauce) or the spinach gnocchi in a fresh tomato-Gorgonzola sauce. Other choices include a huge pizza selection, grilled lamb chops in balsamic vinegar, several types of fresh fish, and luscious desserts. Our personal picks on a stellar menu: garlic spinach topped with Parmesan and pine nuts, polenta with radicchio (the mushrooms and cream sauce are fabulous!), and tiramisu, the best on the island.

INEXPENSIVE

✪ **Café 'O Lei.** Paniolo Courtyard, 3673 Baldwin Ave. ☎ **808/573-9065.** Sandwiches and salads $4.50–$5.95. No credit cards. Mon–Sat 11am–4pm. AMERICAN/ISLAND.

Dana Pastula managed restaurants at Lanai's Manele Bay Hotel and the Four Seasons Resort Wailea before opening her tiny, charming outdoor cafe in this sunlit sliver of Makawao. And the alfresco dining is just part of it: from the sandwiches (roast chicken breast, turkey breast, prosciutto) and salads to the soup of the day, the offerings are homemade and excellent. The chic Makawao shopkeepers who lunch here daily never tire of the quinoa salad, the ginger chicken soup, the curry chicken salad, and the talk of the town—a towering Asian salad of Oriental vegetables, tofu, and baby greens, tossed in a sesame vinaigrette with fresh mint, ginger, and lemongrass, and served over

Chinese noodles. Our favorite? It's the shiitake mushroom soup with chicken long rice and the snow crab–avocado sandwich, too good to be true.

Kitada's Kau Kau Corner. 3617 Baldwin Ave. ☎ **808/572-7241.** Lunch plates $4.50–$8. No credit cards. Mon–Sat 6am–1:30pm. AMERICAN/JAPANESE.

This is saimin central, a combination of Grandma's kitchen and a cowboy diner known for its paniolo-size servings and tasty saimin. Kitada's cheap hamburgers and plate lunches are legendary, and the dry mein, a heap of noodles, is a cross between saimin and Chinese fried noodles. You'll see everyone from upcountry ranch hands to expensively dressed Makawao ladies digging in at this tiny diner brimming with local color and cheap eats. Beef or pork hekka (sukiyaki.)

HALIIMAILE
EXPENSIVE

✪ **Haliimaile General Store.** Haliimaile Rd., Haliimaile. ☎ **808/572-2666.** Reservations recommended. Lunch $6–$14; dinner $14–$28. DC, MC, V. Mon–Fri 11am–2:30pm, Sun 10am–2:30pm (brunch), and daily 5:30–9:30pm. AMERICAN.

The foodie haven in the pineapple fields is still going strong. You'll dine at tables set on old wood floors under high ceilings (sound ricochets fiercely here), in a bustling peach-colored room emblazoned with works by local artists. The food, a blend of eclectic American with ethnic touches, puts an innovative spin on Hawaii Regional Cuisine. Even the fresh-catch sandwich on the lunch menu is anything but prosaic. The house salad, island greens with mandarin oranges, onions, toasted walnuts and blue cheese crumble, is a touch of genius, and the sashimi napoleon (crisp wonton layered with smoked salmon, ahi tartare and sashimi, served with wasabi vinaigrette) is something to write home about. Dinner splurges include the Szechuan salmon, chef Bev Gannon's boboli topped with crab dip, and her famous paniolo ribs in tangy barbecue sauce.

MODERATE

Upcountry Cafe. In the Andrade Building, 7-2 Aewa Place (just off Haleakala Hwy.), Pukalani. ☎ **808/572-2395.** Lunch $5.95–$8.95; most dinner items less than $14.95. AE, MC, V. Daily 6:30am–3pm, and 5:30–9:30pm; Sun 5:30am–1pm. AMERICAN/LOCAL.

Pukalani's inexpensive, casual, and very popular cafe features cows everywhere: on the walls, chairs, menus, aprons, even on the exterior. But the food is the draw: simple, home-cooked comfort food such as meat loaf, roast pork, and humongous hamburgers, plus home-baked bread, oven-fresh muffins, and local faves such as saimin and Chinese chicken salad. Soups and salads (homemade cream of mushroom soup, Cobb and Caesar salads) and shrimp scampi with bow-tie pasta are among the cafe's other pleasures. The signature dessert is the cow pie, a naughty pile of chocolate cream cheese with macadamia nuts in a cookie crust, shaped like you-know-what.

KULA (AT THE BASE OF HALEAKALA NATIONAL PARK)
EXPENSIVE

Kula Lodge. Haleakala Hwy. (Hwy. 377). ☎ **808/878-2517.** Reservations recommended for dinner. Lunch $7.25–$14; dinner main courses $18–$32. AE, JCB, MC, V. Daily 6:30am–9pm, HAWAII REGIONAL/AMERICAN.

Don't let the dinner prices scare you, because the Kula Lodge is equally enjoyable, if not more so, for breakfast and lunch, when the prices are lower and the views through the picture windows have an eye-popping intensity. The million-dollar view through the large picture windows spans the flanks of Haleakala, rolling 3,200 feet down to central Maui, the ocean, and the West Maui Mountains.

The Kula Lodge has always been known for its toe-curling breakfasts: omelettes and a fabulous eggs Benedict, including a vegetarian Benedict with Kula onions, shiitake mushrooms, and scallions. If the legendary banana–mac nut pancakes are too much for you, the tofu scramble with green onions, Kula vegetables, and garlic chives is highly recommended. If possible, go for sunset cocktails and watch the colors change into deep purples and other end-of-day hues. When darkness descends, a roaring fire and lodge atmosphere turn the attention to the coziness of the room. The dinner menu features "small plates" of Thai summer rolls, seared ahi, artichoke and mushroom gratinée, and other starters. Sesame-seared ono, Cuban-style spicy swordfish with rum-soaked bananas, and miso salmon with wild mushrooms are seafood attractions, but there's also pasta, rack of lamb, filet mignon, and free-range chicken breast.

INEXPENSIVE

Café 808. Lower Kula Rd., past Holy Ghost Church, across Morihara Store. ☎ **808/ 878-6874.** Burgers from $3.50, main courses $4.50–$7.50. No credit cards. Daily 6am–8pm. AMERICAN/LOCAL.

Despite its out-of-the-way location (or perhaps because of it), Café 808 has become the universal favorite among upcountry residents of all ages: the breakfast coffee group, the lunchtime crowd, kids after school, and dinner regulars who know they can get tasty home-style cooking with no pretensions. Look for chicken lasagna, smoked salmon omelette, locally famous burgers (teriyaki, hamburger, cheeseburger, garden burger, mahimahi burger, taro), roast pork, smoked turkey, and a huge selection of local-style specials. Regulars rave about the chicken katsu, teriyaki steak burger (on huge fresh buns, with a humongous salad), saimin, and beef stew; even the chicken salad for the deli section is made fresh daily. The few tables are sprinkled around a room with linoleum-tile floors, hardwood benches, plastic patio chairs, and old-fashioned booths—rough around the edges in a pleasing way, the epitome of camp.

Grandma's Coffee House. At the end of Hwy. 37, Keokea (about 6 miles before the Tedeschi Vineyards in Ulupalakua). ☎ **808/878-2140.** Most items less than $8.95. MC, V. Daily 7am–5pm. COFFEEHOUSE/AMERICAN.

Alfred Franco's grandmother started what is now a five-generation coffee business back in 1918, when she was 16 years old. Today, this tiny wooden coffeehouse, still fueled by homegrown Haleakala coffee beans, is the quintessential roadside oasis. Grandma's offers espresso, hot and cold coffees, home-baked pastries, inexpensive pasta, sandwiches (including sensational avocado and garden burgers), homemade soups, fresh juices, and local plate-lunch specials that change daily. Rotating specials include Hawaiian beef stew, ginger chicken, saimin, chicken curry, lentil soup, and sandwiches piled high with Kula vegetables. While the coffee is legendary, we think the real story is the lemon squares and the pumpkin bread.

Kula Sandalwoods Restaurant. Haleakala Hwy. (Hwy. 377). ☎ **808/878-3523.** Most items less than $9. MC, V. Mon–Sat 6:30am–2pm, Sun 6:30am–noon (brunch). AMERICAN.

The chef, Eleanor Loui, a graduate of the Culinary Institute of America, makes hollandaise sauce every morning from fresh upcountry egg yolks, sweet butter, and Myers lemons, which her family grows in the yard above the restaurant. This is Kula cuisine, with produce from the backyard and everything made from scratch: French toast with home-baked Portuguese sweet bread, crab cakes, hotcakes or Belgian waffles with fresh fruit, French baguettes, hamburgers drenched in a special cheese sauce made with grated sharp Cheddar, grilled teriyaki chicken breast, and an outstanding garden veggie burger. The Kula Sandalwoods salad features grilled chicken breast with crimson Kula tomatoes and onions and, when the garden allows, just-picked red-oak, curly-green, and red-leaf lettuces. The omelette is a gourmet treat. You'll dine in one of two separate rooms, in the gazebo, or on the terrace, with dazzling views in all directions, including, in the spring, a yard dusted with lavender jacaranda flowers and a hillside ablaze with fields of orange akulikuli blossoms.

5 East Maui: On the Road to Hana

KUAU & PAIA
EXPENSIVE

Mama's Fish House. 799 Poho Place, just off the Hana Hwy., Kuau. ☎ **808/579-8488.** Reservations recommended. Main courses $22.95–$45. AE, CB, DC, JCB, MC, V. Daily 11am–2:30pm, light menu 2:30–5pm, dinner 5–9:30pm.

The restaurant's entrance, a cove with windsurfers, tide pools, white sand, and a canoe resting under palm trees, is a South Seas fantasy reminiscent of Gauguin. The restaurant's interior features curved lauhala-lined ceilings, walls of split bamboo, lavish arrangements of tropical blooms, and picture windows to let in the view. At sunset the ambience is transcendent. With servers wearing Polynesian prints and flowers behind their ears, and the sun setting in Kuau Cove, the Mama's mood is hard to beat. Menu items include mahimahi laulau with Kula spinach, baked in ti leaves, with kalua pig and lemongrass rice; mahimahi baked in roasted macadamia nuts, stuffed with shrimp and crab; and several fresh fish dishes offered in four preparations. There's also scampi, bouillabaisse, Hawaiian spiny lobster, ginger-teriyaki chicken, crab cakes, and New York steak with wasabi mashed potatoes. *Hint:* We loved the onaga, baked in a mustard crust with Maui onion and herbs.

MODERATE

Jacques Bistro. 89 Hana Hwy., Paia. ☎ **808/579-6255.** Reservations accepted. Main courses $8–$19. MC, V. Daily 5–10pm, bar until later. FRENCH/AMERICAN/ISLAND.

Fresh local seafood with a French touch, served by a chef named Jacques in a room with a 42-foot monkeypod bar and arches, columns, and a garden lanai—it all adds up to Paia's most popular nightspot. And it's such a magnet that it's often hard to get in, especially late at night when the bar is three deep with customers. There are diverse, affordable delights: catch of the day (from Paia fishermen, and a steal at $13.95), ahi poke, rack of lamb, roast chicken, an excellent Tahitian ceviche, curries and pastas, and beaucoup special touches such as seasoned purple potatoes and lightly steamed Kula vegetables. With this setting and menu, they could have jacked up the prices and injected some attitude, but they haven't. For light eaters, the gargantuan Greek salad and perfect ceviche are starters that equal an entree. The garden area is lush with palms, bromeliads, and towering banyan trees. When lit up at night, it's a visual feast as well, at Paia's busiest corner.

Moana Bakery & Café. 71 Baldwin Ave., Paia. ☎ **808/579-9999.** Reservations recommended for dinner. Main courses $7.95–$23.95. MC, V. Daily 8am–9pm. LOCAL/EUROPEAN.

Stylish concrete floors, high ceilings, booths and cafe tables, fairy lights, and fabulous food—this Paia newcomer gets high marks in all departments. Don Ritchey, formerly a chef at Haliimaile General Store, has created the perfect Paia eatery, a casual bakery-cafe that highlights his stellar skills as a chef. All the bases are covered: saimin, omelettes and breakfast wraps, multigrain pancakes and fresh baked goods in the morning; soups, sandwiches, pasta (pesto, basil-tomato), and satisfying Caesar and Thai chicken salads for lunch; and for dinner, varied selections of Asian and European influences and fresh Island ingredients. The lemongrass grilled prawns with green papaya salad are an explosion of flavors and textures; the roasted vegetable napoleon is gourmet fare; and the Thai red curry with coconut milk, with choice of vegetables, seafood, or tofu, is served on jasmine rice with crisped rice noodles and fresh sprouts to cool the fire. Ritchey's Thai-style curries are richly spiced and have strong, intense flavors. We also vouch for his special gift with fish: The nori-sesame crusted opakapaka on rice, with wasabi buerre blanc, was cooked, like the curry, to perfection.

INEXPENSIVE

Bob's on a Roll Deli. 111 Hana Hwy., Paia. ☎ **808/579-8680.** Most items under $8.50. No credit cards. Daily 7am–7pm. DELI/PIZZERIA.

Bob McCarthy's meatball subs and pastrami on rye are famous in Paia. The tiny deli, where friends meet and eat (and crane their necks at the TV set), has only a couple of stools, but there's always take out. Sliced turkey breast and Reuben sandwiches may appeal to carnivores, but vegetarians glom the veggie-ball sub, a savory, wonderful sandwich of vegetarian meatballs, marinara sauce, and provolone cheese. The Paia Cheese steak sandwich, with its roast beef, Maui onions, peppers, and mozzarella cheese, has a legion of fans, and the pizzas, using top quality ingredients, including optional portobello mushrooms, are hugely popular.

Dr. J's Extreme Juice. 42 Baldwin Ave., Paia. ☎ **808/579-6323.** Smoothies and juices under $4.95. No credit cards. Daily 9am–6pm. JUICE BAR.

Dr. J's smoothies are made from fresh-squeezed juices and fresh fruits, and the vegetable juices, made with such things as ginger, radish, carrots, garlic, and kale, are organic. The lemonade is delightful, sweetened with agave nectar, and fresh coconut water can be sipped from a fresh coconut or added to a smoothie. The menu is a map to health, with various smoothies suggested to energize, detoxify, build bone, relieve stress, and help in weight loss and mental performance. Names like Popeye's Potion, Tarzan's Tonic, Funky Monkey Junky, Maui Memories, Pure Passion, and Fat Free Fantasy capture some of the wit and breadth of the offerings here. Some smoothies have seven ingredients, assembled to order with the fresh juice so they're brimming with vitality. The banana cream smoothie was ambrosial and energizing, creamy without being cloying—the best we've ever had.

Milagros Food Company. Hana Hwy. and Baldwin Ave., Paia. ☎ **808/579-8755.** Breakfast about $7; lunch $3–$8; dinner $7–$16. DC, MC, V. Daily 8am–11pm. SOUTHWESTERN/SEAFOOD.

We love Paia, with its tie dyes, beads, and hippie flavor, and this is the front-row seat to it all. Milagros has gained a following with its great home-style cooking, upbeat atmosphere, and highly touted margaritas. Sit outdoors and watch the parade of Willie Nelson look-alikes ambling by as you tuck into the ahi creation of the evening, a combination of Southwestern and Pacific Rim styles and flavors accompanied by fresh veggies and Kula greens. Blackened ahi taquitos, pepper-crusted ono pasta, blue shrimp tostadas, and sandwiches are some of the offerings here. The bountiful chiles-rellenos plate comes with grilled ahi, beans, rice, and Kula greens—a sensation, and generous. For breakfast, don't miss the Olive Oyl spinach omelette or the huevos rancheros, served with home fries. Watch for the happy hour too, with its cheap and fabulous margaritas.

A Worthy Stop

What a delight to stumble across this trio of comforts on the long drive to Hana! On the Hana Highway, at the 28-mile marker, watch for the **Nahiku Coffee Shop, Smoked Fish Stand, and Ti Gallery.** The small coffee shop purveys locally made baked goods, the Ti Gallery sells locally made crafts, and the cast-iron smoker (our favorite part of the operation) puts out smoked and grilled chicken, beef, and fresh local fish, sending seductive aromas out over the moist Nahiku air. The teriyaki-based marinade, made by the owner, adds a special touch to the fish (ono, ahi, marlin) and meats, sold for $3 a skewer. These are not jerkylike smoked meats; the process keeps the kabobs moist while retaining the smoke flavor. The breadfruit—sliced, wrapped in banana leaf, and baked—can be bland and starchy (like a baked potato), but it's a stroke of genius to give visitors a taste of this important Polynesian staple. There are a few roadside picnic tables, or you can take your lunch on the road for a beachside picnic in Hana. No credit cards are accepted. The coffee shop is open daily from 6:30am to 5pm; the fish stand hours are daily 10am to 5pm; and the gallery is open daily from 10am to 5pm.

Paia Fish Market. 110 Hana Hwy. ☎ **808/579-8030.** Lunch and dinner plates $6.95–$18.95. DISC, MC, V. Daily 11am–9:30pm. SEAFOOD.

This really is a fish market, with fresh fish to take home and cooked seafood, salads, pastas, fajitas, and quesadillas to take out or enjoy at the few picnic tables inside the restaurant. It's an appealing and budget-friendly selection: Cajun-style fresh catch, Mexican food with fresh fish, fresh-fish specials (usually ahi or salmon), fresh-fish tacos and quesadillas, and seafood and chicken pastas. You can also order hamburgers, cheeseburgers, and fish-and-chips (shrimp-and-chips, too), and wonderful lunch and dinner plates, cheap and tasty. Peppering the walls are photos of the number-one sport here, windsurfing.

Pic-nics. 30 Baldwin Ave. ☎ **808/579-8021.** Most items less than $6.95. JCB, MC, V. Daily 7am–5pm. SANDWICHES/PICNIC LUNCHES.

Breakfast is terrific here—omelettes, eggs to order, Maui Portuguese sausage, Hawaiian pancakes—and so is lunch. Stop here to refresh yourself with a plate lunch or smoothie for the drive to Hana or Upcountry Maui. Pic-nics is famous for many things, among them the spinach-nut burger, an ingenious vegetarian blend topped with vegetables and Cheddar cheese. A cold version of the nut burger is topped with vegetables and Pic-nics' own homemade nonfat yogurt dressing. The gourmet sandwiches (Kula vegetables, home-baked breast of turkey, Cajun chicken, Cajun fish) are worthy of the most idyllic picnic spot. The rosemary herb–roasted chicken can be ordered as a plate lunch (two scoops of rice and Haiku greens) or as part of the Hana Bay picnic, which includes sandwiches, meats, Maui-style potato chips, and home-baked cookies and muffins. You can order old-fashioned fish-and-chips, too, or shrimp-and-chips, or pastries baked fresh daily. Fresh breads add to the appeal, and several coffee drinks made with Maui-blend coffee may give you the jolt you need.

The Vegan. 115 Baldwin Ave. ☎ **808/579-9144.** Main courses $7.95–$9.95. AE, DC, DISC, JCB, MC, V. Daily noon–9pm. GOURMET VEGETARIAN/VEGAN.

Wholesome foods with ingenious soy substitutes and satisfying flavors appear on a menu that dares you to feel healthy *and* satisfied. Garlic noodles, called Pad Thai noodles, are the best-selling item, cooked in a creamy coconut sauce and generously seasoned with garlic and spices. Curries, grilled polenta, pepper steak made of Seitan (a meat substitute), and organic hummus are among the items that draw vegetarians from around the island. Proving that desserts are justly deserved, Vegan offers a carob cake and coconut milk–flavored tapioca pudding that hint of Thailand yet don't contain dairy milk.

HAIKU

✪ **Pauwela Cafe.** 375 W. Kuiaha Rd. (off Hana Hwy, past Haiku Rd.), Haiku. ☎ **808/ 575-9242.** Most items less than $6.50. No credit cards. Mon–Sat 7am–3pm, Sun 8am–2pm. INTERNATIONAL.

It's easy to get lost trying to find this wonderful cafe, but stick with it. It's a long drive from anywhere, but such a find. We never dreamed we could dine so well with such pleasing informality. The tiny cafe with concrete floors and a few tables indoors and outdoors has a strong local following. Becky Speere, a gifted chef, and her husband, Chris, a food-service instructor at Maui Community College and a former sous chef at the Maui Prince Hotel, infuse every sandwich, salad, and muffin with finesse. All breads are prepared in-house, including rosemary potato, Scottish country, French baguette, and green onion and cheese. The scene-stealing kalua turkey is one success layered on another: warm, smoky, moist shredded turkey, served with cheese on home-baked French bread and covered with a green-chile and cilantro sauce. It gets our vote as the best sandwich on the island. For breakfast, eggs chilaquile are a good starter, with layers of corn tortillas, pinto beans, chiles, cheese, and herbs, topped with egg custard and served hot with salsa and sour cream. For lunch, the Greek salad and veggie burrito are also excellent choices.

6 At the End of the Road in East Maui: Hana

Hana Ranch Restaurant. Hana Hwy. ☎ **808/248-8255.** Reservations required Fri–Sat. Main courses $16.95–$32.95. AE, DC, DISC, JCB, MC, V. Daily, sit-down dining, 7am–10am, 11am–2pm; buffet until 2pm; Fri–Sat 6–8pm. Take-out counter daily 6:30am–10am, 11am–4pm. AMERICAN.

Part of the Hotel Hana-Maui operation, the Hana Ranch Restaurant is the informal alternative to the hotel's dining room. In fact, it's the only other dining room in Hana. Here are some of your dinner choices: New York steak; prawns and pasta; and a few Pacific Rim options, such as spicy shrimp wontons and the predictable fresh-fish poke. Aside from the weekly, warmly received Wednesday Pizza Night, the luncheon buffet is a more affordable prospect: baked mahimahi, pocket pita sandwiches, chicken stir-fry, cheeseburgers, and club and fresh-catch sandwiches. It's not an inspired menu, and the service can be practically nonexistent when the tour buses descend during lunch rush. There are indoor tables as well as two outdoor pavilions that offer distant ocean views. At the take-out stand adjoining the restaurant, the fast-food classics prevail: teriyaki plate lunch, mahimahi sandwich, cheeseburgers, hot dogs, and ice cream.

6

Fun in the Surf & Sun

by Jeanette Foster

This is why you've come to Maui—the sun, the sand, the surf. In this chapter, we'll tell you about the best beaches, from where to soak up the rays to where to plunge beneath the waves for a fish's-eye view of the underwater world. We've covered a range of ocean activities on Maui, as well as our favorite places and outfitters for these marine adventures. Also in this chapter are things to do on dry land, including the best spots for hiking and camping and the greatest golf courses.

1 Beaches

Maui has more than 80 accessible beaches of every conceivable description, from rocky black-sand beaches to powdery golden sand beaches; there's even a rare red-sand beach. What follows is a personal selection of the finest of Maui's beaches, carefully chosen to suit a variety of needs, tastes, and interests.

Hawaii's beaches belong to the people. All beaches (even those in front of exclusive resorts) are public property and you are welcome to visit. Hawaii state law requires all resorts and hotels to offer public right-of-way access (across their private property) to the beach, along with public parking. So just because a beach fronts a hotel doesn't mean that you can't enjoy the water. It does mean that the hotel may restrict certain areas on private property for hotel guests' use only. Generally, hotels welcome nonguests to their facilities. They frown on nonguests using the beach chairs reserved for guests, but if a nonguest has money and wants to rent gear, buy a drink, or eat a sandwich, well, money is money and they will gladly accept it from anyone. For beach toys and equipment, contact the **Rental Warehouse** (☎ **800/ 923-4004;** www.travelhawaii.com), which has branches in Lahaina at 578 Front St., near Prison Street (☎ **808/661-1970**), and in Kihei at Azeka Place II, on the mountain side of Kihei Road near Lipoa Street (☎ **808/875-4050**). Beach chairs rent for $2 a day, coolers (with ice!) for $2 a day, and a host of toys (Frisbees, volleyballs, and more) for $1 a day.

WEST MAUI
✪ D. T. FLEMING BEACH PARK

This quiet, out-of-the-way beach cove, named after the man who started the commercial growing of pineapple on the Valley Isle, is a great place to take the family. The crescent-shaped beach, located north of the Ritz-Carlton Hotel, starts at the 16th hole of the Kapalua golf course (Makaluapuna Point) and rolls around to the sea cliffs at the other side. Ironwood trees provide shade on the land side. Offshore, a shallow sandbar extends to the edge of the surf. The waters are generally good for swimming and snorkeling; sometimes, off on the right side near the sea cliffs, the waves build enough for bodyboarders and surfers to get a few good rides in. This park has lots of facilities: rest rooms, showers, picnic tables, barbecue grills, and a paved parking lot.

✪ KAPALUA BEACH

The beach cove that fronts the Kapalua Bay Hotel is the stuff of dreams: a golden crescent bordered by two palm-studded points. The sandy bottom slopes gently to deep water at the bay mouth; the water is so clear that you can see where the gold sands turn to green, and then deep blue. Protected from strong winds and currents by the lava-rock promontories, Kapalua's calm waters are great for snorkelers and swimmers of all ages and abilities, and the bay is big enough to paddle a kayak around without getting into the more challenging channel that separates Maui from Molokai. Waves come in just right for riding. Fish hang out by the rocks, making it great for snorkeling.

The beach is accessible from the hotel on one end, which provides sun chairs with shades and a beach-activities center for its guests, and a public access way on the other. It isn't so wide that you'll burn your feet getting in or out of the water, and the inland side is edged by a shady path and cool lawns. Outdoor showers are stationed at both ends. You'll also find rest rooms, lifeguards, a rental shack, and plenty of shade.

Parking is limited to about 30 spaces in a small lot off Lower Honoapiilani Road, by Napili Kai Beach Club, so arrive early; next door is a nice but somewhat pricey oceanfront restaurant, Kapalua's Bay Club (see chapter 5 for a review).

✪ KAANAPALI BEACH

Four-mile-long Kaanapali is one of Maui's best beaches, with grainy gold sand as far as the eye can see. The beach parallels the sea channel through most of its length, and a paved beach walk links hotels and condos, open-air restaurants, and Whalers Village shopping center. Because Kaanapali is so long and most hotels have adjacent swimming pools, the beach is crowded only in pockets—there's plenty of room to find seclusion. Summertime swimming is excellent.

There's fabulous snorkeling around **Black Rock,** in front of the Sheraton; the water is clear, calm, and populated with clouds of tropical fish. You might even spot a turtle or two.

Facilities include outdoor showers; you can use the rest rooms at the hotel pools. Various beach-activity vendors line up in front of the hotels, offering nearly every type of water activity and equipment.

Parking is a problem, though. There are two public entrances: At the south end, turn off Honoapiilani Highway into the Kaanapali Resort, and pay for parking there; or continue on Honoapiilani Highway, turn off at the last Kaanapali exit at the stoplight near the Maui Kaanapali Villas, and park next to the beach signs indicating public access (this is a little tricky to find and limited to only a few cars, so to save time you might just head to the Sheraton or Whaler's Village and plunk down your money).

WAHIKULI COUNTY WAYSIDE PARK

This small stretch of beach, adjacent to Honoapiilani Highway between Lahaina and Kaanapali, is one of Lahaina's most popular beach parks. It's packed on weekends, but during the week it's a great place for swimming, snorkeling, sunbathing, and picnics. Offshore, the bottom is composed of rocks and sand, gradually sloping down to deeper

Beaches & Outdoor Pursuits

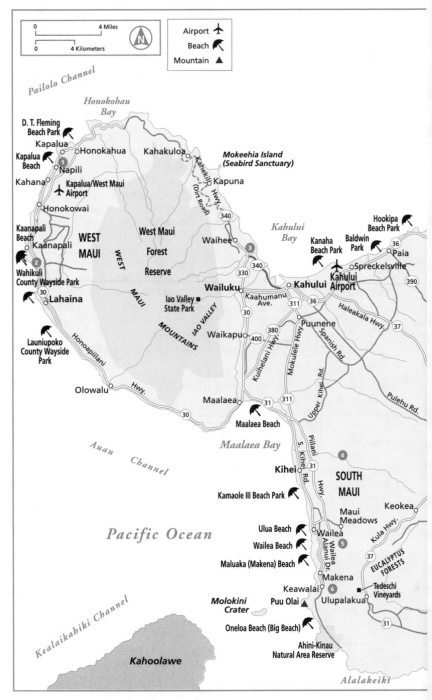

0   4 Miles
0   4 Kilometers

N

Airport ✈
Beach ☂
Mountain ▲

Pailolo Channel

Honokohau Bay

D. T. Fleming Beach Park
Kapalua
Kapalua Beach
Napili
Kahana
Honokohau
Honokowai
Kaanapali Beach
Kaanapali
Wahikuli County Wayside Park
Lahaina
Launiupoko County Wayside Park
Olowalu

Honokahua
Kahakuloa
Kapalua/West Maui Airport

WEST MAUI

West Maui Forest Reserve

WEST MAUI MOUNTAINS

Honoapiilani Hwy.

Mokeehia Island (Seabird Sanctuary)
Kapuna

Kahekili Hwy. (Dirt Road)

340
Waihee
330
340
Wailuku
Iao Valley State Park
Kaahumanu Ave.
IAO VALLEY
Waikapu
400
380
311

Kahului Bay
Kanaha Beach Park
Baldwin Park
Paia
Spreckelsville
Kahului Airport
Puunene
Spanish Rd.
Mokulele Hwy.
Kuihelani Hwy.

Hookipa Beach Park
36
390
Haleakala Hwy.
37

Auau Channel

Maalaea
Maalaea Beach
Maalaea Bay
Kihei
Kamaole III Beach Park
Ulua Beach
Wailea Beach
Maluaka (Makena) Beach

31
311
S. Kihei Rd.
Piilani Hwy.
Wailea Alanui Dr.

Pulehu Rd.
SOUTH MAUI
Maui Meadows
Wailea
Keokea
Kula Hwy.
EUCALYPTUS FORESTS
37

Pacific Ocean

Molokini Crater
Puu Olai ▲
Keawalai
Oneloa Beach (Big Beach)
Ahini-Kinau Natural Area Reserve

Makena
Ulupalakua
Tedeschi Vineyards
31

Kealaikahiki Channel

Kahoolawe

Alalakeiki

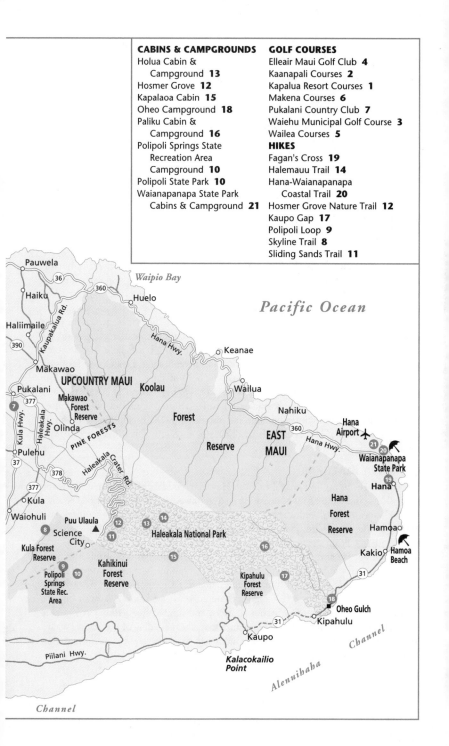

CABINS & CAMPGROUNDS
Holua Cabin &
  Campground **13**
Hosmer Grove **12**
Kapalaoa Cabin **15**
Oheo Campground **18**
Paliku Cabin &
  Campground **16**
Polipoli Springs State
  Recreation Area
  Campground **10**
Polipoli State Park **10**
Waianapanapa State Park
  Cabins & Campgrounds **21**

GOLF COURSES
Elleair Maui Golf Club **4**
Kaanapali Courses **2**
Kapalua Resort Courses **1**
Makena Courses **6**
Pukalani Country Club **7**
Waiehu Municipal Golf Course **3**
Wailea Courses **5**

HIKES
Fagan's Cross **19**
Halemauu Trail **14**
Hana-Waianapanapa
  Coastal Trail **20**
Hosmer Grove Nature Trail **12**
Kaupo Gap **17**
Polipoli Loop **9**
Skyline Trail **8**
Sliding Sands Trail **11**

water. Facilities include paved parking, rest rooms, showers, and small covered pavilions with picnic tables and barbecue grills.

LAUNIUPOKO COUNTY WAYSIDE PARK

Families with children will love this small park off Honoapiilani Highway, just south of Lahaina. A large wading pool for kids fronts the shady park, with giant boulders protecting the wading area from the surf outside. Just to the left is a small sandy beach with good swimming when conditions are right. Offshore, the waves are occasionally big enough for surfing. The view from the park is one of the best: You can see the islands of Kahoolawe, Lanai, and Molokai in the distance. Facilities include paved parking lot, rest rooms, showers, picnic tables, and barbecue grills. It's crowded on weekends.

SOUTH MAUI
KAMAOLE III BEACH PARK

Three beach parks—Kamaole I, II, and III—stand like golden jewels in the front yard of the funky seaside town of Kihei, which all of a sudden is exploding with suburban sprawl. The beaches are the best things about Kihei. All three are popular with local residents and visitors because they're easily accessible. On weekends they're jam-packed with fishermen, picnickers, swimmers, and snorkelers.

The most popular is Kamaole III, or "Kam-3," as locals say. The biggest of the three beaches, with wide pockets of golden sand, it's the only one with a playground for children and a grassy lawn that meets the sand. Swimming is safe here, but scattered lava rocks are toe stubbers at the water line, and parents should watch to make sure that kids don't venture too far out, because the bottom slopes off quickly. Both the north and south shores are rocky fingers with a surge big enough to attract fish and snorkelers, and the winter waves attract bodysurfers. Kam-3 is also a wonderful place to watch the sunset. Facilities include rest rooms, showers, picnic tables, barbecue grills, and lifeguards. There's also plenty of parking on South Kihei Road, across from the Maui Parkshore condos.

✪ WAILEA BEACH

Wailea, which means "water of Lea," the Hawaiian goddess of canoe makers, is the best golden-sand crescent on Maui's sunbaked southwestern coast. One of five beaches within Wailea Resort, Wailea is big, wide, and protected on both sides by black lava points. It's the front yard of the Four Seasons Wailea and the Grand Wailea Resort Hotel and Spa. From the beach, the view out to sea is magnificent, framed by neighboring Kahoolawe and Lanai and the tiny crescent of Molokini, probably the most popular snorkel spot in these parts. The clear waters tumble to shore in waves just the right size for gentle riding, with or without a board. From shore, you can see Pacific humpback whales in season (December through April), and unreal sunsets nightly. Facilities include rest rooms, outdoor showers, and limited free parking at the blue SHORELINE ACCESS sign, on Wailea Alanui Drive, the main drag of this resort. Wailea Resort's beaches might seem off-limits, hidden from plain view by an intimidating wall of luxury resorts, but they're all open to the public.

ULUA BEACH

One of the most popular beaches in Wailea, Ulua is a long, wide, crescent-shaped gold-sand beach between two rocky points. When the ocean is calm, Ulua offers Wailea's best snorkeling; when it's rough, the waves are excellent for bodysurfers. The ocean bottom is shallow and gently slopes down to deeper waters, making swimming generally safe. The beach is usually occupied by guests of nearby resorts; in high season (from Christmas to March and June to August), it's carpeted with beach towels. Facilities include showers and rest rooms. A variety of equipment is available for rent at the nearby Wailea Ocean Activity Center. To find Ulua, look for the new blue SHORELINE ACCESS sign on South Kihei Road, near Stouffer Wailea Beach Resort. A tiny parking lot is nearby.

✪ MALUAKA BEACH (MAKENA BEACH)

On the southern end of Maui's resort coast, development falls off dramatically, leaving a wild, dry countryside of green kiawe trees. The Maui Prince sits in isolated splendor, sharing Makena Resort's 1,800 acres with only a couple of first-rate golf courses and a necklace of perfect beaches. The strand nearest the hotel is Maluaka Beach, often called Makena, notable for its beauty and its views of Molokini Crater, the offshore islet, and Kahoolawe, the so-called "target" island. It's a short, wide, palm-fringed crescent of golden, grainy sand set between two black-lava points and bounded by big sand dunes topped by a grassy knoll. Swimming in this mostly calm bay is considered the best on Makena Bay, which is bordered on the south by Puu Olai cinder cone and historic Keawala'i Congregational Church. Facilities include rest rooms, showers, a landscaped park, lifeguards, and roadside parking. Along Makena Alanui, look for the SHORELINE ACCESS sign near the hotel, turn right, and head down to the shore.

ONELOA BEACH (BIG BEACH)

Oneloa, which means "long sand" in Hawaiian, is one of the most popular beaches on Maui. Locals call it Big Beach—it's 3,300 feet long and more than 100 feet wide. Mauians come here to swim, fish, sunbathe, surf, and enjoy the view of Kahoolawe and Lanai. Snorkeling is good around the north end at the foot of Puu Olai, a 360-foot cinder cone. During storms, however, big waves lash the shore and a strong rip current sweeps the sharp drop-off, posing a danger for inexperienced open-ocean swimmers. There are no facilities except portable toilets, but there's plenty of parking. To get here, drive past the Maui Prince Hotel to the second dirt road, which leads through a kiawe thicket to the beach. On the other side of Puu Olai is **Little Beach,** a small pocket beach where assorted nudists work on their all-over tans, to the chagrin of uptight authorities who take a dim view of public nudity. You can get a real nasty sunburn and a lewd-conduct ticket, too.

EAST MAUI
BALDWIN PARK

Located off the Hana Highway between Sprecklesville and Paia, this beach park draws lots of Maui residents, especially bodyboard enthusiasts. It's easy to see why this place is so popular: The surf breaks along the entire length of the white-sand beach, creating perfect conditions for bodyboarding. On occasion, the waves get big enough for surfing. A couple of swimming areas are safe enough for children: one in the lee of the beach rocks near the large pavilion, and another at the opposite end of the beach, where beach rocks protect a small swimming area. There's a large pavilion with picnic tables and kitchen facilities, barbecue grills, additional picnic tables on the grassy area, rest rooms, showers, a semipaved parking area, a baseball diamond, and a soccer field. The park is well used on weekends; weekdays are much quieter.

HOOKIPA BEACH PARK

Two miles past Paia, on the Hana Highway, you'll find one of the most famous windsurfing sites in the world. Due to constant wind and endless waves, Hookipa attracts top windsurfers and wave jumpers from around the globe. Surfers and fishermen also enjoy this small, gold-sand beach at the foot of a grassy cliff, which provides a natural amphitheater for spectators. Except when international competitions are being held, weekdays are the best time to watch the daredevils fly over the waves. When the water is flat, snorkelers and divers explore the reef. Facilities include rest rooms, showers, pavilions, picnic tables, barbecue grills, and a parking lot.

✪ WAIANAPANAPA STATE PARK

Four miles before Hana, off the Hana Highway, is this beach park, which takes its name from the legend of the Waianapanapa Cave, where Chief Kaakea, a jealous and cruel man, suspected his wife, Popoalaea, of having an affair. Popoalaea left her husband and hid herself in a chamber of the Waianapanapa Cave. She and her attendant ventured out only at night, for food. Nevertheless, a few days later, Kaakea was passing by the area and saw the shadow of the servant. Knowing he had found his wife's hiding place, Kaakea entered the cave and killed her. During certain times of the year, the water in the tide pool turns red as a tribute to Popoalaea, commemorating her death. (Scientists claim, however, that the change in color is due to the presence of small red shrimp.)Waianapanapa State Park's 120 acres have 12 cabins, a caretaker's residence, a beach park, picnic tables, barbecue grills, rest rooms, showers, a parking lot, a shoreline hiking trail, and a black-sand beach (it's actually small black pebbles). This is a wonderful area for both shoreline hikes (bring insect repellent, as the mosquitoes are plentiful) and picnicking. Swimming is generally unsafe, though, due to powerful rip currents and strong waves breaking offshore, which roll into the beach unchecked. Because Waianapanapa is crowded on weekends with local residents and their families, as well as tourists, weekdays are generally a better bet.

✪ HAMOA BEACH

This half moon–shaped, gray-sand beach (a mix of coral and lava) in a truly tropical setting is a favorite among sunbathers seeking rest and refuge. The Hotel Hana-Maui maintains the beach and acts as though it's private, which it isn't—so just march down those lava-rock steps and grab a spot on the sand. James Michener said of Hamoa, "Paradoxically, the only beach I have ever seen that looks like the South Pacific was in the North Pacific—Hamoa Beach . . . a beach so perfectly formed that I wonder at its comparative obscurity." The 100-foot-wide beach is three football fields long and sits below 30-foot black-lava sea cliffs. An unprotected beach open to the ocean, Hamoa is often swept by powerful rip currents. Surf breaks offshore and rolls ashore, making this a popular surfing and bodysurfing area. The calm left side is best for snorkeling in summer. The hotel has numerous facilities for guests; there's an outdoor shower and rest rooms for nonguests. Parking is limited. Look for the Hamoa Beach turnoff from Hana Highway.

2 Hitting the Water

Maui is a haven for every type of water activity for enthusiasts of all kinds, from windsurfers twirling in the ocean breezes to beginners donning a mask and snorkel for the first time to view the dazzling array of underwater life. You can skim across the water on a fast-moving sailing boat, plunge beneath the waves in a high-tech submarine, or soar above the water in a parasail. Whatever your interest, you'll find it on Maui.

BOATING & SAILING

To really appreciate Maui, you need to get off the land and get on the sea. Trade winds off the Lahaina Coast and the strong wind that rips through Maui's isthmus make

Get Away For Less.

Avis features GM cars.

With great offers and services from Avis, you'll get more out of your vacation! And now you can **save $20 on a weekly rental**. All the information you need is on the coupon below. Plus most rentals come with free unlimited mileage to save you even more.

As an added touch you can count on our famous "We try harder." service for a fast, hassle-free rental. Because speed and personal service is what everyone at Avis is dedicated to delivering.

For more information and reservations, call your travel agent or Avis toll free at **1-800-831-8000**.

AVIS®

We try harder.

For You.

Save $20 On A Weekly Rental

Reserve an Avis Intermediate through Full Size 4-Door car for a minimum of five consecutive days. At time of rental, present this coupon at the Avis counter and you can save $20. **An advance reservation is required.** Subject to complete Terms and Conditions below. Rental must begin by 06/30/01.

For reservations and information, call your travel consultant or Avis toll free at **1-800-831-8000**.

Terms and Conditions: Coupon valid on an Intermediate (Group C) through a Full Size 4-Door (Group E) car. Dollars off applies to the cost of the total rental with a minimum of 5 days. A Saturday night overstay is required. Coupon must be surrendered at time of rental; one per rental. Coupon valid at Avis participating locations in the U.S. An advance reservation is required. Cars subject to availability. Taxes, local government surcharges, vehicle licensing and an airport recruitment fee at some locations, optional items such as LDW, additional driver fee and refueling fee are extra. Renter must meet Avis driver and credit requirements. Minimum age is 25 but may vary by location. Rental must begin by 6/30/01.

Coupon #: **MUNA002**

Rental Sales Agent Instructions
At checkout:
In AWD, enter AWD number.
In CPN, enter **MUNA002**.
Complete this information:
RA # _____
Rental location _____
Attach to COUPON tape.

www.avis.com   11/99 DTPP

It's a Whole New World with

Frommer's

Safety Tip

Be sure to see the section "Staying Healthy," in chapter 2, before setting out on your Maui adventures. It includes useful information on hiking, camping, and ocean safety, plus how to avoid seasickness. Even if you just plan to lie on the beach, take a look at our tips on tanning and what to do should you get stung by a jellyfish.

sailing around the island exciting. Many different boats, from a three-masted schooner to spacious trimarans, offer day cruises from Maui. For information on snorkel cruises to Molokini, see "Snorkeling," below. For fishing charters, see "Sportfishing," below. For trips that combine snorkeling with whale watching, see "Whale-Watching Cruises," later in this chapter.

You can experience the thrill of competition sailing with **World Class Yacht Charters,** 107 Kahului Heliport, Kahului, HI 96732 (☎ **800/600-0959** or 808/ 667-7733). There's nothing like it, especially when all you have to do is hold on and cheer. The *World Class,* a 65-foot custom yacht designed for Maui waters, takes 24 passengers for a variety of sailing adventures: 2-hour whale-watching tours for $25; 4-hour morning snorkel sails for $59; high-performance sails for $35; and a 2-hour trade-winds sunset sail for $45. The 2pm high-performance sailing tour is the most exciting. Be prepared to get wet: The captain and crews of this cutter-rigged, high-tech yacht are serious about sailing. All trips leave from Kaanapali Beach.

You can also take a ride on the ***America II,*** Lahaina Harbor, slip 5 (☎ **888/ 667-2133** or 808/667-2195; www.galaxymall.com/stores/americaii), a U.S. contender in the America's Cup. It's a true racing boat: no snorkeling, just the thrill of racing the wind. Trips include a morning sail, an afternoon sail, and a sunset sail, plus a whale-watching sail in the winter. Each trip lasts 2 hours and costs $29.95 to $32.95 for adults, $14.95 to $16.50 for children ages 6 to 12; free for children 5 and under. Complimentary bottled water, soda, and chips are available.

For those not quite so adventuresome on the sea, the ***Navatek II*** (with offices at 330 Hukilike St., Kahului, HI 96732; ☎ **800/852-4183** or 808/873-3475; www.royalhawaiiancruises.com) is for all of you who go out on the sea with patches stuck behind your ears. You couldn't get sick on this boat if you tried. The new and unusual 82-foot SWATH (Small Waterplane Area Twin Hull) vessel is designed to operate in heavy seas without spilling your mai tai. The ship's superstructure (the part you ride on) rests on twin torpedo-like hulls that slash the water, creating a remarkably smooth ride. This comfortable, air-conditioned boat (with spacious outside decks and hot and cold showers) glides through the water so smoothly that you'll forget you're on the sea. They offer a variety of "sails" ranging from a cruise around the island of Lanai ($115 adults, $95 for kids ages 12 to 17, and $75 for children ages 5 to 11) to one of Hawaii's best sunset/dinner cruises (operating Saturday through Thursday, at a price of $87.50 for adults and $55 for kids 2 to 11, including Hawaiian entertainment and a full bar).

Day Cruises to Molokai

The ***Maui Princess,*** Lahaina Harbor slip 3 (☎ **800/275-6969** or 808/667-6165; fax 808/661-5792; www.mauiprincess.com), a 118-foot-yacht certified for 149 passengers, makes the journey from Lahaina to Kaunakakai, on the island of Molokai on Wednesday and Saturday May through December. During whale-watching season, December to May, the vessel runs only on Saturdays. Visitors have three different options: a Walking Tour, which is passage on the boat only, for $73.15 adults, $37.10 children

3 to 12 years, children under 3 free; a Cruise Drive Tour, which includes boat passage and a rental car, for $129 for the first person and $73.15 for each additional person; and the Alii Tour, which includes boat passage, a guided tour of Molokai in a van, and lunch, for $136.75 adults, $83.75 children 3 to 12, children under 3 free. Tours depart Lahaina at 6am, arriving in Molokai at 8am; and leave Molokai at 2pm, arriving in Lahaina at 3:45pm.

DAY CRUISES TO LANAI

Hop aboard ✪ **Trilogy Ocean Sports Lanai's** 50-foot catamaran for a 90-minute sail to Lanai and a fun-filled day of sailing, snorkeling, swimming, and whale watching. This is the only cruise that offers a personalized ground tour of the island. Breakfast (homemade cinnamon buns and freshly brewed Kona coffee) and lunch (a Hawaiian barbecue) are included. The trip is $159 for adults, $79.50 for children ages 3 to 12, and free for children under 3—we think it's worth every penny. Call ☎ **800/ MAUI-800** or 808/628-4800, or point your browser to www.sailtrilogy.com.

The ✪ **Expeditions Lahaina/Lanai Passenger Ferry** (☎ **808/661-3756**) will take you from Maui to Lanai and back for $50 round-trip. The ferry services run daily, five times a day. Before you go, contact **Lanai City Service** (☎ **808/565-7227**) to arrange vehicle and equipment rentals or rides (see chapter 11). A day with **Club Lanai** (☎ **800/531-5262** or 808/871-1144) consists of a catamaran trip departing from Lahaina Harbor, slip 4, at 7:30am to Lanai's eastern shore, where you can spend the day snorkeling, kayaking, bicycling, and relaxing in a hammock at an 8-acre beachfront estate. An all-you-can-eat buffet lunch and an open bar are included in the cost: $89 for adults, $69 for children ages 13 to 20, $29 for children ages 4 to 12, and free for children 3 and under.

Scotch Mist **Sailing Charters** (☎ **808/661-0386**) operates a 50-foot Santa Cruz sailboat anchored in Lahaina Harbor, slip 9, and offers half-day sail-snorkel cruises to Lanai. You won't actually set foot on Lanai, but you'll swim with the fish in its sparkling offshore waters. The price—$55 for adults, $27.50 for children ages 5 to 11, and free for kids under 4—includes snorkel gear, fruit juice, fresh pineapple spears, Maui chips, beer, wine, and soda.

For an amazingly smooth, stable, and swift ride, call the *Maui Nui Explorer* (☎ **800/852-4183** or 808/873-3475). This 48-foot, 49-passenger adventure craft leaves Lahaina Harbor for a 4-hour journey along the coast of Lanai, where you'll be able to swim and snorkel in remote coves and bays. Coffee, juice, and a deli-style lunch (sandwiches, Maui chips, fresh fruit, and cookies) are included, along with snacks, snorkel gear, and whale watching (in season). There's always a Hawaiian cultural specialist/marine-life expert on board to answer questions about the islands and their surrounding waters. The cost is $67 for adults, $60 for juniors (ages 12 to 17), and $51 for children (ages 5 to 11).

BODYBOARDING (BOOGIE BOARDING) & BODYSURFING

Bodysurfing—riding the waves without a board, becoming one with the rolling water—is a way of life in Hawaii. Some bodysurfers just rely on their outstretched hands (or hands at their sides) to ride the waves; others use handboards (flat, paddlelike gloves). For additional maneuverability, try a boogie or bodyboard (also known as belly boards or *paipo* boards). These 3-foot-long vehicles, which support the upper part of your body, are easy to carry and very maneuverable in the water. Both bodysurfing and bodyboarding require a pair of open-heeled swim fins to help propel you through the water. Both kinds of wave riding are very popular in the islands because the equipment is inexpensive and easy to carry, and both sports can be practiced in the small, gentle waves.

You can rent boogie boards and fins for $6.50 a day or $26 a week from **Snorkel Bob's** (www.snorkelbob.com), open from 8am to 5pm daily at three locations: Napili Village Hotel, 5425 Lower Honoapiilani Rd., Napili (☎ **808/669-9603**); 1217 Front St., Lahaina (☎ **808/661-4421**); and Kamaole Beach Center, 2411 S. Kihei Rd., Kihei (☎ **808/879-7449**). The cheapest place to rent boogie boards is the **Activity Warehouse** (☎ **800/923-4004;** www.travelhawaii.com), in Lahaina at 578 Front St., near Prison Street, (☎ **808/661-1970**), or in Kihei at Azeka Place II, on the mountain side of Kihei Road, near Lipoa Street (☎ **808/875-4050**), where they go for as little as $2 a day.

Baldwin Beach, just outside of Paia, has great bodysurfing waves nearly year-round. In winter, Maui's best bodysurfing spot is **Mokuleia Beach,** known locally as Slaughter house because of the cattle slaughterhouse that once stood here, not because of the waves—although they are definitely for expert bodysurfers only. To get to Mokuleia, take Honoapiilani Highway just past Kapalua Bay Resort; various hiking trails will take you down to the pocket beach. Storms from the south bring fair bodysurfing conditions and great boogie boarding to the lee side of Maui: **Oneloa** (Big Beach) in Makena, **Ulua** and **Kamaole III** in Kihei, and **Kapalua** beaches are all good choices.

OCEAN KAYAKING

Gliding silently over the water, propelled by a paddle, seeing Maui from the sea the way the early Hawaiians did—that's what ocean kayaking is all about. One of Maui's best kayak routes is along the Kihei Coast, where there's easy access to calm water. Early mornings are always best, because the wind comes up around 11am, making seas choppy and paddling difficult.

The island's cheapest kayak rentals are at the **Activity Warehouse** (☎ **800/ 923-4004;** www.travelhawaii.com), in Lahaina at 578 Front St., near Prison Street (☎ **808/661-1970**), or in Kihei at Azeka Place II, on the mountain side of Kihei Road, near Lipoa Street (☎ **808/875-4050**), where one-person kayaks are $10 a day and two-person kayaks are $15 a day.

For the uninitiated, our favorite kayak-tour operator is **Makena Kayak Tours** (☎ **808/879-8426**). Professional guide Dino leads the $2^{1}/_{2}$-hour tour from Makena Landing and loves taking first-time kayakers over the secluded coral reefs and into remote coves. His wonderful tour will be the highlight of your trip; it costs $55 per person, including refreshments and snorkel and kayak equipment.

Gordon Godfrey, Suzanne Simmons, and the expert guides of **South Pacific Kayaks,** 2439 S. Kihei Rd., Kihei, HI 96753 (☎ **800/776-2326** or 808/875-4848; fax 808/875-4691; www.maui.net/~kayak), run Maui's oldest kayak-tour company. They offer ocean kayak tours that include lessons, a guided tour, and snorkeling. Tours run from $2^{1}/_{2}$ to 5 hours and range in price from $59 to $89. Kayak rentals start at $30 a day. In Hana, **Hana-Maui Ocean Activities** (☎ **808/248-7711**) runs $2^{1}/_{2}$-hour tours of Hana's coastline on wide, stable "no roll" kayaks (plus snorkeling) for $75 per person.

OCEAN RAFTING

If you're semiadventurous and looking for a more intimate experience with the sea, try ocean rafting. The inflatable rafts hold 6 to 24 passengers, and tours usually include snorkeling and coastal cruising. One of the best (and most reasonably priced) outfitters is **Hawaiian Ocean Raft,** P.O. Box 381, Lahaina, HI 96761 (☎ **888/677-RAFT** or 808/667-2191; fax 808/878-3574; www.ocean-rafting.com), which operates out of Lahaina Harbor. The best deal here is the 5-hour morning tour, which heads over to Lanai, goes searching for dolphins, and includes two snorkeling stops; it costs

$69.95 for adults and $49.95 for children ages 5 to 12 (children under 5 ride free). The all-day (8am to 4pm) tour with eight snorkel stops and lunch costs $109.95 for adults and $79.95 for children ages 5 to 12.

PARASAILING

Soar high above the crowds (at around 400 feet) for a bird's-eye view of Maui. This ocean adventure sport, which is something of a cross between skydiving and water-skiing, involves sailing through the air, suspended under a large parachute attached by a tow line to a speedboat. Keep in mind, though, that parasailing tours don't run during whale season, which is roughly December through May.

We recommend **UFO Parasail** (☎ 800/FLY-4UFO or 808/661-7UFO; www.ufoparasail.com), which picks you up at Kaanapali Beach. The Early Bird Special (arrive by 7am) costs $47 (as opposed to $52) for a 7-minute ride. During whale season, the company converts its 37-foot speedboat into a whale-watching machine, and offers 1¹/₂-hour whale-watching trips for $31 per person.

SCUBA DIVING

Some people come to Maui for the sole purpose of plunging into the tropical Pacific and exploring the underwater world. You can see the great variety of tropical marine life (more than 100 endemic species found nowhere else on the planet), explore sea caves, and swim with sea turtles and monk seals in the clear tropical waters off the island. We recommend going early in the morning. Trade winds often rough up the seas in the afternoon, so most dive operators schedule early-morning dives that end at noon, and then take the rest of the day off.

Unsure about scuba diving? Take an introductory dive; most operators offer no-experience-necessary dives, ranging from $70 to $95. You can learn from this glimpse into the sea world whether diving is for you.

Everyone dives **Molokini,** a marine-life park and one of Hawaii's top dive spots. This crescent-shaped crater has three tiers of diving: a 35-foot plateau inside the crater basin (used by beginning divers and snorkelers), a wall sloping to 70 feet just beyond the inside plateau, and a sheer wall on the outside and backside of the crater that plunges 350 feet. This underwater park is very popular thanks to calm, clear, protected waters and an abundance of marine life, from manta rays to clouds of yellow butterfly fish.

If you're interested in the marine environment and natural history, call **Mike Severns Diving,** P.O. Box 627, Kihei (☎ **808/879-6596;** www.severns.maui.hi.us), for small (12-person maximum, divided into two groups of six people each), personal diving tours on his 38-foot Munson/Hammerhead boat with freshwater shower. Mike and his wife, Pauline Fiene-Severns, are both biologists who make diving not only fun, but also educational (they have a spectacular underwater photography book called *Molokini Island*). In their 20-plus years of operation, they have been accident-free. Two-tank dives are $100 without equipment ($115 with equipment).

If the Severns are booked, contact **Ed Robinson's Diving Adventures** (☎ **800/ 635-1273** or 808/879-3584; fax 808/874-1939; www.mauiscuba.com), another great dive operator. Ed is a widely published underwater photographer who offers specialized charters for small groups (including a new "premiere" trip with just four divers to one guide, setting an even higher standard of personalized service). This is the only Maui company rated in *Scuba Diver* Magazine's top-10 best dive operators for 5 years straight. Most of his business comes from repeat customers. Ed offers two-tank dives for $104 to $145 ($10 extra for equipment); his dive boats depart from Kihei boat ramp.

Stop by any location of the **Maui Dive Shop** (www.mauidiveshop.com), Maui's largest diving retailer, which offers everything from rentals to scuba-diving instruction to dive-boat charters. They'll give you a free copy of the 24-page *Maui Dive Guide*, which has maps and details about the 20 best shoreline and offshore dives and snorkeling sites, all ranked for beginner, intermediate, or advanced snorkelers/divers. This operation has locations in Kihei at Azeka Place II Shopping Center, 1455 S. Kihei Rd. (☎ **808/879-3388**) and at the Kamaole Shopping Center (☎ **808/879-1533**); in Lahaina at the Lahaina Cannery Mall (☎ **808/661-5388**); and in the Honokowai Market Place (☎ **808/661-6166**). Other locations include Whalers Shopping Village, Kaanapali (☎ **808/661-5117**), and Kahana Gateway, Kahana (☎ **808/669-3800**).

SNORKELING

Snorkeling is the main attraction in Maui—and almost anyone can do it. All you need are a mask, a snorkel, fins, and some basic swimming skills. Floating over underwater worlds through colorful clouds of tropical fish is like a dream. In many places, all you have to do is wade into the water and look down.

If you've never snorkeled before, you can take advantage of the snorkeling equipment and lessons offered by most resorts and excursion boats. However, you won't really need lessons; it's plenty easy to figure out for yourself, especially once you're at the beach—everybody around you will be doing it.

Some snorkel tips: Always go with a buddy. Look up every once in a while to see where you are, how far offshore you are, and whether there's any boat traffic. Don't touch anything; not only can you damage coral, but camouflaged fish and shells with poisonous spines might surprise you. Always check with a dive shop, lifeguards, and others on the beach about the area in which you plan to snorkel: Are there any dangerous conditions you should know about? What are the current surf, tide, and weather conditions? If you're not a good swimmer, you may want to wear a life jacket or other flotation device, which you can rent at most places offering water-sports gear.

Snorkel Bob's (www.snorkelbob.com) can rent everything you need at its three Maui locations: 1217 Front St., Lahaina (☎ **808/661-4421**); Napili Village, 5425-C Lower Honoapiilani Hwy., Napili (☎ **808/669-9603**); and Kamaole Beach Center, 2411 Kihei Rd., Kihei (☎ **808/879-7449**). Snorkel gear (fins, mask, and snorkel) rents for $2.50 to $6.50 a day, or $9 to $39 a week.

The **Activity Warehouse** (☎ **800/923-4004**), in Lahaina at 578 Front St., near Prison Street (☎ **808/661-1970**), and in Kihei at Azeka Place II, on the mountain side of Kihei Road, near Lipoa Street (☎ **808/875-4050**), also has everything you need to experience the underwater world. The snorkel sets include mask, fins, snorkel, gear bag, map of great snorkeling areas, no-fog lotion (for your mask), and fish identification chart—just add water and you're ready to go.

Maui's best snorkeling beaches include **Kapalua Beach; Black Rock,** at Kaanapali Beach, in front of the Sheraton; along the Kihei coastline, especially at **Kamaole III Beach Park;** and along the Wailea coastline, particularly at **Ulua Beach.** Mornings are best, because local winds don't kick in until around noon. **Olowalu** has great snorkeling around the **14-mile marker,** where there is a turtle cleaning station about 50 to 75 yards out from shore. Turtles line up here to have cleaner wrasses pick small parasites off.

Ahihi-Kinau Natural Preserve is another terrific place; it requires more effort to reach it, but it's worth it, because it's home to Maui's tropical marine life at its best. You can't miss in Ahihi Bay, a 2,000-acre state natural area reserve in the lee of Cape Kinau, on Maui's rugged south coast, where Haleakala spilled red-hot lava that ran to

An Expert Shares His Secrets: Maui's Best Dives

Ed Robinson, of Ed Robinson's Diving Adventures (see above), knows what makes a great dive. Here are some of his favorites on Maui, and he'll be happy to take you to any or all of them:

Hawaiian Reef   This area off the Kihei-Wailea coast is so named because it has a good cross-section of topography and marine life typical of Hawaiian waters. Diving to depths of 85 feet, you'll see everything from lava formations and coral reef to sand and rubble, plus a diverse range of both shallow and deep-water creatures. You'll see for yourself why this area was so popular with ancient Hawaiian fishermen: Large helmet shells, a healthy garden of large antler coral heads, and large schools of snapper are common.

Third Tank   Located off Makena Beach at 80 feet, this World War II tank is one of the most picturesque artificial reefs you're likely to see around Maui. It acts like a fish magnet: Because it's the only large solid object in the area, any fish or invertebrate looking for a safe home come here. Surrounding the tank is a cloak of schooling snapper and goat fish just waiting for a photographer with a wide-angle lens. For its small size, the Third Tank is loaded with more marine life per square inch than any other site off Maui.

Molokini Crater   The backside is always done as a live boat drift dive. The vertical wall plummets from over 150 feet above sea level to around 250 feet below. Looking down to unseen depths gives you some idea of the vastness of the open ocean. Pelagic fish and sharks are often sighted, and living coral perches on the wall, which is home to lobsters, crabs, and a number of photogenic black coral trees at 50 feet.

There are actually two great dive sites around Molokini crater. Named after common chub or rudder fish, **Enenue Side** gently slopes from the surface to

the sea in 1790. Fishing is strictly *kapu* here, and the fish know it; they're everywhere in this series of rocky coves and black-lava tide pools. The black, barren, lunar-like land stands in stark contrast to the green-blue water. After you snorkel, check out La Pérouse Bay on the south side of Cape Kinau, where the French admiral La Pérouse became the first European to set foot on Maui. A lava-rock pyramid known as Pérouse Monument marks the spot. To get here, drive south of Makena past Puu Olai to Ahihi Bay, where the road turns to gravel and sometimes seems like it'll disappear under the waves. At Cape Kinau, there are three four-wheel-drive trails that lead across the lava flow; take the shortest one, nearest La Pérouse Bay.

If you'd like to head over to Lanai for a day of snorkeling in its pristine waters, see **"Day Cruises to Lanai"** under "Boating & Sailing," above.

SNORKEL CRUISES TO MOLOKINI

Like a crescent moon fallen from the sky, the sunken crater of ✪ **Molokini** sits almost midway between Maui and the uninhabited island of Kahoolawe. Tilted so that only the thin rim of its southern side shows above water in a perfect semicircle, Molokini stands like a scoop against the tide, and it serves, on its concave side, as a natural sanctuary for tropical fish and snorkelers, who commute daily in a fleet of dive boats to this marine-life preserve.

about 60 feet, then drops rapidly to deeper waters. The shallower area is an easy dive, with lots of tame butterfly fish. It's also the home of Morgan Bentjaw, one of our friendliest moray eels. Enenue Side is often done as a live boat drift dive to extend the range of the tour. Diving depths vary. Divers usually do a 50-foot dive, but on occasion advanced divers drop to the 130-foot level to visit the rare boar fish and the shark condos.

Almost every kind of fish found in Hawaii can be seen in the crystalline waters of **Reef's End.** Reef's End is an extension of the rim of Molokini crater, which runs for about 200 yards underwater, barely breaking the surface. Reef's End is shallow enough for novice snorkelers and exciting enough for experienced divers. The end and outside of this shoal drop off in dramatic terraces to beyond diving range. In deeper waters, there are shark ledges at varying depths, and dozens of eels, some of which are tame, including moray, dragon, snowflake, and garden eels. The shallower inner side is home to Garbanzo, one of the largest and first eels to be tamed. The reef is covered with cauliflower coral; in bright sunlight, it's one of the most dramatic underwater scenes in Hawaii.

La Pérouse Pinnacle   In the middle of scenic La Pérouse Bay, site of Haleakala's most recent lava flow, is a pinnacle rising from the 60-foot bottom to about 10 feet below the surface. Getting to the dive site is half the fun: The scenery above water is as exciting as that below the surface. Underwater, you'll enjoy a very diversified dive. Clouds of damselfish and triggerfish will greet you on the surface. Divers can approach even the timid bird wrasse. We find more porcupine puffers here than anywhere else, as well as schools of goatfish and fields of healthy finger coral. La Pérouse is good for snorkeling and long, shallow second dives.

If you'd like take a snorkel boat to Molokini, call the **Ocean Activities Center,** 1847 S. Kihei Rd., Kihei (☎ **800/798-0652** or 808/879-4485), which also operates out of a number of hotels and condos. The best deal is the Maka Kai cruise, which includes continental breakfast, deli lunch, snorkel gear, and instruction; it's $55 for adults and $35 for children ages 3 to 12. The 5-hour cruise departs from Maalaea Harbor, slip 62, at 7am.

You can also try **Maui Classic Charters** (☎ **800/736-5740** or 808/879-8188; www.mauicharters.com). Its snorkel-sail cruises on the 63-foot *Lavengro* leave Maalaea, slip 80, at 7am for a 6-hour journey that includes continental breakfast and deli lunch; it costs $69 for adults and $45 for children ages 3 to 12. This outfitter also has a new boat, *Four Winds II,* a 55-foot glass-bottom catamaran, which offers both 5-hour snorkel trips ($72 for adults, $47 for children ages 3 to 12) and 3¹/₂-hour trips ($40 for adults, $30 for children) with a naturalist on board during whale season.

For an action-packed snorkel-sail experience, check out ***Pride of Maui,*** which operates out of Maalaea Harbor (☎ **877/TO-PRIDE** or 808/875-0955). The 5¹/₂-hour snorkel cruises not only go to Molokini, but also stop at Turtle Bay, off the coast of the Maui Prince Hotel, and in Makena, for more snorkeling. Continental breakfast, barbecue lunch, gear, and instruction are included in the price: $79 for adults, $69 for kids 13 to 17, $49 for kids 3 to 12, and free for kids under 3.

SPORTFISHING

The largest blue marlin taken on a rod and reel in the waters around Maui tipped the scale at more than 1,200 pounds. Marlin, tuna, ono, and mahimahi await the baited hook in Maui's coastal and channel waters. No license is required; just book a sport-fishing vessel out of Lahaina or Maalaea harbors. Most charter boats that troll for big-game fish carry a maximum of six passengers. You can walk the docks, inspecting boats and talking to captains and crews, or book through an activities desk or one of the outfitters recommended below.

Shop around: Prices vary widely according to the boat, the crowd, and the captain. A shared boat for a half-day of fishing starts at $100; a shared full day of fishing starts at around $140. A half-day exclusive (you get the entire boat) is around $300 to $535; a full-day exclusive boat can range from $450 to $900. Also, many boat captains tag and release marlin or keep the fish for themselves (sorry, that's Hawaii style). If you want to eat your mahimahi for dinner or have your marlin mounted, tell the captain before you go.

If you want to fish out of Maalaea, you can spend the day on the 37-foot Tollycraft, the *No Ka Oi III* (☎ 800/798-0652 or 808/879-4485). For other ideas, try the **Maalaea Activities** desk at the harbor (☎ **808/242-6982**).

At Lahaina Harbor, go for one of the following charter companies: **Hinatea Sport-fishing,** slip 27 (☎ **808/667-7548**); **Lucky Strike Charters,** slips 50 and 51 (☎ **808/ 661-4606**); or **Aerial Sportfishing Charters,** slip 2 (☎ **808/667-9089**).

SURFING

The ancient Hawaiian sport of *hee nalu* ("wave sliding") is probably the sport most people picture when they think of the islands. You, too, can be doing some wave sliding—just sign up at any one of the recommended surfing schools listed below.

Always wanted to learn to surf, but didn't know who to ask? Contact the **Nancy Emerson School of Surfing,** P.O. Box 463, Lahaina, HI 96767 (☎ **808/244-SURF** or 808/874-1183; fax 808/874-2581; www.maui.net/~ncesurf/ncesurf.html). Nancy has been surfing since 1961—she was a stunt performer for various movies, including *Waterworld.* She has pioneered a new instructional technique called "Learn to Surf in One Lesson." It's $70 per person for 2 hours with a group; private classes run $125 for 2 hours.

Even if you've never seen a surfboard before, Andrea Thomas claims she can teach you the art of riding the waves. She has instructed thousands at **Maui Surfing School,** P.O. Box 424, Puunene, HI 96784 (☎ **800/851-0543** or 808/875-0625; www.mauisurf.com), including students as young as 3 and as "chronologically gifted" as 70. She backs her classes with a guarantee that she'll get you surfing, or you'll get 110% of your money back. Two-hour lessons are $55, available by appointment.

Surfers on a budget will find the lowest rates on rental boards at **Activity Warehouse** (☎ **800/923-4004**), in Lahaina at 578 Front St., near Prison Street (☎ **808/ 661-1970**), and in Kihei at Azeka Place II, on the mountain side of Kihei Road, near Lipoa Street (☎ **808/875-4050**). "Goober's" boards rent for $10 a day and "shredder's" boards go for $19 a day.

Expert surfers visit Maui in winter when the surf's really up. The best surfing beaches include **Honolua Bay, Lahaina Harbor** (in summer, there'll be waves just off the channel entrance with a south swell), **Maalaea** (a clean, world-class left), and **Hookipa Beach,** where surfers get the waves until noon; after that—in a carefully worked-out compromise to share this prized surf spot—the windsurfers take over.

WHALE WATCHING

Every winter, pods of Pacific humpback whales make the 3,000-mile swim from the chilly waters of Alaska to bask in Maui's summery shallows, fluking, spy hopping, spouting, and having an all-around swell time.

The humpback whale is a cottage industry here. No creature on earth is celebrated in so many ways: you'll see whale posters, T-shirts, jewelry, and art, some of it quite awful. Don't waste your money on whale stuff; go see the real thing. The humpback is the star of the annual whale-watching season, which usually begins in January and lasts, sometimes, until May. About 1,500 to 3,000 humpback whales appear in Hawaii waters each year. Humpbacks are one of the world's oldest, most impressive inhabitants. Adults grow to be about 45 feet long and weigh a hefty 40 tons; when they splash, it looks as though a 747 has hit the drink. Humpbacks are officially an endangered species; in 1997, some of the waters around the state were designated the Hawaiian Islands Humpback Whale National Marine Sanctuary, the country's only federal single-species sanctuary.

WHALE WATCHING FROM SHORE

The best time to whale-watch is between mid-December and April: Just look out to sea. There's no best time of day for whale watching, but the whales seem to appear when the sea is glassy and the wind calm. Once you see one, keep watching in the same vicinity; they might stay down for 20 minutes. Bring a book—and binoculars, if you can. You can rent binoculars for $2 a day at the **Activity Warehouse** (☎ 800/923-4004), in Lahaina at 578 Front St., near Prison Street (☎ 808/661-1970), and in Kihei at Azeka Place II, on the mountain side of Kihei Road, near Lipoa Street (☎ 808/875-4050). Some good whale-watching points on Maui are:

McGregor Point   On the way to Lahaina, there's a scenic lookout at mile marker 9 (just before you get to the Lahaina Tunnel); it's a good viewpoint to scan for whales.

Outrigger Wailea Resort   On the Wailea coastal walk, stop at this resort to look for whales through the telescope installed as a public service by the Hawaiian Island Humpback Whale National Marine Sanctuary.

Olowalu Reef   Along the straight part of Honoapiilani Highway, between McGregor Point and Olowalu, you'll see whales leap out of the water. Sometimes, their appearance brings traffic to a screeching halt: People abandon their cars and run down to the sea to watch, causing a major traffic jam. If you stop, pull off the road so that others can pass.

Puu Olai   It's a tough climb up this coastal landmark near the Maui Prince Hotel, but you're likely to be well rewarded: This is the island's best spot for offshore whale watching. On the 360-foot cinder cone overlooking Makena Beach, you'll be at the right elevation to see Pacific humpbacks as they dodge Molokini and cruise up Alalakeiki Channel between Maui and Kahoolawe. If you don't see one, you'll at least have a whale of a view.

WHALE-WATCHING CRUISES

For a closer look, take a whale-watching cruise. The **Pacific Whale Foundation,** 101 N. Kihei Rd., Kihei, HI 96753 (☎ 800/942-5311 or 808/879-8811; www.pacificwhale.org), is a nonprofit foundation in Kihei that supports its whale research by offering cruises and snorkel tours, some to Molokini and Lanai. They operate a 65-foot power catamaran called the *Ocean Spirit,* a 50-foot sailing catamaran called the *Manute'a,* and a sea kayak. They have 15 daily trips to choose from, and their rates for a 2-hour whale-watch cruise would make Captain Ahab smile (starting at $19.80 for

---

Not So Close! They Hardly Know You _____

In your excitement at seeing a whale or a school of dolphins, don't get too close—both are protected under the Marine Mammals Protection Act. Swimmers, kayakers, and windsurfers must stay at least 100 yards away from all whales, dolphins, and other marine mammals. And yes, they have prosecuted visitors for swimming with dolphins! If you have any questions, call the **National Marine Fisheries Service** (☎ 808/541-2727) or the **Hawaiian Islands Humpback Whale National Marine Sanctuary** (☎ 800/831-4888).

---

adults, $14.90 for children). Cruises are offered from December through May, out of both Lahaina and Maalaea harbors.

The **Ocean Activities Center** (☎ 800/798-0652 or 808/879-4485) runs three 2-hour whale-watching cruises on its spacious 65-foot catamaran, which leaves out of Maalaea Harbor; trips are $30 for adults and $18 for children 3 to 12. Bring a towel and your swimsuit; everything else—fins, mask, snorkel, and usually whales—is provided.

If you want to combine ocean activities, then a snorkel or dive cruise to Molokini, the sunken crater off Maui's south coast, might be just the ticket. You can see whales on the way there, at no extra charge. See "Scuba Diving" and "Boating & Sailing," earlier in this chapter.

WHALE WATCHING BY KAYAK & RAFT

Seeing a humpback whale from an ocean kayak or raft is awesome. The best budget deal for rafting is **Capt. Steve's Rafting Excursions,** P.O. Box 12492, Lahaina, HI 96761 (☎ 808/667-5565), which offers 2-hour whale-watching excursions out of Lahaina Harbor. Take the early bird trip at 7:30am and spot some whales for only $35 per person (regular rates are $45 for adults, $35 for children 12 and under).

Kayakers should call **South Pacific Kayaks,** 2439 S. Kihei Rd., Kihei (☎ 800/776-2326 or 808/875-4848; www.maui.net/~kayak), which leads small groups on 3-hour trips in the calm waters off Maui for $59 per person.

WINDSURFING

Maui has Hawaii's best windsurfing beaches. In winter, windsurfers from around the world flock to the town of **Paia** to ride the waves. **Hookipa Beach,** known all over the globe for its brisk winds and excellent waves, is the site of several world-championship contests. **Kanaha,** west of Kahului Airport, also has dependable winds; when conditions are right, it's packed with colorful butterfly-like sails. When the winds turn northerly, **Kihei** is the spot to be; some days, you can spot whales in the distance behind the windsurfers.

Hawaiian Island Surf and Sport, 415 Dairy Rd., Kahului (☎ 800/231-6958 or 808/871-4981; fax 808/871-4624; www.hawaiianisland.com), offers lessons, rentals, and repairs. Other shops offering rentals and lessons are **Hawaiian Sailboarding Techniques,** 444 Hana Hwy., Kahului (☎ 808/871-5423; www.hstwindsurfing. com), with lessons from $69 and equipment rental from $46 a day; and **Maui Windsurf Co.,** 520 Keolani Place, Kahului (☎ 800/872-0999 or 808/877-4816; www.maui-windsurf.com), which has complete equipment rental (board, sail, rig harness, and roof rack) available from $45 a day and lessons, from beginner to advanced, range in price from $69 to $75 for 1- to 2¹/₂-hour lessons. For daily reports on wind and surf conditions, call the **Wind and Surf Report** at ☎ 808/877-3611.

3 Hiking & Camping

In the past 2 decades, Maui has grown from a rural island to a fast-paced resort destination, but its natural beauty largely remains; there are still many places that can be explored only on foot. Those interested in seeing the backcountry—complete with virgin waterfalls, remote wilderness trails, and quiet meditative settings—should head for Haleakala's upcountry or the tropical Hana coast.

Camping on Maui can be extreme (inside a volcano) or benign (by the sea in Hana). It can be wet, cold, and rainy, or hot, dry, and windy—often all on the same day. If you're heading for Haleakala, remember that U.S. astronauts trained for the moon inside the volcano; bring survival gear. Don't forget both your swimsuit and your rain gear if you're bound for Waianapanapa.

Rental equipment (as well as gear for sale) is available from **The Base Camp,** 3619 Baldwin Ave. (on the way to Haleakala), Makawao (☎ **808/573-2267**). If you need to buy equipment, check out **Gaspro,** 365 Hanakai, Kahului (☎ **808/877-0056**), or **Maui Sporting Goods,** 92 N. Market, Wailuku (☎ **808/244-0011**).

For more information on Maui camping and hiking trails and to obtain free maps, contact **Haleakala National Park,** P.O. Box 369, Makawao, HI 96768 (☎ **808/ 572-4400;** www.nps.gov/hale), and the **State Division of Forestry and Wildlife,** 54 S. High St., Wailuku, HI 96793 (☎ **808/984-8100;** www.hawaii.gov). For information on trails, hikes, and camping, and permits for state parks, contact the **Hawaii State Department of Land and Natural Resources,** State Parks Division, 54 S. High St., Rm. 101, Wailuku, HI 96793 (☎ **808/984-8109;** www.hawaii.gov). For information on Maui County Parks, contact **Maui County Parks and Recreation,** 1580-C Kaahumanu Ave., Wailuku, HI 96793 (☎ **808/243-7380;** www.mauimapp.com).

TIPS ON SAFE HIKING & CAMPING   Water might be everywhere in Hawaii, but it more than likely isn't safe to drink. Most stream water must be treated because cattle, pigs, and goats have probably contaminated the water upstream. The department of health continually warns campers of bacterium leptospirosis, which is found in freshwater streams throughout the state and enters the body through breaks in the skin or through the mucous membranes. It produces flulike symptoms and can be fatal. Make sure that your drinking water is safe by vigorously boiling it, or if boiling is not an option, use tablets with hydroperiodide; portable water filters will not screen out the bacterium leptospirosis. Since firewood isn't always available, it's a good idea to carry a small, light backpacking stove, which you can use both to boil water and to cook meals for your hiking and camping adventures. Remember, there is crime in paradise: Never leave your valuables (wallet, airline ticket, and so on) unprotected. Carry a day pack if you have a campsite, and never camp alone. Some more do's and don'ts: Do bury personal waste away from streams, don't eat unknown fruit, do carry your trash out, and don't forget there is very little twilight in Maui when the sun sets—it gets dark quickly.

GUIDED HIKES   If you would like a knowledgeable guide to accompany you on a hike, contact **Maui Hiking Safaris,** P.O. Box 11198, Lahaina, HI 96761 (☎ **888/ 445-3963** or 808/573-0168; fax 808/572-3037; www.mauihikingsafaris.com). Owner Randy Warner takes visitors on half-day (4 to 5 hours) and full-day (8 to 10 hours) hikes into valleys, rain forests, and coastal areas. Randy has been hiking around Maui for more than 10 years and is wise in the ways of Hawaiian history, native flora and fauna, and volcanology. His rates are $49 for a half day, $89 for a full day (children 13 and under get 10% off on all hikes), and include day packs, rain parkas, snacks, water, and, on full-day hikes, sandwiches.

Maui's oldest hiking-guide company is **Hike Maui,** P.O. Box 330969, Kahului, HI 96733 (☎ **808/879-5270;** www.hikemaui.com), headed by Ken Schmitt, who pioneered guided hikes on the Valley Isle. Hike Maui offers five different hikes a day, ranging from an easy 3½-mile stroll through the rain forest to a waterfall ($85 for adults, $65 for children 15 and under) to a strenuous, full-day hike in the rain forest and along a mountain ridge ($135 for adults, $100 for children 15 and under). Rates include equipment and transportation.

Half-day hikes to lush rain forests in the West Maui Mountains are offered 8am to noon by the not-for-profit **Kapalua Nature Society** (☎ **800/KAPALUA** or 808/ 669-0244). Groups of up to nine can go on guided hiking tours, led by guides from Maui Eco-Adventures and include a continental breakfast and transportation to and from the trails. One of their hikes is the 1¾-mile **Maunalei Arboretum/Puu Kaeo Nature Walk,** which starts at 1,200 feet and goes to the 1,635-foot summit of Puu Kaeo. Hikers will learn about the history of the arboretum and the various plants which call it home. The cost is $70; children must be at least 12. Proceeds go toward the preservation of Puu Kukui rain forest.

HALEAKALA NATIONAL PARK

For complete coverage of the national park, see "House of the Sun: Haleakala National Park," in chapter 7.

INTO THE WILDERNESS: SLIDING SANDS & HALEMAUU TRAILS

Hiking into Maui's dormant volcano is really the best way to see it. The terrain inside the wilderness area of the volcano, which ranges from burnt-red cinder cones to ebony-black lava flows, is simply spectacular. Inside the crater, there are some 27 miles of hiking trails, two camping sites, and three cabins.

The best route takes in two trails: into the crater along **Sliding Sands Trail,** which begins on the rim at 9,800 feet and descends into the belly of the beast, to the valley floor at 6,600 feet; and back out along **Halemauu Trail.** Hardy hikers can consider making the 11.3-mile one-way descent, which takes 9 hours, and the equally long return ascent in 1 day. The rest of us will need to extend this steep but wonderful hike to 2 days. The descending and ascending trails aren't loops; the trailheads are miles (and several thousand feet in elevation) apart, so you'll need to make transportation arrangements in advance. Arrange to stay at least 1 night in the park; 2 or 3 nights will allow you more time to actually explore the fascinating interior of the volcano. See below for details on the cabins and campgrounds in the wilderness area in the valley. Before you set out, stop at park headquarters to get camping and hiking updates. There is no registration for day hikers.

A Word of Warning about the Weather

The weather at nearly 10,000 feet can change suddenly and without warning. Come prepared for cold, high winds, rain, and even snow in winter. Temperatures can range from 77°F down to 26°F (which feels even lower when you factor in the wind chill), and high winds are frequent. Rainfall varies from 40 inches a year on the west end of the crater to more than 200 inches on the eastern side. Bring boots, waterproof gear, warm clothes, extra layers, and lots of sunscreen—the sun shines very brightly up here.

The trailhead for Sliding Sands is well marked and the trail is easy to follow over lava flows and cinders. As you descend, look around: The view is breathtaking. In the afternoon, waves of clouds flow into the Kaupo and Koolau gaps. Vegetation is sparse to nonexistent at the top, but the closer you get to the valley floor, the more vegetation you'll see: bracken ferns, pili grass, shrubs, even flowers. On the floor, the trail travels across rough lava flows, passing rare silversword plants, volcanic vents, and multicolored cinder cones. The Halemauu Trail goes over red and black lava and past vegetation, such as evening primrose, as it begins its ascent up the valley wall. Occasionally, riders on horseback use this trail as an entry and exit from the park. The proper etiquette is to step aside and stand quietly next to the trail as the horses pass.

The descending and ascending trails aren't loops; the trailheads are miles (and several thousand feet in elevation) apart, so you'll need to make advance transportation arrangements to get back to your car, which you'll leave at the beginning of the hike, about a 30- to 45-minute drive from where the Halemauu trail ends. You either arrange with someone to pick you up, hitchhike back up to your car, or hook up with other people doing the same thing and drop off one car at each trailhead. More than a few lifetime friendships have been forged this way.

DAY HIKES FROM THE MAIN ENTRANCE

Aside from the difficult hike into the crater, the park has a few shorter and easier options. Anyone can take a half-mile walk down the **Hosmer Grove Nature Trail,** or you can start down **Sliding Sands Trail** for a mile or two to get a hint of what lies ahead. Even this short hike can be exhausting at the high altitude. A good day hike is **Halemauu Trail** to Holua Cabin and back, an 8-mile, half-day trip. A 20-minute orientation presentation is given daily in the Summit Building at 9:30, 10:30, and 11:30am. The park rangers offer two **guided hikes.** The 2-hour, 2-mile **Cinder Desert Hike** takes place Tuesday and Friday at 10am and starts from the Sliding Sands Trailhead at the end of the Haleakala Visitor Center parking lot. The 3-hour, 3-mile **Waikamoi Cloud Forest Hike** leaves every Monday and Thursday at 9am; it starts at the Hosmer Grove, just inside the park entrance, and traverses through the Nature Conservancy's Waikamoi Preserve.

CAMPING NEAR THE MAIN ENTRANCE

Most people stay at one of two tent campgrounds, unless they get lucky and win the lottery—the lottery, that is, for one of the three wilderness cabins. For more information, contact **Haleakala National Park,** P.O. Box 369, Makawao, HI 96768 (☎ **808/ 572-4400;** www.nps.gov/hale).

CABINS   It can get really cold and windy down in the valley (see "A Word of Warning about the Weather," above), so try for a cabin. They're warm, protected from the elements, and reasonably priced. Each has 12 padded bunks (but no bedding; bring your own), a table, chairs, cooking utensils, a two-burner propane stove, and a wood-burning stove with firewood (you might also have a few cockroaches). The cabins are spaced so that each one is an easy walk from the other: Holua cabin is on the Halemauu Trail, Kapalaoa cabin on Sliding Sands Trail, and Paliku cabin on the eastern end by the Kaupo Gap. The rates are $40 a night for groups of one to six and $80 a night for groups of 7 to 12. The cabins are so popular that the National Park Service has a lottery system for reservations. Requests for cabins must be made 3 months in advance (be sure to request alternate dates). You can request all three cabins at once; you're limited to no more than two nights in one cabin and no more than three nights within the wilderness per month.

CAMPGROUNDS   If you don't win the cabin lottery, all is not lost, as there are three tent-camping sites that can accommodate you: two in the wilderness, and one just outside at Hosmer Grove. There is no charge for tent camping.

Hosmer Grove, located at 6,800 feet, is a small, open grassy area surrounded by a forest. Trees protect campers from the winds, but nights still get quite cold. Hard to believe, but sometimes there's ice on the ground up here. This is the best place to spend the night in a tent if you want to see the Haleakala sunrise, and you don't have to take a long, grueling hike to get here (it's close to the road). Come up the day before, enjoy the park, take a day hike, and then turn in early. The enclosed-glass summit building opens at sunrise for those who come to greet the dawn—a welcome windbreak. Facilities include a covered pavilion with picnic tables and grills, chemical toilets, and drinking water. No permits are needed at Hosmer Grove, and there's no charge—but you can stay for only three nights in a 30-day period.

The two tent-camping areas inside the volcano are **Holua,** just off Halemauu at 6,920 feet; and **Paliku,** just before the Kaupo Gap at the eastern end of the valley, at 6,380 feet. Facilities at both campgrounds are limited to pit toilets and nonpotable catchment water. Water at Holua is limited, especially in summer. No open fires are allowed inside the volcano, so bring a stove if you plan to cook. Tent camping is restricted to the signed area. No camping is allowed in the horse pasture. The inviting grassy lawn in front of the cabin is *kapu*. Camping is free, but limited to 2 consecutive nights, and no more than 3 nights a month inside the volcano. Permits are issued daily at Park Headquarters on a first-come, first-served basis. Occupancy is limited to 25 people in each campground.

The East Maui Section of the Park at Kipahulu (Near Hana)

In the East Maui section of Haleakala National Park, you can set up at **Oheo Campground,** a first-come, first-served, drive-in campground with tent sites for 100 near the ocean, a few tables, barbecue grills, and chemical toilets. No permit is required, but there's a 3-night limit. No food or drinking water is available, so bring your own. Bring a tent as well—it rains 75 inches a year here. Contact **Kipahulu Ranger Station,** Haleakala National Park, HI 96713 (☎ **808/248-7375;** www.nps.gov/hale).

HIKING FROM THE SUMMIT   If you hike from the crater rim down **Kaupo Gap** to the ocean, more than 20 miles away, you'll pass through climate zones ranging from arctic to tropical. On a clear day, you can see every island except Kauai on the trip down.

APPROACHING KIPAHULU FROM HANA   If you drive to Kipahulu, you'll have to approach it from the Hana Highway, as it's not accessible from the summit. Always check in at the ranger station before you begin your hike; the staff can inform you of current conditions and share their wonderful stories about the history, culture, flora, and fauna of the area.

There are two hikes you can take here. The first is a short, easy half-mile loop along the **Kaloa Point Trail** (Kaloa Point is a windy bluff overlooking **Oheo Gulch**), which leads toward the ocean along pools and waterfalls and back to the ranger station. The clearly marked path leaves the parking area and rambles along the flat, grassy peninsula. Crashing surf and views of the Island of Hawaii are a 5-minute walk from the ranger station. Along the way you'll see the remnants of an ancient fishing shrine, a house site, and a lauhala-thatched building depicting an earlier time. The loop stops at the bridge you drove over when you entered the park; this is the best place for a photo opportunity. The pools are above and below the bridge; the best for swimming are usually above the bridge.

The second hike is for the more hardy. Although just a 4-mile round-trip, the trail is steep and you'll want to stop and swim in the pools, so allow 3 hours. Wear hiking boots, as you'll be climbing over rocks and up steep trails. Take water, snacks, swim gear, and insect repellent (to ward off the swarms of mosquitoes). Always be on the lookout for flash-flood conditions. This walk will pass two magnificent waterfalls, the 181-foot **Makahiku Falls** and the even bigger 400-foot **Waimoku Falls.** The trail starts at the ranger station, where you'll walk uphill for a half mile to a fence overlook at the thundering Makahiku Falls. The tired can turn around here, but the true adventurers will press on. Behind the lookout, the well-worn trail picks up again and goes directly to a pool on the top of the Makahiku Falls. The pool is safe to swim in as long as the waters aren't rising; if they are, get out and head back to the ranger station. Back on the trail, you'll cross a meadow and then a creek, where you'll scramble up the rocky bank and head into a bamboo forest jungle. At the edge of the jungle is another creek, but the trail doesn't cross this one. A few minutes more, and the vertical Waimoku Falls will be in sight.

GUIDED HIKES   The rangers at Kipahulu conduct a 1-mile hike to the **Bamboo Forest** at 9am daily; half-mile hikes or orientation talks are given at noon, 1:30, 2:30, and 3:30pm daily; and a 4-mile round-trip hike to **Waimoku Falls** takes place on Saturday at 9:30am. All programs and hikes begin at the ranger station.

SKYLINE TRAIL, POLIPOLI SPRINGS STATE RECREATION AREA

This is some hike—strenuous but worth every step if you like seeing the big picture. It's 8 miles, all downhill, with a dazzling 100-mile view of the islands dotting the blue Pacific, plus the West Maui Mountains, which seem like a separate island. The trail is located just outside Haleakala National Park at Polipoli Springs National Recreation Area; however, you access it by going through the national park to the summit. The Skyline Trail starts just beyond the Puu Ulaula summit building on the south side of Science City and follows the southwest rift zone of Haleakala from its lunarlike cinder cones to a cool redwood grove. The trail drops 3,800 feet on a 4-hour hike to the recreation area, in the 12,000-acre Kahikinui Forest Reserve. If you'd rather drive, you'll need a four-wheel-drive vehicle to access the trail.

There's a **campground** at the recreation area, at 6,300 feet. No fee or reservations are required, but your stay must be limited to five nights. Tent camping is free, but you'll need a permit. One 10-bunk cabin is available for $45 a night for one to four guests ($5 for each additional guest); it has a cold shower, a gas stove, and no electricity. There is no drinking water available, so bring your own. To reserve, contact the **State Parks Division,** 54 S. High St., Rm. 101, Wailuku, HI 96793 (☎ **808/984-8109** between 8am and 4pm Monday through Friday; www.hawaii.gov).

POLIPOLI STATE PARK

One of the most unusual hiking experiences in the state can be found at Polipoli State Park, part of the 21,000-acre Kula and Kahikinui Forest Reserve on the slope of Haleakala. At Polipoli, it's hard to believe that you're in Hawaii. First of all, it's cold, even in summer, because the loop is up at 5,300 to 6,200 feet. Second, this former forest of native koa, ohia, and mamane trees, which was overlogged in the 1800s, was reforested in the 1930s with introduced species: pine, Monterey cypress, ash, sugi, red adler, redwood, and several varieties of eucalyptus. The result is a cool area, with muted sunlight filtered by towering trees.

The **Polipoli Loop** is an easy, 5-mile hike that takes about 3 hours; dress warmly for it. To get here, take the Haleakala Highway (Hwy. 37) to Keokea and turn right onto Highway 337; after less than a half mile, turn on Waipoli Road, which climbs swiftly. After 10 miles, Waipoli Road ends at the Polipoli State Park campground. The well-marked trailhead is next to the parking lot, near a stand of Monterey cypress; the tree-lined trail offers the best view of the island.

Polipoli Loop is really a network of three trails: Haleakala Ridge, Plum Trail, and Redwood Trail. After a half mile of meandering through groves of eucalyptus, black-wood, swamp mahogany, and hybrid cypress, you'll join the Haleakala Ridge Trail, which, about a mile into the trail, joins with the Plum Trail (named for the plums that ripen in June and July). It passes through massive redwoods and by an old Conservation Corps bunkhouse and a rundown cabin before joining up with the Redwood Trail, which climbs through Mexican pine, tropical ash, Port Orford cedar, and—of course—redwood.

Camping is allowed in the park with a permit from the **Division of State Parks,** 54 S. High St., Rm. 101, Wailuku, HI 96793 (☎ **808/984-8109;** www.hawaii.gov). There's one cabin, available by reservation.

KANAHA BEACH PARK CAMPING

The only Maui County camping facility on the island is Kanaha Beach Park, located next to the Kahului Airport. The county has two separate areas for camping: seven tent sites on the beach and an additional 10 tent sites inland. This well-used park is a favorite of windsurfers, who take advantage of the strong winds that roar across this end of the island. Facilities include a paved parking lot, portable toilets, outdoor show-ers, barbecue grills, and picnic tables. Camping is limited to no more than 3 consec-utive days; the permit fee is $3 per person, per night, and can be obtained from the **Maui County Parks and Recreation Department,** 1580-C Kaahumanu Ave., Wailuku, HI 96793 (☎ **808/243-7389;** www.mauimapp.com). The 17 sites book up quickly; reserve your dates far in advance (the county will accept reservations a year in advance).

WAIANAPANAPA STATE PARK

Tucked in a tropical jungle, on the outskirts of the little coastal town of Hana, is Waianapanapa State Park, a black-sand beach set in an emerald forest.

HANA-WAIANAPANAPA COAST TRAIL   This is an easy, 6-mile hike that takes you back in time. Allow 4 hours to walk along this relatively flat trail, which paral-lels the sea, along lava cliffs and a forest of lauhala trees. The best time of day is in either the early morning or the late evening, when the light on the lava and surf makes for great photos. Midday is the worst time; not only is it hot (lava intensifies the heat), but there's no shade or potable water available. There's no formal trailhead; join the route at any point along the Waianapanapa Campground and go in either direction.

Along the trail, you'll see remains of an ancient *heiau* (temple), stands of lauhala trees, caves, a blowhole, and a remarkable plant, *naupaka,* that flourishes along the beach. Upon close inspection, you'll see that the naupaka has only half-blossoms; according to Hawaiian legend, a similar plant living in the mountains has the other half of the blossoms. One ancient explanation is that the two plants represent never-to-be-reunited lovers: As the story goes, the two lovers bickered so much that the gods, fed up with their incessant quarreling, banished one lover to the mountain and the other to the sea.

CAMPING   Waianapanapa has 12 cabins and a tent campground. Go for the cabins, as it rains torrentially here, sometimes turning the campground into a mud-wrestling arena. If you opt to tent-camp, it's free, but limited to 5 nights in a 30-day period. Permits are available from the **State Parks Division,** 54 S. High St., Rm. 101, Wailuku, HI 96793 (☎ **808/984-8109;** fax 808/989-8111; www.hawaii.gov). Facilities include rest rooms, outdoor showers, drinking water, and picnic tables.

HANA: THE HIKE TO FAGAN'S CROSS

This 3-mile hike to the cross erected in the memory of Hana Ranch and Hotel Hana-Maui founder Paul Fagan offers spectacular views of the Hana coast, particularly at sunset. The uphill trail starts across Hana Highway from the Hotel Hana-Maui. Enter the pastures at your own risk; they're often occupied by glaring bulls with sharp horns and cows with new calves, so beware of the bulls, avoid the nursing cows, and don't wear red. Watch your step as you ascend this steep hill on a Jeep trail across open pastures; you'll be rewarded at the cross with the breathtaking view.

KEANAE ARBORETUM

About 47 miles from Kahului, along the Hana Highway and just after the Keanae YMCA Camp (and just before the turnoff to the Keanae Peninsula), is an easy family walk through the Keanae Arboretum, which is maintained by the State Department of Land and Natural Resources, Division of Forestry and Wildlife. The walk, which is just over 2 miles, passes through a forest with both native and introduced plants. Allow 1 to 2 hours; swimming is available, so you might want to stay longer. Take rain gear and mosquito repellent.

Park at the Keanae Arboretum and pass through the turnstile. Walk along the fairly flat Jeep road to the entrance. For a half mile, you will pass by plants introduced to Hawaii (ornamental timber, pomelo, banana, papaya, hibiscus, and more), all with identifying tags. At the end of this section is a taro patch showing the different varieties that Hawaiians used as their staple crop. After the taro, a 1-mile trail leads through a Hawaiian rain forest. The trail crisscrosses a stream as it meanders through the forest. Our favorite swimming hole is just to the left of the first stream crossing, at about 100 yards.

WAIHEE RIDGE

This strenuous 3- to 4-mile hike, with a 1,500-foot climb, offers spectacular views of the valleys of the West Maui Mountains. Allow 3 to 4 hours for the round-trip hike. Pack a lunch, carry water, and pick a dry day, as this area is very wet. There's a picnic table at the summit with great views.

To get here from Wailuku, turn north on Market Street, which becomes the Kahekilii Highway (Hwy. 340) and passes through Waihee. Go just over $2^{1}/_{2}$ miles from the Waihee Elementary School and look for the turnoff to the Boy Scouts' Camp Maluhia on the left. Turn into the camp and drive nearly a mile to the trailhead on Jeep road. About a third of a mile in, there will be another gate, marking the entrance to the West Maui Forest Reserve. A foot trail, kept in good shape by the State Department of Land and Natural Resources, begins here. The trail climbs to the top of the ridge, offering great views of the various valleys. The trail is marked by a number of switchbacks and can be extremely muddy and wet. In some areas, it's so steep that you have to grab onto the trees and bushes for support. There's temporary relief to this climb after about $1^{1}/_{2}$ miles, when the trail crosses a flat area (which can be so wet that it's impassable). After the swampy area, the trail ascends again for about a mile to **Lanilili Peak,** where a picnic table and magnificent views await.

4 Great Golf

In some circles, Maui is synonymous with golf. The island's world-famous golf courses start at the very northern tip of the island and roll right around to Kaanapali, jumping down to Kihei and Wailea in the south. There are also some lesser-known municipal courses that offer challenging play for less than $100.

Golfers new to Maui should know that it's windy here, especially between 10am and 2pm, when winds of 10 to 15 m.p.h. are the norm. Play two to three clubs up or down to compensate for the wind factor. We also recommend bringing extra balls—the rough is thicker here and the wind will pick your ball up and drop it in very unappealing places (like water hazards).

If your heart is set on playing on a resort course, book at least a week in advance. For the ardent golfer on a tight budget: Play in the afternoon, when discounted twilight rates are in effect. There's no guarantee you'll get 18 holes in, especially in winter when it's dark by 6pm, but you'll have an opportunity to experience these world-famous courses at half the usual fee.

If you don't bring your own, rent clubs from the **Rental Warehouse** (☎ 800/923-4004; www.travelhawaii.com), in Lahaina at 578 Front St., near Prison Street (☎ 808/661-1970), or in Kihei at Azeka Place II, on the mountain side of Kihei Road, near Lipoa Street (☎ 808/875-4050), where top-quality clubs go for $15 a day, not-so-top-quality for $10 a day. **Golf Club Rentals** (☎ 808/665-0800; www.maui.net/~rentgolf) offers custom-built clubs for men, women, and juniors in both right- and left-handed versions. Their rates are just $15 a day and they offer delivery island-wide.

For last-minute and discount tee times, call **Stand-by Golf** (☎ 888/645-BOOK in Hawaii, or 808/874-0600 from the mainland) between 7am and 11pm, Hawaii standard time. Stand-by offers discounted (by 10% to 40%) and guaranteed tee times for same-day or next-day golfing.

CENTRAL MAUI

Waiehu Municipal Golf Course. P.O. Box 507, Wailuku, HI 96793. ☎ **808/244-5934.** From the Kahului Airport, turn right on the Hana Hwy. (Hwy. 36), which becomes Kaahumanu Ave. (Hwy. 32). Turn right at the stoplight at the junction of Waiehu Beach Rd. (Hwy. 340). Go another 1¹/₂ miles, and you'll see the entrance on your right.

This public, ocean-side, par-72 golf course is like playing two different courses: The first nine holes, built in 1930, are set along the dramatic coastline, while the back nine holes, added in 1966, head toward the mountains. It's a fun course that probably won't challenge your handicap. The only hazard here is the wind, which can rip off the ocean and play havoc with your ball. Basically, this is a flat and straight course. The only hole that can raise your blood pressure is the 511-yard, par 5, 4th hole, which is very narrow and very long. To par here, you have to hit a long accurate drive, then another long and accurate fairway drive, and finally a perfect pitch over the hazards to the greens (yeah, right).

Facilities include a snack bar, driving range, practice greens, golf-club rental, and clubhouse. Since this is a public course, the greens fees are low—$26 Monday through Friday, $30 on Saturday, Sunday, and holidays—but getting a tee time is tough.

WEST MAUI

✪ **Kaanapali Courses.** Off Hwy. 30, Kaanapali. ☎ **808/661-3691.** At the first stoplight in Kaanapali, turn onto Kaanapali Pkwy.; the first building on your right is the clubhouse.

Both courses at the Kaanapali Resort offer a challenge to all golfers, from high handi-cappers to near-pros. The par-72, 6,305-yard **North Course** (originally called the Royal Lahaina Golf Course) is a true Robert Trent Jones Jr. design: an abundance of wide bunkers; several long, stretched-out tees; and the largest, most contoured greens on Maui. It has a tricky 18th hole (par 4, 435 yd.) with a water hazard on the approach to the green. The par-72, 6,250-yard **South Course** is an Arthur Jack Snyder design; although shorter than the North Course, it requires more accuracy on the narrow, hilly fairways. It, too, has a water hazard on its final hole, so don't tally up your scorecard until the final putt is sunk. Facilities include a driving range, putting course, and clubhouse with dining. Greens fees are $130, $65 after 2pm (for resort guests, $105, $65 after 2pm); weekday tee times are best.

✪ **Kapalua Resort Courses.** ☎ **877/527-2582.** Off Hwy. 30, Kapalua.

The views from these three championship courses are worth the greens fees alone. The first to open was the **Bay Course** (☎ **808/669-8820**), a par-72, 6,761-yard course inaugurated in 1975. Designed by Arnold Palmer and Ed Seay, this course is a bit for-giving with its wide fairways; the greens, however, are difficult to read. The much-photographed 5th hole overlooks a small ocean cove; even the pros have trouble with this rocky par-3, 205-yard hole.

The par-71, 6,632-yard **Village Course** (☎ **808/669-8830**), another Palmer/Seay design, is the most scenic of the three courses; the hole with the best vista is definitely the 6th, which overlooks a lake with the ocean in the distance. But don't get distracted by the view—the tee is between two rows of Cook pines. The **Plantation Course** (☎ **808/669-8877**), scene of the PGA Kapalua Mercedes Championship, was designed by Ben Crenshaw and Bill Coore. A 6,547-yard, par-73 course on a rolling hillside of the West Maui Mountains, this one is excellent for developing your low shots and precise chipping.

Facilities for the three courses include locker rooms, a driving range, and an excellent restaurant. Greens fees for nonguests are $175 ($110 for guests) and twilight rates are $80 after 2pm at the Village and Bay courses; $200 for nonguests ($120 for guests) and $85 twilight rates after 2pm at the Plantation Course. Weekdays are your best bet for tee times.

SOUTH MAUI

✪ **Makena Courses.** On Makena Alanui Dr., just past the Maui Prince Hotel. ☎ **808/879-3344.**

Here you'll find 36 holes of "Mr. Hawaii Golf" (Robert Trent Jones Jr.) at his best. Add to that spectacular views: Molokini islet looms in the background, humpback whales gambol offshore in winter, and the tropical sunsets are spectacular. This is golf not to be missed; the par-72, 6,876-yard **South Course** has a couple of holes you'll never forget. The view from the par-4 15th hole, which shoots from an elevated tee 183 yards downhill to the Pacific, is magnificent. The 16th hole has a two-tiered green that's blind from the tee 383 yards away (that is, if you make it past the gully off the fairway). The par-72, 6,823-yard **North Course** is more difficult and more spectacular. The 13th hole, located partway up the mountain, has a view that makes most golfers stop and stare. The next hole is even more memorable: a 200-foot drop between tee and green.

Facilities include clubhouse, driving range, two putting greens, pro shop, lockers, and lessons. Beware of crowded conditions on weekends. Greens fees are $85 for Makena Resort guests, $140 for nonguests. Twilight rates start after 2pm and are $60 for both guests and nonguests.

Elleair Maui Golf Club (formerly Silversword Golf Club). 1345 Piilani Hwy. (near the Lipoa St. turnoff), Kihei. ☎ **808/874-0777.**

Sitting in the foothills of Haleakala, just high enough to afford spectacular ocean views from every hole, this course is for golfers who love the views as much as the fairways and greens. It's very forgiving, especially for duffers and high handicappers. Just one caveat: Go in the morning. Not only is it cooler, but, more important, it's less windy. In the afternoon, the winds really pick up, blustering down Haleakala with great gusto. This is a fun course to play, with some challenging holes (the par-5 no. 2 is a virtual minefield of bunkers, and the par-5 no.8 shoots over a swale and then up a hill).

Greens fees are $75, with twilight rates after 2pm of $55 and nine-hole rates after 3:30pm of $35.

✪ **Wailea Courses.** Wailea Alanui Dr. (off Wailea Iki Dr.), Wailea. ☎ **888/328-MAUI** or 808/875-7540.

There are three courses to choose from at Wailea. The **Blue Course,** a par-72, 6,700-yard flat, open course designed by Arthur Jack Snyder and dotted with bunkers and water hazards, is for duffers and pros alike. The wide fairways appeal to beginners, and the undulating terrain makes it a course everyone can enjoy. A little more difficult is the par-72, 7,073-yard championship **Gold Course,** with narrow fairways, several tricky dogleg holes, and the classic Robert Trent Jones Jr. challenges: natural hazards, like lava-rock walls, and native Hawaiian grasses. The **Emerald Course,** originally an Arthur Jack Snyder design, was renovated by Robert Trent Jones Jr. into a more challenging course.

With 54 holes to play, getting a tee time is slightly easier here on weekends than at other resorts, but weekdays are best (the Gold Course is usually the toughest to book). Facilities include a pro shop, a restaurant, locker rooms, and a complete golf training facility. Greens fees are $80 to $145, depending on the season and where you're staying. Twilight rates range from $60 to $80. Special deals are available April through December.

UPCOUNTRY

Pukalani Country Club. 360 Pukalani St., Pukalani. ☎ **808/572-1314.** Take the Hana Hwy. (Hwy. 36) to Haleakala Hwy. (Hwy. 37) to the Pukalani exit; turn right onto Pukalani St. and go 2 blocks.

This cool course at 1,100 feet offers a break from the resorts' high greens fees, and it's really fun to play. The par-72, 6,962-yard course has 19 greens. There's an extra green because the third hole offers golfers two different options: a tough iron shot from the tee (especially into the wind), across a gully (yuck!) to the green; or a shot down the side of the gully across a second green into sand traps below. (Most people choose to shoot down the side of the gully; it's actually easier than shooting across a ravine.) High handicappers will love this course; more experienced players can make it more challenging by playing from the back tees. Facilities include club and shoe rentals, practice areas, lockers, a pro shop, and a restaurant. Greens fees, which include the cart fee, are $55.

5 Biking, Horseback Riding & Other Outdoor Pursuits

BIKING

It's not even close to dawn, but here you are, rubbing your eyes awake, riding in a van up the long, dark road to the top of Maui's sleeping volcano. It's colder than you ever thought possible for a tropical island. The air is thin. You stomp your chilly feet while you wait, sipping hot coffee. Then comes the sun, exploding over the yawning Haleakala Crater, which is big enough to swallow Manhattan whole—it's a mystical moment you won't soon forget, imprinted on a palette of dawn colors. Now you know why Hawaiians named it the House of the Sun. But there's no time to linger: Decked out in your screaming yellow parka, you mount your special steed and test its most important feature, the brakes—because you're about to coast 37 miles down a 10,000-foot volcano.

Cruising down Haleakala, from the lunarlike landscape at the top, past flower farms, pineapple fields, and eucalyptus groves, is quite an experience—and you don't have to be an expert cyclist to do it; you just have to be able to ride a bike. This is a safe, comfortable, no-strain bicycle trip, although it requires some stamina in the colder, wetter months between November and March. Wear layers of warm clothing, as there may be a 30° change in temperature from the top of the mountain to the ocean. Generally, tour groups will not take riders under 12, but younger children can ride along in the van that accompanies the groups, as can pregnant women. The trip usually costs between $100 and $140, which includes hotel pickup, transport to the top, bicycle and safety equipment, and meals.

Maui's oldest downhill company is **Maui Downhill,** 199 Dairy Rd., Kahului, HI 96732 (☎ **800/535-BIKE** or 808/871-2155; e-mail: mauidown@gte.net), which has a sunrise-safari bike tour, including continental breakfast and brunch, starting at $104. Haleakala rides for $140 are offered by **Maui Mountain Chasers** in Makawao (☎ **800/232-6284** or 808/871-6014) and for $115 from **Mountain Riders Bike Tours** in Kahului (☎ **800/706-7700** or 808/242-9739).

For bike excursions on other parts of Maui, contact **Chris' Adventures,** P.O. Box 869, Kula, HI 96790 (☎ **800/224-5344** or 808/871-2453). Chris offers various bike tours, with costs ranging from $49 to $110. We recommend the Waihee-Kahakuloa Coastal Adventure ($59), which involves hiking the Waihee Valley or Ridge and then biking along the spectacular northwestern coast, which feels like old Hawaii.

If you want to venture out on your own, cheap rentals—$10 a day for cruisers and $20 a day for mountain bikes—are available from the **Rental Warehouse** (☎ **800/ 923-4004;** www.travelhawaii.com), in Lahaina at 578 Front St., near Prison Street (☎ **808/661-1970**), and in Kihei at Azeka Place II, on the mountain side of Kihei Road, near Lipoa Street (☎ **808/875-4050**).

For information on bikeways and maps, get a copy of the Maui County Bicycle Map, which has information on road suitability, climate, trade wind, mileage, elevation changes, bike shops, safety tips, and various bicycling routes. The map is available for $7.50 ($6.25 for the map and $1.25 postage), bank checks or money orders only, from: Tri Isle R, C, and D Council, Attn: Bike Map Project, 200 Imi Kala St., Suite 208, Wailuku, HI 96793.

A great book for mountain bikers who want to venture out on their own is John Alford's *Mountain Biking the Hawaiian Islands,* published by Ohana Publishing (www.bikehawaii.com).

HORSEBACK RIDING

Maui offers spectacular adventure rides through rugged ranch lands, into tropical forests, and to remote swimming holes. For a 5^1/2-hour tour on horseback—complete with swimming and lunch—call **Adventure on Horseback,** P.O. Box 1419, Makawao, HI 96768 (☎ **808/242-7445** or 808/572-6211); the cost is $175 per person. The day begins over coffee and pastries, while owner Frank Levinson matches the horses to the riders, in terms of both skill and personality. Frank leads small groups across pastures, through thick rain forests, alongside streams, and up to waterfalls and pools. After a hearty lunch, the group retraces its route back. Frank recently has added a "Maui Horse Whisperer Experience," which includes a seminar where you can learn the language of the horse and have a lot of fun in the process, a morning snack, a big lunch, and an afternoon trail ride (from 9am to 5pm) for just $225 per person. No horse lover should pass this up.

If you're out in Hana, **Oheo Stables,** Kipahulu Ranch, Start Route 1, Box 151 A, on Highway 31 (1 mile past Oheo Gulch), Kipahulu (☎ **808/667-2222;** www.maui.net/~ray/index.html), offers two daily rides through the mountains above Oheo Gulch (Seven Sacred Pools). The best deal is the 10:30am ride ($119), which includes brunch and snacks during the 3-hour adventure (2^1/2 hours in the saddle). The ride ventures into the Haleakala National Park, stopping at scenic spots like the Pipiwai lookout, where you can glimpse the 400-foot Waimoku Falls.

If you enjoy your ride, remember to kiss your horse and tip your guide.

HALEAKALA ON HORSEBACK If you'd like to ride down into Haleakala's crater, contact **Pony Express Tours,** P.O. Box 535, Kula, HI 96790 (☎ **808/ 667-2200** or 808/878-6698; fax 808/878-3581), which offers half-day rides down to the crater floor and back up, from $140 to $175 per person. Shorter 1- and 2-hour rides are also offered at Haleakala Ranch, located on the beautiful lower slopes of the volcano, for $45 and $85. Pony Express provides well-trained horses and experienced guides, and accommodates all riding levels. In order to ride, you must be at least 10 years old, weigh no more than 230 pounds, and wear long pants and closed-toe shoes.

WAY OUT WEST ON MAUI: RANCH RIDES We recommend riding with **Mendes Ranch & Trail Rides,** on Kahekili Highway, 4 miles past Wailuku (☎ **808/ 871-5222**). The 300-acre Mendes Ranch is a real-life working cowboy ranch that has all the essential elements of an earthly paradise—rainbows, waterfalls, palm trees, coral-sand beaches, lagoons, tide pools, a rain forest, and its own volcanic peak. Allan Mendes, a third-generation wrangler, will take you from the edge of the rain forest out to the sea. On the way, you'll cross tree-studded meadows where Texas longhorns sit in the shade like surreal lawn statues, and past a dusty corral where Allan's father, Ernest, a champion roper, may be breaking in a wild horse. All the while, Allan keeps close watch, turning often in his saddle on his pinto, Pride, to make sure that everyone is happy. He points out flora and fauna and fields questions, but generally just lets you soak up Maui's natural splendor in golden silence. The morning ride, which lasts 3 hours and ends with a barbecue back at the corral (the perfect ranch-style lunch after a morning in the saddle), is $130; the 2^1/2-hour afternoon ride is $85, including snacks.

SPELUNKING

Most people come to Maui to get outdoors and soak up some Hawaiian sunshine, but don't miss the opportunity to see how the islands were made by exploring a million-year-old underground lava tube/cave. Chuck and Deborah Thorne of **Maui Cave Adventures,** P.O. Box 40, Hana, HI 96713 (☎ **808/248-7308**), offer several tours of this unique geological feature. After more than 10 years of leading scuba tours through underwater caves around Hawaii, Chuck discovered some caves on land that he wanted to show visitors. When the land surrounding the largest cave on Maui went on the market in 1996, Chuck snapped it up and started his own tour company. He'll take you hiking into enormous subterranean passages of a huge, extinct lava tube with 40-foot ceilings. This is a geology lesson you won't soon forget—Chuck is a long-time student of the science of volcano-speleology and can discuss every little formation in the cave, how it came to be, and what its purpose is. All the equipment you'll need (lights, hard hats, gloves, water bottles) is supplied on the tours, which cost $25 for 50 minutes (no children under 7), $50 for the 2-hour Skylight tour (children must be 9 or older), $100 for 4 hours (no children under 16), and $175 for 6 hours (no children under 18). All tours by appointment only. Wear long pants and closed shoes, and bring your camera.

If you want to combine caving with a tour of Hana, contact **Temptation Tours** (☎ **808/877-8888**), which offers not only a 2-hour cave tour, but also an air-conditioned van tour from your hotel to Hana; the $159 cost includes continental breakfast, beachside picnic lunch, and a stop for a swim.

TENNIS

Maui County has excellent tennis courts located all over the island. All are free and available from daylight to sunset; a few are even lit for night play until 10pm. The courts are available on a first-come, first-served basis; when someone's waiting for a court, please limit your play to no more than 45 minutes. For a complete list of all public tennis courts, contact **Maui County of Parks and Recreation,** 1580-C Kaahumanu Ave., Wailuku, HI 96793 (☎ **808/243-7230**).

Private tennis courts are available at most resorts and hotels on the island. The **Kapalua Tennis Garden and Village Tennis Center,** Kapalua Resort (☎ **808/ 669-5677;** www.kapaluamaui.com), is home to the Kapalua Open, featuring the largest purse in the state. Kapalua also provides matchmaking services for those traveling without a tennis partner. Court rentals are $10 an hour for resort guests, $12 for nonguests. In Wailea, the **Wailea Tennis Club,** 131 Wailea Iki Place, Wailea (☎ **808/ 879-1958**), has 11 Plexi-pave courts. Court rentals are $25 per hour for Wailea resort guests, $30 an hour for players not staying in Wailea.

Seeing the Sights

by Jeanette Foster

After a few days of just relaxing on the beach, the itch to explore the rest of Maui sets in: What's on top of Haleakala, looming in the distance? Is the road to Hana really the tropical jungle everyone raves about? What does the inside of a 19th-century whaling boat look like?

There is far more to the Valley Isle than just sun, sand, and surf. Get out and see for yourself the otherworldly interior of a 10,000-foot volcanic crater; watch endangered sea turtles make their way to nesting sites in a wildlife sanctuary; wander back in time to the days when whalers and missionaries fought for the soul of Lahaina; and feel the energy of a thundering waterfall cascade into a serene mountain pool.

1 By Air, Land & Sea: Guided Island Adventures

Admittedly, the adventures below aren't cheap. However, each one offers such a wonderful opportunity to see Maui from a unique perspective that, depending on your interests, you might make one of them the highlight of your trip—it'll be worth every penny.

FLYING HIGH: HELICOPTER RIDES

Only a helicopter can bring you face-to-face with remote sites like Maui's little-known Wall of Tears, up near the summit of Puu Kukui in the West Maui Mountains. A helicopter ride on Maui isn't a wild ride; it's more like a gentle gee-whiz zip into a seldom-seen Eden. You'll glide through canyons etched with 1,000-foot waterfalls, and over dense rain forests; you'll climb to 10,000 feet, high enough to glimpse the summit of Haleakala, and fly by the dramatic vistas at Molokai.

The first chopper pilots in Hawaii were good ol' boys on their way back from Vietnam—hard-flying, hard-drinking cowboys who cared more about the ride than the scenery. But not anymore. Today, pilots, like the ones at Blue Hawaiian (see below), are an interesting hybrid: part Hawaiian historian, part DJ, part tour guide, and part amusement-ride operator. As you soar through the clouds, absorbing Maui's scenic terrain, you'll learn about the island's flora and fauna, history, and culture.

Among the many helicopter-tour operators on Maui, the best is **Blue Hawaiian,** at Kahului Airport (☎ **800/745-BLUE** or 808/871-8844; www.bluehawaiian.com), which not only takes you on the

Especially for Kids

A Submarine Ride   Atlantis Submarines (☎ 800/548-6262) takes the whole family down into the shallow coastal waters off Lahaina in a real sub. The kids will love seeing all the fish—maybe even a shark!—and you'll stay dry the entire time. See "Going Under: Submarine Rides," below, for details.

The Sugarcane Train   This ride will appeal to small kids as well as train buffs of all ages. A steam engine pulls open passenger cars of the Lahaina/Kaanapali & Pacific Railroad on a 30-minute, 12-mile round-trip through sugarcane fields between Lahaina and Kaanapali. The conductor sings and calls out the landmarks, and along the way, you can see Molokai, Lanai, and the backside of Kaanapali. Tickets are $15 for grownups, $8.50 for kids aged 2 to 12; call ☎ **808/661-0089.**

Star Searches   The stars over Kaanapali shine big and bright because the tropical sky is almost entirely free of both pollutants and the interference of big-city lights. Amateur astronomers can probe the Milky Way, see the rings of Saturn's and Jupiter's moons, and scan the Sea of Tranquillity in a 60-minute star search on the world's first recreational computer-driven telescope. This cosmic adventure takes place every night at the **Hyatt Regency Maui,** 200 Nohea Kai Dr. (☎ **808/661-1234**), at 8, 9, and 10pm. It's $20 for adults and $15 for children 12 and under—a bargain for anyone who's starry-eyed.

Sharks, Stingrays & Starfish   Hawaii's largest aquarium, the **Maui Ocean Center** (☎ 808/875-1962), has a range of sea critters—from tiger sharks to tiny starfish—that are sure to fascinate kids of all ages. At this 5-acre facility in Maalaea, visitors can take a virtual walk from the beach down to the ocean depths via the three dozen tanks, countless exhibits, and 100-foot-long, 600,000-gallon main oceanarium.

A Dragonfly's View   Kids will think this is too much fun to be educational. Don a face mask and get the dizzying perspective of what a dragonfly sees as it flies over a mountain stream, or watch the tiny *oopu* fish climb up a stream at the **Hawaii Nature Center** (☎ 808/244-6500) in beautiful Iao Valley, where you'll find some 30 hands-on, interactive exhibits and displays of Hawaii's natural history.

ride of your life, but also entertains, educates, and leaves you with an experience you'll never forget. Flights vary from 45 minutes to a half-day and range from $105 to $230. A keepsake video of your flight is available for $19.95 (so your friends at home can ooh and aah).

If Blue Hawaiian is booked, try **Sunshine Helicopters** (☎ **800/544-2520** or 808/871-0722; www.sunshinehelicopters.com), which offers a variety of flights from short hops around the West Maui Mountains to island tours. Prices range from $105 to $245.

GOING UNDER: SUBMARINE RIDES

Plunge 100 feet under the sea in a state-of-the-art, high-tech submarine and meet swarms of vibrant tropical fish up close and personal as they flutter through the deep blue waters off Lahaina. **Atlantis Submarines,** 665 Front St., Lahaina, HI 96761 (☎ **800/548-6262** or 808/667-7816), offers trips out of Lahaina Harbor, every hour on the hour from 9am to 1pm. Tickets are $79 for adults and $39 for children under 12 (note that children must be at least 3 feet tall). Allow 2 hours for this underwater adventure.

ECOTOURS

Venture into the lush West Maui Mountains with an experienced guide on one of the **Maui Eco-Adventures** (☎ 877/661-7720 or 808/661-7720; www.ecomaui.com) numerous guided hikes. After a continental breakfast, you'll hike by streams and waterfalls, through native trees and plants, and on to breathtaking vistas. The tour stops for a picnic lunch, swims in secluded pools, and there are memorable photo ops. The 6-hour excursion costs $110 per person; they supply the meals, a fanny pack with bottled water, and rain gear, if necessary. No children under 13 allowed.

About 1,500 years ago, the verdant Kahakuloa Valley was a thriving Hawaiian village. Today, only a few hundred people live in this secluded hamlet, but old Hawaii still lives on here. Explore the valley with **Ekahi Tours** (☎ 888/292-2422 or 808/877-9775). Your guide, a Kahakuloa resident and a Hawaiiana expert, walks you through a taro farm, explains the mystical legends of the valley, and gives you a peek into ancient Hawaii. The Kahakuloa Valley Tour is $65 for adults, $50 for children under 12. It starts at 7am daily and lasts $7^1/_2$ hours. A snack, beverages, and hotel pickup are included in the price.

2 Central Maui

Central Maui isn't exactly tourist central; this is where real people live. You'll most likely land here and head directly to the beach. However, there are a few sights worth checking out if you need a respite from the sun 'n' surf.

KAHULUI

Under the airport flight path, next to Maui's busiest intersection and across from Costco and K-mart in Kahului's new business park, is the most unlikely place: **Kanaha Wildlife Sanctuary,** Haleakala Highway Extension and Hana Highway (☎ 808/984-8100). Look for a parking area off Haleakala Highway Extension (behind the mall, across the Hana Highway from Cutter Automotive), and you'll find a 50-yard trail that meanders along the shore to a shade shelter and lookout. Watch for the sign proclaiming this the permanent home of the endangered black-neck Hawaiian stilt, whose population is now down to between 1,000 and 1,500. Naturalists say this is a good place to see endangered Hawaiian Koloa ducks, stilts, coots, and other migrating shorebirds. For a quieter, more natural-looking wildlife preserve, try the **Kealia Pond National Wildlife Preserve** in Kihei (see "South Maui," later in this chapter).

PUUNENE

This town, located in the middle of the Central Maui plains, is nearly gone. Once a thriving sugar-plantation town with hundreds of homes, a school, a shopping area, and a community center, today Puunene is little more than the sugar mill, a post office, and a museum. The Hawaiian Commercial & Sugar Co., owners of the land and the mill, has slowly phased out the rental plantation housing to open up more land to plant sugar.

Alexander & Baldwin Sugar Museum. Puunene Ave. (Hwy. 350) and Hansen Rd. ☎ **808/871-8058.** Admission $4 adults, $2 children 6–17, free for children 5 and under. Mon–Sat 9:30am–4:30pm.

This former sugar-mill superintendent's home has been converted into a museum that tells the story of sugar in Hawaii. Exhibits explain how sugar is grown, harvested, and milled. An eye-opening display shows how Samuel Alexander and Henry Baldwin managed to acquire huge chunks of land from the Kingdom of Hawaii and how they ruthlessly fought to gain access to water on the other side of the island, making sugarcane an economically viable crop.

WAIKAPU

Across the sugarcane fields from Puunene, and about 3 miles south of Wailuku on the Honoapiilani Highway, lies the tiny, one-street village of Waikapu, which has two attractions that are worth a peek, especially if you're trying to kill time before your flight out.

Relive Maui's past by taking a 40-minute narrated tram ride around fields of pineapple, sugarcane, and papaya trees at **Maui Tropical Plantation,** 1670 Honoapiilani Hwy., Waikapu (☎ **800/451-6805** or 808/244-7643). A shop sells fresh and dried fruit. The working plantation is open daily from 9am to 5pm. Admission is free; the tour is $8.50 for adults and $3.50 for kids 5 to 12.

Marilyn Monroe and Frank Lloyd Wright meet for dinner every night (well, sort of) at the **Waikapu Golf and Country Club,** 2500 Honoapiilani Hwy. (☎ **808/244-2011;** fax 808/242-8089), one of Maui's most unusual buildings. Neither actually visited Maui in real life, but the ghosts of these icons of architecture and glamour live on in this paradise setting. Wright designed the place for a Pennsylvania family in 1949, but it was never actually constructed. In 1957, Marilyn and husband, Arthur Miller, wanted to build the structure in Connecticut, but they separated the following year. When Tokyo billionaire Takeshi Sekiguchi went shopping at Taliesen West for a signature building to adorn his 18-hole golf course, he found the blueprints, and he had Marilyn's Wright House cleverly redesigned as a clubhouse. A horizontal in a vertical landscape, it doesn't quite fit into its setting, but it's still the best-looking building on Maui today. You can walk in and look around at Wright's architecture and the portraits of Marilyn in Monroe's, the restaurant.

WAILUKU

This historic gateway to Iao Valley (see below) is worth a visit, if only for a brief stop at the Bailey House Museum and some terrific shopping (see chapter 8).

Bailey House Museum. 2375-A Main St. ☎ **808/244-3326.** Fax 808/244-3920. Admission $5 adults, $4 seniors, $1 7–12, free for children 6 and under. Mon–Sat 10am–4pm.

Missionary and sugar planter Edward Bailey's 1833 home—an architectural hybrid of stones laid by Hawaiian craftsmen and timbers joined in a display of Yankee ingenuity—is a treasure trove of Hawaiiana. Inside, you'll find an eclectic collection, from precontact artifacts like scary temple images, dog-tooth necklaces, and a rare lei made of tree-snail shells to latter-day relics like Duke Kahanamoku's 1919 redwood surfboard and a koa-wood table given to Pres. Ulysses S. Grant, who had to refuse it because he couldn't accept gifts from foreign countries. There's also a gallery devoted to a few of Bailey's landscapes, painted from 1866 to 1896, which capture on canvas a Maui we can only imagine today.

IAO VALLEY

A couple of miles north of Wailuku, past the Bailey House Museum, where the little plantation houses stop and the road climbs ever higher, Maui's true nature begins to reveal itself. The transition between suburban sprawl and raw nature is so abrupt that most people who drive up into the valley don't realize they're suddenly in a rain forest.

The walls of the canyon begin to close around them, and a 2,250-foot needle pricks gray clouds scudding across the blue sky. After the hot tropic sun, the air is moist and cool, and the shade a welcome comfort. This is Iao Valley, a 6.2-acre state park whose great nature, history, and beauty have been enjoyed by millions of people from around the world for more than a century.

Iao ("Supreme Light") Valley, 10 miles long and encompassing 4,000 acres, is the eroded volcanic caldera of the West Maui Mountains. The head of the Iao Valley is a broad circular amphitheater where four major streams converge into Iao Stream. At the back of the amphitheater is rain-drenched Puu Kukui, the West Maui Mountains' highest point. No other Hawaiian valley lets you go from seacoast to rain forest so easily. This peaceful valley, full of tropical plants, rainbows, waterfalls, swimming holes, and hiking trails, is a place of solitude, reflection, and escape for residents and visitors alike.

From Wailuku, take Main Street, then turn right on Iao Valley Road to the entrance to the state park. The park is open daily from 7am to 7pm. Go early in the morning or late in the afternoon, when the sun's rays slant into the valley and create a mystical atmosphere. You can bring a picnic and spend the day, but be prepared at any time for a tropical cloudburst, which often soaks the valley and swells both waterfalls and streams.

For information, contact **Iao Valley State Park,** State Parks and Recreation, 54 S. High St., Rm. 101, Wailuku, HI 96793 (☎ **808/984-8109;** fax 808/984-8111; www.hawaii.gov). The ✪ **Hawaii Nature Center,** 875 Iao Valley Rd. (☎ **808/ 244-6500;** www.hawaiinaturecenter.org), home of the Iao Valley Nature Center, features hands-on, interactive exhibits and displays relating the story of Hawaiian natural history; it's an important stop for all who want to explore Iao Valley. Hours are daily from 10am to 4pm; admission is $6 for adults and $4 for children 4 to 12, under 4 free.

Two paved walkways loop into the massive green amphitheater, across the bridge of Iao Valley Stream, and along the stream itself. The $^1/_3$-mile loop on a paved trail is an easy walk—you can even take your grandmother on this one. A leisurely stroll will allow you to enjoy lovely views of the Iao Needle and the lush vegetation. Others often proceed beyond the state park border and take two trails deeper into the valley, but the trails enter private land, and NO TRESPASSING signs are posted.

The feature known as **Iao Needle** is an erosional remnant composed of basalt dikes. The phallic rock juts an impressive 2,250 feet above sea level. Youngsters play in **Iao Stream,** a peaceful brook that belies its bloody history. In 1790, King Kamehameha the Great and his men engaged in the bloody battle of Iao Valley to gain control of Maui. When the battle ended, so many bodies blocked Iao Stream that the battle site was named Kepaniwai, or "damning of the waters." An architectural heritage park of Hawaiian, Japanese, Chinese, Filipino, and New England–style houses stands in harmony by Iao Stream at **Kepaniwai Heritage Garden.** This is a good picnic spot, as there are plenty of picnic tables and benches. You can see ferns, banana trees, and other native and exotic plants in the **Iao Valley Botanic Garden** along the stream.

3 Lahaina & West Maui

OLOWALU

Most people drive right by Olowalu, on the Honoapiilani Highway 5 miles south of Lahaina; there's little to mark the spot but a small general store and Chez Paul, an expensive, but excellent, French restaurant. Olowalu ("many hills") was the scene of a bloody massacre in 1790. The Hawaiians, fascinated with iron nails and fittings, stole a skiff from the U.S. ship *Eleanora,* took it back to shore here, and burned it for the iron parts. The captain of the ship, Simon Metcalf, was furious and tricked the Hawaiians into sailing out in their canoes to trade with the ship. As the canoes approached, he mowed them down with his cannons, killing 100 people and wounding many others.

Olowalu has great snorkeling around the **14-mile marker,** where there is a turtle-cleaning station about 50 to 75 yards out from shore. Turtles line up here to have cleaner wrasses (small bony fish) pick small parasites off.

HISTORIC LAHAINA

Located between the waving green sugarcane blanketing the West Maui Mountains and the deep azure ocean offshore, Lahaina stands out as one of the few places in Hawaii that has managed to preserve its 19th-century heritage while still accommodating 20th-century guests.

In ancient times, powerful chiefs and kings ruled this hot, dry ocean-side village. At the turn of the 19th century, after King Kamehameha united the Hawaiian Islands, he made Lahaina the royal capital—which it remained until 1845, when Kamehameha III moved the capital to the larger port of Honolulu.

In the 1840s, the whaling industry was at its peak: Hundreds of ships called into Lahaina every year. The streets were filled with sailors 24 hours a day. Even Herman Melville, who later wrote *Moby Dick,* was among the throngs of whalers in Lahaina.

Just 20 years later, the whaling industry was waning, and sugar had taken over the town. The Pioneer Sugar Mill Co., which still exists today, reigned over Lahaina for the next 100 years.

Today the drunken and derelict whalers who wandered through Lahaina's streets in search of bars, dance halls, and brothels have been replaced by hordes of tourists crowding into the small mile-long main section of town in search of boutiques, art galleries, and chic gourmet eateries. Lahaina's colorful past continues to have a profound influence today. This is no quiet seaside village, but a vibrant, cutting-edge kind of place, filled with a sense of history—but definitely with its mind on the future.

See chapter 6 for details on the various cruises and outfitters operating in Lahaina.

Baldwin Home Museum. 696 Front St. (at Dickenson St.). ☎ **808/661-3262.** Admission $3 adults, $2 seniors, $1 children, $5 family. Daily 10am–4:30pm.

The oldest house in Lahaina, this coral-and-rock structure was built in 1834 by Rev. Dwight Baldwin, a doctor with the fourth company of American missionaries to sail around the Horn to Hawaii. Like many missionaries, he came to Hawaii to do good—and did very well for himself. After 17 years of service, Baldwin was granted 2,600 acres for farming and grazing in Kapalua. His ranch manager experimented with what Hawaiians called *hala-kahiki,* or pineapple, on a 4-acre plot; the rest is history. Open for guided tours, the house looks as though Baldwin had just stepped out for a minute to tend a sick neighbor down the street.

Next door is the **Masters' Reading Room,** Maui's oldest building. This became visiting sea captains' favorite hangout once the missionaries closed down all of Lahaina's grog shops and banned prostitution; but by 1844, once hotels and bars started reopening, it lost its appeal. It's now the headquarters of the **Lahaina Restoration Foundation** (☎ **808/661-3262**), a plucky band of historians who try to keep this town alive and antique at the same time. Stop in and pick up a self-guided walking-tour map. You'll learn the stories of those who lived Lahaina's colorful past, from the missionary doctor who single-handedly kept a cholera epidemic from wiping out Maui's people to the boy king who lived on his very own island.

Lahaina

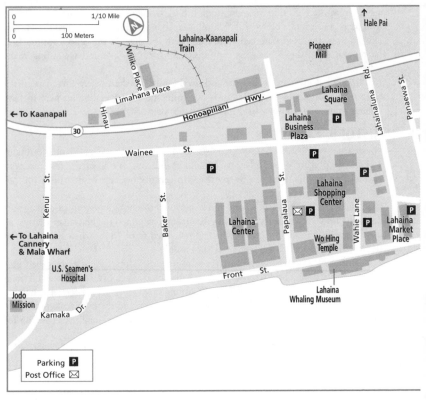

Banyan Tree. At the Courthouse Building, 649 Wharf St.

Of all the banyan trees in Hawaii, this is the biggest, most sheltering of all—so big that you can't get it in your camera's viewfinder. It was only 8 feet tall when it was planted in 1873 by Maui Sheriff William O. Smith to mark the 50th anniversary of Lahaina's first Christian mission; the big old banyan from India is now more than 50 feet tall, has 12 major trunks, and shades ²/₃ acre in the courthouse square.

The Brig *Carthaginian II*. Lahaina Harbor. ☎ **808/661-8527.** Admission $3 adults, $2 seniors, $5 family. Daily 10am–4:30pm.

This authentically restored square-rigged brigantine is an authentic replica of a 19th-century whaling ship, the kind that brought the first missionaries to Hawaii. This floating museum features exhibits on whales and 19th-century whaling life. You won't believe how cramped the living quarters were—they make today's cruise-ship cabins look downright roomy.

Hale Pai. Lahainaluna High School Campus, 980 Lahainaluna Rd. (at the top of the mountain). ☎ **808/661-3262.** Free admission. Mon–Fri by appointment only.

When the missionaries arrived in Hawaii to spread the word of God, they found the Hawaiians had no written language. They quickly rectified the situation by converting the Hawaiian sounds into a written language. They then built the first printing press in order to print educational materials that would assist them on their mission. Hale Pai was the printing house for the Lahainaluna Seminary, the oldest American

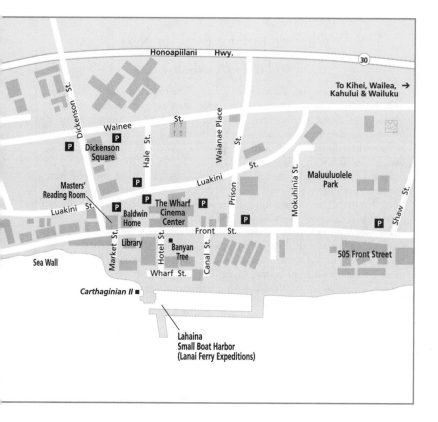

school west of the Rockies. Today Lahainaluna is the public high school for the children of West Maui.

Lahaina Jodo Mission. 12 Ala Moana St. (off Front St., near the Mala Wharf). ☎ **808/ 661-4304.** Free admission. Daily during daylight hours.

This site has long been held sacred. The Hawaiians called it Puunoa Point, which means "the hill freed from taboo." Once a small village named "Mala" ("garden"), Japanese immigrants, who came to Hawaii in 1868 as laborers for the sugarcane plantations, loved to spend time in this peaceful place and eventually built a small wooden temple to worship here. In 1968, on the 100th anniversary of the Japanese in Hawaii, a Great Buddha statue, the largest outside of Japan (some 12 feet high and weighting $3^1/2$ tons) was brought here from Japan. The immaculate grounds also contain a replica of the original wooden temple and 90-foot-tall pagoda.

Lahaina Whaling Museum. At Crazy Shirts, 865 Front St. (near Papalaua St.). ☎ **808/ 661-4775.** Free admission. Daily 9:30am–9pm.

Yankee whalers came to Lahaina to reprovision ships' stores, get drunk, and raise hell with "the girls of old Mowee." Everything was fine and dandy until 1819, when Congregational missionaries arrived and declared the port town "one of the breathing holes of hell." They tried to curb drinking and prostitution, but failed; Lahaina grew ever more lawless until the whaling era came to an end with the discovery of oil in Pennsylvania and the birth of the petroleum industry. That rambunctious era is recalled in this small museum full of art and relics from Lahaina's glory days.

Where to Park for Free—or Next to Free—in Lahaina

Lahaina is the worst place on Maui for parking. The town was created and filled with shops, restaurants, and historic sites before the throngs of tourists (and their cars) invaded. Street parking is hit-or-miss. You can either drive around the block for hours looking for a free place to park on the street or park in one of the nearly 20 parking lots. We've divided the lots into four classes: free; free for customers; discount with validation; and pay.

Free: Of the free lots, the best is the public lot on the south side of Prison Street, between Front and Luakini streets (the lot across the street is pay), which offers 3 hours of free parking. Another free lot is on the corner of Front and Shaw streets, for the users of Maluuluolele Park.

Free for Customers: The three lots on Papalaua Street are all free for customers. The largest is the Lahaina Shopping Center lot, with 2 free hours. Next in size is the Lahaina Center, across the street (which allows 4 hours free, but you must get validation from a store in the Lahaina Center); the smallest is the Lahaina Square lot on Papalaua and Wainee streets, which offers 2 free hours for customers.

Discount with Validation: Customers of the Wharf Cinema Center, located on Front Street, can get a discount by parking at either of the theater's two lots: one on Wainee Street, between Dickenson and Prison streets; and the other on Luakini Street, between Dickenson and Prison streets.

Pay: Lahaina is filled with pay lots ranging from 50¢ for a half hour to all-day parking for $8 to $10. Pay lots on Front Street are located between Papalaua and Lahainaluna streets, on the corner of Dickenson Street, and underground at the 505 Front Street shopping center. Pay lots on Luakini Street are located near the Prison Street intersection and near the Lahainaluna Road intersection. Lahainaluna Road has several pay lots between Wainee and Front streets. Dickenson Street has three pay lots between Wainee and Luakini streets.

Maluuluolele Park. Front and Shaw sts.

At first glance, this Front Street park appears to be only a hot, dry, dusty softball field. But under home plate is the edge of Mokuula, where a royal compound once stood more than 100 years ago, now buried under tons of red dirt and sand. Here, Prince Kauikeaolui, who ascended the throne as King Kamehameha III when he was only 10, lived with the love of his life, his sister Princess Nahienaena. Missionaries took a dim view of incest, which was acceptable to Hawaiian nobles in order to preserve the royal bloodlines. Torn between love for her brother and the new Christian morality, Nahienaena grew despondent and died at the age of 21. King Kamehameha III, who reigned for 29 years—longer than any other Hawaiian monarch—presided over Hawaii as it went from kingdom to constitutional monarchy, and absolute power over the islands began to transfer from island nobles to missionaries, merchants, and sugar planters. Kamehameha died in 1854 at the age of 39. In 1918, his royal compound, containing a mausoleum and artifacts of the kingdom, was demolished and covered with dirt to create a public park. The baseball team from Lahainaluna School now plays games on the site of this royal place, still considered sacred to many Hawaiians.

Wo Hing Temple. Front St. (between Wahie Lane and Papalaua St.). ☎ **808/661-3262.** Admission by donation. Daily 10am–4pm.

The Chinese were among the various immigrants brought to Hawaii to work in the sugarcane fields. In 1909, several Chinese workers formed the Wo Hing society, a chapter of the Chee Kun Tong society, which dates from the 17th century. In 1912, they built this social hall for the Chinese community. Completely restored, the Wo Hing Temple contains displays and artifacts on the history of the Chinese in Lahaina; next door in the old cookhouse is a theater with movies of Hawaii taken by Thomas Edison in 1898 and 1903.

Walking Tour: Historic Lahaina

Back when "there was no God west of the Horn," Lahaina was the capital of Hawaii and the Pacific's wildest port. Today, it's a mild, mollified version of its old self—mostly a hustle-bustle of whale art, timeshares, and "Just Got Lei'd" T-shirts. We're not sure the rowdy whalers would have been pleased. But, if you look hard, you'll still find the historic port town they loved, filled with the kind of history that inspired James Michener to write his best-selling epic novel, *Hawaii.*

Members of the Lahaina Restoration Foundation have worked for three decades to preserve Lahaina's past. They have marked a number of historical sites with brown-and-white markers; below, we've provided explanations of the significance of each site as you walk through Lahaina's historic past.

Getting There: From the Kahului Airport, take the Kuihelani Highway (Hwy. 38) to the intersection of Honoapiilani Highway (Hwy. 30), where you turn left. Follow Honoapiilani Highway to Lahaina and turn left on Lahainaluna Road. When Lahainaluna Road ends, make a left on Front Street. Dickenson Street is a block down (see the box on parking, above).

Start: Front and Dickenson streets.
Finish: Same location.
Time: About an hour.
Best Time: Daylight hours.

Begin your tour at the:

1. **Masters' Reading Room.** This coral-and-stone building looks just as it did in 1834, when Rev. William Richards and Rev. E. Spaulding convinced the whaling-ship captains that they needed a place for the ships' masters and captains, many of whom traveled with their families, to stay while they were ashore. The bottom floor was used as a storage area for the mission; the top floor, from which you could see the ships at anchor in the harbor, was for the visiting ships' officers.

   Next door is the:

2. **Baldwin Home.** Harvard-educated physician Rev. Dwight Baldwin, with his wife of just a few weeks, sailed to Hawaii from New England in 1830. Baldwin was first assigned to a church in Waimea, on the Big Island, and then to Lahaina's Wainee Church in 1838. He and his family lived in this house until 1871. The Baldwin Home and the Masters' Reading Room are the oldest standing buildings in Lahaina, made from thick walls of coral and hand-milled timber. Baldwin also ran his medical office and his missionary activities out of this house. (See the Baldwin Home Museum, above, for information on hours and admission.)

On the other side of the Baldwin Home is the former site of the:

3. **Richards House.** The open field is empty today, but it represents the former home of Lahaina's first Protestant missionary, Rev. William Richards, who had quite an influence on the Kingdom of Hawaii. Richards went on to become the chaplain, teacher, and translator to Kamehameha III. He was also instrumental in drafting Hawaii's constitution and acted as the king's envoy to the United States and England, seeking recognition of Hawaii as an independent nation. After his death in 1847, he was buried in the Wainee Churchyard.

From here, cross Front Street and walk toward the ocean, with the Lahaina Public Library on your right and the green Pioneer Inn on your left, until you see the:

4. **Taro Patch.** The lawn in front of the Lahaina Library was once a taro patch stretching back to the Baldwin Home. The taro plant was a staple of the Hawaiian diet: The root was used to make poi, and the leaves were used in cooking. At one time, Lahaina looked like Venice of the tropics, with streams, ponds, and waterways flooding the taro fields. As the population of the town grew, the water was siphoned off for drinking water.

Walk away from the Lahaina Harbor toward the edge of the lawn, where you'll see the:

5. **Hauola Stone.** Hawaiians believed that certain stones placed in sacred places had the power to heal. Kahunas of medicine used stones like this to help cure illnesses.

Turn around and walk back toward the Pioneer Inn; look for the concrete depression in the ground, which is all that's left of the:

6. **Brick Palace,** begun in 1798 as the first Western-style building in Hawaii. King Kamehameha I had this 20-by-40-foot, two-story brick structure built for his wife, Queen Kaahumanu (who is said to have preferred a grass thatched house nearby). Inside, the walls were constructed of wood and the windows were glazed glass. Kamehameha I lived here from 1801 to 1802, when he was building his war canoe, *Peleleu,* and preparing to invade Kauai. A handmade stone seawall surrounded the palace to protect it from the surf. Amazingly, the building stood for 70 years; in addition to being a royal compound, it was also used as a meeting house, storeroom, and warehouse.

Behind you, dockside of the loading pier of the Lahaina Harbor, is the:

7. **Carthaginian,** a replica of a 19th-century brig, which carried commerce back and forth to Hawaii. It also serves as a museum and exhibit of 19th-century boating and whaling. (For details on hours and fees, see the listing for the Brig *Carthaginian II,* above.)

Directly opposite the Carthaginian is the:

8. **Pioneer Inn,** Lahaina's first hotel and the scene of some wild parties at the turn of the century. George Freeland, of the Royal Canadian Mounted Police, tracked a criminal to Lahaina and then fell in love with the town. He built the hotel in 1901 but soon discovered that Lahaina wasn't the tourist mecca it is today. To make ends meet, Freeland built a movie theater, which was wildly successful. The Pioneer Inn remained the only hotel in all of West Maui until the 1950s. You can stay at this restored building today (see chapter 4).

From the Pioneer Inn, cross Hotel Street and walk along Wharf Street, which borders the harbor. On your left is the:

9. **Banyan Tree,** which has witnessed decades of luaus, dances, concerts, private chats, public rallies, and resting sojourners under its mighty boughs. Hard to believe that this huge tree was once only 8 feet tall. (See complete listing, above.)

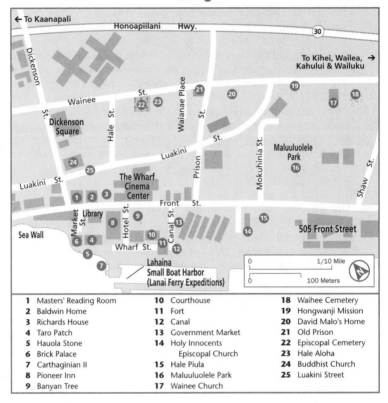

← To Kaanapali

Honoapiilani Hwy.

30

To Kihei, Wailea, →
Kahului & Wailuku

Dickenson St.

Wainee

St.

Waianae Place

21

22 23

20

19

17

18

Dickenson
Square

Hale St.

St.

Luakini

Prison

St.

Mokuhinia St.

Maluuluolele
Park

16

24

25

Luakini   St.

The Wharf
Cinema
Center

1 2 3

Front   St.

Library

8   9

13

15

505 Front Street

6

4

10

14

Shaw St.

Sea Wall

5

Market St.

Hotel St.

Canal St.

11

12

Wharf   St.

7

Lahaina
Small Boat Harbor
(Lanai Ferry Expeditions)

0   1/10 Mile

0   100 Meters

N

1	Masters' Reading Room	10	Courthouse	18	Waihee Cemetery
2	Baldwin Home	11	Fort	19	Hongwanji Mission
3	Richards House	12	Canal	20	David Malo's Home
4	Taro Patch	13	Government Market	21	Old Prison
5	Hauola Stone	14	Holy Innocents	22	Episcopal Cemetery
6	Brick Palace		Episcopal Church	23	Hale Aloha
7	Carthaginian II	15	Hale Piula	24	Buddhist Church
8	Pioneer Inn	16	Maluuluolele Park	25	Luakini Street
9	Banyan Tree	17	Wainee Church		

Continue along Wharf Street; near the edge of the park is the:

10. Courthouse. In 1858, a violent windstorm destroyed about 20 buildings in Lahaina, including Hale Piula, which served as the courthouse and palace of King Kamehameha III. It was rebuilt immediately, using the stones from the previous building; it served not only as courthouse, but also as custom house, post office, tax collector's office, and government offices.

Continue down Wharf Street to Canal Street. On the corner are the remains of the:

11. Fort, which covered an acre and had 20-foot-high walls. In 1830, some whalers fired a few cannonballs into Lahaina in protest of Rev. William Richards's meddling in their affairs. (Richards had convinced Governor Hoapili to create a law forbidding the women of Lahaina from swimming out to greet the whaling ships.) The fort was constructed from 1831 to 1832 with coral blocks taken from the ocean where the Lahaina Harbor sits today. As a further show of strength, cannons were placed along the waterfront, where they remain today. Historical accounts seem to scoff at the "fort," saying it appeared to be more for show than for force. It was later used as a prison, until it was finally torn down in the 1850s; its stones were used for construction of the new prison, Hale Paahao (see no. 21, below).

Cross Canal Street to the:

12. Canal. Unlike Honolulu with its natural deep-water harbor, Lahaina was merely a roadstead with no easy access to the shore. Whalers would anchor in deep water offshore, then board smaller boats (which they used to chase down and harpoon whales) to make the passage over the reef to shore. If the surf were up, coming ashore could be dangerous. In the 1840s, the U.S. consular representative recommended digging a canal from one of the freshwater streams that ran through Lahaina and charging a fee to the whalers who wanted to obtain fresh water. In 1913, the canal was filled in to construct Canal Street.

Next door is the:

13. Government Market. A few years after the Canal was built, the government built a thatched marketplace with stalls for Hawaiians to sell goods to the sailors. Merchants quickly took advantage of this marketplace and erected drinking establishments, grog shops, and other pastimes of interest nearby. Within a few years, this entire area became known as "Rotten Row."

Make a right onto Front Street and continue down the street, past Kamehameha III Elementary School. Across from the park is:

14. Holy Innocents Episcopal Church. When the Episcopal missionaries first came to Lahaina in 1862, they built a church across the street from the current structure. In 1909, the church moved to its present site, which was once a thatched house built for the daughter of King Kamehameha I. The present structure, built in 1927, features unique paintings of a Hawaiian Madonna and endemic birds and plants to Hawaii, executed by DeLos Blackmar in 1940.

Continue down Front Street, and at the next open field look for the white stones by the ocean, marking the former site of:

15. Hale Piula, the "iron-roofed house." In the 1830s, the two-story stone building with a large surrounding courtyard was built for King Kamehameha III. However, the king preferred sleeping in a small thatched hut nearby, so the structure was never really completed. In the 1840s, Kamehameha moved his capital to Honolulu and wasn't using Hale Piula, so it became the local courthouse. The wind storm of 1858, which destroyed the Courthouse on Wharf Street (see no. 10, above), also destroyed the iron-roofed house. The stones from Hale Piula were used to rebuild the Courthouse on Wharf Street.

Continue down Front Street; across from the 505 Front Street complex is:

16. Maluuluolele Park, a sacred spot to Hawaiians and now site of a park and ball field. This used to be a village, Mokuhinia, with a sacred pond that was the home of a *moo* (a spirit in the form of a lizard), which the royal family honored as their personal guardian spirit. In the middle of the pond was a small island, Mokuula, home to Maui's top chiefs. After conquering Maui, Kamehameha I claimed this sacred spot as his own; he and his two sons, Kamehameha II and III, lived here when they were in Lahaina. In 1918, in the spirit of progress, the pond was drained and the ground leveled for a park.

Make a left onto Shaw Street and then another left onto Wainee Street; on the left side, just past the cemetery, is:

17. Wainee Church, the first stone church built in Hawaii (between 1828 and 1832). At one time the church could sit some 3,000 people, albeit tightly packed together, complete with "calabash spittoons" for the tobacco-chewing Hawaiian chiefs and the ship captains. That structure didn't last long—the 1858 wind storm that destroyed several buildings in Lahaina also blew the roof off the original church, knocked over the belfry, and picked up the church's bell and deposited it 100 feet away. The structure was rebuilt, but that too was destroyed—this time by Hawaiians protesting the 1894 overthrow of the monarchy. Again the church was rebuilt, and again it was destroyed—by fire, in 1947. The next incarnation of the church was destroyed by yet another windstorm, in 1951. The current church has been standing since 1953, and so far, so good. Be sure to walk around to the back of the church: The row of palm trees on the ocean side are among the oldest in Lahaina.

Wander next door to the:

18. Waihee Cemetery, the first Christian cemetery in Hawaii. Established in 1823, it tells a fascinating story of old Hawaii, with graves of Hawaiian chiefs, commoners, missionaries and their families (infant mortality was high then), and sailors. Enter this ground with respect, because Hawaiians consider it sacred—many members of the royal family were buried here, including Queen Keopuolani, who was wife of King Kamehameha I, mother of Kings Kamehameha II and III, and the first Hawaiian baptized as a Protestant. Among the other graves are Rev. William Richards (the first missionary in Lahaina) and Princess Nahienaena (sister of Kings Kamehameha II and III).

Continue down Waihee Street to the corner of Luakini Street and the:

19. Hongwanji Mission. The temple was originally built in 1910 by members of Lahaina's Buddhist sect. The current building was constructed in 1927, housing a temple and language school. The public is welcome to attend the New Year's Eve celebration, Buddha's birthday in April (see the calendar in chapter 2), and O Bon Memorial Services in August.

Continue down Wainee Street; just before the intersection with Prison Street, look for the historical marker for:

20. David Malo's Home. Although no longer standing, the house that once stood here was the home of Hawaii's first scholar, philosopher, and well-known author. Educated at Lahainaluna School, his book on ancient Hawaiian culture, *Hawaiian Antiquities,* is considered *the* source on Hawaiiana today. His alma mater celebrates David Malo Day every year in April in recognition of his contributions to Hawaii.

Cross Prison Street; on the corner of Prison and Waihee is the:

21. Old Prison, which the Hawaiians called Hale Paahao ("stuck in irons house"). Sailors who refused to return to their boats at sunset used to be arrested and taken to the old fort (see no. 11, above). In 1851, however, the fort physician told the government that sleeping on the ground at night made the prisoners ill, costing the government quite a bit of money to treat them—so the Kingdom of Hawaii used the prisoners to build a prison from the coral block of the old fort. Most prisoners here had terms of a year or less (those with longer terms were shipped off to Honolulu) and were convicted of crimes like deserting ship, being drunk, or working on Sunday. Today the grounds of the prison have a much more congenial atmosphere, as they are rented out to community groups for parties.

Continue down Waihee Street, just past Waianae Place, to the small:

22. Episcopal Cemetery, which tells another story in Hawaii's history. During the reign of King Kamehameha IV, his wife, Queen Emma, formed close ties with the British Royalty. She encouraged Hawaiians to join the Anglican Church after asking the Archbishop of Canterbury to form a church in Hawaii. This cemetery contains the burial sites of many of those early Anglicans.

Next door is:

23. Hale Aloha. This "house of love" was built in 1858 by Hawaiians in "commemoration of God's causing Lahaina to escape the smallpox, while it desolated Oahu in 1853, carrying off 5,000 to 6,000 of its population." The building served as a church and school until the turn of the century, when it fell into disrepair.

Turn left onto Hale Street and then right onto Luakini Street to the:

24. Buddhist Church. This green, wooden Shingon Buddhist temple is very typical of myriad Buddhist churches that sprang up all over the island when the Japanese laborers were brought to work in the sugarcane fields. Some of the churches were little more than elaborate false "temple" fronts on existing buildings.

On the side of Village Galleries, on the corner of Luakini and Dickenson streets, is the historical marker for:

25. Luakini Street. "Luakini" translates as a heiau or temple where the ruling chiefs prayed and where human sacrifices were made. This street received its unforgettable name after serving as the route for the funeral procession of Princess Harriet Naiehaena, sister of King Kamehameha III. The princess was a victim of the rapid changes in Hawaiian culture. A convert to Protestantism, she had fallen in love with her brother at an early age. Just 20 years earlier, their relationship would have been nurtured in order to preserve the purity of the royal bloodlines. The missionaries, however, frowned on brother and sister marrying. In August 1836, the couple had a son, who only lived a few short hours. Nahienaena never recovered and died in December of that same year (the king was said to mourn her death for years, frequently visiting her grave at the Waihee Cemetery; see no. 18, above). The route of her funeral procession through the breadfruit and koa trees to the cemetery became known as "Luakini," in reference to the gods "sacrificing" the beloved princess.

Turn left on Dickenson and walk down to Front Street, where you'll be back at the starting point.

WINDING DOWN   Ready for some refreshment after your stroll? Head to **Groovy Smoothies,** at 708 Front St. (across the street from the Baldwin Home and from the library; ☎ **808/661-8219**), for tropical smoothies, great espresso, and affordable snacks. Sit in the somewhat funky garden area, or get your drink to go and wander over to the sea wall to watch the surfers.

A WHALE OF A PLACE IN KAANAPALI

Heading north from Lahaina, the next resort area you'll come to is Kaanapali, which boasts a gorgeous stretch of beach. If you haven't seen a real whale yet, go to **Whalers Village,** 2435 Kaanapali Pkwy., a shopping center that has adopted the whale as its mascot. You can't miss it: A huge, almost life-size metal sculpture of a mother whale and two nursing calves greets you. A few more steps, and you're met by the looming, bleached-white bony skeleton of a 40-foot sperm whale; it's pretty impressive.

On the second floor of the mall is the **Whale Center of the Pacific** (☎ **808/661-5992**), a museum celebrating the "Golden Era of Whaling" (1825–60). Harpoons and scrimshaw are on display; the museum has even re-created the cramped quarters of a whaler's seagoing vessel. Open during mall hours, daily from 9:30am to 10pm; admission is free.

THE SCENIC ROUTE FROM WEST MAUI
TO CENTRAL OR UPCOUNTRY MAUI: THE KAHEKILI HIGHWAY

The usual road from West Maui to Wailuku is the Honoapiilani Highway (Hwy. 30), which runs along the coast and then turns inland at Maalaea. But those in search of a back-to-nature driving experience should go the other way, along the **Kahekili**

Highway (Hwy. 340). ("Highway" is a bit of a euphemism for this paved but somewhat precarious narrow road; check your rental-car agreement before you head out. If it is raining or has been raining, skip this road due to mud and rock slides.) It was named after the great chief Kahekili, who built houses from the skulls of his enemies.

You'll start out on the Honoapiilani Highway (Hwy. 30), which becomes the Kahekili Highway (Hwy. 340) after Honokohau, at the northernmost tip of the island. Around this point are twin bays, **Honolua** and **Mokuleia,** which have been designated as Marine Life Conservation Areas (the taking of fish, shells, or anything else is prohibited).

From this point, the quality of the road deteriorates, and you may share the way with roosters, goats, cows, and dogs. The narrow, winding road that weaves along for the next 20 miles, following an ancient Hawaiian coastal footpath, will show you the true wild nature of Maui. If you want views, these are photo opportunities from heaven: steep ravines, rolling pastoral hills, tumbling waterfalls, exploding blowholes, crashing surf, jagged lava coastlines, and a tiny Hawaiian village straight off a postcard.

Just before the 20-mile marker, look for a small turnoff on the mauka side of the road (just before the guardrail starts). Park here and walk across the road, and on your left you'll see a spouting **blow hole.** In winter, this is an excellent spot to look for whales.

About 3 miles farther along the road, you'll come to a wide turnoff providing a great photo op: a view of the jagged coastline down to the crashing surf.

Less than half a mile farther along, just before the 16-mile marker, look for the POHAKU KANI sign, marking the huge, 6-by-6-foot, bell-shaped stone. To "ring" the bell, look on the side facing Kahakuloa for the deep indentations, and strike the stone with another rock.

Along the route, nestled in a crevice between two steep hills, is the picturesque village of **Kahakuloa** ("the tall hau tree"), with a dozen weather-worn houses, a church with a red-tile roof, and vivid green taro patches. From the northern side of the village, you can look back at the great view of Kahakuloa, the dark boulder beach, and the 636-foot Kahakuloa Head rising in the background.

At various points along the drive are artists' studios, nestled into the cliffs and hills. One noteworthy stop is the **Kaukini Gallery,** which features work by more than two dozen local artists, with lots of gifts and crafts to buy in all price ranges. (You may also want to stop here because it has one of the few rest rooms along the drive!)

When you're approaching Wailuku, stop at the **Halekii and Pihanakalani Heiau,** which most visitors rarely see. To get here from Wailuku, turn north from Main Street onto Market Street. Turn right onto Mill Street and follow it until it ends; then make a left on Lower Main Street. Follow Lower Main until it ends at Waiehu Beach Road (Hwy. 340), and turn left. Turn left on Kuhio Street and again at the first left onto Hea Place, and drive through the gates and look for the Hawaii Visitor's Bureau marker.

These two heiau, built in 1240 from stones carried up from the Iao Stream below, sit on a hill with a commanding view of central Maui and Haleakala. Kahekili, the last chief of Maui, lived here. After the bloody battle at Iao Stream, Kamehameha I reportedly came to the temple here to pay homage to the war god, Ku, with a human sacrifice. Halekii ("House of Images") is made of stone walls with a flat grassy top, whereas Pihanakalani ("gathering place of supernatural beings") is a pyramid-shaped mount of stones. If you sit quietly nearby (never walk on any heiau, because that's considered disrespectful), the view alone explains why this spot was chosen.

4 South Maui

MAALAEA

At the bend in the Honopiilani Highway (Hwy. 30), Maalaea Bay runs along the south side of the isthmus between the West Maui Mountains and Haleakala. This is the windiest area on Maui: Trade winds blowing between the two mountains are funneled across the isthmus, and by the time they reach Maalaea, gusts of 25 to 30 miles per hour are not uncommon.

This creates ideal conditions for **windsurfers** out in Maalaea Bay. Surfers are also seen just outside the small boat harbor in Maalaea, which has one of the fastest breaks in the state.

✪ **Maui Ocean Center.** Maalaea Harbor Village, at the triangle between Honoapiilani Hwy. and Maalaea Rd. ☎ **808/875-1962.** www.mauioceancenter.com. Admission $17.50 adults, $12 children 3–12, free for children under 3. Daily 9am–5pm.

This 5-acre facility, which opened in early 1998, houses the largest aquarium in the state and features regional marine life, including one of Hawaii's largest predators: the tiger shark. As you walk past some three dozen tanks and countless exhibits, you'll slowly descend from the "beach" to the deepest part of the ocean, without ever getting wet. Start at the surge pool, where you'll see shallow-water creatures like spiny urchins and cauliflower coral, then move on to the reef tanks, the turtle pool, the "touch" pool (with starfish and sea urchins), and the eagle-ray pool before reaching the star of the show: the 100-foot-long, 600,000-gallon main tank, featuring tiger, gray, and white-tip sharks, as well as tuna, surgeonfish, triggerfish, and numerous other tropicals. The most phenomenal thing about this tank is that the walkway goes right through it—so you'll be surrounded on three sides by marine creatures.

KIHEI

Capt. George Vancouver landed at Kihei in 1778, when it was only a collection of fisherman's grass shacks on the hot, dry, dusty coast (hard to believe, eh?). A **totem pole** stands today where he's believed to have landed, across from Aston Maui Lu Resort, 575 S. Kihei Rd. Vancouver sailed on to what was later known as British Columbia, where a great international city and harbor now bear his name.

West of the junction of Piilani Highway (Hwy. 31) and Mokulele Highway (Hwy. 350) is **Kealia Pond National Wildlife Preserve** (☎ 808/875-1582), a 700-acre U.S. Fish and Wildlife wetland preserve where endangered Hawaiian stilts, coots, and ducks hang out and splash. These ponds work two ways: as bird preserves and as sedimentation basins that keep the coral reefs from silting from runoff. You can take a self-guided tour along a boardwalk dotted with interpretive signs and shade shelters, through sand dunes, and around ponds to Maalaea Harbor. The boardwalk starts at the outlet of Kealia Pond on the ocean side of North Kihei Road (near mile marker 2 on Piilani Hwy.). Among the Hawaiian waterbirds seen here are the black-crowned high heron, Hawaiian coot, Hawaiian duck, and Hawaiian stilt. There are also shorebirds like sanderling, Pacific golden plover, ruddy turnstone, and wandering tattler. From July to December, the hawksbill turtle comes ashore here to lay her eggs.

Kihei has many beaches along its 6-mile coast, plus dozens of restaurants and countless stores in its strip malls. South Kihei Road borders the ocean and goes through the heart of town. If you're bypassing Kihei, take the Piilani Highway (Hwy. 31), which parallels the South Kihei Road, and avoid the hassle of stoplights and traffic.

WAILEA

The dividing line between arid Kihei and artificially green Wailea is distinct. Wailea once had the same kiawe-strewn, dusty landscape as Kihei until Alexander & Baldwin Inc. (of sugarcane fame) began developing a resort here in the 1970s (after piping water from the other side of the island to the desert terrain of Wailea). Today, the manicured 1,450 acres of this affluent resort stand out like an oasis along the normally dry leeward coast.

The best way to explore this golden resort coast is to rise with the sun and head for Wailea's 1 1/2-mile **coastal nature trail,** stretching between the Kea Lani Hotel and the kiawe thicket just beyond the Renaissance Wailea. It's a great morning walk on Maui, a serpentine path that meanders uphill and down past native plants, old Hawaiian habitats, and a billion dollars' worth of luxury hotels. You can pick up the trail at any of the resorts or from clearly marked SHORELINE ACCESS points along the coast. The best time to go is when you first wake up; by midmorning, the coastal trail is too often clogged with joggers, and it grows crowded with beachgoers as the day wears on. As the path crosses several bold black-lava points, it affords new vistas of islands and ocean; benches allow you to pause and contemplate the view across Alalakeiki Channel, which jumps with **whales** in season. Sunset is another good time to hit the trail.

MAKENA

A few miles south of Wailea, the manicured coast turns to wilderness; now you're in Makena ("abundance").

In the 1800s, cattle were driven down the slope from upland ranches, lashed to rafts, and sent into the water to swim to boats that waited to take them to market. Now **Makena Landing** is a beach park with boat-launching facilities, showers, toilets, and picnic tables. It's great for snorkeling and for launching kayaks bound for Pérouse Bay and Ahihi-Kinau preserve.

From the landing, go south on Makena Road; on the right is **Keawali Congregational Church** (☎ 808/879-5557), built in 1855 with walls 3 feet thick. Surrounded by ti leaves, which by Hawaiian custom provides protection, and built of lava rock with coral used as mortar, this Protestant church sits on its own cove with a gold-sand beach. It always attracts a Sunday crowd for its 9:30am Hawaiian-language service. Take some time to wander through the cemetery; you'll see great examples of the old custom of having a ceramic picture of the deceased on the tombstone.

A little farther south on the coast is **La Pérouse Monument,** a pyramid of lava rocks that marks the spot where French explorer Admiral Comte de La Pérouse set foot on Maui in 1786.

The first Westerner to "discover" the island, he described the "burning climate" of the leeward coast, observed several fishing villages near Kihei, and sailed on into oblivion, never to be seen again; some believe he may have been eaten by cannibals in what is now Vanuatu. To get here, drive south past Puu Olai to Ahihi Bay, where the road turns to gravel. Go another 2 miles along the coast to La Pérouse Bay; the monument sits amid a clearing in black lava at the end of the dirt road.

The rocky coastline and sometimes rough seas contribute to the lack of appeal for water activities here; **hiking** opportunities, however, are excellent. Bring plenty of water and sun protection, and wear hiking boots that can withstand walking on lava. From La Pérouse Bay, you can pick up the old King's Highway trail, which at one time circled the island. Walk along the sandy beach at La Pérouse and look for the trail indentation in the lava, which leads down to the lighthouse at the tip of Cape Hanamanioa, about a 3/4-mile round-trip. Or you can continue on the trail as it climbs up the hill for 2 miles, then ventures back toward the ocean, where there are quite a few old Hawaiian home foundations and rocky/coral beaches.

5 House of the Sun: Haleakala National Park

At once forbidding and compelling, ✪ **Haleakala National Park** ("House of the Sun") is Maui's main natural attraction. More than 1.3 million people a year go up the 10,023-foot-high mountain to peer down into the crater of the world's largest dormant volcano. (Haleakala is officially considered to be "active, but not currently erupting," even though it has not rumbled or spewed lava since 1790.) That hole would hold Manhattan: 3,000 feet deep, 7^1/$_2$ miles long by 2^1/$_2$ miles wide, and encompassing 19 square miles.

But there's more to do here than simply stare in a big black hole: Just going up the mountain is an experience in itself. Where else on the planet can you climb from sea level to 10,000 feet in just 37 miles, or a 2-hour drive, without ever leaving the ground? The snaky road passes through big puffy cumulus clouds to offer magnificent views of the isthmus of Maui, the West Maui Mountains, and the Pacific Ocean.

The Hawaiians recognized the mountain as a sacred site. Ancient chants tell of Pele, the volcano goddess, and one of her siblings doing battle on the crater floor where Kawilinau ("Bottomless Pit") now stands. Commoners in ancient Hawaii didn't spend much time here, though. The only people allowed into this sacred area were the kahunas, who took their apprentices to live for periods of time in this intensely spiritual place. Today, New Agers also revere Haleakala as one of the earth's powerful energy points, and even the air force has a not-very-well-explained presence here.

Many drive up to the summit in predawn darkness to watch the **sunrise** over Haleakala; writer Mark Twain called it "the sublimest spectacle" of his life. Others take a trail ride inside the bleak lunar landscape of the wilderness inside the crater, or coast down the 37-mile road from the summit on a bicycle with special brakes (see "Horseback Riding" and "Bicycling," in chapter 6, section 5). Hardy adventurers hike and camp inside the crater's wilderness (see "Hiking & Camping," in chapter 6, section 3). Those bound for the interior bring their survival gear, because the terrain is raw, rugged, and punishing—not unlike the moon. However you choose to experience Haleakala National Park, it will prove memorable—guaranteed.

JUST THE FACTS

Haleakala National Park extends from the summit of Mount Haleakala into the crater, down the volcano's southeast flank to Maui's eastern coast, beyond Hana. There are actually two separate and distinct destinations within the park: **Haleakala Summit** and the **Kipahulu** coast (See "Just Beyond Hana" in section 8, later in this chapter). The summit gets all the publicity, but Kipahulu draws crowds, too—it's lush, green, and tropical, and home to Oheo Gulch (also known as Seven Sacred Pools). No road

Impressions

There are few enough places in the world that belong entirely to themselves. The human passion to carry all things everywhere, so that every place is home, seems well on its way to homogenizing our planet, save for the odd unreachable corner. Haleakala crater is one of those corners.

—Barbara Kingsolver, *The New York Times*

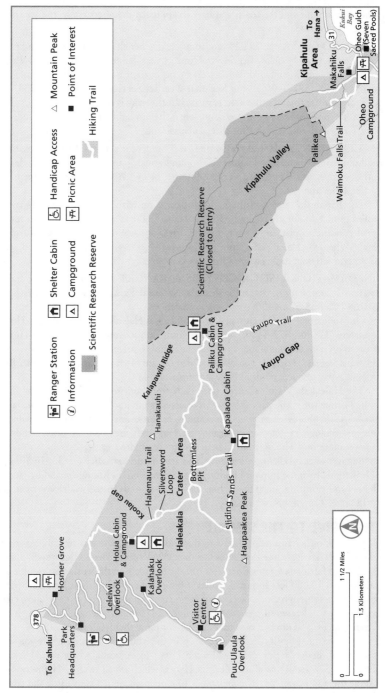

links the summit and the coast; you have to approach them separately, and you need at least a day to see each place.

WHEN TO GO　At the 10,023-foot summit, weather changes fast. With wind chill, temperatures can be below freezing any time of year. Summer can be dry and warm, winters wet, windy, and cold. Before you go, get current weather conditions from the park (☎ 808/572-4400) or the **National Weather Service** (☎ 808/871-5054).

From sunrise to noon, the light is weak, but the view is usually free of clouds. The best time for photos is in the afternoon, when the sun lights the crater and clouds are few. Go on full-moon nights for spectacular viewing.

ACCESS POINTS　**Haleakala Summit** is 37 miles, or about a 2-hour drive, from Kahului. To get here, take Highway 37 to Highway 377 to Highway 378. For details on the drive, see "The Drive to the Summit," below. Pukalani is the last town for water, food, and gas.

The **Kipahulu** section of the national park is on Maui's east end near Hana, 60 miles from Kahului on Highway 36 (the Hana Highway). Due to traffic and rough road conditions, plan on 4 hours for the drive, one way (see "Driving the Road to Hana," below). Hana is the only nearby town for services, water, gas, food, and overnight lodging; some facilities may not be open after dark.

INFORMATION, VISITOR CENTERS & RANGER PROGRAMS　For information before you go, contact **Haleakala National Park,** Box 369, Makawao, HI 96768 (☎ 808/572-4400; www.nps.gov.hale).

One mile from the park entrance, at 7,000 feet, is **Haleakala National Park Headquarters** (☎ 808/572-4400), open daily from 7am to 4pm. You can pick up information on park programs and activities, get camping permits, and, occasionally, see a Hawaiian nene (Hawaiian goose)—one or more are often here to greet visitors. Rest rooms, a pay phone, and drinking water are available.

The **Haleakala Visitor Center,** open daily from sunrise to 3pm, is near the summit, 11 miles from the park entrance. It offers a panoramic view of the volcanic landscape, with photos identifying the various features, and exhibits that explain its history, ecology, geology, and volcanology. Park staff members are often handy to answer questions. The only facilities are rest rooms and water.

Rangers offer excellent, informative, and free **naturalist talks** at 9:30, 10:30, and 11:30am daily in the summit building. For information on **hiking** (including guided hikes) and **camping,** including cabins and campgrounds in the wilderness itself, see "Hiking & Camping," in chapter 6.

THE DRIVE TO THE SUMMIT

If you look on a Maui map, almost in the middle of the part that resembles a torso, there's a black wiggly line that looks like this: WWWWW. That's **Highway 378,** also known as **Haleakala Crater Road**—one of the few roads in the world that climb from sea level to 10,000 feet in just 37 miles. This grand corniche has at least 33 switchbacks; passes through numerous climate zones; goes under, in, and out of clouds; takes you past rare silversword plants and endangered Hawaiian geese sailing through the clear, thin air; and offers a view that extends for more than 100 miles.

Going to the summit takes about 2 hours from Kahului. No matter where you start out, you'll follow Highway 37 (Haleakala Hwy.) to Pukalani, where you'll pick up Highway 377 (which is also Haleakala Hwy.), which you'll take to Highway 378. Along the way, expect fog, rain, and wind. You might encounter stray cattle and downhill bicyclists. Fill up your gas tank before you go—the only gas available is 27 miles below the summit at Pukalani. There are no facilities beyond the ranger stations. Bring your own food and water.

The Legend of the House of the Sun

According to ancient legend, Haleakala got its name from a very clever trick that the demigod Maui pulled on the sun. Maui's mother, the goddess Hina, complained one day that the sun sped across the sky so quickly that her tapa cloth couldn't dry.

Maui, known as a trickster, devised a plan. The next morning, he went to the top of the great mountain and waited for the sun to poke its head above the horizon. Quickly, Maui lassoed the sun, bringing its path across the sky to an abrupt halt.

The sun begged Maui to let go, and Maui said he would on one condition: that the sun slow its trip across the sky to give the island more sunlight. The sun assented. In honor of this agreement, the Hawaiians call the mountain Haleakala, or "House of the Sun."

To this day, the top of Haleakala has about 15 minutes more sunlight than the communities on the coastline below.

Remember, you're entering a high-altitude wilderness area. Some people get dizzy due to the lack of oxygen; you might also suffer lightheadedness, shortness of breath, nausea, or worse: severe headaches, flatulence, and dehydration. People with asthma, pregnant women, heavy smokers, and those with heart conditions should be especially careful in the rarefied air. Bring water and a jacket or a blanket, especially if you go up for sunrise. Or you might want to go up to the summit for sunset instead.

As you go up the slopes the temperate drops about 3° every 1,000 feet, so the temperature at the top can be 30° cooler than it was at sea level. Come prepared with sweaters, jackets, and rain gear.

At the **park entrance,** you'll pay an entrance fee of $10 per car (or $2 for a bicycle). About a mile from the entrance is **Park Headquarters,** where an endangered **nene,** or Hawaiian goose, might greet you with its unique call. With its black face, buff cheeks, and partially webbed feet, the gray-brown bird looks like a small Canada goose with zebra stripes; it brays out "nay-nay" (thus its name), doesn't migrate, and prefers lava beds to lakes. The unusual goose clings to a precarious existence on these alpine slopes. Vast populations of more than 25,000 once inhabited Hawaii, but hunters, pigs, feral cats and dogs, and mongooses preyed on the nene; coupled with habitat destruction, these predators nearly caused its extinction. By 1951, there were only 30 left. Now protected as Hawaii's state bird, the wild nene on Haleakala numbers fewer than 250—and the species remains endangered.

Beyond headquarters are **two scenic overlooks** on the way to the summit. Stop at Leleiwi on the way up and Kalahaku on the way back down, if only to get out, stretch, and get accustomed to the heights. Take a deep breath, look around, and pop your ears. If you feel dizzy or drowsy, or get a sudden headache, consider turning around and going back down.

Leleiwi Overlook is just beyond mile marker 17. From the parking area, a short trail leads you to a panoramic view of the lunar-like crater. When the clouds are low and the sun is in the right place, usually around sunset, you can experience a phenomenon known as the "Specter of the Brocken"—you can see a reflection of your shadow, ringed by a rainbow, in the clouds below. It's an optical illusion caused by a rare combination of sun, shadow, and fog that occurs in only three places on the planet: Haleakala, Scotland, and Germany.

Two miles farther along is **Kalahaku Overlook,** the best place to see a rare **silversword.** You can turn into this overlook only when you are descending from the top. The silversword is the punker of the plant world, its silvery bayonets displaying tiny purple bouquets—like a spacey artichoke with attitude. This botanical wonder proved irresistible to humans, who gathered them in gunnysacks for Chinese potions, for British specimen collections, and just for the sheer thrill of having something so rare. Silverswords grow only in Hawaii, take from 4 to 50 years to bloom, and then, usually between May and October, send up a 1- to 6-foot stalk with a purple bouquet of sunflower-like blooms. They're now very rare, so don't even think about taking one home.

Continue on, and you'll quickly reach the **Haleakala Visitor Center,** which offers spectacular views. You'll feel as if you're at the edge of the earth. But don't turn around here; the actual summit's a little farther on, at **Puu Ulaula Overlook** (also known as Red Hill), the volcano's highest point, where you'll find a mysterious cluster of buildings officially known as Haleakala Observatories, but unofficially called **Science City.** If you do go up for sunrise, the building at Puu Ulaula Overlook, a triangle of glass that serves as a windbreak, is the best viewing spot. After the daily miracle of sunrise— the sun seems to rise out of the vast crater (hence the name "House of the Sun")—you can see all the way across Alenuihaha Channel to the often snowcapped summit of Mauna Kea on the Big Island.

MAKING YOUR DESCENT   Put your car in low gear; that way, you won't suddenly see smoke coming from your brakes, and you won't destroy your brakes by riding them the whole way down.

6 More in Upcountry Maui

Come upcountry and discover a different side of Maui: On the slopes of Haleakala, cowboys, planters, and other country people make their homes in serene, neighborly communities like **Makawao** and **Kula,** a world away from the bustling beach resorts. Even if you can't spare a day or two in the cool upcountry air, there are some sights that are worth a look on your way to or from the crater. Shoppers and gallery hoppers might really want to make the effort; see chapter 8 for details.

On the slopes of Haleakala, Maui's breadbasket has been producing vegetables since the 1800s. In fact, during the gold rush in California, the Hawaiian farmers in Kula shipped so many potatoes that it was nicked named Nu Kaleponi, a sort of pidgin Hawaiian pronunciation of "New California." In the late 1800s, Portuguese and Chinese immigrants, who had fulfilled their labor contracts with the sugarcane companies, moved to this area, drawn by the rural agricultural lifestyle. That lifestyle continues today, among the fancy gentlemen's farms that have sprung up in the past 2 decades. Kula continues to grow the well-known onions, lettuce, tomatoes, carrots, cauliflower, and cabbage. It is also a major source of cut flowers for the state: Most of Hawaii's proteas, as well as nearly all the carnations used in leis, come from Kula.

To experience a bit of the history of Kula, turn off the Kula Highway (Hwy. 37) onto Lower Kula Road. Well before the turnoff, you'll see a white octagonal building with a silver roof, the **Holy Ghost Catholic Church** (☎ 808/878-1091). Hawaii's only eight-sided church, it was built between 1884 and 1897 by Portuguese immigrants. The church resembles something out of Portugal; it's worth a stop to see the hand-carved altar and works of art for the stations of the cross, with inscriptions in Portuguese.

✪ **Kula Botanical Garden.** Hwy. 377, south of Haleakala Crater Rd. (Hwy. 378), ⁷/₁₀ mile from Hwy. 37. ☎ **808/878-1715.** Admission $5 adults, $1 children 6–12. Daily 9am–4pm.

This 5-acre garden offers a good overview of Hawaii's exotic flora in one small, cool place. You can take a self-guided, informative, leisurely stroll through more than 700 native and exotic plants, including three unique collections of orchids, proteas, and bromeliads.

Tedeschi Vineyards and Winery. Off Hwy. 37 (Kula Hwy.); P.O. Box 953, Ulupalakua. ☎ **808/878-6058.** Free tastings. Winery daily 9am–5pm, tours 9:30am–2:30pm.

On the southern shoulder of Haleakala, you'll enter cattle country and the **Ulupalakua Ranch,** more than 20,000 acres once owned by legendary sea captain James Makee, celebrated in the Hawaiian song and dance *Hula O Makee.* Wounded in a Honolulu waterfront brawl in 1843, Captain Makee moved to Maui and bought Ulupalakua. He renamed it Rose Ranch and planted sugar as a cash crop. He grew rich and toasted life until his death, in 1879. Still in operation, the ranch is now home to Maui's only winery, established in 1974 by Napa vintner Emil Tedeschi, who began growing California and European grapes here and producing serious still and sparkling wines, plus a silly wine made of pineapple juice. The rustic grounds are the perfect place for a picnic. Pack a basket before you go, but don't BYOB: There's plenty of great wine to enjoy at Tedeschi. Spread your picnic lunch under the sprawling camphor tree, pop the cork on a Blanc du Blanc, and toast your good fortune in being here.

Across from the winery are the remains of the three smokestacks of the **Makee Sugar Mill,** built in 1878. This is home to Maui artist Reems Mitchell, who carved the mannequins on the front porch of the Ulupakalua Ranch Store: a Filipino with his fighting cock, a cowboy, a farmhand, and a sea captain, all representing the people of Maui's history.

7 Driving the Road to Hana

Top down, sunscreen on, radio tuned to a little Hawaiian music on a Maui morning: It's time to head out to Hana along the Hana Highway (Hwy. 36), a wiggle of a road that runs along Maui's northeastern shore. The drive takes at least 3 hours, but plan to take all day. Going to Hana is about the journey, not the destination.

There are wilder roads and steeper roads and even more dangerous roads, but in all of Hawaii no road is more celebrated than this one. It winds for 50 miles past taro patches, magnificent seascapes, waterfall pools, botanical gardens, and verdant rain forests, and it ends at one of Hawaii's most beautiful tropical places.

The outside world discovered the little village of Hana in 1926, when the narrow coastal road, carved by pickax-wielding convicts, opened with 56 bridges and 600 hairpin switchbacks. The mud-and-gravel road, often subject to landslides and washouts, was paved in 1962, when tourist traffic began to increase; it now sees more than 1,000 cars and dozens of vans a day, according to storekeeper Harry Hasegawa. That equals about 500,000 people a year on this road, which is way too many. Go at the wrong time, and you'll be stuck in a bumper-to-bumper rental-car parade—peak traffic hours are midmorning and midafternoon year-round, especially on weekends.

In the rush to "do" Hana in a day, most visitors spin around town in 10 minutes flat and wonder what all the fuss is about. It takes time to take in Hana, play in the waterfalls, sniff the tropical flowers, hike to bamboo forests, and take in the spectacular scenery; stay overnight if you can, and meander back in a day or two.

However, if you really must do the Hana Highway in a day, go just before sunrise and return after sunset: On a full-moon night, the sea and the waterfalls glow in soft white light, with mysterious shadows appearing in the jungle. And you'll have the road almost to yourself on the way back.

Akamai tips: Forget your mainland road manners. Practice aloha: Give way at the one-lane bridges, wave at oncoming motorists, let the big guys in four-by-fours with pig-hunting dogs in the back have the right of way—it's just common sense, brah. If the guy behind you blinks his lights, let him pass. Oh, yeah, and don't honk your horn—in Hawaii, it's considered rude.

The Road to Hana

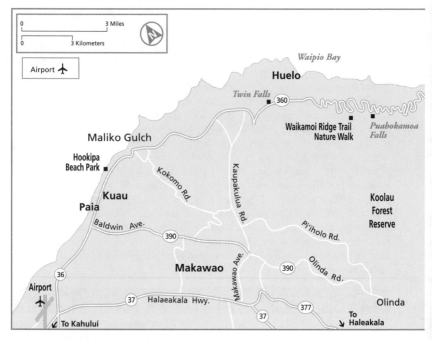

THE JOURNEY BEGINS IN PAIA   Before you even start out, fill up your gas tank. Gas in Paia is very expensive ($2-plus a gallon), and it's the last place for gas until you get to Hana, some 42 miles, 54 bridges, and 600 hairpin turns down the road.

The former plantation village of Paia was once a thriving sugar-mill town. The mill is still here, but the population shifted to Kahului in the 1950s when subdivisions opened there, leaving Paia to shrivel up and die. But the town refused to give up, and it has proven its ability to adapt to the times. Now chic eateries and trendy shops stand next door to the ma-and-pa establishments that have been serving generations of Paia customers.

Plan to be here early, around 7am, when **Charley's,** 142 Hana Hwy. (☎ 808/ 579-9453), opens. Enjoy a big, hearty breakfast for a reasonable price. After your meal, head up Baldwin Avenue; about a half block from the intersection of the Hana Highway and Baldwin Avenue, stop by **Pic-nics,** 30 Baldwin Ave. (☎ 808/ 579-8021), to stock up for a picnic lunch for the road (see chapter 5).

After you leave Paia, just before the bend in the road, you'll pass the Kuau Mart on your left; a small general store, it's the only reminder of the once-thriving sugar plantation community of **Kuau.** The road then bends into an S-turn; in the middle of the S is the entrance to **Mama's Fish House,** depicted by a restored boat with Mama's logo on the side. Just past the truck on the ocean side is the entrance to Mama's parking lot and adjacent small sandy cove in front of the restaurant. Mainly surfers use this treacherous ocean access over very slippery rocks into strong surf, but the beach is a great place to sit and soak up some sun.

WINDSURFING MECCA   A mile from Mama's, just before mile marker 9, is a place known around the world as one of the greatest windsurfing spots on the planet, **Hookipa Beach Park.** Hoopika ("hospitality") is where the top-ranked windsurfers come to test themselves against the forces of nature: thunderous surf and forceful

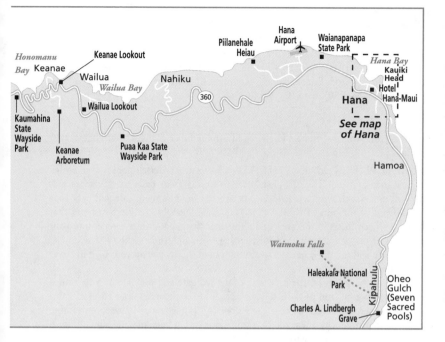

wind. World-championship contests are held here (see "Maui, Molokai & Lanai Calendar of Events," in chapter 2), but on nearly every windy day after noon (the board surfers have the waves in the morning), you can watch dozens of windsurfers twirling and dancing in the wind like colored butterflies. To watch the windsurfers, do not stop on the highway, but go past the park and turn left at the entrance on the far side of the beach. You can either park on the high grassy bluff or drive down to the sandy beach and park alongside the pavilion. The park also has rest rooms, a shower, picnic tables, and a barbecue area.

INTO THE COUNTRY Past Hookipa Beach, the road winds down into **Maliko** ("Budding") **Gulch** at mile marker 10. At the bottom of the gulch, look for the road on your right, which will take you out to **Maliko Bay.** Take the first right, which goes under the bridge and past a rodeo arena (scene of competitions by the Maliko Roping Club in summer) and on to the rocky beach. There are no facilities here except a boat-launch ramp. In the 1940s, Maliko had a thriving community at the mouth of the bay, but its residents rebuilt farther inland after a strong tidal wave wiped it out. The bay may not look that special, but if the surf is up, it's a great place to watch the waves.

Back on the Hana Highway, as you leave Maliko Gulch, you'll see acres of pineapple fields on your left around mile marker 11. Don't be tempted to stop and pick pineapples, because they're the private property of Maui Land & Pineapple Co.; picking is considered stealing. For the next few miles, you'll pass through the rural area of **Haiku,** with banana patches, glimpses of farms, cane grass blowing in the wind, and forests of guava trees, avocados, kukui trees, palms, and Christmas berry. Just before mile marker 15 is the **Maui Grown Market and Deli** (☎ **808/572-1693**), a good stop for drinks or snacks for the ride.

At mile marker 16, the curves begin, one right after another. Slow down and enjoy the view of bucolic rolling hills, mango trees, and vibrant ferns. After mile marker 16,

Travel Tip

If you'd like to know exactly what you're seeing as you head down the road to Hana, we suggest renting a cassette tour, available from **Rental Warehouse** (www.travel-hawaii.com), in Lahaina at 578 Front St., near Prison Street (☎ **808/661-1970**), or in Kihei at Azeka Place II, on the mountain side of Kihei Road near Lipoa Street (☎ **808/875-4050**), for $10 a day.

the road is still called the Hana Highway, but the number changes from Highway 36 to Highway 360, and the mile markers go back to 0.

A GREAT PLUNGE ALONG THE WAY   A dip in a waterfall pool is everybody's tropical-island fantasy. The first great place to stop is **Twin Falls,** at mile marker 2. Just before the wide, concrete bridge, pull over on the mountain side and park (but not in front of the sign that says DO NOT BLOCK DRIVEWAY). Keep in mind that there have been thefts in this area, and remember that a good thief can get into your locked trunk faster than you can with your key. Although there's a NO TRESPASSING sign, no one will mind if you enter; just understand that you're on your own in terms of liability.

Hop over the ladder on the right side of the red gate and walk about 3 to 5 minutes to the waterfall and pool off to your left, or continue on another 10 to 15 minutes to the second, larger waterfall and pool (do not go in if it has been raining recently). If you're lucky, there will be a fruit stand set up here, making fabulous fresh smoothies. What a way to start the trip to Hana.

HIDDEN HUELO   Just before mile marker 4 on a blind curve, look for a double row of mailboxes on the left-hand side by the pay phone. Down the road lies a hidden Hawaii: a Hawaii of an earlier time, where ocean waves pummel soaring lava cliffs and where serenity prevails.

Protruding out of Maui's tumultuous northern coastline, hemmed in by Waipo and Hoalua Bays, is the remote, rural community of **Huelo.** Once, this fertile area supported a population of 75,000; today, only a few hundred live among the scattered homes on this windswept land, where a handful of bed-and-breakfasts and exquisite vacation rentals are known only to a select few travelers (see chapter 4).

The only reason Huelo is even marked is the historic 1853 **Kaulanapueo Church,** which sits in the center of a putting-green–perfect lawn, bordered with hog-wire fence and accessible through a squeaky, metal turnstile. Reminiscent of New England architecture, this coral-and-cement church, topped with a plantation-green steeple and a cloudy gray tin roof, is still in use, although services are held just once or twice a month. It still has the same austere, stark interior of 1853: straight-backed benches, a no-nonsense platform for the minister, and no distractions on the walls to tempt you to not pay attention to the sermon.

Next to the church is a small graveyard, a personal history of this village in concrete and stone. The graves, facing the setting sun and bleached white over the decades, are the community's garden of memories, each well tended and oft visited.

KOOLAU FOREST RESERVE   After Huelo, the vegetation seems lusher, as though Mother Nature had poured Miracle-Gro on everything. This is the edge of the **Koolau Forest Reserve.** Koolau means "windward," and this certainly is one of the greatest examples of a lush windward area: The coastline here gets about 60 to 80 inches of rain a year, and farther up the mountain, the rainfall is 200 to 300 inches a year.

Here you will see 20- to 30-foot-tall guava trees, their branches laden with green (not ripe) and yellow (ripe) fruit. The skin is peeled and the fruit inside of the guava eaten raw, squeezed for juice, or cooked for jams or jellies. Also in this prolific area are mangos, java plums, and avocados the size of softballs. The spiny, long-leafed plants you see are hala trees, which the Hawaiians used for roofing material and for weaving baskets, mats, and even canoe sails.

The very tall trees, up to 200 feet tall, are eucalyptus, brought to Hawaii from Australia to supply the sugarcane mills with power for the wood-burning engines. Unfortunately, in the nearly 100 years since the fast-growing tree was first introduced, it has quickly taken over Hawaiian forests, forcing out native plants and trees.

The 200 to 300 inches of rainfall up the mountain means a waterfall (and one-lane bridge) around nearly every turn in the road from here on out, so drive slowly and be prepared to stop and yield to oncoming cars.

DANGEROUS CURVES   About a half mile after mile marker 6, there's a sharp U-curve in the road, going uphill. The road is practically one lane here, with a brick wall on one side and virtually no maneuvering room. Sound your horn at the start of the U-curve to let approaching cars know you are coming. Take this curve, as well as the few more coming up in the next several miles, very slowly.

Just before mile marker 7 is a forest of waving **bamboo.** The sight is so spectacular that drivers are often tempted to take their eyes off the road. Be very cautious. Wait until just after mile marker 7, at the **Kaaiea** ("breathtaking") **Bridge** and stream below, to pull over and take a closer look at the hand-hewn stone walls. Then turn around to see the vista of bamboo, a photo opportunity that certainly qualifies as "breathtaking."

A GREAT FAMILY HIKE   At mile marker 9, there's a small state wayside area with rest rooms, a pavilion, picnic tables, and a barbecue area. The sign says Koolau Forest Reserve, but the real attraction here is the **Waikamoi Ridge Trail,** an easy 3/4-mile loop that the entire family can do. The start of the trail is just behind the QUIET TREES AT WORK sign. The well-marked trail meanders through eucalyptus (including the unusual paper-bark eucalyptus), ferns, and hala trees.

MORE GREAT PLUNGES   Another great waterfall is **Puohokamoa Falls,** a 30-foot falls that spills into an idyllic pool in a fern-filled amphitheater. Naturalist Ken Schmidt says that its name, loosely translated, means "valley of the chickens bursting into flight"—which is what hot, sweaty hikers look like as they take the plunge.

Park at the bridge at mile marker 11 and take the short walk up the trail, which is lined with stone walls. The spectacular waterfall and deep swimming pool are surrounded by banana trees, colorful heliconias, and sweet-smelling ginger. Bring mosquito repellent. There's a picnic table at the pool.

Back at your car, be sure to check out the view toward the ocean from the bridge: Dozens of varieties of heliconias blanket the valley below.

CAN'T-MISS PHOTO OPPORTUNITIES   Just past mile marker 12 is the **Kaumahina** ("moonrise") **State Wayside Park.** Not only is this a good pit stop (rest rooms are available here) and a wonderful place for a picnic under the tall eucalyptus trees (with tables and barbecue area), but it's also a great vista point. The view of the rugged coastline makes an excellent photo—you can see all the way down to the jutting Keanae Peninsula. Just past the park on the ocean side, there's another scenic turnoff (be careful crossing the oncoming traffic) and great photo opportunity.

Another mile and a couple of bends in the road, and you'll enter the Honomanu Valley ("valley of the bird"), with its beautiful bay. To get down to the **Honomanu Bay County Beach Park,** look for the turnoff on your left, just after mile marker 14, as you begin your ascent up the other side of the valley. The rutted dirt-and-cinder road takes you down to the rocky black-sand beach. There are no facilities here, except for a stone fire pit someone has made in the sand. This is a popular site among surfers and net fishermen. There are strong rip currents offshore, so swimming is best in the stream inland from the ocean. You'll consider the drive down worthwhile as you stand on the beach, well away from the ocean, and turn to look back on the steep cliffs covered with vegetation.

MAUI'S BOTANICAL WORLD Farther along the winding road, between mile markers 16 and 17, is a cluster of bunkhouses composing the YMCA Camp Keanae. A quarter-mile down is the **Keanae Arboretum,** where the region's botany is divided into three parts: native forest; introduced forest; and traditional Hawaiian plants, food, and medicine. You can swim in the pools of Piinaau Stream, or press on along a mile-long trail into Keanae Valley, where a lovely tropical rain forest waits at the end (see "Hiking & Camping," in chapter 6).

KEANAE PENINSULA The old Hawaiian village of **Keanae** stands out against the Pacific like a place time forgot. Here, on an old lava flow graced by an 1860 stone church and swaying palms, is one of the last coastal enclaves of native Hawaiians. They still grow taro in patches and pound it into poi, the staple of the old Hawaiian diet; they still pluck *opihi* (limpet) from tide pools along the jagged coast and cast throw-nets at schools of fish.

The turnoff to the Keanae Peninsula is on the left, just after the arboretum. The road passes by farms and banana bunches as it hugs the peninsula. Where the road bends, there's a small beach where fishermen gather to catch dinner. A quarter-mile farther is the **Kaenae Congregational Church** (☎ **808/248-8040**), built in 1860 of lava rocks and coral mortar, standing out in stark contrast to the green fields surrounding it. Beside the church is a small beach-front park, with false kamani trees against a backdrop of black lava and a roiling turquoise sea.

For an experience in an untouched Hawaii, follow the road until it ends. Park by the white fence and take the short, 5-minute walk along the shoreline over the black lava. Continue along the footpath through the tall California grass to the black rocky beach, separating the freshwater stream, **Pinaau,** which winds back into the Keanae Peninsula, nearly cutting it off from the rest of Maui. This is an excellent place for a picnic and a swim in the cool waters of the stream. There are no facilities here, so be sure you leave no evidence that you were here (carry everything out with you and use rest room facilities before you arrive). As you make your way back, notice the white PVC pipes sticking out of the rocks—they're fishing-pole holders for fishermen, usually hoping to catch ulua.

ANOTHER PHOTO OP: KEANAE LOOKOUT Just past mile marker 17 is a wide spot on the ocean side of the road, where you can see the entire Keanae Peninsula's checkerboard pattern of green taro fields and its ocean boundary etched in black lava. Keanae was the result of a postscript eruption of Haleakala, which flowed through the Koolau Gap and down Keanae Valley and added this geological punctuation to the rugged coastline.

FRUIT & FLOWER STANDS Around mile marker 18, the road widens; you'll start to see numerous small stands selling fruit or flowers. Many of these stands work on the honor system: You leave your money in the basket and select your purchase. We recommend stopping at **Uncle Harry's,** which you'll find just after the Keanae School around mile marker 18. Native Hawaiian Harry Kunihi Mitchell was a legend in his time. An expert in native plants and herbs, he devoted his life to the Hawaiian-rights and nuclear-free movements. Mitchell's family sells a variety of fruit and juices here, Monday through Saturday from 9am to 4pm.

WAILUA   Just after Uncle Harry's, look for the Wailua Road off on the left. This will take you through the hamlet of homes and churches of Wailua, which also contains a shrine depicting what the community calls a "miracle." Behind the pink **St. Gabriel's Church** is the smaller blue-and-white **Coral Miracle Church,** home of the **Our Lady of Fatima Shrine.** According to the story, in 1860, the men of this village were building a church by diving for coral to make the stone. But the coral offshore was in deep water and the men could only come up with a few pieces at a time, making the construction of the church an arduous project. A freak storm hit the area and deposited the coral from the deep on a nearby beach. The Hawaiians gathered what they needed and completed the church. This would make a nice enough miracle story, but there's more—after the church was completed, another freak storm hit the area and swept all the remaining coral on the beach back out to sea.

If you look back at Haleakala from here, on your left you can see the spectacular, near-vertical **Waikani Falls.** On the remainder of the dead-end road is an eclectic collection of old and modern homes. Turning around at the road's end is very difficult, so we suggest you just turn around at the church and head back for the Hana Highway.

Back on the Hana Highway, just before mile marker 19, is the **Wailua Valley State Wayside Park,** on the right side of the road. Climb up the stairs for a view of the Keanae Valley, waterfalls, and Wailua Peninsula. On a really clear day, you can see up the mountain to the Koolau Gap.

For a better view of the Wailua Peninsula, continue down the road about a quarter-mile; on the ocean side, there will be a pull-off area with parking.

PUAA KAA STATE WAYSIDE PARK   You'll hear this park long before you see it, about halfway between mile markers 22 and 23. The sound of waterfalls provides the background music for this small park area with rest rooms, a phone, and a picnic area. There's a well-marked path to the falls and to a swimming hole. Ginger plants are everywhere: Pick some flowers and put them in your car so that you can travel with that sweet smell.

OLD NAHIKU   Just after mile marker 25 is a narrow 3-mile road leading from the highway, at about 1,000 feet elevation, down to sea level—and to the remains of the old Hawaiian community of **Nahiku.** At one time, this was a thriving village of thousands; today, the population has dwindled to fewer than a hundred—including a few Hawaiian families, but mostly extremely wealthy mainland residents who jet in for a few weeks at a time to their luxurious vacation homes. At the turn of the century, this site saw brief commercial activity as home of the Nahiku Rubber Co., the only commercial rubber plantation in the United States. You can still see rubber trees along the Nahiku Road. However, the amount of rainfall, coupled with the damp conditions, could not support the commercial crop; the plantation closed in 1912, and Nahiku was forgotten until the 1980s, when multimillionaires "discovered" the remote and stunningly beautiful area.

At the end of the road, you can see the remains of the old wharf from the rubber-plantation days. Local residents come down here to shoreline fish; there's a small picnic area off to the side. Dolphins are frequently seen in the bay.

HANA AIRPORT   After mile marker 31, a small sign points to the Hana Airport, down Alalele Road on the left. Newly formed commuter airline **Pacific Wings** (☎ **888/575-4546**) offers three flights daily to and from Hana, with connecting flights from Kahului and traveling on to Honolulu. There is no public transportation in Hana. Car rentals are available through **Dollar Rent A Car** (☎ **800/800-4000** or 808/248-8237).

WAIANAPANAPA STATE PARK   At mile marker 32, just on the outskirts of Hana, shiny black-sand Waianapanapa Beach appears like a vivid dream, with bright-green jungle foliage on three sides and cobalt-blue water lapping at its feet. The 120-acre park on an ancient *aa* lava flow includes sea cliffs, lava tubes, arches, and the beach, plus 12 cabins, tent camping, picnic pavilions, rest rooms, showers, drinking water, and hiking trails. If you're interested in staying here, see chapter 4; also see "Beaches" and "Hiking & Camping," in chapter 6.

8   The End of the Road: Heavenly Hana

Green, tropical Hana is a destination all its own, a small coastal village that's probably what you came to Maui in search of.

Here you'll find a rain forest dotted with cascading waterfalls and sparkling blue pools, skirted by red- and black-sand beaches.

Beautiful Hana enjoys more than 90 inches of rain a year—more than enough to keep the scenery lush. Banyans, bamboo, breadfruit trees—everything seems larger than life in this small town, especially the flowers, such as wild ginger and plumeria. Several roadside stands offer exotic blooms for $1 a bunch. Just "put money in box." It's the Hana honor system.

A LOOK AT THE PAST

The Hana coast is rich in Hawaiian history and the scene of many turning points in Hawaiian culture. The ancient chants tell of rulers like the 15th-century **Piilani,** who united the island of Maui and built fish ponds, irrigation fields, paved roads, and the massive **Piilanihale Heiau,** which still stands today. It was Piilani's sons and grandson who finished the heiau and built the first road to Hana from West Maui, not only along the coast, but also up the Kaupo Gap and through the Haleakala Crater.

In 1849, the cantankerous sea captain **George Wilfong** brought commerce to this isolated village when he started the first sugar plantation on some 60 acres. Because his harsh personality and set demands for plantation work did not sit well with the Hawaiians, Wilfong brought in the first Chinese immigrants to work his fields.

In 1864, two Danish brothers, **August and Oscar Unna,** contributed to the growth of the local sugar industry when they established the Hana Plantation. Four years later, they brought in Japanese immigrants to labor in the fields.

By the turn of the century, sugar wasn't the only crop booming in Hana (there were some six plantations in the area): Rubber was being commercially grown in Nahiku, wheat in Kaupo, pineapple in Kipahulu, and tobacco in Ulupalakua.

In the 1920s and 1930s, several self-sufficient towns lined the coast, each with its own general store, school, and churches; some had movie theaters as well. Hana has all of the above plus some 15 stores, a pool hall, and several restaurants.

We can only guess what those towns would have been like today if tragedy hadn't struck. On April 1, 1946, a huge tidal wave hit the state. The damage along the Hana coast was catastrophic: The Keanae Peninsula was swept clear (only the stone church remained), Hamoa was totally wiped out, and entire villages completely disappeared.

After World War II, the labor movement became a powerful force in Hawaii. **C. Brewer,** owner of the largest sugar plantation in Hana, decided to shut down his operation instead of fighting the labor union. The closure of the plantation meant not only the loss of thousands of jobs, but also the loss of plantation-supplied homes and the entire plantation lifestyle. Thankfully, **Paul I. Fagan,** an entrepreneur from San

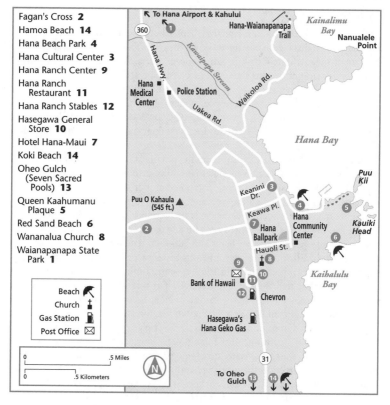

Fagan's Cross **2**
Hamoa Beach **14**
Hana Beach Park **4**
Hana Cultural Center **3**
Hana Ranch Center **9**
Hana Ranch Restaurant **11**
Hana Ranch Stables **12**
Hasegawa General Store **10**
Hotel Hana-Maui **7**
Koki Beach **14**
Oheo Gulch (Seven Sacred Pools) **13**
Queen Kaahumanu Plaque **5**
Red Sand Beach **6**
Wananalua Church **8**
Waianapanapa State Park **1**

Beach
Church
Gas Station
Post Office

0 _____ .5 Miles
0 _____ .5 Kilometers

To Hana Airport & Kahului
Hana-Waianapanapa Trail
360
Kainalimu Bay
Nanualele Point
Hana Hwy
Kawaipapa Stream
Waikoloa Rd.
Hana Medical Center
Police Station
Uakea Rd.
Hana Bay
Puu Kii
Puu O Kahaula (545 ft.)
Keanini Dr.
Keawa Pl.
Hana Community Center
Kauiki Head
Hana Ballpark
Hauoli St.
Bank of Hawaii
Chevron
Hasegawa's Hana Geko Gas
31
Kaihalulu Bay
To Oheo Gulch

Francisco who had purchased the Hana Sugar Co. from the Unna Brothers in the 1930s, became the town's guardian angel.

Fagan wanted to retire here, so he focused his business acumen on the tiny town with big problems. Recognizing that sugar in isolated Hana was no longer economically feasible, he looked at the community and saw other opportunities. He bought 14,000 acres of land in Hana, stripped it of sugarcane, planted grass, and shipped in cattle from his ranch on Molokai.

Next, he did something that was years ahead of his time: He thought tourism might have a future in Hana, so he established an inn in 1946 that later became the **Hotel Hana-Maui.** Fagan also pulled off a public-relations coup: He brought the entire San Francisco Seals baseball team (which he happened to own) to Hana for spring training, and, more important, he brought out the sportswriters as well. The writers loved Hana and wrote glowing reports about the town; one even gave the town a nickname that stuck: "Heavenly Hana."

In 1962, the state paved the Hana Highway. By the 1970s, tourists had not only "discovered" Maui, but they also were willing to make the long trek out to Hana.

The biggest change to the local lifestyle came in December 1977, when television finally arrived—after a local cable operator spent 6 months laying cable over cinder cones, mountain streams, and cavernous gulches from one side of the island to the other. Some 125 homes tuned in to the tube—and the rural Hawaiian community was never the same. Today, Hana is inhabited by 2,500 people, many part Hawaiian.

SEEING THE SIGHTS

Most visitors will zip through Hana, perhaps taking a quick look out their car windows at a few sights before buzzing on down the road. They might think they've "seen" Hana, but they definitely haven't "experienced" Hana. Allow at least 2 or 3 days to really let this land of legends show you its beauty and serenity.

As you enter Hana, the road splits about a half mile past mile marker 33, at the police station. Both roads will take you to Hana, but the lower road, Uakea Road, is more scenic. Just before you get to Hana Bay, you'll see the old wood-frame **Hana District Police Station and Courthouse.** Next door is the **Hana Museum Cultural Center,** on Uakea Road (☎ **808/248-8622;** fax 808/248-8620; www.planet-hawaii.com/hana), open daily from 10am to 4pm (most of the time). This small building has an excellent collection of Hawaiian quilts, artifacts, books, and photos. Also on the grounds are Kauhala O Hana, composed of four *hale* (houses) for living, meeting, cooking, and canoe building or canoe storage.

Catercorner from the cultural center is the entrance to **Hana Bay.** You can drive right down to the pier and park. There are rest rooms, showers, picnic tables, barbecue areas, and even a snack bar here. The 386-foot, red-faced cinder cone beside the bay is **Kauiki Hill,** the scene of numerous fierce battles in ancient Hawaii and the birthplace of Queen Kaahumanu in 1768. A short, 5-minute walk will take you to the spot. Look for the trail along the hill on the wharf side, and follow the path through the ironwood trees; the lighthouse on the point will come into view, and you'll see pocket beaches of red cinder below. Grab onto the ironwood trees for support, because the trail has eroded in some areas. This is a perfect place for a secluded picnic, or you can continue on the path out to the lighthouse. To get to the lighthouse, which sits on a small island, watch the water for about 10 minutes to get a sense of how often and from which direction the waves are coming. Between wave sets, either swim or wade in the shallow, sandy bottom channel or hop across the rocks to the island.

To get to the center of town, leave Hana Bay, cross Uakea Road, and drive up Keawa Place; turn left on Hana Highway, and on the corner will be the **Hotel Hana-Maui,** the once-luxurious hotel established by Paul Fagan in 1946. It has been neglected of late, but new management has taken over, and we're hoping this historic hotel gets the care and maintenance it deserves. On the green hills above Hotel Hana-Maui stands a 30-foot-high white cross made of lava rock. Citizens erected the cross in memory of Paul Fagan, who founded the Hana Ranch as well as the hotel, and helped keep the town alive. The hike up to **Fagan's Cross** provides a gorgeous view of the Hana coast, especially at sunset, when Fagan himself liked to climb this hill. See "Hiking & Camping," in chapter 6, for details.

Back on the Hana Highway, just past Hauoli Road, is the majestic **Wananalua Congregation Church.** It's on the National Historic Register not only because of its age (it was built from 1838 to 1842 from coral stones), but also because of its location, atop an old Hawaiian heiau.

Just past the church on the right side of the Hana Highway is the turnoff to the **Hana Ranch Center,** the commercial center for Hana, with a post office, bank, general store, the Hana Ranch Stables, and a restaurant and snack bar (see chapter 5). But the real shopping experience is across the Hana Highway at the **Hasegawa General Store,** a Maui institution (see chapter 8), which carries oodles of merchandise from soda and fine French wines to fishing line to name-brand clothing, plus everything you need for a picnic or a gourmet meal. This is also the place to find out what's going on in Hana: The bulletin board at the entrance has fliers and handwritten notes advertising everything from fund-raising activities to classes to community-wide activities. You cannot make a trip to Hana without a stop at this unique store.

If you need gas before heading back, note your gas tank, **Chevron Service Station** sits on the right side of the Hana Highway as you leave town.

OUTDOOR PURSUITS

Most day-trippers to Hana can't imagine what there is to do in this tiny community. The answer is: everything. One of the best areas on Maui for ocean activities, it also boasts a wealth of nature hikes, remote places to explore on horseback, waterfalls to discover, and even lava tube caves to investigate.

For more information on the lava tubes, see **Maui Cave Adventures** (☎ 808/ **248-7308**) on page 172. For details on horseback riding, see **Oheo Stables** (☎ 808/ **667-2222**) on page 172. If you're a tennis player, you can take advantage of the free public courts located next to the Hotel Hana-Maui, available on a first-come, first-served basis.

BEACHES & OCEAN ACTIVITIES

Hana's beaches come in numerous varieties: white, black, gray, or red sand; perfectly shaped coves, crescents, or long stretches; and excellent for just about every kind of ocean activity you can think of. Call **Hana-Maui Ocean Activities** (☎ 808/ **248-7711**) if you'd like to snorkel or kayak (see "Ocean Kayaking" under "Hitting the Water," in chapter 6), or venture out on your own at our favorite beaches:

HANA   The waters in the Hana Bay are calm most of the time and great for swimming. There's excellent snorkeling and diving by the lighthouse. Strong currents can run through here, so don't venture farther than the lighthouse. See Hana Bay, above, for more details on the facilities and hikes here.

RED SAND BEACH   The Hawaiian name for this beach is Kaihalulu Beach, which means "roaring sea," and it's easy to understand why: The beach is as red as a Ferrari at a five-alarm fire. It's truly a sight to see. The beach is on the ocean side of Kauiki Hill, just south of Hana Bay, in a wild, natural setting on a pocket cove, where the volcanic cinder cone lost its seaward wall to erosion and spilled red cinders everywhere to create the red sands. Before you put on your bathing suit, there are two things to know about this beach: You have to trespass to get here (trespassing is against the law and you could face charges), and nudity (also illegal in Hawaii—arrests have been made) is common here.

To reach the beach, put on solid walking shoes (no flip-flops) and walk south on Uakea Road, past Haoli Street and the Hotel Hana-Maui, to the parking lot for the hotel's Sea Ranch Cottages. Turn left and cross the open field next to the Hana Community Center. Look for the dirt trail and follow it to the huge ironwood tree, where you turn right (do not go ahead to the old Japanese cemetery). If it's wet, do not attempt to go down the treacherous trail. Use the ironwood trees to maintain your balance as you follow the ever-eroding cinder footpath a short distance along the shoreline, down the narrow cliff trail. The trail suddenly turns the corner, and into view comes the burnt-red beach, set off by the turquoise waters, black lava, and vivid green ironwood trees.

The lava outcropping protects the bay and makes it safe for swimming. Snorkeling is excellent and there's a natural whirlpool area on the Hana Bay side of the cove. Stay away from the surge area where the ocean enters the cove.

KOKI BEACH   One of the best surfing and boogie-boarding beaches on the Hana Coast lies just a couple of miles from the Hasegawa General Store in the Oheo Gulch direction. There is a very strong rip current here, so unless it is dead calm and you are a strong swimmer, do not attempt swimming here. In fact, a sign on the emergency call box, installed after a drowning in 1996, warns of the strong currents. It's a great place, though, to sit on the white sand and watch the surfers. The only facility is a big parking area. To get here, drive toward Oheo Gulch from Hana, where Highway 36 changes to Highway 31. About 1¹/₂ miles outside of Hana, turn left at Haneoo Road.

HAMOA BEACH For one of Hana's best beaches—great for swimming, boogie boarding, and lying out—continue another half mile down the Haneoo Road loop to Hamoa Beach. There is easy access from the road down to the sandy beach, and facilities include a small rest room and an outdoor shower. The large pavilion and beach accessories are for the guests of the Hotel Hana-Maui.

WAIOKA POND Locally, this swimming hole in a series of waterfalls and pools is called Venus Pool, and the rumor is that in ancient Hawaii, only royalty were allowed to use this exquisite site. The freshwater swimming area is a great place to spend a secluded day. Only two warnings here: Don't go to the pond if it has been raining (flash floods), and don't go near the surf at the ocean end of the stream (strong undertow). To get here, park your car well off the Hana Highway at mile marker 48, before the bridge. Hop over the fence on the ocean side of the bridge, and follow the well-worn footpath that parallels the stream. At the stream, turn to your right to take the path down to the smooth rocks above the stream. There's a huge pond just off the white-rock waterfall with a little island you can swim to in the middle.

HIKING

Hana is woven with hiking trails along the shoreline, through the rain forest, and up in the mountains. See "Hiking & Camping," in chapter 6, for a discussion of hiking in Waianapanapa and up to Fagan's Cross.

Another excellent hike leads you to **Blue Pool** and **Piilanihale Heiau.** This easy, 3-mile round-trip takes you to a freshwater, ocean-side waterfall and swimming pool at the halfway point. On the way back, you can tour a tropical botanical garden and see the largest heiau in the state. The hike is on a jeep trail with some climbing over boulders, so wear good hiking boots or tennis shoes (no flip-flops) and bring a swimsuit and mosquito repellent. Go in the morning, when the sun lights up the ocean-side pool, and you'll have plenty of time for a picnic lunch before seeing the garden and heiau in the afternoon.

Turn toward the ocean on Ulaino Road, by mile marker 31. Drive down the paved road (which turns into a dirt road but is still drivable) to the first stream (about 1¹/₂ miles). If the stream is flooded, turn around and go back. If you can forge the stream, cross it and park on the right side of the road by the huge breadfruit trees. The trees are part of the 122-acre **Kahanu Garden** (☎ **808/248-8912**), owned and operated by the National Tropical Botanical Garden (www.ntbg.org), which also has two gardens on Kauai. Call before you go to reserve a spot on the guided tours of the garden and heiau. Tours (limited to 15) are given Monday through Friday at 11am and 1pm, $10 for adults, free for children 12 and under.

After you park your car, walk down the Jeep road that parallels the Kahanu Gardens. You'll have to forge two more streams before the road ends at the beach. Cross the rock-and-gravel beach. If it has been dry, you can just walk along the shoreline. If there has been rain, you will need to cross over the big boulders in the stream. Continue walking down the beach to the 100-foot waterfall on your left with its deep freshwater pool, known locally as **Blue Pool.** After a dip in the bracing spring water, you can sun yourself and eat a picnic lunch on the large boulders.

If you've made reservations for the tour of Kahanu Garden, be back at your car before the 11am or 1pm tour begins. The tour offers a history of Hawaii through a discussion of its native plants, plus the history of the Piilanihale Heiau and a chance to see the rugged coastline of this remote area. The 122 acres encompass plant collections from the Pacific Islands, concentrating on plants of value to the people of Polynesia, Micronesia, and Melanesia. Fringed by a vast native pandanus forest, Kahanu Garden contains the largest known collection of breadfruit cultivars. This collection serves as a germ plasm repository for this important South Pacific food crop, housing cultivars from more than 17 Pacific Island groups and Indonesia, the Philippines, and the Seychelles.

The real draw here is the **Piilanihale Heiau** ("House of Piilani," one of Maui's greatest chiefs—see "A Look at the Past," above). Believed to be the largest in the state, it measures 340 feet by 415 feet, and it was built in a unique terrace design not seen anywhere else in Hawaii. The walls are some 50 feet tall and 8 to 10 feet thick. Historians believe that Piilani's two sons and his grandson built the mammoth temple, which was dedicated to war, sometime in the 1500s.

JUST BEYOND HANA
TROPICAL HALEAKALA: OHEO GULCH AT KIPAHULU

If you're thinking about heading out to the so-called Seven Sacred Pools, out past Hana at the Kipahulu end of Haleakala National Park, let's clear this up right now: There are more than seven pools—about 24, actually—and *all* water in Hawaii is considered sacred. It's all a PR scam that has spun out of control into contemporary myth. Folks here call the attraction by its rightful name, **Oheo Gulch,** and visitors sometimes refer to it as Kipahulu, which is actually the name of the area where Oheo Gulch is located. No matter what you call it, it's a beautiful sight. The dazzling series of waterfall pools and cataracts cascading into the sea is so popular that it now has its own roadside parking lot.

Even though Oheo is part of Haleakala National Park, you cannot drive here from the summit. Even hiking from Halekala to Oheo is tricky: The access trail out of Haleakala is down Kaupo Gap, which ends at the ocean, a good 6 miles down the coast from Oheo. To drive to Oheo, head for Hana, some 60 miles from Kahului on the Hana Highway (Hwy. 36). Oheo is about 30 to 50 minutes beyond Hana, along Highway 31. The Highway 31 bridge passes over pools near the ocean; the other pools, plus magnificent 400-foot Waimoku falls, are reachable via an often-muddy but rewarding, hour-long uphill hike (see "Hiking & Camping," in chapter 6). Expect showers on the Kipahulu coast.

The **Kipahulu Ranger Station** (☎ **808/248-7375**) is staffed from 9am to 5pm daily. Rest rooms are available, but no drinking water. Kipahulu rangers offer safety information, exhibits, books, and a variety of walks and hikes year-round; check at the station for current activities.

There are a number of hikes in the park, and tent camping is allowed. See "Hiking & Camping," in chapter 6, for details.

Check with the Haleakala Park rangers before hiking up to or swimming in the pools, and always keep one eye on the water in the streams; the sky can be sunny near the coast, but flood waters travel 6 miles down from 8,000 acres of Kipahulu Valley and can rise 4 feet in less than 10 minutes.

LINDBERGH'S GRAVE

A mile past Oheo Gulch on the ocean side of the road is **Lindbergh's Grave.** First to fly across the Atlantic Ocean, Charles A. Lindbergh (1902–74) found peace in the Pacific; he settled in Hana, where he died of cancer in 1974. The famous aviator is buried under river stones in a seaside graveyard behind the 1857 **Palapala Hoomau Congregational Church,** where his tombstone is engraved with his favorite words from the 139th Psalm: "If I take the wings of the morning and dwell in the uttermost parts of the sea. . . ."

Even Farther Around the Bend

Those of you who are continuing on around Maui to the fishing village of **Kaupo** and beyond should be warned that Kaupo Road, or Old Piilani Highway (Hwy. 31), is rough and unpaved in parts, often full of potholes and ruts. About 2¹/₂ miles past Oheo Gulch, the pavement ends for about 5 miles—5 very rough miles as the narrow road becomes one lane around blind bends hugging the ocean cliffs, wandering in and out of valleys with sharp rock walls lining the single-car road. You may encounter wild pigs and stray cows. There are no phones or services until you reach **Ulupalakua Ranch** (see "More in Upcountry Maui," above), where there's a winery, general store, and gas station, which is likely to be closed. Before you attempt it, ask around about road conditions, or call the **Maui Public Works Department** (☎ 808/248-8254) or the **Police Department** (☎ 808/248-8311). This road frequently washes out in the rain. You'd really be better off retracing your route through Hana.

About 6 miles and about 60 minutes from Oheo Gulch, you'll see the restored **Huialoha Congregationalist "Circuit" Church,** originally constructed in 1859. Across from the church and down the road a bit is the **Kaupo Store** (☎ 808/ 248-8054), which marks the center of the ranching community of Kaupo. Store hours are officially Monday through Friday from 7:30am to 4:30pm, but in this arid cattle country, posted store hours often prove meaningless. The Kaupo Store is the last of the Soon family stores, which at one time stretched from Kaupo to Keanae.

From the Kaupo Store, the landscape turns into barren, dry desert. In the lee of Haleakala, this area gets little rain. Between mile markers 29 and 30, look for the ancient lava flow that created an arch as it rolled down Haleakala. Keep an eye peeled for cattle, because this is open range country. Eventually the road will wind uphill, and suddenly the forest and greenery of Ulupalakula come into sight. The upcountry town is about 45 minutes from Kahului.

Shops & Galleries

by Jocelyn Fujii

8

Shopping remains a major Maui activity because you can leapfrog from one shopping center to the next simply by following the main road and enjoying the views of Haleakala or the West Maui Mountains in between. As in any popular visitor destination, you'll have to wade through bad art (in this case, oceans of trite marine art) and mountains of trinkets, particularly in Lahaina and Kihei, where touristy boutiques line the streets between rare pockets of treasures. And if you shop in South or West Maui, expect to pay resort prices, clear down to a bottle of Evian or sunscreen. But Maui's gorgeous finds are particularly rewarding.

The island is a center for art, with a large number of resident artists who show their works in dozens of galleries and countless gift shops scattered around the island. Maui is also the queen of specialty products; the area from Kula to Hana is an agricultural cornucopia that produces Kula onions, upcountry protea, Kaanapali coffee, world-renowned potato chips, and many other taste treats that are shipped worldwide.

Central Maui is home to some first-rate boutiques. Our favorite shopping destination here is **Wailuku,** where the new Sig Zane Designs has brought a delightful infusion of creative and cultural energy to a town that is just waking up from a long slumber. Watch Wailuku—it is poised for a resurgence, with plans for a major new promenade/emporium by the end of 2000 and regular festivals and street celebrations that are drawing local residents like never before. The Kaahumanu Center in neighboring **Kahului** is becoming more fashionable by the month. Also in Kahului is the $28 million Maui Arts and Cultural Center, a dream venue for the performing and visual arts, with two theaters and a 3,500-square-foot gallery. Of course there are the big-box retailers in Kahului and a major expansion of the Maui Mall, but the charm of shopping on Maui has never resided in the big stores—it's only in the small, independent shops and galleries that crop up in surprising places.

Another of my favorite shopping spots is upcountry, in **Makawao,** where a string of wonderful boutiques and galleries lines the main street. We've made some lovely finds here, despite some attitude and high prices.

Well-heeled Maui shoppers are expecting many new temptations when **The Shops at Wailea,** a much anticipated shopping-dining complex in the Wailea Resort, opens in late summer 2000. Located between the Grand Wailea Hotel and Outrigger Wailea Resort, the newly rebuilt complex signals a repositioning of the resort as a place of heightened commercial activity. A preview of the tenant list suggests a mix of retailers similar to Kaanapali's **Whalers Village**—mostly upscale, many Euro-mainland chains, with galleries and specialty shops, ice cream and camera shops, clothing and gift boutiques, and of course, the obligatory T-shirt and souvenir stores. (See section 3 of this chapter.)

1 Central Maui

KAHULUI

Kahului's best shopping is concentrated in two places. Almost all of the shops listed below are at one of these centers: Maui Mall and Kaahumanu Center.

The once rough-around-the-edges **Maui Mall,** 70 E. Kaahumanu Ave. (☎ **808/ 877-7559**), is the talk of Kahului. Newly renovated and expanded, it's bigger, it's better, and it has retained some of our favorite stores while adding a 12-screen movie megaplex that has comfortable reclining seats. As for films, the megaplex features current releases and "Academy Art House" films for the avant-garde, ultrahip movie buff. The mall is still a place of everyday good things, from **Long's Drugs** to **Star Market,** and still has **Tasaka Guri Guri,** the decades-old purveyor of inimitable icy treats, neither ice cream nor shaved ice, but something in between.

Kaahumanu Center, 275 Kaahumanu Ave. (☎ **808/877-3369**), a commercial hub only 5 minutes from the Kahului Airport on Highway 32, offers more than 100 shops, restaurants, and theaters. Its new second-floor Plantation District offers home furnishings and accessories (**Twig**), fabulous Naots and Kenneth Cole shoes (**Native Soles**), and new gift and accessories shops. A manageable size, with a thoughtful selection of food and retail shops, Kaahumanu covers all the bases, from the arts and crafts to a **Foodland Supermarket,** with everything in between: a thriving food court; the island's best beauty supply, **Lisa's Beauty Supply & Salon** (☎ **808/877-6463**) and its sister store for cosmetics, **Madison Avenue Day Spa and Boutique** (☎ **808/ 873-0880**); mall standards like **Sunglass Hut, Radio Shack,** and **Local Motion** (surf and beach wear, including the current fad, women's board shorts, a combination of hot pants and men's surf trunks); department store **Liberty House;** and attractive gift shops such as **Maui Hands** and its new sister store of feng shui delights, **Maui Elements,** in the center's new Plantation District. From 11:30am to 1:30pm on the last Friday of every month, there are food demonstrations and samplings, fashion shows, and live entertainment in the center's **Queen's Market Food Court.**

Caswell-Massey. Kaahumanu Center. ☎ **808/877-7761.**

The internationally acclaimed Caswell-Massey remains a Maui store of distinction, due in large part to its Maui-made soaps and bath products that use tropical fragrances and botanicals. America's oldest perfume company, established in 1752, Caswell-Massey triple-mills all its soaps (so they last longer), scents them with natural oils, and uses old-fashioned, tried-and-true methods and ingredients. You can handpick your selection from hundreds of specialty products, from decadent bath salts with 23-karat gold flakes to bath gels, body lotions, sachets, candles, perfume bottles, potpourris, and more. You can also get handsome, custom-designed baskets at no extra charge.

Cost Less Imports. Maui Mall. ☎ **808/877-0300.**

Natural fibers are everywhere in this newly expanded corner of the Maui Mall. Household accessories include lauhala; bamboo blinds; grassy floor and window coverings; shoji-style lamps; burlap yardage; baskets; Balinese cushions; Asian, Indonesian, and Polynesian imports; and top-of-the-line, made-on-Maui soaps and handicrafts. Japanese folk curtains, called noreng, and feng shui accents are among the diverse items you'll find here; it's a good source of tropical and Asian home decor.

Hoaloha Heirlooms. Kaahumanu Center. ☎ **808/873-0461.**

We love this Hawaiian/Polynesian touch in the middle of a mall. Lavish koa ukuleles by Maui Ukulele and leis made of kukui nuts, wiliwili seeds, and Job's tears are part of the Hawaiian offerings at this wonderful gift shop. Paintings, place mats, koa tables, small Hawaiian quilts, children's clothes, muumuus and dresses, hair ornaments, handmade paper, fiber baskets, and hundreds of gift items from Hawaii, Indonesia, and the South Pacific are also sold here.

Lightning Bolt Maui Inc. 55 Kaahumanu Ave. ☎ **808/877-3484.**

There's an excellent selection of women's board shorts, longboards, aloha shirts, swimwear, sandals and shoes, and all necessary accoutrements for fun in the sun. Quality labels such as Patagonia and high-tech, state-of-the-art outdoor gear like Polartec sweaters and moccasins attract adventurers heading for the chilly hinterlands as well as the sun-drenched shores.

Manikin. 55 Kaahumanu Ave. ☎ **808/877-1473.**

Manikin clothing is for women who love washable, flowing designs in silks, rayons, and natural fibers. Easy-care, practical, and good-looking designs can be bought off the rack, but if you don't find what you want in the simple bias-cut designs, you can have it made from the bolts of stupendous washable fabrics lining the walls. Except for a few hand-painted silks, everything in the shop is washable. The fabrics are even washed and dried before they're sewn into your custom design.

Maui Hands. Kaahumanu Center. ☎ **808/877-0368.**

Because it's a consignment shop, you'll find Hawaii-made handicrafts at prices that aren't inflated. The selection includes paintings, prints, jewelry, glass marbles, native-wood bowls, and tchotchkes for every budget. This is an ideal stop for made-on-Maui products and crafts of good quality; 90% of what's sold here was made on the island. There are paintings and prints aplenty, in all price ranges.

The original Maui Hands remains in Makawao at The Courtyard, 3620 Baldwin Ave. (☎ **808/572-5194**). A sister store, **Maui Elements,** opened recently on the center's second floor.

Maui Swap Meet. S. Puunene Ave. (next to the Kahului Post Office). ☎ **808/877-3100.** Admission 50¢. Wed 6am–noon, Sat 5am–noon.

The large and popular Maui Swap Meet is held twice every week. After Thanksgiving and throughout December, the number of booths nearly doubles, to almost 200, and the activity reaches fever pitch. The colorful assortments of Maui specialties include Kula vegetables, vegetables from Keanae, fresh Maui mushrooms, fresh taro, plants, proteas, wood works, crafts, household items, homemade ethnic foods, and baked goods, including some fabulous fruit breads. Early Saturday mornings, vendors spread out their wares in booths, under tarps, in a festival-like atmosphere that is pure Maui with a touch of kitsch. Between the cheap Balinese imports and New-Age crystals and incense, you may find some vintage John Kelly prints and 1930s collectibles. Admission is 50¢, and if you go early while the vendors are setting up, no one will turn you away.

✪ **Summerhouse.** In the Dairy Center, 395 Dairy Rd. ☎ **808/871-1320.**

Summerhouse changes its look and merchandise constantly, but it always stays sleek, chic, and big on style. Easygoing separates by Russ Berens, Johnny Was, FLAX, Kiko, and tencel jeans by Signatur (the best) are among the things we love. Also notable are the hats, accessories, easy-care clothing, and up-to-the-minute evening dresses that Summerhouse carries in abundance. The high-quality T-shirts, always a cut above, will take you from day to evening. The casual selection is well-suited to the island lifestyle.

EDIBLES

The **Star Market** in the Maui Mall, **Foodland** in the Kaahumanu Center, and **Safeway** at 170 E. Kamehameha Ave. will satisfy your ordinary grocery needs. On Wednesday and Saturday, you may want to check out the **Maui Swap Meet** (see above). A few other sources of local specialties, flowers, health foods, and other mighty morsels are worth checking out.

Down to Earth Natural Foods, 305 Dairy Rd. (☎ **808/877-2661**), is a health-food staple, with fresh organic Maui produce, a bountiful salad bar, sandwiches and smoothies, vitamins and supplements, freshly baked goods, chips and snacks, whole grains, and several packed aisles of vegetarian and health foods.

Maui's produce has long been a source of pride for islanders, and **Ohana Farmers Market,** Kahului Shopping Center (next to Ah Fook's Super Market; ☎ **808/878-3189**), is where you'll find a fresh, inexpensive selection of Maui-grown fruit, vegetables, flowers, and plants in season. Crafts and gourmet foods add to the event, and the large monkeypod trees provide welcome shade.

WAILUKU

Located near Iao Valley, the Maui County seat of Wailuku is a town of attractive vintage architecture and a strong feeling of cultural integrity. Iao Theatre (a new performing arts company), antique shops, and mom-and-pop eateries imbue Wailuku with a charm that is noticeably absent in the resort areas of west, south, and upcountry Maui. There is no plastic aloha in Wailuku. We suggest you keep your eyes peeled on this central Maui treasure.

Wailuku is the center of **antiquing** on Maui. Of course there's junk, but a stroll along Main and Market streets usually turns up a treasure or two. It's a mixed bag, but a treasure hunt, too.

✪ **Bailey House Gift Shop.** At the Bailey House Museum, 2375-A Main St. ☎ **808/244-3920.**

Bailey House is a must if you're shopping for high-quality made-in-Hawaii items. You'll browse through compelling and authoritative Hawaiiana at the mouth of Iao Valley, in a museum that's one of the finest examples of missionary architecture, dating from 1833. Gracious gardens, rare paintings of early Maui, wonderful programs in Hawaiian arts and culture, a restored hand-hewn koa canoe, and infinite glimpses of old Hawaii await those who visit this museum.

The shop, a small space of discriminating taste, reflects a high level of integrity in its selection of remarkable gift items, from Hawaiian music albums to exquisite woods, traditional Hawaiian games (konane, checkers, and tick-tack-toe), pareu, and an impressive selection of books. Koa-framed prints by the legendary Hawaii artist Madge Tennent, lauhala hats hanging in midair, hand-sewn pheasant hatbands, jams and jellies, Maui cookbooks, and an occasional Hawaiian quilt are some of the treasures to be found here. Hawaiian music often wafts in from a neighboring room, where a slack-key guitar class may be in session. Classes range from lauhala weaving to gourd-making, slack key guitar, and ukulele.

Bird of Paradise Unique Antiques. 56 N. Market St. ☎ **808/242-7699.**

The owner, Joe Myhand, loves furniture, old Matson liner menus, blue willow china, kimonos for children, and anything nostalgic that happens to be Hawaiian. The furniture in the strongly Hawaiian collection ranges from 1940s rattan to wicker and old koa—those items tailor-made for informal island living and leisurely moments on the lanai. Myhand also collects bottles and mails his license plates all over the world. The collection ebbs and flows with his finds, keeping buyers waiting in the wings for his Depression glass, California pottery from the 1930s and 1940s (Bauer, Metlox, Vernon, the occasional precious Roseville), old dinnerware, perfume bottles, vintage aloha shirts, and vintage Hawaiian music on cassettes.

✪ **Brown-Kobayashi.** 160-A N. Market St. ☎ **808/242-0804.**

Gracious living is the theme of Brown-Kobayashi, whether it's self-adornment or interior design. Prices range from a few dollars to the thousands in this 750-square-foot treasure trove. The owners have added a fabulous selection of antique stone garden pieces that mingle quietly with Asian antiques and old and new French, European, and Hawaiian objects. Although the collection is eclectic, there is a strong cohesive aesthetic that sets Brown Kobayashi apart from other Maui antique stores. Japanese kimono and obi, Bakelite and Peking glass beads, breathtaking Japanese lacquerware, cricket carriers, cloisonné, and a lotus-leaf basket carved of bamboo are among the many treasures here. Exotic and precious Chinese woods (purple sandalwood and huanghauali) glow discreetly from quiet corners, and an occasional monarchy-style lidded milo bowl comes in and flies out.

✪ **Sig Zane Designs Wailuku.** 53 Market St. ☎ **808/249-8997.**

When Hilo-based Sig Zane Designs opened on Wailuku's Market Street, near Iao Theatre, the entire island perked up. Zane and co-owner Punawai Rice have redefined Hawaiian wear by creating an inimitable style in clothing, textiles, furnishings, bedding, and lifestyle accessories. This, their Maui debut, has proven to be an enormously successful reflection of their cohesive aesthetic. Zane's fabrics are compellingly graphic and meaningful, made into aloha shirts and women's wear and used in interiors and furnishings that evoke the gracious Hawaii of an earlier time. As in Hilo, Sig Zane Designs in Wailuku is a cultural outpost, signaling an infusion of joyful creativity to this area.

EDIBLES

Established in 1941, the **Ooka Super Market,** 1870 Main St., Wailuku (☎ **808/ 244-3931**), Maui's ultimate home-grown supermarket, is a mom-and-pop business that has grown by leaps and bounds but still manages to keep its neighborhood flavor. Ooka sells inexpensive produce (fresh Maui mushrooms for a song), fresh island seafood, certified Angus beef, and Maui specialties such as manju and mochi. Proteas cut the same day, freesias in season, hydrangeas, fresh leis, torch ginger from Hana, upcountry calla lilies in season, and multicolored anthuriums are offered at what is one of Maui's finest and most affordable retail flower selections. Prepared foods are also a hit: bentos and plate lunches, roast chicken and laulau, and specialties from all the islands abound.

Located in the northern section of Wailuku, **Takamiya Market,** 359 N. Market St. (☎ 808/244-3404), is much loved by local folks and visitors, who often drive all the way from Kihei to stock up on picnic fare and mouth-watering ethnic foods for sunset gatherings and beach parties. This is for adventurous palates. Unpretentious home-cooked foods from East and West are prepared daily and served on plastic-foam plates from an ethnic smorgasbord. From the chilled-fish counter come fresh sashimi and poke, and in the renowned assortment of prepared foods are mounds of shoyu chicken, tender fried squid, roast pork, kalua pork, laulau, Chinese noodles, fiddlehead ferns, and Western comfort foods, such as cornbread and potato salad.

2 West Maui

LAHAINA

Lahaina's merchants and art galleries go all out from 7 to 9pm on Friday nights, when **Art Night** brings an extra measure of hospitality and conviviality. The Art Night openings are usually marked with live entertainment and refreshments and a livelier-than-usual street scene.

If you're in Lahaina on the second or last Thursday of each month, stroll by the front lawn of the **Baldwin Home,** 696 Front St. (at Dickenson Street), for a splendid look at lei-making and an opportunity to meet the gregarious senior citizens of Lahaina. In a program sponsored by the American Association of Retired Persons, they gather from 10am to 4pm to demonstrate lei-making, to sell their floral creations, and equally important, to socialize.

What was formerly a big, belching pineapple cannery is now a maze of shops and restaurants at the northern end of Lahaina town, known as the **Lahaina Cannery Mall,** 1221 Honoapiilani Hwy. (☎ **808/661-5304**). Find your way through the T-shirt and sportswear shops to **Lahaina Printsellers,** home of antique originals, prints, paintings, and wonderful 18th- to 20th-century cartography. You can follow the scent of coffee to **Sir Wilfred's Coffee House,** or head for **Compadres Bar and Grill,** where the margaritas flow freely and the Mexican food is tasty (see chapter 5 for a review). Crafts, including some hand-turned woods of koa, milo, and tamarind, are displayed in the **Simon-Jon Art and Design Gallery,** where half the gallery displays the landscapes, still lifes, and seascapes of **Julie Taylor Ellingboe.** For film, water, aspirin, groceries, sunscreen, and other things you can't live without, nothing beats **Long's Drugs** and **Safeway,** two old standbys. **Shoes, Sandals & Slippers by Roland's** may surprise you with its selection of footwear, everything from Cole-Haan sophisticates to inexpensive sandals and sports shoes. At the recently expanded international Food Court, the new **Compadres Taqueria** sells Mexican food to go, while **L&L Drive-Inn** sells plate lunches near the Greek and Japanese food booths.

The **Lahaina Center,** 900 Front St. (☎ **808/667-9216**), is fairly new and still a work in progress. It's located north of Lahaina's most congested strip, where Front Street begins. Across the street from the center, the seawall is a much-sought-after front-row seat to the sunset. There's plenty of free validated parking with easy access to more than 30 shops, a hair salon, restaurants, a nightclub, and a four-plex movie-theater complex. Chef Sam Choy opened **Sam Choy's Lahaina** in late January 1999, not long after **Ruth's Chris Steak House** opened its doors in the same center. **Maui Brews** serves lunch and dinner and offers live music nightly except weekends. Among the shopping stops: **Banana Republic,** the **Hilo Hattie Fashion Center** (a dizzying emporium of aloha wear), **McInerny** (wonderfully discounted designer clothes), **ABC Discount Store,** and a dozen other recreational, dining, and entertainment options.

The conversion of 10,000 square feet of parking space into the re-creation of a traditional Hawaiian village is a welcome touch of Hawaiiana at Lahaina Center. With the commercialization of modern Lahaina, it's easy to forget that it was once the capital of the Hawaiian kingdom and a significant historic site. The village, called **Hale Kahiko,** features three main houses, called *hale:* a sleeping house; the men's dining house; and the crafts house, where women pounded lauhala for mats and baskets. Construction of the houses consumed 10,000 feet of ohia wood from the island,

20 tons of pili grass, and more than 4 miles of handwoven coconut sennit for the lashings. Artifacts, weapons, a canoe, and indigenous trees are among the authentic touches in this village, which can be toured privately or with a guide.

David Lee Galleries. 712 Front St. ☎ **808/667-7740.**

The gallery is devoted to the works of David Lee, who uses natural powder colors to paint on silk. The pigments and technique create a luminous, ethereal quality.

Gary's Island. 839-A. Front St. ☎ **808/662-0424.**

You must go through Gary's to enter Woody's, a restaurant hanging over the ocean, and it is a pleasure shopping there. There are mostly aloha shirts, but good ones, including some offbeat styles by Toes on the Nose and the usual top-drawer Tommy Bahama (including exquisite aloha-themed silk ties), Reyn's, and Kahala shirts. Women's dresses and shoes for men and women, from Cole-Haan to gel-soled Sensi's, are also included in this tiny but dynamic shop.

✪ Ka Piko O Lele. 505 Front St. ☎ **808/662-0207.**

This is a wonderful find: a strictly Hawaiian gallery of first-rate works in wood, painting, sculpture, textiles, and crafts. Because it's a fund-raising outlet for the restoration of Moku`ula, considered the spiritual and political power center of the old Hawaiian kingdom in Lahaina, it maintains a cultural integrity that sets it apart from all other Lahaina galleries. Woods by Edward Perreira, Norfolk pine bowls by Todd Campbell, Carla Crow's tapa prints, fabrics by Tutuvi, feather kahili by Jo-Anne Kahanamoku Sterling, paintings by BH Freeland, drawings, quilt cushions, books by the Bishop Museum Press, jewelry, specialty food items—the selection is of top quality, and all by Maui artists. Those looking for authentic made-in-Hawaii treasures and special gifts from Maui will not be disappointed.

Lahaina Arts Society Galleries. Lahaina Center, 900 Front St. ☎ **808/661-0111.**

With its membership of more than 250 Maui artists, the nonprofit Lahaina Arts Society is an excellent community resource. And in its new location, the works of its artist members are more pleasingly displayed than ever before. Two-dimensional art, fiber art, ceramics, sculpture, prints, and all manner of creative endeavor fill the gallery.

This is also the headquarters of the **Live Poets Society,** which holds poetry readings on the last Friday of each month. Every other weekend, near its previous location under the banyan tree at historic Lahaina Courthouse, the Society has its "Art in the Park" fair from 9am to 5pm. Two to three dozen artists display their wares in the shade of the landmark banyan tree planted in 1873 and now covering nearly an acre. In the Lahaina Center gallery, Friday-night Art Night has artists selling their work, occasionally with live entertainment, from 5 to 9pm.

Lahaina Body & Bath. 713 Front St. ☎ **808/661-1076.**
Lei Spa Maui. 505 Front St. ☎ **808/661-1178.**

These two similar stores, which are under the same ownership, are worth a stop. It's a good sign that 95% of the beauty and bath products sold are made on Maui, and that includes Hawaiian Botanical Pikake shower gel; kukui and macadamia-nut oils; Hawaiian potpourris; mud masks with Hawaiian seaweed; and a spate of rejuvenating, cleansing, skin-soothing potions for hair and skin. Aromatherapy body oils and perfumes are popular, as are the handmade Hawaiian soaps and fragrances of torch ginger, plumeria, coconut, tuberose, and sandalwood. Scented candles in coconut shells, inexpensive and fragrant, make great gifts. Lei Spa Maui has expanded to include two massage rooms and shower facilities, making it a day spa with Hawaiian lomi lomi, facials, and other therapies.

Martin Lawrence Galleries. In the Lahaina Market Place, 126 Lahainaluna Rd. ☎ **808/ 661-1788.**

The front is garish, with pop art, kinetic sculptures, and bright, carnivalesque glass objects. Toward the back of the gallery, however, there's a sizable inventory of two-dimensional art and some plausible choices for collectors of Keith Haring, Andy Warhol, and other pop artists. The focus is pop art and national and international artists, with very little art from Maui.

The Old Lahaina Book Emporium. 834 Front St. ☎ **808/661-1399.**

More than 10,000 quality used books are lovingly housed in this 700-square-foot shop, where owner JoAnn Carroll treats books and customers well. Prices are low, the selection is diverse, and if you're a bibliophile looking for that rare first edition, you might find that here too. The specialties include Hawaiiana, fiction, mystery, sci-fi, and military history, with substantial selections in cookbooks, children's books, and philosophy/religion. You could pay as little as $2 for a quality read, or $10, or more.

Totally Hawaiian Gift Gallery. Lahaina Cannery Mall, 1221 Honoapiilani Hwy. ☎ **808/ 667-2558.**

A good browse for its selection of Niihau shell jewelry, excellent Hawaiian CDs, Norfolk pine bowls, and Hawaiian quilt kits. Hawaiian quilt patterns sewn in Asia (at least they're honest about it) are labor-intensive, less expensive, and attractive, although not totally Hawaiian. Hawaiian-quilt patterned gift wraps and tiles, perfumes and soaps, handcrafted Hawaiian dolls, and koa accessories are of good quality. When Christmas rolls around, the Christmas ornament selection is a draw.

✪ **Village Galleries in Lahaina.** 120 and 180 Dickenson St. ☎ **808/661-4402** or 808/661-5559.

The nearly 30-year-old Village Galleries is the oldest continuously running gallery on Maui, and it's highly esteemed as one of the few galleries with consistently high standards. The newer contemporary gallery (with colorful gift items and jewelry) has upped the enjoyment and possibilities. The selection of mostly original two- and three-dimensional art offers a good look at the quality of work emanating from the island. Art collectors know the Village Galleries as a respectable showcase for regional artists.

There's another location in the Ritz-Carlton Kapalua, 1 Ritz-Carlton Dr. (☎ **808/ 669-1800**).

Westside Natural Foods. 193 Lahainaluna Rd. ☎ **808/667-2855.**

A longtime Lahaina staple, Westside is serious about providing tasty food that's healthy and affordable. Its excellent food bar attracts a healthy clientele with vegetarian lasagna, marinated tofu strips, vegetarian pot pie, crisp salads, grains, curries, and gorgeous organic produce. The selection changes regularly.

KAANAPALI

Whalers Village, 2435 Kaanapali Pkwy. (☎ **808/661-4567**), has gone shockingly upscale, but there are some new additions that ease the pain somewhat. It's open daily from 9:30am to 10pm. Our favorite shoe store, **Sandal Tree,** has moved from the Hyatt Regency to Whalers Village next door (see below). It was another good move to get **Martin & MacArthur** and its Hawaii crafts: Larry DeLuz lidded koa bowls, Hawaiian-quilt cushion covers, ceramic anthurium bowls, jewelry, boxes, soaps, books, and a stunning selection of woodworks. You can also find award-winning **Kimo Bean** coffee at a kiosk on the mall, and an expanded **Reyn's** for aloha wear.

Cinnamon Girl, a hit at Honolulu's Ward Warehouse with its matching mother-daughter clothing and accessories, opened its third Hawaii store in Whalers Village. And the welcome return of **Waldenbooks** makes it that much easier to pick up the newest bestseller on the way to Kaanapali Beach. Once you've stood under the authentic whale skeleton or squeezed the plastic whale blubber at the **Whale Center of the Pacific** (see chapter 7), you can blow a bundle at **Tiffany, Prada, Chanel, Ferragamo,** or any of the 70 shops and restaurants that have sprouted up in this beachfront shopping center. The posh Euro trend doesn't bode well; even with the newcomers, there's too little here that's Hawaiian. **The Eyecatcher** has one of the most extensive selections of sunglasses on the island; it's located just across from the busiest **ABC** store in the state. The food court, Leilani's, and Hula Grill are the dining anchors of the village, but the most comforting stop of all is the **Maui Yogurt Company,** where Maui-made Roselani ice cream is sold in mouth-watering flavors, including a bracing mint chocolate chip. The showpiece of the center is the giant **sandcastle** built by Billy Lee, a world champion sandcastle builder, who sprays his architectural marvel with a mild glue solution that purportedly enables his sculpture to withstand 30-mile-per-hour winds and up to 2 inches of driving rain. Impressive, for sure—unless you happen to be within range of the glue spray.

The Hawaii Quilt Company. In the Hyatt Regency Maui, 210 Nohea Kai Dr. ☎ **808/667-7660.**

Rhonda's has increased its made-in-Hawaii selection and has teamed up with The Company Store, specializing in Maui-made crafts. Some T-shirts, tote bags, mouse pads, and Hawaiian quilt designs are designed in-house, but there are also dolls, children's clothing, locally made tiles in Hawaiian quilt patterns, books, stuffed animals, and other eclectic goods in this cheerful store. The assortment includes a small selection of women's clothing among the antique quilts and Americana. The Hawaiian quilts are made both here and, much less expensively, in the Philippines, and all are of high quality. Quilt pillows, supplies, patterns, and kits are sold here, and quilting classes, which include all supplies, are offered on Fridays.

Ki'i Gallery. In the Hyatt Regency Maui. ☎ **808/661-4456.**

Those who love glass in all forms, from hand-blown vessels to jewelry, will love a browse through Ki`i. Some of the works are large and lavish, such as the Toland Sand prisms for just under $5,000 and the John Stokes hand-blown glass. There are many exclusives here, such as the glass jewelry by local artist Mary Kennedy. We found Pat Kazi's work in porcelain and found objects, such as the mermaid in a teacup, to be fantastic and compelling, inspired by fairy tales and mythology. The gallery is devoted to glass and original paintings and drawings, and roughly half of the artists are from Hawaii.

✪ **Sandal Tree.** Whalers Village. ☎ **808/667-5330.**

The Sandal Tree has a flock of footwear fanatics who come here from throughout the islands for their chic kicks. They sell rubber thongs and topsiders, sandals and dressy pumps, athletic shoes and hats, Arche comfort footwear, and much more. Accessories range from fashionable knapsacks to indulgences such as avant-garde geometrical handbags—for town and country, day and evening, kids, women, and men. Prices are realistic, too. The other Maui store is in the Grand Wailea Resort.

KAHANA/NAPILI/HONOKOWAI

Those driving north of Kaanapali toward Kapalua will notice the new **Honokowai Marketplace** on Lower Honoapiilani Road, only minutes before the Kapalua Airport.

A Pacific Cafe is only one of its welcome features; there's the first 1-hour Martinizing dry cleaner in Hawaii, the flagship **Star Market, Pizza Paradiso, Hula Scoops** for ice cream, a gas station, copy shop, a few clothing stores, and the sprawling **Hawaiian Interiorz.** Nearby **Kahana Gateway** is an unimpressive mall built to serve the condominium community that has sprawled along the coastline between Honokowai and Kapalua. If you need women's swimsuits, however, **Rainbow Beach Swimwear** is a find, boldly situated near the waistline-challenging dining mecca, Roy's Kahana Bar and Grill, and a stone's throw from the Fish & Game Brewing Co. & Rotisserie (see chapter 5 for complete reviews of both). At Rainbow, you'll find a selection of suits for all shapes, at lower-than-resort prices, slashed even further during the frequent sales.

Also in Kahana Gateway, **Hutton's Fine Jewelry** is a breath of fresh air for lovers of fine jewelry. High-end jewelry from designers around the country (a lot of platinum and diamonds) reflect discerning taste for those who can afford it. Tahitian black pearls and jade (some hundreds of years old, all certified) are among Hutton's specialties, but we love the Carleton Kinkade oil paintings hanging on the walls.

KAPALUA

Honolua Store. 502 Office Rd. (next to the Ritz-Carlton Kapalua). ☎ **808/669-6128.**

Walk on the old wood floors peppered with holes from golf shoes and find your everyday essentials: bottled water, stationery, jackets, chips, wine, soft drinks, paper products, fresh fruit and produce, and aisles of notions and necessities. With picnic tables on the veranda and a take-out counter offering deli items—more than a dozen types of sandwiches; salads; and a budget-friendly breakfast of eggs, biscuits, and gravy—there are always long lines of customers. Cheap breakfasts are big with surfers on their way out to the surf, and at lunch, the salad bar attracts the health-conscious. Golfers and surfers love to come here for the morning paper and coffee.

Kapalua Shops. At the Kapalua Bay Hotel and Villas. ☎ **808/669-1029.**

Shops have come and gone in this small, exclusive, and once-chic shopping center, now much quieter than in days past. Tiny **Mandalay** still sells East-West luxe with its silk clothing and handful of interior accents. Mostly, though, it's logo wear, jewelry, and real estate offices—and of course, Maui's dining phenomenon, Sansei.

✪ **Village Galleries.** In the Ritz-Carlton Kapalua, 1 Ritz-Carlton Dr. ☎ **808/669-1800.**

Maui's finest exhibit their works here and in the other two Village Galleries in Lahaina. Take heart, art lovers: There's no clichéd marine art here. Translucent, delicately turned bowls of Norfolk pine gleam in the light, and George Allan, Betty Hay

---

A Creative Way to Spend the Day

Make a bowl from clay or paint a premade one, then fire it and take it home. Or paint a picture, or learn ballet, or learn to sketch like the masters at the **Art School at Kapalua** (☎ **808/665-0007**), West Maui's only art school, featuring local and visiting instructors. It's open daily for people of all ages and skill levels. Projects, programs, classes, and workshops at this not-for-profit organization highlight creativity in all forms. Classes in using your camera, sketching, figure drawing, ceramics, landscape painting, painting on silk, throwing at the potter's wheel, and the performing arts (ballet, creative dramatics, yoga, creative movement, Pilates stretch) are offered in a charming 1920s plantation building that was part of an old cannery operation in the heart of the Kapalua resort. The classes are inexpensive. Call the school to see what's scheduled while you're on Maui.

Freeland, Fred KenKnight, Joyce Clark, and Pamela Andelin are included in the pantheon of respected artists represented in the tiny gallery. Watercolors, oils, sculptures, handblown glass, Niihau shell leis, jewelry, and all media are represented. The Ritz-Carlton's monthly Artist-in-Residence program features Village Gallery artists in demonstrations and special hands-on workshops—free, including materials.

3 South Maui

KIHEI

Kihei is one long strip of strip malls. Most of the shopping to be done here is concentrated in the **Azeka Place Shopping Center** on South Kihei Road. Fast foods abound at Azeka's, as do tourist-oriented clothing shops like **Crazy Shirts** and the overly tropical **Tropical Tantrum.** Across the street, **Azeka Place II** houses several prominent attractions, including the popular restaurant called **A Pacific Cafe, General Nutrition Center,** the **Coffee Store,** and a cluster of specialty shops with everything from children's clothes to shoes, sunglasses, beauty services, a nail salon, and swimwear. Also on South Kihei Road is the **Kukui Mall,** with its movie theaters, **Waldenbooks,** and **Whaler's General Store.**

Aloha Books. In the Kamaole Beach Center, 2411 S. Kihei Rd. ☎ **808/874-8070.**

Having added a coffee/espresso bar with indoor-outdoor seating and live music, poetry, and theatrical performances, Tom Holland can once again concentrate on his first love: used books, especially Hawaiiana. This is a bookstore with character—a community bookstore—and it has only gotten better with the years. You'll find an impressive selection of books on Hawaiiana (particularly antiques, collectibles, and art), health, metaphysics, cooking, music, film, travel, and history. The walls are draped with vintage Hawaiian and Polynesian art. There are new, used, and rare books, and although this isn't a big bookstore, the titles cover a range of tastes, from popular fiction to historic novels and Dick Francis whodunits. There's even a shelf full of old LPs, including most of the Beatles albums. If there's an out-of-print Don Blanding or an old John Kelly print to be found in the neighborhood, it's likely to be here.

✪ **Hawaiian Moons Natural Foods.** 2411 S. Kihei Rd. ☎ **808/875-4356.**

Hawaiian Moons is actually a health minisupermarket, with one of the best selections of made-on-Maui products we've encountered on the island. The Mexican tortillas are made on Maui (and good!), and much of the produce here, such as organic vine-ripened tomatoes and organic onions, is grown in the fertile upcountry soil of Kula. There's also locally grown organic coffee, Maui teas, gourmet salsas, Maui shiitake mushrooms, organic lemongrass and okra, Maui Crunch bread, free-range Big Island turkeys and chickens (no antibiotics or artificial nasties), and fresh Maui juices. Cosmetics are also top-of-the-line; it is a staggering and wonderful selection of health-conscious sunblocks, fragrant floral oils, kukui-nut oil from Waialua on Oahu, and the Island Essence made-on-Maui mango-coconut and vanilla-papaya skin lotions, the ultimate in body pampering.

Maui Sports & Cycle. 1215 S. Kihei Rd. ☎ **808/875-8448.**

These upbeat water-sports retail and rental shops are a hit among beachgoers and water-sports enthusiasts. Plans call for the addition of golf clubs, tennis racquets, and binoculars to the rental department. A friendly, knowledgeable staff helps you choose from among the mind-boggling selection of snorkel gear, boogie boards, kayaks, beach umbrellas, coolers, and view boards for "snorkeling lying down." You'll find swimwear and mountain bikes, too, and gear for riding on land or sea. There's high-quality snorkel gear, with a selection so extensive you can tailor your choice to your budget as well as your fit. Prescription masks are available, as are underwater cameras, sunscreens and lotions, jewelry, T-shirts, postcards, and hats and visors by the bushel.

Old Daze. In Azeka I, 1280 S. Kihei Rd. ☎ **808/875-7566.**

Nineteenth-century Americana and Hawaiian collectibles are nicely married in this charming shop. The collection features a modest furniture selection, Hawaiian pictures, 1960s ashtrays, Depression glass, old washboards, souvenir plates from county fairs, and an eclectic assortment of items for table and home. Choices range from hokey to rustic to pleasantly nostalgic, with many items for the kitchen. Some recent finds: an 1850s German sideboard, a Don Blanding teapot, old Noritake tea set, Royal Worcester china, 1940s head vases, a turn-of-the-century pie safe, antique kimonos, framed vintage music sheets, and Hawaiian silver collectible spoons.

Pua's Lei Stand. Kihei Kalama Village, 1941 S. Kihei Rd.

Surprise! Fresh plumeria lei in hot Kihei! Located at the far mauka (mountainside) end of the shopping village, Pua's Lei Stand is an oasis of fragrance, freshness, and the spirit of Hawaii. There are fresh plumeria lei in a refrigerated section, lavish wiliwili and seed lei, hula implements, Hawaiian-printed flaxseed eye pillows, Hawaiian angels made from fibers found in Kihei, and all manner of made-on-Maui gems. This is the only place in the Kalama Village that carries Maui Herbal soaps. They're generous blocks of soap in fragrances of pikake, tuberose, guavaberry, tropical sea, and my favorite, plumeria. These are fabulously fragrant, hard-to-find soaps that lather richly and contain pure ingredients, and whose simple packaging belie the fact that they are top quality. Buy three and you get a free lauhala basket to pack them in.

Tuna Luna. Kihei Kalama Village, 1941 S. Kihei Rd. ☎ **808/874-9482.**

There are treasures to be found in this small cluster of tables and booths where Maui artists display their work. Ceramics, exotic wood photo albums, jewelry, candle holders and soaps, handmade paper, and fiber accessories make great gifts to go. Something to watch for: Maui Metal hand-crafted journals, aluminum books with designs of hula girls, palms, fish and seahorses, $15. Koa paddles and implements, beautiful koa books and photo albums, and fiber-art picture frames make terrific Maui mementos.

WAILEA

As tony as Kihei is tacky, Wailea consists of resort shops that sell expensive souvenirs, gift items, clothing, and accessories for a life of perpetual vacations. **Sandal Tree** (see Kaanapali, above), with its affordable-and-up designer wear, raises the footwear banner at the Grand Wailea Resort, while stores like **Mandalay,** in the Grand Wailea Shops and the Four Seasons Resort Maui, specialize in sumptuous Thai silks and Asian imports, from resort wear to the very dressy.

The Shops at Wailea, due to open in late summer 2000, promises to infuse this west Maui resort with a substantial dose of upscale shopping. Four new restaurants have signed on at the time of this writing, and the shops number in the dozens. Most of them are upscale (Louis Vuitton, Tiffany & Co., Fendi, Dolce & Gabbana, Bally, Cartier, Coach—you get the picture), and some of them, like Banana Republic and The Gap, are mainland chains. **Tommy Bahama,** the mainland tropical sportswear line, will open a cafe-emporium that combines its distinctive aloha wear with tropical-style dining. The $70 million complex is located between the Outrigger Wailea Resort and Grand Wailea Resort.

Grand Wailea Shops. At the Grand Wailea Resort, 3850 Wailea Alanui Dr. ☎ **808/875-1234.**

The sprawling Grand Wailea Resort is known for its long arcade of shops and galleries tailored to hefty pocketbooks. However, gift items in all price ranges can be found at **Lahaina Printsellers** (the premier store for old maps and prints), **Dolphin Galleries, H. F. Wichman, Sandal Tree,** and **Napua Gallery,** which houses the private collection of the resort owner. And these are only some of the shops that line the arcade.

Ki'i Gallery (☎ **808/871-4557**) is slightly larger than a corner, but what a corner it is. Sleek and taut, the gallery is luminous with studio glass and the warm glow of exquisitely turned woods. If you love ceramics and the Japanese aesthetic, go to the flower shop in the lobby and its adjoining minigallery, a small, quiet, unsigned corner called **Gentoku.** It is like a small Zen temple, serene and beautiful, with distinctive ceramics and pictures of the Daihonzan Chozen-Ji temple in Kalihi, Oahu.

4 Upcountry Maui

MAKAWAO

Equally beloved by shoppers and artists, Makawao is the home of the island's most prominent arts organization, the ✪ **Hui No'eau Visual Arts Center,** 2841 Baldwin Ave. (☎ **808/572-6560**). Designed in 1917 by C. W. Dickey, one of Hawaii's most prominent architects, the two-story, Mediterranean-style stucco home that houses the center is located on a sprawling, manicured, 9-acre estate called Kaluanui. A legacy of Maui's prominent *kamaaina* (native-born residents), Harry and Ethel Baldwin, the estate became an art center in 1976 and remains a complete aesthetic experience. Visiting artists offer lectures, classes, and demonstrations, all at reasonable prices, in basketry, jewelry-making, ceramics, printmaking, painting, and diverse media. Half-day classes on Hawaiian art, culture, and history are available to visitors and residents. The Hui is one of the few facilities available on Maui for independent art study and studios. Call ahead for schedules and details. The exhibits here are drawn from a wide range of disciplines and multicultural sources, and include both contemporary and traditional art from established and emerging artists. Maui artists consider this the most prestigious of venues. There's also a unique gift shop worth a special stop, featuring many one-of-a-kind works by local artists and artisans. Open Monday to Saturday from 10am to 4pm.

✪ **Collections.** 3677 Baldwin Ave. ☎ **808/572-0781.**

Collections is a longtime Makawao attraction that shows renewed vigor after more than 2 decades on Baldwin Avenue. Its selection of sportswear, soaps, jewelry, candles, and tasteful, marvelous miscellany reflects good sense and style. Dresses, separates, home and bath accessories, sweaters, and a shop full of good things make this a Makawao must.

Cuckoo for Coconuts. 1158 Makawao Ave. ☎ **808/573-6887.**

The owner, a professional clown called Cuckoo, expresses her quirky sense of humor in every inch of this tiny shop. Though barely bigger than a large walk-in closet, it brims with vintage collectibles, gag gifts, silly coconuts, 1960s and '70s aloha wear, tutus, sequined dresses, vintage wedding gowns, and all sorts of oddities. Things we've seen there: an Elvira wig, very convincing; a raffia hat looking suspiciously like a nest, with blue eggs on top; stained Billy-Bob teeth that fit well and are baaaaad; and some vintage aloha shirts that would make a collector drool.

Gallery Maui. 3643A Baldwin Ave. ☎ **808/572-8092.**

Since it moved here in 1999 from its obscure location down the street, the gallery has been reborn. Follow the sign down the shaded pathway to a cozy gallery of topnotch, mostly Maui fine artists and fine crafts in furniture and fiber. All the works here are local except for glass and ceramics, and the quality is outstanding. The 30 artists represented in the gallery include Wayne Omura and his Norfolk pine bowls; Pamela Hayes and her watercolors; and wonderful paintings by Martha Vockrodt. A dresser of curly koa and ebony, made by Steve Hynson, and a desk and rocking chair of koa are stunning examples of the hand-rendered excellence the gallery owners look for.

Gecko Trading Co. Boutique. 3621 Baldwin Ave. ☎ **808/572-0249.**

The eclectic, ever-changing selection could include St. John's Wort body lotion one day, and mesh T-shirts in a dragon motif, Provence soaps, and antique lapis jewelry the next. You never know what you'll find in this tiny boutique; we've seen everything from hair scrunchies to handmade crocheted bags from New York, clothing from Spain and France, collectible bottles from four different lifetime collectors, T-shirts, toys, shawls, and Mexican hammered-tin candle holders. The prices are reasonable, the service is friendly, and it's not as self-consciously stylish as other local boutiques.

Holiday & Co. 3681 Baldwin Ave. ☎ **808/572-1470.**

Attractive women's clothing in natural fibers hangs from racks, while jewelry to go with it beckons from the counter. Holiday's large selection of Citron dresses and separates, leather Dansko clogs, shawls, shoes, soaps, aloha shirts, books, picture frames and jewelry will appeal to those with discerning tastes. The Holiday signature: the latest in comfortable clothing and interchangeable styles in easy-care fabrics.

Hot Island Glassblowing Studio & Gallery. 3620 Baldwin Ave. ☎ **808/572-4527.**

You can watch the artist transform molten glass into works of art and utility in this cordial studio in Makawao's Courtyard. An award-winning family of glassblowers built its own furnaces here and opened the studio to public view. It's fascinating to watch the shapes emerge from glass melted at 2,300°F. The colorful works displayed in the studio range from small paperweights to large vessels and are shipped around the world. Four to five artists participate in the demonstrations, which begin when the furnace is heated, about half an hour before the studio opens at 9am.

Hurricane. 3639 Baldwin Ave. ☎ **808/572-5076.**

This split-level boutique carries clothing, gifts, accessories, and books that are two steps ahead of the competition. Tommy Bahama silk pique aloha shirts and aloha print dresses, hats, art by local artists, and hard-to-find, eccentric books and home accessories are part of the Hurricane appeal. Sigrid Olsen's three different collections per month include morning-to-evening attire, from business suits and extraordinary silk tank dresses (expensive but wonderful) to T-shirts and soft, washable Tencel jeans. There's also an intoxicating selection of fragrance and bath products.

✪ The Mercantile. 3673 Baldwin Ave. ☎ **808/572-1407.**

Mercantile's devotion to the good life encompasses jewelry, home accessories (especially the Tiffany-style glass-and-shell lamps), dinnerware, Provencçal and made-on-Maui soaps, Italian linens, plantation-style furniture, and clothing. Soothing eye pillows filled with flaxseeds, handmade designer dolls, hand-carved armoires, down-filled furniture and slip covers, and a large selection of Kiehl's products will make it easy to part with your time and money. The clothing selection—comfortable cottons and upscale European linens—is for men and women, as are the soaps, which include Maui Herbal Soap products and some unusual finds from France.

✪ Ola's Makawao. In the Paniolo Building, 1156 Makawao Ave. ☎ **808/573-1334.**

Chosen as Maui's "up-and-coming business" in 1999 and nominated for *Niche* magazine's "top retailer of American craft" award, Ola's is on a roll. You'll always find a Doug Britt painting or two here, which is reason enough to find Ola's. Britt's scintillating paintings and furniture assemblages (vanities and lockers made of found wood) are among the great art finds of Hawaii. Big Island artist Ira Ono has added to the Ola's mix his beautiful objects of found art (twisted spoons and forks from the Kauai dump) and handmade paper. Owners Cindy Heacock and Shari O'Brien add a personal touch to the delightful environment they've created. The handmade art by more than 160 artists includes Hawaii's best in glassware, ceramics, wood, jewelry, two-dimensional art, paper, books, and other media. Enjoy the studio glass, porcelain vases, koa chopsticks, outrageous martini glasses, seed leis, toys, letter openers, dolls, silks, sumptuous bath products, and art, but don't forget Bella's at Ola's, a line of fourth-generation handmade chocolates, offered in 12 pricey but irresistible varieties.

Tropo. 3643 Baldwin Ave. ☎ **808/573-0356.**

Tropo is a magnet for stylish, sensitive, *and* rugged men searching for tasteful aloha wear and comfortable basics. Books, clothing, Tilley hats, and Crabtree & Evelyn products are among the finds here. Men can shop for Tommy Bahama silk pique trousers and shorts, tasteful T-shirts, stylish winter wovens by Toes on the Nose, and aloha shirts by Reyn Spooner, Tori Richards, Que, and Kahala. The paintings of Maui artist Avi Kiriaty are immensely popular.

✪ **Viewpoints Gallery.** 3620 Baldwin Ave. ☎ **808/572-5979.**

The island's only fine-arts cooperative showcases the work of 20 of Maui's most established artists in an airy, attractive gallery located in a restored theater with a courtyard, glassblowing studio, and restaurants. This is a delightful trip through the creative atmosphere of Maui. The gallery features two-dimensional art, jewelry, fiber art, stained glass, papermaking, sculpture, and other media. A high degree of professionalism is maintained because the artists involved have passed a rigorous screening and are award-winning in their media. This is a fine example of what can happen in a collectively supportive artistic environment.

EDIBLES

Working folks in Makawao come to the **Rodeo General Store,** 3661 Baldwin Ave. (☎ **808/572-7841**), to pick up spaghetti and lasagna, sandwiches, salads, and changing specials from the deli. Even in their plastic-wrapped paper trays, the pastas are tasty. You can also pick up all the necessary accompaniments here—fresh produce, soft drinks, paper products, baked goods, deli items, and sweets. At the far end of the store is the oenophile's bonanza, a superior wine selection housed in its own temperature-controlled cave.

Down to Earth Natural Foods, 1169 Makawao Ave. (☎ **808/572-1488**), always has fresh salads and sandwiches, a full section of organic produce (Kula onions, strawberry papayas, mangos, and litchis in season), bulk grains, supplements, beauty aids, herbs, juices, snacks, condiments, tofu, seaweed, soy products, and aisles of vegetarian and health foods—canned, packaged, prepared, and fresh. Whether it's a smoothie or a salad, Down to Earth has fresh, healthy vegetarian offerings.

In the more than 6 decades that the **T. Komoda Store and Bakery,** 3674 Baldwin Ave. (☎ **808/572-7261**), has spent in this spot, untold numbers have creaked over the wooden floors to pick up Komoda's famous cream puffs. Old-timers know to come early, or they'll be sold out. Then the cinnamon rolls, doughnuts, pies, chocolate cake, and assorted edibles take over, keeping the aromas of fresh baking wafting through the old store. Pastries are just the beginning; poi, macadamia-nut candies and cookies, and small bunches of local fruit keep the customers coming.

FRESH FLOWERS IN KULA (AT THE BASE OF HALEAKALA NATIONAL PARK)

Proteas, a Maui trademark (like anthuriums on the Big Island), grow abundantly on Haleakala's rich volcanic slopes. The sturdy blooms also travel well, dry beautifully, and can be shipped worldwide with ease. Among Maui's most prominent sources is **Sunrise Protea** (☎ 808/876-0200) in Kula. It has a walk-through garden and gift shops, and provides friendly service and a larger-than-usual selection. Freshly cut flowers arrive from the fields on Tuesday and Friday afternoons. You can order individual blooms, baskets, arrangements, or wreaths for shipping all over the world. Next door, the Sunrise Country Market offers fresh local fruits, snacks, and sandwiches, with picnic tables for lingering. **Proteas of Hawaii** (☎ 808/878-2533), another reliable source, offers regular walking tours of the University of Hawaii Extension Service gardens across the street in Kula.

For flower shopping in other parts of Maui, **Ooka Super Market** and the Saturday-morning **Maui Swap Meet** (see section 1 of this chapter) are among the best and least expensive places for tropical flowers of every stripe.

5 East Maui

ON THE ROAD TO HANA: PAIA

Biasa Rose Boutique. 104 Hana Hwy. ☎ **808/579-8602.**

You'll find unusual gift items and clothing with a tropical flair: floating plumeria candles, retro fabrics, dinnerware, handbags and accessories, and stylish vintage-inspired kids' clothes for boys and girls. If the aloha shirts don't get you, the candles in the shape of nude males and females will surely catch your eye. Eighty percent of the items are locally made. You can also custom-order clothing from a selection of washable rayons.

Big Bugga Sportswear. 18 Baldwin Ave. ☎ **808/579-6216.**

You have to be microsized or ultrahuge to shop at Big Bugga, Maui's only large-size clothing store for sumo-sized men. Togs for tots are a small part of the inventory of T-shirts and surf wear; the rest begins at L and goes up to 10X, with aloha shirts as large as 7X. Sorry, mediums and larges, there's nothing for you here. But there is a great selection of sportswear, from shorts for 40- to 60-inch waistlines to T-shirts for the ultra-ample girth. You can even make special orders for sweatpants and -shirts up to size 10X.

Hemp House. 16 Baldwin Ave. ☎ **808/579-8880.**

Clothing and accessories made of hemp, a sturdy and sensible fiber, are finally making their way into the mainstream in stylish and practical selections. The Hemp House has as complete a selection as you can expect to see in Hawaii, with "denim" hemp jeans, lightweight linenlike hemp trousers, dresses, shirts, and the full range of sensible, easy-care wear. We were impressed with the selection of jeans and shirts in all weights and designs.

✪ **Maui Crafts Guild.** 43 Hana Hwy. ☎ **808/579-9697.**

The old wooden storefront at the gateway to Paia houses local crafts of high quality and in all price ranges, from pit-fired raku to bowls of Norfolk pine and other Maui woods, fashioned by Maui hands. Artist-owned and operated, the guild claims 25 members who live and work on Maui. Basketry, hand-painted silks and fabrics, jewelry, beadwork, traditional Hawaiian stonework, prints, pressed flowers, fused glass, stained glass, copper sculpture, banana bark paintings, pottery of all styles, and hundreds of items are displayed in the two-story gift gallery. Upstairs, sculptor Arthur Dennis Williams displays his breathtaking work in wood, bronze, and stone. Everything can be shipped, and all artists are selectively screened. **Aloha Bead Co. (☎ 808/579-9709)** in the back of the gallery is a treasure trove for beadworkers.

Moonbow Tropics. 36 Baldwin Ave. ☎ **808/579-8592.**

If you're looking for a tasteful aloha shirt, go to Moonbow. The selection consists of a few carefully culled racks of the top labels in aloha wear, in fabrics ranging from the finest silks and linens to Egyptian cotton and spun rayons. Silk pants, silk shorts, vintage print neckwear, and an upgraded women's selection are the Moonbow offerings. There are also shorts, a few purses, and a growing jewelry collection of individual and one-of-a-kind pieces. Tahitian black pearls, emeralds, rubies, moonstone, tanzanite, and other stones are mounted in unique settings made on property. As for the aloha shirts, they cover the best: Tommy Bahama, Tori Richards, Paradise Found, Kahala, Kamehameha, Reyn's, and other name brands, in good-quality fabrics.

HANA

✪ **Hana Coast Gallery.** Hotel Hana-Maui. ☎ **808/248-8636.**

This gallery is a good reason for going to Hana; it's an esthetic and cultural experience that informs as it enlightens. Tucked away in the lush folds of this historic hotel, the gallery is known for its high level of curatorship and commitment to the cultural art of Hawaii. "There are no jumping whales or dolphins here," curator Patrick Robinson notes proudly. Except for a section of European and Asian masters (Renoir, Japanese woodblock prints), the 3,000-square-foot gallery is devoted entirely to Hawaii artists; 60% of the painters and about 15% of the crafters are from Maui. More than the numbers, it's the quality of the work that makes this a revered cultural resource of the island. Dozens of well-established Hawaiian artists display their sculptures, paintings, prints, feather work, stonework, carvings, and three-dimensional works in displays that are so natural they could well exist in someone's home.

Hasegawa General Store. Hana Hwy. ☎ **808/248-8231.**

Established in 1910, immortalized in song since 1961, burned to the ground in 1990, and back in business since 1991, this legendary store is indefatigable and more colorful than ever in its fourth generation in business. The aisles are choked with merchandise: Hana-blend coffee specially roasted and blended for the store, Ono Farms organic dried fruit, fishing equipment, every tape and CD that mentions Hana, the best books on Hana to be found, T-shirts, beach and garden essentials, mugs, baseball caps, film, baby food, napkins, and other necessities for the Hana life.

Maui After Dark

by Jocelyn Fujii

The buzz on Maui is all about **'Ulalena,** an extraordinary production that tells the story of Hawaii in chant, song, original music, acrobatics, and dance, using state-of-the-art technology and some of the most creative staging to be seen in Hawaii. A local and international cast performs this $9.5 million production at the new **Maui Myth & Magic Theatre** in Lahaina (see below).

Centered in the $32 million **Maui Arts and Cultural Center** in Kahului (☎ **808/242-7469**), the performing arts are alive and well on this island. The MACC remains the island's most prestigious entertainment venue, a first-class center for the visual and performing arts. Bonnie Raitt has performed here, as have Hiroshima, Pearl Jam, Ziggy Marley, Kenny Loggins, Lou Rawls, and Tony Bennett, not to mention the Maui Symphony Orchestra and the finest in local and Hawaii talent. The center is as precious to Maui as the Met is to New York, with a visual-arts gallery, an outdoor amphitheater, offices, rehearsal space, a 300-seat theater for experimental performances, and a 1,200-seat main theater. Whether it's hula, the Iona Pear Dance Company, Willie Nelson, or Hawaiian-music icon Keali'i Reichel, only the best appear at the Maui Arts and Cultural Center. The center's activities are well publicized locally, so check the *Maui News* or ask your hotel concierge what's going on during your visit.

IN SEARCH OF HAWAIIAN, JAWAIIAN & MORE

Nighttime revelers on Maui head for Casanova in Makawao, Hapa's in Kihei, Tsunami in Wailea, and Maui Brews in Lahaina (see below for details on all). As they are all in different parts of this spread-out island, you'll either have to drive a great distance to these clubs or explore what's happening in the major hotels near you. The hotels often have lobby lounges offering generic Hawaiian music, soft jazz, or hula shows beginning at sunset.

If **Hapa, Willie K. and Amy Gilliom,** and the soloist **Keali'i Reichel** are playing anywhere on their native island, don't miss them; they're among the finest Hawaiian musicians around today. Most clubs with dance floors play a combination of Hawaiian and reggae, called Jawaiian, with a heated-up rhythm that dancers love.

To see what's happening in Jawaiian music, reggae, and funk, look in at **Hapa's Brew Haus** (☎ **808/879-9001**) in Kihei (see below). Even with 300 seats, the place fills up for dancing. A DJ spins dance music several times a week, and when there's live music, such as Willie K., the place is packed.

The only place on Maui for jazz is the highly recommended **Pizazz Café** in Kihei (see below).

AT THE MOVIES

Movie buffs are rejoicing over the new 12-screen movie megaplex at the **Maui Mall,** 70 E. Kaahumanu Ave. (☎ **808/877-7559**), which comes complete with comfortable reclining seats! As for films, the megaplex features current releases and "Academy Art House" films for the avant-garde, ultra-hip movie buff.

Film buffs can check the local newspapers to see what's playing at the other theaters around town: the **Kaahumanu Theatres** in the Kaahumanu Center in Kahului (☎ 808/873-3133); the **Maui Theatre** in the Kahului Shopping Center (☎ 808/ 877-3560); the **Kukui Mall Theater** at 1819 S. Kihei Rd. in Kihei (☎ 808/ 875-4533); and the **Wallace Theatres** in Lahaina (☎ 808/661-3347), at the Wharf Cinema Center, 658 Front St., and the **Front Street Theatres** at the Lahaina Center, 900 Front St.

1 West Maui: Lahaina

Maui Brews, 900 Front St. (☎ **808/667-7794**), is open daily from 11:30am, with happy hour from 3 to 6pm and a nightclub from 9pm to 1:30am. Hawaiian, salsa, reggae, rock and roll, R&B, and late-night jams draw the crowds to this 5,000-square-foot nightclub, adjoining a bistro/bar with indoor-outdoor seating in a sidewalk-cafe ambience. Whether it's live entertainment or dancing to a DJ, there's something going on every night at Maui Brews. Ladies Night is on Thursdays, and every Friday from 5 to 9pm, the Maui Brews highlight—"the best thing we do," claims the manager—is The Jonah Livin Band, which fills the place with contemporary rock and nostalgic riffs (Eagles, Beatles), with no cover charge. Sixteen draft beers and the full range of tropical libations are among the brews of Maui Brews.

The **Hard Rock Café,** 900 Front St. (☎ **808/667-7400**), occasionally offers live music, so it wouldn't hurt to call them to see if something's up. Usually they feature mainland bands, such as Burrito Brothers and Silver River Wrestlers, and normally on weekends after 10pm.

Longhi's, 888 Front St. (☎ **808/667-2288**), features live entertainment from 9:30pm to 1:30am Friday nights. Usually it's jazz or rock, but call ahead to confirm. Other special gigs can be expected if rock 'n' rollers or jazz musicians who are friends of the owner happen to be passing through.

You won't have to ask what's going on at **Cheeseburger in Paradise,** 811 Front St. (☎ **808/661-4855**), the two-story green-and-white building at the corner of Front and Lahainaluna streets. Just go outside and you'll hear it. Loud, live, and lively tropical rock blasts into the streets and out to sea daily from 4:30 to 11pm.

A NIGHT TO REMEMBER: LUAU, MAUI STYLE

Most of the larger hotels in Maui's major resorts offer luaus on a regular basis. You'll pay about $65 to $69 to attend one. To protect yourself from disappointment, don't expect it to be a homegrown affair prepared in the traditional Hawaiian way. There are, however, commercial luaus that capture the romance and spirit of the affair with quality food and entertainment in outdoor settings.

Maui's best luau is indisputably the nightly ✪ **Old Lahaina Luau** (☎ **808/ 667-1998**), which plans to bring hula and Hawaii to the Macy*s Thanksgiving Day Parade for the first time in the parade's 74-year history. The planned appearance of 24 dancers from Old Lahaina Luau in 2000 will mark the first time a hula troupe has had its own float in the parade, and the first time that hula will be performed in front of

It Begins with Sunset . . .

Nightlife in Maui begins at sunset, when all eyes turn westward to see how the day will end. Sunset viewers seem to bond in the mutual enjoyment of a natural spectacle. And what better way to take it all in than over cocktails? Maui is a haven for lovers of both. With its view of Molokai to the northwest and Lanai to the west, Kaanapali and the west Maui destinations boast panoramic vistas unique to this island. In south Maui's Wailea and Makena, tiny Kahoolawe and the crescent-shaped Molokini islet are visible as familiar forms on the horizon, and the West Maui Mountains look like an entirely separate island. No matter what your vantage point, you are likely to be treated to an astonishing view.

Sunset viewers along south and west Maui shorelines need only head for the ocean and find a seat. Our favorite sunset watering holes begin toward the north with **The Bay Club at Kapalua** (☎ 808/669-5656), where a pianist plays nightly and the northwesterly view of Molokai and Lanai is enhanced by the elegant surroundings. It's quiet here, removed from the hubbub that prevails in the more populated Kaanapali Beach Resort to the south.

In Kaanapali, park in Whalers Village and head for **Leilani's** (☎ 808/661-4495) or **Hula Grill** (☎ 808/667-6636), next to each other on the beach. Both have busy, upbeat bars and tables bordering the sand. These are happy places for great people watching, gazing at the lump of Lanai that looks to be a stone's throw away, and enjoying end-of-day rituals like mai tais and margaritas. Hula Grill's Barefoot Bar appetizer menu is a cut above, offering such treats as macadamia-nut/crab wontons, fresh fish-and-chips, and pizza. Leilani's has live music daily from 2:30 to 6pm, while Hula Grill offers hula from 3 to 5pm and at 6:30pm.

Now, Lahaina: It's a sunset-lover's nirvana, lined with restaurants that hang over the ocean and offer fresh fish in a multitude of preparations—and mai tais elevated to an art form. If you love loud rock, head for **Cheeseburger in Paradise** (☎ 808/661-4855). A few doors away, the **Lahaina Fish Company** (☎ 808/661-3472) and **Kimo's** (☎ 808/661-4811) are magnets all day long and especially at sunset, when their open decks fill up with revelers. These three restaurants occupy the section of Front Street between Lahainaluna Road and Papalaua Street.

At the southern end of Lahaina, in the 505 Front Street complex, **Pacific'o** (☎ 808/667-4341) is a solid hit, with a raised bar, seating on the ocean, and a backdrop of Lanai across the channel. Besides the view and the friendly service, the food is notable, having won many awards for seafood. A few steps away from

Macy*s during the parade. It is, after all, a megahit at its 1-acre site just ocean-side of the Lahaina Cannery, a perennial award-winner as "best Maui luau," not only with us but in local Maui publications as well. From food to entertainment to service and setting, it is peerless. We've seen guests become literally giddy with it all: the brilliant sunset, the throbbing drums and powerful dancing, the fragrances of flowers, the sounds of rustling fiber skirts. Local craftspeople display their wares only a few feet from the ocean. Seating is provided on lauhala mats for those wishing to dine as the traditional Hawaiians did, but there are tables for everyone else. There's no fire-dancing in the program, but you don't even miss it. (For that, you go to the Feast at Lele; see chapter 5 for a full review.) Thatched buildings, amphitheater seating, excellent food and

Pacific'o, sister restaurant Ió shares the same drop-dead-gorgeous view, with an appetizer menu and a techno-curved bar that will wow you as much as the view.

Moving south toward Wailea, the harbor stop called Maalaea is famous for its whale sightings during the winter months. We haven't seen it yet, but culinary wizard Peter Merriman's soon-to-open Merriman's **Bamboo Bistro** will have a view of Maalaea, and will no doubt be something to watch for. Year-round, **Buzz's Wharf** (☎ 808/244-5426) is a formula restaurant with a superb ocean view and continuous service between lunch and dinner. Those are the basic makings of a sunset-viewing way station. Add an ice-cold beer or mai tai and a steaming order of fish-and-chips, and the sunset package is complete.

In Wailea, **Ferraro's** and **Pacific Grill** (☎ 808/874-8000), both at the Four Seasons Resort Wailea, have great sunset views, and no doubt the restaurants at The Shops at Wailea will be trying to outdo them. In Makena resort farther south, you can't beat the Maui Prince's **Molokini Lounge** (☎ 808/874-1111), with its casual elegance and unequalled view of Molokini islet on the ocean side and, on the mauka side, a graceful, serene courtyard with ponds, rock gardens, and lush foliage. Adding to the setting is the appetizer menu, which comes from the esteemed Prince Court kitchen. From 5:30pm nightly, the pupu menu features a Prince Court sampler platter: Kona lobster cakes, sugarcane-speared grilled prawns with tropical fruit relish, and kalua duck lumpia with mango chile vinaigrette. The live Hawaiian entertainment runs nightly from 6 to 10:30pm, beginning with a mini hula show from 6pm on Monday, Wednesday, and Friday and the contemporary Hawaiian melodies of Mele Ohana or Ron Kuala'au from 6:45pm on.

Don't forget the upcountry view, a kick-ass way to end the day if you don't mind the drive. **Kula Lodge** (☎ 808/878-2517) is making some big changes with its new executive chef, Dan Saito, formerly of the Manele Bay Hotel, Spago, and Masa's in San Francisco. Along with one of the most seductive views on the island, from 3,200 feet high on the slopes of Haleakala, you can enjoy Saito's menu of upcountry comfort food. From 3 to 4:45pm daily, the appetizer-only menu includes a host of gourmet salads (the farmers are a stone's throw away); ahi carpaccio and steamed clams; the Kula poke tower (seared and raw poke on a bed of wasabi mashed potatoes); and a host of dishes to accompany the wine selection and the views. There's more glass than wood in the dining room, so the view encompasses Kihei, Kahului, and the West Maui Mountains—south and central Maui in its jaw-dropping magnificence.

entertainment, and the backdrop of a Lahaina sunset are among its unforgettable features.

This is the consummate luau, with a healthy balance of entertainment, showmanship, authentic high-quality food, educational value, and sheer romantic beauty. (No watered-down mai tais, either; these are the real thing.) The luau begins at sunset and features Tahitian and Hawaiian entertainment, including ancient hula, hula from the missionary era, modern hula, and an intelligent narrative on the dance's rocky course of survival into modern times. The entertainment is riveting, even for jaded locals. The food, which is served from an open-air thatched structure, is as much Pacific Rim as authentically Hawaiian: imu-roasted kalua pig, baked mahimahi in Maui onion

'Ulalena: Hula, Myth & Modern Dance

The highly polished **'Ulalena,** staged in the Maui Myth and Magic Theatre, 878 Front St., Lahaina (☎ **808/661-9913**), is the talk of the town, a riveting production that weaves Hawaiian mythology with drama, dance, and state-of-the-art multimedia capabilities in a brand-new, multimillion-dollar theater.

A local and international cast performs Polynesian dance, original music, acrobatics, and chant to create an evocative experience that often leaves the audience speechless. It is interactive, with dancers coming down the aisles, drummers and musicians in surprising corners, and mind-boggling stage and lighting effects that draw the audience in. In one scene, sugarcane is shown growing on the stage, projected on mesh curtains as if by time-lapse photography. Some special moments: the goddess dancing on the moon, the white sail signaling the coming of the first Europeans, the wrath of the volcano goddess Pele (the stage effects depicting lava are unforgettable), and the despairing labors of the field worker immigrants. The effects of the modern choreography and traditional hula, a fusion of genres, are surprisingly evocative and emotional. The story unfolds seamlessly and at the end, you are shocked to realize that not a single word of dialogue has been spoken.

Tickets are $35 for adults, $25 for children; shows are at 6:30 and 9pm Tuesday through Saturday.

cream sauce, guava chicken, teriyaki sirloin steak, lomi salmon, poi, dried fish, poke, Hawaiian sweet potato, sautéed vegetables, seafood salad, and the ultimate taste treat, taro leaves with coconut milk. The cost is $69 plus tax for adults, $39 for children.

On the same shore at the southern end of Lahaina, the owners of the Old Lahaina Luau have created the ✪ **Feast at Lele,** 505 Front St. (☎ **808/667-5353**), which offers Polynesian entertainment (from Hawaii, Tonga, Tahiti, and Samoa), while gourmet versions of the native cuisines are served, first by the light of sunset, then by candlelight. The romantic setup features restaurant seating, and the sunsets are as bright as the fire-dancing. This dinner show is offered on Tuesday, Thursday, and Saturday nights; reservations are strongly recommended. The price is $89 for adults, $59 for children ages 2 to 12. See chapter 5, "Dining," for a complete review.

2 South Maui

KIHEI

Hapa's Brew Haus, Lipoa Shopping Center, 41 E. Lipoa St. (☎ **808/879-9001**), is the only game in town, with local icon Willie K. usually packing them in every Monday night from 9:30pm to 1:30am. The intimate environment, tiered seating, and state-of-the-art sound and lighting show off to great advantage his virtuoso guitar playing and unmistakable vocals. As of this writing, a DJ plays Top 40 music on Tuesday nights, Wednesday is gay night, Thursday is ladies' night, and Friday night features live Hawaiian bands, such as Ehukai, Kapena, Fiji, Hoomau, and Hapa. On Saturdays, the program is a live broadcast with Q103, a hot Maui station that brings in five DJs who play for the live audience and islandwide broadcast. Themes frequently change, so call ahead to confirm what's on the night you plan to visit.

The **Pizazz Café,** 1279 S. Kihei Rd., Azeka Place II (☎ **808/891-2123**), is the jazz nexus of Maui, with live jazz 7 nights a week. Latin jazz by Joyce and Gordon, George Benson, the Artist Formerly Known as Prince, and other known and unknown artists have graced the stage of the 100-seat club. The Pizazz All That Jazz Band, in which the owner is the bass player, is a house specialty, but there are nights when rhythm and blues and an occasional Motown riff takes over momentarily. Mostly it's straight-up jazz, though, and Pizazz, open since December 1998, has a loyal following that comes regularly to dance, listen, or tuck into the jambalaya, catfish, fried chicken, and other Southern and Cajun specialties served at the cafe. There's a $5 cover charge for after-dinner entertainment; the cafe is open daily 11am to midnight, with dinners starting at 4:30pm and entertainment at 7:30pm. For jazz lovers, it's the only game in town.

WAILEA

The Grand Wailea Resort's **Tsunami,** 3850 Wailea Alanui Dr. (☎ **808/875-1234**), Maui's most high-tech club, happens to be South Maui's best-known nightspot for dancing. But the recent addition of shuffleboard and pool tables has changed the mix considerably, turning Tsunami into a game room on Sundays through Tuesdays and a nightclub with a live DJ the rest of the nights. The 10,000-square-foot room, with its marble, laser lights, huge video screens, and futuristic decor, hosts some well-dressed partygoers on Wednesday through Saturday nights, when a DJ plays everything from 1980s hits to Top 40 tunes. Tsunami is open daily from 9pm to 1am, with a $5 cover charge Wednesday through Saturday nights.

3 Upcountry Maui

Upcountry in Makawao, the partying never ends at **Casanova** (☎ **808/572-0220**), the popular Italian ristorante (see chapter 5 for a complete dining review) where the good times roll with the pasta. If a big-name mainland band is resting up on Maui following a sold-out concert on Oahu, you may find its members setting up for an impromptu night here. DJs take over on Wednesday (ladies' night), and Thursday night is the night of surprises. It could be anything from world beat to experimental music to techno and new bands, all live. Thursday is also smoke-free day at Casanova, whether for dinner or dancing; and on Friday, when the live entertainment is usually salsa, mambo, and Latin rhythms, nonsmokers can also breathe easier. Saturday night is the time for big local names in contemporary Hawaiian music. Among the big-timers who have taken the Casanova stage are Taj Mahal, Jesse Colin Young, Three Plus, and Hoomau. Over-all, expect good blues, rock 'n' roll, reggae, jazz, Hawaiian, and the top names in local and visiting entertainment. The show starts at 9:45pm and continues to 1:30am, with a usual cover charge of $5.

10 Molokai, the Most Hawaiian Isle

Born of volcanic eruptions 1¹/₂ million years ago, Molokai remains a time capsule at the dawn of the 21st century. It has no deluxe resorts, no stoplights, and no buildings taller than a coconut tree. Fortunately for adventure travelers and peace-seekers, Molokai is the least developed, most "Hawaiian" of all the islands.

Molokai lives up to its reputation as the most Hawaiian place chiefly through its lineage; there are, in fact, more people here of Hawaiian blood than anywhere else. This slipper-shaped island was the cradle of Hawaiian dance (the hula was born here) and the ancient science of aquaculture. An aura of ancient mysticism clings to the land here, and the old ways still govern life. The residents survive by taking fish from the sea and hunting wild pigs and axis deer on the range. Some folks still catch fish in throw nets and troll the reef for squid, a traditional Hawaiian delicacy. Families are important, friendship is cherished, and the Hawaiian concept of taking care of the land remains a priority. The modern Hawaii of high-rise hotels and shopping centers hasn't been able to gain a foothold here—one lone low-rise resort, Kaluakoi, built more than 25 years ago, is Molokai's token attempt at contemporary tourism.

The only "new" developments since Kaluakoi are the Molokai Ranch's ecotourism project of upscale "camping" in semipermanent "tentalows" (a combination of a bungalow and a tent) and an expensive 22-room lodge on the 53,000-acre ranch. The focus of both is on outdoor recreation and adventure, with all the comforts of home.

The slow-paced, simple life here attracts those in search of the "real" Hawaii. These visitors stand in awe of this little island's natural wonders: Hawaii's highest waterfall and greatest collection of fishponds; the world's tallest sea cliffs; and sand dunes, coral reefs, rain forests, hidden coves—and empty, gloriously empty, beaches.

EXPLORING THE "MOST HAWAIIAN" ISLE

Only 38 miles from end to end and just 10 miles wide, Molokai stands like a big green wedge in the blue Pacific. It has an east side, a west side, a backside, and a topside. This long, narrow island is like yin and yang: one side is a flat, austere, arid desert; the other is a lush, green, steepled tropical Eden. Three volcanic eruptions formed Molokai; the third produced the island's "thumb"—a peninsula jutting out of the steep cliffs of the north shore, like a punctuation mark on the island's geological story.

Molokai

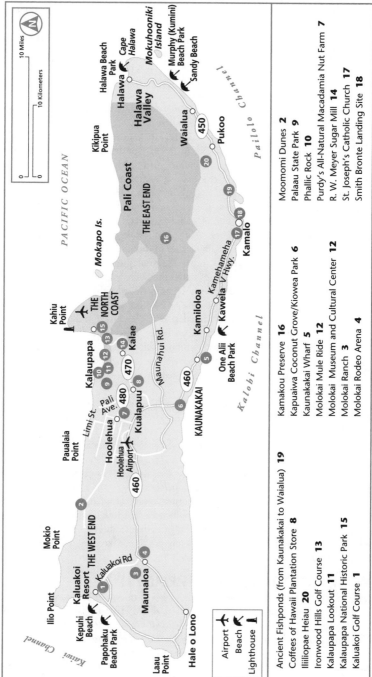

Ancient Fishponds (from Kaunakakai to Waialua) 19
Coffees of Hawaii Plantation Store 8
Ililiopae Heiau 20
Ironwood Hills Golf Course 13
Kalaupapa Lookout 11
Kalaupapa National Historic Park 15
Kaluakoi Golf Course 1

Kamakou Preserve 16
Kapuaiwa Coconut Grove/Kiowea Park 6
Kaunakakai Wharf 5
Molokai Mule Ride 12
Molokai Museum and Cultural Center 12
Molokai Ranch 3
Molokai Rodeo Arena 4

Moomomi Dunes 2
Palaau State Park 9
Phallic Rock 10
Purdy's All-Natural Macadamia Nut Farm 7
R. W. Meyer Sugar Mill 14
St. Joseph's Catholic Church 17
Smith Bronte Landing Site 18

Airport ✈
Beach ⛱
Lighthouse 🗼

On the red-dirt southern plain, where most of the island's 6,000 residents live, the rustic village of **Kaunakakai** looks like the set of an old Hollywood Western, with sun-faded clapboard houses and horses tethered in tall grass on the side of the road. At mile marker 0, in the center of town, the island is divided dramatically into east and west; an arid cactus desert lies on one side, and a lush coco-palm jungle on the other.

Travelers eastbound, along the **coastal highway** named for King Kamehameha V, are able to see Gauguin-like, palm-shaded cottages set on small coves or near fish-ponds; spectacular vistas that take in Maui, Lanai, and Kahoolawe; and a fringing coral reef visible through the crystal-clear waves.

Out on the sun-scorched west end is the island's lone destination resort, **Kaluakoi,** overlooking a gold-sand beach too big to fit on a postcard with water usually too rough to swim in. The old hilltop plantation town of **Maunaloa** has been razed and rebuilt as a gentrified plantation community, complete with an expensive country lodge with a pricey dining room. Cowboys still ride the range on Molokai Ranch, a 53,000-acre spread, while adventure travelers and outdoor recreation buffs stay at the tentalows on the ranch property and spend their days mountain biking, kayaking, horseback riding, sailing, hiking, snorkeling, and just vegetating on the endless white-sand beaches (see "Hiking & Camping," later in this chapter).

Elsewhere around the island, in hamlets like **Kualapuu,** old farmhouses with pick-up trucks in the yards and sleepy dogs under the shade trees stand amid row crops of papaya, coffee, and corn—just like farm towns in Anywhere, USA.

But that's not all there is. The "backside" of Molokai is a rugged wilderness of spec-tacular beauty. On the outskirts of **Kaunakakai,** the land rises gradually from sea-level fishponds to cool uplands and the Molokai Forest, long ago stripped of sandalwood for the China trade. All that remains is an indentation in the earth that natives shaped like a ship's hull, a crude matrix that gave them a rough idea of when they'd cut enough sandalwood to fill a ship (it's identified on good maps as Luanamokuiliahi, or Sandalwood Boat).

The land inclines sharply to the lofty mountains and the nearly mile-high summit of Mount Kamakou, then ends abruptly with emerald-green cliffs, which plunge into a lurid aquamarine sea dotted with tiny deserted islets. These breathtaking 3,250-foot **sea cliffs,** the highest in the world, stretch 14 majestic miles along Molokai's north shore, laced by waterfalls and creased by five Eden-like valleys—Halawa, Papalaua, Wailau, Pelekunu, and Waikolu—once occupied by early Hawaiians who built stone terraces and used waterfalls to irrigate taro patches.

Long after the sea cliffs were formed, a tiny volcano erupted out of the sea at their feet and spread lava into a flat, leaflike peninsula called **Kalaupapa**—the 1860s leper exile where Father Damien de Veuster of Belgium devoted his life caring for the afflict-ed. A few people remain in the remote colony by choice, keeping it tidy for the daily company that arrives on mules and by small planes.

WHAT A VISIT TO MOLOKAI IS *REALLY* LIKE

There's plenty of aloha on Molokai, but the so-called "friendly island" remains ambivalent about vacationers. One of the least visited Hawaiian islands, Molokai wel-comes about 80,000 visitors annually, on its own take-it-or-leave-it terms and makes few concessions beyond that of gracious host; it never wants to attract too much of a crowd, anyway. A sign at the airport offers the first clue: SLOW DOWN, YOU ON MOLOKAI NOW—wisdom to heed on this island, where life proceeds at its own pace.

Rugged, red-dirt Molokai isn't for everyone, but those who like to explore remote places and seek their own adventures should love it. The best of the island can only be seen on foot, bicycle, mule, or horse, or via kayak or boat. The sea cliffs are only accessible by sea in the summer, when the Pacific is calm, or via a 10-mile trek through the Wailau Valley—an adventure only a handful of hardy hikers attempt each year. The great Kamakou Preserve is open just once a month, by special arrangement with the Nature Conservancy. Even Moomomi, which holds bony relics of prehistoric flightless birds and other Lost World creatures, requires a guide to divulge the secrets of the dunes.

Those in search of nightlife have come to the wrong place; Molokai shuts down after sunset. The only public diversions are softball games under the lights of Mitchell Pauole Field, movies at Maunaloa, and the few restaurants that stay open after dark, often serving local brew and pizza.

The "friendly" island may strike you as the "real" Hawaii. On the other hand, you may leave with your head shaking, never to return. It all depends on how you approach Molokai: with an open heart to what it offers or a closed mind to what it doesn't offer. Either way, take it slow.

1 Orientation

by Jeanette Foster

ARRIVING

BY PLANE   Molokai has two airports, but you'll most likely fly into the one at Hoolehua Airport, which everyone calls "the Molokai Airport." It's located on a dusty plain about 6 miles from Kaunakakai town. Airlines with flights from Honolulu to Molokai include: **Island Air** (☎ **800/323-3345** from the mainland, 800/652-6541 interisland; www.alohaair.com), which offers 11 direct flights a day from Honolulu and four direct flights from Maui; **Molokai Air Shuttle** (☎ **808/545-4988**); **Hawaiian Airlines** (☎ **800/367-5320** or 808/553-3644; www.hawaiianair.com); and **Pacific Wings** (☎ **888/575-4546** from the mainland, 808/873-0877 from Maui; www.pacificwings.com), which has flights from both Honolulu and Maui in eight-passenger, twin-engine Cessna 402-C aircraft.

BY BOAT   You can travel across the seas from Lahaina Harbor on Maui to Kaunakakai Wharf on Molokai on the *Maui Princess* (☎ **800/275-6969** or 808/667-6165; fax 808/661-5792; www.mauiprincess.com). The 118-foot yacht (certified for 149 passengers) makes the journey from Maui's Lahaina to Molokai's Kaunakakai on Wednesday and Saturday May through December. During whale-watching season, December to May, it runs only on Saturday. You can book your passage three different ways. Their Walking Tour is passage on the boat only, for $73.15 for adults, $37.10 for children 3 to 12 years, free for children under 3. The Cruise Drive Tour, which includes boat passage and a rental car, costs $129 for the first person and $73.15 for each additional person. And the Alii Tour includes boat passage, a guided tour of Molokai in a van, and lunch, for $136.75 adults, $83.75 for children ages 3 to 12, and free for children under 3. Tours depart Lahaina at 6am, arriving in Molokai at 8am; they leave Molokai at 2pm, arriving in Lahaina at 3:45pm.

VISITOR INFORMATION

Look for a sun-faded, yellow building on the main drag, Kamehameha V Highway (Hwy. 460), on the right just past the town's first stop sign, at mile marker 0; it houses the **Molokai Visitors Association,** P.O. Box 960 Kaunakakai, HI 96748 (☎ **800/ 800-6367,** 808/553-3876 in the U.S. mainland and Canada, 800/553-0404 or 808/553-3876 interisland; www.molokai-hawaii.com). The staff can give you all the information you need on what to see and do while you're on the Friendly Isle.

THE ISLAND IN BRIEF

KAUNAKAKAI Dusty vehicles, mostly pickup trucks, are parked diagonally along Ala Malama Street. It could be any small town, except it's Kaunakakai, where Friendly Isle Realty and Friendly Isle Travel offer islanders dream homes and vacations; Rabang's Filipino Food posts bad checks in the window; antlered deer-head trophies guard the grocery aisles at Misaki's Market; and Kanemitsu's, the town's legendary bakery, churns out fresh loaves of onion-cheese bread daily.

Once an ancient canoe landing, Kaunakakai was the royal summer residence of King Kamehameha V. The port town bustled when pineapple and sugar were king, but those days, too, are gone. With its Old West–style storefronts laid out in a 3-block grid on a flat, dusty plain, Kaunakakai is a town from the past. Molokai's main settlement may appear rustic, but the spirit of aloha still reigns. At the end of Wharf Road is Molokai Wharf, a picturesque place to fish, photograph, and just hang out.

THE NORTH COAST Upland from Kaunakakai, the land tilts skyward and turns green, with scented plumeria in yards and glossy coffee trees all in a row, until it blooms into a true forest—and then abruptly ends at a great precipice, falling 3,250 feet to the sea. The green sea cliffs are creased with five V-shaped crevices so deep that light is seldom seen (to paraphrase a Hawaii poet). The North Coast is a remote, forbidding place, with a solitary peninsula—**Kalaupapa**—once the home for exiled lepers (it's now a national historical park). This region is easy on the eyes, difficult to visit.

THE WEST END This end of the island, home to Molokai Ranch, is miles of stark desert terrain, bordered by the most beautiful white-sand beaches in Hawaii. The rugged rolling land slopes down to Molokai's only destination resort, Kaluakoi, a cul-de-sac of condos clustered around a 25-year-old seafront hotel near 3-mile-long Papohaku, the island's biggest beach. On the way to Kaluakoi, you'll find Maunaloa, a 1920s-era pineapple plantation town that's in the midst of being transformed into a master-planned community, Maunaloa Village, with an upscale lodge, triplex theater, restaurants, and shops.

THE EAST END The area east of Kaunakakai becomes lush, green, and tropical, with golden pocket beaches and a handful of cottages and condos that are popular with thrifty travelers. Beyond Kaunakakai, the two-lane road curves along the coast past piggeries, palm groves, and a 20-mile string of fishponds as well as an ancient heiau, Damien-built churches, and a few contemporary condos by the sea. The road ends in the earthly paradise of **Halawa Valley,** one of Hawaii's most beautiful valleys.

FAST FACTS: MOLOKAI

Molokai, like Lanai, is part of Maui County. For **local emergencies,** call ☎ **911.** For nonemergencies, call ☎ **808/553-5355** for **police,** ☎ **808/553-5601** for **fire,** and ☎ **808/553-5331** for **Molokai General Hospital,** in Kaunakakai.

Downtown Kaunakakai also has a **post office** (☎ **808/553-5845**) and several banks, including the **Bank of Hawaii** (☎ **808/553-3273**), which has a 24-hour ATM. **Molokai Drugs,** in the Kamoi Professional Center (☎ **808/553-5790**), has a pharmacy and over-the-counter medicines.

2 Getting Around

by Jeanette Foster

Getting around Molokai isn't easy if you don't have a rental car, and rental cars are often hard to find here. On holiday weekends—and remember, Hawaii celebrates different holidays than the rest of the United States (see "When to Go," in chapter 2)—car-rental agencies simply run out of cars. Book before you go. There's no municipal transit or shuttle service, but a 24-hour taxi service is available.

CAR-RENTAL AGENCIES Rental cars are available from **Budget** (☎ **800/ 527-0700** or 808/567-6877 locally; www.budgetrentacar.com) and **Dollar** (☎ **800/ 800-4000** or 808/567-6156 locally; www.dollarcar.com); both agencies are located at the Molokai Airport.

We recommend **Island Kine** car rental (☎ **808/553-5242;** fax 808/553-3880; e-mail: cars@molokai-aloha.com). Not only are the cars cheaper, but Barbara Shonely and her son, Steve, give personalized service. They meet you at the Molokai Airport and take you to their office in Kaunakakai. Barbara spends time recommending which outfitters to choose for your activities ("I know who does a good job and who does a poor job"). The used cars are in perfect condition ("I would drive every one of them with my grandkids") and are air-conditioned. They also rent six- and seven-passenger vans, as well as pickup trucks.

TAXI & TOUR SERVICES Molokai Off-Road Tours & Taxi (☎ 808/ 552-2218) offers regular taxi service and island tours. **Kukui Tours** (☎ 808/ 552-2282) offers airport shuttle service and two tours. The $3^{1}/_{2}$-hour tour of West End includes Kaluakoi, Molokai Ranch lands, and Purdy's Mac Nut Farm, then goes up to Kalae for a view of the North Coast, and then returns to Kaunakakai; it costs $30 per person, minimum of three passengers. Kukui's 7-hour grand tour includes the West End tour, with a stop for lunch, plus a tour of the East End out to Halawa Valley; the cost is $50 each, with a minimum of three passengers.

3 Accommodations

by Jeanette Foster

Molokai is Hawaii's most affordable island, especially for hotels. Plus, because the island's restaurants are few, most hotel rooms and condos come with kitchens, which can save you a bundle on dining costs.

There aren't a ton of options on Molokai—mostly B&Bs, condos, a few quaint oceanfront vacation rentals, an aging resort, and a very expensive lodge. I've listed my top picks below; you may want to contact the **Molokai Visitors Association** (☎ **800/800-6367** in the U.S. mainland, 800/553-0404 interisland, or 808/553-3879 on Molokai; www.molokai-hawaii.com) for additional recommendations.

Note: Taxes of 11.42% will be added to your hotel bill. Parking is free everywhere.

KAUNAKAKAI
MODERATE

Molokai Shores Suites. Kamehameha V Hwy. (P.O. Box 1037), Kaunakakai, HI 96748. ☎ **800/535-0085** or 808/553-5954. Fax 808/553-5954. www.marcresorts.com. 100 units. TV. $144 1-bedroom apt (for up to 4); $189 2-bedroom apt (for up to 6). Discounted rates for weekly and extended stays, plus corporate, military, and senior discounts. AE, DC, JCB, MC, V.

This quiet complex of recently painted three-story Polynesian-style buildings is less than a mile from Kaunakakai. It consists of bright, clean, basic units with kitchens and large lanai facing a small gold-sand beach and the ocean beyond. Alas, the beach is mostly for show (offshore, it's shallow mud flats underfoot), fishing, or launching kayaks, but the swimming pool and barbecue area come with an ocean view. Well-tended gardens, spreading lawns, and palms frame a restful view of fishponds, offshore reefs, and neighbor islands. The central location can be a plus, minimizing driving time from the airport or town, and it's convenient to the mule ride, as well as the lush East End countryside. There are coin-operated laundry facilities but no daily maid service.

INEXPENSIVE

A'ahi Place. P.O. Box 528, Kaunakakai, HI 96748. ☎ **808/553-5869.** www.molokai-aloha. com/aahi. 1 unit. $75 double. Rate includes continental breakfast. Extra person $20. 2-night minimum. No credit cards.

Just outside of the main town of Kaunakakai, and located up a small hill, lies this wonderful cottage, complete with a white wicker-filled sitting area, a full kitchen, and two full-sized beds in the bedroom. The entire property is surrounded by tropical plants, flowers, and fruit trees. Two lanai (one in the front and one in the back) are great places to just sit and enjoy the stars at night. Hostess Meridith Potts puts a great continental breakfast (home-grown Molokai coffee, fresh baked goods, and fruit from the property) in your kitchen so you can enjoy it at your leisure. For those who want peace and quiet (no phone or television to distract you), this is the place. And for those who want to explore Molokai, the central location is perfect.

Hotel Molokai. Kamehameha V Hwy. (P.O. Box 1020), Kaunakakai, HI 96748. ☎ **800/367-5004** in the U.S. mainland, 800/272-5275 in Hawaii, or 808/553-5347. Fax 800/477-2329. www.castle-group.com. 45 units. TV TEL. $78–$128 double, $130 suite with kitchenette (sleeps 4). Extra bed/crib $17. AE, CB, DC, DISC, JCB, MC, V.

This place isn't the Ritz; it's more along the lines of a nostalgic Hawaiian motel. The complex is composed of a series of modified A-frame units, nestled under coconut palms along a gray-sand beach with a great view of Lanai. The rooms are basic (be sure to ask for one with a ceiling fan), with tub/shower combos, refrigerators, and lanai. The mattresses are on the soft side, the sheets are thin, and the bath towels are rough, but this is Molokai and this is the only hotel in Kaunakakai. The kitchenettes, with coffeemaker, toaster, pots, and two-burner stoves, can save you money on eating out. On the property is a freshwater swimming pool, an activities desk, laundry facilities, a gift shop, a restaurant (see "Dining," below), and a cocktail lounge. The front desk is only open 7am to 8pm; late check-ins or people with problems have to go to security.

Ka Hale Mala Bed and Breakfast. 7 Kamakana Pl. (P.O. Box 1582), Kaunakakai, HI 96748. ☎ and fax **808/553-9009.** www.molokai-bnb.com. 1 unit. TV. $70 double. Extra person $10; breakfast $5 additional. No credit cards.

In a subdivision just outside of town (off Kamehameha V Highway, before the 5-mile marker), you'll find this large, four-room unit, with a private entrance through the garden, and a Jacuzzi just outside. Inside, the decor consists of white rattan furnishings, room enough to sleep four, and a full kitchen. The owners will happily share their homegrown organic produce. We recommend having the breakfast here. The helpful owners, Jack Pugh and Cheryl Corbeil, meet all guests at the airport like long-lost relatives. They can also supply a couple of bikes and snorkel and picnic gear.

THE WEST END

Also consider **Kaluakoi Villas,** Kaluakoi Resort, 1131 Kaluakoi Rd., Maunaloa, HI 96770 (☎ **800/367-5004** or 808/552-2721; fax 800/477-2329 or 808/552-2201). These aging, Polynesian-style units are comfortable but could definitely use some work ($128 to $154 studio; $155 to $185 one-bedroom apartment; $206 cottage).

Another option is the **Kaluakoi Hotel & Golf Club,** Kaluakoi Resort, Kepuhi Beach (P.O. Box 1977), HI 96770 (☎ **888/552-2550** or 808/552-2555; fax

808/552-2821), the only resort hotel on the island, with a faultless location. As we went to press, the hotel was in escrow with a new owner. Hopefully the new owner will renovate this aging 25-year-old resort and restore it to its former glory. Rates are $155 to $170 studio; $185 to $195 one-bedroom condo; $220 one-bedroom cottage; $275 two-bedroom cottage.

Very Expensive

Molokai Ranch Lodge. P.O. Box 259, Maunaloa, HI 96770. ☎ **877/726-4656** or 808/660-2722. Fax 808/660-2724. www.molokai-ranch.com. 22 units. A/C TV TEL. $295–$350 double. Extra person $75. AE, CB, DC, DISC, JCB, MC, V. Airport shuttle service $20 round-trip.

If this upscale lodge were priced moderately, we'd give it a star and recommend it, but at $295 a night, you can do much better, not only on Molokai, but anywhere in Hawaii.

Molokai Ranch opened this lovely little two-story lodge in 1999. Located in a cool upcountry climate, it's 6 miles and a half-hour shuttle ride from the nearest beach. Designed to resemble a Hawaii ranch owner's private home from the 1920s and 1930s, it's architecturally attractive and sits on 8 nicely landscaped acres. When you first glance through the etched glass double-door entry into the spacious "Great Room," the Lodge appears magnificent, with huge wooden beams, panoramic views, and lots of detail to make it look and feel like a real ranch (gnarled, scuffed cowboy boots next to the door, lots of old books lining the shelves, and nostalgic memorabilia sprinkled about).

But on closer inspection, the grand turns out to be not so grand: The finish construction on the beams is beyond rough; the view is sweeping, but it overlooks dreary, arid pasture; and the bookshelves are not filled with great works and coffee-table books, but an eclectic collection of used-book sale remainders. It has the feel of a great project that ran short of capital just before the finishing touches were put in place.

The guests rooms, each with individual country decor, are of two types: deluxe ($295) and luxury ($350). The luxury rooms are all spacious corner units and feature either greenhouse-type skylights or cozy king-size day beds nestled in comfy alcoves. The luxury room we stayed in looked wonderful: a free-standing four-poster bed, with a 270° view out curving windows and a TV set that hydraulically lifted out of a credenza, then disappeared magically. However, there were some real practical and aesthetic problems, such as no reading lights near the bed (and the light switches were all the way across the room). The fan in the bathroom was noisier than a hurricane, and a light fixture dangled off the wall (and remained that way for days, despite calls to maintenance).

We point out these details because this is the most expensive place to stay on Molokai; it's priced as high as oceanfront resorts on Maui. Despite some nice features, the lodge cannot compete with the amenities (not to mention the beach location) offered by other Hawaii resorts at the same price. And it certainly doesn't come close to the excellent quality and service of Hawaii's other upcountry lodge, The Lodge at Koele on Lanai.

Dining/Diversions: The Maunaloa Room offers three expensive meals a day. The chef calls the fare "Molokai regional cuisine," with interesting signature dishes, but the service in the first 6 months was painfully slow. (See "Dining," below, for a full review). We hope that as the restaurant matures this will improve. Also on property are a lounge with a "paniolo" (cowboy) theme and a pool bar. The large open hall called the "Great Room," with a cozy fireplace, hosts wonderful local entertainment in the evening (even if you don't stay here, come for the free entertainment).

Amenities: Reading library; game room with cable TV; gorgeous "infinity" pool heated to a perfect temperature for the cool climate; one-room workout center; limited spa with massage room; high-speed data ports (both in odd places in the guest rooms and in other areas of the lodge); concierge. A complimentary shuttle will take you to the Molokai Ranch for activities (horseback riding, mountain biking, hiking, kayaking, snorkeling, and beach activities, ranging in price from $25 to $125), to the beach, and to other recreational areas. The airport shuttle costs $20 round-trip.

EXPENSIVE

Molokai Ranch. P.O. Box 259, Maunaloa, HI 96770. ☎ **877/726-4656** or 808/660-2722. Fax 808/660-2724. www.molokai-ranch.com. 3 semipermanent camping sites of 20–40 units each. $145–$245 double. Rates include breakfast. Extra person $40–$50. Children 12 and under stay free. AE, CB, DC, DISC, JCB, MC, V. Airport shuttle service $20 round-trip.

This was a great idea, an unique ecoadventure that combines camping and outdoor activities with the amenities of a resort. The Ranch developed three camping areas (two near the beach and one up near chilly Maunaloa town) with very upscale accommodations in bungalow/tents called *tentalows* (safari-type tents mounted on wooden platforms) at two camps and *yurts* (circular canvas shelters on platforms) at one site. This is yuppie camping: All the tents and yurts have queen-size or twin beds, ceiling fans, solar-powdered lights, private bathrooms with composting toilets, and solar hot-water showers, plus a big deck with lounge chairs and a picnic table outside. There's even daily maid service!

When the ranch first opened, these "camps" had an all-inclusive price, which included all meals plus many outdoor activities (horseback riding, mountain biking, hikes, sailing, snorkeling, kayaking, and other adventures). There were some glitches, but generally it was worth it. Today the prices have risen to $145 to $245 for the tentalow/yurt, with breakfast only (you now have to pay for other meals and all activities on an à la carte basis). We feel this is way too expensive, not only for what you get, but also considering the multitude of logistical problems that have plagued the camps since they opened.

These problems, some of which we experienced firsthand during a recent stay and others of which we've heard about via reader letters, include unreliable transportation from one camp to another, and from one activity to another (even getting back to the airport has been iffy). Sometimes there has even been a shortage of food (we quickly learned to be at the dining pavilion on time because several times in our stay they completely ran out of food); requests for special meals due to dietary considerations were frequently ignored or just "forgotten." There seems to be a lack of a friendly, helpful attitude among the staff (virtually every request was answered with a sigh and an attempt to talk the guest out of the request).

MODERATE

Ke Nani Kai Resort. Kaluakoi Resort, Kaluakoi Rd., off Hwy. 460 (P.O. Box 289), Maunaloa, HI 96770. ☎ **800/535-0085** or 808/552-2761. Fax 808/552-0045. www.marcresorts.com. 100 apts. TV TEL. $149–$159 1-bedroom apt (sleeps up to 4); $179–$199 2-bedroom apt (sleeps up to 6). AE, CB, DISC, DC, JCB, MC, V.

This place is great for families, who'll like the space and quiet. These large apartments have real kitchens, washer/dryers, VCRs, attractive furnishings, and breezy lanai. There's a huge pool, a volleyball court, tennis courts, and golf on the neighboring Kaluakoi course. These condos are farther from the sea than other local accommodations, but it's still just a brief walk down to the beach. The two-story buildings are surrounded by parking and garden areas.

✪ **Paniolo Hale.** Next door to Kaluakoi Resort, Lio Place (P.O. Box 190), Maunaloa, HI 96770. ☎ **800/367-2984** or 808/552-2731. Fax 808/552-2288. www.lava.net/paniolo. 77 units. TV. $95–$205 double studio; $115–$230 1-bedroom apt (sleeps up to 4); $145–$265 2-bedroom apt (sleeps up to 6). Extra person $10. 2-night minimum, 1-week minimum Dec 20–Jan 5. Ask about weekly rates and condo/car packages. AE, MC, V.

This is far and away Molokai's most charming lodging, and probably its best value—be sure to ask about discounts and special packages when booking your reservations here. The two-story Old Hawaii ranch-house design is airy and homey, with oak floors and walls of folding glass doors that open to huge screened verandas, doubling your living space. The one- and two-bedrooms come with two bathrooms, so they accommodate three or four people easily. Some have hot tubs on the lanai. Units are spacious, comfortably furnished, and well equipped, with full kitchens and washer/dryers.

The whole place overlooks the Kaluakoi Golf Course, a green barrier that separates these condos from the rest of Kaluakoi Resort. Hotel shops, a restaurant, and a lounge are just across the fairway, as is Kepuhi Beach, which is a scenic place to walk and beachcomb, though the waters are too hazardous for most swimmers. A pool, paddle tennis, and barbecue facilities are on the property, which adjoins open grassland countryside.

THE EAST END
MODERATE

✪ **Dunbar Beachfront Cottages.** Kamehameha V Hwy., past mile marker 18. Reservations c/o Kip and Leslie Dunbar, HC01 Box 901, Kaunakakai, HI 96748. ☎ **800/673-0520** or 808/558-8153. Fax 808/558-8153. www.molokai-aloha.com/kainalu. 2 cottages (each sleeps up to 4). TV TEL. $125 per night, $938 per week. 3-night minimum. AE, MC, V.

This is one of the most peaceful, comfortable, and elegant properties on Molokai's East End, and the setting is simply stunning. Each of these green-and-white plantation-style cottages sits on its own secluded beach—you'll feel like you're on your own private island. The Puunana Cottage has a king bed and two twins; the Pauwalu has a queen and two twin beds. Both have full kitchens, VCRs, washer/dryers, ceiling fans, comfortable tropical furniture, large furnished decks, and views of Maui, Lanai, and Kahoolawe across the channel. In the winter, the decks are perfect places for whale watching.

Moanui Beach House. Kamehameha V. Hwy., at mile marker 20. Reservations c/o Glenn and Akiko Foster, HC01, Box 300, Kaunakakai, HI 96748. ☎ and fax **808/558-8326.** www.molokai.com/kamalo. TV TEL. 1 unit. $140 double. Extra person $20. 3-night minimum. No credit cards.

The owners have lived in the islands for many years and have run the popular Kamalo Plantation Bed and Breakfast (see below). Recently they purchased this two-bedroom beach house right across the street from a secluded white-sand cove beach and totally renovated it. The A-frame house has a shaded lanai facing the ocean view, plus another screened-in lanai on the side, giving you plenty of outdoor living space protected from the elements. The house has a bedroom upstairs and another downstairs, a full kitchen, and an ocean view that's worth the price all by itself. The Fosters leave a "starter supply" of breakfast for guests, with a fruit basket, home-baked bread, tropical fruit juices, and tea and coffee. If you want a quiet, remote beach house, this is it. The only drawback is the lack of laundry facilities.

INEXPENSIVE

Country Cottage at Puu O Hoku Ranch. Kamehameha V Hwy., at mile marker 25. Reservations: P.O. Box 1889, Kaunakakai, HI 96748. ☎ **808/558-8109.** Fax 808/558-8100. www.puuohoku.com. 1 cottage (sleeps up to 5). $85 double. Extra person $10. 2-night minimum. No credit cards.

ⓕ Family-Friendly Accommodations

Ke Nani Kai Resort (*see p. 242*)   Located in Kaluakoi Resort, these one- and two-bedroom condo units offer lots of space, with complete kitchens, washer/dryers, VCRs, attractive furnishings, and breezy lanai. For active families, there's a huge pool, a volleyball court, tennis courts, and golf at neighboring Kaluakoi.

Molokai Shores (*see p. 239*)   At this great central location, just outside of Kaunakakai, families can choose from large one- and two-bedroom units in a tropical garden complex with great views of the fishponds, offshore reefs, and neighbor islands. Amenities include a swimming pool and laundry facilities.

Dunbar Beachfront Cottages (*see p. 243*)   Here, you'll find private two-bedroom cottages located on the beach in the lush East End—the perfect spot for a family getaway vacation. Each cottage sits on its own secluded beach and features complete kitchens, washer/dryers, VCRs, large decks, and breathtaking views (great for watching whales in the winter).

Country Cottage at Puu O Hoku Ranch (*see p. 243*)   Take the kids to a working cattle ranch. *Puu o Hoku* ("Star Hill"), located at least an hour's drive from Kaunakai, nearly at Halawa Valley, has plenty of room for the kids to spread out and play, plus your own secluded, private beach on the shoreline. If you have a really big family (or a family reunion), there's an 11-room lodge on the property also.

Escape to a working cattle ranch! *Puu o Hoku* ("Star Hill") Ranch, which spreads across the East End of Molokai on 14,000 acres of pasture and forests, is the last place to stay before Halawa Valley—it's at least an hour's drive from Kaunakai along the shoreline. Two acres of tropically landscaped property circle the ranch's rustic cottage, which has breathtaking views of rolling hills and the Pacific Ocean. The wooden cottage features comfortable country furniture, a fully equipped kitchen, two bedrooms (one with double bed, one with two twins), two bathrooms, a big living area, and a separate dining room on the enclosed lanai. TVs and VCRs are available on request. You'll stargaze at night, watch the sunrise in the morning, and play in the afternoon: croquet, hiking, swimming, or just roaming the grounds. For larger parties, there's an 11-room lodge on the property.

Honomuni House. Kamehameha V Hwy., just after mile marker 17 (HC-01, Box 700), Kaunakakai, HI 96748. ☎ **808/558-8383.** 1 cottage. TV. $85 double. Extra person $10 adult, $5 child. 2-night minimum. No credit cards.

Old stonework taro terraces and house foundations testify that Honomuni Valley was popular with early Hawaiians, whose groves of breadfruit, coconut, fruit, ginger, and coffee still flourish in the wilderness. Modern folks can sample this miniparadise at a remote cottage—$17^1/_2$ miles from Kaunakakai, a mile or more from the nearest public beach area—set in the forest along the foot of the East End upslope. Freshwater prawns and native fish hide out in the stream that carved the valley. Experienced hikers will enjoy exploring upstream, where they'll find pools for swimming and watching (or catching) prawns and, farther up, a waterfall of their very own. The small cottage has a full kitchen, one separate bedroom, a bathroom, and an outside shower for rinsing off the sand from the beach. You're welcome to enjoy the tropical fruits growing right on the premises, which are dominated by a huge monkeypod tree. The cottage does sit right on the road, but there's generally little traffic after dark.

✪ **Kamalo Plantation Bed & Breakfast.** Kamehameha V Hwy., just past mile marker 10 (HC01, Box 300), Kaunakakai, HI 96748. ☎ and fax **808/558-8236.** www.molokai.com/ kamalo. 1 unit. TV. $85 cottage. Rates include continental breakfast. Extra person $10. 2-night minimum. No credit cards.

Glenn and Akiko Foster's 5-acre spread includes an ancient heiau ruin in the front yard, plus leafy tropical gardens and a working fruit orchard. Their Eden-like property is easy to find: It's right across the East End road from Father Damien's historic St. Joseph church. The plantation-style cottage is tucked under flower trees and surrounded by swaying palms and tropical foliage. It has its own lanai, a big living room with a queen-size pull-out couch, and a separate bedroom with a king-size bed, so it can sleep four comfortably. The kitchen is fully equipped (it even has spices), and there's a barbecue outside. A breakfast of fruit and freshly baked bread is served every morning.

Kumu'eli Farm B&B. Kamehameha V. Hwy., just past mile marker 10, P.O. Box 1829, Kaunakakai, HI 96748. ☎ and fax **808/558-8284.** www.visitmolokai.com/kumueli. 1 unit. TV. $100 double. Rates include complete breakfast. 2-night minimum. No credit cards.

Nestled on an 8-acre farm and surrounded by gardens, lies this large private cottage with hardwood floors, a big bedroom with floor-to-ceiling windows, and a huge bathroom with enough space to dance. It comes complete with a kitchenette (microwave, refrigerator, and coffeemaker), a VCR, and all the peace and quiet in the world. Daily breakfast with hostess Dorothy Curtis consists of waffles or omelettes and just-out-of-the-oven homemade bread. Outside is a 75-foot lap pool, beautiful gardens for sitting, and miles of hiking trails.

4 Dining

by Jocelyn Fujii

When the Molokai Ranch Lodge opened in September 1999, it introduced two firsts: Molokai's first elevator and the island's first upscale restaurant, the Maunaloa Room, an attractive dining room with a deck, a view, and a menu they've dubbed "Molokai Regional Cuisine." Miles away in Kaunakakai, the reopening of the renovated Hotel Molokai unveiled a tropical fantasy of an oceanfront dining room that quickly became the island's busiest restaurant.

These additions to the otherwise spare culinary offerings of the island are in the uplands of Maunaloa and the seaside of Kaunakakai—two different and complementary locales. In between, Molokai's offerings are dominated by small mom-and-pop eateries, nothing fancy, most of them fast-food or take-out places and many of them with a home-cooked touch.

Even with these new developments, one of the best things about Molokai is its glacial pace of change. Lovers of the fast lane might consider this aspect of the island's personality a con rather than a pro, but they wouldn't choose to come here, anyway. Molokai is for those who want to get away from it all, who consider the lack of high-rises and traffic lights a welcome change from the urban chaos that keeps nibbling at the edges of the more popular and populated islands. Sybarites, foodies, and pampered oenophiles had best lower their expectations upon arrival, or turn around and leave the island's natural beauty to nature lovers.

Personally, we like the unpretentiousness of the island; it's an oasis in a state where plastic aloha abounds. Most Molokai residents fish, collect seaweed, grow potatoes and tomatoes, and prepare for backyard luaus. Unlike Lanai, which is small and rural but offers some of the finest dining in the islands, Molokai provides no such mix of innocence and sophistication. You must meet this island on its own terms. Except for the significant cultural departure presented by the Molokai Ranch Lodge, Molokai doesn't pretend to be anything more than a combination of old ways and an informal lifestyle that's close to the land.

You'll even find a certain defiant stance against the trappings of modernity. Although some of the best produce in Hawaii is grown on this island, you're not likely to find much of it served in its restaurants, other than in the take-out items at Outpost Natural Foods, or at the Molokai Pizza Café (one of the most pleasing eateries on the island), the Hotel Molokai, and the Maunaloa Room. The rest of the time, content yourself with ethnic or diner fare, or fresh fish from the Molokai Ice House—or cook for yourself. The many visitors who stay in condos find that it doesn't take long to sniff out the best sources of produce, groceries, and fresh fish to fire up at home when the island's other dining options are exhausted. The "Edibles" sections in "Shopping," later in this chapter, will point you to the shops and markets where you can pick up foodstuffs for your own island-style feast.

Except for the Maunaloa Room, Molokai's restaurants are inexpensive or moderately priced, and several of them do not accept credit cards. Regardless of where you eat, you certainly won't have to dress up on Molokai. In most cases, we've listed just the town rather than the street address, because as you'll see, street addresses are as meaningless on this island as fancy cars and sequins. Reservations are not accepted unless otherwise noted.

KAUNAKAKAI

Codi's Lunch Wagon. 16 Kamoi St. ☎ **808/553-3443.** $4.75–$5.50. No credit cards. Mon–Fri 10:30am–1:30pm. LOCAL.

Only days after its opening in March 1998, residents were touting the spare ribs, oxtail soup, and pork adobo served up at this tiny, modest lunch wagon. The four different plate lunches a day are served with rice, macaroni salad, and kimchi—a good value. The rotating menu includes chicken broccoli, chicken papaya, roast pork, meat loaf, shrimp curry, and other ethnic fare. But Codi's isn't for everyone: If you're scared off by a modest exterior, obscure location (on a side street in front of a car repair shop), and a very local menu, head for something more mainstream and accessible.

Hotel Molokai. Kamehameha V. Hwy. ☎ **808/553-5347.** Reservations recommended for dinner. Lunch main courses $6.50–$8.50, dinner main courses $11–$15. AE, CB, DC, JCB, MC, V. Daily 7am–10am, 11am–2pm, and 5–9pm; bar open until 10:30pm. AMERICAN/ISLAND.

This hotel dining room evokes the romance of the quintessential South Seas fantasy. Right on the ocean, with a view of Lanai, torch flickering under palm trees, and tiny fairy lights line the room and the neighboring pool area. It's a casual room, and since its 1999 reopening, it has provided the only nightlife in Kaunakakai (see "Molokai After Dark," at the end of this chapter).

Lunch choices stick to the basics and are most promising in salads (Big Island organic greens are a nice touch) and sandwiches, from roast beef to boneless chicken and grilled mahimahi. As the sun sets and the torches are lit for dinner, the room is at its most romantic and the menu turns to heavier meats, ribs, fish, and pasta. We had high hopes for the Molokai coconut shrimp, made with shrimp from an aquaculture venture on the island, but it was a disappointment, too heavy on the batter and too light on the shrimp. We had better luck with the charbroiled garlic chicken breast, fork tender, and the New York steak, topped with sautéed Maui onions and mushrooms. Temper your expectations of culinary excellence and you're sure to enjoy a pleasing but not perfect dinner in an atmosphere that is unequalled on the island.

Kamoi Snack-N-Go. Kamoi Professional Center. ☎ **808/553-3742.** Ice cream $1.65–$3.40. No credit cards. Mon–Sat 9am–9pm, Sun noon–9pm. ICE CREAM/SNACKS.

The Kamoi specialty: sweets and icy treats. Ice cream made by Dave's on Oahu comes in flavors such as green tea, litchi sherbet, ube (a brilliant purple, made from Okinawan sweet potato), haupia, mango, and many other tropical and traditional flavors. Schoolchildren and their parents line up for the ice cream cones, shakes, floats, sundaes, and the popular Icee floats served at this tiny snack shop. No tables, but there are aisles of candies.

Kanemitsu's Bakery & Restaurant. 79 Ala Malama St. ☎ **808/553-5855.** Most items less than $5.50. No credit cards. Restaurant Wed–Sun 5:30–11:30am; bakery Wed–Mon 5:30am–6:30pm. BAKERY/DELI.

Morning, noon, and night, this local legend fills the Kaunakakai air with the sweet smells of baking. Taro lavosh is the hot seller, joining Molokai bread—developed in 1935 in a cast-iron, kiawe-fired oven—as a Kanemitsu signature. Flavors range from apricot-pineapple to mango (in season), but the classics remain the regular white, wheat, cheese, sweet, and onion-cheese breads. The bread mixes (regular, sweet, and macadamia-nut) offer a way to take Molokai home. In the adjoining coffee shop/deli, all sandwiches come on their own freshly baked buns and breads. The hamburgers, egg-salad sandwiches, mahi burgers, and honey-dipped fried chicken are popular and cheap.

Kanemitsu's has a life after dark, too. Whenever anyone on Molokai mentions "hot bread," he's talking about the hot bread run at Kanemitsu's, the late-night ritual for die-hard bread lovers. Those in the know line up at the bakery's back door beginning at 10:30pm, when the bread is whisked hot out of the oven and into waiting hands. You can order your fresh bread with butter, jelly, cinnamon, cream cheese, or "whatever," say the bakers, and they'll cut the hot loaves down the middle and slather on the works so it melts in the bread. A hand will pop out of the half-door with your order, your payment is accepted (usually around $3.25), and the person shuffles back into the dark interior. Eventually your change appears, thrust out of the half-door to complete this surreal, wonderful, only-on-Molokai experience. *Hint:* The cream cheese and jelly bread makes a fine substitute for dessert.

Molokai Drive-Inn. Kaunakakai. ☎ **808/553-5655.** Most items less than $6. No credit cards. Mon–Fri 5:30am–10pm, Sat–Sun 6am–10:30pm. AMERICAN/TAKEOUT.

The $6 plate-lunch prices are a bit steep at this greasy spoon, but it's one of the rare drive-up places with fresh *akule* (mackerel) and ahi (when available), and fried saimin at budget-friendly prices. The honey-dipped fried chicken is a favorite among residents, who also come here for the floats, shakes, and other artery-clogging choices. But don't expect much in terms of ambience: This is a fast-food take-out counter with the smells of frying in the surrounding air—and it doesn't pretend to be otherwise.

Molokai Mango. 93-D Ala Malama St. ☎ **808/553-3981.** MC, V. Mon–Sat 9am–7:30pm. DELI/AMERICAN.

The former owner of JoJo's restaurant in Maunaloa opened this video store and popular sandwich shop in downtown Kaunakakai, where he sells sandwiches and nachos from the take-out counter. Turkey, ham, and roast beef (Angus beef) are served on five different breads, and all are popular. The inexpensive nachos are a big hit, too, for those evenings at home with a rented movie. Molokai Mango also rents and sells videos, games, and equipment, including TV sets.

✪ **Molokai Pizza Cafe.** At Kahua Center, on the old Wharf Rd. ☎ **808/553-3288.** Large pizzas $12.60–$22.15. No credit cards. Sun 11am–10pm, Mon–Thurs 10am–10pm, Fri–Sat 10am–11pm. PIZZA.

This place was the talk of the town when it opened—"Molokai has pizza now," the locals announced proudly—and its excellent pizzas and sandwiches have made it a Kaunakakai staple as well as one of our favorite eateries on the island. The best-selling pies: the Molokai (pepperoni and cheese), the Big Island (pepperoni, ham, mushroom, Italian sausage, bacon, and vegetables), and the Molokini (simple, individual cheese slices). Pasta, sandwiches, and specials (garden burger to huli huli chicken) round out the menu. Our personal fave is the vegetarian Maui pizza, but others tout the fresh baked submarine and pocket sandwiches and the gyro pocket with spinach pie. Sunday is prime rib day, Wednesday is Mexican, and Hawaiian plates are sold on Thursdays. Coin-operated cars and a toy airplane follow the children's theme, but adults should feel equally at home with the very popular barbecued baby-back rib plate and the fresh fish dinners. Children's art and letters in the tiled dining room add an entertaining and charming touch. Free delivery to the Hotel Molokai is a nice new touch.

✪ **Outpost Natural Foods.** 70 Makaena Place. ☎ **808/553-3377.** Most items less than $5. No credit cards. Sun–Fri 10am–3pm. VEGETARIAN.

The healthiest and freshest food on the island is served at the lunch counter of this health-food store, around the corner from the main drag on the makai (toward the sea) side of Kaunakakai town. The tiny health food store abounds in Molokai papayas, bananas, herbs, potatoes, watermelon, and other local produce, complementing its selection of vitamins, cosmetics, and health aids, as well as bulk and shelf items. But the real star is the closet-size lunch counter. The salads, burritos, tempeh sandwiches, vegetarian pot pie and tofu-spinach lasagna specials, and mock chicken, turkey, and meat loaf (made from oats, sprouts, seeds, and seasonings) will likely dispel the notion most folks have about vegetarian food being boring. For health-conscious diners and shoppers, a must.

Rabang's. Kaunakakai. ☎ **808/553-5841.** Most items less than $4.50; combination plate $6. No credit cards. Daily 7am–9pm. FILIPINO.

Specialties here include sweet-and-sour turkey tail prepared Ilocano style (as opposed to Tagalog) and a Filipino dish called *pinat bet*—a mixture of eggplant, string beans, pumpkin, lima beans, and other vegetables, with a smidgen of pork and some assertive seasonings. This diner is a bit more in the thick of things and more inviting than Oviedo's down the street, but it's still extremely casual, with only a few tables that are always full at lunchtime. The Friday Hawaiian plate, barbecued chicken plate, and sweet-and-sour pork are among the Molokai favorites, but all in all, this is a place for adventurous palates.

Sundown Deli. 145 Puali St. (across the street from Veteran's Memorial Park). ☎ **808/553-3713.** Sandwiches, soups, and salads $3.95–$7.50. AE, MC, V. Mon–Fri 10:30am–5pm, Sat 10:30am–2pm. DELI.

From "gourmet saimin" to spinach pie, Sundown's offerings are home-cooked and healthy, with daily specials that include vegetarian quiche, spanakopita, vegetarian lasagna, and club sandwiches. The sandwiches (like smoked turkey and chicken salad) and several salads (Caesar, Oriental, stuffed tomato) are served daily, with a soup that changes by the day (it might be clam chowder, Portuguese bean, or cream of broccoli). Vitamins, T-shirts, and snacks are sold in this tiny two-table cafe, but most of the business is take-out.

THE WEST END

Maunaloa Room. In Molokai Ranch Lodge, Maunaloa. ☎ **808/660-2725.** Reservations recommended for dinner. Main courses $19–$39. AE, CB, DC, DISC, MC, V. Daily 6–10am, 11am–1:30pm, and 6–9pm; Sun brunch 11am–1:30pm. MOLOKAI REGIONAL.

Thirty-dollar entrees on Molokai? It's an oxymoron if ever there were one. Clearly emulating the highly successful Lodge at Koele on Lanai, the Molokai Ranch Lodge is out of its league. This laid-back island has never had anything resembling fine dining, but with the island's first upscale hotel, a 22-room lodge fashioned after a ranch owner's private home in the cool hills of Maunaloa, the first baby steps have been taken on the long and rocky road to luxury. How successful the restaurant will be remains to be seen; my dining experience required an attitude adjustment, but was pleasing.

The menu honors fresh Molokai ingredients in cross-cultural preparations, including "Molokai red dirt bread," reddened with health-giving 'alae (clay) and paprika; freshwater prawns; farm-raised Molokai white shrimp; 'opihi (limpets) from local fishermen; and Molokai sweet corn and onions. The 'opihi come atop cubed cucumbers and tomatoes in saimin spoons that are fanned out across the plate, with a small mound of seaweed between each spoon. Although seasoned 'opihi lovers prefer more 'opihi and less of everything else, this presentation is ideal for the uninitiated. The bamboo-steamed moi (threadfish) with black beans was succulent, and the special of the evening, a tower of mahimahi, lobster, and guava coulis on a corn cake, was contained vertically in nori, and was excellent.

The room's rustic, lodgey ambience fits the paniolo surroundings, and Hawaiian proverbs stenciled on the walls are a nice cultural touch. From the hotel you can see Oahu (Diamond Head under the best of conditions) past the rolling ranchlands and the ocean. It remains to be seen whether Molokai outdoor enthusiasts, who often pack nothing dressier than a T-shirt and jeans, will take to this retooling of the Molokai image and the much higher prices that accompany it.

The Village Grill. Maunaloa. ☎ **808/552-0012.** Reservations recommended for dinner. Main courses $19.50–$21.50. AE, CB, DC, DISC, MC, V. Mon–Fri 11:30am–1:30pm, daily 6–9pm. STONE GRILL/LOCAL/AMERICAN.

The plantation architecture of the original building remains, with a wraparound veranda and indoor dining room around an antique bar. On a clear day, you can see Oahu from the deck—the back side of Diamond Head is a surprising sight from Molokai.

At lunch it's plate-lunch, order-at-the-counter, Styrofoam-style, with local favorites and daily specials such as Korean chicken and oxtail soup, at prices around $6 and under. At dinner, flat heated stones (700°) do the cooking at your table in a method called "stone grill dining." Porterhouse steak, lamb, chicken, seafood, and combinations, some of them marinated, sizzle to a lower-fat doneness in front of you and are served with vegetables or salads. With the orders thus seared to personal tastes, the method is touted as a freshly grilled healthy meal. For loyalists, the old Pistol Pete's 10-ounce prime rib is still available for $19.50, on Fridays and Saturdays only, and the fresh catch of the day, for $21.95.

THE EAST END

Neighborhood Store 'N Counter. Pukoo. ☎ **808/558-8498.** Most items less than $6.50. No credit cards. Daily 8am–6pm. AMERICAN.

The Neighborhood Store is nothing fancy, and that's what we love about it. This store/lunch counter appears like a mirage near mile marker 16 in the Pukoo area en route to the East End. Picnic tables under a royal poinciana tree are a cordial sight, and the food does not disappoint. The place serves omelettes, Portuguese sausage, and other breakfast specials (the brunch is very popular), then segues into sandwiches, salads, mahimahi plates, and varied over-the-counter lunch offerings. Favorites include the mahimahi plate lunch, the chicken katsu, and the Mexican plate, tried and true and each one with a home-cooked flavor. There are daily specials, ethnic dishes, and some vegetarian dishes, as well as burgers (including a killer veggie burger), saimin, and legendary desserts. Made-on-Maui Roselani ice cream is a featured attraction, and we hear raves over the Portuguese donut dessert, a deep-fried donut filled with ice cream. This is a great stop on the east end, a Molokai treasure. (Also see "Shopping," later in this chapter.)

5 Beaches

by Jeanette Foster

With imposing sea cliffs on one side and lazy fishponds on the other, Molokai has little room for beaches along its 106-mile coast. Still, a big gold-sand beach lies on the West End, and you'll find tiny pocket beaches on the East End. The emptiness of Molokai's beaches is both a blessing and a curse: The welcome seclusion means no lifeguards.

KAUNAKAKAI'S BEACH: ONE ALII BEACH PARK

This thin strip of sand, once reserved for the *alii* (chiefs), is the oldest public beach park on Molokai. You'll find One Alii Beach Park (*One* is pronounced *O-nay*, not *won*) by a coconut grove on the outskirts of Kaunakakai. Safe for swimmers of all ages and abilities, it's often crowded with splashy families on weekends, but it can be all yours on weekdays. Facilities include outdoor showers, rest rooms, and free parking.

WEST END BEACHES
✪ PAPOHAKU BEACH

Nearly 3 miles long and 100 yards wide, gold-sand Papohaku Beach is one of the biggest in Hawaii (17-mile-long Polihale Beach on Kauai actually takes that prize). It's great for walking, beachcombing, picnics, and sunset-watching year-round. The big surf and rip tides make swimming risky except in the summer, when the waters are calmer. Go early in the day when the tropical sun is less fierce and the winds are calm. The beach is so big that you may never see another soul except at sunset, when a few people gather on the shore in hopes of spotting the elusive green flash, a natural wonder that takes place when the horizon is cloud-free. Facilities include outdoor showers, rest rooms, picnic grounds, and free parking.

KEPUHI BEACH

Golfers see this picturesque golden strand in front of the Kaluakoi Resort and Golf Course as just another sand trap, but sunbathers like the semiprivate grassy dunes; they're seldom, if ever, crowded. Beachcombers often find what they're looking for here, but swimmers have to dodge lava rocks and risk rip tides. And oh, yes—look out for errant golf balls. There are no facilities or lifeguards, but cold drinks and rest rooms are handy at the resort.

EAST END BEACHES
✪ SANDY BEACH

Molokai's most popular swimming beach—ideal for families with small kids—is a roadside pocket of gold sand, protected by a reef, with a great view of Maui and Lanai.

You'll find it off the King Kamehameha V Highway (Hwy. 450) at mile marker 20. There are no facilities—just you, the sun, the sand, and the surf.

MURPHY BEACH PARK (KUMIMI BEACH PARK)

In 1970, the Molokai Jaycees wanted to create a sandy beach park with a good swimming area for the children of the East End. They chose a section known as Kumimi Beach, which was owned by the Puu o Hoku Ranch. The beach was a dump, literally. The ranch owner, George Murphy, immediately gave his permission to use the site as a park; the Jaycees cleaned it up and built three small pavilions, plus picnic tables and barbecue grills. Officially, the park is called the George Murphy Beach Park (shortened to Murphy Beach Park over the years), but some old-timers still call it Kumimi Beach, and just to make things real confusing, some people call it Jaycees Park.

No matter what you call it, this small park is shaded by ironwood trees that line a white-sand beach. Generally it's a very safe swimming area. On calm days, snorkeling and diving are great outside the reef. Fishermen are also frequently spotted here looking for papio and other island fish.

HALAWA BEACH PARK

At the foot of scenic Halawa Valley is this beautiful black-sand beach with a palm-fringed lagoon, a wave-lashed island offshore, and a distant view of the West Maui Mountains across the Pailolo Channel. The swimming is safe in the shallows close to shore, but where the waterfall stream meets the sea, the ocean is often murky and unnerving. A winter swell creases the mouth of Halawa Valley on the north side of the bay and attracts a crowd of local surfers. Facilities are minimal; bring your own water. To get here, take King Kamehameha V Highway (Hwy. 450) east to the end.

6 Hitting the Water

by Jeanette Foster

The best place to rent beach toys (snorkels, boogie boards, surf boards, beach chairs, fishing poles) is from **Molokai Outdoor Activities,** located in the lobby of the Hotel Molokai, just outside of Kaunakakai (☎ **877/553-4477** or 808/553-4477; www.molokai-outdoors.com). They not only have everything you need, but can give you advice on where to find a great swimming beach, or where the waves are breaking. Another option is **Molokai Fish & Dive** (☎ **808/553-5926**), in Kaunakakai, a mind-boggling store filled with outdoor gear. You can rent snorkeling gear, fishing gear, and even ice chests here ($4 a day). This is also a hotspot for fishing news and tips on what's running where.

For details on the activities listed below, see chapter 6, "Fun in the Surf & Sun."

BODYBOARDING (BOOGIE BOARDING) & BODYSURFING

Molokai only has three beaches that offer ridable waves for bodyboarding and bodysurfing: Papohaku, Kepuhi, and Halawa. Even these beaches are only for experienced bodysurfers, due to the strength of the rip currents and undertows. You can rent boogie boards ($5.95 a day or $23.95 a week) and fins ($2.95 a day or $11.95 a week) from **Molokai Outdoor Activities** (see above for contact information).

OCEAN KAYAKING

During the summer months, when the waters on the north shore are calm, Molokai offers some of the most spectacular kayaking in Hawaii. You can paddle from remote valley to remote valley, spending a week or more exploring the exotic terrain.

❂ Frommer's Favorite Molakai Experiences

Ride a Mule into Kalaupapa. Don't pass up the opportunity to see this hauntingly beautiful peninsula. Buzzy Sproats's mules go up and down the 2.9-mile trail (with 26 switchbacks, it can be a bit tricky) to Molokai's famous leper colony. The views are breathtaking: You'll see the world's highest sea cliffs (taller than a 300-story skyscraper) and waterfalls plunging thousands of feet into the ocean. If you're afraid of heights, catch the views from the Kalaupapa Lookout.

Travel Back in Time on the Pepeopae Trail. This awesome hike takes you through the Molokai Forest Reserve and back a few million years in time. Along the misty trail (actually a boardwalk across the bog), expect close encounters of the flora kind: mosses, sedges, violets, lichens, and knee-high ancient ohias.

Stroll the Sands at Papohaku. Go early, when the tropical sun isn't so fierce, and stroll this 3-mile stretch of unspoiled golden sand—it's one of the longest beaches in Hawaii. The big surf and rip currents make swimming somewhat risky, but Papohaku is perfect for walking, beachcombing, and in the evening, sunset-watching.

Soak in the Warm Waters off Sandy Beach. On Molokai's East End, about 20 miles outside of Kaunakakai—just before the road starts to climb to Halawa Valley—lies a small pocket of white sand known as Sandy Beach. Submerging yourself here in the warm, calm waters (an outer reef protects the cove) is a sensual experience par excellence.

Snorkel Among Clouds of Butterfly Fish. The calm waters off Kumimi Beach, on the East End, are perfect for snorkelers. Just don your gear and head to the reef, where you'll find lots of exotic tropical fish, including long-nosed butterfly fish, saddle wrasses, and convict tangs.

Venture Into the Garden of Eden. Drive the 30 miles of road along Molokai's East End. Take your time. Stop to smell the flowers and pick guavas by the side of the road. Pull over for a swim. Wave at every car you pass and every person you see. At the end of the road, stand on the beach at Halawa Valley and see Hawaii as it must have looked in A.D. 650, when the first people arrived in the islands.

Celebrate the Ancient Hula. Hula is the heartbeat of Hawaiian culture, and Molokai is the birthplace of the hula. While most visitors to Hawaii never get to see the real thing, it's possible to see it here—once a year, on the third Saturday in May, when Molokai celebrates the birth of the hula at its ❂ **Molokai Ka Hula Piko Festival.** The day-long affair at Papohaku Beach Park includes dance,

However, Molokai is for the experienced kayaker only. You must be adept in paddling through open ocean swells and rough waves.

Molokai Outdoor Activities (see above for contact information) offers kayak tours of the ancient Hawaii fish ponds and the inshore reefs for beginners for $35 per person and coastline tours for more experienced kayakers for $45. They also rent kayaks: $8 an hour single ($25 a day) and $10 an hour double ($30 a day).

SAILING

Molokai Charters (☎ **808/553-5852**) offers a variety of sailing trips on *Satan's Doll*, a 42-foot sloop: 2-hour sunset sails for $40 per person, a half-day of sailing music, food, and crafts; see "Maui, Molokai & Lanai Calendar of Events" in chapter 2 for details.

Kayak Along the North Shore. This is the Hawaii of your dreams: waterfalls thundering down sheer cliffs, remote sand beaches, miles of tropical vegetation, tropical seabirds soaring overhead, and the sound of the sea splashing on your kayak and of the wind whispering in your ear. The best times to go are during the brief window in early spring, around March to April, and during the summer months, especially August to September, when the normally galloping ocean lies down flat.

Sample the Local Brew. Saunter up to the Espresso Bar at the Coffees of Hawaii Plantation Store in Kualapuu for a fresh cup of java made from beans that were grown, processed, and packed on this 450-acre plantation. While you sip, survey the vast collection of native crafts.

Taste Aloha at a Macadamia Nut Farm. It could be the owner, Tuddie Purdy, and his friendly disposition that make the macadamia nuts here taste so good. Or it could be his years of practice in growing, harvesting, and shelling them on his 1$^{1}/_{2}$-acre farm. Either way, Purdy produces a perfect crop. You can see how he does it on a short, free tour of Purdy's All Natural Macadamia Nut Farm in Hoolehua, just a nut's throw from the airport.

Talk Story with the Locals. The number-one favorite pastime of most islanders is "talking story," or exchanging experiences and knowledge. It's an old Hawaiian custom that brings people, and generations, closer together. You can probably find residents more than willing to share their wisdom with you while fishing from the wharf at Kaunakakai, hanging out at Molokai Fish & Dive, or having coffee at any of the island's restaurants.

Post a Nut. Why send a picturesque postcard to your friends and family back home when you can send a fresh coconut? The Hoolelua Post Office will supply the free coconuts, if you'll supply the $3 postage fee.

Watch the Sunset from a Coconut Grove. Kapuaiwa Coconut Beach Park, off Maunaloa Highway (Hwy. 460), is a perfect place to watch the sunset. The sky behind the coconut trees fills with a kaleidoscope of colors as the sun sinks into the Pacific. Molokai's tropical sunsets—often red, sometimes orange, always different—are an everyday miracle that stop people in their tracks. Be careful where you sit, though: Falling coconuts could have you seeing stars well before dusk.

and whale-watching for $50, and a full-day sail to Lanai with swimming and snorkeling for $90 (which includes lunch, cold drinks, snacks, and all equipment). Owners Richard and Doris Reed have been sailing visitors around Molokai's waters since 1975.

They also offer **whale-watching cruises** from mid-December to mid-March, when humpback whales frequent the waters around Molokai.

SCUBA DIVING

Want to see turtles or manta rays up close? How about sharks? Molokai resident Bill Kapuni has been diving the waters around Molokai his entire life; he'll be happy to show you whatever you're brave enough to encounter. **Bill Kapuni's Snorkel and Dive,** Kaunakakai (☎ 808/553-9867), can provide gear, a boat, and even instruction. Two-tank dives in his 22-foot Boston whaler cost $110 and include Bill's voluminous knowledge of the legends and lore of Hawaii.

SNORKELING

When the waters are calm, Molokai offers excellent snorkeling; you'll see a wide range of butterfly fish, tangs, and angelfish. Most Molokai beaches are too dangerous for snorkeling in the winter, when big waves and strong currents are generated by storms that sweep down from Alaska. From mid-September to April, stick to Murphy Beach Park (also known as Kumimi Beach Park; see above) on the East End. In summer, roughly May to mid-September, when the Pacific Ocean takes a holiday and turns into a flat lake, the whole west coast of Molokai opens up for snorkeling.

Mike Holmes, of Molokai Ranch & Fun Hogs, says that these are the best spots:

- **Kawaikiunui, Ilio Point, and Pohaku Moiliili** (West End): These are all special places seldom seen even by those who live on Molokai. You can reach Kawaikikunui and Pohaku Moiliili on foot after a long, hot, dusty ride in a four-wheel-drive vehicle, but it's much easier and quicker to go by sea.

- **Kapukahehu or Dixie Maru** (West End): This gold-sand family beach is well protected, and the reef is close and shallow. The name Dixie Maru comes from a 1920s Japanese fishing boat stranded off the rocky shore. One of the Molokai Ranch cowboys hung the wrecked boat's nameplate on a gate by Kapukahehu Beach, and the name Dixie Maru stuck. To get here, take Kaluakoi Road to the end of the pavement, and then take the footpath 100 yards to the beach.

- **Murphy Beach Park** (East End): This beach (also called Kumimi Beach) is located between mile markers 20 and 21, off Kamehameha V Highway. The reef here is easily reachable, and the waters are calm year-round.

During the calm summer months, **Molokai Outdoor Activities** (see above for contact information) offers 2-hour snorkel excursions on the west side for $45, which includes guide, equipment, and beverages. They also have the least expensive snorkel gear for rent at $5.95 a day or $23.95 a week.

Molokai Fish & Dive in Kanakakai (☎ 808/553-5926) rents snorkeling gear for $8.98 a day; the staff will also point out that day's best snorkeling spots. Snorkeling tours of $2^1/2$ hours are available for $55 from **Bill Kapuni's Snorkel & Dive** (☎ 808/553-9867), which also rents snorkeling gear for $9 a day (see "Scuba Diving," above).

Walter Naki of **Molokai Action Adventures** (☎ 808/558-8184) offers snorkeling, diving, and swimming trips in his 21-foot Boston whaler for $100 per person for a 4- to 6-hour custom tour. **Fun Hogs of Hawaii** (☎ 808/567-6789) offers snorkeling excursions in a 27-foot sportfishing boat for $50 per person, which includes all snorkeling equipment.

SPORTFISHING

Molokai's waters can provide prime sporting opportunities, whether you're looking for big-game sportfishing or bottom fishing. When customers are scarce, Captain Joe Reich, who has been fishing the waters around Molokai for 2 decades, goes commercial fishing, so he always knows where the fish are biting. He runs *Alyce* **C Sportfishing** out of Kaunakakai Harbor (☎ 808/558-8377). A full day of fishing for up to six people is $400, three-quarters of a day is $350, and a half-day is $300. You can persuade him to do a whale-watching cruise during the winter months.

For fly-fishing or light-tackle reef-fish trolling, contact Walter Naki at **Molokai Action Adventures** (☎ **808/558-8184**). Walter has been fishing his entire life and loves to share his secret spots with visiting fishermen—he knows *the* place for bone-fishing on the flats. A half-day trip in his 21-foot Boston whaler is $50 per person (minimum two people), $100 per person for a full day.

For deep-sea fishing, **Fun Hogs Hawaii** (☎ **808/567-6789**) has fishing excursions on a 27-foot, fully equipped sportfishing vessel. Priced at $350 for six passengers for a 6-hour excursion and $400 for six people for the 8-hour trip.

If you just want to try your luck casting along the shoreline, **Molokai Outdoor Activities** (see above for contact information) rents fishing poles for $6.95 a day and probably can tell you where they're biting.

SURFING & WINDSURFING

Molokai Outdoor Activities (see above for contact information) has surfing lessons ($50 per person) and windsurfing lessons ($50 per person), as well as surf boards for rent ($20 to $30 a day).

7 Hiking & Camping

by Jeanette Foster

HIKING MOLOKAI'S PEPEOPAE TRAIL

Molokai's most awesome hike is the **Pepeopae Trail,** which takes you back a few million years. On the cloud-draped trail (actually a boardwalk across the bog), you'll see mosses, sedges, native violets, knee-high ancient ohias, and lichens that evolved in total isolation over eons. Eerie intermittent mists blowing in and out will give you an idea of this island at its creation.

The narrow boardwalk, built by volunteers, protects the bog and keeps you out of the primal ooze. Don't venture off it; you could damage this fragile environment or get lost. The 3-mile round-trip takes about 90 minutes to hike—but first you have to drive about 20 miles from Kaunakakai, deep into the Molokai Forest Preserve on a four-wheel-drive road. (Don't try this with a regular rental car.) No permit is required for this easy hike. You should call ahead (☎ **808/537-4508** or 808/553-5236 on Molokai) to check on the condition of the ungraded four-wheel-drive red-dirt road that leads to the trailhead and to let people know that you'll be up there. Plan a full day for this outing. Better yet, go on a guided nature hike with **The Nature Conservancy of Hawaii,** which guards this unusual ecosystem. For information, write to the Conservancy at 1116 Smith St., Suite 201, Honolulu, HI 96817.

To get there, take Highway 460 west from Kaunakakai for 3¹/₂ miles and turn right before the Maunawainui Bridge onto the unmarked Molokai Forest Reserve Road (sorry, there aren't any road signs). The pavement ends at the cemetery; continue on the dirt road. After about 2 to 2¹/₂ miles, you'll see a sign telling you that you are now in the Molokai Forest Reserve. At the Waikolu Lookout and picnic area, which is just over 9 miles on the Molokai Forest Reserve Road, sign in at the box near the entrance. Continue on the road for another 5 miles to a fork in the road with the sign Puu Kolekole pointing to the right side of the fork. Do not turn right; instead, continue straight at the fork, which will lead to the clearly marked trailhead.

HIKING TO KALAUPAPA

This hike to the site of Molokai's famous leper colony is like going down a switchback staircase with what seems like a million steps. You don't always see the breathtaking

If it's action you're looking for, call **Molokai Action Adventures** (☎ 808/ 558-8184). Island guide Walter Naki will take you skin diving, reef trolling, kayaking, hunting, or hiking into Molokai's remote hidden valleys. Hiking tours are $50 per person for 4 hours; the number of participants is limited to no more than four. Not only does Walter know Molokai like the back of his hand, but he also loves being outdoors and "talking story" with visitors; he tells them about the island, the people, the politics, the myths, and anything else his guests want to know.

view, because you're too busy watching your step. It's easier going down (surprise!)— in about an hour, you'll go 2¹/₂ miles, from 2,000 feet to sea level. The trip up sometimes takes twice as long. The trailhead starts on the mauka (inland) side of Highway 470, just past the Mule Barn (you can't miss it). Check in there at 7:30am, get a permit, and go before the mule train departs. You must be 16 or older (it's an old state law that kept kids out of the leper colony) and should be in good shape. Wear good hiking boots or sneakers; you won't make it past the first turn in zoris.

CAMPING

One of the best year-round places to camp on Molokai is **Papohaku Beach Park** on the island's West End. This drive-up seaside site makes a great getaway. Facilities include rest rooms, drinking water, outdoor showers, barbecue grills, and picnic tables. Groceries and gas are available in Maunaloa, 6 miles away. Kaluakoi Resort is a mile away. Obtain camping permits by contacting **Maui County Parks Department,** P.O. Box 526, Kaunakakai, HI 96748 (☎ 808/553-3204). Camping is limited to 3 days, but if nobody else has applied, the time limit is waived. The cost is $3 a person per night.

At the end of Highway 470 is the 234-acre piney woods known as **Palaau State Park,** home to the Kalaupapa Lookout (the best vantage point for seeing the historic leper colony if you're not hiking or mule-riding in). It's airy and cool in the park's ironwood forest, where many love to camp at the designated state campground. Camping is free here, but you need a permit from the **State Division of Parks** (☎ 808/ 567-6618). For more on the park, see "Seeing the Sights," below.

8 Golf, Biking, Horseback Riding & Tennis

by Jeanette Foster

GOLF

Golf is one of Molokai's best-kept secrets; it's challenging and fun, tee times are open, and the rates are lower than your score will be. Most popular is the par-72, 6,564-yard **Kaluakoi Golf Course** (☎ 808/552-2739). The course is cut along the ocean (six holes are along the shoreline) and through the woods (pheasants, axis deer, and wild turkeys freely roam the fairways). The hilly, wooded fairways are bisected by ravines. The par-3, 16th hole, called "The Gorge," plays 190 yards over a deep ravine to a two-tiered green. When you finish that, both the 17th and 18th holes are very long par-4s, with greens blind from the tee. Facilities include driving range, putting green, pro shop, and restaurant. It's rarely crowded here. Greens fees are $45 for Kaluakoi Hotel

Resort guests, $60 for guests in the condos at Kaluakoi, and $80 for nonguests; twilight rates are $43 for nonguests and $35 for guests.

The real find in golf courses is the **Ironwood Hills Golf Course,** off Kalae Highway (☎ **808/567-6000**). It's located just before the Molokai Mule Ride Mule Barn, on the road to the Lookout. One of the oldest golf courses in the state, Ironwood Hills (named after the two predominant features of the course, ironwood trees and hills) was built in 1929 by Del Monte Plantation for its executives. This unusual course, which sits in the cool air at 1,200 feet, delights with its rich foliage, open fairways, and spectacular views of the rest of the island. If you play here, use a trick developed by the local residents: After teeing off on the 6th hole, just take whatever clubs you need to finish playing the hole and a driver for the 7th hole, and park your bag under a tree. The climb to the 7th hole is steep—you'll be glad that you're only carrying a few clubs. Greens fees are $10 for 9 holes, $14 for 18 holes. Cart fees are $7 for 9 holes, $14 for 18. You can also rent a hand cart for just $2.50. Club rentals are $7 for nine holes and $12 for 18.

BIKING

Molokai Outdoor Activities, HC 01, Box 28, located in the lobby of the Hotel Molokai, just outside of Kaunakakai (☎ **877/553-4477** or 808/553-4477; www.molokai-outdoors.com), has "tours of the top" of the Kamakou Forest Reserve for $70, including lunch and bicycle. They'll rent you everything from a beach cruiser ($15 a day) to an MTB front shock ($23 a day), including complimentary bike racks for your rental.

Molokai Ranch (☎ **877-726-4656** or 808/552-2797, ext. 234; www.molokai-ranch.com) has excellent mountain bike tours for riders of all abilities on the 53,000-acre ranch property for $40 per person.

HORSEBACK RIDING

One of the most scenic places to go horseback riding on Molokai is **Pu'u-O-Hoku Ranch** (☎ **808/558-8109;** e-mail: hoku@aloha.net), about 25 miles outside of Kaunakakai on the East End. Guided trail rides pass through green pastures on one of the largest working ranches on Molokai and head up into the high mountain forest. Don't forget your camera; there are plenty of scenic views of waterfalls, the Pacific Ocean, and Maui and Lanai in the distance. Rates are $75 for a 2-hour ride and $105 for a 4-hour ride.

For those looking for a little more than just a horseback ride, **Molokai Ranch** (☎ **877/726-4656** or 808/552-2797, ext. 234; www.molokai-ranch.com) offers a "Paniolo Roundup," where you learn horsemanship from the ranch's working cowboys and compete in traditional rodeo games. It's $90 for the 2-hour adventure. Or you can participate in an actual cattle trail drive with the ranch, where you will learn how to herd cattle; lunch is included in the $90 price.

TENNIS

The only two tennis courts on Molokai are located at the **Mitchell Pauole Center** in Kaunakakai (☎ **808/553-5141**). Both have night lights and are available free on a first-come, first-served basis, with a 45-minute time limit if someone is waiting. You can rent tennis rackets for $4.95 a day or $19.95 a week from **Molokai Outdoor Activities,** located in the lobby of the Hotel Molokai, just outside of Kaunakakai (☎ **877/553-4477** or 808/553-4477; www.molokai-outdoors.com).

9 Seeing the Sights

by Jeanette Foster

IN & AROUND KAUNAKAKAI

Kapuaiwa Coconut Grove/Kiowea Park. Along Maunaloa Highway (Hwy. 460), 2 miles west of Kaunakakai.

This royal grove of 1,000 coconut trees on 10 acres was planted in 1863 by the island's high chief Kapua'iwa (later, King Kamehameha V). It's a major roadside attraction. The shoreline park, 2 miles west of Kaunakakai, is a favorite subject of sunset photographers and visitors who delight in a hand-lettered sign that warns DANGER: FALLING COCONUTS. In its backyard, across the highway, stands Church Row: seven churches, each a different denomination, clear evidence of the missionary impact on Hawaii.

Post-A-Nut. Hoolehua Post Office, Puu Peelua Ave. (Hwy. 480), near Maunaloa Highway (Hwy. 460). ☎ **808/567-6144.** Mon–Fri 7:30–11:30am and 12:30–4:30pm.

Postmaster Margaret Keahi-Leary will help you say "Aloha" with a dried Molokai coconut. Just write a message on the coconut with a felt-tip pen, and she'll send it via U.S. mail over the sea. Coconuts are free, but postage is $3.20 for a mainland-bound 2-pound coconut.

Purdy's All-Natural Macadamia Nut Farm (Na Hua O'Ka Aina). Lihipali Rd. (behind Molokai High School), Hoolehua. ☎ **808/567-6601.** www.visitmolokai.com. Mon–Fri 9:30am–3:30pm, Sat 10am–2pm. Free admission.

The Purdys have made macadamia nut–buying an entertainment event. They offer tours of the 1 1/2-acre homestead and give lively demonstrations of nutshell-cracking in the shade of their towering trees. The tour of the 70-year-old nut farm explains the growth, bearing, harvesting, and shelling processes, so that by the time you bite into the luxurious macadamia nut, you'll have more than a passing knowledge of its entire life cycle.

EN ROUTE TO THE NORTH COAST

Most people never get a chance to see Hawaii's most dramatic coast in its entirety, but nobody should miss the opportunity to glimpse it from the **Kalaupapa Lookout** at Palauu State Park. On the way, there are a few diversions, including **Coffees of Hawaii,** on Highway 480 near the junction of Highway 470. See "Shops & Galleries," later in this chapter, for complete details. You can get the caffeine jolt you need, buy gifts, and even tour this former pineapple plantation in a mule-drawn wagon (tours are offered at 10am and 1pm).

Molokai Museum and Cultural Center. Meyer Sugar Mill, Hwy. 470 (just after the turnoff for the Ironwood Hills Golf Course, and 2 miles below Kalaupapa Overlook), Kaunakakai. ☎ **808/567-6436.** Admission $2.50 adults, $1 students. Mon–Thurs 10am–4:30pm, Fri–Sat 10am–2pm.

En route to the California Gold Rush in 1849, Rudolph W. Meyer, a German professor, came to Molokai, married the high chiefess Kalama and, after planting corn, wheat, and potatoes, began to operate a small sugar plantation near his home. Now on the National Register of Historic Places, this restored 1878 sugar mill, with its century-old steam engine, mule-driven cane crusher, copper clarifiers, and redwood evaporating pan (all in working order), is the last of its kind in Hawaii. The mill also houses a museum that traces the history of sugar-growing on Molokai and features

---

ⓘ Especially for Kids

Flying a Kite (*see p. 261*)   Not only can you get a guaranteed-to-fly kite at the **Big Wind Kite Factory** (☎ 808/552-2634) in Maunaloa, but kite designer Jonathan Socher offers free kite-flying classes to kids, who'll learn how to make their kites soar, swoop, and most important, stay in the air for more than 5 minutes.

Spending the Day at Murphy Beach Park (*see p. 251*)   Just beyond Wailua on the East End, Murphy Beach Park (also known as Kumini Beach Park) is a small wayside park that's perfect for kids. Swimming is safe, and there's plenty of shade from the ironwood trees. Useful facilities include small pavilions with picnic tables and barbecue grills.

Riding a Wagon (*see p. 262*)   Kids will love being in a wagon drawn by two horses as it traverses a dirt trail through a mango grove bound for an ancient temple of sacrifice on Molokai's East End.

Watching Whales (*see p. 252*)   From mid-December to mid-March, kids of all ages can go whale-watching on Molokai Charters' 42-foot sloop, *Satan's Doll*.

---

special events, such as wine tastings every 2 months, taro festivals, an annual music festival, and occasional classes in ukulele making, loom weaving, and sewing. Call for a schedule.

THE NORTH COAST
PALAAU STATE PARK

This 234-acre piney-woods park, 8 miles out of Kaunakakai at the end of Highway 470, doesn't look like much until you get out of the car and take a hike, which really puts you between a rock and a hard place. Go right, and you end up on the edge of Molokai's magnificent sea cliffs, with its panoramic view of the well-known Kalaupapa leper colony; go left, and you come face to face with a stone phallus.

If you have no plans to scale the cliffs on mule or foot (see "Hiking & Camping," above), the ❂ **Kalaupapa Lookout** is the only place from which to see the former place of exile. The trail is marked, and there are historic photos and interpretive signs to explain what you're seeing.

It's airy and cool in the ironwood forest, where camping is free at the designated state campground. You'll need a permit from the **State Division of Parks** (☎ 808/567-6618). Not many people seem to camp here, probably because of the legend associated with the **Phallic Rock.** Six feet high, pointed at an angle that means business, Molokai's famous Phallic Rock is a legendary fertility tool that appears to be working today. According to Hawaiian legend, a woman who wishes to become pregnant need only spend the night near the rock and . . . Voilà! It's probably just a coincidence, of course, but Molokai does have a growing number of young pregnant women.

Phallic Rock is at the end of a well-worn uphill path that passes an ironwood grove and several other rocks that vaguely resemble sexual body parts. No mistaking the big guy, though. Supposedly, it belonged to Nanahoa, a demigod who quarreled with his wife, Kawahuna, over a pretty girl. In the tussle, Kawahuna was thrown over the cliff, and both husband and wife were turned to stone. Of all the phallic rocks in Hawaii and the Pacific, this is the one to see. It's featured on a postcard with a tiny, awestruck Japanese woman standing next to it.

THE LEGACY OF FATHER DAMIEN:
KALAUPAPA NATIONAL HISTORIC PARK

An old tongue of lava that sticks out to form a peninsula, Kalaupapa became infamous because of man's inhumanity to victims of a formerly incurable contagious disease.

On January 6, 1866, King Kamehameha V sent the first lepers—nine men and three women—into exile on this lonely shore, at the base of ramparts that rise like temples against the Pacific. More than 11,000 lepers came here between 1865 and 1874, dispatched to disfigure and die in one of the world's most beautiful and lonely places. They called Kalaupapa "The Place of the Living Dead."

Leprosy is actually one of the world's least contagious diseases, transmitted only by direct, repetitive contact over a long period of time. It's caused by a germ, Mycobacterium leprae, that attacks the nerves, skin, and eyes, and is found mainly, but not exclusively, in tropical regions. American scientists found a cure for leprosy in the 1940s.

Before science intervened, there was Father Damien. Born to wealth in Belgium, Joseph de Veuster traded a life of excess for a missionary life, and eventually for exile among lepers; he devoted himself to caring for the afflicted at Kalaupapa. Father Damien, as he became known, volunteered to go out to the Pacific in place of his ailing brother when he was 33. Horrified at the conditions in the leper colony, Father Damien worked at Kalaupapa for 11 years, building houses, schools, and churches, and giving hope to his patients. He died on April 15, 1889, in Kalaupapa, of leprosy. He was 49.

A hero who's been nominated for Catholic sainthood (the process is still pending), Father Damien is buried not in his tomb next to St. Philomena Church, but in his native Belgium. His hand was recently returned to Molokai, however, and was reinterred at Kalaupapa as a relic of his martyrdom.

This small peninsula is probably the final resting place of more than 11,000 souls. The sand dunes are littered with grave markers, sorted by the religious affiliation—Catholic, Protestant, Lutheran, Buddhist—of those who died here. But so many are buried in unmarked graves that no census of the dead is believed to be accurate or complete.

Kalaupapa (☎ **808/567-6802;** www.nps.gov/kala) is now a National Historic Park and one of Hawaii's richest archaeological preserves, with sites that date from A.D. 1000. About 60 former patients chose to remain in the tidy village of whitewashed houses with statues of angels in the yards. The original name for their former affliction, "leprosy," was officially banned in Hawaii by the state legislature in 1981. It is now called "Hansen's disease," for Dr. Gerhard Hansen of Norway, who discovered the germ in 1873. The few remaining residents of Kalaupapa still call their disease leprosy, although none are too keen on being called lepers.

Kalaupapa welcomes visitors who arrive on foot, by mule, or by small plane. Father Damien's St. Philomena church, built in 1872, is now open to visitors, who can see it from a yellow school bus driven by resident tour guide Richard Marks, an ex-seaman

---

Impressions

In the chronicle of man there is perhaps no more melancholy landing than this . . .
—Robert Louis Stevenson, on Kalaupapa

Smile. It No Broke Your Face.
—Sign at Kalaupapa

---

and sheriff who survived the disease. You won't be able to roam freely, and you'll only be allowed to enter the museum, the craft shop, and the church.

✪ MULE RIDES TO KALAUPAPA   The first turn's a gasp, and it's all downhill from there. You can close your eyes and hold on for dear life, or slip the reins over the pommel and sit back, letting the mule do the walking down the precipitous path to Kalaupapa National Historic Park.

Even if you have only 1 day to spend on Molokai, spend it on a mule. This is a once-in-a-lifetime ride. The cliffs are taller than a 300-story skyscraper, but Buzzy Sproat's mules go safely up and down the narrow 2.9-mile trail daily, rain or shine. Starting at the top of the nearly perpendicular ridge (1,600 feet high), the surefooted mules step down the muddy trail, pausing often on the 26 switchbacks to calculate their next move—and always, it seems to me, veering a little too close to the edge. Each switchback is numbered; by the time you get to number four, you'll catch your breath, put the mule on cruise control, and begin to enjoy Hawaii's most awesome trail ride.

The mule tours are offered once daily starting at 8am, and they last until about 3:30pm. It's $150 per person for the all-day adventure, which includes the round-trip mule ride, a guided tour of the settlement, a visit to Father Damien's church and grave, lunch at Kalawao, and souvenirs. To go, you must be at least 16 years old and physically fit, and there's a weight limitation of 250 lbs. Contact **✪ Molokai Mule Ride,** 100 Kalae Hwy., Suite 104, on Hwy. 470, 5 miles north of Hwy. 460 (☎ **800/ 567-7550** or 808/567-6088 between 8 and 10pm; fax 808/567-6244; www.muleride. com). Advance reservations (at least 2 weeks) are required.

SEEING KALAUPAPA BY PLANE   Instead of getting to Kalaupapa via mule or on foot, you can get there faster and more easily by hopping on a plane (from Honolulu or Maui) and zipping to Kalauapapa airport. From there, you can pick up the regular tour of Kalaupapa (which the mule riders and hikers take). **Father Damien Tours,** P.O. Box 1, Kalaupapa, HI 96742 (☎ and fax **808/567-6171**), picks you up at Kalaupapa airport and takes you to some of the area's most scenic spots, including Kalawao, where Father Damien's church still stands, and the town of Kalaupapa. The $30 fee includes the tour of Kalaupapa and the permit to enter this secluded area. Airfare is additional: $49.90 round-trip on **Molokai-Lanai Air Shuttle** (☎ **808/ 567-6847**), from Molokai Airport (in Hoolelua). **Island Air** (☎ **800/652-6541**) has round trips from either Honolulu or Molokai Airport for $180 (AAA members get special fare of $136); and **Paragon Air** (☎ **808/244-3356**), on Maui, offers a package deal of airfare from Kahului Airport on Maui to Kalaupapa, plus the 4¹/₂-hour tour, with lunch and drinks, for $199. All visitors must be at least 16 years old.

THE WEST END
MAUNALOA

In the first and only instance of urban renewal on Molokai, the 1920s-era pineapple-plantation town of Maunaloa is being reinvented. Streets are getting widened and paved, and curbs and sidewalks are going in to serve a new tract of houses. Historic Maunaloa is becoming Maunaloa Village—there's already a town center with a park, a restaurant, a triplex movie theater, a gas station, a Kentucky Fried Chicken, and an upscale lodge.

This master-planned village will also have a museum and artisan's studios—uptown stuff for Molokai. Jonathan Socher's Big Wind Kite Factory (see "Shopping," below) is keeping its kites and books wrapped in cellophane against constant clouds of red dust raised by construction crews.

ON THE NORTHWEST SHORE: MOOMOMI DUNES

Undisturbed for centuries, the Moomomi Dunes, on Molokai's northwest shore, are a unique treasure chest of great scientific value. The area may look like just a pile of sand as you fly over on the final approach to Hoolehua Airport, but Moomomi Dunes is much more than that. Archaeologists have found adz quarries, ancient Hawaiian burial sites, and shelter caves; botanists have identified five endangered plant species; and marine biologists are finding evidence that endangered green sea turtles are coming out from the waters once again to lay eggs here. The greatest discovery, however, belongs to Smithsonian Institute ornithologists, who have found bones of prehistoric birds, some of them flightless, that existed nowhere else on earth.

Accessible by Jeep trails that thread downhill to the shore, this wild coast is buffeted by strong afternoon breezes. It's hot, dry, and windy, so take water, sunscreen, and a windbreaker. At Kawaaloa Bay, a 20-minute walk to the west, there's a broad golden beach that you can have all to yourself. Stay out of the water. The 920-acre preserve is accessible via monthly guided nature tours led by **The Nature Conservancy of Hawaii;** call ☎ **808/553-5236** or 808/524-0779 for an exact schedule and details.

To get to Moomomi Dunes, take Highway 460 (Maunaloa Hwy.) from Kaunakakai; turn right onto Highway 470, and follow it to Kualapuu. At Kualapuu, turn left on Highway 480 and go through Hoolehua Village; it's 3 miles to the bay.

THE EAST END

The East End is a cool and inviting green place that's worth a drive to the end of King Kamehameha V Highway (Hwy. 450). Unfortunately, the trail that leads into the area's greatest natural attraction, **Halawa Valley,** is now off-limits.

AN ADVENTURE FOR EVERYONE:
A WAGON RIDE OR HORSEBACK RIDE TO ILIILIOPAE HEIAU

In a wagon drawn by two horses, or on horseback, you bump along a dirt trail through an incredible mango grove, bound for an ancient temple of human sacrifice. This temple of doom—right out of an Indiana Jones movie—is Ili'ili'opae, a huge rectangle of stone made of 90 million rocks, overlooking the once-important village of Mapulehu and four ancient fishponds. The wagon glides under the perfumed mangoes, then heads uphill through a kiawe forest filled with Java plums to the heiau, which stands across a dry stream-bed under cloud-spiked Kaunolu, the 4,970-foot island summit.

Hawaii's most powerful *heiau* (temple) attracted *kahuna* (priests) from all over the islands. They came to learn the rules of human sacrifice at this university of sacred rites. Contrary to Hollywood's version, historians say that the victims here were always men, not young virgins, and that they were strangled, not thrown into a volcano, while priests sat on lauhala mats watching silently. Spooky, eh?

This is the biggest, oldest, and most famous heiau on Molokai. The massive, 22-foot-high stone altar is dedicated to Lono, the Hawaiian god of fertility. The heiau resonates with *mana* (power) strong enough to lean on. Legend says Ili'ili'opae was built in a single night by a thousand men who passed rocks hand over hand through the Wailau Valley from the other side of the island; each received a shrimp (*'opae*) in exchange for the rock (*ili'ili*). Others say it was built by *menehunes,* mythic elves who accomplished Herculean feats.

After the visit to the temple, the horse-drawn wagon or your own horse takes you back to the mango grove.

Contact **Molokai Wagon Rides,** P.O. Box 1528, King Kamehameha V Highway (Hwy. 450), at the 15-mile marker, Kaunakakai, HI 96748 (☎ **808/558-8380**). The tour via wagon is $35 per person or $40 per person on horseback. The hour-long ride goes up to the heiau, then beyond it to the top of the mountain for those breathtaking views, and finally back down to the beach.

KAMAKOU PRESERVE

It's hard to believe, but close to the nearly mile-high summit here, it rains more than 80 inches a year—enough to qualify as a rain forest. The Molokai Forest, as it was historically known, is the source of 60% of Molokai's water. Nearly 3,000 acres from the summit to the lowland forests of eucalyptus and pine are now held by the Nature Conservancy, which has identified 219 Hawaiian plants that grow here exclusively. The preserve is also the last stand of the endangered Molokai thrush (*olomao*) and Molokai creeper (*kawawahie*).

To get to this Nature Conservancy preserve, take the Forest Reserve jeep road from Kaunakakai. It's a 45-minute, four-wheel-drive trip on a dirt trail to Waikolu Lookout Campground; from there, you can venture into the wilderness preserve on foot across a boardwalk on a 1¹/₂-hour hike (see "Hiking Molokai's Pepeopae Trail," above). For more information, contact **The Nature Conservancy** at ☎ **808/553-5236.**

EN ROUTE TO HALAWA VALLEY

No visit to Molokai is complete without at least a passing glance at the island's **ancient fishponds,** a singular achievement in Pacific aquaculture. With their hunger for fresh fish and lack of ice or refrigeration, Hawaiians perfected aquaculture in 1400, before Christopher Columbus "discovered" America. They built gated, U-shaped stone and coral walls on the shore to catch fish on the incoming tide, and would then raise them in captivity. The result: A constant, ready supply of fresh fish.

The ponds stretch for 20 miles along Molokai's south shore and are visible from Kamehameha V Highway (Hwy. 450). Molokai's fishponds offer insight into the island's ancient population. It took something like 1,000 people to tend a single fishpond, and more than 60 ponds once existed on this coast. All the fishponds are named; a few are privately owned. Some are silted in by red-dirt runoff from South Coast gulches; others have been revived by folks who raise fish and seaweed.

The largest, 54-acre **Keawa Nui Pond,** is surrounded by a 3-foot-high, 2,000-foot-long stone wall. **Alii Fishpond,** reserved for kings, is visible through the coconut groves at One Alii Beach Park (see "Beaches," above). From the road you can see **Kalokoeli Pond,** 6 miles east of Kaunakakai on the highway.

Our Lady of Sorrows Catholic Church, one of five built by Father Damien on Molokai and the first outside Kalaupapa, sits across the highway from a fishpond. Park in the church lot (except on Sundays) for a closer look.

St. Joseph's Catholic Church. King Kamehameha V Hwy. (Hwy. 450), just after mile marker 10.

The afternoon sun strikes St. Joseph's Church with such a bold ray of light that it looks as if God is about to perform a miracle. This little 1876 wood-frame church is one of four Father Damien built "topside" on Molokai. Restored in 1971, the church stands beside a seaside cemetery, where feral cats play under the gaze of a Damien statue amid gravestones decorated with flower leis.

Smith Bronte Landing Site. King Kamehameha V Hwy. (Hwy. 450), at mile marker 11, on the *makai* (ocean) side.

In 1927, Charles Lindbergh soloed the Atlantic Ocean in a plane called *The Spirit of St. Louis* and became an American hero. That same year, Ernie Smith and Emory B. Bronte took off from Oakland, California, on July 14 in a single-engine Travelair aircraft named *The City of Oakland,* headed across the Pacific Ocean for Honolulu, 2,397 miles away. The next day, after running out of fuel, they crash-landed upside-down in a kiawe thicket on Molokai, but emerged unhurt. They were the first civilians to fly to Hawaii from the U.S. mainland. The 25-hour, 2-minute flight landed Smith and Bronte a place in aviation history—and on a roadside marker on Molokai.

HALAWA VALLEY

Of the five great valleys of Molokai, only Halawa, with its two waterfalls, golden beach, sleepy lagoon, great surf, and offshore island, is easily accessible. Access to the trail through Halawa Valley, a fertile valley that was inhabited for centuries, and on to the 250-foot Moaula Falls has been closed for some time. There is one operator who is conducting very expensive tours, but we have received so many letters of complaints (plus our own experience of being stood up by him after a confirmed reservation), we no longer recommend you use him.

You can spend a day at the county beach park, but do not venture into the valley on your own. In a kind of 21st-century "kapu," the private landowners in the valley worry about slip-and-fall law suits and have posted NO TRESPASSING signs on their private property.

To get to Halawa Valley, drive north from Kaunakakai on Highway 450 for 30 miles along the coast to the end of the road, which descends into the valley past Jersalema Hou Church. If you'd just like a glimpse of the valley on your way to the beach, there's a scenic overlook along the road: After Puuo Hoku Ranch at mile marker 25, the narrow two-lane road widens at a hairpin curve, and you'll find the overlook on your right; it's 2 miles more to the valley floor.

10 Shops & Galleries

by Jocelyn Fujii

KAUNAKAKAI

Molokai Surf, Molokai Island Creations, Molokai Imports (which has great, inexpensive lauhala bags and local lemons), and **Lourdes** are clothing and gift shops in close proximity to each other in downtown Kaunakakai, where most of the retail shops sell T-shirts, muumuus, surf wear, and informal apparel. Serious shoppers will be disappointed, unless they love kites or native wood vessels. The following are Kaunakakai's notable stores.

Imamura Store. ☎ **808/553-5615.**

Wilfred Imamura, whose mother founded the store (she died in 1990 at age 97), has assembled a marvelous amalgam of precious old-fashioned things. Rubber boots, Hawaiian-print tablecloths, Japanese tea plates, ukulele cases, plastic slippers, and even coconut bikini tops line the shelves. Recently we found a pair of tatami sandals with red velvet thongs, a treasure for $19. But it's not all nostalgia. The Molokai T-shirts, jeans, and palaka shorts are of good quality and inexpensive, and the pareu fabrics are a find.

Molokai Drugs. In the Kamoi Professional Center. ☎ **808/553-5790.**

David Mikami, whose father-in-law founded the pharmacy in 1935, has made this more than a drugstore. It's a gleaming, friendly stop full of life's basic necessities, with generous amenities such as a phone and a rest room for passersby (!). You'll find the best selection of guidebooks, books about Molokai, and maps here, as well as greeting cards, paperbacks, cassette players, flip-flops, and every imaginable essential. The

Mikamis are a household name on the island not only because of their pharmacy, but also because the family has shown exceptional kindness to the often economically strapped Molokaians.

Molokai Fish & Dive. ☎ 808/553-5926.

Get ready for merchandising overload: This is the island's largest selection of T-shirts and souvenirs, crammed in among fishing, snorkeling, and outdoor gear that you can rent or buy. Find your way among the fishnets, boogie boards, diving equipment, bamboo rakes, beach towels, postcards, juices and soft drinks, disposable cameras, and the staggering miscellany of this chockablock store. One entire wall is lined with T-shirts, and the selection of Molokai books and souvenirs is extensive. The store also rents snorkel gear; for visitors, the staff will also point out the best snorkeling spots of the day. *Caveat:* The entire store smells of rubber.

Molokai Surf. 130 Kamehameha V. Hwy. ☎ 808/553-5093.

The brand-new, freestanding brown wooden building now houses Molokai Surf and its selection of skateboards, surf shorts, sweatshirts, sunglasses, T-shirts, footwear, boogie boards, backpacks, and broad range of clothing and accessories for life in the surf and sun.

Take's Variety Store. ☎ 808/553-5442.

If you need luggage tags, buzz saws, toys, candy, cloth dolls, canned goods, canteens, camping equipment, hardware, signs, batteries, candles, paints, pipe fittings, fishing supplies—whew!—and other products for work and play, this 51-year-old variety store may be your answer. You may suffer from claustrophobia in the crowded, dusty aisles, but Take's carries everything.

EDIBLES

Another good source of healthy foods is **Outpost Natural Foods,** 70 Makaena Place (☎ 808/553-3377); see "Dining," earlier in this chapter, for details.

Friendly Market Center. ☎ 808/553-5595.

Friendly's is the best place on the island for groceries. You can't miss this salmon-colored wooden storefront on the main drag of "downtown" Kaunakakai, where people of all generations can be found at all times of the day just "talking story" in the Molokai way. Friendly's has an especially good selection of produce and healthy foods—whether it's local poi or Glenlivet, they'll have it. Blue-corn tortilla chips, soy milk, organic brown rice, a good pasta sauce selection, and Kumu Farms macadamia-nut pesto (the island's stellar gourmet food) are among the items that surpass standard grocery-store fare.

Misaki's Grocery and Dry Goods. ☎ 808/553-5505.

Established in 1922, this third-generation local legend is one of Kaunakakai's two grocery stores. Some of its notable items: chopped garlic from Gilroy, California; fresh luau leaves (taro greens); fresh okra; Boca Burgers; large Korean chestnuts in season; and gorgeous bananas. The fish section includes akule and ahi, fresh and dried, but the stock mostly consists of meats, produce, baking products, and a humongous array of soft drinks. Liquor, stationery, candies, and paper products round out the selection.

Molokai Ice House. At the end of Kaunakakai Wharf Rd. ☎ 808/553-3054.

This fishermen's co-op opened its doors as a fish market in 1994—and it's a find. Gathered daily from the fishing boats at the wharf, the seafood comes in all forms—sashimi, poke (seasoned raw fish), lomi (mixed, seasoned, and worked with the fingers), salmon, and squid, oysters, seaweed, and teriyaki marlin fillets. Seafood can't come any fresher, and everything's skillfully seasoned and reasonably priced. Locals come here for their fresh fish, whole or in fillets. The lomi 'o'io and the lomi ahi (yellowfin tuna) may look like mashed raw fish, but they're delicacies much appreciated by Molokaians and neighbor islanders. Various seasoned shrimp and octopus dishes, and frequent surprise catches make this an ever-changing adventure. The prepared foods are perfect for no-fuss cooking or a quiet lunch at the wharf. In true Hawaiian spirit, the place sells poi to go with the fish.

Molokai Wines & Spirits. ☎ **808/553-5009.**

This is your best bet on the island for a decent bottle of wine. The shop offers hundreds of labels, and *Wine Spectator* reviews are tacked to some of the selections, which always helps. The snack offerings include Cambozola gourmet cheeses, salami, and Carr's biscuits. Frozen burritos, canned tuna, chips, and prepackaged nibbles are on the shelves for the impromptu happy-hour gathering.

EN ROUTE TO THE NORTH COAST

Coffees of Hawaii. The Plantation Store. Kualapuu. ☎ **800/709-BEAN** or 808/567-9023.

This is a fairly slick—for Molokai—combination coffee bar, store, and gallery for more than 30 artists and craftspeople from Molokai, Maui, and the Big Island. Malulani Estate and Muleskinner coffees are sold here; they're grown, processed, and packed on the 500-acre plantation surrounding the shop. (A tour of the plantation is offered weekdays at 10am and 1pm and, upon special request, Saturdays at 10am.) You may find better prices on coffee at other retail outlets, but the gift items are worth a look: pikake and plumeria soaps from Kauai; perfumes and pure beeswax candles from Maui; koa bookmarks and hair sticks; and pottery, woods, and baskets.

Kualapuu Market. Kualapuu. ☎ **808/567-6243.**

This market, in its third generation, is a stone's throw from the new Coffees of Hawaii Store. It's a scaled-down, one-stop shop with wine, food, and necessities—and a surprisingly presentable, albeit small, assortment of produce, from Molokai sweet potatoes to Ka'u navel oranges in season.

Molokai Museum Gift Shop. At the old R. W. Meyer Sugar Mill, Kalae. ☎ **808/567-6436.**

The restored 1878 sugar mill sits 1,500 feet above the town of Kualapuu (see "Seeing the Sights," earlier in this chapter). It's a considerable drive from town, but a good cause for those who'd like to support the museum and the handful of local artisans who sell their crafts, fabrics, cookbooks, quilt sets, and other gift items in the tiny shop. There's also a modest selection of cards, T-shirts, coloring books, and handmade ornaments at Christmas, made of lauhala and koa.

THE WEST END

A Touch of Molokai. Kaluakoi Hotel & Golf Club. ☎ **808/552-0133.**

We were pleasantly surprised by the selection of gift items in this hotel shop. The surf shorts and aloha shirts were better than the norm, with attractive, up-to-date choices by Jams, Quiksilver, and other name brands. Tencel dresses, South Pacific shell necklaces (up to $400), and a magnificent, hand-turned milo bowl were among the items that caught our attention. Most impressive were the wiliwili, kamani, and soap-berry leis and a handsome array of lauhala bags, all made on Molokai.

MAUNALOA

Big Wind Kite Factory & the Plantation Gallery. Maunaloa. ☎ **808/552-2634.**

Jonathan and Daphne Socher, kite designers and inveterate Bali-philes, have combined their interests in a kite factory/import shop that dominates the commercial landscape of Maunaloa, the reconstituted plantation town. Maunaloa's naturally windy conditions make it ideal for kite-flying classes, which are offered free when conditions are right. The adjoining Plantation Gallery features local handicrafts such as milo-wood bowls, locally made T-shirts, Hawaii-themed sandblasted glassware, baskets of lauhala and other fibers, and Hawaiian-music CDs. The shop is overflowing with Balinese handicrafts, from jewelry to clothing and fabrics.

Maunaloa General Store. ☎ **808/552-2346.**

Maunaloa's only general store sells everything from paper products to batteries, dairy products, frozen and fresh meats, wine, canned goods, and a cross-section of necessities.

Molokai Ranch Outfitter Provisions. ☎ **808/552-2791.**

Located next to the ranch's bicycle rentals in a newly renovated wooden building, this shop could, indeed, outfit you for life's great adventures. North Face parkas, Bullfrog sunscreens, saddle blankets, socks, Teva sandals, bicycle helmets, swimwear, T-shirts, kites, walking sticks, and camping gear for all kinds of conditions line the shelves. The food items and souvenirs are also diverse: mugs, magnets, CDs and cassettes, Buckeye corn bread, pasta, Molokai Ranch toffees, mobiles, toys, plastic buckets, lidded koa boxes, Dr. Bronner's soaps, Muleskinner coffees, coconut shell soap dishes, picture frames, and other attractive gifts to go.

THE EAST END

The Neighborhood Store 'N Counter. Pukoo. ☎ **808/554-8498.**

The Neighborhood Store, the only grocery on the East End, sells batteries, film, aspirin, cookies, beer, Molokai produce, candies, paper products, and other sundries. There's good food pouring out of the kitchen for the breakfast and lunch counter, too.

11 Molokai After Dark

by Jocelyn Fujii

The **Hotel Molokai** in Kaunakakai offers live entertainment Sunday through Thursday night in the dining room and music by the pool on Friday and Saturday, 7:30 to 10:30pm. This means that there's music nightly at the hotel. With its South Seas ambiance and poolside setting, it has become the island's premier venue for local and visiting entertainers.

Up in Maunaloa, the **Molokai Ranch Hotel** offers live music nightly in the lounge, ranging from Zachary Helm and his lively falsetto to keiki hula, Phil Stevens and his acoustic classical guitar, and contemporary Hawaiian music.

Molokai musicians to watch for: **Pound for Pound,** a powerful group of artists, each over 250 pounds: lead vocalist Jack Stone, Shane Dudoit, Danny Reyes, John Pele, and Alika Lani. As popular off-island as on, they play Hawaiian, reggae, country, and contemporary Hawaiian numbers, many of them originals. Their CD, "100% Molokai," is a local legend.

Darryl Labrado is a teen phenom, the island's rising star, who sings and plays the ukulele to a huge local following. And **Pa'a Pono,** with its contemporary Hawaiian and reggae sounds, is a familiar name in the local nightlife circuit. "Molokai Now," a CD anthology of original music from Molokai, is a terrific memento for those who love the island and its music.

Movie fans finally have a place to call their own on Molokai. **Maunaloa Cinemas** (☎ **808/552-2707**) is a triplex theater that shows first-run movies in the middle of Maunaloa town—four screenings a day at each of the three theaters, beginning with the matinee.

Lanai: A Different Kind of Paradise

Lanai is not an easy place to reach. There are no direct flights from the mainland, and most air carriers route flights onto the island from Honolulu. It is almost as if this quiet, gentle oasis that's known, paradoxically, for both its small-town feel and its celebrity appeal, demands that its visitors go to great lengths to get here to ensure that those who come will appreciate it.

Lanai (pronounced lah-*nigh*-ee), Hawaii's sixth largest island and the nation's biggest defunct pineapple patch, now claims to be one of the world's top tropical destinations. It's a bold claim, since there are no stoplights, barely 30 miles of paved road, no fast-food joints, no strip malls, no taxis—in short, none of what you usually find in a tourist destination. Instead, what you have here is something quite rare: an almost virgin island, unspoiled by what passes for progress, except for a tiny 1920s-era plantation village—and, of course, its fancy new neighbors, two first-class luxury hotels where room rates hover around $400 a night.

As soon as you arrive, you'll feel the blanket of coziness of a small town: People wave to every car, residents stop to "talk story" with their friends, taking time to fish or work in the garden is considered a priority in life, and leaving the keys in your car's ignition is standard practice.

For generations, Lanai was little more than a small village, owned and operated by the pineapple company, surrounded by acres of pineapple fields. The few visitors to the island were either relatives of the mainly Filipino residents or occasional weekend hunters. Life in the 1960s was pretty much the same as in the 1930s.

But all that changed in 1990, when the Lodge at Koele, a 102-room hotel resembling an opulent English Tudor mansion, opened its doors, followed a year later by the 250-room Manele Bay Hotel, a Mediterranean-style luxury resort overlooking Hulopoe Bay. Overnight, the isolated island was transformed: Corporate jets streamed into the tiny Lanai Airport, former pineapple-plantation workers were retrained in the art of serving gourmet meals, and the population of 2,500 swelled with transient visitors and outsiders coming to work in the island's new hospitality industry. Microsoft billionaire Bill Gates chose the island for his lavish wedding, buying up all of its hotel rooms to fend off the press—and uncomplicated Lanai went on the map as a place where the rich and powerful vacation.

But it's also a place where people come looking for dramatic beauty, quiet, solitude, and an experience with nature away from the bright lights of Waikiki, the development of Maui, and the hoopla surrounding most resorts. The sojourners who find their way to Lanai come seeking the dramatic views, the tropical stars at night, and the chance to be alone with the elements.

They also come for the wealth of activities: snorkeling and swimming in the sapphire waters of Hulopoe Bay; hiking on a hundred miles of remote trails that canvass the 141-square-mile island; talking story with the friendly locals; and beachcombing and whale watching along a stretch of otherwise deserted sand. For the adventurous, there's horseback riding in the mist of the forest, scuba diving in caves, playing golf next to scenic ocean views, or renting a four-wheel-drive vehicle for the day and discovering wild plains where spotted deer run free and a rich cultural history comes alive in the ruins of a once-vibrant village.

In a single decade, a plain red-dirt pineapple patch has become one of Hawaii's most unusual destinations. But the real Lanai is a multifaceted place that's so much more than just another luxury resort—and it's the traveler who comes to discover the island's natural wonders, local lifestyle, and other inherent joys who's bound to have the most genuine island experience.

THE PINEAPPLE ISLAND'S UNUSUAL PAST

This old shield volcano in the rain shadow of Maui has a history of resisting change in a big way. Early Polynesians, fierce Hawaiian kings, European explorers, 20th-century farmers—the island has seen them all and sent most of them packing, empty-handed and broken. The ancient Hawaiians believed that the island was haunted by spirits so wily and vicious that no human could survive here. The "cannibal spirits" were finally driven off around A.D. 1400, and people settled in.

But those spirits never really went away, it seems. In 1778, just before Captain Cook "discovered" Hawaii, the king of the Big Island, Kalaniopuu, invaded Lanai in what was called "the war of loose bowels." His men slaughtered every warrior, cut down trees, and set fire to all that was left except a bitter fern whose roots gave them all dysentery.

In 1802, Wu Tsin made the first attempt to harvest on the island, but he ultimately abandoned his cane fields and went away. Charles Gay acquired 600 acres at public auction to experiment with pineapple as a crop, but a 3-year drought left him bankrupt. Others tried in vain to grow cotton, sisal, and sugar beets; they started a dairy and a piggery, and raised sheep for wool. But all enterprises failed, mostly for lack of water.

Harry Baldwin, a missionary's grandson and Massachusetts Institute of Technology grad, was the first to do okay for himself. He bought Lanai for $588,000 in 1917, developed a 20-mile water pipeline between Koele and Manele, and sold the island 5 years later to Jim Dole for $1.1 million.

Dole planted and irrigated 18,000 acres of pineapple, built Lanai City, blasted out a harbor, and turned the island into a fancy fruit plantation. For a half-century, he enjoyed great success. Even Dole was ultimately vanquished, however; cheaper pineapple production in Asia brought an end to Lanai's heyday.

The island still resembles old photographs taken in the glory days of Dole. Any minute now, you half expect to look up and see old Jim Dole himself rattling up the road in a Model-T truck with a load of fresh-picked pineapples. Only now, there's a new lord of the manor, and his name is David Murdock.

Of all who have looked at Lanai with a gleam in their eye, nobody has succeeded quite like David Murdock, a self-made billionaire who acquired the island in a merger more than a decade ago. About 97% of it is now his private holding.

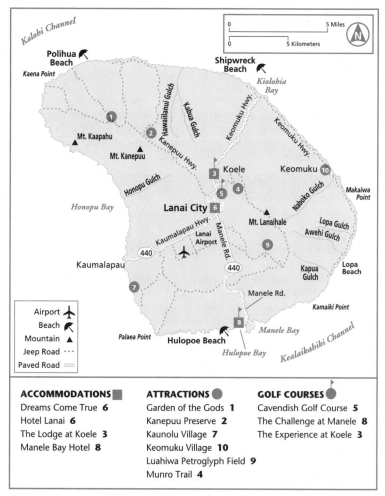

ACCOMMODATIONS ■
Dreams Come True **6**
Hotel Lanai **6**
The Lodge at Koele **3**
Manele Bay Hotel **8**

ATTRACTIONS ●
Garden of the Gods **1**
Kanepuu Preserve **2**
Kaunolu Village **7**
Keomuku Village **10**
Luahiwa Petroglyph Field **9**
Munro Trail **4**

GOLF COURSES ⚐
Cavendish Golf Course **5**
The Challenge at Manele **8**
The Experience at Koele **3**

After declaring Lanai's plantation era over, Murdock spent $400 million to build two grand hotels on the island: the Lodge at Koele, which resembles an English country retreat, and the Manele Bay Hotel, a green tile-roofed Mediterranean palazzo by the sea. Murdock recycled the former field hands into wait staff, even summoning a London butler to school the natives in the fine art of service, and carved a pair of daunting golf courses out of the island's interior and along the wave-lashed coast. He then set out to attract tourists by touting Lanai as "the private island."

Murdock is now trying to make all this pay for itself by selling vacation homes and condos next door to the two resorts. Hardly Thoreau's cabin in the woods, the homes and condos start at around $500,000 and carry an upward price tag of $3 million.

The redevelopment of this tiny rock should have been a pushover for the big-time tycoon, but island-style politics have continually thwarted his schemes. GO SLOW, a sun-faded sign at Dole's old maintenance shed once said. Murdock might have heeded the warning, because his grandiose plans are taking twice as long to accomplish as he had expected. Every permit he has sought has stuck in the tropic heat like a damp cotton shirt. Lanai is under the political thumb of many who believe that the island's precious water supply shouldn't all be diverted to championship golf courses and Jacuzzis, and there remains opposition from Lanaians for Sensible Growth, who advocate affordable housing, alternative water systems, and civic improvements that benefit residents.

Lanai residents, who might have lived in a rural setting, certainly haven't been isolated. Having watched the other islands in Hawaii attempt the balancing act of economic growth and the maintenance of an island lifestyle, the residents of Lanai are cautiously welcoming visitors, but at a pace that is still easy for this former plantation community to digest.

1 Orientation

by Jeanette Foster

ARRIVING

BY PLANE   No matter which island you're coming from, you'll have to make a connection in Honolulu, where you can easily catch a small plane for the 25-minute flight to Lanai's airport. Jet service to Lanai is now available, but only on **Hawaiian Airlines** (☎ **800/367-5320** or 808/565-6977; www.hawaiianair.com), which offers two flights a day. Twin-engine planes take longer and are sometimes bumpier, but they offer great views since they fly lower. **Island Air** (☎ **800/652-6541** or 808/565-6744; www.alohaair.com) offers 9 to 12 flights a day. For more details on these airlines—including details on how to get the cheapest fares—see "Getting There & Getting Around" and "Money-Saving Package Deals" in chapter 2.

Prop or jet, you'll touch down in Puuwai Basin, once the world's largest pineapple plantation; it's about 10 minutes by car to Lanai City and 25 minutes to Manele Bay.

BY BOAT   A round-trip on **Expeditions Lahaina/Lanai Passenger Ferry** (☎ **808/ 661-3756**) takes you between Maui and Lanai for $50. The ferry service runs five times a day, 365 days a year, between Lahaina and Lanai's Manele Bay harbor. The ferry leaves Lahaina at 6:45am, 9:15am, 12:45pm, 3:15pm, and 5:45pm; the return ferry from Lanai's Manele Bay Harbor leaves at 8am, 10:30am, 2pm, 4:30pm, and 6:45pm. The 9-mile channel crossing takes 45 minutes to an hour, depending on sea conditions. Reservations are strongly recommended. Baggage is limited to two checked bags and one carry-on.

VISITOR INFORMATION

Destination Lanai (☎ **800/947-4774** or 808/565-7600; fax 808/565-9316) and the **Hawaii Visitors and Convention Bureau** (☎ **800/GO-HAWAII** or 808/923-1811; www.gohawaii.com) will both provide you with brochures, maps, and island guides. For a free *Road and Site Map* of hikes, archaeological sites, and other sights, contact **The Lanai Company,** P.O. Box 310, Lanai, HI 96763 (☎ **808/565-3812**).

THE ISLAND IN BRIEF

Inhabited Lanai is divided into three parts—Lanai City, Koele, and Manele—and two distinct climate zones: hot and dry, and cool and misty.

Lanai City (population 2,800) sits at the heart of the island at 1,645 feet above sea level. This is the only place on the island where you'll find services. Built in 1924, this plantation village is a tidy grid of quaint tin-roofed cottages in bright pastels, with roosters penned in tropical gardens of bananas, lilikois, and papayas. Many of the residents are Filipino immigrants who worked the pineapple fields and imported the art, culture, language, food, and lifestyle of the Philippines. Their clapboard homes, now worth $125,000 or more, are excellent examples of historic preservation; the whole town looks like it has been preserved under a bell jar.

Around Dole Park Square, a charming village square lined with towering Norfolk and Cook Island pines, plantation buildings house general stores with basic necessities, as well as a U.S. post office (where people stop to chat), two banks, and a police station with a jail that consists of three bright blue-and-white wooden outhouse-sized cells with padlocks.

In the nearby cool upland district of **Koele** is The Lodge at Koele, standing by itself on a knoll overlooking pastures and the sea at the edge of a pine forest, like a grand European manor. The other bastion of indulgence, the Manele Bay Hotel, is on the sunny southwestern tip of the island at **Manele.** You'll get more of what you expect from Hawaii here—beaches, swaying palms, mai tais, and the like.

FAST FACTS: LANAI

In an emergency, call ☎ **911** for police, fire, and ambulance services; call ☎ **800/362-3585** for the Poison Control Center.

For nonemergencies, call the **Lanai Police** at ☎ **808/565-6428.**

If you need nonemergency medical attention, call **Lanai Family Health Center** at ☎ **808/565-6423** or the Lanai Community Hospital at ☎ **808/565-6411.** (There is no pharmacy on Lanai. The emergency room and doctor's office can dispense some medicines, but as for regular prescription drugs, you'd better bring 'em with you.)

For dental care, call **Dr. Nick's Family Dentistry** at ☎ **808/565-7801.**

For a weather report, call the **National Weather Service** at ☎ **808/565-6033.**

Lanai has two banks, the Bank of Hawaii and First Hawaiian Bank, both of which have ATMs.

2 Getting Around

by Jeanette Foster

With so few paved roads here, you'll need a four-wheel-drive vehicle if you plan on exploring the island's remote shores, its interior, or the summit of Mount Lanaihale. Even if you only have one day on Lanai, rent one and explore. You could also arrange a 4X4 adventure tour with the **Lanai EcoAdventure Centre;** see "Seeing the Sights," later in this chapter.

A larger fleet of rental vehicles is available at the **Dollar Rent-A-Car** desk at **Lanai City Service,** 1036 Lanai Ave. (☎ **808/565-7227** for Lanai City Service; www.dollarcar.com). Dollar has both cars and four-wheel-drive vehicles. Expect to pay about $60 a day for the least expensive car available, a Nissan Sentra, and $129 to $145 a day for a four-wheel-drive vehicle (both these rates drops 10% if you rent for a week or more).

Adventure Lanai EcoCentre, P.O. Box 1394, Lanai City, HI 96763 ☎ **808/565-7373;** www.adventurelanai.com), also has 4X4 Jeep and Suburban rentals for $89 to $129, which includes an ice chest, snorkel gear, bodyboard, and day packs, so you are ready to explore the island.

Be warned: Gas is expensive on Lanai, and those four-wheel-drive vehicles don't get good gas mileage. Since everything in Lanai City is within walking distance, it makes sense to rent a Jeep just for the day (or days) that you want to explore the island.

The two big resort hotels run shuttle vans around the island, but you can only use them if you're staying at one of the hotels. **Lanai City Service** (☎ **808/565-7227**) will provide shuttle service from the airport to Lanai City for $5 per person, and will also transport you from Lanai City to Hulopoe Beach for $10 per person one way. Whether or not you rent a car, sooner or later you'll find yourself at Lanai City Service. This all-in-one grocery store, gas station, rental-car agency, and souvenir shop serves as the island's Grand Central Station; here you can pick up information, directions, maps, and all the local gossip.

3 Accommodations

by Jeanette Foster

Most accommodations are located "in the village," as residents call Lanai City. Above the village is the luxurious Lodge at Koele, while down the hill at Hulopoe Bay are two options: the luxurious Manele Bay Hotel or tent camping under the stars at the park.

In addition to the choices listed below, also consider the B&B accommodations offered by **Delores Fabrao** (☎ **808/565-6134**), who has two guest rooms in her home: a double with a shared bathroom, and a family room that sleeps up to six ($55 double, $100 for four) with a private bathroom. She doesn't provide breakfast, but you'll have the run of the entire house, including the kitchen.

At **Hale Moe** (☎ **808/565-9520**), host and Lanai native Momi Suzuki makes three bedrooms in her Lanai City home available to guests; all have private bathrooms ($80 to $90 double). Guests are welcome to use the entertainment center, large deck, and Momi's two bicycles.

For a fully equipped, two-bedroom vacation rental that sleeps up to six, call **Hale O Lanai** in Lanai City (☎ **808/247-3637**); rates range from $95 to $125.

Don't forget to add 11.42% in taxes to all accommodation bills. Parking is free at all the choices described here.

VERY EXPENSIVE

✪ **The Lodge at Koele.** P.O. Box 310, Lanai City, HI 96793. ☎ **800/321-4666** or 808/565-7300. Fax 808/565-3868. www.lanai-resorts.com. 107 units. A/C MINIBAR TV TEL. $375–$550 double, $700–$2,000 suite. Extra person $60. Children under 15 stay free in parent's room. Numerous packages (5th night free, adventure package, golf package, wedding package) available. AE, CB, DC, MC, V. Airport shuttle $10 round-trip.

This is the place to stay for a quiet vacation in the cool mist of the mountains. Most guests who stay here are looking for relaxation: sitting out on the porch, reading or watching the turkeys mosey across the manicured lawns; strolling through the Japanese hillside garden; or watching the sun sink into the Pacific and the stars light up at night. The Lodge, as folks here call it, stands in a 21-acre grove of Norfolk Island pines at 1,700 feet above sea level, 8 miles inland from any beach. The atmosphere is informal during the day, more formal after sunset.

The 102-room resort resembles a grand English country estate (Lanai City, at nearly 2,000 feet in the clouds, is not very tropical, so the architecture actually fits in). Inside, heavy timbers, beamed ceilings, and the two huge stone fireplaces of the Great Hall complete the look. Overstuffed furniture sits invitingly around the fireplaces and richly patterned rugs adorn the floor, while museum-quality art hangs on the walls. Cushioned wicker chairs on the long porches are perfect for a long afternoon with a good book. The guest rooms continue the English theme with four-poster beds, sitting areas (complete with window seats for reading), flowery wallpaper, formal writing desks, and luxury bathrooms with oversized tubs. Some of the rooms even offer butler service. There are plenty of activities here and at the sister resort down the hill, Manele Bay, so you'll have the best of both hotels.

Dining/Diversions: A formal dining room, where men are required to wear jackets at night, serves dinner; a less formal interior terrace is open all day. Both use local island ingredients, and both are reviewed in "Dining," later in this chapter. Entertainment is limited to quiet, live music; hula; and periodic guest appearances by celebrities who chat informally in a drawing-room setting about their work (see "Lanai After Dark," at the end of this chapter). Guests enjoy complimentary coffee and tea in the lobby, and formal tea every afternoon. There's a game room, a bar, and a music room.

Amenities: Swimming pool; complimentary shuttle to the golf courses, beach, and Manele Bay Hotel; an 18-hole championship Greg Norman/Ted Robinson–designed golf course called the Experience at Koele; executive putting green; twice-daily maid service; evening turndown; croquet lawns; stables; tennis courts; bikes; upcountry hiking trails; garden walks; library. Guests have access to the Manele Bay facilities as well.

✪ **Manele Bay Hotel.** P.O. Box 310, Lanai City, HI 96793. ☎ **800/321-4666** or 808/565-7700. www.lanai-resorts.com. 250 units. A/C MINIBAR TV TEL. $350–$650 double, $700–$2,000 suite. Extra person $60. Children under 15 stay free in parent's room. Numerous packages (5th night free, adventure package, golf package, wedding package) available. AE, CB, DC, MC, V. Airport shuttle $10 round-trip.

If you want to stay at the beach instead of the mountains, come to this sun-washed bluff overlooking Hulopoe Beach, one of Hawaii's best stretches of golden sand. Much less formal than its sibling, the Lodge at Koele, it attracts more families, and because it's warmer here, people wander through the lobby in shorts and T-shirts. The U-shaped hotel steps down the hillside to the pool and that great beach, then fans out in oceanfront wings separated by gardens with lush flora, manmade waterfalls, lotus ponds, and streams. On the other side, it's bordered by golf greens on a hillside of dry land scrub. The place is a real oasis against the dry Arizona-like heat of Lanai's arid South Coast.

This is a traditional luxury beachfront hotel: open, airy, and situated so that every room has a peek at the big blue Pacific. The lobby is filled with murals depicting scenes from Hawaiian history, sea charts, potted palms, soft camel-hued club chairs, and handwoven kilim rugs. The oversized guest rooms are done in the style of an English country house on the beach: sunny chintz fabrics, mahogany furniture, Audubon prints, huge marble bathrooms, and semiprivate lanais. Thirteen of the suites feature butler service.

Dining/Diversions: Do not miss Chef Edwin Goto's creations in the Ihilani, the specialty dining room. Hulopoe Court features innovative Hawaii Regional Cuisine and ocean views. Both are reviewed in "Dining," later in this chapter. Entertainment is limited to quiet, live music; hula; and periodic guest-lecture appearances by celebrities (see the "'Talk Story' with the Greats" box near the end of this chapter).

Amenities: Water sports at the neighboring beach; swimming pool; tennis; spa with massage and other treatments; bicycling; complimentary shuttle service to the golf courses, the Lodge at Koele, and Manele Boat Harbor; game room; library; historic tours and Jeep tours; twice-daily maid service; turndown. There's golf at the Jack Nicklaus–designed Challenge at Manele, a seaside layout in nice contrast to the upland Experience (see "The Lodge at Koele," above). Guests can also enjoy the amenities at The Lodge at Koele.

MODERATE

Hotel Lanai. 828 Lanai Ave. (P.O. Box 520), Lanai City, HI 96763. ☎ **800/795-7211** or 808/565-7211. Fax 808/565-6450. www.onlanai.com. 11 units. $95–$105 double, $140 cottage double. 2-bedroom house (sleeps 6) nearby $200. Rates include continental breakfast. Extra person $10. AE, MC, V. Airport shuttle $10 round-trip.

This hotel lacks the facilities of the above two resorts, but it's perfect if you can't afford to spend $300 to $400 a night. Just a few years ago, the Hotel Lanai, on a rise overlooking Lanai City, was the only place to stay and eat unless you knew someone who lived on the island. Built in the 1920s for VIP plantation guests, this clapboard plantation-era relic has retained its quaint character and lives on as a country inn. A well-known chef from Maui, Henry Clay Richardson, is the inn's owner and executive chef in the dining room (see "Dining," below).

The rooms are extremely small, but are clean and newly decorated, with Hawaiian quilts, wood furniture, and ceiling fans. The most popular are the lanai rooms, which feature a shared lanai with the room next door. The small, one-bedroom cottage on the property is perfect for a small family. All rooms have ceiling fans and bathrooms with shower only. Only the cottage has a TV and bathtub.

The hotel serves as a down-home crossroads where total strangers meet local folks on the lanai to drink beer and "talk story" or play the ukulele and sing into the dark, tropic night. Often, a curious visitor in search of an authentic experience will join the party and discover Lanai's very Hawaiian heart.

An excellent restaurant is open for continental breakfast for guests only and open to the public for dinner daily. Guests have the use of the complimentary shuttle service to the Lodge at Koele, the Manele Bay Hotel, the golf courses (at which they also get the same low rates given to the guests at the two resorts), and the beach.

INEXPENSIVE

✪ **Dreams Come True.** 547 12th St. (P.O. Box 525), Lanai City, HI 96763. ☎ **800/ 566-6961** or 808/565-6961. www.go-native.com/Inns/0117.html. 3 units. $86–$110 double. Rates include continental breakfast. Extra person $20. AE, DISC, MC, V.

This quaint plantation house is tucked away among papaya, banana, lemon, and avocado trees in the heart of Lanai City, at 1,620 feet. Hosts Susan and Michael Hunter have filled their house with Southeast Asian antiques collected on their travels. Both are jewelers, and they operate a working studio on the premises. Two of the three bedrooms feature a four-poster canopied bed, with an additional single bed (perfect for a small family), while the third has just one queen bed. The common area looks out on the garden and is equipped with both TV and VCR. Breakfast usually consists of freshly baked bread with homemade jellies and jams, tropical fruit, juice, and coffee. The Hunters also rent nearby two-, three- and four-bedroom homes for $220 to $350 a night.

4 Dining

By Jocelyn Fujii

Lanai is heaven for foodies. The island remains a curious mix of innocence and sophistication, with strong cross-cultural elements that liven up its culinary offerings. On this island of three hotels, a handful of stores, and fewer than 3,000 residents, you can go from a greasy-spoon breakfast to a five-star dinner in less than a mile and a few hundred feet in altitude. You can dine like a sultan on this island, but be prepared for high prices. The tony hotel restaurants require deep pockets (or bottomless expense accounts), and there are only a handful of other options.

EXPENSIVE

✪ **Formal Dining Room.** In The Lodge at Koele. ☎ **808/565-4580.** Reservations required. Jackets requested for men. Main courses $32–$40. AE, DC, JCB, MC, V. Daily 6–9:30pm. RUSTIC AMERICAN/UPCOUNTRY HAWAIIAN.

After crossing a gargantuan lobby with immense fireplaces and soaring ceilings, you'll come upon the hotel's dining room, which has its own fireplace and bountiful sprays of orchids. Well-dressed women in pearls sit facing men in jackets, with wine buckets tableside. The elegant, octagonal-shaped room was designed for intimate dining, and the menu, highlighting rustic American favorites (rack of lamb, grilled tenderloin, roasted venison), is an ideal match. Executive chef Andrew Manion-Copley (who has replaced wunderkind Edwin Goto) favors local ingredients simply prepared, but with intense flavors. The seasonally changing menu features braised meats and stews in the winter, and overall, a heightened emphasis on venison and local seafood. Although you won't find any cream sauces, the food can still be rich (foie gras, butter, pancetta). During fall and winter months, expect to see pumpkins, beans, ragouts, and braised items offered in creative seasonal preparations. Roast rack of lamb and Lanai venison top the list for game lovers, and the fish au courant, moi, is a year-round attraction.

Hulopoe Court. In the Manele Bay Hotel. ☎ **808/565-7700.** Reservations recommended. Collared shirt required for men. Main courses $21–$30. AE, DC, JCB, MC, V. Daily 7–11am and 6–9:30pm. HAWAII REGIONAL.

Casual compared to the hotel's fine dining room, Ihilani, but more formal than the Pool Grille, the hotel's lunchtime spot, Hulopoe, has gone Polynesian, with a new menu highlighting Hawaiian and Polynesian cookery. To wit: the Hulopoe Luau plate for two, a dinner selection of kalua pig wrapped in ti leaves with local sweet potatoes; lomi tomatoes; and an upscale take on chicken adobo, a popular Filipino dish served with coconut rice. The seared moi is served with cooled local vegetables, and the "braised and confused tofu" is spiced up with soy and sweet chile sauce and served over tamaki rice, the smaller, rounder, glossier (and more expensive) grain that is the rage among rice connoisseurs. Having gone through several incarnations in style, Hulopoe is still defining itself; let's hope the ethnic approach takes.

✪ **Ihilani.** In the Manele Bay Hotel. ☎ **808/565-2290.** Reservations required. Jackets requested for men. Main courses $38–$44; set menu $85 without wine, $115–$125 with wine. AE, DC, JCB, MC, V. Daily 6–9:30pm. FRENCH-MEDITERRANEAN.

The Manele Bay's formal dining room sits across the lobby from Hulopoe Court; its lower ceilings (beautifully painted with bird-of-paradise murals) and pleasing design permit an ocean view and a clubby, darker, more intimate ambience. There are three sections to the split-level dining room: the terrace, overlooking the ocean and pool; the indoor middle area next to the terrace; and the elevated dining area with banquettes and private niches. The recent arrival of award-winning chef Edwin Goto from The Lodge at Koele has made a good menu even better. Some standouts: Molokai sweet potato and lobster chowder with saffron; ahi carpaccio with Beluga caviar and hazelnut aioli; braised mahimahi; and steamed Kona lobster with portobello-shiitake risotto. Pheasant is a new menu item, and the fish preparations have been upgraded: braised mahimahi is presented with Hudson Valley foie gras and Madeira truffle sauce. For dessert, the gourmet cheeses and walnut bread cannot be beat, unless, of course, it's the paradise chocolate cake with Maui coffee bean sauce and Valrhona chocolate sorbet.

The Terrace. In The Lodge at Koele. ☎ **808/565-4580.** Reservations recommended. Breakfast items $7.25–$14.50, lunch main courses $9.75–$14, dinner main courses $16–$27. AE, DC, JCB, MC, V. Daily 6am–9:30pm. AMERICAN.

Located between the 35-foot-high Great Hall and a wall of glass looking out over prim English gardens, The Terrace is hardly your typical hotel dining room. The food may be fancy for comfort food, but it does, indeed, comfort. Hearty breakfasts of waffles and cereals, fresh pineapple from the nearby Palawai Basin, frittata, and Eggs Polihua (on blue crab cakes with watercress-tomato hollandaise) are a grand start to the day.

At lunch the fresh catch is presented on flavorful nori bread, served with bacon chips, fries, and a coleslaw too elegant for its name. There are vegetable wraps and turkey burgers too. Dinner choices are the American classics, with some Mediterranean touches: skillet-roasted chicken; polenta "pizza" with roasted eggplant, leeks, portobellos, and goat cheese; grilled and roasted vegetables; and seafood, venison, and pork entrees. Not surprisingly, this is the most sophisticated full-service hotel dining room in the Islands.

MODERATE

✪ **Henry Clay's Rotisserie.** In the Hotel Lanai, 828 Lanai Ave., Lanai City. ☎ **808/565-7211.** Main courses $11.95–$36.95. JCB, MC, V. Daily 5:30–9pm. COUNTRY CUISINE.

Lanai has been infused with a hefty dose of New Orleans spice, thanks to Henry Clay Richardson, a New Orleans native who has made some welcome changes in the island's dining landscape. His rustic inn in Lanai City is always full and is arguably the island's most popular restaurant. It's the only restaurant on Lanai to occupy the vast gap between deli-diner and upscale-luxe.

The menu focuses on American country cuisine: fresh meats, seafood, and local produce in assertive preparations. The meats, which could be rabbit, quail, venison, osso bucco, beef, and chicken, are spit-roasted on the rotisserie. Appetizers and entrees reflect Cajun, regional, and international influences, particularly the Rajun Cajun Clay's shrimp, a fabulous, fiery concoction of hefty shrimp in a heavily spiced tomato reduction. From the rotisserie come herb-marinated chicken and Louisiana-style pork ribs, while gourmet pizzas and salads occupy the lighter end of the spectrum. Diners rave about the fresh catch in a lemon butter caper sauce; we adored the eggplant creole, presented with perfect sugar snap peas on a bed of herbed angel hair pasta. There are plates on the pine-paneled walls, chintz curtains, a friendly bartender, and fireplaces in both rooms.

Manele Bay Clubhouse. Challenge at Manele Clubhouse. ☎ **808/565-2222.** Reservations recommended. Main courses $12–$15. AE, DC, JCB, MC, V. Sun–Mon 11am–5pm, Tues–Sat 11am–4pm, 5–9pm. PACIFIC RIM.

The view here may be the best on the island, encompassing Kahoolawe, Haleakala on Maui and, on an especially clear day, the peaks of Mauna Kea and Mauna Loa on the Big Island. And the alfresco dining takes advantage of the ocean view. Lighter fare prevails at lunch: salads and sandwiches, burgers, Caesar salad with chicken, herbed chicken sandwich on sourdough, fish-and-chips. Despite the candlelight and tablecloths at dinner, this place remains casual, serving only chilled and warm pupu, such as sashimi, rock shrimp cocktail with green papaya salad, and various types of ravioli, dim sum, and grilled fish cakes with exotic dressings.

Pool Grille. In the Manele Bay Hotel. ☎ **808/565-7700.** Main courses $6–$15. AE, DC, JCB, MC, V. Daily 11am–5pm. ECLECTIC.

At this, the most casual of the hotel's restaurants, you'll dine poolside under beach umbrellas, feasting on huge hamburgers (homemade buns, of course) and gourmet salads in a sea of well-oiled, suntanned bodies. Salad choices include marinated grilled vegetables with Big Island goat cheese, spicy chicken, and Caesar salad with shrimp. The grilled ahi and the tuna pita are among the popular sandwich choices.

INEXPENSIVE

Blue Ginger Cafe. 409 Seventh St., Lanai City. ☎ **808/565-6363.** Most items less than $12. No credit cards. Daily 6am–9pm. COFFEE SHOP.

This is a very local, very casual, and moderately priced alternative to Lanai's fancy hotel restaurants. The four tables on the front porch face the cool Norfolk pines of Dole Park and are always filled with locals who "talk story" from morning to night. The tiny cafe is often jammed from 6 to 7am with construction workers on their way to work. The offerings are solid, no-nonsense, everyday fare: fried saimin (no MSG, a plus), the very popular hamburgers on homemade buns, and the mahimahi with capers in a white-wine sauce. Blue Ginger also serves a tasty French toast of homemade bread, a vegetable lumpia (the Filipino version of a spring roll), and inexpensive home-made omelettes. The Mexican specials are popular, and the stir-fry vegetables—a heaping platter of fresh, perfectly cooked veggies, including summer squash and fresh mushrooms—make a sensible lunch for two.

✪ **Pele's Other Garden.** On Dole Park, 811 Houston St. ☎ **808/565-9628.** Most items less than $7. AE, DISC, JCB, MC, V. Mon–Sat 11am–8:30pm. DELI/PIZZERIA/JUICE BAR.

Healthy, tasty eats come streaming across the counter at this New York–style deli, which offers outdoor seating and plans to expand into the space next door. It breaks all the rules: It's healthy *and* delicious, and it's not expensive. Sandwiches, daily soup and menu specials, salads, pizza, fresh organic produce, fresh juices, and special touch-es such as top-quality black-bean burritos, roasted red peppers, and stuffed grape leaves are some of the features that make Pele's Other Garden a Lanai City must. There are dozens of cheese choices for your orders. Our vegetarian pizza came with fresh shi-itake mushrooms and vegetarian pepperoni, and it was excellent. Sandwiches are made with whole wheat, rye, sourdough, or French bread, baked on the island and delivered fresh daily. The turkey is free-range. The food is mostly takeout, but there are a cou-ple of tables on the veranda, facing the tree-shaded square. Most menu items are made from natural and organic ingredients, and even the meats—roast beef, pastrami, corned beef—are top quality. Plans call for the addition of pastas, daily specials, seafood, and chicken to the menu.

Tanigawa's Restaurant. 419 Seventh St., Lanai City. ☎ **808/565-6537.** Reservations not accepted. Breakfast less than $7. No credit cards. Thurs–Tues 6:30am–1pm. LOCAL FOOD.

Formerly S. T. Properties, Tanigawa's has changed its name but remains the landmark that it's been since the 1920s. In those days, the tiny storefront sold canned goods and cigarettes; the 10 tables, hamburgers, and Filipino food came later. Jerry Tani-gawa has kept his hole-in-the-wall a local institution, with a reputation for serving a good local-style breakfast. The fare—saimin, plate lunches, beef stew, and omelettes—is a nod to sentiment, more greasy spoon than gourmet, and friendliest above all to the pocketbook.

5 Beaches

by Jeanette Foster

If you like big, wide, empty beaches, with golden sands and crystal-clear, cobalt-blue water full of bright tropical fish—and who doesn't?—go to Lanai. With 18 miles of sandy shoreline, Lanai has some of Hawaii's least crowded and most interesting beach-es. One in particular is perfect for swimming, snorkeling, and watching spinner dol-phins play: Hulopoe Beach, Lanai's best.

✪ HULOPOE BEACH

In 1997, Stephen Leatherman, the University of Maryland's "Dr. Beach," ranked Hulopoe the best beach in the United States. It's easy to see why. This palm-fringed, gold-sand beach is bordered by black-lava fingers, protecting swimmers from the serious ocean currents that sweep around Lanai. In summer, Hulopoe is perfect for swimming, snorkeling, or just lolling about; the water temperature is usually in the mid-70s. Swimming is usually safe, except when swells kick up in the winter. The bay at the foot of the Manele Bay Hotel is a protected marine preserve, and the schools of colorful fish know it. So do the spinner dolphins that come here to play, and the Pacific Humpback whales that cruise by in winter. Hulopoe is also Lanai's premier beach park, with a grassy lawn, picnic tables, barbecue grills, rest rooms, showers, and ample parking. You can also camp here.

Some of the best lava-rock **tide pools** in Hawaii are found along the south shore of Hulopoe Bay. These miniature Sea Worlds are full of strange creatures: asteroids (sea stars) and holothurians (sea cucumbers), not to mention spaghetti worms, Barber Pole shrimp, and Hawaii's favorite local delicacy, the opihi, a tasty morsel also known as the limpet. Youngsters enjoy swimming in the enlarged tide pool at the eastern edge of the bay.

When you explore tide pools, do it at low tide. Never turn your back on the waves. Wear tennis shoes or reef walkers, as wet rocks are slippery. Collecting specimens in this marine preserve is forbidden, so don't take any souvenirs home.

SHIPWRECK BEACH

This 8-mile-long windswept strand from Polihua Beach to Kahokunui—named for the rusty ship, *Liberty,* stuck on the coral reef—is a sailor's nightmare and a beachcomber's dream. The strong currents yield all sorts of flotsam, from Japanese handblown-glass fish floats and rare pelagic paper nautilus shells to lots of junk. This is also a great place to spot whales from December to April, when the Pacific humpbacks cruise in from Alaska to winter in the calm offshore waters. The road to the beach is paved most of the way, but you really need a four-wheel-drive to get down here.

POLIHUA BEACH

This deserted north shore beach is at the end of Polihua Road, a 4-mile Jeep trail. So many sea turtles once hauled themselves out of the water to lay their eggs in the sun-baked sand on Lanai's northwestern shore that Hawaiians named the beach here *Polihua,* or "egg nest." Although Hawaii's endangered green sea turtles are making a comeback, they're seldom seen here now. You're more likely to spot an offshore whale (in season) or the perennial litter that washes up on shore. There are no facilities except fishermen's huts and driftwood shelters. Bring water and sunscreen. Swimming here is unsafe, because of the strong currents, but this strand is ideal for beachcombing (those little green-glass Japanese fishing-net floats often show up here), fishing, or just being alone.

6 Hitting the Water

by Jeanette Foster

Lanai has Hawaii's best water clarity, because it lacks major development and has low rainfall and runoff, and because its coast is washed clean daily by the sea current known as "The Way to Tahiti." But the strong sea currents pose a threat to swimmers, and there are few good surf breaks. Most of the aquatic adventures—swimming, snorkeling, and scuba diving—are centered on the somewhat protected south shore, around Hulopoe Bay.

✪ Frommer's Favorite Lanai Experiences

Snorkel Hulopoe Beach. This beach is one of Hawaii's best. There are tide pools to explore, waves to play in, and other surprises—like a pod of spinner dolphins that often makes a splashy entrance. The crystal-clear water teems with brilliant tropical fish.

Explore the Garden of the Gods. Eroded by wind, rain, and time, these geologic badlands are worth visiting at sunrise or sunset, when the low light plays tricks on the land—and your mind.

Hike the Munro Trail. The 11-mile Munro Trail is a lofty, rigorous hike along the rim of an old volcano. You'll get great views of the nearby islands. You can also take a four-wheel-drive vehicle, to spend more time on top of the island.

Four-Wheel It. Four-wheeling is a way of life on Lanai, since there are only 30 miles of pavement. Plenty of rugged trails lead to deserted beaches, abandoned villages, and valleys filled with wild game. No other island offers off-road adventures like this one.

Camp under the Stars. The campsites at Hulopoe Beach Park are about as close to the heavens as you can get. The sound of the crashing surf will lull you to sleep at night; the sound of chirping birds will wake you in the morning. If you're into roughing it, this is a great way to experience Lanai.

Beachcomb at Shipwreck Beach. This 8-mile stretch along the northeastern shore is a great place to dig up treasures of the sea. Occasionally, a glass ball from a Japanese fishing boat will float in—in Hawaii, this is considered the greatest beachcombing treasure you can find.

Watch the Whales at Polihua Beach. This north-shore beach—which gets its name from the turtles that nested here—is a great place to spend the day scanning the ocean for whales during the winter months.

BODYBOARDING (BOOGIE BOARDING), BODYSURFING & BOARD SURFING

When the surf's up on Lanai, it's a real treat. Under the right conditions, Hulopoe and Polihua are both great for catching waves. You've got to bring your own board, as the beach shack at Hulopoe Beach has complimentary boogie boards for guests of the Manele Bay Hotel and The Lodge at Koele only.

OCEAN KAYAKING

The **Lanai EcoAdventure Centre,** P.O. Box 1394, Lanai City, HI 96763 (☎ **808/ 565-7737** or 565-7373; www.kayakhawaii.com), offers half-day sea kayak/snorkeling adventures (as well as kayak/scuba trips; see below) aimed at introducing beginners to the world of ocean kayaking. The Centre provides state-of-the-art kayaks (with lightweight graphite paddles and full back-support seats), life vests, the latest in snorkel equipment, dry bags, towels, water, and snacks. After instructions on how to kayak, the group sets off to explore the waters around Lanai, with stops for snorkeling, snacks, and beachcombing. The 4-hour trip costs $69. The Centre also rents kayaks, starting at $39.95 a day.

SCUBA DIVING

Two of Hawaii's best-known dive spots are found in Lanai's clear waters, just off the south shore: **Cathedrals I and II,** so named because the sun lights up an underwater grotto like a magnificent church. **Trilogy Charters** (☎ 888/MAUI-800; www.sail-trilogy.com), offers sailing, diving, and snorkeling trips on its catamarans. The cost is $95 for snorkelers and $140 for certified scuba divers for a two-tank dive. The trip, which goes from 8:45am to 1pm, includes continental breakfast and all snorkeling and diving equipment.

   Lanai EcoAdventure Centre, P.O. Box 1394, Lanai City, HI 96763 (☎ 808/565-7737 or 808/565-7373; www.kayakhawaii.com), offers kayak-scuba adventures for $69 to $89 for one-tank dives. Their store in Lanai City, **Adventure Lanai Eco-Centre,** 338 8th St., Lanai City (☎ 808/565-7373; www.adventurelanai.com), has scuba gear for rent from $49.

SNORKELING

Hulopoe is Lanai's best snorkeling spot. Fish are abundant and friendly in the marine-life conservation area. Try the lava-rock points at either end of the beach and around the lava pools. Snorkel gear is free to guests of the two resorts, and also can be rented from **Lanai EcoAdventure Centre,** 338 8th St., Lanai City (☎ 808/565-7737 or 808/565-7373; www.kayakhawaii.com), for $9.95 a day. Also see above for information on the Centre's ocean kayaking/snorkeling trips.

SPORTFISHING

Jeff Menze will take you out on the 28-foot Omega boat *Spinning Dolphin* (☎ 808/565-6613). His fishing charters cost $400 for six people for 4 hours, or $600 for six people for 8 hours. He also has exclusive 4-hour whale-watching/snorkeling charters, which cost $400 for six passengers.

WHALE WATCHING

From late December to March, **Trilogy Charters** (☎ 800/874-2666 or 808/565-9303; www.sailtrilogy.com) offers 3-hour whale-watching adventures, either on a 50-plus foot catamaran or on a 34-foot, 26-passenger rigid-hulled inflatable boat. The cost is $75 and includes snacks.

7 Hiking & Camping

by Jeanette Foster

HIKES

A LEISURELY MORNING HIKE

The 3-hour **Koele Nature Hike** starts by the reflecting pool in the backyard of the Lodge at Koele and takes you on a 5-mile loop trail through a cathedral of Norfolk Island pines, into Hulopoe Valley, past wild ginger, and up to Koloiki Ridge, with its panoramic view of Maunalei Valley and Molokai and Maui in the distance. You're welcome to take the hike even if you're not a guest at the Lodge. The trailhead isn't obvious—just keep going *mauka* (inland) toward the trees. The path isn't clearly marked, but the concierge will give you a free map.

THE CHALLENGING MUNRO TRAIL

This tough, 11-mile (round-trip) uphill climb through the groves of Norfolk pines is a lung-buster, but if you reach the top you'll be rewarded with a breathtaking view of

Molokai, Maui, Kahoolawe, the peaks of the Big Island, and—on a really clear day—Oahu in the distance. Figure on 7 hours. The trail begins at Lanai Cemetery along Keomoku Road (Hwy. 44) and follows Lanai's ancient caldera rim, ending up at the island's highest point, Lanaihale. Go in the morning for the best visibility. After 4 miles, you'll get a view of Lanai City. The weary retrace their steps from there, while the more determined go the last $1^1/_3$ miles to the top. Diehards go down Lanai's steep south-crater rim to join the highway to Manele Bay. For more details on the Munro Trail—including information on four-wheel-driving it to the top—see "Seeing the Sights," below.

A SELF-GUIDED NATURE TRAIL

This self-guided nature trail is in the Kanepuu Preserve. The trailhead is clearly marked on the Polihua Road on the way to the Garden of the Gods. The trail is about a 10- to 15-minute walk through eight stations, with interpretive signs explaining the natural or cultural significance of what you see. Kanepuu is one of the last remaining examples of the type of forest that once covered the dry lowlands throughout the state. There are some 49 plant species here that are found only in Hawaii (such as sandalwood and Hawaiian gardenia, both listed as endangered species). The Nature Conservancy conducts guided hikes every month; call ☎ **808/565-7430.**

GUIDED HIKES

The **Lanai EcoAdventure Centre,** 338 8th St., Lanai City (☎ **808/565-7737** or 808/565-7373; www.kayakhawaii.com), offers a 4X4 Adventure Trek that combines hiking and four-wheeling. The trips include such destinations as the Munro Trail, Poiaiwa Gulch, Garden of the Gods, and others. The cost is $69 per person, and includes fruit, drinks, snacks, and transportation.

CAMPING AT HULOPOE BEACH PARK

There is only one place to "legally" camp on Lanai: Hulopoe Beach Park, which is owned by The Lanai Company. To camp in this exquisite beach park, with its crescent-shaped, white-sand beach bordered by kiawe trees, contact the **Lanai Company,** P.O. Box 310, Lanai City, HI 96763 (☎ **808/565-3982;** www.lanai-resorts.com). There is a $5 registration fee, plus $5 per person, per night. Holupoe has six campsites, each of which can accommodate up to six people. Facilities include rest rooms, running water, showers, barbecue areas, and picnic tables.

You can rent camping equipment from the **Lanai EcoAdventure Centre,** 338 8th St., Lanai City (☎ **808/565-7737;** www.kayakhawaii.com), which has everything from backpacks to tents. A set of camping gear starts at $19.95 a day. The Lanai Company recommends a tent (rain can be expected year-round), a cooking stove or hibachi (the number of barbecues are limited), and insect repellent (mosquitoes are plentiful).

8 Biking, Golf, Horseback Riding & Tennis

by Jeanette Foster

BIKING

Road bike treks are available through **Lanai EcoAdventure Centre,** 338 8th St., Lanai City (☎ **808/565-7737** or 808/565-7373; www.kayakhawaii.com), for $69 per person. The $3^1/_2$-hour tours are perfect for beginners and are all downhill. A 4X4 van meets you at the bottom with snacks and takes you on a tour of the petroglyphys, then gives you a ride back up to the top. There are also trips for more advanced riders. The Centre rents 21-speed suspension mountain bikes starting at $20 a day.

For general information about bike trails, check out **www.bikehawaii.com.**

GOLF

Cavendish Golf Course. Located next to the Lodge at Koele in Lanai City. No phone.

This quirky par-36, nine-hole public course not only has no clubhouse or club pros, but also no tee times, scorecards, or club rentals. To play, just show up, put a donation into the little wooden box next to the first tee ($5 to $10 would be nice), and hit away. The 3,071-yard, E. B. Cavendish–designed course was built by the Dole plantation in 1947 for its employees. The greens are a bit bumpy, but the views of Lanai are great, and the temperatures are usually quite mild.

✪ **The Challenge at Manele.** Located next to the Manele Bay Hotel in Holopoe Bay (P.O. Box 310, Lanai City, HI 96763). ☎ **800/321-4666** or 808/565-2222.

This target-style, desert-links course, designed by Jack Nicklaus, is one of the most challenging courses in the state. Check out the local rules: "No retrieving golf balls from the 150-foot cliffs on the ocean holes 12, 13, or 17," and "All whales, axis deer, and other wild animals are considered immovable obstructions." That's just a hint of the uniqueness of this course routed among lava outcroppings, archaeological sites, kiawe groves, and ilima trees. The five sets of staggered tees give everyone, from the casual golfer to the pro, a challenging game.

Rates are $135 for guests of Manele Bay Hotel, Koele Lodge, or Hotel Lanai, and $185 for nonguests. You can play both this course and The Experience at Koele for $185 for hotel guests and $235 for nonguests, plus $25 for the cart rental for the second round. Twilight play after 2pm is $70. Facilities include clubhouse, pro shop, rentals, practice area, lockers, and showers.

✪ **The Experience at Koele.** Located next to the Lodge at Koele in Lanai City (P.O. Box L, Lanai City, HI 96763). ☎ **800/321-4666** or 808/565-4600.

This traditional par-72 course, designed by Greg Norman with fairway architecture by Ted Robinson, has a very different front and back nine holes. Mother Nature reigns throughout: You'll find Cook Island and Norfolk pines, indigenous plants, and water—lots of water, including seven lakes, flowing streams, cascading waterfalls, and one green (the 17th) completely surrounded by a lake. All goes well until you hit the signature hole, number 8, where you tee off from a 250-foot elevated tee to a fairway bordered by a lake on the right and trees and dense shrubs on the left. After that, the back nine holes drop dramatically through ravines filled with pine, koa, and eucalyptus trees. The grand finale, the 18th, a par five, features a green rimmed by waterfalls that flow into a lake on the left side. To give golfers a break, there are four different sets of tees to level the playing field.

Rates are $135 for guests of Manele Bay Hotel, Koele Lodge, or Hotel Lanai and $185 for nonguests. You play at both this course and The Challenge at Manele for $185 for hotel guests and $235 for nonguests, plus $25 for the cart rental for the second round. Twilight play after 2pm is $70. Facilities include clubhouse, pro shop, rentals, practice area, lockers, and showers.

HORSEBACK RIDING

Horses can take you to many places in Lanai's unique landscape that are otherwise unreachable, even in a four-wheel-drive vehicle. **The Stables at Koele** (☎ **808/ 565-4424**) offer various rides, starting at $40 for a 1-hour trip. We recommend the 2-hour **Paniolo Trail Ride,** which takes you into the hills surrounding Koele. You'll meander through guava groves and patches of ironwood trees, catch glimpses of axis deer, quail, wild turkeys, and Santa Getrudis cattle, and end with panoramic views of Maui and Lanai. The cost is $65. Long pants and shoes are required; safety helmets are provided. Carry a jacket, as the weather is chilly and rain is frequent. Children must be at least 9 years old and 4 feet tall. The maximum weight is 250 pounds.

TENNIS
Public courts, lit for night play as well as day, are available in Lanai City at no charge; call ☎ **808/565-6979** for reservations. Guests staying at the Lodge at Koele or the Manele Bay Hotel have complimentary tennis privileges at either the Tennis Center at Manele, with its six Plexi-paved courts, a fully equipped pro shop, and tournament facilities; or at the courts at Koele. Instruction is available for a fee. For information, call ☎ **808/565-2072.**

9 Seeing the Sights

by Jeanette Foster

You'll need a four-wheel-drive vehicle to reach all the sights listed below. Renting a Jeep is an expensive proposition on Lanai—from $89 to $145 a day—so rent one just for the day (or days) you plan on sightseeing; otherwise, it's easy enough to get to the beach and around Lanai City without your own wheels. For details on how to rent a Jeep, see "Getting Around," above.

For a guided 4X4 tour, contact **Lanai EcoAdventure Centre,** 338 8th St., Lanai City (☎**808/565-7737** or 808/565-7373; www.kayakhawaii.com), which offers 3- to 4-hour off-road tours for $69 per person.

✪ GARDEN OF THE GODS
A dirt 4X4 road leads out of Lanai City, through the now uncultivated pineapple fields, past the Kanepuu Preserve (a dry-land forest preserve teeming with rare plant and animal life), to the so-called Garden of the Gods, out on Lanai's north shore. This place has little to do with gods, Hawaiian or otherwise. It is, however, the ultimate rock garden: a rugged, barren, beautiful place full of rocks strewn by volcanic forces and shaped by the elements into a variety of shapes and colors: brilliant reds, oranges, ochers, and yellows.

Ancient Hawaiians considered this desolate, windswept place an entirely supernatural phenomenon. Scientists, however, have other, less colorful explanations. Some call the area an "ongoing posterosional event;" others say it's just "plain and simple badlands." Take a four-wheel-drive ride out here and decide for yourself.

Go early in the morning or just before sunset, when the light casts eerie shadows on the mysterious lava formations that dot the amber- and ocher-colored ground. Drive west from the Lodge on Polihua Road; in about 2 miles, you'll see a hand-painted sign that'll point you in the right direction, left down a one-lane, red-dirt road through a kiawe forest and past sisal and scrub to the site.

✪ FIVE ISLANDS AT A SINGLE GLANCE: THE MUNRO TRAIL
In the first golden rays of dawn, hop into your rented 4X4 and head out on the two-lane blacktop toward Mt. Lanaihale, the 3,370-foot summit of Lanai. Your destination is the Munro Trail, the narrow, winding ridge trail that runs across Lanai's razorback spine to the summit. From here, hopefully, you'll get a rare Hawaii treat: On a clear day, you can see all the main islands in the Hawaiian chain except Kauai.

When it rains, the Munro Trail becomes slick and boggy with major washouts. Rainy-day excursions often end with a rental Jeep on the hook of the island's lone tow truck—and a $250 tow charge. You could even slide off into a major gulch and never be found, so don't try it. But in late August and September, when trade winds stop

Adventures for Kids (& Kids at Heart)

Explore Hulopoe Tide Pools (*see p. 280*)   An entire world of marine life lives in the tide pools on the eastern side of Hulopoe Bay. Everything in the waters, including the tiny fish, is small—kid-size. After examining the wonders of the tide pool, check out the larger swimming holes in the lava rock, perfect for children.

Hunt for Petroglyphs (*see below*)   The Luahiwa Petroglyphs Field, located just outside Lanai City, is spread out over a 3-acre site. Make it a game: Whoever finds the most petroglyphs gets ice cream from the Pine Isle Market.

Listen to Storytelling at the Lanai Library   Check with the Lanai Library (Fraser Ave., near Fifth St., Lanai City; ☎ **808/565-6996**) to see if any storytelling or other activities for children are scheduled. The events are usually free and open to everyone.

and the air over the islands stalls in what is called a *kona* condition, Mt. Lanaihale's suddenly visible peak becomes an irresistible attraction.

When you're on Lanai, look to the summit. If it's clear in the morning, get a four-wheel-drive vehicle and take the Munro Trail to the top. Look for a red-dirt road off Manele Road (Hwy. 440), about 5 miles south of Lanai City; turn left and head up the ridge line. No sign says, "Summit 3,370 feet," so you have to keep an eye out. Look for a wide spot in the road and a clearing that falls sharply to the sea.

The islands stand in order on the flat blue sea: Kahoolawe, Maui, the Big Island of Hawaii, even Molokini's tiny crescent. Even the summits show. You can also see the silver domes of Space City on Haleakala in Maui; Puu Moaulanui, the tongue-twisting summit of Kahoolawe; and Mauna Kea on the Big Island looming above the clouds. At another clearing farther along the thickly forested ridge, all of Molokai, including the 4,961-foot summit of Kamakou, and the faint outline of Oahu (more than 30 miles across the sea) are visible. You actually can't see all five in a single glance anymore, because a thriving pine forest blocks the view. For details on hiking the trail, see "Hiking & Camping," above.

LUAHIWA PETROGLYPH FIELD

Lanai is second only to the Big Island in its wealth of prehistoric rock art, but you'll have to search a little to find it. Some of the best examples are on the outskirts of Lanai City, on a hillside site known as Luahiwa Petroglyph Field. The characters you'll see incised on 13 boulders in this grassy 3-acre knoll include a running man, a deer, a turtle, a bird, a goat, and even a rare, curly-tailed Polynesian dog (a latter-day wag has put a leash on him—some joke).

To get here, take the road to Hulopoe Beach. About 2 miles out of Lanai City, look to the left, up on the slopes of the crater, for a cluster of reddish-tan boulders (believed to form a rain *heiau,* or shrine, where people called up the gods Ku and Hina to nourish their crops). A cluster of spiky century plants marks the spot. As you are driving, look for the Norfolk pine trees on the left hand side of the highway, turn left on the dirt road that veers across the abandoned pineapple fields. Watch your odometer, at just about one mile, take a sharp left by the water tanks. Drive for another half mile and then veer to the right at the "v" in the road. Stay on this upper road for about $^1/_3$ mile where you will come to a large cluster of boulders on the right side. It's just a short walk up the cliffs (wear walking or hiking shoes) to the petro-glyphs. Exit the same way you came. Go between 3pm and sunset for ideal viewing and photo ops.

KAUNOLU VILLAGE

Out on Lanai's nearly vertical, Gibraltar-like sea cliffs is an old royal compound and fishing village. Now a national historic landmark and one of Hawaii's most treasured ruins, it's believed to have been inhabited by King Kamehameha the Great and hundreds of his closest followers about 200 years ago. It's a hot, dry, dusty, slow-going, 3-mile 4X4 drive from Lanai City to Kaunolu, but the miniexpedition is worth it. Take plenty of water, don a hat for protection against the sun, and wear sturdy shoes.

Ruins of 86 house platforms and 35 stone shelters have been identified on both sides of Kaunolu Gulch. The residential complex also includes the Halulu Heiau temple, named after a mythical man-eating bird. His majesty's royal retreat is thought to have stood on the eastern edge of Kaunolu Gulch, overlooking the rocky shore facing Kahekili's Leap, a 62-foot-high bluff named for the mighty Maui chief who leaped off cliffs as a show of bravado. Nearby are burial caves, a fishing shrine, a lookout tower, and many warriorlike stick figures carved on boulders. Just offshore stands the telltale fin of little Shark Island, a popular dive spot.

Excavations are underway to discover more about how ancient Hawaiians lived, worked, and worshipped on Lanai's leeward coast. Who knows? The royal fishing village may yet yield the bones of King Kamehameha. His burial site, according to legend, is known only to the moon and the stars.

KANEPUU PRESERVE

Don't expect giant sequoias big enough to drive a car through; this ancient forest on the island's western plateau is so fragile that you can only visit once a month. Kanepuu, which has 48 species of plants unique to Hawaii, including the endangered Hawaiian gardenia (*na'u*) and the once-plentiful sandalwood (*iliahi*), survives under the Nature Conservancy's protective wing. Botanists say the 590-acre forest is the last dry lowland forest in Hawaii; the others have all vanished, trashed by axis deer, agriculture, or "progress." Among the botanical marvels of this dry forest are the remains of *olopua* (native olive), *lama* (native ebony), *mau hau hele* (a native hibiscus), and the rare *'aiea* trees, which were used for canoe parts.

Due to the forest's fragile nature, guided hikes are led only 12 times a year, on a monthly, reservations-only basis. Contact the **Nature Conservancy Oahu Land Preserve** manager at 1116 Smith St., Suite 201, Honolulu, HI 96817 (☎ **808/537-4508**), to reserve.

OFF THE TOURIST TRAIL: KEOMOKU VILLAGE

If you're sunburned lobster red, have read all the books you brought, and are starting to get island fever, take a little drive to Keomoku Village, on Lanai's East Coast.

You're really off the tourist trail now. All that's in Keomoku, a ghost town since the mid-1950s, is a 1903 clapboard church in disrepair, an overgrown graveyard, an excellent view across the 9-mile Auau Channel to Maui's crowded Kaanapali Beach, and some really empty beaches that are perfect for a picnic or a snorkel. This former ranching and fishing village of 2,000 was the first non-Hawaiian settlement on Lanai, but it dried up after droughts killed off the Maunalei Sugar Company. The village, such as it is, is a great little escape from Lanai City. Follow Keomoku Road for 8 miles to the coast, turn right on the sandy road, and keep going for 5.7 miles.

10 Shops & Galleries

by Jocelyn Fujii

Gifts with Aloha. On Dole Park, 363 Seventh St. ☎ **808/565-6589.**

Phoenix and Kimberly Dupree have assembled a store of treasures, offering T-shirts, swimwear, quilts, Jams World dresses, children's books and toys, Hawaii-themed books, pareus, candles, aloha shirts, picture frames, handbags, ceramics, hats, and art by local artists. The sumptuous white lehua honey from the Big Island is sold here, as well as jams and jellies by Lanai's Fabrao House. The made-on-Maui soaps and bath products are in gardenia, pikake, and plumeria fragrances, and are sublime.

International Food & Clothing. 833 Ilima Ave. ☎ **808/565-6433.**

Here's a place for the basics: groceries, a few housewares, T-shirts, hunting and fishing supplies, over-the-counter drugs, wine and liquor, paper goods, and hardware. We were pleasantly surprised by the extraordinary candy and bubble-gum section, the beautiful local bananas in the small produce section, the surprisingly extensive selection of yuppie soft drinks, and the best knife-sharpener we've seen—handy for the Lanai lifestyle.

Lanai Art Program. 339 Seventh St. ☎ **808/565-7503.**

Located between the Laundromat and the community college office, the Lanai Art Program displays and sells a small selection of made-on-Lanai crafts: jewelry, ceramics, scarves, fused glass, watercolors, woodworks, and other two- and three-dimensional pieces. This is the retail space for a not-for-profit arts program that supports and showcases Lanai artists, so the inventory fluctuates and can, at times, be minimal. Classes are also offered for children and adults. Because it's staffed by volunteers, hours vary; it's best to call ahead.

Lanai Marketplace. Dole Sq.

Gardens are big on Lanai, where everyone seems to be a backyard farmer. From 7 till 11am or noon on Saturday, they all head to this shady square to sell their dewy-fresh produce, home-baked breads, plate lunches, and handicrafts. This is Lanai's version of the green market: petite in scale (like the island) but charming, and growing.

Dolores Fabrao's jams and jellies, under the Fabrao House label (☎ **808/565-6134,** if you want to special order), are a big seller at the market and at the resort gift shops where they're sold. The exotic flavors include pineapple-coconut, pineapple-mango, papaya, guaivi (strawberry guava), poha (gooseberry) in season, passion fruit, Surinam cherry, and the very tart karamay jelly. All fruits are grown on the island. Gift packs and bags are available.

The Local Gentry. 363 7th St. ☎ **808/565-9130.**

Open since December 1999, Jenna Gentry's wonderful boutique is the first of its kind on the island: a shop of clothing and accessories that are not the standard resort-shop fare. (Lanai women make a beeline for this store.) So you'll find fabulous silk aloha shirts by Iolani in Hiroshige-type prints; Putumayo separates (perfect for Hawaii) in easy-care fabrics; the Tommy Bahama line for men and women; loose linens and high-quality T-shirts; swimwear; jewelry; bath products; picture frames; jeans; and chic sunglasses and offbeat sandals.

"Talk Story" with the Greats:
Lanai's Visiting Artist Program

Not so very long ago, before CNN, e-mail, faxes, and modems, news spread in person, on the lips of those who chanced by these remote islands. Visitors were always welcome, especially if they had a good story to tell. The *ha'i mo'olelo,* or storyteller, was always held in high regard. In Hawaiian pidgin, this tale-telling is called "talk story."

The tradition continues today at The Lodge at Koele. Its Lanai Visiting Artists Program is dedicated to bringing the literati of America to Lanai, in a new version of "talk story." On any given weekend, you could find yourself in the company of poets, musicians, writers, actors, filmmakers, chefs, and other creative types. You might find yourself vacationing with, say, classical pianist André Watts, humorist Dave Barry, author Tom Robbins, "A Prairie Home Companion" host Garrison Keillor, or who knows which Pulitzer Prize or Academy Award winner, each sharing his or her talent and insights in a casual, living-room atmosphere.

The program takes place about 14 or 15 times a year at both the Lodge and the Manele Bay Hotel. It's free and open to everyone. There's a constantly changing schedule, so call either of those resorts to see who's visiting while you're on Lanai (☎ **800/321-4666** or www.lanai-resorts.com).

—Jeanette Foster

Pele's Garden. 811 Houston St. ☎ **808/565-9629.**

Even if nothing ails you, Pele's Garden is the Eden of the island for health products, with a health-giving assortment of vitamins, herbs, homeopathics, and supplements. Shop here for health-related reference books, greeting cards and magazines, natural and organic groceries, baby food, and a natural health-and-beauty-aid section. Owner Beverly Zigmond, a naturopathic doctor, has assembled a wide-ranging inventory of products promoting health of body, mind, and spirit. With the addition of Pele's Other Garden (Zigmond's brother's deli) serving up guiltless gourmet fare in the front section of the store, this corner of Lanai is a place you'd want to find.

Pine Isle Market. 356 Eighth St. ☎ **808/565-6047.**

A two-generation local landmark, Pine Isle specializes in locally caught fresh fish. You can also shop here for fresh herbs and spices from Pete Felipe's garden, canned goods, electronic games, ice cream, toys, zoris, diapers, paint, cigars, and other basic essentials of work and play. The fishing section is outstanding, with every lure imaginable.

Richard's Shopping Center. 434 Eighth St. ☎ **808/565-6047.**

The Tamashiros' family business has been on the square since 1946, and except for the merchandise, not much has changed. This "shopping center" is, in fact, a general store with a grocery section, paper products, ethnic foods, liquor, toys, film, cosmetics, fishing gear, sunscreens, clothing, kitchen utensils, T-shirts, and other miscellany. Half of a wall is lined with fish hooks and anglers' needs, and even the fashion-conscious can find some treasures: aloha-printed zoris, quirky Japanese wooden getas with velvet thongs (a steal at $13), and lauhala mats that fold flat and have handles for carrying like handbags. Aloha shirts, inexpensive brocade-covered writing tablets, and gourmet breads from the Lanai Bake Shop are some good things from Richard's.

11 Lanai After Dark

by Jocelyn Fujii

Once, when we inquired about nightlife on Lanai, an island woman raised her eyebrows in mock umbrage. "Oh," she said, "that's personal." Except for special programs such as the annual **Pineapple Festival** in May, when some of Hawaii's best musicians arrive to show their support for Lanai (see "Maui, Molokai & Lanai Calendar of Events" in chapter 2), the only regular nightlife venues are the Lanai Playhouse, at the corner of Seventh and Lanai avenues in Lanai City, and the two resorts, the Lodge at Koele and Manele Bay Hotel.

The **Lanai Playhouse** (☎ 808/565-7500) is a historic 1920s building that has won awards for its renovations. When it opened in 1993, the 150-seat venue stunned residents by offering first-run movies with Dolby sound—quite contemporary for anachronistic Lanai. Lanai Playhouse usually, but not always, shows two movies each evening from Friday to Tuesday (to Wednesday during the summer), at 6:30pm and 8:30pm, with occasional Sunday afternoon and Monday morning matinees. If a 3-hour movie is on, it's shown at 7:30pm. Tickets are $7 for adults and $4.50 for kids and seniors. The playhouse is also the venue for occasional special events.

Except for special programs, the Hotel Lanai has discontinued its weekend program of live music, but the Lodge at Koele has stepped up its live entertainment. In the **Lodge's Great Hall,** in front of its manorial fireplaces, visiting artists bring contemporary Hawaiian, jazz, Broadway, classical, and other genres to listeners who sip port and fine liqueurs while sinking into plush leather chairs. The special programs take place on weekends, but throughout the week, some form of nightly entertainment takes place in the Great Hall from 7 to 10pm. In the lounge area near the main lobby of the **Manele Bay Hotel,** above Ihilani, a pianist plays on Tuesday to Saturday evenings from 5:30 to 9:30pm.

Both the Lodge at Koele and Manele Bay Hotel are known for their **Visiting Artist Program** (see box above), which brings acclaimed literary and performing artists from across the country to this tiny island. These are scheduled throughout the year, usually on a monthly or bimonthly basis.

Other than that, what happens after dark in Lanai is really up to you. Dinner becomes leisurely extended entertainment. Afterwards, you can repair to your room with a book or find an after-dinner crowd in the Tea Room at Koele or a game of billiards at Manele. And the local folks out on the veranda of the Hotel Lanai will be happy to welcome you.

Appendix: Maui in Depth

Maui is the only island in the Hawaiian chain named after a god—well, actually a demigod (half man, half god). Hawaiian legends are filled with the escapades of Maui, who had a reputation as a trickster. In one story, Maui is credited with causing the birth of the Hawaiian Islands when he threw his "magic" fish hook down to the ocean floor and pulled the islands up from the bottom of the sea. Another legend tells how Maui lassoed the sun to make it travel more slowly across the sky—so that his mother could more easily dry her clothes. Maui's status as the only island to carry the name of a deity seems fitting, considering its reputation as the perfect tropical paradise, or as Hawaiians say, *Maui no ka oi* ("Maui is the best").

1 Maui Today

by Jeanette Foster

Since the 1970s, Maui has seen a rapid increase in the number of visitors to this sleepy, agrarian community, which found itself suddenly designated the in place to visit. The islanders spent the 1970s trying to adjust not only to this sudden influx of visitors, but also to the fact that the visitors liked what they saw and wanted to stay. Seemingly overnight, a massive building campaign began, with condominiums mushrooming along the coastline.

By the 1980s, the furious pace of building had slowed, but the new visitors to the island were no longer content to just sit on the beach: They wanted snorkeling and sailing trips, bike rides down Haleakala, and guided tours to Hana. A new industry developed to service these action-oriented vacationers.

In the 1990s, Hawaii's state economy went into a tailspin following a series of events: First, the Gulf War severely curtailed air travel to the island; then, Hurricane Iniki slammed into Kauai, crippling its infrastructure; and finally, sugarcane companies across the state began shutting down, laying off thousands of workers. Maui, however, seemed to be able to weather this turbulent economic storm. As the rest of the state struggled with the stormy economy, the outlook remained sunny and clear on Maui.

What did Maui have that the other islands didn't? According to experts, the farsightedness to build up the island's name recognition in the fickle tourism industry, coupled with a diversified economy. Not only had Maui started planning "destination resort areas" in the 1960s, with Kaanapali the first planned resort area outside of Waikiki, but the island's tourism industry also knew that a reputation for the ability to deliver was the key calling card to success. Or as one expert put it: "Maui has been unbelievably successful at name recognition. You'd be hard-pressed to find someone in the U.S. or Canada over 20 years old who has not heard of Maui."

In addition, Maui did not put all its eggs into the visitor-industry basket. Instead, island leaders continued to nurture Maui's agricultural roots, but instead of wooing giant agribusiness, they courted small niche farming: organic farmers, the flower industry, herb growers. The island also branched out into various high-tech fields, including the rapidly growing Internet industry. It's no coincidence that just as the World Wide Web was starting to become a household word, Maui's visitor industry—from tiny, two-bedroom B&Bs to megaresorts—had one of the highest rates of Web sites per capita in the United States.

Maui has seen centuries of change since Captain Cook first cruised by. The island, once populated only by Hawaiians, is today home to a diverse mix of Asians, Pacific Islanders, Caucasians, and African Americans. L.A.-style traffic jams and strip malls have arrived, though the island still maintains its natural beauty, with golden beaches, tropical waterfalls, and misty upcountry hills. The population continues to learn lessons in balance: how to nurture the visitor industry without destroying the very product that visitors come to see.

2 Life & Language

by Jeanette Foster

Plantations brought so many different people to Hawaii that the state is now a rainbow of ethnic groups. No one group is a majority; everyone's a minority. Living here are Caucasians, African Americans, American Indians, Eskimos, Aleuts, Japanese, Chinese, Filipinos, Koreans, Tahitians, Asian Indians, Vietnamese, Hawaiians, Samoans, Tongans, and other Asian and Pacific Islanders. Add to that a few Canadians, Dutch, English, French, German, Irish, Italians, Portuguese, Scottish, Puerto Ricans, and Spanish.

More than a century ago, W. Somerset Maugham noted: "All these strange people live close to each other, with different languages and different thoughts; they believe in different gods and they have different values; two passions alone they share: love and hunger." More recently, noted travel journalist Jan Morris said of Hawaii's population: "Half the world's races seem to be represented and interbred here, and between them they have created an improbable microcosm of human society as a whole."

In combination, it's a remarkable potpourri. Many people seem to retain an element of the traditions of their homeland. Some Japanese Americans of Hawaii, even three and four generations removed from the homeland, are more traditional than the Japanese of Tokyo. And the same is true of many Chinese, Koreans, Filipinos, and the rest of the 25 or so ethnic groups that make Hawaii a kind of living museum of various Asian and Pacific cultures.

THE HAWAIIAN LANGUAGE

Almost everyone here speaks English, so except for pronouncing place names, you should have no trouble communicating on Maui. Many folks in Hawaii now speak Hawaiian, for the ancient language is making a comeback. Everybody who visits Hawaii, in fact, will hear the words *aloha* and *mahalo* (thank-you). If you've just arrived, you're a *malihini*. Someone who's been here a long time is a *kamaaina*. When you finish a job or your meal, you are *pau* (over). On Friday it's *pau hana* (work over). When you go *pau hana*, you put a *pupu* in your mouth (that's Hawaii's version of hors d'oeuvres).

The Hawaiian alphabet, created by the New England missionaries, has only 12 letters—the five regular vowels (*a, e, i, o,* and *u*) and seven consonants (*h, k, l, m, n, p,* and *w*). The vowels are pronounced in the Roman fashion, that is, *ah, ay, ee, oh,* and *oo* (as in "too")—not *ay, ee, eye, oh,* and *you,* as they are in English. For example, *huhu* is pronounced *who-who.* Almost all vowels are sounded separately, although some are pronounced together, as in *Kalakaua: Kah-lah-cow-ah.*

WHAT *HAOLE* MEANS When Hawaiians first saw Western visitors, they called the pale-skinned, frail men *haole,* because they looked so out of breath. In Hawaiian, *ha* means breath, while *ole* means an absence of what precedes it. In other words, a lifeless-looking person. Today, the term *haole* is generally a synonym for Caucasian or foreigner; it's used casually without intending any disrespect. However, if uttered by an angry stranger who adds certain adjectives like "stupid" or "dumb," the term *haole* can be construed as a mild racial slur.

SOME HAWAIIAN WORDS Here are some basic Hawaiian words that you'll often hear in Hawaii and see throughout this book. For a more complete list of Hawaiian words, point your Web browser to www.geocities.com/~olelo/hltableofcontents.html or www.hisurf.com/hawaiian/dictionary.html.

akamai smart
alii Hawaiian royalty
aloha greeting or farewell
halau school
hale house or building
heiau Hawaiian temple or place of worship
hui club, assembly
kahuna priest or expert
kamaaina old-timer
kapa tapa, bark cloth
kapu taboo, forbidden
keiki child
lanai porch or veranda
lomilomi massage
mahalo thank you
makai a direction, toward the sea
malihini stranger, newcomer
mana spirit power
mauka a direction, toward the mountains
muumuu loose-fitting gown or dress
nene official state bird, a goose
ono delicious
pali cliff
wiki quick

PIDGIN: 'EH FO'REAL, BRAH

If you venture beyond the tourist areas, you might hear another local tongue: pidgin English. A conglomeration of slang and words from the Hawaiian language, pidgin was developed by sugar planters as a method to communicate with their Chinese laborers in the 1800s. Today it's used by people who grew up in Hawaii to talk with their peers.

"Broke da mouth" (tastes really good) is the favorite pidgin phrase and one you might hear; "'Eh fo'real, brah" means "It's true, brother." You could be invited to hear an elder "talk story" (relating myths and memories), or to enjoy local treats like "shave ice" (a tropical snow cone) and "crack seed" (highly seasoned preserved fruit). But since pidgin is really the province of the locals, your visit to Maui is likely to pass without your hearing much pidgin at all.

3 A Taste of Maui

by Jocelyn Fujii

On Maui, a great lunch or dinner can lure a foodie halfway across the island. Whether it's haute cuisine, local-style diners, small mom-and-pops, or sunset appetizers in Kaanapali and Wailea, dining matters a lot on this island made for sybarites. Although Maui's restaurant kitchens are at the leading edge of Hawaii's maturing regional cuisine, the small-town charms remain, and countless gastronomic discoveries await the adventurous.

THE NEW GUARD: HAWAII REGIONAL CUISINE

Since the mid-1980s, when Hawaii Regional Cuisine (HRC) ignited a culinary revolution, Hawaii has elevated its standing on the global epicurean map to bona-fide star status. Fresh ideas and sophisticated menus have made the islands a culinary destination, applauded and emulated nationwide. (In a tip of the toque to island tradition, *ahi*—a word ubiquitous in Hawaii—has replaced *tuna* on many chic New York menus.)

Waves of new Asian residents have planted the food traditions of their homelands in the fertile soil of Hawaii, resulting in unforgettable taste treats true to their Thai, Vietnamese, Japanese, Chinese, and Indo-Pacific roots. Like the peoples of Hawaii, traditions are mixed and matched—and when combined with the fresh harvests from sea and land for which Hawaii is known, these ethnic and culinary traditions take on renewed vigor and a cross-cultural, uniquely Hawaiian quality.

This is good news for the eager palate. From the five-star restaurant to the informal neighborhood gathering place, from the totally eclectic to the purely Japanese to the multiethnic plate lunch, dining in Hawaii is one great culinary joyride.

Expect to encounter Indonesian sates, Polynesian imu-baked foods, and guava-smoked meats in sophisticated presentations in the finest dining rooms on Maui. If there's pasta or risotto or rack of lamb on the menu, it could be nori (seaweed) linguine with opihi (limpet sauce), or risotto with local seafood served in taro cups, or a rack of lamb in cabernet and hoisin sauce (fermented soybean, garlic, and spices), or with macadamia nuts and coconut. Watch for ponzu sauce, too; it's lemony and zesty, much more flavorful than the soy sauce it resembles, and a welcome new staple on local menus.

While on Maui, you'll encounter many labels that embrace the fundamentals of HRC and the sophistication, informality, and nostalgia it encompasses. Euro-Asian, Pacific Rim, Pacific Edge, Euro-Pacific, fusion cuisine, hapa cuisine—by whatever name, Hawaii regional cuisine has evolved as Hawaii's singular cooking style, what some say is this country's current gastronomic, as well as geographic, frontier. It highlights the fresh seafood and produce of Hawaii's rich waters and volcanic soil, the cultural traditions of Hawaii's ethnic groups, and the skills of well-trained chefs who broke ranks with their European predecessors to forge new ground in the 50th state. Among those in the vanguard of HRC are Beverly Gannon (Haliimaile General Store), Roy Yamaguchi (Roy's on Oahu, Maui, Hawaii, and Kauai), Peter Merriman (Merriman's on the Big Island and Hula Grill on Maui), George Mavrothalassitis (Chef Mavro Restaurant in Honolulu), and Jean-Marie Josselin (A Pacific Cafe on Kauai, Maui, and Oahu). Some of Hawaii's most prominent chefs, such as David Paul (David Paul's Lahaina Grill) were not original HRC members but have gone ahead to form their own strong culinary identities.

Fresh ingredients are foremost, and farmers and fishermen work together to provide steady supplies of just-harvested seafood, seaweed, fern shoots, vine-ripened tomatoes, goat cheese, lamb, herbs, taro, and gourmet lettuces. Countless harvests from land and sea wind up in myriad forms on ever-changing menus, prepared in Asian and Western culinary styles. Exotic fruits introduced by recent Southeast Asian immigrants, such as sapodilla, mangosteen, soursop, and rambutan, are beginning to appear regularly in Chinatown markets. Aquacultured seafood, from seaweed to salmon to lobster, is a staple on many menus. Additionally, fresh-fruit salsas and sauces (mango, litchi, papaya, pineapple, guava), ginger-sesame-wasabi flavorings, corn cakes with sake sauces, tamarind and fish sauces, coconut-chile accents, tropical-fruit vinaigrettes, and other local and newly arrived seasonings from Southeast Asia and the Pacific impart unique qualities to the preparations.

Here's a sampling of what you can expect to find on a Hawaii regional menu: seared Hawaiian fish with lilikoi shrimp butter; taro-crab cakes; Molokai sweet-potato or breadfruit vichyssoise; Ka'u orange sauce and Kahua Ranch lamb; fern shoots from Waipio Valley; Hawaiian bouillabaisse with fresh snapper, Kona crab, and fresh aquacultured shrimp; blackened ahi summer rolls; and gourmet Waimanalo or Kula greens, picked that day. Menus often change daily, and since the leading chefs have an unquenchable appetite for cooking on the edge, possibilities abound on Maui for once-in-a-lifetime dining adventures.

PLATE LUNCHES & MORE: LOCAL FOOD

At the other end of the spectrum is the vast and endearing world of "local food." By that we mean plate lunches and poke, shave ice and saimin, bento lunches and manapua—cultural hybrids all.

Reflecting a polyglot population of many styles and ethnicities, Hawaii's idiosyncratic dining scene is eminently inclusive. Consider surfer chic: barefoot in the sand, in a swimsuit, you chow down on a plate lunch ordered from a lunch wagon, consisting of fried mahimahi, "two scoops rice," macaroni salad, and a few leaves of green, typically julienned cabbage or iceberg lettuce. (Generally, teriyaki beef or shoyu chicken are options, too.) Heavy gravy is often the accompaniment of choice, accompanied by a soft drink in a paper cup. Like saimin—the local version of noodles in broth topped with scrambled eggs, green onions, and, sometimes, pork—the plate lunch is Hawaii's version of high camp.

Because this is Hawaii, at least a few licks of *poi*—the Hawaiian staple of cooked, pounded taro (the local tuber)—and other examples of indigenous cuisine are de rigueur, if not at a corny luau, then at least in a Hawaiian plate lunch. The native samplers include foods from before and after Western contact, such as *laulau* (pork, chicken, or fish steamed in ti leaves), *kalua* pork (pork cooked in a Polynesian underground oven known here as an *imu*), *lomi* salmon (salted salmon with tomatoes and green onions), squid *luau* (octopus

Ahi, Ono & Opakapaka:
A Hawaiian Seafood Primer

The fresh seafood in Hawaii has been described as the best in the world. In the pivotal book *The New Cuisine of Hawaii,* by Janice Wald Henderson, acclaimed chef Nobuyuki Matsuhisa (chef/owner of Matsuhisa in Beverly Hills and Nobu in Manhattan and London) writes, "As a chef who specializes in fresh seafood, I am in awe of the quality of Hawaii's fish; it is unparalleled anywhere else in the world." And why not? Without a doubt, the islands' surrounding waters, the waters of the remote northwestern Hawaiian Islands, and a growing aquaculture industry are fertile grounds for this most important of Hawaii's food resources.

The reputable restaurants in Hawaii buy fresh fish daily at predawn auctions or from local fishermen. Some chefs even spear-fish their ingredients themselves. "Still wiggling" is the ultimate term for freshness in Hawaii. The fish can then be grilled over *kiawe* (mesquite) or prepared in innumerable ways.

Although most menus include the Western description for the fresh fish used, most often the local nomenclature is listed, turning dinner for the uninitiated into a confusing, quasiforeign experience. To help familiarize you with the menu language of Hawaii, here's a basic glossary of island fish:

ahi   yellowfin or bigeye tuna, important for its use in sashimi and poke, at sushi bars, and in Hawaii regional cuisine

aku   skipjack tuna, heavily used by local families in home cooking and poke

ehu   red snapper, delicate and sumptuous, yet lesser known than opakapaka (see below)

hapuupuu   grouper, a sea bass whose use is expanding from ethnic to nonethnic restaurants

hebi   spearfish, mildly flavored and frequently featured as the "catch of the day" in upscale restaurants

cooked in coconut milk and taro tops), *poke* (cubed raw fish seasoned with onions and seaweed, and the occasional sprinkling of roasted *kukui* nuts), *haupia* (creamy coconut pudding), and *kulolo* (steamed pudding of coconut, brown sugar, and taro).

Bento, another popular choice for the dine-and-dash set, is also available throughout Hawaii. The compact, boxed assortment of picnic fare usually consists of neatly arranged sections of rice, pickled vegetables, and fried chicken, beef, or pork. Increasingly, however, the bento is becoming more streamlined and health-conscious, as in macrobiotic bento lunches or vegetarian brown-rice bentos. A derivative of the modest lunch box for Japanese immigrants who once labored in the sugar and pineapple fields, bentos are dispensed ubiquitously throughout Hawaii, everywhere from Longs Drugs and Japanese stores to corner delis and supermarkets.

Also from the plantations come *manapua,* a bready, doughy round with tasty fillings of sweetened pork or sweet beans. In the old days, the Chinese

kajiki Pacific blue marlin, also called *au,* with a firm flesh and high fat content that make it a plausible substitute for tuna in some raw fish dishes, and as a grilled item on menus

kumu goatfish, a luxury item on Chinese and upscale menus, served en papillote or steamed whole, Oriental style, with sesame oil, scallions, ginger, and garlic

mahimahi dolphin fish (the game fish, not the mammal) or dorado, a classic sweet, white-fleshed fish requiring vigilance among purists because it is often disguised as fresh when it's actually "fresh-frozen"—a big difference

monchong big-scale or sickle pomfret, an exotic, tasty fish, scarce but gaining a higher profile on Hawaiian Island menus

nairagi striped marlin, also called *au;* good as sashimi and in poke, and often substituted for ahi in raw-fish products

onaga ruby snapper, a luxury fish, versatile, moist, and flaky; top-of-the-line

ono wahoo, firmer and drier than the snappers, often served grilled and in sandwiches

opah moonfish, rich and fatty, and versatile—cooked, raw, smoked, and broiled

opakapaka pink snapper, light, flaky, and luxurious, suited for sashimi, poaching, sautéing, and baking; the best-known upscale fish

papio jack fish, light, firm, and flavorful, and favored in island cookery

shutome broadbill swordfish, of beeflike texture and rich flavor

tombo albacore tuna, with a high fat content, suitable for grilling and sautéing

uhu parrot fish, most often encountered steamed, Chinese style

uku gray snapper of clear, pale-pink flesh, delicately flavored and moist

ulua large jack fish, firm-fleshed and versatile.

"manapua man" would make his rounds with bamboo containers balanced on a rod over his shoulders. Today, you'll find white or whole-wheat manapua containing chicken, vegetables, curry, and other savory fillings.

The daintier Chinese delicacy, dim sum, is made of translucent wrappers filled with fresh seafood, pork hash, and vegetables, served for breakfast and lunch in Chinatown restaurants. The Hong Kong–style dumplings are ordered fresh and hot from bamboo steamers from invariably brusque servers who move their carts from table to table. Much like hailing a taxi in Manhattan, you have to be quick and loud for dim sum.

TASTY TREATS: SHAVE ICE & MALASSADAS

For dessert or a snack, the prevailing choice is shave ice, the island version of a snow cone. Particularly on hot, humid days, long lines gather for the rainbow-colored cones heaped with finely shaved ice and topped with sweet tropical syrups. (The sweet-sour *li hing mui* flavor is a current rage.) The fast-melting mounds requiring prompt, efficient consumption are quite the local summer ritual for those with a sweet tooth. Aficionados order shave ice with ice cream and sweetened adzuki beans plopped in the middle.

You might also encounter *malassadas,* the Portuguese version of doughnuts, and if you do, it's best to eat them immediately. A leftover malassada has all the appeal of a heavy, lumpen, cold doughnut. When fresh and hot, however, as at school carnivals (where they attract the longest lines) or at bakeries and roadside stands, the sugary, yeasty doughnut-without-a-hole is enjoyed by many as one of the enduring legacies of the Portuguese in Hawaii.

PINEAPPLES, PAPAYAS & OTHER ISLAND FRUITS

Lanai isn't growing pineapples commercially anymore, but low-acid, white-fleshed, wondrously sweet Hawaiian Sugar Loaf pineapples are being commercially grown, on a small scale, on Kauai as well as the Big Island. That's just one of the developments in the rapidly changing agricultural landscape in Hawaii. The litchilike Southeast Asian *rambutan; longan* (Chinese dragon's-eye litchis); 80-pound Indian jackfruits; the starfruit; the luscious, custardy mangosteen; and the usual mangoes, papayas, guava, and *lilikoi* (passion fruit) make up the dazzling parade of fresh island fruits that come and go with the seasons.

Papayas, bananas, and **pineapples** grow year-round, but pineapples are always sweetest, juiciest, and most yellow in the summer. Although new papaya hybrids are making their way into the marketplace, the classic bests include the fleshy, firm-textured Kahuku papayas, the queen of them all; the Big Island's sweet Kapoho and Puna papayas; and the fragile, juicy, and reddish-orange Sunrise papayas from Kauai. Those who have transferred their allegiance from Puna to Sunrise claim they're sweeter, juicier, and more elegant than all others. Also called strawberry papayas, the Sunrise variety is easily misjudged and often served overripe; delicate inside and out, these papayas are easily bruised and fragile in texture, yet robust in flavor. Apple bananas are smaller, firmer, and tarter than the standard, and they are a local specialty that flourish throughout the islands.

Litchis and **mangoes** are long-awaited summer fruit. Mangoes begin appearing in late spring or early summer and can be found at roadside fruit stands, markets, and health-food stores (where the high prices may shock you). Our favorite is the white pirie—rare and resinous, fiberless, and so sweet and juicy it makes the high-profile Hayden seem prosaic. A popular newcomer is the Rapoza mango, only a few years in the islands yet already earning raves for its sweetness, resilience, and fiberless, 2-pound fruit.

Watermelons are a summer hit and a signature of Molokai and Oahu. The state of Hawaii, which consumes more watermelons per capita than any other in the country, also produces top-notch fruit for its loyal clientele. Kahuku watermelons, available in the summer months, give the popular Molokai variety a run for its money. Juicy, fleshy, and sweet, Kahuku watermelons are now grown primarily in Waialua on Oahu's north shore, while production of the Molokai variety has expanded to central Oahu. Most markets sell these bulging orbs of refreshment throughout summer and early fall.

In the competitive world of **oranges,** the Kau Gold navel oranges from the southern Big Island put Sunkist to shame. Grown in the volcanic soil and sunny conditions of the South Point region (the southernmost point in the United States), the "Ugly Orange" is brown, rough, and anything but pretty. But the browner and uglier they are, the sweeter and juicier. Because the thin-skinned oranges are tree-ripened, they're fleshy and heavy with liquid, and they will spoil you for life. Although these oranges have traditionally been a winter fruit, they're appearing more abundantly year-round.

4 The Natural World: An Environmental Guide to Maui

by Jeanette Foster

Born of violent volcanic eruptions from deep beneath the ocean's surface, the first Hawaiian islands emerged about 70 million years ago—more than 200 million years after the major continental land masses formed. Two thousand miles from the nearest continent, Mother Nature's fury began to carve beauty from barren rock. Untiring volcanoes spewed forth curtains of fire that cooled into stone, while severe tropical storms, some with hurricane-force winds, battered and blasted the cooling lava rock into a series of shapes. Ferocious earthquakes flattened, shattered, and reshaped the islands into precipitous valleys, jagged cliffs, and recumbent flatlands. Monstrous surf and gigantic tidal waves rearranged and polished the lands above and below the reaches of the tide.

It took millions upon millions of years for nature to chisel the familiar form of Maui's majestic Haleakala peak, to create the waterfalls on Molokai's northern side, to shape the reefs of Hulopoe Bay on Lanai, and to establish the lush rain forests of the Hana coastline. The result is an island-chain-within-a-chain like no other on the planet—rich in unique flora and fauna, surrounded by a vibrant underwater world that will haunt you forever.

THE FLORA OF MAUI

Maui radiates with the sweet smell of flowers, lush vegetation, and exotic plant life.

AFRICAN TULIP TREES Even from afar, you can see the flaming red flowers on these large trees, which can grow to be more than 50 feet tall. Children in Hawaii love them because the buds hold water—they use the flowers as water pistols.

ANGEL'S TRUMPETS These small trees can grow up to 20 feet tall, with an abundance of large (up to 10 inches in diameter) pendants—white or pink flowers that resemble, well, trumpets. The Hawaiians call them *nana-honua,* which means "earth gazing." The flowers, which bloom continually from early spring to late fall, have a musky scent. However, beware: All parts of the plant are poisonous and contain a strong narcotic.

ANTHURIUMS One of Hawaii's most popular cut flowers, anthuriums originally came from the tropical Americas and the Caribbean islands. There are more than 550 species, but the most popular in Hawaii are the heart-shaped red, orange, pink, white, and even purple flowers with tail-like spathes. Look for the heart-shaped green leaves in shaded areas. These exotic plants have no scent but will last several weeks as cut flowers.

BIRDS OF PARADISE These natives of Africa have become something of a trademark of Hawaii. They're easily recognizable by the orange and blue flowers nestled in gray-green bracts, looking somewhat like birds in flight.

BOUGAINVILLEA Originally from Brazil and named for the 18th-century French explorer Louis Antoine de Bougainville, these colorful, tissue-thin bracts (ranging in color from majestic purple to fiery orange) hide tiny white flowers.

BROMELIADS   The pineapple plant is the best-known bromeliad; native to tropical South America and the islands of the Caribbean, bromeliads comprise more than 1,400 species. "Bromes," as they're affectionately called, are generally spiky plants ranging in size from a few inches to several feet in diameter. They are popular not only for their unusual foliage but also for their strange and wonderful flowers, which range from colorful spikes to delicate blossoms resembling orchids. Bromeliads are widely used in landscaping and as interior decoration, especially in resort areas.

COFFEE   Hawaii is the only state that commercially produces coffee. Coffee is an evergreen shrub with shiny, waxy, dark-green, pointed leaves. The flower is a small, fragrant white blossom that develops into half-inch berries that turn bright red when ripe. Look for coffee plants in Kaanapali on Maui and in Kualapuu on Molokai.

GINGER   Some of the most fragrant flowers in Hawaii are white and yellow ginger. Usually found in clumps, and growing 4 to 7 feet tall in areas blessed by rain, these sweet-smelling, 3-inch-wide flowers are composed of three dainty petal-like stamens and three long, thin petals. Both white and yellow ginger are so prolific that many people assume they are native to Hawaii; actually, they were introduced in the 19th century from the Indonesia-Malaysia area. Look for white and yellow ginger from late spring to fall. If you see them on the side of the road (especially on the Hana Highway), stop and pick a few blossoms—your car will be filled with a divine fragrance for the rest of the day. The only downside is that, once picked, the flowers will live only briefly.

Other members of the ginger family frequently seen in Hawaii (there are some 700 species) include red, shell, and torch gingers. Red ginger consists of tall, green stalks with foot-long red "flower heads." The red "petals" are actually bracts; inch-long white flowers are protected by the bracts and can be seen if you look down into the red head. Red ginger, which does not share the heavenly smell of white ginger, will last a week or longer when cut. Look for red ginger from spring through late fall. Cool, wet mountain forests are ideal conditions for shell ginger; natives of India and Burma, these plants, with their pearly white, clamshell-like blossoms, bloom from spring to fall.

Perhaps the most exotic ginger is the red or pink torch ginger. Cultivated in Malaysia as seasoning (the young flower shoots are used in curries), torch ginger rises directly out of the ground; the flower stalks, which are about 5 to 8 inches in length, resemble the fire of a lighted torch. This is one of the few types of ginger that can bloom year-round.

HELICONIA   Some 80 species of the colorful heliconia family came to Hawaii from the Caribbean and Central and South America. The bright yellow, red, green, and orange bracts overlap and appear to unfold like origami birds. The most obvious heliconia to spot is the lobster claw, which resembles a string of boiled crustacean pincers—the brilliant crimson bracts alternate on the stem. Another prolific heliconia is the parrot's beak; growing to about hip height, it's composed of bright-orange flower bracts with black tips, not unlike the beak of a parrot. Look for parrot's beak in the spring and summer, when it blooms in profusion.

HIBISCUS   One variety of this year-round blossom, the yellow hibiscus, is the official state flower. The 4- to 6-inch hibiscus flowers come in a range of colors, from lily white to lipstick red. The flowers resemble crepe paper, with stamens and pistils protruding spirelike from the center. Hibiscus hedges can grow up to 15 feet tall. Once plucked, the flowers wither quickly.

JACARANDA   Beginning around March and sometimes lasting until early May, these huge, lacy-leafed trees metamorphose into large clusters of spectacular lavender-blue sprays. The bell-shaped flowers drop quickly, leaving a majestic purple carpet beneath the tree.

NIGHT-BLOOMING CEREUS   Look along rock walls for this spectacular night-blooming flower. Originally from Central America, this vinelike member of the cactus family has green scalloped edges and produces foot-long white flowers that open as darkness falls and wither as the sun rises. The plant also bears a red fruit that is edible.

ORCHIDS   To many minds, nothing says Hawaii more than orchids. The orchid family is the largest in the entire plant kingdom. The most widely grown variety—and the major source of flowers for leis and garnish for tropical libations—is the vanda orchid. The vandas used in Hawaii's commercial flower industry are generally lavender or white, but they grow in a rainbow of colors, shapes, and sizes. The orchids used for corsages are the large, delicate cattleya; the ones used in floral arrangements—you'll probably see them in your hotel lobby—are usually dendrobiums.

PLUMERIA   Also known as frangipani, this sweet-smelling, five-petal flower, found in clusters on trees, is the most popular choice of lei makers. The Singapore plumeria has five creamy-white petals, with a touch of yellow in the center. Another popular variety, ruba—with flowers from soft pink to flaming red—is also used in leis. When picking plumeria, be careful of the sap from the flower, as it is poisonous and can stain clothes.

PROTEAS   Originally from South Africa, this unusual plant comes in more than 40 varieties. Proteas are shrubs that bloom into a range of flower types. Different species of proteas range from those resembling pincushions to a species that looks just like a bouquet of feathers. Proteas are long-lasting cut flowers; once dried, they will last for years.

FRUIT TREES

BANANA   Edible bananas are among the oldest of the world's food crops. By the time Europeans arrived in the islands, the Hawaiians had planted more than 40 types of bananas. Most banana plants have long green leaves hanging from the tree, with the flowers giving way to fruit in clusters.

BREADFRUIT   A large tree, more than 60 feet tall, with broad, sculpted, dark-green leaves, the famous breadfruit produces a round, head-size green fruit that is a staple in the diets of all Polynesians. When roasted or baked, the whitish-yellow meat tastes somewhat like a sweet potato.

LYCHEE   This evergreen tree, which can grow to well over 30 feet across, originated in China. Small flowers grow into panicles about a foot long in June and July. The round, red-skinned fruit appears shortly afterward.

MACADAMIA   A transplant from Australia, macadamia nuts have become a commercial crop in recent decades in Hawaii, especially on Maui and the Big Island. The large trees, up to 60 feet tall, bear a hard-shelled nut encased in a leathery husk, which splits open and dries when ripe.

MANGO   From Indonesia and Malaysia comes the delicious mango, a fruit with peachlike flesh. Mango season usually begins in the spring and lasts through the summer, depending on the variety. The trees can grow to more than 100 feet tall. The tiny reddish flowers give way to a green fruit that turns red-yellow when ripe. Some people enjoy unripe mangoes, either thinly sliced or in chutney, a traditional Indian preparation. Note that mango sap can cause a skin rash on some people.

PAPAYA   One of the sweetest of all tropical fruits, the pear-shaped papaya turns yellow or reddish pink when ripe. They are found at the base of the large, scalloped-shaped leaves on a pedestal-like, nonbranched tree whose trunk is hollow. Papayas ripen year-round.

OTHER TREES & PLANTS

BANYAN   Among the world's largest trees, banyans have branches that grow out and away from the trunk, forming descending roots that grow down to the ground to feed and form additional trunks, making the tree very stable during tropical storms. The banyan in the courtyard next to the old Court House in Lahaina is an excellent example of a spreading banyan—it covers $2/3$ acre.

MONKEYPOD   The monkeypod is one of Hawaii's most majestic trees; it grows more than 80 feet tall and 100 feet across. Seen near older homes and in parks, the leaves of the monkeypod drop in February and March. The wood is a favorite of woodworking artisans.

SILVERSWORD   This very uncommon and unusual plant is seen only on the Big Island and in the Haleakala Crater on Maui. Once a year, this rare relative of the sunflower family blooms between July and September. Resembling a pinecone more than a sunflower, the silversword in bloom is a fountain of red-petaled, daisylike flowers that turn silver soon after blooming.

TARO   Around pools, near streams, and in neatly planted fields, you'll see the green heart-shaped leaves of taro, whose dense roots are a Polynesian staple. The ancient Hawaiians pounded the roots into poi. Originally from Sri Lanka, taro is grown not only as a food crop, but also as an ornamental.

MARIJUANA   This not-so-rare-and-unusual plant—called *pakalolo*, or "crazy weed"—is grown throughout the islands. You probably won't see it as you drive along the roads, but if you go hiking, you might glimpse the feathery green leaves with tight clusters of buds. Despite years of police effort to eradicate the plant, the illegal industry continues. Don't be tempted to pick a few buds, as the purveyors of this nefarious industry don't take kindly to poaching.

THE FAUNA OF MAUI

When the first Polynesians arrived in Hawaii between A.D. 500 and A.D. 800, scientists say they found some 67 varieties of endemic Hawaiian birds, a third of which are now believed to be extinct. What's even more astonishing is what they didn't find—there were no reptiles, amphibians, mosquitoes, lice, fleas, or even cockroaches.

There were only two endemic mammals: the hoary bat and the monk seal. The small **hoary bat** must have accidentally blown to Hawaii at some point, from either North or South America. It can still be seen today on its early evening forays.

The **Hawaiian monk seal,** a relative of warm-water seals found in the Caribbean and Mediterranean, was nearly slaughtered into extinction for its skin and oil during the 19th century. These seals have recently experienced a minor population explosion, forcing relocation of some males from their protected homes in the islets north of the main Hawaiian Islands. Periodically, these endangered animals turn up at various beaches throughout the state. They are protected under federal law by the Marine Mammals Protection Act.

Geckos are harmless, soft-skinned, insect-eating lizards that come equipped with suction pads on their feet, enabling them to climb walls and windows to reach tasty insects like mosquitoes and cockroaches. You'll see these little guys on windows outside a lighted room at night or hear their cheerful chirp. Don't be scared!

If you're fortunate enough to see a monk seal, just look; don't disturb one of Hawaii's living treasures.

The first Polynesians brought a few animals from home: dogs, pigs, and chickens (all were for eating), as well as rats (stowaways). All four animals are still found in the Hawaiian wild today.

BIRDS

More species of native birds have become extinct in Hawaii in the past 200 years than anywhere else on the planet. Of the 67 native species, 23 are extinct and 30 are endangered. Even the Hawaiian crow, **alala,** is threatened.

The **aeo,** or Hawaiian stilt, a 16-inch-long bird with a black head, a black coat, a white underside, and long pink legs, can be found in protected wetlands like the Kanaha Wild Life Sanctuary (where it shares its natural habitat with the Hawaiian coot) and the Kealia Pond.

Endemic to the islands, the **nene** is Hawaii's state bird. It's currently being brought back from the brink of extinction through captive breeding and by strenuous protection laws. A relative of the Canada goose, the nene stands about 2 feet high and has a black head and yellow cheek, a buff neck with deep furrows, a grayish-brown body, and clawed feet. It gets its name from its two-syllable, high nasal call, "nay-nay." The approximately 500 nenes in existence can be seen at Haleakala National Park.

The Hawaiian short-eared owl, **pueo,** which grows to between 12 and 17 inches in size, can be seen at dawn and dusk, when the black-billed, brown-and-white bird goes hunting for rodents. Pueos are highly regarded by Hawaiians; according to legend, spotting a pueo is a good omen.

SEALIFE

Approximately 680 species of fish are known to inhabit the waters around the Hawaiian Islands. Of those, approximately 450 species stay close to the reef and inshore areas.

CORAL The reefs surrounding Hawaii are made up of various coral and algae. The living coral grows through sunlight that feeds a specialized algae, which in turn allows the development of the coral's calcareous skeleton. The reefs, which take thousands of years to develop, attract and support fish and crustaceans, which use them for food, habitat, mating, and raising their young. Mother Nature can batter the fragile reefs with a strong storm or large waves, but humans, through seemingly innocuous acts such as touching the coral, have proven far more destructive.

The corals most frequently seen around Maui are hard, rocklike formations named for their familiar shapes: antler, cauliflower, finger, plate, and razor coral. Wire coral looks just like its name—a randomly bent wire growing straight out of the reef. Some corals appear soft, such as tube coral, which can be found in the ceilings of caves. Black coral, which resembles winter-bare trees or shrubs, is found at depths of more than 100 feet.

REEF FISH   Of the approximately 450 reef fish, about 27% are native to Hawaii and are found nowhere else in the world. As the islands were born from erupting volcanoes, evolving over millions of years, ocean currents, mainly from Southeast Asia, carried the larvae of thousands of marine animals and plants to Hawaii's reef. Of those, approximately 100 species not only adapted, but thrived.

Some species are much bigger and more plentiful than their Pacific cousins, and many developed unique characteristics. Some, like the lemon or milletseed butterfly fish, are not only particular to Hawaii but also unique within their larger, worldwide family in their specialized schooling and feeding behaviors. Another surprising thing about Hawaii endemics is how common some of the native fish are; you can see the saddleback wrasse, for instance, on virtually any snorkeling excursion or dive in Hawaiian waters. You're likely to spot one or more of the following reef fish while underwater.

Angel fish, often mistaken for butterfly fish, can be distinguished by the spine, located low on the gill plate. Angel fish are very shy; several species live in colonies close to coral for protection.

Blennies are small, elongated fish, ranging from 2 to 10 inches long, with the majority in the 3- to 4-inch range. Blennies are so small that they can live in tide pools; you might have a hard time spotting one.

Butterfly fish, among the most colorful of the reef fish, are usually seen in pairs (scientists believe they mate for life) and appear to spend most of their day feeding. There are 22 species of butterfly fish, of which three (blue-stripe, lemon or milletseed, and multiband or pebbled butterfly fish) are endemic. Most butterfly fish have a dark band through the eye and a spot near the tail resembling an eye, meant to confuse their predators (the moray eel loves to lunch on them).

Moray and conger **eels** are the common eels seen in Hawaii. Morays are usually docile unless provoked, or if there's food or an injured fish around. Unfortunately, some morays have been fed by divers and, being intelligent creatures, associate divers with food; thus, they can become aggressive. But most morays like to keep to themselves, hidden in their hole or crevice. While morays may look menacing, conger eels look downright happy, with big lips and pectoral fins (situated so they look like big ears) that give them the appearance of a perpetually smiling face. Conger eels have crushing teeth so they can feed on crustaceans; in fact, since they're sloppy eaters, they usually live with shrimp and crabs that feed off the crumbs they leave.

One of the largest and most colorful of the reef fish, the **parrot fish** can grow up to 40 inches long. Parrot fish are easy to spot—their front teeth are fused together, protruding like buck teeth and resembling a parrot's beak. These unique teeth allow them to feed by scraping algae from rocks and coral. The rocks and coral pass through the parrot fish's system, resulting in fine sand. In fact, most of the white sand found in Hawaii is parrot-fish waste; one large parrot fish can produce a ton of sand a year. Hawaiian native parrot-fish species include yellowbar, regal, and spectacled.

Scorpion fish are what scientists call "ambush predators." They hide under camouflaged exteriors and ambush their prey when they come along. Several sport a venomous dorsal spine. These fish don't have a gas bladder, so when they stop swimming, they sink—that's why you usually find them "resting" on ledges and on the ocean bottom. Although they're not aggressive, an inattentive snorkeler or diver could feel the effects of those venomous spines—so be very careful where you put your hands and feet in the water.

Surgeonfish, sometimes called *tang,* get their name from the scalpel-like spines located on each side of their bodies near the base of their tails. Some surgeonfish have a rigid spine, while others have the ability to fold their spine against their body until it's needed for defense purposes. Some surgeon fish, like the brightly colored yellow tang, are boldly colored; others are adorned in more conservative shades of gray, brown, or black. The only endemic surgeonfish—and the most abundant in Hawaiian waters—is the convict tang, a pale white fish with vertical black stripes (like a convict's uniform).

Wrasses are a very diverse family of fish, ranging in size from 2 to 15 inches. Several wrasses are brilliantly colored and change their colors through aging and sexual dimorphism (sex changing). Wrasses have the ability to change gender with maturation, from female (when young) to male. Several types are endemic to Hawaii: the Hawaiian cleaner, shortnose, belted, and gray (or old woman).

GAME FISH Hawaii is known around the globe as *the* place for big-game fish—marlin, swordfish, and tuna—but its waters are also great for catching other offshore fish, such as mahimahi, rainbow runner, and wahoo; coastal fish, such as barracuda and scad; bottom fish, such as snappers, sea bass, and amberjack; and inshore fish, like trevally and bonefish.

Six kinds of **billfish** are found in the offshore waters around the islands: Pacific blue marlin, black marlin, sailfish, broadbill swordfish, striped marlin, and shortbill spearfish. Hawaii billfish range in size from the 20-pound shortbill spearfish and striped marlin to an 1,805-pound Pacific blue marlin, the largest marlin ever caught on rod and reel anywhere in the world.

Tuna ranges in size from small (a pound or less) mackerel tuna used as bait (Hawaiians call them *oioi*) to 250-pound yellowfin ahi tuna. Other species of tuna found in Hawaii are bigeye, albacore, kawakawa, and skipjack.

Some of the best fish for eating are also found in offshore waters: **mahimahi** (also known as dolphin fish or dorado), in the 20- to 70-pound range; **rainbow runner** (*kamanu*), from 15 to 30 pounds; and **wahoo** (*ono*), from 15 to 80 pounds. Shoreline fishers are always on the lookout for **trevally** (the state record for giant trevally is 191 pounds), **bonefish, ladyfish, threadfin, leatherfish,** and **goatfish.** Bottom fishers pursue a range of **snappers**—red, pink, gray, and others—as well as **sea bass** (the state record is a whopping 563 pounds) and **amberjack,** which weigh up to 100 pounds.

WHALES The most popular visitors to Hawaii come every year around December and stay until spring (April or so), when they return to their summer home in Alaska. Humpback whales—some as big as a city bus and weighing many tons—migrate to the warm, protected Hawaiian waters in the winter to mate and calve.

You can take whale-watching cruises that will let you observe these magnificent leviathans up close, or you can spot their signature spouts of water from shore as they expel water off in the distance. Humpbacks grow to up to 45 feet long, so when they breach (propel their entire body out of the water) or even wave a fluke, you can see it for miles.

Humpbacks are among the biggest whales found in Hawaiian waters, but other whales—like pilot, sperm, false killer, melon-headed, pygmy killer, and beaked—can be seen year-round. These whales usually travel in pods of 20 to 40 animals and are very social, interacting with one another on the surface.

SHARKS Yes, there *are* sharks in Hawaii, but more than likely you won't see a shark unless you specifically go looking for one. The ancient Hawaiians had great respect for these animals and believed that some sharks were reincarnated relatives who had returned to assist them.

About 40 different species of shark inhabit the waters surrounding Hawaii, ranging from the totally harmless whale shark (at 60 feet, the world's largest fish), which has no teeth and is so docile that it frequently lets divers ride on its back, to the not-so-docile, infamous, and extremely uncommon, great white shark. The most common sharks seen in Hawaii are white-tip reef sharks, gray reef sharks (about 5 feet long), and black-tip reef sharks (about 6 feet long).

MAUI'S ECOSYSTEM PROBLEMS

Maui might be paradise, but even paradise has its problems. The biggest threat facing Maui's natural environment is human intrusion—simply put, too many people want to experience paradise firsthand. From the magnificent underwater world to the breathtaking rain forest, the presence of people isn't always benign, no matter how cautious or environmentally aware they may be.

MARINE LIFE   Hawaii's beautiful and abundant marine life has attracted so many visitors that they threaten to overwhelm it. A great example of this over-enthusiasm is **Molokini,** a small, partially submerged, half-moon–shaped crater off the coast of Maui. In the 1970s, residents made the area a conservation district to protect the unique aquarium-like atmosphere of the waters inside the arms of the crater. Unfortunately, once it was protected, everyone wanted to come here just to see what was worth special protection. Twenty-five years ago, one or two small six-passenger boats made the trip once a day to Molokini; today, it's not uncommon to sight 20 or more boats, each carrying 20 to 49 passengers, moored inside the tiny crater. One tour operator has claimed that on some days, it's so crowded that you can actually see a slick of suntan oil floating on the surface of the water.

People who fall in love with the colorful **reef fish** and want to see them all the time back home are also thought to be impacting the health of Hawaii's reefs. Because of the popularity of home and office aquariums, more and more collectors are taking a growing number of reef fish from Hawaiian waters.

The **reefs** themselves have faced increasing ecological problems over the years. Runoff of soil and chemicals from construction, agriculture, erosion, and even heavy storms can blanket and choke a reef, which needs sunlight to survive. In addition, the intrusion of foreign elements, like breaks in sewage lines, can cause problems for Hawaii's reef. Human contact with the reef can upset the ecosystem as well. Coral, the basis of the reef system, is very fragile; snorkelers and divers grabbing on to it can break off pieces that took decades to form. Feeding the fish can also upset the balance of the ecosystem (not to mention upsetting the digestive systems of the fish). One glass-bottom boat operator reported that divers fed an eel for years, considering it their "pet" eel. One day the eel decided that he wanted more than just the food being offered and bit the diver's fingers. Divers and snorkelers report that in areas where the fish are fed, the fish have become more aggressive; clouds of normally shy reef fish surround divers, demanding food.

FLORA   One of Hawaii's most fragile environments is the rain forest. Any intrusion—from a hiker carrying seeds on his shoes to the rooting of wild boars—can upset the delicate balance in these complete ecosystems. In recent years, development has moved closer and closer to the rain forest.

FAUNA   The biggest impact on the fauna in Hawaii is the decimation of native birds by feral animals, which have destroyed the birds' habitats, and by mongooses that have eaten the birds' eggs and young. Government officials are vigilant about snakes because of the potential damage tree snakes can do to the remaining bird life.

Index

See also Accommodations and Restaurant indexes, below.

General Index

General Index

General Index

FROMMER'S® COMPLETE TRAVEL GUIDES

Alaska
Amsterdam
Arizona
Atlanta
Australia
Austria
Bahamas
Barcelona, Madrid &
  Seville
Beijing
Belgium, Holland &
  Luxembourg
Bermuda
Boston
British Columbia & the
  Canadian Rockies
Budapest & the Best of
  Hungary
California
Canada
Cancún, Cozumel &
  the Yucatán
Cape Cod, Nantucket &
  Martha's Vineyard
Caribbean
Caribbean Cruises & Ports
  of Call
Caribbean Ports of Call
Carolinas & Georgia
Chicago
China
Colorado
Costa Rica
Denmark
Denver, Boulder & Colorado
  Springs
England
Europe

European Cruises & Ports
  of Call
Florida
France
Germany
Greece
Greek Islands
Hawaii
Hong Kong
Honolulu, Waikiki &
  Oahu
Ireland
Israel
Italy
Jamaica
Japan
Las Vegas
London
Los Angeles
Maryland & Delaware
Maui
Mexico
Miami & the Keys
Montana & Wyoming
Montréal & Québec City
Munich & the Bavarian
  Alps
Nashville & Memphis
Nepal
New England
New Mexico
New Orleans
New York City
New Zealand
Nova Scotia, New Brunswick
  & Prince Edward Island
Oregon
Paris

Philadelphia & the
  Amish Country
Portugal
Prague & the Best of the
  Czech Republic
Provence & the Riviera
Puerto Rico
Rome
San Antonio & Austin
San Diego
San Francisco
Santa Fe, Taos & Albuquerque
Scandinavia
Scotland
Seattle & Portland
Singapore & Malaysia
South Africa
Southeast Asia
South Pacific
Spain
Sweden
Switzerland
Thailand
Tokyo
Toronto
Tuscany & Umbria
USA
Utah
Vancouver & Victoria
Vermont, New Hampshire
  & Maine
Vienna & the Danube Valley
Virgin Islands
Virginia
Walt Disney World &
  Orlando
Washington, D.C.
Washington State

FROMMER'S® DOLLAR-A-DAY GUIDES

Australia from $50 a Day
California from $60 a Day
Caribbean from $70 a Day
England from $70 a Day
Europe from $60 a Day

Florida from $60 a Day
Hawaii from $70 a Day
Ireland from $60 a Day
Italy from $70 a Day
London from $85 a Day

New York from $80 a Day
Paris from $85 a Day
San Francisco from $60 a Day
Washington, D.C.,
  from $60 a Day

FROMMER'S® PORTABLE GUIDES

Acapulco, Ixtapa &
  Zihuatanejo
Alaska Cruises & Ports of Call
Bahamas
Baja & Los Cabos
Berlin
California Wine Country
Charleston & Savannah
Chicago

Dublin
Hawaii: The Big Island
Las Vegas
London
Maine Coast
Maui
New Orleans
New York City
Paris

Puerto Vallarta, Manzanillo
  & Guadalajara
San Diego
San Francisco
Sydney
Tampa & St. Petersburg
Venice
Washington, D.C.

FROMMER'S® NATIONAL PARK GUIDES

Family Vacations in the
  National Parks
Grand Canyon

National Parks of the
  American West
Rocky Mountain

Yellowstone & Grand Teton
Yosemite & Sequoia/
  Kings Canyon
Zion & Bryce Canyon

FROMMER'S® MEMORABLE WALKS

Chicago
London

New York
Paris

San Francisco
Washington D.C.

FROMMER'S® GREAT OUTDOOR GUIDES

New England
Northern California

Southern California & Baja
Southern New England

Washington & Oregon

FROMMER'S® BORN TO SHOP GUIDES

Born to Shop: China
Born to Shop: France

Born to Shop: Italy
Born to Shop: London

Born to Shop: New York
Born to Shop: Paris

FROMMER'S® IRREVERENT GUIDES

Amsterdam
Boston
Chicago
Las Vegas

London
Los Angeles
Manhattan
New Orleans

Paris
San Francisco
Seattle & Portland
Vancouver

Walt Disney World
Washington, D.C.

FROMMER'S® BEST-LOVED DRIVING TOURS

America
Britain
California

Florida
France
Germany

Ireland
Italy
New England

Scotland
Spain
Western Europe

THE UNOFFICIAL GUIDES®

Bed & Breakfasts in
  California
Bed & Breakfasts in
  New England
Bed & Breakfasts in
  the Northwest
Beyond Disney
Branson, Missouri
California with Kids
Chicago

Cruises
Disneyland
Florida with Kids
Golf Vacations in the
  Eastern U.S.
The Great Smoky &
  Blue Ridge
  Mountains
Inside Disney

Hawaii
Las Vegas
London
Miami & the Keys
Mini Las Vegas
Mini-Mickey
New Orleans
New York City
Paris

Safaris
San Francisco
Skiing in the West
Walt Disney World
Walt Disney World
  for Grown-ups
Walt Disney World
  for Kids
Washington, D.C.

SPECIAL-INTEREST TITLES

Frommer's Britain's Best Bed & Breakfasts and
  Country Inns
Frommer's Britain's Best Bike Rides
The Civil War Trust's Official Guide
  to the Civil War Discovery Trail
Frommer's Caribbean Hideaways
Frommer's Food Lover's Companion to France
Frommer's Food Lover's Companion to Italy
Frommer's Gay & Lesbian Europe
Frommer's Exploring America by RV
Hanging Out in Europe
Israel Past & Present

Mad Monks' Guide to California
Mad Monks' Guide to New York City
Frommer's The Moon
Frommer's New York City with Kids
The New York Times' Unforgettable
  Weekends
Places Rated Almanac
Retirement Places Rated
Frommer's Road Atlas Britain
Frommer's Road Atlas Europe
Frommer's Washington, D.C., with Kids
Frommer's What the Airlines Never Tell You